P9-EKC-999

Violence in War and Peace

Blackwell Readers in Anthropology

As Anthropology moves beyond the limits of so-called area studies, there is an increasing need for texts that attempt to do the work of both synthesizing the literature and of challenging more traditional or subdisciplinary approaches to anthropology. This is the object of the exciting new series, *Blackwell Readers in Anthropology*.

Each volume in the series offers what have emerged as seminal readings on a chosen theme, and provides the finest, most thought-provoking recent works in the given thematic area. A number of these volumes bring together for the first time a body of literature on a certain topic. Inasmuch, these books are intended to become more than definitive collections, they demonstrate the very ways in which anthropological inquiry has evolved and is evolving.

Violence in War and Peace

Edited by

Nancy Scheper-Hughes and Philippe Bourgois

Blackwell Publishing

BLACKWELL PUBLISHING
350 Main Street, Malden, MA 02148-5020, USA
9600 Garsington Road, Oxford OX4 2DQ, UK
550 Swanston Street, Carlton, Victoria 3053, Australia

First published 2004 by Blackwell Publishing Ltd

10   2011

Library of Congress Cataloging-in-Publication Data

Violence in war and peace: an anthology/edited by Nancy Scheper-Hughes and Philippe Bourgois.
    p. cm.–(Blackwell readers in anthropology; 5)
  Includes bibliographical references and index.
  ISBN 978-0-631-22348-1 (alk. paper)–ISBN 978-0-631-22349-8 (pbk.: alk. paper)
   1. Violence. 2. Genocide. 3. Political violence. I. Scheper-Hughes, Nancy. II. Bourgois,
  Philippe I., 1956-III. Series.

GN495.2.V56 2004
303.6–dc21

2003045324

A catalogue record for this title is available from the British Library.

Typeset in 9 on 11 pt Sabon
by Kolam Information Services Pvt. Ltd, Pondicherry, India.
Printed and bound in Singapore
by Fabulous Printers Pte Ltd

The publisher's policy is to use permanent paper from mills that operate a sustainable forestry policy,
and which has been manufactured from pulp processed using acid-free and elementary chlorine-free
practices. Furthermore, the publisher ensures that the text paper and cover board used have met
acceptable environmental accreditation standards.

For further information on
Blackwell Publishing, visit our website:
www.blackwellpublishing.com

Contents

About the Editors

Nancy Scheper-Hughes is Professor of Anthropology at the University of California, Berkeley where she also directs doctoral studies in "Medicine, Science and the Body". Scheper-Hughes's lifework concerns the violence of everyday life from analyses of the suffering of "leftover" bachelor farmers in rural Ireland; the madness of hunger and the experience of mothering in Northeast Brazil; AIDS and sexual citizenship in Cuba and Brazil; violence, "truth," and justice in the New South Africa; death squad executions of Brazilian street children, to the global traffic in human organs. She is best known for her ethnographies, *Death Without Weeping* (1992) and *Saints, Scholars and Schizophrenics* (1979, new, updated edition 2000). She has been the recipient of many awards and prizes including a Guggenheim, the Staley Prize, the Margaret Mead Award, the Wellcome Medal, the Bryce Wood Book Award, the Harry Chapin Media Award, and the Pietre Prize.

Philippe Bourgois is Professor and Chair of the Department of Anthropology, History and Social Medicine at the University of California, San Francisco. He is best known for his ethnographies *Ethnicity at Work: Divided Labor on a Central American Banana Plantation* (1989) and *In Search of Respect: Selling Crack in El Barrio* (1995, new, updated edition in 2003). He has received several awards, including the C. Wright Mills Prize and the Margaret Mead Award. He also conducted fieldwork among the Miskitu Amerindians during the Sandinista Revolution, FMLN guerrilla fighters during the Salvadoran civil war, and street children in Bolivia. His academic and popular media articles address political and intimate violence, ethnic conflict, poverty, and the phenomenon of "US inner city apartheid". He is currently conducting fieldwork among homeless heroin injectors and crack smokers in San Francisco. www.ucsf.edu/dahsm/pages/faculty/bourgois.html

Acknowledgments

We are very grateful to the Harry Frank Guggenheim Foundation for a publications grant that made this volume possible. Lisa Stevenson, Rennie Salomon, Jennifer S. Hughes, and Ann Magruder were extremely, helpful, at various stages, in the preparation of the manuscript. Three cohorts of graduate students who participated in our UCB/UCSF Medical Anthropology advanced seminar on violence, genocide, and social suffering over the past few years provided critical and thoughtful feedback that influenced the shape of the anthology. Jeff Schonberg selected most of the photographs. The Open Society Institute of New York City (the Soros Foundation) provided research support to Nancy Scheper-Hughes; the National Institutes on Health R01-DA10164 as well as the Wenner-Grenn Foundation for Anthropological Research provided research funds to Philippe Bourgois. Our steadfast editors at Blackwell – Jane Huber and Angela Cohen – are much appreciated. Cameron Laux was a patient and careful copy-editor.

1. Conrad, Joseph. 1999 [1902]. (excerpt) From, *Heart of Darkness*, pp. 20–30. New York: Penguin.

2. Taussig, Michael. 1984. (abridged) "Culture of Terror – Face of Death: Roger Casement's Putumayo Report and the Explanation of Torture." *Comparative Studies in Society and History* 26(1): 467–97. Reprinted by permission of Cambridge University Press.

3. Kroeber, Theodora. 1961. (abridged) "Episodes in Extermination." From *Ishi in Two Worlds*, pp. 79–85, 90–100. Berkeley: University of California Press. Reproduced by permission of Theodora Kroeber and Jed Riffe & Associates. © 1961 The Regents of the University of California; © Renewed 1989 John Quinn. Reproduced by permission of Jed Riffe & Associates on behalf of the John Quinn Trust of 1992.

4. Scheper-Hughes, Nancy. 2001. (abridged) "Ishi's Brain, Ishi's Ashes." *Anthropology Today* 17(1): 12–18. © Royal Anthropological Institute of Great Britain and Ireland.

5. Ferguson, Brian. 1992. (abridged) "Tribal Warfare." *Scientific American* 266(1): 108–13. Reprinted by permission of the author and the publisher. Copyright © 2003 by Scientific American, inc. All rights reserved.

6. Gordon, Robert. 1992. (abridged) From *The Bushmen Myth: The Making of a Namibian Underclass*, pp. 212–17, 269–85. Boulder, CO: Westview Press. Reprinted by permission of Westview Press, a member of Perseus Books, LLC.

7. Foucault, Michel. 1978. (excerpt) "The Right of Death and Power Over Life." From *History of Sexuality*, pp. 135–44. New York: Random House. Copyright © Random House 1978, Inc., New York. Originally published in French as *La Volonté du savoir*. Copyright © Editions Gallimard 1976. Reprinted by permission of Georges Borchardt, Inc., for the Editions Gallimard.

8. Levi, Primo. 1988. (excerpt) "The Gray Zone." From *The Drowned and the Saved*, pp. 37–58. New York: Simon & Schuster. From "The Gray Zone." Abridged and reprinted with permission of Simon & Schuster Adult Publishing Group. Translated from the Italian by Raymond Rosenthal. English translation Copyright © 1988 by Simon & Schuster Inc.

9. Arendt, Hannah. 1963. (abridged) "Judgement, Appeal, and Execution." From *Eichmann in Jerusalem: A Report on the Banality of Evil*, pp. 21, 25–6, 46–55, 135, 137–8, 148, 252. New York: Penguin Books. Copyright © 1963, 1964 by Hannah Arendt. Used by permission of Viking Penguin, a division of Penguin Putnam Inc.

10. Browning, Christopher. 1993. (abridged) "Initiation to Mass Murder: The Józefów Massacre." From *Ordinary Men: Reserve Police Battalion 101 and the Final Solution in Poland*, pp. 55–70, 234–7. New York: Harper Perennial. Copyright © 1992, 1998 by Christopher Browning. Reprinted by permission of HarperCollins Publishers Inc.

11. Borowski, Tadeusz. 1967 [1959]. (excerpt) From *This Way for the Gas, Ladies and Gentlemen*, pp. 29–49. New York: Penguin Books. Translated by Barbara Vedder. Copyright © 1967 by Penguin Books Ltd. Original text copyright © 1959 by Maria Borowski. Used by permission of Viking Penguin, a division of Penguin Putnam Inc.

12. Spiegelman, Art. 1991. (excerpt) From: *Maus II: A Survivor's Tale: And Here My Troubles Began*, pp. 65–7. New York: Pantheon Books. Copyright © 1986, 1989, 1990, 1991 by Art Spiegelman. Used by permission of Pantheon Books, a division of Random House, Inc.

13. Litwack, Leon. 2000. (abridged) "Hellhounds." From: *Without Sanctuary, Lynching Photography in America*, pp. 8–14, 17–18, 20–4, 26, 30, 35–7, 206–7. Santa Fe, NM: Twin Palms Publishers. Reprinted by permission of Leon F. Litwack.

14. Malkki, Liisa. 1995. (abridged) "The Mythic History." From *Purity and Exile: Violence, Memory and National Cosmology*, pp. 53–5, 78–80, 84–5, 87–95, 325–44. Chicago: University of Chicago Press. Reprinted by permission of University of Chicago Press ©.

15. Gourevitch, Philip. 1998. (excerpt) From *We Wish to Inform You That Tomorrow We Will Be Killed With Our Families: Stories from Rwanda*, pp. 85–100. New York: Farrar, Strauss & Giroux. Copyright © 1998 by Philip Gourevitch. Reprinted by permission of Farrar, Straus & Giroux LLC.

16. Milgram, Stanley. 1974. (abridged) "Behavioral Study of Obedience." In Zack Rubin, ed., *Doing Unto Others: Joining, Molding, Conforming, Helping, Loving*, pp. 98–108. Englewood Cliffs, NJ: Prentice Hall, 1974.

17. Rosaldo, Renato. 1989. (abridged) "Grief and a Headhunter's Rage." From *Culture and Truth: The Remaking of Social Analysis*, pp. 1–11, 16–20, 26–8. Boston: Beacon Press. From *Culture and Truth: The Remaking of Social Analysis* by Renato Rosaldo. Reprinted by permission of Beacon Press, Boston; Routledge (UK).

18. Hinton, Alexander. 1998. (abridged) "Why did You Kill?: The Cambodian Genocide and the Dark Side of Face and Honor." *The Journal of Asian Studies* 57(1): 93–122. Reprinted with permission of the Association for Asian Studies, Inc.

19. Taussig, Michael. 1992. (abridged) "Talking Terror." From *The Nervous System*, pp. 29–35, 184. New York: Routledge. Copyright © 1992. Reproduced by permission of Routledge Inc., part of The Taylor & Francis Group.

20. Scheper-Hughes, Nancy. 1992. (abridged) "Bodies, Death and Silence." From *Death Without Weeping*, pp. 216–33. Berkeley: University of California Press. Reproduced with permission of the University of California Press.

21. Green, Linda. 1998. (abridged) "Living in a State of Fear." From *Fear as a Way of Life*, pp. 60–79. New York: Columbia University Press. © 1998 Columbia University Press. Reprinted with the permission of the publisher.

22. Franco, Jean. 1985. (abridged) "Killing Priests, Nuns, Women, Children." In Marshall Bonsky, ed. On Signs, pp. 414–20. Baltimore: John Hopkins Press. Reproduced with permission of the author.

23. Robben, Antonius. 1999. (abridged) "The Fear of Indifference: Combatants' Anxieties about the Political Identity of Civilians during Argentina's Dirty War." From K. Koonings and D. Kruijt, eds., *Societies of Fear: The Legacy of Civil War, Violence and Terror in Latin America*, pp. 125–40. London: Zed Books. Reproduced by permission of Zed Books Ltd.

24. Feldman, Allen. 1994 (abridged) "On Cultural Anesthesia: From Desert Storm to Rodney King." *American Ethnologist* 21(2): 404–18. Reproduced by permission of the author and the American Anthropological Association from *American Ethnologist*. Not for sale or further reproduction.

25. Chomsky, Noam. 2001. (abridged) "The New War Against Terror." From "An Evening with Noam Chomsky." http://www.zmag.org/GlobalWatch/chomskymit.html. Copyright © 2001 and 2003 by Noam Chomsky. This chapter is an excerpted transcript of a lecture given at the Massachusetts Institute of Technology (MIT) Technology and Culture forum, October 18, 2000.

26. Scheper-Hughes, Nancy. 2002. (abridged) "Violence Foretold: Reflections on 9/11." *IDEAS Journal of the National Humanities Center*, 9(1): 56–8, 61. Reprinted with permission of The National Humanities Center.

27. Sartre, Jean-Paul. 1963. (excerpt) "Preface." From Frantz Fanon, *Wretched of the Earth*, pp. 7–31. New York: Grove Press. © 1963 Jean-Paul Sartre. Reprinted by permission of HarperCollins Publishers Ltd.

28. Arendt, Hannah. 1969. (excerpt) From *On Violence*, chapter 1, pp. 35–56. New York: Harcourt, Brace and Company.

29. Aretxaga, Begoña. 1995. (abridged) "Dirty Protest: Symbolic Over-determination and Gender in Northern Ireland Ethnic Violence". *Ethos* 23(2): 123–41, 144–8. Reproduced by permission of the American Anthropological Association. Not for sale or further reproduction.

30. Scheper-Hughes, Nancy. 1995 (abridged) "Who's the Killer?" *Social Justice* 22(3): 143–64 © Social Justice.

31. Taussig, Michael. 1992. (abridged) "Terror as Usual: Walter Benjamin's Theory of History as State of Siege." From *The Nervous System*, pp. 11–16, 195–9. New York: Routledge. Reproduced by permission of Routledge, Inc., part of The Taylor & Francis Group.

32. Bourdieu, Pierre and Loïc Wacquant. 1992. "Symbolic Violence." From *An Invitation to Reflective Sociology*, pp. 167–8, 170–3. Chicago: University of Chicago Press. © The University of Chicago Press.

33. Scheper-Hughes, Nancy. 1992. (excerpt) "Two Feet Under and a Cardboard Coffin," pp. 268–9, 286–96. From *Death Without Weeping*. Berkeley: University of California Press. Reproduced with permission of the University of California Press.

34. Farmer, Paul. 1997. (abridged) "On Suffering and Structural Violence: A View from Below." From Arthur Kleinman, Veena Das, and Margaret Lock, eds., *Social Suffering*, pp. 261–83. Berkeley: University of California Press. Reproduced by permission of The University of California Press.

35. Quesada, Jim. 1998. (abridged) "Suffering Child: An Embodiment of War and its Aftermath in Post-Sandinista Nicaragua." *Medical Anthropology Quarterly* 12(1): 51–73. Reproduced by permission of the American Anthropological Association. Not for sale or further reproduction.

36. Orwell, George. 1937. "The Lower Classes Smell." From *The Road to Wigan Pier*. New York: Harcourt Brace Jovanovich.

37. Bourgois, Philippe. 2002. (abridged) "US Inner City Apartheid: The Contours of Structural and Interpersonal Violence." From *In Search of Respect: Selling Crack in El Barrio*. New York: Cambridge University Press, 1995. Reprinted by permission of Cambridge University Press.

38. Klinenberg, Eric. 1999. (abridged) "Denaturalizing Disaster: A Social Autopsy of the 1995 Chicago Heat Wave." *Theory and Society* 28: 239–42, 244, 246–50, 254–62, 269–76, 283–92. Published with kind permission of Kluwer Academic Publishers.

39. Wacquant, Loïc. 2000. (abridged) "The New 'Peculiar Institution': On the Prison as Surrogate Ghetto." *Theoretical Criminology* 4(3): 377–89.

40. Das, Veena, 1997. (abridged) "Language and Body: Transactions in the Construction of Pain." From Arthur Kleinman, Veena Das, and Margaret Lock, eds., *Social Suffering*, pp. 67–73, 75–8, 82–91. Berkeley, CA: University of California Press. Reproduced by permission of the University of California Press.

41. Danner, Mark. 1993. (abridged) From *The Massacre at El Mozote: A Parable of the Cold War*, pp. 74–84. New York: Vintage Books. Copyright © 1994 by Mark Danner. Used by permission of Random House Inc.

42. Bourdieu, Pierre. 2001. (abridged) "Gender and Symbolic Violence." From *Masculine Domination*, pp. 34–42. Stanford: Stanford University Press. Adapted from Bourdieu, Pierre, *Domination masculine*. Copyright © Editions du Seuil; translation © 2001 Polity Press. With the permission of Stanford University Press, www.sup.org.

43. Bourgois, Philippe. 2002. (abridged) "The Everyday Violence of Gang Rape." From *In Search of Respect: Selling Crack in El Barrio*. New York: Cambridge University Press, 1995. Reprinted with the permission of Cambridge University Press.

44. Donaldson, Stephen. (abridged) "Hooking Up: Protective Pairing for Punks," Stop Prisoner Rape, Los Angeles, CA 90048.

45. Cohn, Carol. 1987. (abridged) "Sex and Death in the Rational World of Defense Intellectuals." *Signs: Journal of Woman in Culture and Society* 12(4): 690–6, 699–705, 707–13, 716–18. © The University of Chicago.

46. Scarry, Elaine. 1985. (excerpt) From *The Body in Pain: The Making and Unmaking of the World*, pp. 3–5, 28–30. New York: Oxford University Press. Copyright © 1985 by Oxford University Press Inc. Used by permission of Oxford University Press, Inc.

47. Herman, Judith Lewis. 1992. (abridged) "A New Diagnosis." *Trauma and Recovery*, chapter 6, pp. 115–22, 255–6. New York: Basic Books. Copyright © 1992 by Basic Books. Reprinted by permission of Basic Books, a member of Perseus Books, LLC.

48. Krog, Antjie. 1999. (excerpt) "The Wet Bag and Other Phantoms." From *Country of My Skull: Guilt, Sorrow, and the Limits of Forgiveness in the New South Africa*, pp. 70–8. New York: Three Rivers Press. Copyright © 1998 by Antjie Samuel; Introduction copyright © 1999 by Carlayne Hunter-Gault. Used by permission of Times Books, a division of Random House, Inc.

49. Suarez-Orozco, Marcelo M. 1987. (abridged) "The Treatment of Children in the Dirty War: Ideology, State Terrorism, and the Abuse of Children in Argentina." From N. Scheper-Hughes, ed.,

Child Survival, pp. 227–43, 245–6. Kluwer Publishing Company. Published with kind permission from Kluwer Academic Publishers.

50. Spiegelman, Art. 1991. (excerpt) *Maus II: A Survivor's Tale: And Here My Troubles Began*; see (12) above.

51. Starn, Orin. 1992. (abridged) "Missing the Revolution: Anthropologists and the War in Peru." From George Marcus, ed., *Re-reading Cultural Anthropology*, pp. 152–4, 159–60, 164–9, 173, 175–80. Durham: Duke University Press. Reproduced by permission of the American Anthropological Association from *Cultural Anthropology* 6(1). Not for sale or further reproduction.

52. Pedelty, Mark. 1995. (excerpt) From *War Stories: The Culture of Foreign Correspondents*, pp. 1–4, 6–12, 20, 24–5. London: Routledge.

53. Swedenburg, Ted. 1995. (abridged) "Prisoners of Love: With Genet in the Palestinian Field." From C. Nordstrom and A. Robben, eds., *Fieldwork Under Fire*, pp. 25–40. Berkeley: University of California Press. Reproduced by permission of The University of California Press.

54. Zulaika, Joseba. 1995. (abridged) "The Anthropologist as Terrorist." From C. Nordstrom and A. Robben, eds., *Fieldwork Under Fire*, pp. 207–10, 219–22. Berkeley: University of California Press. Copyright © 1995 The Regents of the University of California. Reproduced with permission of the University of California Press.

55. Binford, Leigh. 1996. (abridged) "An Alternative Anthropology: Exercising the Preferential Option for the Poor." From *The El Mozote Massacre*, pp. 192–206. Tucson, AZ: University of Arizona Press. © 1996 The Arizona Board of Regents. Reprinted by permission of the University of Arizona Press.

56. Bourgois, Philippe. 2001. (abridged) "The Power of Violence in War and Peace: Post-Cold War Lessons from El Salvador." *Ethnography* 2(1): 5–34. © 2001 Sage Publications Ltd. Reprinted by permission of Sage Publications.

57. Agamben, Giorgio. 1999 (abridged) "The Witness." From *Remnants of Auschwitz: The Witness and the Archive*, chapter 1, pp. 15–26. New York: Zone Books. Reproduced with permission of Blackwell Publishing.

58. Fanon, Frantz. 1963. (abridged) "Colonial War and Mental Disorders." From *Wretched of the Earth*, pp. 249, 251, 254–61, 264–75, 306–10. New York: Grove Press. Copyright © 1963 by Présence Africaine. Used by permission of Grove/Atlantic Inc.

59. Sachs, Albie. 2000. (abridged) From *The Soft Vengeance of a Freedom Fighter*, pp. 7–14, 205–11. Berkeley: University of California Press. Reproduced by permission of the University of California Press.

60. Scheper-Hughes, Nancy. 1998. (abridged) "Undoing – Social Suffering and the Politics of Remorse in the New South Africa." *Social Justice* 1998 25(4): 126–39. © Social Justice.

61. Mamdani, Mahmood. 2001. (excerpt) From *When Victims Become Killers: Colonialism, Nativism, and the Genocide in Rwanda*, pp. 266–8, 270–6, 280–3. Princeton, NJ: Princeton University Press. Copyright © 2001 by Princeton University Press. Reprinted by permission of Princeton University Press.

62. Soyinka, Wole. 1999. (excerpt) From *The Burden of Memory: The Muse of Forgiveness*, pp. 23–36. New York: Oxford University Press. Copyright © 1998 by Wole Soyinka. Used by permission of Oxford University Press, Inc.

Every effort has been made to trace copyright holders and to obtain their permission for the use of copyright material. The authors and publishers will gladly receive any information enabling them to rectify any error or omission in subsequent editions.

Plate 1: Serra Pelada Mine, Pará, Brazil 1986. Photo © Sebastião Salgado, Contact Press Images.

Introduction: Making Sense of Violence

Nancy Scheper-Hughes and Philippe Bourgois

Violence is a slippery concept – nonlinear, productive, destructive, *and* reproductive. It is mimetic, like imitative magic or homeopathy. "Like produces like," that much we know. Violence gives birth to itself. So we can rightly speak of chains, spirals, and mirrors of violence – or, as we prefer – a continuum of violence. We all know, as though by rote, that wife beaters and sexual abusers were themselves usually beaten and abused. Repressive political regimes resting on terror/fear/torture are often mimetically reproduced by the same revolutionary militants determined to overthrow them (see Bourgois, Chapter 56; Scheper-Hughes, Chapter 30; and Fanon, Chapter 58). Structural violence – the violence of poverty, hunger, social exclusion and humiliation – inevitably translates into intimate and domestic violence (Scheper-Hughes, Chapter 33; Bourgois, Chapter 37). Politically motivated torture is amplified by the symbolic violence that trails in its wake, making those who were tortured feel shame for their "weakness" in betraying their comrades under duress. Rape survivors – especially those who were violated with genocidal or sadistic political intent during civil wars (Danner, Chapter 41) often become living-dead people, refusing to speak of the unspeakable, and are often shunned or outcasted by kin and community, and even by comrades and lovers (Das, Chapter 40 and Fanon, Chapter 58).

Violence can never be understood solely in terms of its physicality – force, assault, or the infliction of pain – alone. Violence also includes assaults on the personhood, dignity, sense of worth or value of the victim. The social and cultural dimensions of violence are what gives violence its power and meaning. Focusing exclusively on the physical aspects of torture/terror/violence misses the point and transforms the project into a clinical, literary, or artistic exercise, which runs the risk of degenerating into a theatre or pornography of violence in which the voyeuristic impulse subverts the larger project of witnessing, critiquing, and writing against violence, injustice, and suffering.

The sadistic Boer cop, Jeffrey Benzien (Krog, Chapter 48), a pathetic minor player in the last stages of apartheid, became a key symbol of apartheid's inhumanity and cruelty during the South African Truth and Reconciliation amnesty hearings in Cape Town when he demonstrated before television cameras his signature torture technique, the "wet bag" which he used to force victims to give up the names of their comrades in the anti-apartheid struggle. Meanwhile, the deep structures of apartheid violence that consigned 80 percent of the African population to rural bantustands and to squalid squatter camps and worker hostel barracks in urban areas – social institutions that resembled concentration camps – were left virtually unexamined by the South African TRC (see Scheper-Hughes, Chapter 60; Sachs, Chapter 59; and Soyinka, Chapter 62). The elderly victim of apartheid who stood before the TRC seeking restitution for the grove of fruit trees uprooted from his yard by security police was treated as a sweet distraction amidst the serious work of the Commission. But the old man spoke to the very heart of apartheid's darkness and to the more inclusive meanings of state and political violence treated in this volume.

Despite our work in putting together this expansive, eclectic, anthropologically informed anthology, in the end we cannot say that now we "know" exactly what violence is. "It" cannot be readily objectified and quantified so that a "check list" can be drawn up with positive criteria for defining any particular act as violent or not. Of course, police, social workers, and family-court judges *must* decide whether spanking a child with a hand, a hairbrush, or a leather strap, or throwing a child across a room, or slamming him or her against a wall is a violent act or a culturally defined legitimate expression of parental authority and responsibility. World courts need to decide whether to include "dirty wars" and "ethnic cleansings" under the legalistic rubric of genocide. We have our own political views on these issues and we state these clearly.

Violence itself, however, defies easy categorization. It can be everything and nothing; legitimate or illegitimate; visible or invisible; necessary or useless; senseless and gratuitous or utterly rational and strategic. Revolutionary violence, community-based massacres, and state repression are often painfully graphic and transparent. The *everyday* violence of infant mortality, slow starvation, disease, despair, and humiliation that destroys socially marginalized humans with even greater frequency are usually invisible or misrecognized (Scheper-Hughes 1992 and Chapter 20). Dom Helder Camara, the "little red archbishop" of Recife, Brazil, railed fearlessly against the military government's attacks on "violent" landless peasants by reminding those in power of the "violence of hunger" and the "atomic bombs" of sickness and destitution (see Farmer, Chapter 34).

Rather than *sui generis*, violence is in the eye of the beholder. What constitutes violence is always mediated by an expressed or implicit dichotomy between legitimate/illegitimate, permissible or sanctioned acts, as when the "legitimate" violence of the militarized state is differentiated from the unruly, illicit violence of the mob or of revolutionaries (see Swedenburg, Chapter 53 and Zulaika, Chapter 54). Depending on one's political-economic position in the world (dis)order, particular acts of violence may be perceived as "depraved" or "glorious," as when Palestinian suicide bombers and the World Trade Center attackers are alternatively viewed as martyrs or terrorists or when Israeli settlers and the US military forces in the Middle East are alternatively viewed as heroic patriots/liberators or violent oppressors. Violent acts may be denounced as "freakish" (e.g., the cannibalistic serial killer) or ignored as "banal" (e.g., the college date rapist). Violence (like power) corrupts absolutely, except when it is said to "ennoble" or liberate the perpetrator, as when Jean-Paul Sartre (Chapter 27) states that colonized subjects can only regain their humanity through acts of revolutionary violence. Perhaps the most one can say about violence is that like madness, sickness, suffering, or death itself, it is a human condition. Violence is present (as a capability) in each of us, as is its opposite – the rejection of violence.

Our readers will note a conspicuous absence in the organization of our selections. We have rejected the commonsense view of violence as an essential, universal, sociobiological or psychobiological entity, a residue of our primate and prehistoric evolutionary origins as a species of hunter-killers. Our incisors are, after all, very small. Our nails can inflict pain, but not death. Our minds and our cultural inventiveness, more than our hominid bodies, are our ecological niche. We *are* social creatures. Cultures, social structures, ideas, and ideologies shape all dimensions of violence, *both* its expressions and its repressions. Torturing and killing are as cultural as nursing the sick and wounded or burying and mourning the dead. We reject the view that violence is fundamentally a question of hard-wiring, genes or hormones, while certainly accepting that these contribute to human behavior, accelerating, amplifying, or modifying human emotions. But *brute* force is a misnomer, and it is the very *human* face of violence that we are trying to unravel here. Sadly, most violence is not "senseless" at all.

Both of us, as editors of this volume, have been involved for many years as active field-workers, teachers, and political advocates in the field of violence. Our collective experiences have shaped the organization of this volume, which we see as a basic reader for conceptualizing violence studies from a multidisciplinary but anthropologically informed perspective.

Bourgois's focus on violence began through his work in Central America from 1979 through the mid-1980s. His first formal fieldwork site among the Miskitu Amerindians of Nicaragua became the center of a bloody ethnic insurrection that was drawn to the center of Cold War power politics. He had taken a leave of absence from graduate school to work for the Sandinista Ministry of Agrarian Reform. Had he not been expelled by the Sandinista government for coauthoring an article (CIERA 1981: 89–149) advocating regional autonomy for the Miskitu, he may not have finished his doctorate in anthropology. A year later, before beginning his actual doctoral fieldwork on the abusive labor practices of a US multinational banana plantation, he was placed on probation by his graduate program for visiting villages controlled by Salvadoran guerrillas and denouncing US complicity in human rights violations in that country without the approval of his institution's committee for research with human subjects (Bourgois 1991). Members of his dissertation committee admonished him to choose between "being an anthropologist, a human rights activist, or a journalist."[1]

Bourgois is best known for his ethnographic work on crack dealers in East Harlem, which addresses the interface between interpersonal "delinquent violence," including self-destructive substance abuse and the gendered dynamics of brutality in the family and of adolescent gang rape, with the larger structural violence of what he calls US inner-city apartheid. His analysis of the United States allows him to reinterpret the everyday violence he witnessed in revolutionary Central America, especially its gendered contours, which he had not yet explored when he focused instead on the direct, physically assaultive turmoil of political repression, resistance, human rights violations, and organized class struggles and cultural mobilizations.

Scheper-Hughes gradually came to the realization that the family is one of the most violent of social institutions. But the family system – whether it concerned the scape-goating, exploitation, and social death inflicted on the farm-inheriting bachelor sons of County Kerry, Ireland (Scheper-Hughes [1979] 2000) or the hastened deaths of "angel babies" in the Northeast of Brazil (Scheper-Hughes 1993) – was in each instance responding to larger social-political-economic exclusions which made the "violent" behavior seem like the only possible recourse. While studying the "dark interiors" of family life during the mid-1970s in a small mountain community of western Ireland, Scheper-Hughes paid scant attention to the activities of Matty Dowd, from whom she rented a cottage in the mountain hamlet of Ballynalacken. She turned a blind eye to the installation of a small arsenal of guns and explosives in the attic of her rented cottage that Matty and a few of his Sinn Fein buddies were then running to fuel the fires in Northern Ireland. And so, she left unexamined, until recently (see Scheper-Hughes 2000, epilogue), the links between political violence in Northern Ireland and the family dramas of captive farmers on failed farms that certainly had a violence of their own. Even while conducting fieldwork in Brazil during some of the harshest periods of the military dictatorship (1964–84) Scheper-Hughes did not begin to study state violence until the half-grown sons of her friends and neighbors in the shantytown of Alto do Cruzeiro began to "disappear" – their mutilated bodies turning up later, the handiwork of police-infiltrated local death squads (Scheper-Hughes 2003).

Up until that time Scheper-Hughes believed that the analysis of political violence occurring in the context of military dictatorships and police states, in times of revolutionary transition during and after civil wars and wars of liberation, was best left to journalists. Anthropologists were too slow, too hesitant, too reflective; and the ethnographic knowledge that was produced was too local. Political events were altogether too fast and unstable, so that by the time the anthropologists had something to say it was usually long after the fact. But as Brazilian newspapers insisted on printing stories about the "dangerousness" and the "violence" of shantytown dwellers (especially of poor, young Afro-Brazilians), a public slander that made the work of the death squads seem like a necessary defense against the anarchy of the *favela*, she came to see that anthropological interventions were absolutely necessary to contest the dangerous half-truths of the media. At that time, she also entered a more frankly activist and political struggle in Northeast Brazil against the hegemony of the death squads, which operated in many cases with the tacit support of the police and political leaders. Later, Scheper-Hughes began to study political violence among the "young lions" during the anti-apartheid struggle and the paradoxes involved in national and personal programs of reconciliation designed primarily to disarm Black South Africans and to help them to "get over" apartheid in face of the frank impossibility of "un-doing" its collective damages. (See Chapters 30 and 60.)

Violence in War and Peace strives, above all, to "trouble" the distinctions between public and private, visible and invisible, legitimate and illegitimate forms of violence in times that can best be described as neither war nor peacetime in so many parts of the world.

Teaching Violence

When violence is addressed in the university curriculum, it is often "safely" cordoned off in military training courses (ROTC), or in the few alternative "Peace and Conflict Studies" programs still surviving at American universities. By and large, however, within the general liberal arts undergraduate curriculum, violence as an object of study makes only cameo appearances. Worse yet, in the natural and behavioral sciences classes (biology, psychology, physical anthropology) where violence *is* addressed, it tends to be subsumed under biologized notions of "human aggression," reduced to a discussion of drives and instincts, the XYY genotype, and the fight/flight response. Alternatively, violence is often individualized and pathologized as "deviance" in psychology and sociology classes (as for example in discussions of the criminally insane). When the subject is raised in women's studies classes, usually violence against women and children, it still often remains trapped in a medicalized/psychologized framework or confined to a totalizing discourse on patriarchy and its aberrations.

These ideological approaches misrecognize the extent to which structural inequalities and power relations are naturalized by our categories and conceptions of what violence really is. They also fail to address the totality and range of violent acts, including those which are part of the normative fabric of social and political life. Structural violence is generally invisible because it is part of the routine grounds of everyday life and transformed into expressions of moral worth. Most importantly in this volume, we want to demonstrate how often the most violent acts consist of conduct that is socially permitted, encouraged, or enjoined as a moral right or a duty. Most violence is not deviant behavior, not disapproved of, but to the contrary is defined as virtuous action in the service of generally applauded conventional social, economic, and political norms.

For this reason, our anthology is organized around a cluster of readings that constantly juxtapose the routine, ordinary, and normative violence of everyday life ("terror as usual") with sudden eruptions of extraordinary, pathological, excessive, or "gratuitous" violence (genocides, communal violence, ethnic cleansings, state terror, dirty wars, revolutions, guerrilla wars, and vigilante justice). Many selections grapple with the relations and continuities between political and criminal violence, state violence and "communal" violence, and the relations between social inequalities and individual and collective pathologies of power.

A few generative key words and terms inform our anthology and serve as a kind of map through the maze of disparate readings. These include Bourdieu's "symbolic violence" and his related notion of "misrecognition," Taussig's "culture of terror, space of death," and Benjamin's "modern history as a state of siege"; Conrad's "fascination of the abomination"; Arendt's "banality of evil"; Primo Levi's "gray zone," Basaglia's "peace-time crimes"; Scheper-Hughes's "everyday violence" and "invisible genocides," Farmer's "structural violence" and "pathologies of power"; Kleinman's "social suffering," Agamben's "impossibility of witnessing," Foucault's "bio-power"; and, finally, our "violence continuum."

Our selections draw upon the social sciences, moral and political philosophy, psychiatry, literature, and journalism. All the selections are infused with an ethnographic, anthropological sensibility in which scientific observation is combined with moral and political witnessing.

Tristes Anthropologiques:
Anthropology's Heart of Darkness

We open this anthology with "Conquest and Colonialism" because of the historic centrality of these processes in shaping contemporary patterns of violence across the world. The treatment of colonial violences opens the door to a critique of the categories of civilization and savagery, progress, underdevelopment, and modernity. As cultural anthropologists we feel that an examination of the colonial and imperialist violence that "produced" the very subjects of our discipline – the so-called primitive, indigenous, traditional, nonindustrialized peoples of the world – is a necessary place to begin. The lives, suffering, and deaths of these "people without history" – as Eric Wolf (1982) described with critical irony those indigenous populations first decimated by Europe and then by the United States – have provided generations of anthropologists with their livelihood.

Genocide and ethnocide constitute anthropology's primal scene. Despite this history – and the privileged position of the anthropologist-ethnographer as eye-witness to some of these events – the discipline, until quite recently, has been largely mute on the subject. Ethnocide, when treated at all, is divorced from its colonial context.

To this day most early-warning signs concerning genocidal sentiments, gestures, and acts come from political journalists rather than from ethnographers in the field. Most theories of the causes, meanings, and consequences of mass violence and genocide come from other disciplines – history, psychology and psychiatry, theology, comparative law, human rights, and political science. In all, anthropology is a late arrival to the field, and this anthology, published in 2003, represents an opening gambit in an attempt to establish an anthropologically informed field of violence studies.

As Orin Starn (see Chapter 51) notes, violence is not a natural subject for anthropologists. Everything in our disciplinary training predisposes us *not* to see the blatant and manifest forms of violence that so often ravage the lives of our subjects. The term and modern conception of "genocide" were first coined by Raphael Lemkin (1944) following and in response to the Jewish Holocaust, but genocides and other forms of mass killing have existed prior to modernity and in societies relatively untouched by western "civilization." The characteristic avoidance of violence by most twentieth-century anthropologists was based on a legitimate fear that study and analyses of *indigenous* forms of human cruelty and mass killing (which certainly exist) would only exacerbate Western stereotypes of primitivity, savagery, and barbarism that took modern anthropology more than half a century to dislodge.

Less charitably, anthropology's theoretical formulations, epistemological orientations, and the bourgeois identity of most of its practitioners steered the discipline away from facing structural violence and the pathologies of power. Instead, the discipline continued its relentless and ahistoric pursuit of the exotic other with literary, philosophical, and descriptive precision, recording the symbol systems, kinship structures, and salvaged remnants in the vacuum of a fictitious ethnographic present.

Meanwhile, those few cultural anthropologists who have dealt directly with violence and cruelty – either arguing from untenable universal premises derived from evolutionary sociobiology (like Napoleon Chagnon [1968] on the "fierce" Yanomami of Venezuela/Brazil) or from a crude form of cultural materialism (like Harris and Ross [1987] on the "wild-ing" effects of meat protein hunger on male violence toward females, including female infanticide and the collective kidnapping/rape of women across a wide arc of tribal societies) or from an atheoretical, populist ethnographic sensationalism (such as Colin Turnbull [1972] on the cruel to the point of socially pathological Ik people of Uganda) – proved an embarrassing sideshow to the field.[2]

Like so many inverse bloodhounds on the scent of the good in the societies they studied, traditionally, anthropologists saw, heard, and reported no violence from the field. Violence was not considered a proper subject for the discipline.[3] Consequently, the contribution of anthropology to understanding *all* levels of violence – from individual sexual abuse and homicide to state-sponsored political terrorism and "dirty" wars to genocide is extremely modest.[4] And those who have deviated from the golden rule of moral relativism are often saddled with accusations of victim-blaming by advocates of a bourgeois politics of representation interacting with new versions of cultural nationalism and cultural fundamentalism.

In his professional memoir, *After the Fact*, Clifford Geertz (1995) notes somewhat wryly that he always had the uncomfortable feeling of arriving too early or too late to observe the really large and significant political events and the violent upheavals that descended on his respective fieldsites in Morocco and Java. But, in fact, he also writes that he consciously avoided the conflicts, moving back and forth between his respective fieldsites during relative periods of calm, always managing to "miss the violence, the genocide, the revolution" (see Starn, Chapter 51) as it were.

And so there is nothing in Geertz's ethnographic writings hinting at the "killing fields" that were beginning to engulf Indonesia soon after he had departed from the field, a massacre of suspected Communists by Islamic fundamentalists in 1965 that rivaled the 1994 genocide in Rwanda (see Gourevitch, Chapter 15). What Geertz missed was a blood-bath, a political massacre of more than 500,000 Indonesians, carried out with diplomatic support from the US government, following an unsuccessful Marxist-inspired coup in 1965 (though one could interpret Geertz's celebrated analysis of the Balinese cock fight as a coded expression of the fierce aggression that he perceived as lying just beneath the surface of a people whom he otherwise described as among the most poised, controlled, and decorous in the world). When asked at a presentation he gave at the Russell Sage Foundation in the winter of 1991 why he did not publicly denounce the loss of life and the human rights violations of the families and villagers he studied (especially in light of his own government's complicity), Geertz responded that he had not wanted to distract attention away from the theoretical points he was making by engaging in a media fray or a politics of advocacy.

In other quarters of anthropology a new mood of political and ethical engagement and of "witnessing" (see Part X) resulted in considerable soul-searching, even exemplified toward the end of the life of the Polish aristocrat, anthropology's very own Conrad of colonial anthropology, Bronislaw Malinowski. Malinowski began his anthropological career under considerable duress as an "enemy-alien," a Polish-born Austrian citizen detained in Australia while en route to his first fieldwork expedition during the outbreak of the First World War. Granted *libera custodia* by the Australian government, Malinowski was permitted to conduct his ethnographic research in New Guinea as long as the war continued. This artificially expanded his intended term of fieldwork. His famous field diary, covering the period 1914–18, published posthumously, records the anthropologist's conflicting emotions and identities as a European gentleman, a child of Western imperialism, and a natural scientist trying to reinvent himself and carve out a new science and method for recording and understanding human and cultural difference. Malinowski's own sympathies were initially aligned with the values of his own European civilization, and in a desperate or very likely ironic entry to his Trobriand diary, Malinowski repeats the words of the savage colonizer, Kurtz, from Joseph Conrad's Heart of Darkness (see Conrad, Chapter 1): "My feelings toward the natives are [on the whole] decidedly tending to 'exterminate the brutes' " (Malinowski 1967: 69). Here, the anthropologist, dedicated eth-nographer, and racist imperialist become kindred spirits.

When Malinowski finally sat down to reflect on Western imperialism and the moral obligation of his discipline, he wrote that "the duty of the anthropologist is to be a fair and true interpreter of the Native and . . . to register that Europeans [have at times] exterminated whole island peoples; that they expropriated most of the patrimony of savage races; that they introduced slavery in a specially cruel and pernicious form" (1945: 3–4, cited by James 1973: 66). Finally, Malinowski sided with the anticolonialist revolutions of mid-twentieth century. He argued passionately against the anthropologist as a neutral and objective observer and "bystander" to the history of colonial violence and the suffering that it visited upon the people and cultures with whom anthropology had cast its lots.

These tentative forays by Malinowski into an engaged and politicized applied anthropology were roundly dismissed by his peers as the irresponsible deviations of an old man past his intellectual prime. Instead, "salvage anthropology" continued to be the acceptable, politically blind, and culturally relative approach taken by twentieth-century anthropologists toward the destruction of indigenous populations. Even Margaret Mead, whose sense of urgency – "We must study them before they disappear!" – was dictated by the accelerating die-outs of indigenous peoples and their languages and cultures.

Hence, we open this anthology with several readings on the violence of Western conquest and on the weak supporting role of anthropologists *vis-à-vis* Western colonialism. We begin with Joseph Conrad, whose *Heart of Darkness* has haunted anthropological writings for the past century. There are many anthropological Conrads, from Malinowski to Michael Taussig (see Taussig, Chapter 2) and many dangerous liaisons and brushes in the field between anthropologists and Kurtzian type postcolonials and later-day racists, exemplified in Robert Gordon's critique of the Bushman myth (see Gordon, Chapter 6). So called "applied anthropology" is especially tainted by history. Born as a stepchild of colonialism (see James 1973; Feuchtwang 1973; Johnson 1982), it came of age during the Cold War (see Nader 1997a; Wakin 1992; Gow 1993; Hymes 1972) only to find itself maturing into a partisan of neoliberal globalization in the name of a kinder, gentler cultural sensitivity and sometimes more openly as cost-effective market-based research.

While genocides predate the spread of Western "civilization," the colonization of Africa, Asia, and the New World incited some of the worst genocides of the eighteenth to late twentieth centuries (the role, for example, of colonialist tropes of biological racism that settled and infected relations between the Tutsi and the Hutu in Central Africa). The modern history of native North America is a particularly egregious case of Taussig's culture of terror/space of death, and we have included here two selections dealing with the anthropological record responding to the die-outs of entire populations of native Californians in massacres and bounty-hunts by Anglo ranchers and gold miners (Kroeber, Chapter 3; Scheper-Hughes, Chapter 4). Tellingly, of the two Kroebers – Alfred and Theodora – it was the anthropological *spouse*, Theodora, who dealt directly and humanely in her writings with the ongoing history of Northern California Indian genocide so studiously avoided by Alfred, the distinguished father of California Anthropology.

The history of anthropology's intellectual complicity, intended or not, in the erasure of genocide in California's history may seem minor compared to the role that cultural and physical anthropology played in providing a scientific rationale and conceptual "toolkit" for the Jewish Holocaust (see Arnold 2001; Schafft 2001) or to South African apartheid (see Boonzaier and Sharp 1988). But the reification of the "last" Yahi Indian, Ishi, as a living public spectacle in the University of California museum of Anthropology and the preservation of his brain as an object of scientific curiosity – even if mislaid for half a century in a tank of formaldehyde – is on a par with the naked display of Saartjie Baartman, the so called "Hottentot Venus" of South Africa, in circuses in Western Europe and the preservation of her remains until 1976[5] as a "sexual curiosity" in a Parisian museum, the Musée de l'Homme. These are misrecognized acts of violence that suggest a genocidal impulse – to destroy, to possess, and to display "aboriginal" human remains in the name of science. Again, one is reminded of Conrad's Kurtz and the collection of shrunken heads on poles surrounding his compound in the heart of [colonial] darkness (see Ferguson, Chapter 3). Within the framework of a genocidal continuum, it is essential to recognize the ease with which the abnormal is normalized and the death of "anthropology's" indigenous subjects is accepted as inevitable or routine, even when seen as a scientific or (as in the case of Ishi) a sentimental loss.

One could supply many other instances of the misuse of anthropological ideas and practices in fostering structural, political, and symbolic violence. There are also numerous examples of anthropological ideas and methods used as tools of human liberation in opposition to state projects of mass killing and genocide, such as Maybury-Lewis's Cultural Survival movement, or the structural Marxist tradition of social anthropology that was taught at the Universities of Witswatersrand and Cape Town, South Africa, in defiance of apartheid. Meanwhile, the courageous work of forensic anthropologist, Claude Snow, in collaboration with Mary Clare King, offers yet another example of scientific practice in defense of humanity and human rights in the face of mass killings and genocide (see Sanford 2003). Snow helped to organize and to train the *Equipo Argentino de Antropologia Forense* of Buenos Aires, one of the first groups to use the technology of DNA to identify the politically disappeared from the remains exhumed from mass graves.

It is also good to recall that if some anthropological concepts – from Lowie's notion of culture to Ruth Benedict's "configurationalism" to Mead's notions of national character –

were expropriated and applied (as during apartheid) to advance "scientific racism" and genocidal policies, these same concepts have been used at other times and places to foster cultural and human rights. Finally, as this volume illustrates, there were at the turn of the twentieth century a growing number of younger anthropologists who did not "miss the revolution" or turn their scientific gaze away from emerging genocides. They have positioned themselves squarely on the side of the victims and survivors of political and ethnic violence and have designed their research to foster human survival (see Part X, especially Pedelty, Chapter 52; Swedenburg, Chapter 53; and Binford, Chapter 55; and also Nordstrom 1997; Nordstrom and Robben 1995; Sluka 1999; Leyton 1998; Mahmood 1996; Hinton 2002).

The Modernity of Genocide – The Holocaust

We devote an entire section of this volume to the Nazi Holocaust because of its deep symbolic resonance, occurring as it did in the heart of the most modern of all European nations and because of the catastrophically tragic, industrialized scale of human death and destruction. We also wanted to acknowledge the massive quantity and the exceptional quality of historical documentation, autobiographical reflection, and critical thinking that this distinctive genre of post-Second World War/Holocaust literature has spawned. This in and of itself poses a quandary, for it is partly through these writings that the Holocaust lives on in history. A few scholars have argued passionately[6] that the best response to the Holocaust would be a purposeful silence, an active *obliteration*, which is the opposite of merely "forgetting."

The prominence given to this section might seem to imply that the Nazi Holocaust is in some way *sui generis* and beyond cross-cultural understanding, comparison, or reckoning. But to the contrary, the goal of this anthology is to draw links between forms of violence and terrorism that are normally kept apart and compartmentalized, as well as to make public the other kinds of genocides that are so easily transformed into "public secrets" or normalized into invisibility. Indeed, we want to treat the Holocaust as the outer limit, the extreme pole along a continuum that spans communal violence (Part III), mass killings and disappearances (Hinton, Chapter 18; Taussig, Chapter 19; Green, Chapter 21; Robben, Chapter 23; Danner, Chapter 41; Suarez-Orozco, Chapter 49; Pedelty, Chapter 52) to structural violence (Scheper-Hughes, Chapter 33; Farmer, Chapter 34; Bourgois, Chapter 37;), including public policies of imprisonment and rape (Wacquant, Chapter 39; Donaldson, Chapter 44) and the violently masculine and deceptively technical language of nuclear weapons researchers (Cohn, Chapter 45).

In this section on the Holocaust we have assembled readings drawn from philosophy (Foucault, Chapter 7; Arendt, Chapter 9), autobiography (Levi, Chapter 8), history (Browning, Chapter 10), and fiction (Borowski, Chapter 11) – including comic strip art (see Spiegelman, Chapter 12). Foucault, with whom we open the discussion, analyzes racialized mass murder as the workings of the ultimate logic of biopower. Governments utilize scientific and moral discourses to manage the biological quality and the "stock" of their citizens, by sanitizing the population to eliminate "polluting" elements – as when the Nazis destroyed millions of Jews, hundreds of thousands of gypsies, disabled people, homosexuals and an assorted melange of communists, Jehovah's Witnesses, nationalists, resistance fighters, and prisoners of war – in the interest of social hygiene and moral order.

Foucault's analysis anticipates Zygmunt Bauman's thesis that industrial-style mass murder is a product of modernist efficiency, engineering, and morality. Certainly, the Nazis disabused an arrogant Eurocentric world of its confidence in progress and the superiority of Western civilization. The industrial scale and systematic logic for Nazi crimes against humanity render self-evident the postmodern critiques of the Enlightenment in all its guises, including the humanities and social sciences, especially cultural anthropology. At the same time, however, the urgent need to document all aspects of the Nazi concentration camps, in light of the persistence of Holocaust deniers and revisionists – some of them candidates for high office in Europe at the turn of the twenty-first century – painfully reveals the political dangers, ethical weakness, and historical limits of postmodernism's embrace of partial truths, multiple and fragmented realities, literary deconstructionism, and moral relativism.

Foucault (Chapter 7), Hannah Arendt (Chapter 9), Christopher Browning (Chapter 10), and Tadeusz Borowski (Chapter 11) all attribute to the Holocaust a mad triumph of rational efficiency, a distorted end-product of the increasing rationalization of late modernity. Eichmann, the SS guard who arranged thousands of deportations and deaths, emerges as an unusually shallow and simple soul, a man concerned primarily with doing a good job, fitting in, not making waves, promoting bureaucratic efficiency, and rising up in the firm, so to speak. Eichmann really cared about being promoted. He was, for Arendt (Chapter 9) a prototype of the "banality of evil" which she took to be the primary characteristic and lesson of the Holocaust. More recently, Agamben (Chapter 57), drawing on Foucault, identified the Nazi concentration camp as the prototype of late modern biopolitics in its creation of a population of "living dead" – known in camp argot as "muselmanner" or muslims – people whose bodies and lives could be taken by the state at will or at whim, neither for (religious) sacrifice nor for crimes committed (capital punishment), but merely because of their "availability" for execution.

In all, the Holocaust is something of a misnomer. What happened in those camps, gas chambers, and ovens had nothing to do with religion or with human sacrifice and burnt offerings to placate angry gods. Rather – if Agambem is correct – the genocide of the Jews was about actualizing the "readiness" of certain vulnerable and targeted populations to be killed, a dangerous theory reminiscent of Arendt's (Chapter 9) controversial depiction of Jewish leaders collaborating with the Nazis. One thinks of the "muselmann" who had given up hope and the last shreds of their humanity and who existed only as "a staggering corpse, a bundle of physical functions in its last convulsions" (Agamben, Chapter 57). The Muselmanner bore witness to "the total triumph of power over the human being" (ibid.). Their horrifyingly reduced condition led to their social abandonment by others in the camps.

The Gray Zone

Primo Levi, the Italian Jewish survivor of the IG Farben Petrochemical plant at Auschwitz, developed the concept of the gray zone which bears some family resemblance to Michael Taussig's space of death. Concentration camp inmates – like those who are disappeared, tortured or starving – are often forced into a morally ambiguous space of mutual betrayal and complicity with the enemy in exchange for the smallest personal advantage. The gray zone is populated by "a thousand sealed off monads" engaged in "a desperate, covert and continuous struggle" to survive (see Levi, Chapter 8).

Levi, an uncompromising moralist, dares to question Holocaust survivors, those like himself who did not die in the camps along with all the others because they were in some sense "privileged prisoners" (Levi 1988: 40). Such a relentless and unforgiving view of the survivor-as-betrayer can be understood as deriving from enormous grief and rage as well as survivor guilt. But Levi had something else in mind. He raises the question of how any one of us might have behaved in the camps. Would you or I have gone along with the ruse, deluding ourselves with the belief that I, at least, will be selected to work rather than to die? What would I be capable of doing in order to survive? Would I rather die a dehumanized "mummy-man" than make the mortal compromises necessary to stay alive?

Brazilian peasants from that country's drought and famine plagued Northeast states are, like Levi, aware that the "good" die young and that the ability to survive a natural or a manmade disaster requires "a knack for life" and a willingness to cheat death. The tactics used are not always morally upright ones. They comment of themselves as survivors, "None of us is innocent here."

While working on this anthology, Bourgois tape-recorded his father, who had always been reluctant to talk about his Second World War experiences. The elder Bourgois was a "civilian" (as Levi called such inmates) who was deported from the South of France to labor at the same IG Farben petrochemical plant as Levi, downwind from the gas chambers and crematoria. Finally, Bourgois senior relented and gave his son the following painfully rendered reflections:

"If there is anything I feel guilty about it's not knowing what was going on. I think all the time of this young Frenchman from the Jewish camp who worked with us during the day. We weren't allowed to talk to the Jewish prisoners, but when the guard wasn't looking, I spoke with him. He was about 22 or 24 years old and we were riding on the back of a flatbed truck. We crouched forward so the guard, a little old German with a big gun wouldn't hear... [whispering] 'They are starving us,' he told me, [lifting his pant leg to reveal his knee]. The joint of his knee was all swollen [pointing to the articulations of his own knee]. You could see the outline of the tibia meeting the base of the knee, visible through the skin.

"He told me that he had been taken from the 'champ de courses' to Auschwitz. And it is horrible to say, but I thought that he was a little bit stupid, 'Why the hell did this guy go to the horse races in the middle of the war in Paris?' Because when he said 'champ de courses' I thought he meant Longchamp where they race horses. I thought that he had been rounded up while exiting the races. But he was trying to tell me that he had been rounded up in the Vélodrome de Drancy where they race bicycles. I couldn't conceive that the French were rounding up the Jews into stadiums for deportation to work in Germany, let alone for extermination... That was in May of 1944. [pausing] Do you think that man could have survived?

"I too felt a little stupid because I had been picked up coming out of a movie theater in Nice at a routine checkpoint for identity papers. But I had a privileged job and I wasn't meant to die. I wasn't Jewish... The chief of my block liked me and used to serve me soup first and he dipped deeply from the bottom of the pot. When one of the others complained he threw his knife into the middle of the table, saying, 'I'm in command here and the little guy eats first.'

"The other non-Jewish workers used to joke when the smoke from the crematorium blew our way. They're burning pigs again today'... I didn't consciously reject anyone telling me that the Jews were being gassed, but when I escaped and told my friends in Paris – even the ones in the Resistance who were feeding me and helping me hide – that the Nazis were starving and working the Jews to death in huge camps, they thought I was exaggerating. When I tried to tell my father, he told me to shut up. He said, 'Certaines choses ne se dissent pas' [Certain things are best left unsaid]."

Forced collaboration in the Gray Zone does not always guarantee survival, of course, and very few of the "privileged" prisoners of the Sonderkommando survived. Sonderkommando were the Jews who were charged with responsibility for maintaining and administering the gas chambers. They lived in separate barracks; they ate better and they dressed more warmly than the common concentration camp inmates. We selected a short story by a Communist survivor, Tadeusz Borowski (Chapter 11), on one day in the life of a new Sonderkommando member at the Auschwitz train station. Sonderkommando represent the ultimate collaborators conflating victims and victimizer. Their first task was always to cremate the bodies of their predecessors. Levi sees the gray zone as the final moral challenge, and it recalls the imperative "to defend our souls when a similar test should once more loom before us, even if we only want to understand what takes place in a big, industrial factory" (Levi 1988: 40).

A similar message emerges from Spiegelman's comic-strip book *Maus*, with which we close this difficult section. Spiegelman, the son of an Auschwitz survivor, opens his book with his father warning him, "Friends? Your Friends? If you lock them together in a room with no food for a week then you could see what it is, friends!" (Spiegelman 1986: 5). The human capacity for infinite petty cruelty is not a particularly original lesson to come out of the Holocaust. Much more important is the implication that the preparation and schooling in "how to behave" during a holocaust or genocide takes place in very normal social contexts and institutions unfolding around us every day.

The Politics of Communal Violence

Bauman's (1989) thesis linking genocide to a specific level of state formation, technological efficiency, rationality and subjectivity is belied in many of the ethnographic examples included in this anthology. While the legal concept of genocide is new, the "eliminationist" impulse can be found under premodern as well as modern and late modern conditions. A spiritual charter for genocide appears in the Old Testament when God the Creator turns into Conan the Destroyer and unleashes his rage in a flood to destroy the world (save Noah and his family). The destruction of Sodom and Gomorra and King Herod's decree ordering the destruction of *all* first-born infant sons in Judea are other Biblical allusions to mass killing-as-usual.

Genocides and communal massacres have been attributed to "weak states" (Bayart 1993; Reno 1998) and to statelessness, as in Robert Kaplan's (1994) controversial "coming of anarchy" thesis to explain the political chaos and violence that has periodically erupted in postcolonial equatorial Africa, such as in Angola, Sierra Leone, and Congo. Conversely, genocides have been linked to strong, authoritarian, and bureaucratically efficient states, like Germany at mid-twentieth century (see Goldhagen 1997; Arendt, Chapter 9). Of course, genocides have also been identified as the products of individualism (Eichmann, for example) as well as its converse, communalism and obedience to authority (Gourevitch, Chapter 15).

Witch-hunts and witch burnings in parts of Africa and highland New Guinea have at times led to die-outs and to demographic collapse verging on genocide (see Knauft 1985; 1987). The impulse to identify and to eliminate all witches, seen as disease objects in some, especially horticultural, societies is motivated by a similar kind of "social hygiene" characteristic of genocide in modern, industrial states (see Douglas 1970). Indeed, mass killing, genocides, and provoked die-outs of scapegoated populations have occurred in pre-state societies, and in ancient as well as modern states.

In Part III on communal violence we are exploring another model of modern genocide – one based on proximity and intimacy (rather than on the bureaucratically impersonal) – in which there is a face-to-face and hand-to-hand mass murder of former neighbors, coworkers, and compatriots. Gourevitch (Chapter 15) sees the Hutu genocide of Rwandan Tutsis as a perverse "exercise in community building." We "balance," or rather, supplement this against Liisa Malkki's (Chapter 14) sympathetic portrait of Hutu refugees who are both former victims and future perpetrators of genocide. The circular chain of violence (cf. Mamdani, Chapter 61) is suggested in the sad, angry narratives of a devastated people "rearming" themselves in a Tanzanian relocation camp for battle as future *genocidaires* against their Tutsi enemies. Malkki presents her Hutu informants as taking heart from a "mythopoetic" history replete with race libels and blood vengeance. Do the ethnographer's cultural relativism and empathy with escaping Hutu refugees detract from the brewing genocide or do they offer a profound context-ualization – or both?

We accept the term "communal violence," but we argue against the Weberian false dichotomy that it suggests between modern, high-tech, hyperrationalized, and impersonal genocides versus premodern, low-tech, intimate, personal, and "charismatic" genocides. Hence, we included in the previous section (Part II) a detailed account by the historian Christopher Browning (Chapter 10) of the activities of the *Einsatzgruppen*, an elite group of German soldiers charged at an early stage in the Holocaust with the particularly gory command of marching tens of thousands of Jews into the woods, surrounding their villages, and shooting them at point blank range in the head or neck. It is a description that resembles the Rwandan hand-to-hand, face-to-face approach to genocide. It was only later into the Holocaust that the efficient, bureaucratized – even sanitized – higher-tech model of genocide, using the pesticide Zyclon B in the gas chambers, was implemented to assassinate millions more people, more rapidly, less bloodily, and out of the public view. The ultimate bureaucratization of genocide fostered not only the banality of Eichmann the Nazi factotum, but also the "gray zone" of mutual betrayals by victims. It produced a frightening normalization of everyday life in the camps such as Sunday soccer matches between Sonderkommando and SS guards, as recorded in the survivors' accounts of Levi and Borowski, and revisited by Agamben (Chapter 57).

Our selection and juxtaposition of articles also suggests the need to understand community-based killings in their relationship to weak central states and ideologies of racism. Hence, we place side by side an article on the lynching of African Americans in small towns of the rural south in the United States at the turn of the century (Litwack, Chapter 13) with one on the massacres of Tutsis in Rwanda and Hutus in Burundi in the 1980s and 1990s in equatorial Africa (Malkki, Chapter 14 and Gourevitch, Chapter 15). We are mindful, however, of the danger of evoking notions of irrational savagery in a vacuum of state power, postcoloniality, and the global political economy.

What Makes Genocide Possible?

With the shocking reappearance of mass killings in the late twentieth century – in Central Africa (Gourevitch and Malkki in this volume), South Asia (Das 1990; Daniels 1997), Eastern Europe (Olujic 1998), and in Central and South America (Danner, Chapter 41; Green, Chapter 21; Suarez-Orozco, Chapter 49; Pedelty, Chapter 52; and Robben, Chapter 23) – the world has witnessed the recurrence of what moral philosophers once thought could not happen again, following the Holocaust. The recurrence of atrocities forces us to revisit the question that so vexed a generation of post-Holocaust social theorists: *What makes genocide possible?* What, after all, can we say about the limits and capacities of human nature? How do we explain the complicity of ordinary people, the proverbial bystanders, during outbreaks of genocidal violence? Adorno and the post-Second World War Frankfurt School suggested that participation in genocidal acts requires a strong childhood conditioning that produces almost mindless obedience to authority figures. More recently Goldhagen (1997) argued to the contrary, that thousands of ordinary Germans participated willingly, even eagerly, in the Holocaust, not out of fear of punishment or retribution by authority figures but because they *chose* to do so, guided by sociopathological race hatred alone. What conditions made the unthinkable plausible and, worse, doable?

Modern theorists of genocide have proposed certain social-structural, political-economic, and cultural and psychological prerequisites necessary to mass participation in genocides. Indeed, mass killings rarely appear on the scene unbidden. They evolve. There are usually identifiable starting points or instigating circumstances, but they are never as linear, discrete, or predictable as theorists are wont to imply, and these preconditions do not "cause" genocides to occur. Genocides are often preceded by social upheavals, a radical decline in economic conditions, political disorganization, or precipitous sociocultural changes leading to an undermining of traditional values and widespread anomie, or normlessness. Conflict between competing groups over material resources – land, and water – can sometimes also escalate into mass slaughters when combined with social sentiments that question or denigrate the basic humanity of the opposing group. Extreme forms of "us" versus "them" can result in a social self-identity predicated on a stigmatized, devalued notion of the other as enemy.

The German example has alerted a generation of post-Second World War scholars to the pathologies of social conformity and the repression of dissent. More recently, the conflict in the Middle East, in the former Yugoslavia, and in many postcolonial societies of sub-Saharan Africa, has suggested that a past history of social suffering and woundedness, especially a history of racial victimization, leads to a vulnerability to explosions of retaliatory mass violence. A kind of collective post-traumatic stress disorder may predispose certain "wronged" populations to a hypersensitivity and hypervigilance that can lead to another cycle of slaughtering in "self defense" (cf. Mamdani, Chapter 61).

Ritual sacrifice and the search to identify a generative scapegoat – a social class or ethnic or racial group on which to pin the blame for the social and economic problems that arise – is also a common precondition in the evolution of genocide. Finally, there must be a shared ideology, a blueprint for living, a vision of the world and how to live that defines certain obstacles to the good or holy life in the form of certain kinds of people who must be removed, eliminated, wiped out. There is the belief that everyone will benefit from this social cleansing, even the dead themselves.

Finally, there must be a broad constituency of ordinary citizens who behave as bystanders either (as in the case of white South Africa) "allowing" race-hostile policies to continue without significant civil disobedience or (as in Nazi Germany and in Rwanda) who allow themselves obediently to be recruited in public acts of genocidal violence. Far less well analyzed, is the role of external or global "bystanders" including strong nation-states, and international and nongovernmental agencies, like the United Nations whose delays or refusals to intervene can aid and abet genocides at times when the tide could still be reversed. In the case of Rwanda, for example, UN peace-keepers were explicitly instructed to do nothing. Similarly, during the Holocaust and during the worst phases of apartheid's program of political terror, a great many US corporations, such as IBM, continued to do business-as-usual with the perpetrators of mass violence, and US Customs barred entry of Jewish refugees, deporting them back to face genocide. The origins and evolution of genocide are complex and multifaceted, but they are not inscrutable or unpredictable even if they are never reducible to our neat categories of political-economic, social-structural, cultural, or psychological preconditions.

Why Do People Kill?

There is something dangerously seductive about this question: the idea that killing can be explained by or linked to a specific set of biopsychological universals. And, indeed, everything from meat protein hunger to unbalanced sex ratios to faulty genes to male hormones to (most recently) the corrosive and explosive effects of social shame (Gilligan 1996) have been invoked in an attempt to answer this question. Such arguments understand pleasure in eating, in sex, in nursing a newborn, in social interaction, and in hunting and killing – as precultural, human attributes.

But to the cultural anthropologist there is no such thing as unmediated *natural* passions or emotions, for without our cultures we would hardly know how or what to feel. Scheper-Hughes has, for example, described Irish bachelors entering the bridal chambers with fear and trembling. She watched Brazilian shantytown mothers recoiling from offering a breast to a newborn, and she spoke with "dangerous" young lions who fled from ANC military camps in Angola because they could not imagine themselves killing another human being. Killing (like any other powerful human act) has to be learned. But once learned, the resistance to killing (like resistance to sex for those perennial shy Irish bachelors) can be readily overcome – or so the historical and anthropological record suggests.

In his frequently cited book, *On Killing* (which we found useful, but did not include in this anthology), Lt. Col. David Grossman, a former soldier and a professor of psychology at the US Military Academy at West Point, draws on his own battle experience as well as on interviews with veterans of American wars since the Second World War. The real trauma of war, he argues, is not about being killed but about killing, and he records the difficulty most new soldiers face in overcoming a profound disinclination to take the life of another person, even an enemy. But Grossman trades in simplistic biological universals when he posits the existence of a "violence immune system" as a natural human safety mechanism which any military must confront and overcome in training its new soldiers. Grossman argues that by and large human beings are profoundly uninterested in killing and when confronted for the first time with the command to do so often behave like "conscientious objectors" on the battlefield.

Indeed, in her conversations with young anti-apartheid militants in a South African shantytown, Scheper-Hughes was frequently told that killing was unnatural to most young anti-apartheid warriors and that township thugs ("skollies" and "totsies") had to be recruited into the military wings of the local ANC and PAC branches to perform the violent acts that most of the politicized young men could not bear to undertake themselves. "Do you think that Temba here [pointing to a local ANC political leader] would have the courage to burn a person alive with petrol? Poor as he is, he is not *born* to do that! He will never do that! But a born skollie has got the courage. He can attack a man in broad daylight. He has the ability to rape and to murder in front of all the people. Yes! He has got that crazy kind of courage. It is in his blood! So, we said, 'Give him the petrol! Give him the matches! He'll do the job for us! He will do what we could NEVER do!'" (Scheper-Hughes 1997: 492).

Additionally, a great deal of human fighting among those peoples considered to be exceptionally "prone" to violence often turns out to be staged, dramaturgical, and mock aggression, a kind of "locking horns" that inflicts relatively little damage. In the murderous urban shantytowns of Brazil (where homicide rates are among the highest in the world), when a serious knife fight is about the break out, the aggressors readily allow themselves to be restrained by their relatives and friends. And, as it turns out, up to a third of all reported homicides for urban Brazil are, in fact, the handiwork of the police. Amidst the recent accusations that Napoleon Chagnon's and Timothy Ash's ethnographic films of Yanomami aggression and warfare were staged by the anthropologist (see Tierney 2000), no one has raised the more obvious insight that Yanomami forms of warfare are largely dramaturgical events, based on posturing and dramatic displays of fierceness, entailing relatively little bloodshed. Chagnon and Ash's films are far more useful in demonstrating "sham" aggression than the "sham" anthropology that Tierney would have us see.

Sham killing was also characteristic of the great World Wars of Europe when it was discovered that the majority of new soldiers shot their rifles into the air well above their enemy targets. If David Grossman (1995) is correct, it was only during the Vietnam War that a conscripted military was effective in applying the principles of behavior modification and operant conditioning – repetition, desensitization tactics, rewards and punishment for hitting human-like decoys and targets such as watermelons painted like heads that explode in a spray of red liquid when hit directly by a bullet. US soldiers were successfully taught to overcome their inhibitions to killing Vietnamese communists and "gooks."

On the other hand, Stanley Milgram's classic behavioral experiment on blind obedience to authority (Chapter 16), with which we open Part IV, argues, to the contrary, for the enormous power of authoritative institutions to elicit incredibly cruel behavior from naive subjects, especially when conducted in the name of science. Milgram's laboratory study was designed in the historical shadow of the Nazi Holocaust to demonstrate how and why normally decent human beings – in this case ordinary Yale University students – could be recruited to commit an atrocity. In this instance, not a single volunteer research participant refused to administer severe electric shocks to counterfeit subjects, when instructed to do so by a scientist in a white coat.

Certainly by the time of the Vietnam War in the mid-twentieth century, American soldiers had learned not only to shoot to kill enemy fighters, but even to obey orders to massacre civilians. These resulted in other transgressive terrorist acts, including gang rape and the mutilation of the bodies of the enemy. Vietnam vets came home laden with war trophies taken from the killing fields, including scalps, gold teeth, and skulls. Girlfriends were sent bullets and bloodied handkerchiefs to wear as necklaces or ankle bracelets. This Bakhtinian "carnivalization" of sadistic death on the battlefield has long vexed anthropologists and other social scientists.

Here, Renato Rosaldo's (Chapter 17) painfully self-reflexive, almost literary, discussion of Ilongot headhunting is apropos. Rosaldo could not at first understand the blood lust and deep sense of enjoyment over taking a human head expressed by the ordinarily gentle horticultural villagers of the remote tribe in the Philippines. In this classic piece, Rosaldo argues that powerful emotions – especially the anger and grief following loss – are a primary motivating force in human action. This major figure in symbolic anthropology and a pioneer of the reflexive turn in cultural studies, evokes with great sensitivity the cultural logics that inform Ilongot enjoyment in killing their neighbors and preserving their heads. But like his mentor Geertz he neglects to supply the missing colonial historical context. He says almost nothing about the destruction of the Ilongot's jungle horticultural ecosystem under the guise of national "development" and their persecution under the Marcos dictatorship.

Hinton's article (Chapter 18) on the Cambodian genocide under Pol Pot draws explicitly from psychological anthropology and emphasizes the role of hierarchy, "face," and honor. In all, this section highlights the institutional relations and the larger social contexts that have consistently enabled humans to inflict so much systematic brutality on one another across historical epochs and in dramatically distinct cultural contexts.

The State Amok – Dirty Wars

Late modern history is disaster-haunted by world wars, guerrilla wars, civil wars, wars of liberation, and – most pervasively, even if invisibly – by dirty wars in which governments turn in fury against their own citizens suspected of harboring the seeds of subversion – state-terror-as-usual. Part V focuses primarily on Latin America in the 1980s and 1990s, but also explores links to the US government and military "state terrorism," especially relevant following 9/11 and the destruction of the World Trade Center in New York.

We open this section with Taussig's (Chapter 19) "talking terror" piece which harkens back to his essay (Chapter 2) on the cruelty of international rubber barons in the Colombian

Amazon, denounced in Casement's Putumayo report. In the context of a Colombian dirty war, victims and victimizers are conflated and power is exercised through the circulation of terror, but in the 1990s the perpetrator is the modern state itself. The terror operates quietly and secretly, below and between the lines, as it were, and in the blatant contradictions between "the official story" and what actually happens on the ground. The chaos and the terror are disguised behind a façade of normalcy, and the culture of terror moves between the space of death and the space of everyday life. In fact, everyday life is truly terrifying, whether in the form of political kidnappings and torture (as in Argentina [Robben, Chapter 23; Suarez-Orozco, Chapter 49], El Salvador [Bourgois, Chapter 56; Pedalty, Chapter 52] or Guatemala [Green, Chapter 21; Franco, Chapter 22], Colombia [Taussig, Chapter 19]), or in the daily experiences of the shantytown poor of northeast Brazil (Scheper-Hughes, Chapter 20), who live just one step away from the public morgue and the collective grave and whose only act of subversion is that they have managed to survive at all.

We have brought 9/11 into this section because we see another version of the state amok in the anarchic terrorist attacks. The most powerful military and economic state on earth, the United States, refuses to see, let alone attend to, the human suffering caused by its global economic and political policies (Chomsky, Chapter 25; Scheper-Hughes, Chapter 26).

Revolutionary Violence

Violence and political resistance on the cusp of the twenty-first century recall the classic debates of the mid-twentieth century about the necessity and glorious inevitability of violent revolutions to achieve national liberation in the context of anticolonial, socialist struggles in Africa, Asia, and Latin America. In Part VI we also explore more recent revolutionary mobilizations in the very different contexts of Northern Ireland and South Africa.

In the 1950s through the early 1980s, anticolonial struggles, inspired by ideals of socialist justice for peasants and workers in the nonindustrialized Third World emerging nations translated into a veritable celebration of armed struggle and revolutionary violence. The most articulate expression of this view was that of the Martiniquan psychiatrist, Frantz Fanon, in writing about his adopted country, Algeria, in *The Wretched of the Earth* (Chapter 58), seconded by Jean-Paul Sartre (Chapter 27).

The public debate between the two leading French public intellectuals of the day – Albert Camus (himself a colonial subject of France born and raised in an illiterate, white settler family in Algeria) and Jean-Paul Sartre (then an active member of the French Communist Party) – over the legitimacy of political violence and terror in the revolutionary struggle in Algeria remains one of the most painful and traumatic philosophical rifts in late modern times. Camus, a Christian humanist, rejected a form of violence that would harm naive bystanders. Forced to choose between a glorious ideal (the anticolonial struggle, which he otherwise supported) and his mother, Camus famously opted for nonviolence in the face of terrorism. "At this moment bombs are being thrown in the trolleys of Algiers and my mother might find herself in one of these trolleys, and if that's your justice, I prefer my mother to justice" (cited in Todd 1997: 379). Sartre (Chapter 27), in contrast, championed Third World revolutionary liberation struggles not merely by any means necessary, but preferably through bloody catharsis.

Inspired by Fanon-the-psychiatrist's extraordinary documentation of the internalization of structural and political violence – especially colonial racism – among Algerians, Sartre amplified Fanon's insistence that only acts of revolutionary violence could possibly emancipate the wretched of the earth, allowing them to become leaders of their own history: "In the first days of the revolt you must kill: to shoot down a European is to kill two birds with one stone, to destroy an oppressor and the man he oppresses at the same time: there remain a dead man, and a free man" (Sartre, Chapter 27, p. 229).

The Algerian revolution and the embrace of anticolonial armed struggle ushered in an optimistic period in which the colonized – and the *lumpen proletariat* more broadly – were celebrated as the organic vanguard of a new and just global order. From the revolt of Wounded Knee on the Sioux reservation in the northern plains of the United States to the struggles of the IRA in Northern Ireland (Begoña, Chapter 29) to the guerrilla revolutions of Nicaragua and El Salvador (Quesada, Chapter 35; Bourgois, Chapter 56) to the mobilization of the Black Panthers in inner-city Oakland in the early 1970s, and, finally, to the student–worker anarchist protests in Paris in May 1968 and in Italy a few months later, the global revolution of the New Left seemed almost at hand.

Hannah Arendt, one of the late twentieth century's most eminent political theorists, addressed some of the key questions confronting political theory during this period – from the origins of totalitarianism (Stalinism and Fascism) to the rationales for political violence in the colonial world to the ultra-leftist student movements of the late 1960s. Never a very comfortable or politically correct thinker, Arendt was an elitist who was rarely moved by political revolutionary arguments based on the problem of unmet basic human needs. While tolerant of the French student movement and the Vietnam antiwar movement, Arendt was a harsh critic of the American Black Power Movement. Her broadsheet *On Violence* (see Chapter 28) expressed her response to the student/worker revolutionary struggles of the mid-1960s *against the background* of the anticolonial revolutions of mid-twentieth century. *On Violence* was a frontal attack on "The New Left," and its embrace of the politics of armed struggle. She questioned the conventional view of political violence as the "most flagrant manifestation of power" and she argued instead that violence was the very antithesis and failure of power.

Indeed, almost four decades later, and following broad disillusionment with the failures and betrayals of national liberation revolutionary movements and socialist experiments in Europe, Asia, Africa, and Central America, a hegemony emerged around the desirability of a global economic system based on principles of democracy, human rights, and free markets (see Soros 1999). Meanwhile, violence and terrorism as expressions of political resistance have continued to proliferate from the Palestinian Intifada to the holy wars of Islamic fundamentalists poised against an exploitative world capitalist system and against Western, secular political and cultural dominance.

The righteous political demands of rural guerrilla fighters and urban rebels unified marginalized populations. Initially at least, the mobilization eradicated many everyday forms of violence which were acted out on the interpersonal level often by neighbors and spouses killing each other in drunken rages with machetes. At the end of the wars, however, and when peace was reestablished and overt political violence virtually disappeared, the everyday violence of suicide, and interpersonal and delinquent beatings of loved ones, neighbors, and crime victims often resumed with a vengeance (Quesada, Chapter 35; Bourgois, Chapter 56).

Even during the height of revolutionary struggles, when large numbers of people mobilized in support of national liberation movements, new forms of everyday interpersonal and (especially) gender-based violence reared their ugly heads, sometimes hidden in the rhetoric of liberation (Lancaster 1988; 1992). Some of it took the form of revolutionary or popular justice in which comrades and companheiros killed one another over perceptions and accusations of treachery, complicity with the police state, or even over different interpretations of political strategy (See Begoña, Chapter 29; Scheper-Hughes, Chapter 30). Ironically, revolutionary interpersonal relations are sometimes mimetic of state repression, operating both in response to, and as a reflection of, the logic of the same political repression that the revolutionaries were suffering at the hands of the government which they were trying to overthrow.

At the dawn of the twenty-first century, with the spread of a neoliberal social order across the globe, political violence has become passé among intellectuals even if actively practiced by millions of desperately angry people across the globe. Of central concern is a better understanding of the transition from popular political violence in revolutionary situations to the anomie of delinquent violence in the neoliberal social order that has occurred in so many settings. In the case of El Salvador, Bourgois (see Chapter 56) was unprepared for the rapidity and ease of the transition from political violence to crimnal and interpersonal violence in the neoliberal context of structural and symbolic violence. Retrospectively this allowed him to discover that the boundary between freedom fighter and coward is often ambiguous and inconsistent in counterinsurgency warfare. Yet again, a "liminal space of death" (Taussig 1987) or "gray zone" (Levi 1988) obfuscates responsibility from those primarily responsible for the terror that constitutes everyday life.

Peacetime Crimes

This large and at first sight "messy" Part VII is central to this anthology's thesis. It encompasses everything from the routinized, bureaucratized, and utterly banal violence of children dying of hunger and maternal despair in Northeast Brazil (Scheper-Hughes, Chapter 33) to elderly African Americans dying of heat stroke in Mayor Daly's version of US apartheid in Chicago's South Side (Klinenberg, Chapter 38) to the racialized class hatred expressed by British Victorians in their olfactory disgust of the "smelly" working classes (Orwell, Chapter 36). In these readings violence is located in the symbolic and social structures that overdetermine and allow the criminalized drug addictions, interpersonal bloodshed, and racially patterned incarcerations that characterize the US "inner city" to be normalized (Bourgois, Chapter 37 and Wacquant, Chapter 39). Violence also takes the form of class, racial, political self-hatred and adolescent self-destruction (Quesada, Chapter 35), as well as of useless (i.e. preventable), rawly embodied physical suffering, and death (Farmer, Chapter 34).

Absolutely central to our approach is a blurring of categories and distinctions between wartime and peacetime violence. Close attention to the "little" violences produced in the structures, habituses, and *mentalités* of everyday life shifts our attention to pathologies of class, race, and gender inequalities. More important, it interrupts the voyeuristic tendencies of "violence studies" that risk publicly humiliating the powerless who are often forced into complicity with social and individual pathologies of power because suffering is often a solvent of human integrity and dignity. Thus, in this anthology we are positing a violence continuum comprised of a multitude of "small wars and invisible genocides" (see also Scheper-Hughes 1996; 1997; 2000b) conducted in the normative social spaces of public schools, clinics, emergency rooms, hospital wards, nursing homes, courtrooms, public registry offices, prisons, detention centers, and public morgues. The violence continuum also refers to the ease with which humans are capable of reducing the socially vulnerable into expendable nonpersons and assuming the license – even the duty – to kill, maim, or soul-murder.

We realize that in referring to a violence and a genocide *continuum* we are flying in the face of a tradition of genocide studies that argues for the absolute uniqueness of the Jewish Holocaust and for vigilance with respect to restricted purist use of the term genocide itself (see Kuper 1985; Chaulk 1999; Fein 1990; Chorbajian 1999). But we hold an opposing and alternative view that, to the contrary, it is absolutely necessary to make just such existential leaps in purposefully linking violent acts in normal times to those of abnormal times. Hence the title of our volume: *Violence in War and in Peace*. If (as we concede) there is a moral risk in overextending the concept of "genocide" into spaces and corners of everyday life where we might not ordinarily think to find it (and there is), an even greater risk lies in failing to sensitize ourselves, in misrecognizing protogenocidal practices and sentiments daily enacted as normative behavior by "ordinary" good-enough citizens.

Peacetime crimes, such as prison construction sold as economic development to impoverished communities in the mountains and deserts of California, or the evolution of the criminal industrial complex into the latest peculiar institution for managing race relations in the United States (Waquant, Chapter 39), constitute the "small wars and invisible genocides" to which we refer. This applies to African American and Latino youth mortality statistics in Oakland, California, Baltimore, Washington DC, and New York City. These are "invisible" genocides not because they are secreted away or hidden from view, but quite the opposite. As Wittgenstein observed, the things that are hardest to perceive are those which are right before our eyes and therefore taken for granted.

In this regard, Bourdieu's partial and unfinished theory of violence (see Chapters 32 and 42) as well as his concept of misrecognition is crucial to our task. By including the normative everyday forms of violence hidden in the minutiae of "normal" social practices – in the architecture of homes, in gender relations, in communal work, in the exchange of gifts, and so forth – Bourdieu forces us to reconsider the broader meanings and status of violence, especially the links between the violence of everyday life and explicit political terror and state repression.

Similarly, Basaglia's notion of "peacetime crimes" – *crimini di pace* – imagines a direct relationship between wartime and peacetime violence. Peacetime crimes suggests the possibility that war crimes are merely ordinary, everyday crimes of public consent applied systematically and dramatically in the extreme context of war. Consider the parallel uses of rape during peacetime and wartime, or the family resemblances between the legalized violence of US immigration and naturalization border raids on "illegal aliens" versus the US government-engineered genocide in 1938, known as the Cherokee "Trail of Tears." Peacetime crimes suggests that everyday forms of state violence make a certain kind of domestic peace possible. Internal "stability" is purchased with the currency of peacetime crimes, many of which take the form of professionally applied "strangle-holds."

Everyday forms of state violence during peacetime make a certain kind of domestic "peace" possible. It is an easy-to-identify peacetime crime that is usually maintained as a public secret by the government and by a scared or apathetic populace. Most subtly, but no less politically or structurally, the phenomenal growth in the United States of a new military, postindustrial prison industrial complex has taken place in the absence of broad-based opposition, let alone collective acts of civil disobedience. The public consensus is based primarily on a new mobilization of an old fear of the mob, the mugger, the rapist, the Black man, the undeserving poor. How many public executions of mentally deficient prisoners in the United States are needed to make life feel more secure for the affluent? What can it *possibly* mean when incarceration becomes the "normative" socializing experience for ethnic minority youth in a society, i.e., over 33 percent of young African American men (Prison Watch 2002).

In the end it is essential that we recognize the existence of a genocidal capacity among otherwise good-enough humans and that we need to exercise a defensive hypervigilance to the less dramatic, permitted, and even rewarded everyday acts of violence that render participation in genocidal acts and policies possible (under adverse political or economic conditions), perhaps more easily than we would like to recognize. Under the violence continuum we include, therefore, all expressions of radical social exclusion, dehumanization, depersonalization, pseudospeciation, and reification which normalize atrocious behavior and violence toward others. A constant self-mobilization for alarm, a state of constant hyperarousal is, perhaps, a reasonable response to Benjamin's view of late modern history as a chronic "state of emergency" (Taussig, Chapter 31).

We are trying to recover here the classic anagogic thinking that enabled Erving Goffman, Jules Henry, C. Wright Mills, and Franco Basaglia among other mid-twentieth-century radically critical thinkers, to perceive the symbolic and structural relations, i.e., between inmates and patients, between concentration camps, prisons, mental hospitals, nursing homes, and other "total institutions." Making that decisive move to recognize the continuum of violence allows us to see the capacity and the willingness – if not enthusiasm – of ordinary people, the practical technicians of the social consensus, to enforce genocidal-like crimes against categories of rubbish people. There is no primary impulse out of which mass violence and genocide are born, it is ingrained in the common sense of everyday social life.

The mad, the differently abled, the mentally vulnerable have often fallen into this category of the unworthy living, as have the very old and infirm, the sick-poor, and, of course, the despised racial, religious, sexual, and ethnic groups of the moment. Erik Erikson referred to "pseudo-speciation" as the human tendency to classify some individuals or social groups as less than fully human – a prerequisite to genocide and one that is carefully honed during the unremarkable peacetimes that precede the sudden, "seemingly unintelligible" outbreaks of mass violence.

Collective denial and misrecognition are prerequisites for mass violence and genocide. But so are formal bureaucratic structures and professional roles. The practical technicians of everyday violence in the backlands of Northeast Brazil (Scheper-Hughes, Chapter 33), for example, include the clinic doctors who prescribe powerful tranquilizers to fretful and frightfully hungry babies, the Catholic priests who celebrate the death of "angel-babies," and the municipal bureaucrats who dispense free baby coffins but no food to hungry families.

Everyday violence encompasses the implicit, legitimate, and routinized forms of violence inherent in particular social, economic, and political formations. It is close to what Bourdieu (1977, 1996) means by "symbolic violence," the violence that is often "mis-recognized" for something else, usually something good. Everyday violence is similar to what Taussig (1989) calls "terror as usual." All these terms are meant to reveal a public secret – the hidden links between violence in war and violence in peace, and between war crimes and "peace-time crimes."

Bourdieu (1977) finds domination and violence in the least likely places – in courtship and marriage, in the exchange of gifts, in systems of classification, in style, art, and culinary taste – the various uses of culture. Violence, Bourdieu insists, is everywhere in social practice. It is misrecognized because its very everydayness and its familiarity render it invisible. Lacan identifies "méconnaissance" as the prerequisite of the social. The exploitation of bachelor sons, robbing them of autonomy, independence, and progeny, within the structures of family farming in the European countryside that Bourdieu escaped is a case in point (Bourdieu, Chapter 42; see also Scheper-Hughes, 2000b; Favret-Saada, 1989).

Following Gramsci, Foucault, Sartre, Arendt, and other modern theorists of power-violence, Bourdieu treats direct aggression and physical violence as a crude, uneconomical mode of domination; it is less efficient and, according to Arendt (1969), it is certainly less legitimate. While power and symbolic domination are not to be *equated* with violence – and Arendt argues persuasively that violence is to be understood as a failure of power – violence, as we are presenting it here, is more than simply the expression of illegitimate physical force against a person or group of persons. Rather, we need to understand violence as encompassing all forms of "controlling processes" (Nader 1997b) that assault basic human freedoms and individual or collective survival. Our task is to recognize these gray zones of violence which are, by definition, not obvious.

Once again, the point of bringing into the discourses on genocide everyday, normative experiences of reification, depersonalization, institutional confinement, and acceptable death is to help answer the question: What makes mass violence and genocide possible? In this volume we are suggesting that mass violence is part of a continuum, and that it is socially incremental and often experienced by perpetrators, collaborators, bystanders – and even by victims themselves – as expected, routine, even justified. The preparations for mass killing can be found in social sentiments and institutions from the family, to schools, churches, hospitals, and the military. They harbor the early "warning signs" (Charney 1991), the "priming" (as Hinton, ed., 2002 calls it), or the "genocidal continuum" (as we call it) that push social consensus toward devaluing certain forms of human life and lifeways from the refusal of social support and humane care to vulnerable "social parasites" (the nursing home elderly, "welfare queens," undocumented immigrants, drug addicts) to the militarization of everyday life (super-maximum-security prisons, capital punishment; the technologies of heightened personal security, including the house gun and gated communities; and reversed feelings of victimization).

Gendered Violence

Because it is difficult to conceive of violence without addressing its almost inevitably gendered contours, a separate category for gendered violence risks obscuring the extent to which gender operates throughout all forms of violence. We developed this separate Part VIII, however, to address a range of gender violences – some obviously visible, cruel, and bloody such as wartime rape (Das, Chapter 40; Danner, Chapter 41) and peacetime rape (Bourgois, Chapter 43; Donaldson, Chapter 44), and others deeply structural and symbolic (Cohn, Chapter 45). In each example, however, the violence is structured to harness cultural notions of femininity, masculinity, procreation, and nurturance and to put them into the service of state wars and mass murder or to fuel peacetime forms of domination that make the subordinate participate in their own socially imposed suffering (Bourdieu, Chapter 42).

Carol Cohn's (Chapter 45) semiotic and ethnographic analysis of how the horrors of nuclear warfare can be normalized through the clean professional languages of science and technology gives new meaning to Benjamin's perception of modernity as a constant state of siege. Our selections on the uses and meanings of rape purposefully span both peacetime and wartime, as well as male and female victims on the battlefield, in prison and in the inner city. Their juxtaposition demonstrates the normalization and institutionalization of this most extreme form of gendered violence.

Whether male or female bodies are being raped, whether individually or collectively, whether in times of conflict or peace, rape is an act of violence against the female or the feminized male body and against the male owners and supposed protectors of those same bodies. The interface of the three bodies – individual, social, political – (Scheper-Hughes and Lock 1987) is shown to be at stake in the sexual assault on female bodies as war booty (Das, Chapter, 40; Danner, Chapter 41), as expression of adolescent rage (Bourgois, Chapter 43), and as involuted institutional hierarchy. Bourdieu considers gendered oppression to be a classic example of symbolic violence whereby hierarchies are naturalized into a common sense discourse shared by the dominated and the dominant. Once again, Bourdieu forces us to recognize the continuum that links the gendered violence of war rape of a deceptively trivial patriarchal aesthetic that makes women want to marry taller men.

Torture and Modernity

The Foucauldian narrative, spelled out most clearly in his *Discipline and Punish*, would have us believe that over the past 200 years torture has been superseded as a legitimate tool of the state. It has allegedly been replaced by more efficient, softer methods for extracting confessions of guilt as well as instilling popular "consent" to the authority of the state by obedient citizens. The black hooded torturer/executioner and the black robed Inquisitioner of the *ancien régime* has given way – or so Foucault suggests – to new social techniques and technicians of governmentality – labor management specialists, urban planners, media technicians, educators, civil servants, and, of course, doctors, counselors, psychiatrists, and social workers. But *pace* Foucault, during the latter half of the twentieth century there was a repugnant modernization and bloody escalation of the official uses of physical and psychological torture (Fanon, Chapter 58) – epitomized in the phenomenon of the disappeared (Suarez-Orozco, Chapter 49; Taussig, Chapter 19).

In the southern cone of South America during the 1970s and 1980s state torture was used in a new way – preventively and as a kind of political inoculation designed to nip threatening, "contaminating," or subversive ideas in the bud. In Argentina, Chile, Uruguay, and Brazil, those who were kidnapped, detained, tortured, and killed often had nothing to confess save their innocence and, failing that their own unwillingness to be killed (Weschler 1990). Consequently, forced confessions, suspect since the Enlightenment, once again became "credible" forms of eliciting truth (see *New York Times*, March 3, 2003).

In the late twentieth century, more refined and efficient forms of state torture were invented to wrest absolute and unconditional consent to the state, such as the torture of children in front of their parents and vice versa (Suarez-Orozco, Chapter 49). Torture reemerged as a tolerated political tactic, not only in authoritarian states like South Africa under apartheid, or Argentina during the Dirty War years, but in democratizing states like Brazil in the mid-1980s, and, more subtly, as a public secret in "mature" democracies like the US, in the aftermath of 9/11 or in the use of solitary confinement as a routinized punishment within new "super max" facilities built to contain an ever-expanding number of petty, drug-related offenders in the early twenty-first century (see Rhodes in press; Gilmore in press). Following the Al Qaeda attack on the Twin Towers of the World Trade Center and the Pentagon, public debates, unimaginable before "9/11," have emerged about the possible uses of torture to solicit information from terrorists about future planned attacks in order "to save thousands of lives" (see CBS, *60 Minutes*, Sunday, Sept. 21, 2002).

How are we to understand the late modern uses of state-level torture? Torture resides, of course, not only in explicit acts of bodily violence and violation but also in the reversals and interruptions of the expected and the predictable, striking terror in the ontological security of one's lifeworld. As Elaine Scarry (Chapter 46) has famously described it, torture silences and wrecks language, obliterating words and writing, and thereby *de-scribing* experience. Torture inverts and destroys the given, the commonsense reality, including one's taken-for-granted experience of embodiment, casting doubt on one's very existence ("Am I real? Is this *really* happening to me? Is this a dream?" [see Strejilevich 1997]). Torture produces a profound sort of existential nausea and silence cemented by terror and/or shame for not having remained silent.

Paraphrasing Maurice Blanchot (1995), it is not so much what one undergoes in torture as what *goes under* with it – i.e., everything that structures human existence: time, space, touch, the senses, and the sentient world. More important, torture obliterates hope and erases the possibility of a future with its long-term traumatic sequel – especially when the shame and guilt of having given up the names of comrades continually assaults survivors of tortures as an ongoing dynamic of symbolic violences. Torture breaks all limits. It is the ultimate spoiler that takes and ruins everything in its path while seeming to leave everything intact.

The apartheid government's security forces "reinvented" "primitive" witch burnings and they discarded their political enemies by slowly burning them – sometimes while still alive – over barbecue pits fashioned after the traditional Afrikaner family picnic known as the briaii (Scheper-Hughes, Chapter 60). The accused "terrorists" (i.e. politicized young Black men) were kidnapped and brought into peaceful forest clearings where they were made to gather sticks and to build the bonfires over which succulent Afrikaner sausages would be roasted and eaten while cold bottles of beer and coca-cola were passed around the fire until the time came for the suspect to be interrogated, tortured, killed, and roasted as well (see Feldman 2002). The Brazilian and Argentinean military's "parrot's perch" for breaking backs and for suffocating could be a tool and technique straight out of the Catholic Inquisition. True, the Argentine military did use modern planes to dispose of the dead bodies produced by their medieval tortures, air-dropping them into the ocean.

Meanwhile, the presumably modern invention of political "disappearances" are spoken about by the terrorized populations subject to these roundups for mass slaughter in the premodern idiom of "body snatching," "blood and organ stealing" (Scheper-Hughes 2001). In Argentina during the Dirty War, for example, widespread rumors of adult- and child-stealing for organs were readily denied by public officials representing INCUCAI, the national system in place for harvesting and distributing human organs from the brain dead. Meanwhile, however, mutilated bodies of the profoundly mentally retarded were later discovered on the grounds of Montes de Oca public mental asylum, also reputed to be a site for the detainment and torture of political prisoners (Scheper-Hughes 2003).

Modern torture is, above all, "smart torture" carefully designed to leave no physical scars, no tell-tale marks on the body. At the trial in 1994 of the township youths charged in the stoning death of American student Amy Biehl at the Cape Town Supreme Court, the three young men singled out as the ring leaders of a spontaneous mob, protested that their signed confessions (the *only* evidence available to the apartheid state in transition) had been ex-tracted through police torture. The responsible Afrikaner police officer, Mr. Du Plessey, responded to the charge by subjecting the young men to a careful, forensic medical examin-ation to prove (he said) that the many scars and marks on the bodies of the accused were old wounds resulting from *domestic* rather than *police* violence and from township brawls and knife fights, untreated skin infections, and badly set broken bones. In short, the public spectacle of those bodies revealed only the ordinary wounds of the everyday and structural violences of township life under apartheid. No politically inflicted "fresh wounds" caused by police interrogation could be identified to support the young men's defense, according to officer Du Plessey.

An especially sadistic South African security officer known for his theatrical, bipolar swings from "good" to "bad" cop, badgered one of his victims during the South African Truth and Reconciliation hearings: "Don't you remember the good times we had together? Once, on the road to Vakplas [the brutal police interrogation and torture center] we stopped at the

'Kentucky Fry' shop and you ate more chicken, you said, than you had ever eaten at one time in all your life. We stopped the car and we rough-housed in an open field? Don't you remember that?" The victim conceded that he was half starving and had, indeed, enjoyed the finger-licking good chicken, but not the sadistic game of chicken – a form of torture – that preceded and followed that brief interlude.

Another form of torture as psychological warfare appears in the claims made by police torturers (see Krog, Chapter 48) and other such officially sanctioned sadists to the "sickness exception" (see Parsons 1972). Through the cover offered in post-traumatic stress disorder (PTSD). This phenomenon, which evolved out of the "war neuroses," "battle fatigue," and "shell shock" cases of the two World Wars (Young 1995), was enlarged and expanded, following the 1960s, to include other populations exposed to severely traumatizing experiences, from kidnap to rape to police interrogation. Judith Herman (Chapter 47), a radical feminist psychotherapist, is one of the strongest advocates of PTSD being applied in the context of domestic violence and rape, now understood as a gendered form of torture during war and peacetime alike.

But we do have to ask what kind of social and political morality is created by a diagnosis (PTSD) that can fall equally on the victim and the executioner – on Vietnam war criminals (see Young 1995), police torturers (Antjie Krog, Chapter 48) *and* their victims? Scarry (Chapter 46) via Bourdieu (Chapter 42) reveals another dimension of the disabling and reproductive symbolic violence that emerges from focusing on the torturer rather than the tortured. In the archives of the Supreme Court of Cape Town Scheper-Hughes read through many transcripts in which police interrogators, increasingly on the defense, at the close of the apartheid state, looked for sympathy from a newly conscience-struck court: "We suffered too. Do you think it is easy to stay awake for 24 hours interrogating a terrorist? We skipped meals and went without sleep too." Sergeant Benzien, the man behind the infamous "wet bag" torture technique, defended his lapses in memory, his chaotic emotions, his rage, and his tears as the symptoms of PTSD through the pitifully amateurish testimony of his clinical psychologist, Ria Kotze. Benzien claimed he could not remember exactly what he had done to whom. At various moments during his long hearing before the South African TRC (not covered in Krog's brief report) Benzien presented himself as just another victim of apartheid. To the outside observer Benzien remains an unreconstituted political monster, but to Justice Albie Sachs (Chapter 59) there is room in the New South Africa even for the likes of Sergeant Benzien.

Perhaps the real contribution of medicalized approaches to the traumatic residues of torture and abuse is that they recognize links between perpetrator and victim. Torturer and tortured participate in the other's world, not only in terms of bad faith and false consciousness, but also when Sergeant Benzien identifies with Tony Yengeni, as his double, his Conradian secret sharer. Perhaps one of the great insights of the post-Holocaust twentieth century is that we can no longer assume an absolute incommensurability between victims and perpetrators. We have finally entered the gray zone.

Ethnographic Witnessing

Section X on "Witnessing/Writing Violence" is posed as a basic challenge to twenty-first-century modern anthropology. Only one nonanthropologist – a comic-strip writer – is featured in this section, which is meant to be an unabashed clarion for frank political engagement in situations of genocide and chronic structural violence. Contrary to Taussig's view that writing against violence might be impossible (or actually backfire), we are willing to strike a compromise, recognizing the weakness and limitations of ethnography but suggesting a more human role of engaged witness over that of scientific spectator. This requires a certain wariness of the ways that naive fieldworkers can fall prey to delusions of political activist grandeur or to becoming pornographers of violence. Here we are thinking of Clifford Geertz's insightful critique of the privilege of first-world ethnographic authority (as "I-witnessing") and, by analogy, of the images of the AIDS sufferer that Benetton used on billboards to advertise their line of clothing. There is always the intellectual trap of ethnographic realist writing posing as political activism *per se*.

Anthropologists who make their living observing and recording the misery of the world have a special obligation to reflect critically on the impact of the brutal images of human suffering that they foist on the public. As medical anthropologists our terrain is the suffering body. The texts and images we present to the world are often profoundly disturbing. When we report and write in an intimate way about scenes of violence, genocide, and extreme social suffering, our readers have the right to react with anger and to ask just what we are after (after all)? Indeed, what do we want from our audience? To shock? To evoke pity? To create new forms of totalizing narrative through an "aesthetic" of misery? What of the people whose suffering is being made into a public spectacle for the sake of the theoretical argument?

Our years of observing many different forms of misery, violence, and chronic social suffering has shown us that the more frequent and ubiquitous the images of sickness, suffering, and death, the more likely they are to become invisible. Shock reactions to blood and violence are readily extinguished. People everywhere have an enormous capacity to absorb the hideous and go on with life and business as usual. As Taussig (Chapter 19) notes, humans have an uncanny ability to hold terror and misery at arm's length, even when it occurs very close to home.

Those for whom the representation of hunger, misery, and violence is central to their life's work, need to continually resensitize their audiences as well as themselves to the state of emergency in which we live. To do so we must locate the proper distance from our subjects. Not so distant so as to objectify their suffering, and not so close that we turn the sufferer into an object of pity, contempt, or public spectacle. We need to avoid the aestheticization of misery as much as a descent into political rhetoric and polemics.

In a rural squatter camp in South Africa Scheper-Hughes was invited to record (and to photograph) the wounded bodies of three young thieves who had been flogged almost to their deaths (Scheper-Hughes, Chapter 30). When she tried to back away, her field assistant, Sidney Khamalo countered: "You must do it for evidence." And this record was, in fact, used at several open-air meetings in the Chris Hani squatter camp during an acrimonious debate on the role and place of popular justice, discipline, and punishment in the context of the new democratic South Africa. After defying the codes of rough justice that obtained in the camp, Scheper-Hughes brought one of the flogged thieves to a nearby hospital for treatment. Death threats ensued and she was, ultimately, brought to a camp meeting where she was asked to justify her actions, probably the most terrifying moment in an anthropological career marked by a certain degree of political contentiousness.

Anthropological witnessing obviously positions the anthropologist inside human events as a responsive, reflexive, and morally or politically committed being, a person who can be counted on to "take sides" when necessary and to eschew the privileges of neutrality. This stance flies directly in the face of academic non-engagement. The gift of the ethnographer remains, however, some combination of thick description, eye-witnessing, and radical juxtaposition based on cross-cultural insight. But the rules of our living-in and living-with peoples in dramatic flux, often on the verge of extermination, remain as yet unwritten, perhaps even unspoken. There is no appropriate distance to take from our subjects during torture, lynching, or rape. What kinds of participant-observation, what sort of eye-witnessing, are adequate to scenes of genocide and its aftermath, or even to structural violence and ethnocide? When the anthropologist is witness to crimes against humanity mere scientific empathy is not sufficient. At what point does the anthropologist as eye witness become a bystander or even a co-conspirator?

These remain vexing and unresolved issues. But the original mandate of anthropology and ethnography remains clear: to put ourselves and our discipline squarely on the side of humanity, world-saving, and world-repair, even though we may not always be certain about exactly what this means or what is being asked of us at any particular moment. In the final analysis we can only hope that our time-honored methods of empathic and engaged witnessing, of "being with" and "being there" – as tired as these old concepts may seem – will provide us with the tools necessary for anthropology to emerge as a small practice of human liberation.

Aftermaths: Getting Over

This leads quite naturally into our final Part, "Aftermaths," which corrects the celebratory impulse and contradicts banal assertions of personal and political closure and reconciliation. Instead, these readings open a Pandora's box of ongoing conflict in states poised between war and peace. South Africa's much-heralded political transition offers a classic case in point. In the first decade of the new South Africa the political violence of the anti-apartheid struggle metamorphosed into criminal and delinquent violence arising in the economically marginalized shantytowns that are the legacy of apartheid. Talk of reconciliation and of restorative justice side-track the legitimate demand for *redistributive* justice, a call that strikes terror into the hearts and minds of those who still believe in the trickle-down effects of global capitalism. Similarly, in El Salvador, criminal violence killed more people than wartime violence during the 10 years following the peace accords and the end of the civil war in 1991.

Many wounded nations and populations – from post-military-dictatorship Chile to post-apartheid South Africa to post-genocide Rwanda and Guatemala – have put their faith in international tribunals or in independent truth commissions to deal with the ghosts of the past. At times this has meant uncovering mass graves and reburying the unquiet dead. At other times – as in the South African Truth and Reconciliation Commission – this has meant a complicated political gamble in which justice is traded for truth. But the very idea that individuals and nations can heal and ultimately recover from violence falls prey to inappropriate and impoverished medical and psychological metaphors. The history of human violence teaches us that there are few happy endings. The only answer to violence resides in the struggle to maintain a constant state of hypervigilance and a steadfast refusal to turn into the very same enemy and *genocidaire* that one most fears and hates.

NOTES

1   In testimony presented to a United Nations Forum organized by the World Council of Churches, Bourgois had to remove at the insistence of his anthropology graduate program his photographic evidence of massacred civilians, lest he violate an interpretation of anthropological ethics mandating the unconditional anonymity of research subjects/collaborators (United Nations Economic and Social Council 1982; see also Bourgois 1991).

2   See, for example, the controversy surrounding *Darkness in El Dorado* by Patrick Tierney (Tierney 2000; American Anthropological Association 2002).

3   For a notable exception to this rule see the edited volume *Sanctions for Evil* edited by Nevitt Sanford and Craig Comstack, 1971, a project organized in response to the My Lai massacre during the Vietnam War and to which a few anthropologists contributed.
4   This point, made by Elliott Leyton at the plenary session of the Canadian Anthropological Society in 1997, belies the substantial contributions he has made to ethnographies of violence – from the structural violence of mining (Leyton 1975) to the pathological hatred that drives serial murderers [Hunting Heads] to collective responses to African genocide (Leyton 1998).
5   On August 9, 2002, the remains of Ms. Baartmann, who was sold in 1810, and paraded in England and France in local freakshows, were buried with honor in Hankey, South Africa, following a long struggle by South Africa's "colored" community over her repatriation.
6   The late canon law scholar, David Daube, who had himself escaped Nazi Germany and later helped several of his relatives to escape the camps as well, once told Scheper-Hughes that in answer to a naive question from a young grandchild about who this man Hitler was, and whether he was a good man or bad, he responded: "It doesn't matter." When questioned about the logic of this response David replied that it pleased him enormously that the memory of the Holocaust was dying in the younger generation so that they could be free of the terrible burden of the memory.

REFERENCES

American Anthropological Association. 2002. "El Dorado Taskforce Papers." Electronic document, http://www.aaanet.org/edtf/final/preface.htm. Accessed March 6, 2003.

Arendt, Hannah. 1963. *Eichmann in Jerusalem: A Report on the Banality of Evil*. New York: Viking Press.

——. 1969. *On Violence*. New York: Harcourt, Brace and World, Inc., pp. 3–87.

Arnold, Betinna. 2002. "Justifying Genocide: Archaeology and the Construction of Difference." In A. Hinton, ed., *Annihilating Difference: The Anthropology of Genocide*. Berkeley: University of California Press, pp. 95–116.

Asad, Talal, ed. 1973. *Anthropology and the Colonial Encounter*. New York: Humanity Books.

Basaglia, Franco. 1987. "Institutions of Violence." *Psychiatry Inside Out: Selected Writings of Franco Basaglia*, ed. Nancy Scheper-Hughes. New York: Columbia University Press, pp. 59–85.

Bauman, Zygmunt. 1989. *Modernity and the Holocaust*. Ithaca, NY: Cornell University Press.

Bayart, Jean-François. 1993. "The Politics of the Belly." *The State in Africa: The Politics of the Belly*. London: Longman, pp. 228–59.

Benjamin, Walter. 1968 [1940]. *Illuminations: Essays and Reflections*, ed. Hannah Arendt. New York: Schocken Books.

Blanchot, Maurice. 1995. *The Writing of the Disaster*. Lincoln and London: University of Nebraska Press.

Boonzaier, Emile and John Sharp, eds. 1988. *South African Key Words*. Cape Town, South Africa: Phillips.

Borneman, John. 1997. *Settling Accounts: Violence, Justice, and Accountability in Postsocialist Europe*. Princeton: Princeton University Press.

Bourdieu, Pierre. 1977. "Symbolic Power," trans. Colin Wringe. In Denis Gleeson, ed. *Identity and Structure: Issues in the Sociology of Education*. Driffield, England: Nafferton Books, pp. 112–19.

——. 1997. *Pascalian Meditations*. Stanford: Stanford University Press.

Bourgois, Philippe. 1982. "Running for My Life in El Salvador: An American Caught in a Government Attack that Chiefly Killed Civilians." *The Washington Post*. Feb. 14, pp. C1, C5.

——. 1991. "Confronting the Ethics of Ethnography: Lessons from Fieldwork in Central America." In Faye Harrison, ed., *Decolonizing Anthropology: Moving Further Toward an Anthropology for Liberation*. Washington, DC: American Anthropological Association, pp. 110–26.

——. 1995. *In Search of Respect: Selling Crack in El Barrio*. New York: Cambridge University Press, pp. 198–212 and pp. 267–76.

——. 1999. "Reconfronting Violence in El Salvador and the US Inner City with a Cold War Hangover." Paper presented to the Society for Cultural Anthropology, San Francisco, May 1999.

Camus, Albert. 1960. "The Artist and His Time." In *Resistance, Rebellion and Death*. New York: Alfred A. Knopf, pp. 181–9.

Centro de Investigación y Estudios de la Reforma Agraria (CIERA) [Bourgois, Philippe and Georg Grünberg]. 1981. "Informe de una Investigación Rural en la Costa Atlántica norte." In *La Mosquitia en la Revolución*. Managua, Nicaragua: CIERA, Coleccion Blas Real Espinales, pp. 89–149.

Chagnon, Napoleon A. 1968. *Yanomamo: The Fierce People*. New York: Holt Rinehart and Winston.

Chaulk, Frank. 1999. "Redefining Genocide." In L. Chorbajian and G. Shirinian, eds., *Studies in Comparative Genocide*. New York: St. Martin's Press, pp. 47–63.

Chorbajian, Levon. 1999. "Introduction." In L. Chorbajian and G. Shirinian, eds., *Studies in Comparative Genocide*. New York: St. Martin's Press, pp. xv–xxxv.

Churchill, Ward. 1997. *A Little Matter of Genocide: Holocaust and Denial in the Americas, 1492 to the Present*. San Francisco: City Lights Books.

Daniel, Valentine E. 1996. *Charred Lullabies: Chapters in an Anthropology of Violence*. Princeton: Princeton University Press.

Das, Veena. 1990. "Our Work to Cry: Yours Work to Listen." In Veena Das, ed., *Mirrors of Violence*. Delhi: Oxford University Press, pp. 345–98.

Douglas, Mary. 1970. *Natural Symbols*. London: Barrie & Rockliff.

Favret-Saada, Jeanne. 1989. "Unbewitching as Therapy." *American Ethnologist* 16(1): 40–56.

Fein, Helen. 1990. "Genocide – A Sociological Perspective." *Current Sociology* 38: 23–35.

Feitlowitz, Marguerite. 1998. *A Lexicon of Terror: Argentina and the Legacies of Torture*. New York: Oxford University Press, pp. 48–62.

Feldman, Alan. 1991. *Formations of Violence: The Narrative of the Body and Political Terror in Northern Ireland*. Chicago: University of Chicago Press.

——. 2002. "Strange Fruit: The South African Truth Commission and the Demonic Economies of Violence." *Social Analysis* 46(3):234–65.

Feuchtwang, Stephan. 1982. "The Colonial Formation of British Social Anthropology." In Talal Asad, ed., *Anthropology and the Colonial Encounter*. New York: Humanity Books.

Foucault, Michel. 1979. *Discipline and Punish: The Birth of the Prison*. New York: Vintage.

Geertz, Clifford. 1973 [1972]. "Deep Play: Notes on the Balinese Cockfight." In *The Interpretation of Cultures*. New York: Basic Books.

——. 1995. *After the Fact: Two Countries, Four Decades, One Anthropologist*. Cambridge, MA: Harvard University Press.

Gilligan, James. 1996. *Violence: Reflections on a National Epidemic*. New York: Basic Books.

Gilmore, Ruthie. In press. *Golden Gulag: Labor, Land, State, and Opposition in Globalizing California*. Berkeley: University of California Press.

Gladwell, Malcom. 1996. "The Tipping Point." *The New Yorker*, June 3, 1996.

Goldhagen, Daniel Jonah. 1997. *Hitler's Willing Executioners: Ordinary Germans and the Holocaust*. New York: Vintage.

Gourevitch, Philip. 1998. *We wish to inform You That Tomorrow We Will Be Killed with Our Families: Stories from Rwanda*. New York: Farar, Strauss and Giroux.

Gow, David. 1993. "Doubly Damned: Dealing with Power and Praxis in Development Anthropology." *Human Organization* 52(4): 380.

Green, Linda. 1999. *Fear as a Way of Life*. New York: Columbia University Press.

Grossman, David. 1995. *On Killing: The Psychological Cost of Learning to Kill in War and Society*. Boston: Little, Brown and Co.

Harris, Marvin and Eric B. Ross. 1987. *Food and Evolution: Toward a Theory of Human Food Habits*. Philadelphia: Temple University Press.

Herman, Judith. 1992. *Trauma and Recovery*. New York: Basic Books.

Hinton, Alexander, ed. 2002. *Annihilating Difference: The Anthropology of Genocide*. Berkeley: University of California Press.

Human Rights Watch. 2000. *Out of Sight: Super-Maximum Security Confinement in the United States*. Vol. 12, no. 1 (G), Feb.

Hymes, Dell. 1972. *Reinventing Anthropology*. New York: Pantheon.

James, Wendy. 1973. "The Anthropologist as Reluctant Imperialist." In Talal Asad, ed., *Anthropology and the Colonial Encounter*. New York: Humanity Books.

Jaspers, Karl. 1961. *The Question of German Guilt*. New York: Capricorn Books.

Jefferys-Jones, Rhodi. 1989. *The CIA and American Democracy*. New Haven: Yale University Press.

Johnson, Douglas H. 1982. "Evans-Pritchard, the Nuer, and the Sudan Political Service." *African Affairs* 81: 231–46.

Kaplan, Robert. 1994. "The Coming of Anarchy." *The Atlantic Monthly*, Feb.: 44–76.

Kleinman, Arthur and Joan Kleinman. 1997. "The Appeal of Experience; The Dismay of Images: Cultural Appropriations of Suffering in Our Times." In A. Kleinman, V. Das, and M. Lock, eds., *Social Suffering*. Berkeley: University of California Press.

Knauft, Bruce M. 1985. *Good Company and Violence: Sorcery and Social Action in a Lowland New Guinea Society.* Berkeley: University of California Press.

——. 1987. "Reconsidering Violence in Simply Human Societies: Homicide Among the Gebusi of New Guinea." *Current Anthropology* 28: 457–500.

Kroeber, Alfred L. 1911a. "The Ellusive Mill Creeks: A Band of Wild Indians Roaming in Northern California Today." *Travel* XVII (4): 510–13,548,5550. New York.

——. 1911b. "Ishi, the Last Aborigine." *World's Work Magaine*, XXIV (3): 304–8. New York.

Kroeber, Theodora, 1961. *Ishi in Two Worlds.* Berkeley: University of California Press.

Krog, Antjie. 1998. *Country of My Skull.* South Africa: Random House.

Kuper, Leo. 1982. *Genocide: Its Political Use in the Twentieth Century.* New Haven, CT.: Yale University Press.

——. 1985. *The Prevention of Genocide.* New Haven, CT.: Yale University Press.

Lancaster, Roger Nelson. 1988. *Thanks To God and the Revolution.* New York: Columbia University Press.

——. 1992. *Life is hard: Machismo, Danger and the Intimacy of Power in Nicaragua.* Berkeley: University of California Press.

Lassalle, Yvonne and Maureen O'Dougherty. 1997. "In Search of Weeping Worlds: Economies of Agency and Politics of Representation in the Ethnography of Inequality." *Radical History Review* 69:243–60.

Lemkin, Raphael. 1944. *Axis Rule in Occupied Europe: Laws of Occupation, Analysis of Government, Proposals for Redress.* Washington, DC: Carnegie Endowment for International Peace.

Levi, Primo. 1988. *The Drowned and the Saved.* New York: Vintage.

Leyton, Elliott. 1975. *The One Blood: Kinship and Class in an Irish Village.* St. John: Institute of Social and Economic Research.

——. 1995. *Men of Blood: Murder in Everyday Life.* Toronto: McClelland and Stewart.

——, with Greg Locke. 1998. *Touched by Fire: Doctors Without Borders in a Third World Crisis.* Toronto: McClelland and Stewart.

Mahmood, Cynthia Keppley. 1996. *Fighting for Faith and Nation: Dialogues with Sikh Militants.* Philadelphia: University of Pennsylvania Press.

Malinowski, Bronislaw. 1967. *A Diary in the Strict Sense of the Term.* New York and London: Routledge.

Nader, Laura. 1997a. "The Phantom Factor: Impact of the Cold War on Anthropology." In *Cold War and the University*, vol. 1. New York: New Press.

——. 1997b. "Controlling Processes: Tracing the Dynamic Components of Power." *Current Anthropology* 38(5): 711–37.

Nagengast, Carole. 2002. "Inoculations of Evil: Symbolic Violence and Ordinary People: An Anthropological Perspective on Genocide." In Alex Hinton, ed., *Annihilating Differences: The Anthropology of Genocide.* Berkeley: University of California Press.

Nelson, Diane. 1999. *A Finger in the Wound: Body Politics in Quincentennial Guatemala.* Berkeley: University of California Press.

Nordstrom, Carolyn. 1997. *A Different Kind of War Study.* Berkeley: University of California Press.

——, and Robben, A., eds. 1995. *Fieldwork Under Fire.* Berkeley: University of California Press.

Olujic, Maria B. 1998. "Children in Extremely Difficult Circumstances: War and Its Aftermath in Croatia." In N. Scheper-Hughes and Carolyn Sargent, eds., *Small Wars: The Cultural Politics of Childhood.* Berkeley: University of California Press, pp. 318–30.

Parsons, Talcott. 1972. "Definitions of Health and Illness in Light of American Values and Social Structure." In *Patients and Physicians*, 2nd ed., ed. E. Gartley Jaco. New York: Free Press, pp. 107–27.

Reno, William. 1998. "The Distinctive Political Logic of Weak States." In *Warlord Politics and African States.* Boulder, CO: Lynn Rienner.

Rhodes, Lorna. In press. *Total Confinement: Rationality, Insanity, and the Maximum Security Prisons.* Berkeley: University of California Press.

Sanford, Victoria. 2003. *Buried Secrets: Truth and Human Rights in Guatemala.* New York: Palgrave Macmillan.

Sartre, Jean-Paul. 1952. "Reply to Camus." In *Situations*, tr. Benita Eisler. London: Hamish Hamilton, pp. 88–105.

Schafft, Gretchen E. 2002. "Scientific Racism in Service of the Reich: German Anthropologists in the Nazi Era." In A. Hinton, ed., *Annihilating Difference: The Anthropology of Genocide.* Berkeley: University of California Press, pp. 117–36.

Scheper-Hughes, Nancy. 1993. *Death Without Weeping: The Violence of Everyday Life in Brazil.* Berkeley: University of California Press.

——. 1994. "The Last White Christmas: The Heidelberg Pub Massacre." *American Anthropologist* 96(4): 805–32.

——. 1995. "The Primacy of the Ethical: Propositions for a Militant Anthropology." In *Current Anthropology* 36(3): 409–40.

——. 1996. "Small Wars and Invisible Genocides." *Social Science & Medicine* 43: 889–900.

——. 1997. "Peace-Time Crimes." *Social Identities* 3(3): 471–97.

——. 1998. "Un-Doing: Social Suffering and the Politics of Remorse in the New South Africa." *Social Justice* 25(4): 114–42.

——. 2000a. *Saints, Scholars and Schizophrenics: Mental Illness in Rural Ireland*. New ed. Berkeley: University of California Press.

——. 2000b. "The Genocide Continuum." In Jeannette Mageo, ed., *Power and the Self*. Cambridge: Cambridge University Press, pp. 29–47.

——. 2003. "Death Squads and Democracy in Northeast Brazil: Mobilizing Human Rights Discourses in the Defense of Children." In *HFG Review* (Harry Frank Guggenheim Foundation, New York City), spring.

—— and Margaret Lock. 1987. "The Mindful Body: A Prolegomenon to Future Work in Medical Anthropology." *Medical Anthropology Quarterly* 1(1): 6–41.

Sennett, Richard and Jonathan Cobbs. 1975. *The Hidden Injuries of Class*. New York: Vintage, pp. 53–150.

Sluka, Jeffrey A., ed. 2000. *Death Squad: The Anthropology of State Terror*. Philadelphia: University of Pennsylvania Press.

Soros, George. 1999. *The Crisis of Global Capitalism*. New York: Public Affairs.

Spiegelman, Art. 1986. *Maus: A Survivor's Tale*. New York: Pantheon.

Stoll, David. 1993. *Between Two Armies in the Ixil Towns of Guatemala*. New York: Columbia University Press, pp. xi–xviii (Preface) and pp. 61–91 (chap. 3).

Strejilevich, Nora. 1997. *Una Sola Muerte Numerosa*. Miami: North-South Center Press.

Taussig, Michael. 1987. *Shamanism, Colonialism and the Wildman*. Chicago: University of Chicago Press, pp. 3–73 (Chaps. 1–3).

Tierney, Patrick. 2000. *Darkness in El Dorado: How Scientists and Journalists Devastated the Amazon*. New York: W. W. Norton.

Todd, Olivier. 1997. *Albert Camus: A Life*, tr. Benjamin Ivry. New York: Alfred Knopf.

Turnbull, Colin. 1972. *The Mountain People*. New York: Simon and Schuster.

United Nations Economic and Social Council. 1982. Commission on Human Rights, 38th Session, Agenda Item 12. E/CN.4/1982/NGO/15. Feb. 12, 1982. New York: United Nations.

Wakin, Eric. 1992. *Anthropology Goes to War: Professional Ethics and Counterinsurgency in Thailand*. Madison: University of Wisconsin Press.

Wechsler, Lawrence. 1990. *A Miracle, A Universe: Settling Accounts with Torturers*. New York: Viking.

Williams, Raymond. 1976. "Violence." In *Keywords*. New York: Oxford University Press, pp. 329–31.

Wolf, Eric. 1982. *Europe and the People without History*. Berkeley: University of California Press.

Wooden, Wayne and Jay Parker. 1982. "The Punks in Prison." *Men Behind Bars: Sexual Exploitation in Prison*. New York: Da Capo Press.

Young, Allan. 1995. *The Harmony of Illusions: Inventing Post-Traumatic Stress Disorder*. Princeton: Princeton University Press.

Part I

Conquest and Colonialism

Plate 2: Indian Killers and Bounty Hunters, Mill Creek, California circa 1869. Photo Credit: Native Daughters Museum, Oroville, California, courtesy of Department of Anthropology, University of California, Berkeley. Photographer unknown.

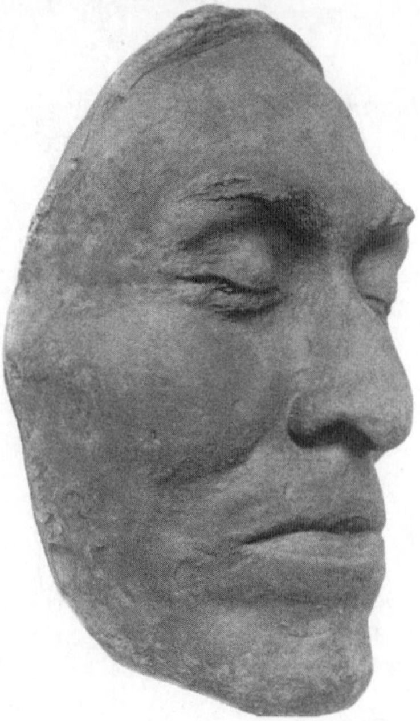

Plate 3: Death Mask of Ishi, California, March 1916. Photo Credit: Alexander Pope, courtesy of Department of Anthropology, University of California, Berkeley.

1

From *Heart of Darkness*

Joseph Conrad

'I left in a French steamer, and she called in every blamed port they have out there, for, as far as I could see, the sole purpose of landing soldiers and custom-house officers. I watched the coast. Watching a coast as it slips by the ship is like thinking about an enigma. There it is before you – smiling, frowning, inviting, grand, mean, insipid, or savage, and always mute with an air of whispering, Come and find out. This one was almost feature-less, as if still in the making, with an aspect of monotonous grimness. The edge of a colossal jungle, so dark-green as to be almost black, fringed with white surf, ran straight, like a ruled line, far, far away along a blue sea whose glitter was blurred by a creeping mist. The sun was fierce, the land seemed to glisten and drip with steam. Here and there greyish-whitish specks showed up, clus-tered inside the white surf, with a flag flying above them perhaps – settlements some centuries old, and still no bigger than pin-heads on the un-touched expanse of their background. We pounded along, stopped, landed soldiers; went on, landed custom-house clerks to levy toll in what looked like a God-forsaken wilderness, with a tin shed and a flag-pole lost in it; landed more soldiers – to take care of the custom-house clerks, presumably. Some, I heard, got drowned in the surf; but whether they did or not, nobody seemed particularly to care. They were just flung out there, and on we went. Every day the coast looked the same, as though we had not moved; but we passed various places – trading places – with names like Gran' Bassam, Little Popo, names that seemed to belong to some sordid farce acted in front of a sinister backcloth. The idleness of a passenger, my isolation amongst all these men with whom I had no point of contact, the oily and languid sea, the uniform sombreness of the coast, seemed to keep me away from the truth of things, within the toil of a mournful and senseless delusion. The voice of the surf heard now and then was a positive pleasure, like the speech of a brother. It was something natural, that had its reason, that had a meaning. Now and then a boat from the shore gave one a momentary contact with reality. It was paddled by black fellows. You could see from afar the white of their eyeballs glistening. They shouted, sang; their bodies streamed with perspiration; they had faces like grotesque masks – these chaps; but they had bone, muscle, a wild vitality, an intense energy of movement, that was as natural and true as the surf along their coast. They wanted no excuse for being there. They were a great comfort to look at. For a time I would feel I belonged still to a world of straightforward facts; but the feeling would not last long. Something would turn up to scare it away. Once, I remember, we came upon a man-of-war anchored off the coast. There wasn't even a shed there, and she was shelling the bush. It appears the French had one of their wars going on there-abouts. Her ensign dropped limp like a rag; the muzzles of the long eight-inch guns stuck out all over the low hull; the greasy, slimy swell swung her up lazily and let her down, swaying her thin masts. In the empty immensity of earth, sky, and water, there she was, incomprehensible, firing into a continent. Pop, would go one of the eight-inch guns; a small flame would dart and vanish, a little white smoke would disappear, a tiny projectile would give a feeble screech – and nothing happened. Nothing could happen. There was a touch of insanity in the proceeding, a sense of lugubrious drollery in the sight; and it was not dissipated by somebody on board assuring me earnestly there was a camp of natives – he called them enemies! – hidden out of sight somewhere.

'We gave her her letters (I heard the men in that lonely ship were dying of fever at the rate of three a-day) and went on. We called at some more places with farcical names, where the merry dance of death and trade goes on in a still and earthy atmosphere as of an overheated catacomb; all along the formless coast bordered by dangerous surf, as if Nature herself had tried to ward off intruders; in and out of rivers, streams of death in life, whose banks were rotting into mud, whose waters, thickened into slime, invaded the contorted mangroves, that seemed to writhe at us in the extremity of an impotent despair. Nowhere did we stop long enough to get a particularised impression, but the general sense of vague and oppressive wonder grew upon me. It was like a weary pilgrimage amongst hints for nightmares.

'It was upward of thirty days before I saw the mouth of the big river. We anchored off the seat of the government. But my work would not begin till some two hundred miles farther on. So as soon as I could I made a start for a place thirty miles higher up.

'I had my passage on a little sea-going steamer. Her captain was a Swede, and knowing me for a seaman, invited me on the bridge. He was a young man, lean, fair, and morose, with lanky hair and a shuffling gait. As we left the miserable little wharf, he tossed his head contemptuously at the shore. 'Been living there?' he asked. I said, "Yes." "Fine lot these government chaps – are they not?" he went on, speaking English with great precision and considerable bitterness. "It is funny what some people will do for a few francs a-month. I wonder what becomes of that kind when it goes up country?" I said to him I expected to see that soon. "So-o-o!" he exclaimed. He shuffled athwart, keeping one eye ahead vigilantly. "Don't be too sure," he continued. "The other day I took up a man who hanged himself on the road. He was a Swede, too." "Hanged himself! Why, in God's name?" I cried. He kept on looking out watchfully. "Who Knows? The sun too much for him, or the country perhaps."

'At last we opened a reach. A rocky cliff appeared, mounds of turned-up earth by the shore, houses on a hill, others, with iron roofs, amongst a waste of excavations, or hanging to the declivity. A continuous noise of the rapids above hovered over this scene of inhabited devastation. A lot of people, mostly black and naked, moved about like ants. A jetty projected into the river. A blinding sunlight drowned all this at times in a sudden recrudescence of glare. "There's your Company's station," said the Swede, pointing to three wooden barrack-like structures on the rocky slope. "I will send your things up. Four boxes did you say? So. Farewell."

'I came upon a boiler wallowing in the grass, then found a path leading up the hill. It turned aside for the boulders, and also for an undersized railway-truck lying there on its back with its wheels in the air. One was off. The thing looked as dead as the carcass of some animal. I came upon more pieces of decaying machinery, a stack of rusty rails. To the left a clump of trees made a shady spot, where dark things seemed to stir feebly. I blinked, the path was steep. A horn tooted to the right, and I saw the black people run. A heavy and dull detonation shook the ground, a puff of smoke came out of the cliff, and that was all. No change appeared on the face of the rock. They were building a railway. The cliff was not in the way or anything; but this objectless blasting was all the work going on.

'A slight clinking behind me made me turn my head. Six black men advanced in a file, toiling up the path. They walked erect and slow, balancing small baskets full of earth on their heads, and the clink kept time with their footsteps. Black rags were wound round their loins, and the short ends behind wagged to and fro like tails. I could see every rib, the joints of their limbs were like knots in a rope; each had an iron collar on his neck, and all were connected together with a chain whose bights swung between them, rhythmically clinking. Another report from the cliff made me think suddenly of that ship of war I had seen firing into a continent. It was the same kind of ominous voice; but these men could by no stretch of imagination be called enemies. They were called criminals, and the outraged law, like the bursting shells, had come to them, an insoluble mystery from over the sea. All their meagre breasts panted together, the violently dilated nostrils quivered, the eyes stared stonily up-hill. They passed me within six inches, without a glance, with that complete, deathlike indifference of unhappy savages. Behind this raw matter one of the reclaimed, the product of the new forces at work, strolled despondently, carrying a rifle by its middle. He had a uniform jacket with one button off, and seeing a white man on the path, hoisted his weapon to his shoulder with alacrity. This was simple prudence, white men being so much alike at a distance that he could not tell who I might be. He was speedily reassured, and with a large, white, rascally grin, and a glance at his charge, seemed to take me into partnership in his exalted trust. After all, I also was a part of the great cause of these high and just proceedings.

'Instead of going up, I turned and descended to the left. My idea was to let that chain-gang get out of sight before I climbed the hill. You know I am not particularly tender; I've had to strike and to fend off. I've had to resist and to attack sometimes – that's only one way of resisting – without counting the exact cost, according to the demands of such sort of life as I had blundered into. I've seen the devil of violence, and the devil of greed, and the devil of hot desire; but, by all the stars! these were strong, lusty, red-eyed devils, that swayed and drove men – men, I tell you. But as I stood on this hillside. I foresaw that in the blinding sunshine of that land I would become acquainted with a flabby, pretending, weak-eyed devil of a rapacious and pitiless folly. How insidious he could be, too, I was only to find out several months later and a thousand miles farther. For a moment I stood appalled, as though by a warning. Finally I descended the hill, obliquely, towards the trees I had seen.

'I avoided a vast artificial hole somebody had been digging on the slope, the purpose of which I found it impossible to divine. It wasn't a quarry or a sandpit, anyhow. It was just a hole. It might have been connected with the philanthropic desire of giving the criminals something to do. I don't know. Then I nearly fell into a very narrow ravine, almost no more than a scar in the hillside. I discovered that a lot of imported drainage-pipes for the settlement had been tumbled in there. There wasn't one that was not broken. It was a wanton smash-up. At last I got under the trees. My purpose was to stroll into the shade for a moment; but no sooner within than it seemed to me I had stepped into the gloomy circle of some Inferno. The rapids were near, and an uninterrupted, uniform, head-long, rushing noise filled the mournful stillness of the grove, where not a breath stirred, not a leaf moved, with a mysterious sound – as though the tearing pace of the launched earth had suddenly become audible.

'Black shapes crouched, lay, sat between the trees, leaning against the trunks, clinging to the earth, half coming out, half effaced within the dim light, in all the attitudes of pain, abandonment, and despair. Another mine on the cliff went off, followed by a slight shudder of the soil under my feet. The work was going on. The work! And this was the place where some of the helpers had withdrawn to die.

'They were dying slowly – it was very clear. They were not enemies, they were not criminals, they were nothing earthly now, – nothing but black shadows of disease and starvation, lying confusedly in the greenish gloom. Brought from all the recesses of the coast in all the legality of time contracts, lost in uncongenial surroundings, fed on unfamiliar food, they sickened, became inefficient, and were then allowed to crawl away and rest. These moribund shapes were free as air – and nearly as thin. I began to distinguish the gleam of eyes under the trees. Then, glancing down, I saw a face near my hand. The black bones reclined at full length with one shoulder against the tree, and slowly the eyelids rose and the sunken eyes looked up at me, enormous and vacant, a kind of blind, white flicker in the depths of the orbs, which died out slowly. The man seemed young – almost a boy – but you know with them it's hard to tell. I found nothing else to do but to offer him one of my good Swede's ship's biscuits I had in my pocket. The fingers closed slowly on it and held – there was no other movement and no other glance. He had tied a bit of white worsted round his neck – Why? Where did he get it? Was it a badge – an ornament – a charm – a propitiatory act? Was there any idea at all connected with it? It looked startling round his black neck, this bit of white thread from beyond the seas.

'Near the same tree two more bundles of acute angles sat with their legs drawn up. One, with his chin propped on his knees, stared at nothing, in an intolerable and appalling manner: his brother phantom rested its forehead, as if over-come with a great weariness; and all about others were scattered in every pose of contorted collapse, as in some picture of a massacre or a pestilence. While I stood horror-struck, one of these creatures rose to his hands and knees, and went off on all-fours towards the river to drink. He lapped out of his hand, then sat up in the sunlight, crossing his shins in front of him, and after a time let his woolly head fall on his breastbone.

'I didn't want any more loitering in the shade, and I made haste towards the station. When near the buildings I met a white man, in such an unexpected elegance of get-up that in the first moment I took him for a sort of vision. I saw a high starched collar, white cuffs, a light alpaca jacket, snowy trousers, a clear silk necktie, and varnished boots. No hat. Hair parted, brushed, oiled, under a green-lined parasol held in a big white hand. He was amazing, and had a penholder behind his ear.

'I shook hands with this miracle, and I learned he was the Company's chief accountant, and that all the book-keeping was done at this station. He had come out for a moment, he said, "to get a breath of fresh air." The expression sounded wonderfully odd, with its suggestion of sedentary desk-life. I wouldn't have mentioned the fellow to you at all, only it was from his lips that I first heard the name of the man who is so indissolubly connected with the memories of that time. Moreover, I respected the fellow. Yes; I respected his collars, his vast cuffs, his brushed hair. His appearance was certainly that of a hairdresser's dummy; but in the great demoralisation of the land he kept up his appearance. That's backbone. His starched collars and got-up shirt-fronts were achievements of character. He had been out nearly three years; and, later on, I could not help asking him how he managed to sport such linen. He had just the faintest blush, and said modestly, "I've been teaching one of the native women about the station. It was difficult. She had a distaste for the work." Thus this man had verily accomplished something. And he was devoted to his books, which were in apple-pie order.

2

Culture of Terror – Space of Death: Roger Casement's Putumayo Report and the Explanation of Torture

Michael Taussig

This essay is about torture and the culture of terror, which for most of us, including myself, are known only through the words of others. Thus my concern is with the mediation of the culture of terror through narration – and with the problems of writing effectively against terror.

Jacobo Timerman ends his recent book, *Prisoner without a Name, Cell without a Number*, with the imprint of the gaze of hope in the space of death.

Have any of you looked into the eyes of another person, on the floor of a cell, who knows that he's about to die though no one has told him so? He knows that he's about to die but clings to his biological desire to live, as a single hope, since no one has told him he's to be executed.

I have many such gazes imprinted upon me....

Those gazes which I encountered in the clandestine prisons of Argentina and which I've retained one by one, were the culminating point, the purest moment of my tragedy.

They are here with me today. And although I might wish to do so, I could not and would not know how to share them with you.[1]

The space of death is crucial to the creation of meaning and consciousness, nowhere more so than in societies where torture is endemic and where the culture of terror flourishes. We may think of the space of death as a threshold, yet it is a wide space whose breadth offers positions of advance as well as of extinction. Sometimes a person goes through it and returns to us to tell the tale, like Timerman, who entered it, he says, because he believed the battle against military dictatorship had to be fought.[2]

Timerman fought with words, with his newspaper *La Opinion*, in and against the silence imposed by the arbiters of discourse who beat out a new reality in the prison cells where the torturers and the tortured came together. "We victims and victimizers, we're part of the same humanity, colleagues in the same endeavor to prove the existence of ideologies, feelings, heroic deeds, religions, obsessions. And the rest of humanity, what are they engaged in?"[3]

The construction of colonial reality that occurred in the New World has been and will remain a topic of immense curiosity and study – the New World where the Indian and the African became subject to an initially far smaller number of Christians. Whatever conclusions we draw as to how that hegemony was so speedily effected, we would be most unwise to overlook or underestimate the role of terror. And by this I mean us to think through terror, which as well as being a physiological state is also a social fact and a cultural construction whose baroque dimensions allow it to serve as the mediator *par excellence* of colonial hegemony. The space of death is one of the crucial spaces where Indian, African, and white gave birth to the New World.

This space of death has a long and rich culture. It is where the social imagination has populated its metamorphosing images of evil and the underworld: in the Western tradition, Homer, Virgil, the Bible, Dante, Bosch, the Inquisition, Baudelaire, Rimbaud, *Heart of Darkness*; in Northwest Amazonian tradition, zones of visions, communication between terrestrial and supernatural beings, putrefaction, death, rebirth, and genesis, perhaps in the rivers and land of maternal milk bathed eternally in subtle green light of coca leaves.[4] With European conquest and colonization, these spaces of death blend as a common pool of key signifiers or caption points binding the culture of the conqueror with that of the conquered. The space of death is preeminently a space of transformation: through the experience of death, life; through fear, loss of self and conformity to a new reality; or through evil, good. Lost in the dark woods, then journeying through the underworld with his guide, Dante achieves paradise only after he has mounted Satan's back. [. . .]

From Timerman's chronicle and texts like Miguel Angel Asturias's *El señor presidente* it is abundantly clear that cultures of terror are based on and nourished by silence and myth in which the fanatical stress on the mysterious side of the mysterious flourishes by means of rumor and fantasy woven in a dense web of magical realism. It is also clear that the victimizer needs the victim for the purpose of making truth, objectifying the victimizer's fantasies in the discourse of the other. To be sure, the torturer's desire is also prosaic: to acquire information, to act in concert with large-scale economic strategies elaborated by the masters and exigencies of production. Yet equally if not more important is the need to control massive populations through the cultural elaboration of fear.

That is why silence is imposed, why Timerman, the publisher, was so important, why he knew when to be silent and close off reality in the torture chamber. "Such silence," he tells us,

begins in the channels of communication. Certain political leaders, institutions, and priests attempt to denounce what is happening, but are unable to establish contact with the population. The silence begins with a strong odor. People sniff the suicides, but it eludes them. Then silence finds another ally: solitude. People fear suicides as they fear madmen. And the person who wants to fight senses his solitude and is frightened.[5]

Hence, there is the need for us to fight that solitude, fear, and silence, to examine these conditions of truth-making and culture-making, to follow Michel Foucault in "seeing historically how effects of truth are produced within discourses which are in themselves neither true nor false."[6] At the same time we not only have to see, we also have to see anew through the creation of counterdiscourses.

If effects of truth are power, then the question is raised not only concerning the power to speak and write, but as to what form shall that counterdiscourse take. This issue of form has lately been of much concern to those involved in writing histories and ethnographies. But faced with the endemicity of torture, terror, and the growth of armies, we in the New World are today assailed with a new urgency. There is the effort to understand terror, in order to make *others* understand. Yet the reality at stake here makes a mockery of understanding and derides rationality, as when the young boy Jacobo Timerman asks his mother, "Why do they hate us?" And she replies, "Because they do not understand." And after his ordeal, the old Timerman writes of the need for a hated object and the simultaneous fear of that object – the almost magical inevitability of hatred. "No," he concludes, "there can be no doubt my mother was the one who was mistaken. It is not the anti-Semites who must be made to understand. It is we Jews."[7]

Hated and feared, objects to be despised, yet also of awe, the reified essence of evil in the very being of their bodies, these figures of the Jew, the black, the Indian, and woman herself, are clearly objects of cultural construction, the leaden keel of evil and of mystery stabilizing the ship and course that is Western history. With the cold war we add the communist. With the time bomb ticking inside the nuclear family, we add the feminists and the gays. The military and the New Right, like the conquerors of old, discover the evil they have imputed to these aliens, and mimic the savagery they have imputed.

What sort of understanding – what sort of speech, writing, and construction of meaning by any mode – can deal with and subvert that?

On one thing Timerman is clear. To counterpose the eroticization and romanticization of violence by the same means or by forms equally mystical is a dead end. Yet to offer one or all of the standard rational explanations of the culture of terror is similarly pointless. For behind the search for profits, the need to control labor, the need to assuage frustration, and so on, lie intricately construed long-standing cultural logics of meaning – structures of feeling – whose basis lies in a symbolic world and not in one of rationalism. Ultimately there are two features; the crudest of empirical facts such as the electrodes and the mutilated human body, and the experience of going through torture. In his text Timerman does create a powerful counterdiscourse, precisely because, like torture itself, it moves us through that space of death where reality is up for grabs, to confront the hallucination of the military. [...]

Conrad's way of dealing with the terror of the rubber boom in the Congo was *Heart of Darkness*. There were three realities there, comments Frederick Karl: King Leopold's, made out of intricate disguises and deceptions; Roger Casement's studied realism; and Conrad's, which, to quote Karl, "fell midway between the other two, as he attempted to penetrate the veil and yet was anxious to retain its hallucinatory quality."[8]

This formularization is sharp and important: *to penetrate the veil while retaining its hallucinatory quality*. It evokes Paul Ricoeur's two hermeneutics in his major discussion of Freud: that of suspicion (or reduction) and that of revelation.[9] As to the political effect of *Heart of Darkness*, while Ian Watt regards it as the enduring and most powerful literary indictment of imperialism,[10] I am not so sure that its strikingly literary quality and hallucinatory filminess do not finally blind and stun the reader into a trance, drowning in a sea-storm of imagery. The danger here lies with aestheticizing horror, and while Conrad manages to stop short of doing that, we must realize that just to the side lurks the seductive poetics of fascism and the imaginative source of terror and torture embedded deep within us all. The political and artistic problem is to engage with that, to maintain that hallucinatory quality, while effectively turning it against itself. That would be the true catharsis, the great counterdiscourse whose poetics we must ponder in the political terrain now urgently exposed today; the form wherein all that appeals and seduces in the iconography and sensuality of the underworld becomes its own force for self-subversion. Foucault's concept of discourse eludes this aspiration and concept of dialectically engaged subversion. But it is with this poetics that we must develop the cultural politics appropriate to our times.

Casement offers a useful and startling contrast to Conrad, all the more vivid because of the ways their paths crossed in the Congo in 1890, because of the features common to their political backgrounds as exiles or quasi-exiles from imperialized European societies, Poland and Ireland, and because of an indefinable if only superficial similarity in their temperaments and love of literature. Yet it was Casement who resorted to militant action on behalf of his native land, organizing gun running from Germany to the rebels at Dublin for Easter Sunday 1916, and was hung for treason, while Conrad resolutely stuck to his task as an artist, bathed in nostalgia and guilt for Poland, lending his name but otherwise refusing to assist Casement in the Congo Reform Society, claiming he was but a "wretched novelist." [...]

Casement's reports on the Congo and the Putumayo did much to stop the pervasive brutality there and, in Edmund Morel's opinion, "innoculated the diplomacy of this country [Britain] with a moral toxin" such that "historians will cherish these occasions as the only two in which British diplomacy rose above the commonplace."[11]

In addition to the coincidences of imperialist history, what brings Casement and Conrad together is the problem they jointly create concerning the rhetorical power and political effect of social realism and mythic realism. Between the emotional consul-general who wrote effectively on the side of the colonized as a realist and a rationalist, and the great artist who did not, lie many of the crucial problems concerning the domination of culture and cultures of domination.

The Putumayo Report

At this point it is instructive to analyze briefly Casement's Putumayo report, which was submitted to Sir Edward Grey, head of the British Foreign Service, and published by the House of Commons on 13 July 1913 when Casement was forty-nine years old.

At the outset it should be noted that Casement's attachment to the cause of Irish home rule and his anger at British imperialism made his almost life-long work as a British consul extremely fraught with contradiction; in addition, he felt his experiences in Africa and South America increased his understanding of the effects of the colonialism in Ireland, which in turn stimulated his ethnographic and political sensibilities regarding conditions south of the equator. He claimed, for example, that it was his knowledge of Irish history which allowed him to understand the Congo atrocities, whereas the Foreign Office could not because the empirical evidence made no sense to them. In a letter to his close friend Alice Green he noted:

I knew the Foreign Office would not understand the thing, for I realized that I was looking at this tragedy with the eyes of another race of people once hunted themselves, whose hearts were based on affection as the root principle of contact with their fellow men, and whose estimate of life was not something eternally to be appraised at its market price.[12]

[...] The essence of his 136-page Putumayo report, based on seven weeks of travel in 1910 through the rubber-gathering areas of the jungles of the Caraparaná and Igaraparaná affluents of the middle reaches of the Putumayo river, and on some six months in the Amazon basin, lay in its detail of the terror and tortures together with Casement's explanation of causes and his estimate of the toll in human life. Putumayo rubber would be unprofitable were it not for the forced labor of local Indians, principally those called Huitotos. For the twelve years from 1900, the Putumayo output of some 4,000 tons of rubber cost thousands of Indians their lives. Deaths from torture, disease, and possibly flight had decreased the population of the area by around 30,000 during that time.

The British government felt obliged to send Casement as its consular representative to the Putumayo because of the public outcry aroused in 1909 by a series of articles in the London magazine, *Truth*; the series depicted the brutality of the rubber company, which since 1907 had been a consortium of Peruvian and British interests in the region. Entitled "The Devil's Paradise: A British Owned Congo," these articles were the work of a young "engineer" and adventurer from the United States named Walter Hardenburg, who had with a companion entered the remote corner of the Amazon basin from the Colombian Andes in 1907 and had been taken prisoner by the Peruvian Rubber Company founded by Julio César Arana in

1903. Hardenburg's chronicle is to an important extent an elaboration on a text basic to the Putumayo saga, an article published in the Iquitos newspaper *La Sanción* shortly before its publication was suspended by the Peruvian government and Arana.

Asserting that the rubber trees are in rapid decline and will be exhausted in four years' time because of the rapacity of the production system, the article continues by declaring that the peaceful Indians work night and day collecting rubber without the slightest remuneration. They are given nothing to eat or wear. Their crops, together with the women and children, are taken for the pleasure of the whites. They are inhumanly flogged until their bones are visible. Given no medical treatment, they are left to die after torture, eaten by the company's dogs. They are castrated, and their ears, fingers, arms, and legs are cut off. They are also tortured by means of fire, water, and crucifixion tied head-down. The whites cut them to pieces with machetes and dash out the brains of small children by hurling them against trees and walls. The elderly are killed when they can no longer work. To amuse themselves, company officials practice shooting, using Indians as targets, and on special occasions such as Easter Saturday – Saturday of Glory – shoot them down in groups or, in preference, douse them in kerosene and set them on fire to enjoy their agony.[13]

In a letter written to Hardenburg by an employee of the company we read how a "commission" was sent out by a rubber-station manager to exterminate a group of Indians for not bringing in sufficient rubber. The commission returned in four days with fingers, ears, and several heads of Indians to prove the orders had been carried out.[14] On another occasion, the manager called in hundreds of Indians to assemble at the station:

He grasped his carbine and machete and began the slaughter of these defenseless Indians, leaving the ground covered with over 150 corpses, among them men, women, and children. Bathed in blood and appealing for mercy, the survivors were heaped with the dead and burned to death, while the manager shouted, "I want to exterminate all the Indians who do not obey my orders about the rubber that I require them to bring in."

"When they get drunk," adds the correspondent, "the upper-level employees of the company toast with champagne the man who can boast of the greatest number of murders."[15]

The drama perhaps most central to the Putu-mayo terror, quoted from an Iquitos newspaper article in 1908, and affirmed as fact by both Case-ment and Hardenburg, concerns the weighing-in of rubber brought by the Indians from the forest:

The Indian is so humble that as soon as he sees that the needle of the scale does not mark the ten kilos, he himself stretches out his hands and throws himself on the ground to receive the punishment. Then the chief [of the rubber station] or a subordinate advances, bends down, takes the Indian by the hair, strikes him, raises his head, drops it face downwards on the ground, and after the face is beaten and kicked and covered with blood, the Indian is scourged. This is when they are treated best, for often they cut them to pieces with machetes.[16]

In the rubber station of Matanzas, continues the writer, "I have seen Indians tied to a tree, their feet about half a yard above the ground. Fuel is then placed below, and they are burnt alive. This is done to pass the time."

Casement's report to the House of Commons is staid and sober, somewhat like a lawyer arguing a case and in marked contrast to his diary covering the same experience. He piles fact on brutal fact, suggests an over-all analysis, and makes his recom-mendations. His material comes from three sources: what he personally witnessed; testimony of 30 Barbados blacks who, with 166 others, were contracted by the company during 1903–4 to serve as overseers, and whose statements occupy 85 published foolscap pages; and, interspersed with Casement's direct observations, numerous stories from local residents and company employees.

Early on in the report, in a vivid throwaway line, he evokes the banality of the cruelty. "The employ-ees at all the stations passed the time when not hunting Indians, either lying in their hammocks or in gambling."[17] The unreal atmosphere of ordin-ariness, of the ordinariness of the extraordinary, can be startling. "At some of the stations the prin-cipal flogger was the station cook – two such men were directly named to me, and I ate the food they prepared, while many of their victims carried my baggage from station to station, and showed often terrible scars on their limbs inflicted at the hands of these men."[18]

From the evidence of scarring, Casement found that the "great majority" (perhaps up to 90 per-cent) of the more than 1,600 Indians he saw had

been badly beaten.[19] Some of the worst affected were small boys, and deaths due to flogging were frquent, either under the lash, or more frequently, a few days later when the wounds became maggot infested.[20] Floggings occurred when an Indian brought in insufficient rubber and were most sad-istic for those who dared to flee. Flogging was mixed with other tortures such as near drowning, "designed," as Casement points out, "to just stop short of taking life while inspiring the acute mental fear and inflicting much of the physical agony of death."[21] Casement was informed by a man who had himself often flogged Indians that he had seen mothers flogged because their little sons had not brought in enough rubber. While the boy stood terrified and crying at the sight, his mother would be beaten "just a few strokes" to make him a better worker.[22]

Deliberate starvation was resorted to repeat-edly, sometimes to frighten, more often to kill. Men and women were kept in the stocks until they died of hunger. One Barbadian related how he had seen Indians in this situation "scraping up the dirt with their fingers and eating it." Another declared he had seen them eating the maggots in their wounds.[23]

The stocks were sometimes placed on the upper verandah or residential part of the main dwelling house of the rubber stations, in direct view of the manager and his employees. Children, men, and women might be confined in them for months, and some of the Barbados men said they had seen women raped while in the stocks.[24]

Much of the surveillance and punishment was carried out by the corps of Indian guards known as the *muchachos*. Members of this armed corps had been trained by the company from an early age, and were used to control *salvajes* other than those to whom they were kin. Casement thought them to be generally every bit as evil as their white masters.[25] When Barbados men were present, they were fre-quently assigned the task of flogging, but, Case-ment emphasizes, "no monopoly of flogging was enjoyed by any employee as a right. The chief of the section frequently himself took the lash, which, in turn, might be wielded by every member of the civilized or 'rational staff.'"[26]

"Such men," reports Casement, "had lost all sight or sense of rubber-gathering – they were simply beasts of prey who lived upon the Indians and delighted in shedding their blood." Moreover, the station managers from the areas where

Casement got his most precise information were in debt (despite their handsome rates of commission), running their operations at a loss to the company which in some sections ran to many thousands of pounds sterling.[27]

It is necessary at this point to note that although the Indians received the brunt of the terror, whites and blacks were also targets. Whether as competitors for Indian rubber gatherers, like the independent Colombian rubber traders who first conquered the Putumayo and were then dislodged by Arana's company in 1908, or as employees of the company, extremely few escaped the ever-present threat of degradation and torture. Asked by Casement if he did not know it to be wrong to torture Indians, one of the Barbados men replied that he was unable to refuse orders, "that a man might be a man down in Iquitos, but 'you couldn't be a man up there.'"[28] In addition, most of the company's white and black employees were themselves trapped in a debt-peonage system, but one quite different from the one the company used in controlling its Indians.

From the testimony of the Barbados men it is clear that dissension, hatred, and mistrust ran riot among all members of the company – to the degree that one has to consider seriously the hypothesis that only in their group ritualization of torturing Indians could such anomie and mistrust be held in check, thus guaranteeing to the company the solidarity required to sustain it as an effective social unit.

To read Casement's secondhand and Hardenburg's eyewitness accounts of the company attacks against independent white Colombian traders is to become further aware of the ritualistic features which assured the violence of the Putumayo rubber boom of its success as a culture of terror.

Casement's Analysis

Casement's main line of analysis lies with his argument that it was not rubber but labor that was scarce in the Putumayo, and that this scarcity was the basic cause of the use of terror. Putumayo rubber was of the lowest quality, the remoteness of its source made its transport expensive relative to rubber from other zones, and wages for free labor were very high. Hence, he reasons, the company resorted to the use of forced labor under a debt-peonage system, and used torture to maintain labor discipline.

The problem with this argument, which assumes the purported rationality of business and the capital-logic of commodities (such as labor), is that it encounters certain contradictions and, while not exactly wrong, strikes me as giving insufficient weight to two fundamental considerations. The first consideration concerns the forms of labor and economic organization that local history and Indian society made available, or potentially available, to world capitalism in the jungles of the Putumayo. The second, put crudely, is that terror and torture do not derive only from market pressure (which we can regard here as a trigger) but also from the process of cultural construction of evil as well. "Market pressure" assumes the paradigm of scarcity essential to capitalist economism and capitalist socioeconomic theory. Leaving aside the question of how accurate a depiction of capitalist society results from this paradigm, it is highly dubious that it reveals much of the reality of the Putumayo rubber boom where the problem facing capitalist enterprise was precisely that there were no capitalist social institutions and no market for abstract labor into which capital could be fed and multiplied. Indeed, one could go further to develop an argument which begins with the premise that it was just this lack of commoditized social relationships, in interaction with commodity forces emanating from the world rubber market, that accounts for the production of torture and terror. We can say that the culture of terror was functional to the needs of the labor system, but that tells us little about the most significant contradictions to emerge from Casement's report, namely, that the slaughter of this precious labor was on a scale vast beyond belief, and that, as Casement himself states, not only were the station managers costing the company large sums of money but that "such men had lost all sight or sense of rubber-gathering – they were simply beasts of prey who lived upon the Indians and delighted in shedding their blood." To claim the rationality of business for this is to claim and sustain an illusory rationality, obscuring our understanding of the way business can transform the use of terror from the means into an end in itself.

The consideration of local history and economic organization requires far fuller treatment than can be attempted here. But it should be noted in passing that "scarcity" of labor cannot refer to a scarcity of Indians, of whom there seems to have been an abundance, but rather to the fact that the Indians would not work in the regular and dependable manner necessary to a large-scale capitalist enterprise. Casement downplayed this phenomenon, now often referred to as "the backward sloping supply curve of labor," and did so even though in the Congo he had himself complained that the problem was that the natives would not work;[29] he felt sure that if paid with more goods, the Indians would work to the level required by the company without force. Many people with far longer experience in the Putumayo denied this naive assertion and pointed out, with logic as impeccable as Casement's, that the scarcity of labor and the ease with which the Indians could live off the forest obliged employers elsewhere in the Putumayo to treat them with consideration.[30] In either case, however, with or without use of coercion, the labor productivity obtained fell far short of what employers desired.

The contradictions mount further on close examination of the debt-peonage system, which Casement regards as slavery. It was a pretext, he says, that the Indian in such a relation was in debt, for the Indian was bound by physical force to work for the company and could not escape.[31] One then must ask why the company persisted in this pretense, especially given the means of coercion at its disposal. [...]

Pretext as it was, the debt which ensured peonage was nonetheless real, and as a pretense its magical realism was as essential to the labor organization of the Putumayo rubber boom as is the "commodity fiction" Karl Polanyi describes for a mature capitalist economy.[32] To analyze the construction of these fictional realities we need now to turn to some of their more obviously mythic features, enclosed as they are in the synergistic relation of savagery and business, cannibalism and capitalism. Interrogated by the British Parliamentary Select Committee on Putumayo in 1913, Julio César Arana, the driving force of the rubber company, was asked to clarify what he meant when he stated that the Indians had resisted the establishment of civilization in their districts, that they had been resisting for many years, and had practiced cannibalism. "What I mean by that," he replied, "is that they did not admit of exchange, or anybody to do business with them – Whites, for example."[33]

Jungle and Savagery

There is a problem that I have only hinted at in all of the accounts of the atrocities of the Putumayo rubber boom. While the immensity of the cruelty is beyond question, most of the evidence comes through stories. The meticulous historian would seize upon this fact as a challenge to winnow out truth from exaggeration or understatement. But the more basic implication, it seems to me, is that *the narratives are in themselves evidence of the process whereby a culture of terror was created and sustained.*

Two interlacing motifs stand out: the horrors of the jungle, and the horrors of savagery. All the facts are bent through the prism formed by these motifs, which, in keeping with Conrad's theory of art, mediate effective truth not so much through the dissemination of information as through the appeal of temperaments through sensory impressions. Here the European and colonist image of the primeval jungle with its vines and rubber trees and domination of man's domination stands forth as the colonially apt metaphor of the great space of terror and deep cruelties. (Europe – late nineteenth century, penetrating the ancient forests of the tropics.)[...]

In *Heart of Darkness*, the narrator, Marlow, sits back, like a Buddha, introducing his yarn, prefiguring the late-nineteenth-century colonial exploitation of the Congo by evoking a soldier of imperial Rome, moving through the marshes of the Thames.

Land in a swamp, march through the woods, and in some inland post feel the savagery, the utter savagery, had closed around him, – all that mysterious life of the wilderness that stirs in the forest, in the jungles, in the hearts of wild men. There's no initiation either into such mysteries. He has to live in the midst of the incomprehensible, which is also detestable. And it has a fascination, too, that goes to work upon him. The fascination of the abomination – you know, imagine the growing regrets, the longing to escape, the powerless disgust, the surrender, the hate.

[...] Father Francisco de Vilanova addresses the same vexing problem, only here it is the Putumayo jungle which constitutes the great figure of savagery. In a book describing Capuchin endeavors among the Huitotos from the 1920s on, we read:

It is almost something unbelievable to those who do not know the jungle. It is an irrational fact that enslaves those who go there. It is a whirlwind of savage passions that dominates the civilized person who has too much confidence in himself. It is a degeneration of the spirit in a drunkenness of improbable but real circumstances. The rational and civilized man loses respect for himself and his domestic place. He throws his heritage into the mire from where who knows when it will be retrieved. One's heart fills with morbidity and the sentiment of savagery. It becomes insensible to the most pure and great things of humanity. Even cultivated spirits, finely formed and well educated, have succumbed.[34]

But of course it is not the jungle but the sentiments men project into it that is decisive in filling their hearts with savagery. And what the jungle can accomplish, so much more can its native inhabitants, the wild Indians, like those tortured into gathering rubber. It must not be overlooked that the colonially constructed image of the wild Indian here at stake was a powerfully ambiguous image, a seesawing, bifocalized, and hazy composite of the animal and the human. In their human or human-like form, the wild Indians could all the better reflect back to the colonists the vast and baroque projections of human wildness that the colonists needed to establish their reality as civilized (not to mention business-like) people. And it was only because the wild Indians were human that they were able to serve as labor – and as subjects of torture. For it is not the victim as animal that gratifies the torturer, but the fact that the victim is human, thus enabling the torturer to become the savage.

How Savage were the Huitotos?

The savagery of the wild Indians occupied a key role in the propaganda of the rubber company. Hardenburg writes that the Huitotos "are hospitable to a marked degree," and that while the Church improves their morals, in the company's domain, priests have been carefully excluded. "Indeed," he continues, "in order to frighten people and thus prevent them from entering the region, the company has circulated the most blood curdling reports of the ferocity and cannibalism of these helpless Indians, whom travellers such as myself have found to be timid, peaceful, mild, industrious and humble."[35] Father Pinell has published a document from Peru describing a film commissioned by Arana's company in 1917. Shown in the cinemas of Lima, it portrayed the civilizing effect of the company on "these savage regions that as recently as 25 years ago were peopled entirely by cannibals. Owing to the energy of this tireless struggler

[Arana] they have been converted into useful elements of labor."[36]

Propaganda usually flowers only where the soil has been long and well prepared, and it seems to me that Arana's was no exception since the mythology of savagery dates from times long before his. Yet, the passions unleashed by the rubber boom invigorated this mythology with a seductive power. Before probing further into the ways the rubber company acquired the savagery it imputed to the Indians, it is necessary to pause and examine the colonists' mythology and folklore concerning the Upper Amazon forest people.

Time and again Casement tells us that the Huitotos and all Upper Amazon Indians were gentle and docile. He downplays their cannibalism, says that they were thoughtless rather than cruel, and regards their docility as a *natural* and remarkable characteristic. This helps him to explain the ease with which they were conquered and forced to gather rubber.

An Indian would promise anything for a gun, or for some of the other tempting things offered as inducements to him to work rubber. Many Indians submitted to the alluring offer only to find that once in the "conquistadores" books they had lost all liberty, and were reduced to unending demands for more rubber and varied tasks. A cacique or "capitán" might be bought over to dispose of the labor of his clan, and as the cacique's influence was very great and the natural docility of the Indian a remarkable characteristic of Upper Amazon tribes, the work of conquering a primitive people and reducing them to a continual strain of rubber-finding was less difficult than might at first be supposed.[37]

Yet, on the other hand, such docility makes the violence of the whites even harder to understand. [...]

Alfred Simson, an Englishman who travelled the Putumayo and Napo rivers in the 1880s and spent far more time there than Casement, conveys a picture quite different from Casement's. An example is his description of the Zaparos, who, like the Huitotos, were considered by the whites to be wild Indians. Noting that they raided other groups and abducted their children for sale to white traders, Simson goes on to state:

When unprovoked they are, like really wild Indians, very shy and retiring, but are perfectly fearless, and will suffer no one, either whites or others, to employ force with them. They can only be managed by tact, good treatment, and sometimes simple reasoning: otherwise resenting ill-treatment or an attempt to resort to blows, [they react] with the worst of violence.... At all times they are changeable and unreliable, betraying under different circumstances, and often apparently under the same, in common with so many of their class, all the most opposite traits of character, excepting perhaps servility – a true characteristic of the old world – and stinginess, which I have never observed in them. The absence of servility is typical of all the independent Indians of Ecuador.[38]

And he observes that "they also gain great enjoyment from the destruction of life. They are always ready to kill animals or people, and they delight in it."[39]

Simson was employed on the first steam launch to ascend the Putumayo, that of Rafael Reyes, later a president of Colombia. Hence he witnessed the opening of the region to modern commerce, and was in a special position to observe the institutionalization of ideologies concerning race and class. Not only does he present a contrary and more complex estimate of Indian toughness than does Casement: he also provides the clue and ethnographic motif necessary to understand why such contrary images coexist and flourish, how Indian images of wildness come halfway, as it were, to meet and merge with white colonial images of savagery, and, finally, how such imagery functions in the creation of terror.

It is first necessary to observe that the inhabitants of the Putumayo were, according to Joaquin Rocha at the turn of the century, divided into two great classes of social types: whites and savage Indians. The category, whites (also referred to as "rationals," Christians, and "civilized"), included not only people phenotypically white, but also mestizos, negros, mulattos, Zambos, and Indians "of those groups incorporated into civilization since the time of the Spanish conquest."[40] Simson takes us further into this classification, and although his remarks here pertain to the *montaña* region at the headwaters of the rivers, they seem to me generally applicable to the middle reaches of the Putumayo as well, and are certainly relevant to the understanding of colonist culture.

Simson notes that what he calls the "pure Indians of the forest" are divided, by whites and Spanish-speaking Indians, into two classes; Indians (*Indios*) and heathens (*infieles*). The *Indios* are Quichua-speaking, salt-eating, semi-Christians, while the heathens, also known as *aucas*, speak distinct languages, eat salt rarely, and know nothing of baptism or of the Catholic Church.[41] In passing it should be observed that today, if not in times long past, the term *auca* also connotes cannibals who roam the forest naked, are without marriage rules, and practice incest. [...]

It is crucial to grasp the dialectic of sentiments involved here by the appelation *auca*, a dialectic enshrouded in magic and composed of both fear and contempt – identical to the mysticism, hatred, and awe projected onto the Zionist socialist Timerman in the torture chambers of the military. In the case of the *aucas*, this projection is inseparable from the imputation of their resistance to sacred imperial authority and the further imputation of magical power possessed by lowland forest dwellers as a class and by their oracles, seers, and healers – their shamans – in particular. Moreover, this indigenous, and what may well be a pre-Colombian, construction blends with the medieval European mythology of the Wild Man brought to the Andes and the Amazon by the Spaniards and Portuguese. Today, in the upper reaches of the Putumayo with which I am acquainted, the mythology of *auca* and Wild Man underlies the resort to Indian shamans by white and black colonists who seek cure from sorcery and hard times, while these very same colonists despise Indians as savages.[42] In the rubber boom, with its desperate need for Indian labor, the same mythology nourished incalculable cruelty and paranoia on the part of the whites. It is to this mythic endowment inherited by world capitalism in the jungles of the Putumayo that we need to pay attention if we are to understand the irrational "excesses" of the terror and torture depicted by Casement.

Fear of Indian Rebellion

Casement mentions the possibility that, in addition to their drive for profit, the whites' fear of Indian rebellion impelled them toward viciousness. But in keeping with his stress on Indian docility, he gives four reasons why Indian rebellion was unlikely. Indian communities were disunited long before the advent of the rubber boom, while the whites were armed and well organized. The Indians were poorly armed and their blowpipes, bows, and lances had been confiscated. Most important in his opinion was the fact that the elders had been systematically murdered by the company for the crime of giving "bad advice."[43]

Rocha, who was in the area some seven years before Casement, thought differently. He claims that the whites feared the consequences of the Indians' hatred and that this fear was central to their policies and thought. "Life for the Whites in the land of the Huitotos," he declares, "hangs by a thread." Small uprisings were common, and he provides an account of one of these.

In 1903 the Colombian Emilio Gutiérrez navigated up the Caquetá from Brazil searching for Indians to use to establish a rubber station. Reaching the area whose conquest he desired, he sent the bulk of his men back to carry in merchandise, and he and three others remained. While asleep, Gutiérrez and the companions were killed by wild Indians. Hearing the news, other whites prepared to retaliate when news reached them that thirty of Gutiérrez's civilized Indian work force had also been killed, all at the same time yet in different parts of the jungle. Indians working for whites were set in pursuit of the rebels; some were caught and killed outright, some were taken as prisoners for the whites, and the majority escaped. A few were captured and eaten by the Indian mercenaries – so the tale goes.[44]

In 1910 Casement heard the same episode from a Peruvian, who introduced his story by saying that the methods used by Colombian conquerors were very bad. In this version, the rebel Indians decapitated Gutiérrez together with an unstated number of other whites and exposed their skulls on the walls of their "drum house," keeping the limbless bodies in water for as long as possible to show them off to other Indians. Casement's informant said he had found the bodies of twelve others tied to stakes, assuring Casement that the reason they had not been eaten was that Indians "had a repugnance to eating white men, whom they hated too much." Terrible reprisals subsequently fell upon the Indians, notes Casement.[45]

Considered separately, and especially in relation to Rocha's version, this account of Casement's establishes the point that the white fear of Indian rebellion was not unjustified, but that, in addition, such rebellion was perceived in a mythic and colonially paranoid vision in which the image of dismemberment and cannibalism glowed vividly.

Fear of Cannibalism

Cannibalism acquired great ideological potency for the colonists from the beginning of the European conquest of the New World. The figure of the cannibal was elaborated and used for many sorts of ends, responding as it did to some of the most powerful symbolic forces known to humankind. It could be used to justify enslavement and as such was apparently important in the early economy of Brazil,[46] thereby affecting even the headwaters of the Amazon such as the Putumayo where cannibalism was kept luridly alive in the imagination of the whites down to the era of the rubber boom.

Rocha provides many examples. He signals his arrival at Huitoto territory writing of "this singular land of the cannibals, the land of the Huitotos conquered by a dozen valiant Colombians repeating the heroism of their Spanish ancestors."[47] The rubber traders, he emphatically asserts, have tried to stamp out cannibalism with severe punishments. Yet cannibalism is an addiction. The Huitotos think they can deceive the whites about this, but "they succumb to the satisfaction of their beastly appetites."[48] The most notorious of the modern *conquistadores*, the Colombian Crisóstomo Hernandez (a Colombian highlands mulatto who had fled the police and sought refuge in the jungle), had, so Rocha was told, killed all the children, women, and men of an Indian long house because they practiced cannibalism – a surprising story given the need for labor, yet typical of white folk tales in the Putumayo. [. . .]

The story which most impressed Rocha was the one about the Huitoto rite of judicial murder, or capital punishment. One can easily imagine the chords of exotic terror it provoked among the colonists and employees of the rubber company listening to it in the chit-chat of a jungle night.

All the individuals of the nation that has captured the prisoner retire to an area of the bush to which women are absolutely prohibited, except for one who acts a special role. Children are rigorously excluded also. In the center, a pot of cooked tobacco juice is placed for the pleasure of the men, and in a corner seated on a little bench and firmly bound is the captive.

Clasping each other's arms, the savages form a long line, and to the sound of drum beats advance dancing very close to the victim. They retreat and advance many times, with individuals separating to drink from the pot of tobacco. Then the drum stops for the dancing cannibals, and so that the unfortunate victim can see how much he is going to lose by dying, the most beautiful girl of the tribe enters, regally attired with the most varied and brilliant feathers of the birds of these woods. The drum starts again, and the beautiful girl dances alone in front of and almost touching him. She twists and advances, showering him with passionate looks and gestures of love, turning around and repeating this three or four times. She then leaves, terminating the second act of this solemn occasion. The third follows with the same men's dance as before, except that each time the line of dancers approaches the prisoner, one of the men detaches himself and declaims something like this: "Remember when your people killed Jatijiko, man of our nation whom you couldn't take prisoner because he knew how to die before allowing himself to be dragged in front of your people? We are going to take vengeance of his death in you, you coward, that doesn't know how to die in battle like he did." Or else: "Remember when you and your people surprised my sister Jifisino bathing, captured her and while alive made a party of her flesh and tormented her until her last breath? Do you remember? Now you god-cursed man we are going to devour you alive and you won't die until all traces of your bloody flesh have disappeared from around our mouths."

Following this is the fourth and last act of the terrifying tragedy. One by one the dancers come forward and with his knife each one cuts a slice of meat off the prisoner, which they eat half roasted to the sound of his death rattle. When he eventually dies, they finish cutting him up and continue roasting and cooking his flesh, eating him to the last little bit.[49]

Narrative Mediation: Epistemic Murk

It seems to me that stories like these were the groundwork indispensable to the formation and flowering of the colonial imagination during the Putumayo rubber boom. "Their imagination was diseased," wrote the Peruvian judge Rómulo Paredes in 1911, referring to the rubber-station managers, "and they saw everywhere attacks by Indians, conspiracies, uprisings, treachery etc.: and in order to save themselves from these fancied perils... they killed, and killed without compassion."[50] Far from being trivial daydreams indulged in after work was over, these stories and the imagination they sustained were a potent political force

without which the work of conquest and of supervising rubber gathering could not have been accomplished. What is essential to understand is the way in which these stories functioned to create, through magical realism, a culture of terror dominating both whites and Indians.

The importance of this fabulous work extends beyond the epic and grotesque quality of its content. The truly crucial feature lies in creating an uncertain reality out of fiction, a nightmarish reality in which the unstable interplay of truth and illusion becomes a social force of horrendous and phantasmic dimensions. To an important extent all societies live by fictions taken as reality. What distinguishes cultures of terror is that the epistemological, ontological, and otherwise purely philosophical problem of reality-and-illusion, certainty-and-doubt, becomes infinitely more than a "merely" philosophical problem. It becomes a high-powered tool for domination and a principal medium of political practice. And in the Putumayo rubber boom this medium of epistemic and ontological murk was most keenly figured and objectified as the space of death.

In his report, Paredes tells us that the rubber-station managers lived obsessed with death. They saw danger everywhere and thought solely of the fact that they were surrounded by vipers, tigers, and cannibals. It is these ideas of death, he writes, which constantly struck their imaginations, making them terrified and capable of any act. Like children who read the *Arabian Nights*, he goes on to say, they had nightmares of witches, evil spirits, death, treason, and blood. The only way they could live in such a terrifying world, he observes, was by themselves inspiring terror.[51]

Sociological and Mythic Mediation: The *Muchachos*

If it was the telling of tales which mediated inspiration of the terror, then it behooves us to inquire a little into the sociological agency which mediated this mediation, namely, the corps of Indian guards trained by the company and known as the *muchachos*. For in Rómulo Paredes's words, they were "constantly devising executions and continually revealing meetings of Indians 'licking tobacco' – which meant an oath to kill white men – imaginary uprisings which never existed, and other similar crimes."[52]

Mediating as civilized or rational Indians between the savages of the forest and the whites of the rubber camps, the *muchachos* personified all the critical distinctions in the class and caste system of rubber production. Cut off from their own kind, whom they persecuted and betrayed and in whom they inspired envy and hatred, and now classified as civilized yet dependent on whites for food, arms, and goods, the *muchachos* wrought to perfection all that was horrifying in the colonial mythology of savagery – because they occupied the perfect sociological and mythic space to do so. Not only did they create fictions stoking the fires of white paranoia, they embodied the brutality which the whites feared, created, and tried to harness to their own ends. In a very literal sense, the *muchachos* traded their identity as savages for their new social status as civilized Indians and guards. As Paredes notes, they placed at the disposal of the whites "their special instincts, such as sense of direction, scent, their sobriety, and their knowledge of the forest."[53] Just as they bought rubber from the wild Indians of the forest, so the whites also bought the *auca*-like savage instincts of the Indian *muchachos*.

Yet, unlike rubber, these savage instincts were manufactured largely in the imaginations of the Whites. All the *muchachos* had to do in order to receive their rewards was to objectify and through words reflect back to the whites the phantoms that populated colonist culture. Given the centuries of colonial mythology concerning the *auca* and the Wild Man, and given the implosion of this mythology in the contradictory social being of the *muchachos*, the task was an easy one. The *muchachos*' stories were, in fact, stories within a much older story encompassing the *muchachos* as objects of a colonialist discourse rather than as its authors.

The trading system of debt-peonage established by the Putumayo rubber boom was thus more than a trade in white goods for rubber gathered by the Indians. It was also a trade in terrifying mythologies and fictional realities, pivoted on the mediation of the *muchachos*, whose storytelling bartered betrayal of Indian realities for the confirmation of colonial fantasies.

The Colonial Mirror

I began this essay stating that my concern was with the mediation of the culture of terror through narration, and with the problems of writing against terror. In part my concern stemmed from my problems in evaluating and interpreting the "facts" constituted in the various accounts of the Putumayo atrocities. This problem of interpretation grew ever larger, eventually bursting into the realization that that problem is precisely what is central to the culture of terror – not only making effective talking and writing against terror extremely difficult, but, even more to the point, making the terrible reality of the death squads, disappearances, and torture all the more effectively crippling of people's capacity to resist.

While much attention is given to "ideology" in the social sciences, virtually none as far as I know is given to the fact that people delineate their world, including its large as well as its microscale politics, in stories and story-like creations and very rarely, if ever, in ideologies (as customarily defined). Surely it is in the coils of rumor, gossip, story, and chit-chat where ideology and ideas become emotionally powerful and enter into active social circulation and meaningful existence. So it was with the Putumayo terror, from the accounts of which it seems clear that the colonists and rubber company employees not only feared but also themselves created through narration fearful and confusing images of savagery – images which bound colonial society together through the epistemic murk of the space of death. The systems of torture they devised to secure rubber mirrored the horror of the savagery they so feared, condemned – and fictionalized. Moreover, when we consider the task of creating counterrepresentations and counterdiscourses, we must take stock of the way that most if not all the narratives reproduced by Hardenburg and Casement, referring to and critical of the atrocities, were similarly fictionalized, drawing upon the same historically moulded source that men succumbed to when torturing Indians.

Torture and terror in the Putumayo were motivated by the need for cheap labor. But labor *per se* – labor as a commodity – did not exist in the jungles of the Caraparaná and Igaraparaná affluents of the Putumayo. What existed was not a market for labor but a society and culture of human beings whom the colonists called Indians, irrationals, and savages, with their very specific historical trajectory, form of life, and modes of exchange. In the blundering colonial attempt to dovetail forcibly the capitalist commodity-structure to one or the other of the possibilities for rubber gathering offered by these modes of exchange, torture, as Casement alludes, took on a life of its own: "Just as the appetite comes in the eating so each crime led on to fresh crimes."[54] To this we should add that, step by step, terror and torture became *the* form of life for some fifteen years, an organized culture with its systematized rules, imagery, procedures, and meanings involved in spectacles and rituals that sustained the precarious solidarity of the rubber company employees as well as beating out through the body of the tortured some sort of canonical truth about Civilization and Business.

It was not commodity fetishism but debt fetishism drenched in the fictive reality of the debt-peonage institution, with its enforced "advances" and theater-like farce of business exchanges, that exercised the decisive force in the creation of terror, transforming torture from the status of a means to that of the mode if not, finally, the very aim of production.

From the reports of both Timerman and Casement it is obvious that torture and institutionalized terror is like a ritual art form, and that far from being spontaneous, *sui generis*, and an abandonment of what are often called "the values of civilization," such rites have a deep history deriving power and meaning from those values. What demands further analysis here is the mimesis between the savagery attributed to the Indians by the colonists and the savagery perpetrated by the colonists in the name of what Julio César Arana called civilization.[55]

This reciprocating yet distorted mimesis has been and continues to be of great importance in the construction of colonial culture – *the colonial mirror* which reflects back onto the colonists the barbarity of their own social relations, but as imputed to the savage or evil figures they wish to colonize. It is highlighted in the Putumayo in the colonist lore as related, for instance, through Joaquin Rocha's lurid tale of Huitoto cannibalism. And what is put into discourse through the artful story telling of the colonists is the same as what they practiced on the bodies of Indians.[56]

Tenaciously embedded in this artful practice is a vast and mystifying Western history and iconography of evil in the imagery of the inferno and the savage – wedded to and inseparable from paradise, utopia, and the good. It is to the subversion of that apocalyptic dialectic that all of us would be advised to bend our counterdiscursive efforts, in a quite different poetics of good-and-evil whose cathartic force lies not with cataclysmic resolution of contradictions but with their disruption.

Post-Enlightenment European culture makes it difficult if not impossible to penetrate the hallucinatory veil of the heart of darkness without either succumbing to its hallucinatory quality or losing that quality. Fascist poetics succeed where liberal rationalism self-destructs. But what might point a way out of this impasse is precisely what is so painfully absent from all the Putumayo accounts, namely, the narrative and narrative mode of the Indians which does de-sensationalize terror so that the histrionic stress on the mysterious side of the mysterious (to adopt Benjamin's formula) is indeed denied by an optic which perceives the everyday as impenetrable, the impenetrable as everyday.[57] At least this is the poetics of the sorcery and shamanism I know about in the upper reaches of the Putumayo, but that is another history for another time, not only of terror but of healing as well.

NOTES

1 Jacobo Timerman, *Prisoner without a Name, Cell without a Number* (New York: Vintage Books, 1982), 164.
2 Timerman, *Prisoner*, 28.
3 Timerman, *Prisoner*, 111.
4 Gerardo Reichel-Dolmatoff, *Amazonian Cosmos: The Sexual and Religious Symbolism of the Tukano Indians* (Chicago: University of Chicago Press, 1971).
5 Timerman, *Prisoner*, 52.
6 Michel Foucault, "Truth and Power" in *Power/Knowledge*, Colin Gordon, ed. (New York: Pantheon, 1980), 118.
7 Timerman, *Prisoner*, 62, 66.
8 Frederick R. Karl, *Joseph Conrad: The Three Lives* (New York: Farrar, Straus and Giroux, 1979), 286.
9 Paul Ricoeur, *Freud and Philosophy: An Essay on Interpretation* (New Haven and London: Yale University Press, 1970).
10 Ian Watt, *Conrad: In the Nineteenth Century* (Berkeley and Los Angeles: University of California Press, 1979), 161.
11 Brian Inglis, *Roger Casement* (London: Hodder, 1974), 46.
12 Ibid., 131.
13 Walter Hardenburg, *The Putumayo: The Devil's Paradise. Travels in the Peruvian Amazon Region and an Account of the Atrocities Committed upon*

the Indians Therein (London: T. Fisher Unwin, 1912), 214.

14   Hardenburg, *Putumayo*, 258.

15   Ibid., 260, 259.

16   Ibid., 236. Also cited by Casement in his Putumayo report to Sir Edward Grey. There Casement declares that this description was repeated to him "again and again ... by men who had been employed in this work." Roger Casement, "Correspondence respecting the Treatment of British Colonial Subjects and Native Indians employed in the Collection of Rubber in the Putumayo District," *House of Commons Sessional Papers*, 14 February 1912 to 7 March 1913, vol. 68 (hereafter cited as Casement, *Putumayo Report*), p. 35.

17   Casement, *Putumayo Report*, p. 17.

18   Ibid., p. 34.

19   Ibid., pp. 33, 34.

20   Ibid., p. 37.

21   Ibid., p. 39.

22   Ibid., p. 37.

23   Ibid., p. 39.

24   Ibid., p. 42.

25   Ibid., p. 31. From various estimates it appears that the ratio of armed supervisors to wild Indians gathering rubber was somewhere between 1:16 and 1:50. Of these armed supervisors, the *muchachos* outnumbered the whites by around 2:1. See Howard Wolf and Ralph Wolf, *Rubber: A Story of Glory and Greed* (New York: Covici, Friede, 1936), 88; US Consul Charles C. Eberhardt, *Slavery in Peru*, 7 February 1913, report prepared for US House of Representatives, 62d Cong., 3d Sess., 1912, H. Doc. 1366, p. 112; Roger Casement, British Parliamentary Select Committee on Putumayo, *House of Commons Sessional Papers*, 1913, vol. 14, p. xi; Casement, *Putumayo Report*, p. 33.

26   Casement, *Putumayo Report*, p. 33.

27   Ibid., pp. 44–5.

28   Ibid., p. 55.

29   Inglis, *Roger Casement*, 29.

30   Joaquin Rocha, *Memorandum de un viaje* (Bogotá: Editorial el Mercurio, 1905), 123–4, asserts that because the Indians are "naturally loafers" they postpone paying off their advances from the rubber traders, thus compelling the traders to use physical violence. Eberhardt, *Slavery in Peru*, p. 110, writes that "the Indian enters the employ of some rubber gatherer, often willingly, though not infrequently by force, and immediately becomes indebted to him for food etc. ... However, the scarcity of labor and the ease with which the Indians can usually escape and live on the natural products of the forest oblige the owners to treat them with some consideration. The Indians realize this and their work is not at all satisfactory, judging from our standards. This was particularly noticeable during a recent visit I made to a mill where "cachassa" or aguadiente is extracted from cane. The men seemed to work when and how they chose, requiring a liberal amount of the liquor each day (of which they are all particularly fond), and if this is not forthcoming or they are treated harshly in any way they run to the forests. The employer has the law on his side, and if he can find the runaway he is at liberty to bring him back; but the time lost and the almost useless task of trying to track the Indian through the dense forests and small streams makes it far more practical that the servant be treated with consideration in the first place."

31   Casement, British Parliamentary Select Committe on Putumayo, *House of Commons Sessional Papers*, 1913, vol. 14, p. 113, no. 2809.

32   Karl Polanyi, *The Great Transformation* (Boston: Beacon Press, 1957), 72. Cf. Michael Taussig, *The Devil and Commodity Fetishism in South America* (Chapel Hill: University of North Carolina Press, 1980).

33   Julio César Arana, Evidence to the British Parliamentary Select Committee on Putumayo. *House of Commons Sessional Papers*, 1913, vol. 14, p. 488, no. 12,222.

34   P. Francisco de Vilanova, introduction to P. Francisco de Igualada, *Indios Amazonicas: Coleccion Misiones Capuchinas*, vol. VI (Barcelona: Imprenta Myria, 1948).

35   Hardenburg, *Putumayo*, 163.

36   Father Gaspar de Pinell, *Un viaje por el Putumayo el Amazonas* (Bogotá: Imprenta Nacional, 1924), 196.

37   Casement, *Putumayo Report*, pp. 27–8.

38   Alfred Simson, *Travels in the Wilds of Ecuador and the Exploration of the Putumayo River* (London: Samson Low, 1886), 170.

39   Simson, *Travels*, 170–1.

40   Rocha, *Memorandum de un viaje*, 138.

41   Simson, *Travels*, 58.

42   Michael Taussig, "Folk Healing and the Structure of Conquest," *Journal of Latin American Lore*, 6:2 (1980), 217–78.

43   Casement, *Putumayo Report*, p. 45.

44   Rocha, *Memorandum de un viaje*, 125–6.

45   Casement, *Putumayo Report*, 30.

46   An excellent discussion of this is to be found in David Sweet, "A Rich Realm of Nature Destroyed: The Middle Amazon Valley, 1640–1750" (Ph.D. diss., University of Wisconsin, 1975), I, 113–14, 116, 120, 126, 130–1, 141, 347.

47   Rocha, *Memorandum de un viaje*, 92–3.

48   Ibid., p. 118.

49   Ibid., 116–17.

50   Rómulo Paredes, "Confidential Report to the Ministry of Foreign Relations, Peru," September 1911, translated in Eberhardt, *Slavery in Peru*, p. 146.

51 Paredes, "Confidential Report," in Eberhardt, *Slavery in Peru*, p. 158.

52 Ibid., p. 147. One should not omit the role of the blacks recruited in Barbados, mediating between the whites and the Indians. In much the same way as the British army from the mid-nineteenth century on deployed different colonial and ethnic groups so as to maximize reputations for ferocity and checking one against the other, the British and Peruvian rubber companies used its "ethnic soldiers" in the Putumayo.

53 Paredes, "Confidential Report," in Eberhardt, *Slavery in Peru*, p. 147.

54 Casement, *Putumayo Report*, p. 44.

55 See note 33 above, and text.

56 Illustrations of the way in which this following of the letter of the tale was enacted in the torture of Indians can be found in the rare instances of dialogue that Casement allows his witnesses in the section of his report given over to testimony by men recruited in Barbados, as, for example:

"And you say you saw the Indians burnt?" Consul-General Casement asked Augustus Walcott, born in the Caribbean island of Antigua but twenty three years before.
"Yes."
"Burnt alive?"
"Alive."
"How do you mean? Describe this."
"Only one I see burnt alive."
"Well, tell me about that one?"
"He had not work 'caucho,' he ran away and he kill a 'muchacho,' a boy, and they cut off his two arms and legs by the knee and they burn his body. . . ."
"Are you sure he was still alive – not dead when they threw him on the fire?"
"Yes, he did alive. I'm sure of it – I see him move – open his eyes, he screamed out. . . ."
"Was Aurelio Rodriguez [the rubber-station manager] looking on – all the time?"
"Yes, all the time."
"Giving directions?"
"Yes, Sir."
"He told them to cut off the legs and arms?"
"Yes."

There was something else the Consul-General could not understand and he called Walcott back to explain what he meant by saying, "because he told the Indians that we was Indians too, and eat those –." What he meant, Casement summarized, was that the station manager, Señor Normand, in order "to frighten the Indians told them that the negroes were cannibals, and a fierce tribe of cannibals who eat people, and that if they did not bring in rubber these black men would be sent to kill and eat them." (Casement, *Putumayo Report*, pp. 115, 118.)

Another, more complicated, example follows:
"Have you ever seen Aguero kill Indians?" the Consul-General asked Evelyn Bateson, aged twenty five, born in Barbados, and working in the rubber depôt of La Chorrera.
"No, Sir; I haven't seen him kill Indians – but I have seen him send 'muchachos' to kill Indians. He has taken an Indian man and given him to the 'muchachos' to eat, and they have a dance of it. . . ."
"You saw the man killed?"
"Yes, Sir. They tied him to a stake and they shot him, and they cut off his head after he was shot and his feet and hands, and they carried them about the section – in the yard and they carries them up and down and singing, and they carries them to their house and dances. . . ."
"How do you know they ate them?"
"I heard they eat them. I have not witnessed it, Sir, but I heard the manager Señor Aguero tell that they eat this man."
"The manager said all this?"
"Yes, Sir, he did." (Casement, *Putumayo Report*, p. 103.)

This sort of stimulation if not creation of cannibalism by colonial pressure is also recorded in missionaries' letters concerning King Leopold's Congo Free State and the gathering of rubber there. See, for example, the account of Mr. John Harris in the work by Edmund Morel, *King Leopold's Rule in Africa* (New York: Funk and Wagnalls, 1905), 437–41.

57 Walter Benjamin, "Surrealism: The Last Snapshot of the European Intelligentsia," in the collection of his essays entitled *Reflections*, trans. E. Jephcott, ed. P. Demetz (New York: Harcourt Brace Jovanovich, 1978), esp. pp. 189–90.

3

From *Ishi in Two Worlds: A Biography of the Last Wild Indian in North America*

Theodora Kroeber

The Long Concealment

The middle sixties and early seventies – the era of the Civil War, of Lincoln's assassination, and of the invasion of the South by an army of carpet-baggers – were the years when the clash between Indians and whites in California reached a climax of fear and fury.

These years were also the time when the small boy, Ishi, was being taught Yahi skills, language, manners, law, and religion by his parents and the old men of the tribe. It was to be Ishi's fate to remember Yahi life only within the terror which encompassed and finally engulfed his people. Those Yahi who survived the first decade of the gold rush lived still in their old villages, but they were exposed and vulnerable as never before. Their near neighbors south of Deer Creek were dead or scattered; and to the north, from Mill Creek all the way to the old Yahi border across Montgomery Creek, the ancient Yana world was destroyed: its villages despoiled, its land invaded, its people murdered. In a lonely and lengthy last stand the Yahi contrived to prolong for another half century what may be called the tribal history of the Yana.

The lives of the Yahi and of the white ranchers whose land lay in the valley below and who pastured their stock in the Yana hills were, by this time, geographically interposed one on the other and at hopeless and deadly cross purpose. The white pressure was such that the Yahi were confined to the parts of their country which were inaccessible to stock or to a man on horseback. This meant that to live they were reduced to constant raiding and stealing. When they could not find livestock, they took the food which was stored in sheds or cabins for use at roundup time: they took whatever they could get their hands on. And on a raiding trip one or more of their number, a half-grown boy or one of their able bodied young men or women were as like as not to be picked off with a shot from the gun of a rancher or a herder, or one of the sheriff's men out on a scouting party – an attrition the Yahi could not at all afford. Occasionally the Indians succeeded in a raid of some size. They would take several head of stock or several sacks of grain, or perhaps in their turn they would murder a white woman or a child or a man. This always meant reprisals which were in the event disastrous to the dwindling tribelet.

The Workman ranch was on lower Concow Creek, far below the Yahi. There, Mrs. Workman, her hired man John Banks known as "Scotch John," and a young woman newly arrived from England, Rosanna Smith, were unaccountably murdered, on August 15, 1865. Two days earlier, the peaceful Maidu Indians at Big Meadows had been attacked and some of their young women and girls kidnaped. That a small band as hard pressed as were the Yahi should have undertaken two simultaneous and madcap projects would at this distance seem most improbable. They were believed, however, to have been responsible for both, their guilt attested to by scouts who claimed to have picked up one trail from the Workman ranch and another from Big Meadows, leading straight to Mill Creek. An avenging party of seventeen armed men, among them the wrought-up neighbors of the Workmans, put themselves under Anderson's and Good's leadership.

We might imagine that the Yahi, if only just returned from two bloody expeditions, would have been doubly on their guard. Such was not the case. Anderson and his men made their roundabout way undetected into Mill Creek above the gorge not far from Bruff's old camp – a site much favored by Anderson because its three knolls gave him a natural hiding place from which he overlooked a stretch of the creek and one of the largest of the Yahi villages. Under cover of a moonless night, Anderson deployed his men in two parties, leading one of them up a steep detour which brought them out onto the three knolls where their gunfire would cover the upstream retreat from the village. Good and the remaining men hid themselves close beside the downstream entrance to the village, which position further commanded the only ford by which the creek could be readily crossed.

Anderson knew to a nicety the terrain, the special features of each village, and the probable behavior of the villagers under surprise attack; these things and more he had learned in the campaigns against the Central and Northern Yana. His execution of the Three Knolls attack was so successful that it almost ended what he called "the scourge of the Mill Creeks," before dawn of August sixteenth. Waiting only until there was light enough for his men to see where they were shooting, Anderson directed a continuous stream of gunfire down from above onto the sleeping village. As he had surmised, the Yahi ran downstream making for the open ford which brought them under Good's fire from below. The terrified Indians leapt into Mill Creek, but the rapid current was a sorry protection. They became targets there for Good's guns, and Mill Creek ran red with the blood of its people. Anderson reported that "many dead bodies floated down the rapid current."

This was, all in all, Anderson's most brilliantly successful attack. Beyond the customary taking of scalps, it may also have had some atrocity embellishments not usual under his command. He does not detail any, but he does suggest them in a single laconic sentence, "The Concow people were intensely wrought up over the horrible atrocities

[also never made specific] practiced by the Indians on the white women whom they killed, and I had told them [the Concow people] that they were at liberty to deal with the Indians as they saw fit."[1]

A few Yahi escaped, the small child Ishi and his mother among them. Ishi remembered the morning attack, but he did not talk about it in after years; it may have been then that his father was killed. The attackers ransacked the wrecked village and went triumphantly home, dangling it is not known how many scalps from their belts. Good took with him also a small child whom he found unharmed under a sheepskin blanket when they looted the village. The little boy had six toes on each foot – a peculiarity which seemed to endear him to Good.

Long, long after that August morning, the scarred ground where the village had been remained a shambles of wrecked summer shelters, of overturned food baskets, broken harpoons, and bows amidst the exposed and rotting bodies and at last the whitened bones of the dead. This unnatural neglect of their dead by the Yahi is alone sufficient evidence of how desperate was their condition. They were being attacked again and again at their center, at one or another of their larger villages situated on Mill Creek, from Bay Tree village downstream to the vicinity of Black Rock upstream. This was a concentrated and by Yahi standards a populous area of barely fifteen to twenty miles along the creek and never far from its banks or open fords or overhanging caves and bluffs. Plainly the Yahi were close to the end of their career as trouble makers, their numbers so reduced that any clash, or the loss of a single one of their depleted band made their total annihilation imminent.

It is in Sim Moak's recollections that another punishing attack by Anderson, this one in 1866, is described in much detail. The Yahi must have been desperate, because they were incautious enough to raid a ranch house at midday. The rancher's wife, Mrs. Silva, and a hired man were hiving bees near the house and looked up to see several Yahi, loaded with provisions of one sort and another, climbing out of a window. They got away, but within a few hours Anderson was in pursuit with a number of his regulars, trailing them over Deer Creek Flats and to the far side of the creek despite some delay in making the crossing. The Yahi had taken the precaution of dislodging the logs on which they crossed, which floated away downstream so that the pursuers were forced to rig a precarious and hop-scotch sort of temporary bridge between boulders as a crossing. Perhaps the Indians discounted the white men's competence to do this, and indeed one of the posse barely made it over; perhaps the Yahi did not know they were being followed. In any case, as they neared their home, they kept no rear guard. Without warning, Anderson came over the brow of a ravine above Mill Creek so little behind the Indians that they were dotted along the steep incline below him in a pattern of perfect and helpless targets.

Their slaughter was complete even to the one of their number who was farthest downhill and who took refuge behind a waterfall in the creek. Jake Moak, Sim's brother, could see the outline of a person crouched behind the tumbling spray, and continued to pour shot through the water until he saw the figure collapse into the basin of the falls. This expedition was as sheerly disastrous for the Yahi as it was plain good fun for the Moak brothers. Besides the waterfall episode, with its detail of Jake's going into the stream to retrieve his dead quarry from behind the falls and drag him out onto the bank by his long hair, there is the story of the flower-covered hat and the trip home. Here it is as Sim tells it:

We all took a load of plunder [which included a flower-bedecked hat stolen from the Workman house and retrieved by Anderson] and packed it out to the valley. Anderson was riding a very small white mule and as we were coming down the stage road one of the party said that Anderson must wear the flowered hat. We untied it from the top of the pack and Anderson being such a large man we had to tie it on his head. We then took a scalp and fastened it on the mule's rump. We met several emigrant wagons going to Oregon. The drivers would stop and the canvas would part, and the women's and children's heads would poke out. It was a sight to see that large man riding such a small mule, the long rifle laid across in front of him and the flowered bonnet and the long haired scalp.

Either in 1867 or 1868, Anderson and his men tracked to a cave a considerable number of Yahi. The different accounts agree neither about the exact date nor about the particular reason alleged for the massacre, but as nearly as can be made out, it was in reparation for a murder. Mrs. Allen's and Mrs. Dirsch's names come up again in this connection but their murder was earlier, and had already motivated the completion of the wiping out of the Central and Northern Yana. All that is known is that the Yahi were tracked to a cave at Campo Seco, north of Mill Creek, and there thirty-three of them were murdered and scalped, making this cave another charnel house of whitening bones to be avoided by whites and Indians.

Neither Robert Anderson, Hiram Good, nor any other of the guards participated in the final mass massacre of Yahi. A party of four vaqueros, J. J. Bogart, Jim Baker, Scott Williams, and Norman Kingsley, were camped at Wild Horse Corral engaged in a roundup of cattle from the Yana hills. One morning toward the end of the roundup they came on a trail of blood. Guessing it was that of a wounded steer, they followed the blood trail which led them in the direction of upper Mill Creek. They found a broken arrow and, a little beyond, the remains of the carcass of a steer. The hunters who had killed the steer had been too pressed to skin it in their usual fashion, and had instead hurriedly hacked off chunks of meat, as much as they could carry, and thrown the rest into the brush to be retrieved no doubt if there was opportunity later.

Having found this much, the vaqueros went back to their own camp, but the next day, with dogs this time, they picked up the trail again and followed it into Mill Creek and upstream to a large cave. In this remote and seemingly safe spot were gathered more than thirty Yahi including young children and babies, well supplied with food, even to fresh and dried meat. They were helpless against the four armed men who forthwith killed them all. Norman Kingsley, as he explained afterwards, changed guns during the slaughter, exchanging his .56-caliber Spencer rifle for a .38-caliber Smith and Wesson revolver, because the rifle "tore them up so bad," particularly the babies. There is today a Kingsley Cave, only about two trail miles from Wild Horse Corral. This is presumably the cave of the last massacre.

With this morning's work done, it was generally believed that the Yahi – the stubborn Mill Creeks whom Anderson and Good had sworn to exterminate – had been killed to the last woman and child. Silence brooded over Mill Creek whose caves had become truly the tombs of its ancient peoples.

Except that the bodies of the victims of this final massacre disappeared complete and clean from the cave.

That the few survivors of the Kingsley Cave disaster might have resorted to burial instead of cremation rites for its victims suggests itself as a possibly necessary compromise, owing to the risk of detection from the smoke of a funeral pyre, or rather from the series of pyres needed for so many corpses. Archaeological evidence within the cave is not conclusive, nor is there other evidence. Ishi implied in any reluctant reference he ever made to deaths or funerary rites that the bodies of the Yahi dead were always cremated according to correct and usual practice. After cremation it was the custom to collect the bones and ashes from the pyre and put them in a shallow hollow among the rocks where a rock cairn was built up to mark the place and also to prevent dogs or wild animals from digging up the bones. The soil of Mill Creek canyon and its caves is thin and not easily dug to any depth with primitive tools. Solomon Gore reported to Waterman that he, in company with a number of other white men, visited the cave soon after the violence there and that there were no bodies, or exposed bones, nor was there evidence of recently dug graves which they could find. Perhaps the customary cremation had, somehow, been managed. [. . .]

Ishi was a little child three or four years old at the time of the Three Knolls massacre, old enough to remember terror-fraught experiences. He was eight or nine when the Kingsley Cave massacre took place, old enough, possibly, to have taken some part in the cleaning up of the cave and in the ritual disposition of its victims. He entered the concealment in which he would grow up at not more than ten years of age. [. . .] Stephen Powers wrote about the Yahi during the first years of the concealment. He arrived at an imaginatively prophetic projection of the tragi-drama the concealment was to become:

They [the Yahi] seem likely to present a spectacle which is without parallel in human history – that of a barbaric race resisting civilization with arms in their hands, to the last man, and the last squaw, and the last papoose. They were once a numerous and thrifty tribe. Now there are only five of them left – two men, two women, and a child. [Powers was mistaken in the numbers left at the time he was writing but again he was accurately prophetic of what would be the numbers and composition of the band a few years later.] No human eye ever beholds them, except now and then some lonely hunter, perhaps, prowling and crouching for days over the volcanic wastes and scraggy forests which they inhabit. Just at nightfall he may catch a glimpse of a faint camp-fire, with figures flitting about it; but before he can creep within rifle-range of it the figures have disappeared, the flame wastes slowly out, and he arrives only to find that the objects of his search have indeed been there before him, but are gone. They cooked there their hasty evening repast, but they will sleep somewhere else, with no camp-fire to guide a lurking enemy within reach. For days and weeks together they never touch the earth, stepping always from one volcanic stone to another. They never leave a broken twig or a disturbed leaf behind them. Probably no day of the year ever passes over their heads but some one of their doomed nation of five sits crouching on a hillock or in a tree-top within easy eye-shot of his fellows; and not a hare can move upon the earth beneath without its motions being heeded and recorded by the watcher's eye. There are men in and around Chico who have sworn a great oath of vengeance that these five Indians shall die a bloody death; but weeks, months, and years have passed away, and brought for their oaths no fulfillment.

Withdrawal and retreat had been a Yahi pattern since 1850; the period of concealment meant their commitment to the pattern as a total way of life. The problem is to try to understand what motivated the prolonged concealment, their "almost disembodied life" as Powers called it, in the light of the person Ishi showed himself to be when he finally renounced the known agony for an unknown fate.

Withdrawal is a response congenial to much in the American Indian temperament which leans toward the Yogi not the Commissar, being Eastern and not Western in its orientation: fatalistic, introspective, and introverted. The Hopi Indians, remote on their almost impregnable mesas, responded to both Spaniards and Anglo-Americans by excluding them, a withdrawal psychologically comparable to the Japanese nation's 250 years of exclusion; nor has there yet appeared a Perry to breach those mesa ramparts of the Hopi. The Zuni Indians, living in seven accessible villages, were gathered together by the Spaniards into a single large community organized around a mission church. The Zuni continue to live where the Spaniards re-placed them, and they continue to bury their dead in the mission churchyard; otherwise the Spanish-Christian influence has faded except for a single Christian saint who has been allowed living space within the pantheon of Zuni Gods.

Given the intimate separatism of the Californians, it is reasonable to surmise that they would have maintained their identities, some as have the Hopi, some as the Zuni, had there been for them, too, time and place to do so. There was neither; they were visited with annihilation, not interpenetration. Individuals survived sometimes; cultures did not, except along the Colorado River area whose remoteness saved its peoples and their culture for nearly a century longer than elsewhere in the state. It would be sentimentalization to read into the years of desperate concealment a chosen way of life: such choice was never the Yahi's to make. Their choice was between submission with certain loss of identity and probable loss of life, and a finish fight. They chose to fight, withdrawal and concealment being merely the final phase of the unequal fight.

That we know in some detail certain aspects of the concealment and nothing at all of others, is due neither to lack of curiosity and zeal on the part of Ishi's white friends, nor to any uncooperativeness in Ishi, but rather to inhibiting circumstances, some linguistic, some cultural and very "Yana," very "Indian," some humane. It was incorrect and dangerous to the living and the dead for Ishi to use the name of a dead relative or friend, and circumlocutions were impossibly difficult to Ishi's limited English confronted with his friends' limited Yahi. Any, however informal, census-taking was thus ruled out. Had Ishi's measure of life been longer, he would no doubt have transgressed somewhat the taboo against speaking of the dead, in order to preserve something of their history. This would have come naturally with time as his English and his friends' Yahi became more fluent, all the more since he had a strong sense for participation in whatever was of importance to those about him.

Ishi remembered almost everything that had happened in his lifetime. He was a willing autobiographer, patient and conscientious, yet there is not preserved for the present record the "human interest," the tragical, personal accounts in the detail and circumstantiality which he could have given them, and which some readers will be disappointed not to find. But to be questioned and to talk at length and with any intimacy of his family and people at whose death from starvation or old age or sickness he had stood by, a helpless witness and unhappy survivor, left Ishi depressed and distressed. His friends, seeing how it was with him, forebore to question him, contenting themselves with picking up so much as from time to time Ishi might, unasked, volunteer. And in his own time

and way, he told more than a little about certain aspects of the concealment.

We know, for example, only approximately how many people undertook the concealment, and at what ages; we do not know how many of them were men, how many, women; nor do we know the name of a single individual of that small company, not even Ishi's, for Ishi is not a personal name; it means simply, "man."

When Stephen Powers, writing in the *Overland Monthly* of May, 1874, described the escape of the Indians from Hiram Good's cabin as having occurred in the summer of 1870, placing it in time with these words, "There is now wanting only a month of four years since they have been seen together," the two accounts, Powers' and Segraves', agree as to the year. They are within weeks of each other as to the month, and they fit Ishi's description of himself as a child "this high," which again corresponds with the best estimate Doctor Saxton Pope could make from medical evidence of Ishi's age in 1911. The late spring or early summer of 1870 is, then, a time datum firmer than most that we have. It is of help in unraveling the relative chronologies, and it is from this agreement that any estimate of the population numbers of the concealed must take off.

The twelve adults who presented themselves to Segraves are the certainly known Yahi survivors – and the child Ishi – who made up the original group. Waterman, Dr. Pope, and others who were as informed as it was possible to be about the probable numbers, estimated that there may have been as many as fifteen or sixteen in all; that Ishi's cousin or sister, who was not much older (or younger) than Ishi himself, and two or three old people were probably hiding in the brush during the Five Bows parley, unseen by Segraves and the other white men, but close enough at hand to join the twelve upon their retreat from Good's cabin.

There was current in 1915, as in preceding years, a romantic version of the concealment which had it that only five Indians were involved, and the same five, from the beginning. The number had been given the sanction of print by Powers in 1874. Powers' sources for details of the Five Bows incident were second-hand and confused in certain of their parts with other events, or were wrongly reported. According to this version there were two men two women, and a small boy, who would have been Ishi. Since, as will be seen, there were five and only five survivors for many of the forty years, this stretching to make it for the whole of the time becomes in retrospect not much more unlikely than was the concealment itself.

If any births ever for a time augmented the numbers of those hiding, Ishi mentioned none. The population curve was inevitably and presumably only downward. The survival of the Yahi, with restoration of something more than parity of births over deaths would have been risky and dubious at best, so long as they remained sealed off from other human beings. A species which drops seriously below its customary group numbers and swings far from its usual age and sex distributions only rarely and under unusually favorable life conditions is able to survive long enough to rehabilitate itself and to increase. But the Yahi were not, after all, a "species." They were a macrocosmic nation victimized by the common killers: invasion, war, famine, and intolerance.

Beyond the agreement among those best able to judge what was the probable population of the concealment, there are compelling psychological and physiological reasons for believing that it could not have been undertaken by more than a handful of people. There is the question: In a given situation and circumstance, how many people *can* hide as a single unit? With the disadvantages of the Yahi situation, the answer is: Very few. The Yahi limit would seem to have been only as many as would inhabit one of their smaller villages, a larger number being almost sure to bring down upon itself some drastic debacle, such as another Kingsley Cave massacre.

There is the question: Could the Yana hills, or any land so nearly marginal, support life, with the best hunting and gathering grounds unavailable or despoiled? The answer is: Probably not. This leads to the further question: Was this because there was too little, or because so much time and energy had to be diverted to the elaborate and eternal routines of remaining hidden whatever the activity? And the answer is, surely: Both. [...]

The phenomenon of the sealed-off community is a rare but recurrent one in human history. It may be said categorically that it is doomed because of the nature of man, which is social, intermingling, and generalized. A baby raised without hearing human speech or experiencing normal emotional expression and exchange would probably die early, and would in no case develop either speech or other distinctively human and cultural attributes, these being matters which are taught by

example and transmitted through imitation and learning. Nor do adults thrive in solitude – we are not hibernating or singly-living animals. And since we are as men the superficially variant members of a single species, an ingrown, inward-looking, and too-specialized community begins to lose health and adherents after a single generation, or goes to pieces through exacerbation of tempers and temperaments which impinge too nearly and too exclusively one upon another.

But these occasional retreats vary enormously in their origins, in their successes, and in the nature of their ultimate failures. The Long Concealment failed in its objective to save a peoples' life, but it would seem to have been brilliantly successful in its psychology and techniques of living. Ishi's group was master of the difficult art of communal and peaceful coexistence under permanent threat of alarm, and in a tragic and deteriorating prospect. We know from Ishi that men took on "women's work" and *vice versa* according to need. The sick, the dying, and the bedridden were cared for; the dead were sent on their way with ritual formality, nor did the living neglect to mourn for them.

It is a curious circumstance that some of the questions which arise about the concealment are those for which in a different context psychologists and neurologists are trying to find answers for the submarine and outer space services today. Some of these are: What makes for morale under confining and limiting life conditions? What are the presumable limits of claustrophobic endurance? What temperament and build should be sought for these special and confining situations? It seems that the Yahi might have qualified for outer space had they lasted into this century. They were not too large, nor were they awkward or clumsy or restless; they were skilled and resourceful with whatever materials and means were at hand; they were self-sufficient; and their outlook was duly fatalistic.

In contrast to the Forty-niners whom Bruff describes, whose morality and morale had crumbled, Ishi and his band remained incorrupt, humane, compassionate, and with their faith intact even unto starvation, pain, and death. The questions then are: What makes for stability? For psychic strength? For endurance, courage, faith?

Some of the Yahi sources of strength might be said to be that they were on home ground and that they were already skilled in what they had to do to live. That these were not aspects of first import- ance Ishi's later ready adaptation to changed locale and culture would suggest. Of very great import- ance to their psychic health was the circumstance that their sufferings and curtailments arose from wrongs done to them by others. They were not guilt ridden, nor were they "alienated from their culture." Their aims were modest, reasonable, realistic; their egos and ambitions uninflamed; and the American Indian *mystique*, pervasive and unconscious, stood them in good stead.

The twelve years from 1872 to 1884 were with- out incident or rumor. The concealment for those twelve years was complete. No horses or stock were hunted, no cabins were rifled, no grain stolen; not a footprint, not a telltale bit of ash, or wisp of smoke from a fire was seen; not a single broken arrowshaft or a lost spear point or a rem- nant of a milkweed rope snare was found on a forest or meadow floor as a sign that Indians were about. Stephen Powers prefigured this hidden life back in 1874, but not even he foresaw that it might go on so long.

The years of Ishi's total disconnection from his- tory were most of the years of his life: a long interlude of stillness. The senses strain to under- stand what must have been the waking and the sleeping of that time; and if Ishi could not light up for us its traumas and tragedies, he could and did describe and reënact for us, something of its day-to-day living.

The hidden ones fished with the harpoon and the net, and hunted with the bow and arrow, and by setting snares – silent weapons all. They gathered acorns in the autumn, enough if possible to see them through the winter. They ate green clover in April, and brodiaea bulbs in early summer. In mid- summer they went to Waganupa, four nights' jour- ney, to its cooler air and deeper shade and more abundant game. For the rest, they lived on upper Mill Creek in small houses camouflaged so that from above, the only direction from which they could have been seen, the bent branches which covered them looked like nature's work. Nearby were storage shelters disguised in the same way, and containing drying frames, baskets of dried meat and fish and acorns, and utensil baskets, tools, and hides. They traveled sometimes for long distances by leaping from boulder to boulder, their bare feet leaving no print; or they walked up or down stream, making of their creeks a highroad. Each footprint on the ground was covered over with dead leaves, obliterated. Their trails went under the heavy chaparral, not through it, and they traveled them on all fours. A cow could not find such trails; even deer sought more open ones. If a branch was in the way it was gradually bent back farther and farther, and if need be severed by charring and wearing through with a crude tool made from splitting a boulder, a slow but silent process. They never chopped, the sound of chopping being the unmistakable announcement of human presence. They kept their fires small so that the smoke dissipated harmlessly through the brush without rising beaconwise above the bay tree canopy, and they covered the site of a campfire with broken rock as soon as the fire was out. They went up and down the perpendicular cliffs of Mill Creek canyon on ropes of milkweed fiber – a quick and safe way down, since the canyon was well screened by trees that overhung its rim. They could bring up a catch of fish or a basket of water, or let themselves down for a swim with far less trouble and time than it took to scramble up and down the little branching trails which led to the water's edge. Also, they preferred to use these trails sparingly so that they would not become too plainly marked but continue to appear to be no more than the runways of rabbits or weasels. They ground their acorns to flour on smooth stones and made the staple mush, cooking it in baskets. They wore capes of deerskin and wildcat, occasionally of bearskin. And they slept under blankets of rabbitskins. Ethnologists are agreed that they pursued a way of life the most totally aboriginal and primitive of any on the con- tinent, at least after the coming of the white man to America.

NOTE

1   *Editors' note*: the two bracketed interpolations in the passage are Kroeber's.

4

Ishi's Brain, Ishi's Ashes: Anthropology and Genocide

Nancy Scheper-Hughes

Modern anthropology was built up in the face of colonial and postcolonial genocides, ethnocides, population die-outs, and other forms of mass destruction visited on the 'non-Western' peoples whose lives, suffering and deaths provide the raw material for much of our work. Yet despite this history – and the privileged position of the ethnographer as eye-witness to some of these events – anthropology has been, until quite recently, relatively mute on the subject. Although predisposed by our training not to see the political or manifest forms of violence that so often ravage the lives of our subjects, anthropologists are somewhat better at analyzing psychological (see Devereux 1961; Edgerton 1992; Scheper-Hughes 2000 [1979]) and symbolic forms of violence (see Bourdieu and Waquant 1992: 111–205) that underlie so many ordinary human institutions and social interactions.

A basic premise guiding twentieth-century ethnographic research was, quite simply, to see, hear, and report no evil after returning from the field. But the moral blinkers that we wore in one instance spilled over into a kind of hermeneutic generosity in other and less appropriate instances – for example, toward Western colonizers, police states, and other social and political institutions of mass violence.

Today the world, the objects of our study, and the uses of anthropology have changed considerably. Those privileged to observe human events close up and over time, who are thereby privy to local, community, and even state secrets that are generally hidden from view until much later, after the collective graves have been discovered and the body counts completed, are beginning to recognize another ethical position – that of naming and identifying the sources, structures, and institutions of mass violence. This new mood of political and ethical engagement has resulted in considerable soul-searching, even if long after the fact (see Geertz 1995).

Claude Lévi-Strauss (1995), for example, opened his recently published photographic memoir, *Saudades do Brasil* (*Homesickness for Brazil*), with a sobering caveat. He warned that the lyrically beautiful images of 'pristine' rainforest Brazilian Indians about to be presented – photos taken by him between 1935 and 1939 – should not be trusted. The images were illusory for the world they portray no longer exists. The images of starkly beautiful, seemingly timeless Nambikwara, Caduveo, and Bororo bear no resemblance to the reduced populations one might find today camped out by the sides of busy truck routes or loitering in urban villages. The indigenous populations have been decimated by wage labor, gold prospecting, prostitution and the diseases of cultural contact – smallpox, TB, AIDS, syphilis.

But the old master's confession goes further. These early photos capturing simple, naked Indians sleeping on the ground under shelters of palm leaves have nothing to do (he now says) with a state of pristine humanity that has since been lost. The 1930s photos already show the effects of a savage European colonization on the once populous civilizations of Central Brazil and the

Amazon. Following contact these civilizations were destroyed, leaving behind a people not so much 'primitive' as 'stranded,' stripped of their material and symbolic wealth. Lévi-Strauss's camera had captured images of an 'invisible genocide' (see Scheper-Hughes 1996), of the magnitude of which the anthropologist was at the time unaware.

Earlier, Lévi-Strauss (1966: 126) had described the quandary that demands that anthropology be a 'vocation' (see also Sontag 1964: 68–81) rather than just a scholarly pursuit: 'Anthropology is not a dispassionate science like astronomy, which springs from the contemplation of things at a distance. It is the outcome of a historical process which has made the larger part of mankind subservient to the other, and during which millions of innocent human beings have had their resources plundered and their institutions and beliefs destroyed whilst they themselves were ruthlessly killed, thrown into bondage, and contaminated by diseases they were unable to resist. Anthropology is the daughter to this era of violence.'

His statement is an indictment of those anthropologists who served as bystanders, silent and useless witnesses to the genocides and die-outs they encountered in the course of pursuing their science.

Kroeber and Ishi: Last of Their Tribes

Alfred Kroeber, however, died before he could imagine a radically different role for the anthropologist as engaged witness rather than disinterested spectator to scenes of cultural destruction and genocide. When Kroeber arrived in San Francisco in 1901 to take up the post of museum anthropologist at the University of California it was at the tail-end of a horrendous, wanton, and officially sanctioned extermination of Northern California Indians that began during the Gold Rush and culminated in the early decades of the twentieth century, during which the native population of California experienced a 90 percent reduction of their pre-contact numbers.

The die-out was the cumulative result of disease epidemics, military campaigns, massacres, bounty hunts, debt peonage, child kidnapping, land grabbing, and enclosures by the Anglo settlers that began during the California Gold Rush in the mid-nineteenth century and lasted through the

first decades of the twentieth century (see Castillo 1978, Churchill 1997, Cook 1978, Heizer 1978, Riddell 1978). The devastation suffered by the Maiduan community of Northern California is illustrative of a general pattern of invisible genocide. In 1850 there were between 3,500 and 4,500. By 1910 there were only 900 Maidu people remaining (Riddell 1978: 386). The ethnocides continue to this day, though in different forms, the toll exacted from generations of structural violence – poverty, racism, social exclusion and geopolitical displacement, chronic unemployment, ill health, and family disorganization resulting from alcohol and drug addictions.

Kroeber, like most anthropologists of his day, dedicated himself early on to what was then called 'salvage ethnography' – an attempt to document the cultures of rapidly disappearing indigenous peoples. It was North American anthropology's weak response to genocide, although it was never explicitly recognized as such. But by the time Kroeber completed his monumental *Handbook of the Indians of California* in 1917 he had come to view salvage ethnography – which he once described as gathering the remnants from survivors in blue-jeans living in ruined and 'bastardized' cultures (Kroeber 1948: 427) – as less than satisfying work, and he took up more theoretical writings focusing on the collective 'genius' of a given cultural tradition to which the individual was largely irrelevant. Kroeber saw the destruction of entire small populations of Natives as a side-bar in the *longue durée* of social evolutionary time. He once described the genocide which reduced the indigenous population of California from 300,000 in the mid-1840s to less than 20,000 people at the close of the century as a thing of small import, 'a little history . . . of pitiful events' (Buckley 1996).

Perhaps confronting the suffering, devastation, and culture deaths of his Native California informants was too difficult for Kroeber to bear and he retreated into the safety zone of an abstract theory that put their losses into a broader cultural historical perspective. Kroeber admitted to an 'unusual personal resistance' to 'vehement' emotions, and he once confided to A. R. Pilling, another specialist in Yurok ethnography, that he did not delve into his informants' experiences of the contact era because he 'could not stand all the tears' (Buckley 1996: 277). Moreover, he did not consider the Native California genocide an appropriate anthropological topic. 'After some hesitation', Kroeber wrote in 1925, 'I have omitted all directly historical treatment...of the relations of the natives with the whites and of the events befalling them after such contact was established. It is not that this subject is unimportant or uninteresting, but that I am not in a position to treat it adequately. It is also a matter that has comparatively slight relation to aboriginal civilization' (cited by Buckley 1996: 274). Vanquished peoples could cast little light on the 'authentic' aboriginal civilizations that preceded them, which Kroeber viewed as the true subject of his discipline.

Kroeber's retreat into theory may alternatively have expressed his deep faith in science (see Kroeber 1948b: 22–4). But, like Freud who made a similar move away from the social reality of his women patients in favor of a general theory of the unconscious (see Masson 1984), Kroeber's turning away from the suffering of his living informants in favour of a general theory of culture history that 'had no people in it' (see Wolf 1981) could be seen as a betrayal.

This much is certain. The arrival of the Yahi Indian, Ishi, into Kroeber's life and therefore into our anthropological and historical consciousness was uncannily overdetermined. In the first of two pieces that Kroeber (1911a and b) wrote about the Yahi Indians in the summer of 1911, he described the 'discovery' in 1908 by California surveyors of a rag-tag band of Mill Creek Indian survivors. The surveyors came upon a cleverly concealed campsite, now believed to be the last hiding place of Ishi and his few remaining family members. After frightening the Indians away the surveyors carried off all the blankets, tools, bows and arrows, and other supplies from the Yahi encampment. (These 'artefacts' are still 'housed' in the Hearst Museum of Anthropology.) Ishi's state of near starvation when he was later captured may have resulted from the confiscation of his tools of subsistence.

Writing for popular consumption and supporting the lesser of two evils – death being the other alternative – Kroeber argued for the capture of the Mill Creek Indians by a posse of US soldiers and their integration with the other 'survivors of landless tribes that have lived for many years as scattered outcasts on the fringes of civilization.' Otherwise, the future was grim: 'If the Indians are ever caught in the act of marauding it may go hard with them, for the rancher in these districts

rarely has his rifle far from his hand *and can scarcely be blamed for resorting to violence* [italics supplied] when his belongings have been repeatedly seized' (p. 8).

Then, on 29 August 1911, the last living member of that Yahi Mill Creek band, the man that Kroeber would later call 'Ishi' (the Yahi word for 'human'), appeared in Oroville, California. Possibly driven by hunger and desperation, the Indian emerged from hiding in the foothills of Mt. Lassen and was discovered cowering in the corner of a slaughterhouse. He was held at the local jail until Kroeber and a young linguist, Tom Waterman, were summoned and they identified him as a Yahi Indian. Ishi was cold, frightened, and hungry, but he refused to accept food or water. In the first photo taken just hours after his capture Ishi seemed startled and was in a state of advanced emaciation. His hair was clipped or singed close to his head in a traditional sign of Yahi mourning. His cheeks cling fast to the bones and accentuate his deep-set eyes. The photo shows a man of intelligence and of deep sorrow.

After Ishi's 'rescue' by Kroeber, he lived out his final years (1911–15) as a salaried assistant janitor, key informant, and 'living specimen' at the Museum of Anthropology at the University of California, then located in San Francisco near the medical school. Ishi was given his own private quarters, but his room was located next to a large collection of human skulls and bones that depressed him. Nonetheless, Ishi conveyed to his anthropological and medical 'guardians' that he wished to remain at the museum rather than face uncertainty elsewhere. He could not go home: his territory was occupied by the ghosts and spirits of his kin who had not died a peaceful death nor been given a proper funeral.

During the period that Ishi lived among whites (doctors and anthropologists), he served as a willing informant to Kroeber and other local and visiting anthropologists, including Edward Sapir whom Waterman accused of overworking Ishi, already weak from illness. Like other 'first contact' peoples, Ishi contracted tuberculosis, an urban disease, although his condition was not diagnosed until the final weeks of his life. Kroeber feared this outcome, as his first wife, Henriette, was felled by the same disease two years after Ishi arrived at the Museum. Ishi succumbed in March 1916 while Kroeber was away in New York City on sabbatical leave.

Ishi has been described as northern California's Anne Frank. Cruelly hunted, his group was reduced to five, then to three, and finally to one when Ishi was discovered and captured. Some local Indians speculate that Ishi may have been in search of refuge at the nearby Feather River (Maidu Indian) rancheria. The Maidu were known to offer sanctuary to escaping Yahi. 'Ishi wasn't crazy,' Art Angle, head of the Butte County Native American Cultural Committee in Oroville, told me. 'He knew where he was headed.' But, betrayed by barking guard dogs, Ishi fell into the hands of whites instead. One Pit River man thought that Ishi had perhaps lost his bearings. 'Too many years alone,' others said. 'Ishi didn't really trust anyone – white or Indian.'

The unlettered Ishi did not (like Anne Frank) write his own diary, but he told some parts of his life story to Alfred Kroeber, who recorded these fragments by hand and captured Ishi's rendition of Yahi myths, origin stories, and folktales on primitive wax cylinders, many of which have since melted. However, Ishi refused to talk about the death of his relatives and his last years of solitary hiding around Deer Creek. In the second of two popular articles on the Yahi, Kroeber described Ishi's arrival in San Francisco on Labor Day in 1911. 'Ishi was a curious and pathetic figure in those [first] days. Timid, gentle, an almost ever-pervading fear... concealed to the best of his ability, he startled and leaped at the slightest sudden sound. A new sight, or the crowding around of half a dozen people, made his limbs rigid. If his hand had been held and was released, his arm remained frozen in the air for several minutes. The first boom from a cannon fired in the artillery practice at the Presidio several miles away, raised him a foot from his chair... His one great dread, which he overcame but slowly, was of crowds. It is not hard to understand this in light of his lonely life in a tribe of five.'

In this passage Kroeber describes what would today be considered the clinical symptoms of PTSD, post-traumatic stress disorder. Ishi's startle reflex, his phobias, his mobilization for flight are similar to the symptoms reported by many victims of sustained terror and warfare (see Herman 1992). Yet despite Ishi's physical and psychological vulnerability and his fear of crowds, Kroeber allowed Ishi to perform as a living exhibit at the Museum of Anthropology and at the San Francisco Panama-Pacific Trade Exhibition.

When Kroeber left for a sabbatical year in New York City he suspected that Ishi was gravely ill and that this might be his final leave-taking. When his worst fears were confirmed by a letter from Dr. Saxton Pope that Ishi was dying, Kroeber sent urgent telegrams demanding timely postings on his friend's deteriorating condition. He also demanded that Ishi's body be treated respectfully and according to the Indian's request to be cremated intact. 'If there is any talk about the interests of science,' Kroeber wrote in a letter to Gifford dated 24 March 1916, 'say for me that science can go to hell.' But with Kroeber far away, a standard autopsy was performed on Ishi's body during which his brain was removed 'for science.'

By the time Kroeber returned to Berkeley his ire had cooled considerably. He even arranged for Ishi's brain to be packaged and shipped to the Smithsonian and to the care of Ales Hrdlicka, a physical anthropologist of the 'old school' dedicated to collecting and measuring brain 'specimens' from various orders of primates and human 'exotics.'[1] Why Kroeber made such an about-face I can only speculate. Perhaps he thought that it was too late for 'sentimental' reservations. Ishi was dead and the damage to his body was irreversible.

Or perhaps – and to my mind this is the most probable explanation – Kroeber's behavior was an act of disordered mourning. Grief can be expressed in a myriad of inchoate and displaced ways ranging from denial and avoidance, as in the Yahi taboo on speaking the names of the dead, to the insistence that the death and loss experienced is a minor one (see Scheper-Hughes 1992 on 'death without weeping' among Brazilian shantytown mothers), to the glee and rage of the Illonget headhunter intent on getting an enemy's head to 'kill' the loss experienced on the death of a loved one, as described by Rosaldo (1989). Freud's (1957) classic essay on 'mourning and melancholia' certainly comes to mind with respect to Kroeber 's own 'swallowed grief' following the deaths of his first wife and then, soon afterwards, of his friend and key informant, Ishi, both from the same disease. Added to this was the the disturbing impact of the First World War on a German-American who was certainly sensitive to how the war might influence others' interpretation of his work. Support for the depression and mourning thesis comes from Kroeber's second wife, Theodora Kroeber (1970: 87), who gives an account of her husband's long period of depression and self-doubt between 1915 and 1922. A. L. Kroeber himself characterized this unsettling period in his mid-life as a '*hegira*' – a dark period of journey, soul-searching, and melancholia. The depression was marked by severe psychosomatic symptoms that led to a period of psychoanalysis in New York City, following which Kroeber became a practising psychotherapist himself for a few years, taking a leave of absence from teaching.

Consequently, Kroeber did not write the definitive history of Ishi and his people. After Ishi's death, Kroeber generally avoided talking about him. In her biography, Theodora Kroeber writes that the subject of Ishi caused Alfred considerable psychological pain and so was generally avoided in the Kroeber household. Perhaps Kroeber was observing the Yahi custom that forbade naming and speaking of the dead. I like to think so. But many years later Kroeber allowed Theodora to use him as a key informant on Ishi's last years. And so it was Theodora who told the story that her husband could not bear to write.

Alternatively, Kroeber may have sent Ishi's brain for 'work-up' at the Smithsonian because he believed that the science of anthropology to which he had dedicated his life might benefit from the tragedy of his friend's death. If so, it was a triumph of science over sentiment. Kroeber was not totally naive. In fact, he had been through a similar situation when, as a 21-year-old neophyte student of Franz Boas at Columbia University, he was given full responsibility for ethnographic and linguistic work-up on a small party of captive Eskimos brought to Boas by the Arctic explorer Robert Peary. When one of the Eskimo adults died of tuberculosis, members of his group were brought to mourn before a traditional earth mound that covered a counterfeit corpse made from a log. Without telling his indigenous mourners, the real body of the Eskimo 'specimen' had been immediately whisked away to Bellevue Hospital's College of Physicians and Surgeons for autopsy and study (see Thomas 2000: 77). But there is no evidence that the results of Ishi's autopsy (see Pope 1920) or his severed brain were ever included in any scientific study. The brain was simply forgotten and abandoned in a Smithsonian warehouse.

Art Angle, a Maidu Indian leader, kept alive his family's 'folklore' about Ishi's remains. And in the mid-1990s he decided to pursue the case, locate the brain, and return it, together with Ishi's cremated ashes, to Mt. Lassen for reburial. Angle enlisted the help of other tribal leaders and the skills of Nancy Rockafellar, a UCSF medical historian, and Orin Starn, a cultural anthropologist from Duke University. It was Starn who located the valuable correspondence in the Bancroft Collection at UC Berkeley that confirmed the transactions between Kroeber and Hrdlicka.

It is easy today, with the advantage of hindsight, to identify the blind spots of our anthropological predecessors, including Kroeber's failure to recognize the ongoing genocide of Indians in northern California, or to deal more humanely with Ishi. Is it fair to ask what Kroeber might have done differently? What options did he have? Before Ishi became mortally ill might Kroeber have broached the topic of where Ishi had been headed when he was caught on the run? If it was indeed to find sanctuary among related Native peoples, might that have been a possible solution? After Ishi's health began to fail, were the museum and hospital the best places for him?

To this day there is a strong investment in believing that Ishi was a happy man who enjoyed his life among his white friends and was content in his roles of museum janitor and Sunday exhibit. Perhaps he was. But the evidence (see especially Heizer and T. Kroeber 1979) suggests another interpretation – that Ishi was simply at the end of his existential rope. The Museum of Anthropology was his end of the line. Though not of his choosing, Ishi accepted his final destiny with patience, good humor, and grace. He was exceptionally learned in the art of waiting.

Ishi's Brain

The final chapter of this story opened in the spring of 1999 with the rediscovery of Ishi's brain. Anthropologists at Berkeley differed in their opinions of what, if anything, should be said or done. Some were embarrassed by the initial denials by the Hearst Museum of Anthropology and the UC administration. An official letter from the University of California to Art Angle stated: 'There is no historical support for the idea that his brain was maintained as a scientific specimen.' Following the official news release indicating that Ishi's brain had, indeed, been traced to the Smithsonian, a departmental meeting was held and a proposed statement was debated, many times revised, and finally accepted as the collective response of the Department of Anthropology at Berkeley. While falling short of the apology to Northern California Indians that a majority of the faculty had signed in an earlier draft, the final unanimous statement read:

The recent recovery of a famous California Indian's brain from a Smithsonian warehouse has led the Department of Anthropology at the University of California Berkeley to revisit and reflect on a troubling chapter of our history. Ishi, whose family and cultural group, the Yahi Indians, were murdered as part of the genocide that characterized the influx of western settlers to California, lived out his last years at the original museum of anthropology at the University of California. He served as an informant to one of our department's founding members, Alfred Kroeber, as well as to other local and visiting anthropologists. The nature of the relationships between Ishi and the anthropologists and linguists who worked with him for some five years at the museum were complex and contradictory. Despite Kroeber's lifelong devotion to California Indians and his friendship with Ishi, he failed in his efforts to honor Ishi's wishes not to be autopsied and he inexplicably arranged for Ishi's brain to be shipped to and to be curated at the Smithsonian. We acknowledge our department's role in what happened to Ishi, a man who had already lost all that was dear to him. We strongly urge that the process of returning Ishi's brain to appropriate Native American representatives be speedily accomplished. We are considering various ways to pay honor and respect to Ishi's memory. We regard public participation as a necessary component of these discussions and in particular we invite the peoples of Native California to instruct us in how we may better serve the needs of their communities through our research related activities. Perhaps, working together, we can ensure that the next millennium will represent a new era in the relationship between indigenous peoples, anthropologists, and the public.

I read the full statement, including the original and deleted apology – 'We are sorry for our department's role, however unintentional, in the final betrayal of Ishi, a man who had already lost all that was dear to him at the hands of Western colonizers and we recognize that the exploitation and betrayal of Native Americans is still commonplace in American society' – into the record of the California state legislature repatriation hearings held in Sacramento, California on 5 April 1999.

Some Indian leaders who were present accepted the apology, seeing it as a 'big step' for anthropology and for the University of California. Others dismissed the apology as 'too little and too late.' Obviously, the mistrust between Native Americans and anthropologists founded in the history of genocide (and genocide ignored) requires more than an apology or a scholarly conference to honor Ishi. But the return of Ishi's brain from the Smithsonian to representatives of the Pit River tribe on 8 August 2000, and the two-day celebration at Summit Lake on Mt. Lassen – communal feasting and healing dancing – a few weeks after the secret burial,[2] represented an essential first step toward more constructive engagement between anthropologists and the survivors of California's genocides. At one of the 'talking circle' events, Alfred Kroeber was forgiven. [. . .]

In the end, what can be said about Kroeber and the man called Ishi? Not all Native Californians spoke well of Ishi, especially in years past. Some resented the fact that he accepted sanctuary with whites and the 'anthros.' Young people, in particular, were quick to judge him. But as they grew older they began to imagine how they themselves might behave in similar circumstances. And today they recognize in Ishi one way of surviving a holocaust. 'We need to think in a good way now and to find ways to honor our grandfather Ishi.' Anthropologists also need to 'think in a good way' now. We also need to respect our ancestors, including 'grandfather' Kroeber, recognizing that it is not always clear what is required at particularly fraught historical moments. Perhaps we all need to apologize and forgive each other as we once again go about reinventing anthropology as a tool and practice of human freedom.

NOTES

1 Kroeber wrote to Hrdlicka on 27 October 1916 (Bancroft Library, Records of the Department and Museum of Anthropology, CU-23): 'I find that with Ishi's death last spring his brain was removed and preserved. There is no one here who can put it to scientific use. If you wish it, I would be pleased to deposit it in the National Museum collection.' Hrdlicka replied on 12 December 1916 that he would be 'very glad' to receive the brain and he would have it 'properly worked up'. In another letter dated 20 December 1916 Hrdlicka gave precise dir-

ections for the preparation of the brain for shipping: 'The brain should be packed in plenty of absorbent cotton saturated with the liquid in which it is preserved, and the whole should be enclosed in a piece of oiled cloth...' Then, in a letter dated 20 February 1917, the Curator of the Museum of Anthropology at the University of California, confirmed the transaction: 'Ishi's brain was sent to the National Museum as a gift with the compliments of the University of California... If you will enter the donor as the *Department of Anthropology* of [said] University, I think your record will be as accurate as you can make it.'

2 Thomas W. Killion, the archaeologist and director of the Smithsonian Institution's repatriation program, was extremely helpful to various leaders of California tribes once the Smithsonian decided (after an initial denial) that it did have the brain. Killion and his committee designated the Pit River tribe of Redding Rancheria over the Maidu Indians of Enterprise Rancheria, who made the initial claim for Ishi's brain, on the grounds of greater linguistic affinities between the Pit River and the 'disappeared' Yahi. The ceremonial delivery of the brain that took place at the Smithsonian and the ritual events surrounding the reburial of Ishi's brain and his ashes (and the location of the burial site) remain secret, at the request of the Northern California Indians.

REFERENCES

Bourdieu, Pierre and Loïc Waquant. 1992. *Invitation to Reflexive Sociology*. Chicago: University of Chicago Press.

Buckley, Thomas. 1996. 'The little history of pitiful events': the epistemological and moral contexts of Kroeber's Californian ethnology. In George Stocking (ed.), *Volkgeist as Method and Ethic: Essays on Boasian Ethnography and the German Anthropological Tradition*. History of Anthropology series, vol. 8. Madison: University of Wisconsin Press.

Castillo, Edward. 1978. The impact of Euro-American exploration and settlement. In Heizer (ed.), *California*, pp. 99–127. Vol. 8. Washington: Smithsonian Institution.

Churchill, Ward. 1997. *A Little Matter of Genocide: Holocaust and Denial in the Americas: 1492 to the Present*. San Francisco: City Lights Books.

Cook, Sherburne F. 1978. Historical demography. In Heizer (ed.), *California*, pp. 91–8. Vol. 8. Washington: Smithsonian Institution.

Devereux, George. 1961. *Mohave Ethnopsychiatry and Suicide*. Washington: Smithsonian Institution, Bureau of American Ethnology, Bulletin No. 175.

Edgerton, Robert B. 1992. *Sick Societies: Challenging the Myth of Primitive Harmony*. New York: The Free Press.

Freud, Sigmund. 1957. 'Mourning and melancholia'. *In Standard Edition of the Complete Psychological Works of Sigmund Freud*, vol. 14, 243–58. London: Hogarth.

Geertz, Clifford. 1995. *After the Fact: Two Countries, Four Decades, One Anthropologist*. Cambridge, MA: Harvard University Press.

Heizer, Robert F. 1978. *California*. Vol. 8. Washington: Smithsonian Institution.

——and Theodora Kroeber. 1979. *Ishi the Last Yahi: A Documentary History*. Berkeley: University of California Press.

Herman, Judith. 1992. *Trauma and Recovery*. New York: Basic Books.

Kroeber, Alfred L. 1911a. The elusive Mill Creeks: A band of wild Indians roaming in northern California today. *Travel* XVII(4): 510–13, 548, 550. New York.

——1911b. Ishi, the last aborigine. *World's Work Magazine*, XXIV (3):304–8. New York.

——1925. *Handbook of the Indians of California*. Smithsonian Institution. Bureau of American Ethnology. Bulletin 78. Washington: US Government Printing Office.

——1948. *Anthropology: Race, Language, Culture, Psychology and Prehistory*. New York: Harcourt, Brace and Company.

——1948b. My faith. In *The Faith of Great Scientists: A Collection from the American Weekly*, pp. 22–4. New York: Hearst Publishing Company.

Kroeber, Theodora, 1964. *Ishi, Last of his Tribe*. Berkeley: Parnassus Press.

——1970. *Alfred Kroeber: A Personal Configuration*. Berkeley: University of California Press.

Lévi-Strauss, Claude. 1966. *Tristes tropiques*. (Tr. by John Russell) New York: Atheneum, 1967.

——1995. *Saudades do Brasil: A Photographic Memoir*. Seattle and London: University of Washington Press.

Masson, Jeffrey, 1984. *The Assault on Truth: Freud's Suppression of the Seduction Hypothesis*. New York: Harper.

Pope, Saxton, 1920. The medical history of Ishi. *University of California Publications in American Archaeology and Ethnology* 13(5): 175–213.

Riddell, Francis A. 1978. Maidu and Konkow. In Heizer (ed.), *California*, pp. 370–86. Vol. 8. Washington: Smithsonian Institution.

Rosaldo, Renato. 1989. Grief and a headhunter's rage. In Rosaldo, R. (ed.), *Culture and Truth: The Making of Social Analysis*, pp. 1–21. Boston: Beacon Press.

Scheper-Hughes, Nancy. 1992. *Death without Weeping: The Violence of Everyday Life in Brazil*. Berkeley: University of California Press.

——1996. Small wars and invisible genocides. *Social Science & Medicine* 43(5): 889–900.

——2000 [1979]. *Saints, Scholars and Schizophrenics: Mental Illness in Rural Ireland*. Berkeley: University of California Press.

Sontag, Susan 1964. The anthropologist as hero. In *Against Interpretation*, pp. 68–81. New York: Dell Publishing Company.

Thomas, David Hurst. 2000. *Skull Wars*. New York: Basic Books.

Wolf, Eric. 1981. Alfred L. Kroeber. In Silverman, Sydel (ed.), *Totems and Teachers: Perspectives on the History of Anthropology*. New York: Columbia University Press.

5

Tribal Warfare

R. Brian Ferguson

When the philosopher Thomas Hobbes wrote in 1651 of the primeval war of "every man against every man," he observed that "the savage people in many places of America ... live at this day in that brutish manner." Accepted wisdom even now holds that "primitive" cultures are typically at war and that the primary military effect of contact with the West is the suppression of ongoing combat.

In fact, the initial effect of European colonialism has generally been quite the opposite. Contact has invariably transformed war patterns, very frequently intensified war and not uncommonly generated war among groups who previously had lived in peace. Many, perhaps most, recorded wars involving tribal peoples can be directly attributed to the circumstances of Western contact. [. . .]

Trade in manufactured goods has dominated the interaction of states and their nonstate neighbors since the time of Mesopotamia, but industrial production puts European expansion in a class by itself. Steel tools, for example, are several times more efficient than are stone implements. The acquisition of axes and machetes enabled many Amazonian groups to expand their forest gardens and to begin production of manioc for trade with Brazilian woodsmen.

In most of the New World, metal tools passed along indigenous trade networks far ahead of the Europeans themselves. The passage of large quantities of such valuable items restructured those trade systems, and the exploitative terms imposed by native groups who had a monopoly on the supply of European goods often generated violent disputes. Other items besides steel rapidly became necessities in indigenous societies, in particular guns and ammunition. Guns were not always superior to native arms in the early centuries of contact (as many Europeans learned), but they nonetheless led in many situations to a marked intensification of the killing.

Epidemics, ecological change and new technologies can precede face-to-face contact. The actual presence of Europeans adds even more complexity to the tribal zone. One especially complicating factor is the number of states attempting to operate in the same area. The simultaneous presence of English and French colonial agents in eighteenth-century North America, for example, gave the local population more political latitude in which to maneuver, but it also embroiled them in foreign rivalries. [. . .]

Paradoxically, there is strong evidence that much of the tribal structure recorded by Europeans was in fact called into being by their presence. State agents have great difficulty dealing with indigenous people as they are often organized – without authoritative leaders or fixed group identities. So they strive to create both, appointing chiefs and imposing cultural and political boundaries. These artificial boundaries in turn quickly become integrated into the fabric of native society because they are instrumental in the crucial matter of interacting with state agents. [. . .]

This is illustrated in a number of well-studied cases, ranging from shortly after the time of Columbus to the present. The published narrative of Hans Staden, held captive around 1550 by the Tupinamba of the Brazilian coast, titillated Europe with images of savagery. Even by this early date, however, the Tupinamba had been enlisted as allies in wars between the Portuguese and the French, embroiled in raids to capture slaves for the Europeans, impoverished by loss of land to colonialists and deliberately encouraged in factionalism and vengeance by settlers who were following a divide-and-rule policy.

Another people made infamous in early reports were the Carib, notorious for cannibalism and slave raiding. Although both practices do appear in the earliest contact reports, as my colleague Neil Whitehead has shown, the Carib reputation for cannibalism was deliberately inflated. The more careful and less self-serving accounts show that cannibalism was a limited ritual practice in which warriors ate small portions of individuals they captured. Because Spanish law made cannibal tribes fair game for immediate enslavement, Europeans employed stories of huge cannibal buffets as a pretext.

Similarly, the limited information about captives not eaten suggests that they were generally well treated and integrated into the captor society. Only after contact with the West was the sporadic taking of captives transformed into a massive and far-reaching industry supplying the colonial markets.

Late in the nineteenth century the Mundurucu of the Upper Tapajos River had the reputation of being the most warlike tribe in all of Amazonia. It is not coincidental that they also had the reputation of being the greatest friends of the Portuguese. Indeed, their ferocious long-distance raiding was directed by the Portuguese, who paid them to attack more troublesome peoples and encouraged the warriors to bring back trophy heads.

A few decades later the description of "most warlike" passed to the Jivaro of the Andean foothills, a reflection of their renown for producing shrunken heads. By this time, burgeoning demand in Europe and North America had made the ancient, ritualistic practice of headshrinking a major export business. The standard payment to the Jivaro, one gun for one head, set off a deadly internecine arms race and led to virtually indiscriminate slaughter.

North America saw similar reorientations of warfare. Probably the best-known case is that of the Great Plains tribes. The introduction of horses and guns transformed their entire way of life, and the subsequent intertribal conflicts were closely linked to this continuing upheaval. Encroaching settlements and the growth of trade in buffalo pelts stimulated competition for buffalo rangeland. Raiding for horses contributed to a constant state of war, and peoples such as the Blackfoot and Cheyenne relied on force to preserve their monopolistic access to Western traders.

In the Pacific Northwest, groups such as the Kwakiutl, Haida, and Tsimshian had established a centuries-old pattern in which residents of localities with few resources raided those who controlled major salmon rivers and other prime fishing grounds. These hostilities subsided after European contact, as epidemics killed a third or more of the native population. The intensity of war, however, increased as the development of a fur trade incited battles to control the trade. In addition, the growing wealth of some successful tribes stimulated a local demand for slaves. Slave raiding intensified as some local groups found slaves to be the only commodity they could barter for the firearms they needed for self-defense.

In the Northeastern woodlands, competition over fur trading sparked long-distance warfare between the Iroquois and the Huron. The tribes fought to obtain access to trading posts and prime beaver-hunting areas, and they plundered each other's trade goods and pelts. The British and the French, meanwhile, encouraged native warfare as a way of advancing their own competing colonial ambitions.

In other parts of North America, particularly the Southeast and the Southwest, a similar pattern manifested itself. In response to the European demand for slaves, the Cherokee raided tribes to their west, the Pima raided the Yavapai and yet other groups raided the Navaho.

The same factors that can be seen in the historical record still influence war in the tribal zone today. Possibly the best contemporary case study is the Yanomami, a relatively unacculturated people traditionally inhabiting the highlands separating Venezuela and Brazil. In recent years the Yanomami have been victimized by settlers seeking to mine minerals in their territory. They are currently the subject of international efforts to protect their lands from further incursions.

The **TRIBAL ZONE** is a region extending outward from state boundaries in which the life of tribal groups is disrupted. It is often marked by war, epidemic and ecological change. This zone is the scene both of direct conflicts between settlers and natives and of hostilities between native groups fleeing state influence or competing for access to trade groups.

The Yanomami are also known for their seemingly chronic warfare. In the widely read works of anthropologist Napoleon A. Chagnon of the University of California at Santa Barbara, they are portrayed as a virtual type case of savage ferocity. Chagnon cites the Yanomami as an exemplar of Hobbes's primeval state of war and asserts that their society is typical of pre-state conditions.

Chagnon's interpretation has been challenged by William J. Smole of the University of Pittsburgh, the Brazilian anthropologist Alcida R. Ramos and others who have conducted field research among the Yanomami. These researchers have found his reports of violence inapplicable to the people they studied.

Others have contested the claim that Yanomami conflicts result from male competition over women. Marvin Harris of the University of Florida at Gainesville, for example, has long argued that the disputes over women are themselves a result of other problems. He contends that the scarcity of nutritionally necessary game animals creates a sexually charged competition among hunters. The resulting violence, Harris asserts, reduces population growth and leads to a closer match between people and available game. Revenge and belief in witchcraft have also been suggested as explanations for chronic war among the Yanomami.

I believe that all these factors are of secondary importance compared with the continuing effects of "civilized" incursions. Contrary to most scholarly opinion, the Yanomami are not an isolated people. Their location in the rugged Parima highlands appears to be a reaction to slave raids going back to the early seventeenth century, and their staple food, the plantain, is generally, though not universally, believed to be a European introduction. Slave raids occurred again during the eighteenth and nineteenth centuries, and the rubber-tapping industry entered Yanomami territory in force around the turn of the twentieth century. The most recent period of direct contact with outsiders is therefore the fourth or fifth wave, not the first.

By examining all available reports of war or peace among all Yanomami from the early 1800s to the 1980s, I have found that in the overwhelming majority of cases, instances of war followed abruptly on some significant change in the Western presence – either a new penetration, a withdrawal or a change in location. Constancy in the presence or absence of Westerners is usually accompanied by peace.

Although many factors are involved in this association, access to Western manufactured goods, especially steel tools, has proved critical to explaining the actual patterns of combat. The Yanomami find steel tools roughly 10 times as efficient as stone axes. They rapidly become necessities for many basic subsistence tasks, such as clearing gardens and gathering firewood.

The Yanomami place extraordinary value on these tools and on other Western manufactured goods used for utilitarian and ornamental purposes. These items are scarce and unequally available. The Yanomami have made hazardous treks and repeatedly relocated villages in their effort to obtain better access to suppliers of Western goods.

Although the Yanomami sometimes raided Western settlements or other villages to obtain goods, plundering is a risky, short-term solution. It is far better to establish a position that allows access to a regular source of goods either by moving the village along a trade route or, even better, by settling next to a mission or some other Western outpost. A powerful group in such a location can obtain a relative abundance of new Western trade goods. Furthermore, a group can derive great benefits by acting as monopolistic middlemen in trade to more remote villages.

Such a group often trades Western goods after they have been worn down by use. In return, they receive a wide variety of valuable local products, such as spun cotton, woven hammocks, bows, quivers, curare-tipped arrows, dogs, and food. They also gain an advantage in the intermarriage between villages. Remote villages wishing to establish a trade connection often do so by ceding a wife to the middlemen. In these marriages, middlemen substitute manufactured goods for the years of onerous labor, or bride service, that the groom would normally owe his father-in-law. Those who control access to the Westerners rise in status and in political and military reputation, both because of their control of trade and because of (usually well-armed) Western support.

In this context, collective aggression can accomplish several ends. For Yanomami separated from a source of Western goods, raids or an assault on a trading party can force out a middleman or establish a presence along a trade route. For established middlemen, violence can protect their position by keeping a potential competitor from moving in or by thwarting an attempt to travel around their area of control. Within an existing trade relationship, bellicose confrontations in the form of club fights can alter the direction of trade or the rate of exchange for Western goods.

Almost invariably, force is used soon after some change in the source of the goods. Most commonly a more remote group attacks a village located between them and the source. Whether the distant group is successful in driving out the middlemen or whether the middlemen consolidate their position by successful retaliation, a new power relationship tends to be established quickly. Active raiding between two villages rarely lasts more than two years.

The distribution of sources of Western goods can explain major variations in the pattern of combat, but that is not the whole story. The Yanomami around the confluence of the Orinoco and Mavaca rivers, well described by Chagnon and several others, displayed a greater readiness to resort to aggression in the mid-1960s than they did in the early 1940s, at the start of the current wave of contact. The threshold at which conflict turns to war was lower, and factors in addition to trade antagonism were very much implicated in the increased violence.

These and other aspects of life in the tribal zone – including some suggested as the root cause of Yanomami warfare – fit together to create a war complex that pervades society and makes these Yanomami appear to be "the fierce people." Foremost among them is disease – malaria and measles as well as pulmonary and gastrointestinal illness. A series of epidemics began with the current wave of European contact soon after 1940 and has continued with terrible frequency over subsequent decades. As many as 40 percent of the people in a village may die in a single epidemic. Such a catastrophe disrupts the family-based social system, shattering the carefully crafted balance of marriages that once existed.

Over these same decades, large villages anchored near missions have depleted the local supply of game. This loss has led to a decrease in the communal sharing of meat, a practice that serves as the primary basis of solidarity between families in more mobile villages. Epidemics and the disappearance of plentiful game have combined to undermine social solidarity. In its place is an atomistic and competitive situation in which a disposition to violence plays a key role in daily interactions.

The villages that reconstituted themselves after these disruptions were accommodated to the atmosphere of warfare. They were much larger than more traditional villages and so able to field more fighters. The married men tended to remain with their natal kin, rather than moving in with the wife's family as some other Yanomami do. As a result, they were able to mobilize rapidly to defend their interests. Village leaders were elevated in power by the exigencies of war, by their key role as trade controllers and by the support of local Westerners. Usually unobtrusive in traditional villages, some headmen became almost despotic. In addition, relations among villages were structured by possibilities of trade and took on the character of formal military alliances.

These changes ramified through the Yanomami's system of values and beliefs. Status became a central concern, as any perceived slight could signify the beginning of a disastrous erosion of one's position in war and trade. As a result, the Yanomami encouraged belligerence in the young. Those seeking to persuade others of a course of military action skillfully manipulated the idioms of witchcraft and revenge.

Even mythology was adapted to the social climate. The Orinoco-Mavaca Yanomami have an origin myth in which their violence is explained as a result of the blood of a wounded moon falling to the earth. Yanomami in more pacific areas are unfamiliar with this myth.

Perhaps all societies have their origin myths for war. Western civilization has that of Hobbes. Certainly tribal peoples of the Americas knew war before the arrival of Columbus. Militaristic states such as the Inca and Aztec had their own tribal zone, although these areas were probably less turbulent than those created by European colonialism. Even in the absence of any state, archaeology provides unmistakable evidence of war among sedentary village peoples, sometimes going back thousands of years.

Yet the wild violence noted by Hobbes was not an expression of "man in the state of nature" but a reflection of contact with Hobbes's Leviathan – the states of western Europe. To take the carnage as revealing the fundamental nature of human existence is to pass through the looking glass. [...]

If this scenario is true – and it has been played out many times in the succeeding five centuries – it would mean that the destabilizing, violence-provoking impact of European contact in the New World began as early as 1493.

6

From *The Bushman Myth: The Making of a Namibian Underclass*

Robert J. Gordon

The Changing Image of Bushmen and the Culture of Terror

One can start in this regard with the cultural values expressed in the talk of the settlers, namely that of "taming" "wild" Bushmen. Implicit in such rhetoric is the notion, not of development or peaceful coexistence, but of subjugation. Taming suggests a fundamental difference between those defined as tame and wild; between "civilized" and "barbarian"; between those who live by the law and those who are outside the law; between humans and animals. This fragile and at times highly flexible, but important, mental line, is also a cerebral frontier. And indeed settlers see themselves as living in a frontier situation. [...]

The distinction between "wild" and "tame" was not so much a descriptive distinction as a principle of colonization. In another sense the Bushman image in frontier areas was a flexible one. One day they might be seen as vermin of the veld, but the following day a woman might be regarded as human enough to be taken to bed or set up as a concubine. This suggests that the image was not meant to provide an ideological justification for intended behavior as much as a rationalization for past actions. The discursive power of the settlers and their kindred is dramatically demonstrated in their ability to switch their stereotypes of the Bushmen almost at will. That phenomenon is perhaps the most mundane indicator of Bushman underclass status. It is the underclass status of Bushmen

that exaggerates their cultural ambiguity and makes them susceptible to genocide when they are enveloped by the state. This ambiguity has also led the Western imagination to develop a long cultural "tradition" about them, resplendent with metamorphosing images of evil (Taussig 1984: 468). And it is this cultural construction of evil, coupled with market pressure, that leads to terror in northeastern Namibia.

The frontier is a "zone of death," an area of unpredictability. Nothing can be taken for granted. People and even symbols find their ambiguity amplified with attributions of animalesque powers and drug enhancements. Such a milieu provides a surface explanation and makes credible allegations of atrocities committed by the terrorizers. Analytically, the theoretical assemblage that immediately suggests itself is Victor Turner's notion of liminality and antistructure. "Liminality" is a concept developed from van Gennep's classic analysis of rites of passage. Undergoing this rite the subject "becomes ambiguous, neither here nor there, betwixt and between all fixed points of classification; he passes through a symbolic domain that has few or none of the attributes of his past or coming state" (Turner 1974: 232). In a similar analysis Leach (1976, 1977) has illustrated the situation with a Euler diagram in terms of "Situation A" and "Situation Not A." In the center is a gray area of ambiguity. People placed in this area are *in* but not *of* the world. They are different but alike, despised yet held in awe. They have both animal and human qualities and possess both secular and mystical power. It is not only the whites and, more recently, the young troopers in the South African army who have attributed mystical qualities to both their opponents and their own supporting cast of Bushmen. On the contrary, such a discourse is intrinsic to the imperial process.

The attributed ambiguity of Bushmen served at once to shield them and to lay them open to acts of destruction, epitomized by the almost random stereotyping. It was not only Europeans and settlers and troopers who imprint mysticism onto Bushmen. Other colonized groups have also engaged in such exercises of the cultural imagination. Herero and Tswana often employed Bushman healers and trancers in times of illness (Shostak 1983: 219; Lee 1979). Botswana Bushmen attached to the settlement of Kgalagadi patrons not only did the menial labor of watering cattle, cleaning the kraal and fetching firewood but were also called upon to act as ritual functionaries, dance for rain and treat the sick (Kuper 1970: 45). Similarly, on the settler farms of Botswana's Ghanzi district, Bushmen served as ritual experts for the African farmers and farm workers (Guenther 1985). [. . .]

In many ways the marginal status of Bushmen resembles that of peripatetic minorities found in other parts of the world (Rao 1987). A key difference, however, is that the peripatetic niche of Bushmen occurred in a frontier zone. Frontiers, in the words of some of the foremost southern Africanist historians, are "zones of interaction between people either subject to different political authorities or engaged in different modes of production, or indeed recognizing no formal authority at all" (Marks and Atmore 1980: 8). Could it be that the invention of the Bushmen is a product of our own frontiers?

The parallels between these events and those that happened in Nazi Germany are striking, and indeed Hannah Arendt has argued (see Gann and Duignan 1977 for a critique of her thesis) for lodging the origins of totalitarianism in the colonial experience. Certainly events in Namibia *anticipated* those in Nazi Germany to an extraordinary degree. Indeed a number of criticisms of Arendt's thesis are voided when it is noted that, like anthropologists, colonial administrators differentiated between *Buschleute* and *Eingeborene* in their discourses.

The Bushman discourse was premised on the alleged fundamental *unassimilability* of Bushmen,

in which genital distinctiveness played a central, if at times submerged, role. This debate was especially dominant from 1906 to 1914, a period when it was explicit German colonial policy to wipe out Bushmen. As a largely male-dominated discourse, Bushman studies demonstrated in a Foucaultian mode the discourse and display of the power of *man*. Surely there can be no better display of the deployment of power in nineteenth- and twentieth-century Europe than making people strip to have their genitals measured? George Mosse argued that this male fixation was intimately connected to the nature of bourgeois respectability and German nationalism (Mosse 1985). Interestingly, most of the participants in the great Bushman debate rapidly established radical conservative credentials. Franz Seiner, Rudolph Pöch and Siegfried Passarge were well-known activists for restoring greater Germany, and many of the most prominent Nazi racial hygienists cut their academic teeth on the Bushman debate (Proctor 1988; Muller-Hill 1989). Indeed, the last scientific article that the most renowned Nazi racial hygienist, Eugen Fischer, wrote concerned Bushman genitalia.

Portrayals and policies toward Bushmen and Jews are frighteningly similar, and there are striking parallels of Bushman and Jewish imagery in this scientific discourse. Muller-Hill (1988) has noted that the sexuality of mental patients and Gypsies alarmed and frightened German scientists for a long time and argued that hating and exterminating Jews had its origins in ill-comprehended aspects of sexuality, which is why the extermination of Jews and Gypsies took on an almost ritual-like quality, while the Slavs were worked to death (Muller-Hill 1989).

On Forgetting and Anthropological Arrogance

Science, especially anthropology, has contributed toward the shaping of this image. Indeed, science has a vested interest in the Bushmen, for, as Trefor Jenkins said, from the vantage point of science, the Bushmen are "southern Africa's model people" (Jenkins 1979: 280). Whereas film-makers and journalists were the Bushman image makers par excellence, it was scientific research that lent credibility to their enterprise. Indeed in a sense they were simply the popularizers and amplifiers of the scientific colloquy. Their discourse on Bushmen exemplifies our fascination with strange customs, the search for laws of development and the enchantment of misunderstanding. Anthropological publications were readily misused by popularizers and politicians alike. As Alexander Leighton said, "Their findings are used like a drunk uses a lamppost, for support not illumination." Among contemporary anthropologists, few have suffered more from such misreadings than Richard Lee, who as an active opponent to the apartheid regime had to bear the indignity of having his work misused by the SADF in a totally different context to justify their Bushman "recruitment policy." Lee's dilemma is not only a personal one but a central one to the practice of anthropology. Undoubtedly there are many reasons why the Bushmen became an attractive field for study. [...]

Periodically one finds reports that yet another last group of "wild Bushmen" has been rediscovered. This tradition is especially strong in the filmographic treatment of Bushmen (most recently demonstrated in Paul Myburgh's *People of the Sandface* [see Gordon 1990 for a critique]). It is also found among administrators and especially those ego boosters of scientists, the press. Scholars also engaged in such claims. Dunn is typical. One of his articles started with this ringing revelation: "I am perhaps the only survivor of those who came in contact with the true Bushman, and saw him in his own country, living in his natural way" (Dunn 1937: 1050). Dunn was not the first nor will he be the last to claim to have had contact with the last of the "wild Bushmen" (see, e.g., Peringuey 1911; Wilmsen and Denbow 1990). Such claims engender a sense of importance in scientific documents of this type.

Despite the extensive research on Bushmen in recent years (Tobias 1978), covering many aspects of their biology, psychology, language and culture, their image has not changed much; in fact, at the risk of oversimplification, I would suggest that there is little difference between the current scientific and the popular image of the Bushmen. For whether we portray them as living in "primitive affluence" or "struggling to survive," the overwhelming textbook image is that they are *different* from us in terms of physiognomy, social organization, values and personality. When we were lounging with a smug sense of ethnocentric superiority in the Victorian era, we saw the Bushmen as the epitome of savagery. But later, in the turmoil of the 1960s, when students were asking serious questions about the nature of Western society,

social scientists reified the Bushmen's egalitarianism and generosity, virtues seen to be seriously lacking in Western society. If Bushmen did not exist, we would surely have invented them.

REFERENCES

Dunn, Edward J. 1937. "The Bushman." *South African Journal of Science* 33: 1050–4.

Gann, Lewis, and Peter Duignan. 1977. *The Rulers of German Africa*. Stanford: Stanford University Press.

Gordon, Robert J. 1990. "People of the Sandface: People of the Great White Lie?" *Commission on Visual Anthropology Review.*

Guenther, Mathias G. 1985. "From Foragers to Miners and Bands to Bandits. On the Flexibility and Adaptability of Bushman Band Societies." *Sprache und Geschichte in Afrika.* 7(1): 133–59.

Jenkins, Trefor, 1979. "Southern Africa's Model People." *South African Journal of Science* 75: 280–2.

Kuper, Adam. 1970. *Kalahari Village Politics.* New York: Cambridge University Press.

Leach, Edmund R. 1976. *Culture and Communication.* New York: Cambridge University Press.

——. 1977. *Custom, Law and Terroristic Violence.* Edinburgh: University Press.

Lee, Richard B. 1979. *The Kung San.* New York: Cambridge University Press.

Marks, Shula and Anthony Atmore, eds. 1980. *Economy and Society in Preindustrial South Africa.* London: Longman.

Mosse, George. 1985. *Nationalism and Sexuality.* Madison: University of Wisconsin Press.

Muller-Hill, Benno. 1989. *Murderous Science.* New York: Oxford University Press.

Peringuey, Louis. 1911. "The Stone Ages of South Africa." *Annals of the South African Museum* (Cape Town) 8.

Proctor, Robert. 1988. *Racial Hygiene.* Cambridge, MA: Harvard University Press.

Rao, Aparna, ed. 1987. *The Other Nomads.* Cologne: Bohlau Verlag.

Shostak, Marjorie. 1983. *Nisa, the Life and Words of a !Kung Woman.* New York: Vintage.

Taussig, Michael. 1984. "Culture of Terror – Space of Death. Roger Casement's Putumayo Report and the Explanation of Torture." *Comparative Studies in Society and History* 26(2): 467–97.

Tobias, Philip V., ed. 1978. *The Bushmen: San Hunters and Herders of South Africa.* Cape Town: Human & Rousseau.

Wilmsen, Edwin and James Denbow. 1990. "Almost Free as Birds: Pre-Harvard History of San-speaking Peoples and 'Post-Modern' Attempts at Reconstruction." *Current Anthropology* 31(5).

Part II

The Holocaust

Plate 4: SS officer Eichelsdoerfer, the commandant of the Kaufering IV concentration camp, Germany April 27 – April 30, 1945, Hurlach, Bavaria. Photo Credit: Arnold Bauer Barach, courtesy of USHMM Photo Archives.

7

Right of Death and Power Over Life

Michel Foucault

For a long time, one of the characteristic privileges of sovereign power was the right to decide life and death. In a formal sense, it derived no doubt from the ancient *patria potestas* that granted the father of the Roman family the right to "dispose" of the life of his children and his slaves; just as he had given them life, so he could take it away. By the time the right of life and death was framed by the classical theoreticians, it was in a considerably diminished form. It was no longer considered that this power of the sovereign over his subjects could be exercised in an absolute and uncondi- tional way, but only in cases where the sovereign's very existence was in jeopardy: a sort of right of rejoinder. If he were threatened by external en- emies who sought to overthrow him or contest his rights, he could then legitimately wage war, and require his subjects to take part in the defense of the state; without "directly proposing their death," he was empowered to "expose their life": in this sense, he wielded an "indirect" power over them of life and death.[1] But if someone dared to rise up against him and transgress his laws, then he could exercise a direct power over the offender's life: as punishment, the latter would be put to death. Viewed in this way, the power of life and death was not an absolute privilege: it was conditioned by the defense of the sovereign, and his own survival. Must we follow Hobbes in seeing it as the transfer to the prince of the natural right possessed by every individual to defend his life even if this meant the death of others? Or should it be regarded as a specific right that was mani- fested with the formation of that new juridical

being, the sovereign?[2] In any case, in its modern form – relative and limited – as in its ancient and absolute form, the right of life and death is a dissymmetrical one. The sovereign exercised his right of life only by exercising his right to kill, or by refraining from killing; he evidenced his power over life only through the death he was capable of requiring. The right which was formulated as the "power of life and death" was in reality the right to *take* life or *let* live. Its symbol, after all, was the sword. Perhaps this juridical form must be referred to a historical type of society in which power was exercised mainly as a means of deduction (*prélève- ment*), a subtraction mechanism, a right to appro- priate a portion of the wealth, a tax of products, goods and services, labor and blood, levied on the subjects. Power in this instance was essentially a right of seizure: of things, time, bodies, and ultim- ately life itself; it culminated in the privilege to seize hold of life in order to suppress it.

Since the classical age the West has undergone a very profound transformation of these mechan- isms of power. "Deduction" has tended to be no longer the major form of power but merely one element among others, working to incite, reinforce, control, monitor, optimize, and organize the forces under it: a power bent on generating forces, making them grow, and ordering them, rather than one dedicated to impeding them, making them submit, or destroying them. There has been a parallel shift in the right of death, or at least a tendency to align itself with the exigencies of a life-administering power and to define itself accordingly. This death that was based on the right of the sovereign is now manifested as simply the reverse of the right of the social body to ensure, maintain, or develop its life. Yet wars were never as bloody as they have been since the nineteenth century, and all things being equal, never before did regimes visit such holocausts on their own populations. But this formidable power of death – and this is perhaps what accounts for part of its force and the cynicism with which it has so greatly expanded its limits – now presents itself as the counterpart of a power that exerts a positive influence on life, that endeavors to administer, optimize, and multiply it, subjecting it to precise controls and comprehensive regulations. Wars are no longer waged in the name of a sovereign who must be defended; they are waged on behalf of the existence of everyone; entire populations are mobilized for the purpose of wholesale slaughter in the name of life necessity: massacres have become vital. It is as managers of life and survival, of bodies and the race, that so many regimes have been able to wage so many wars, causing so many men to be killed. And through a turn that closes the circle, as the technology of wars has caused them to tend increasingly toward all-out destruction, the decision that initiates them and the one that terminates them are in fact increasingly informed by the naked question of survival. The atomic situation is now at the end point of this process: the power to expose a whole population to death is the underside of the power to guarantee an individual's continued existence. The principle underlying the tactics of battle – that one has to be capable of killing in order to go on living – has become the principle that defines the strategy of states. But the existence in question is no longer the juridical existence of sovereignty; at stake is the biological existence of a population. If genocide is indeed the dream of modern powers, this is not because of a recent return of the ancient right to kill; it is because power is situated and exercised at the level of life, the species, the race, and the large-scale phenomena of population.

On another level, I might have taken up the example of the death penalty. Together with war, it was for a long time the other form of the right of the sword; it constituted the reply of the sovereign to those who attacked his will, his law, or his person. Those who died on the scaffold became fewer and fewer, in contrast to those who died in wars. But it was for the same reasons that the latter became more numerous and the former more and more rare. As soon as power gave itself the function of administering life, its reason for being and the logic of its exercise – and not the awakening of humanitarian feelings – made it more and more difficult to apply the death penalty. How could power exercise its highest prerogatives by putting people to death, when its main role was to ensure, sustain, and multiply life, to put this life in order? For such a power, execution was at the same time a limit, a scandal, and a contradiction. Hence capital punishment could not be maintained except by invoking less the enormity of the crime itself than the monstrosity of the criminal, his incorrigibility, and the safeguard of society. One had the right to kill those who represented a kind of biological danger to others.

One might say that the ancient right to *take* life or *let* live was replaced by a power to *foster* life or *disallow* it to the point of death. This is perhaps what explains that disqualification of death which marks the recent wane of the rituals that accompanied it. That death is so carefully evaded is linked less to a new anxiety which makes death unbearable for our societies than to the fact that the procedures of power have not ceased to turn away from death. In the passage from this world to the other, death was the manner in which a terrestrial sovereignty was relieved by another, singularly more powerful sovereignty; the pageantry that surrounded it was in the category of political ceremony. Now it is over life, throughout its unfolding, that power establishes its dominion; death is power's limit, the moment that escapes it; death becomes the most secret aspect of existence, the most "private." It is not surprising that suicide – once a crime, since it was a way to usurp the power of death which the sovereign alone, whether the one here below or the Lord above, had the right to exercise – became, in the course of the nineteenth century, one of the first conducts to enter into the sphere of sociological analysis; it testified to the individual and private right to die, at the borders and in the interstices of power that was exercised over life. This determination to die, strange and yet so persistent and constant in its manifestations, and consequently so difficult to explain as being due to particular circumstances or individual accidents, was one of the first astonishments of a society in which political power had assigned itself the task of administering life.

In concrete terms, starting in the seventeenth century, this power over life evolved in two basic forms; these forms were not antithetical, however;

they constituted rather two poles of development linked together by a whole intermediary cluster of relations. One of these poles – the first to be formed, it seems – centered on the body as a machine: its disciplining, the optimization of its capabilities, the extortion of its forces, the parallel increase of its usefulness and its docility, its integration into systems of efficient and economic controls, all this was ensured by the procedures of power that characterized the *disciplines*: an *anatomo-politics of the human body*. The second, formed somewhat later, focused on the species body, the body imbued with the mechanics of life and serving as the basis of the biological processes: propagation, births and mortality, the level of health, life expectancy and longevity, with all the conditions that can cause these to vary. Their supervision was effected through an entire series of interventions and *regulatory controls: a biopolitics of the population*. The disciplines of the body and the regulations of the population constituted the two poles around which the organization of power over life was deployed. The setting up, in the course of the classical age, of this great bipolar technology – anatomic and biological, individualizing and specifying, directed toward the performances of the body, with attention to the processes of life – characterized a power whose highest function was perhaps no longer to kill, but to invest life through and through.

The old power of death that symbolized sovereign power was now carefully supplanted by the administration of bodies and the calculated management of life. During the classical period, there was a rapid development of various disciplines – universities, secondary schools, barracks, workshops; there was also the emergence, in the field of political practices and economic observation, of the problems of birthrate, longevity, public health, housing, and migration. Hence there was an explosion of numerous and diverse techniques for achieving the subjugation of bodies and the control of populations, marking the beginning of an era of "bio-power." [...]

This bio-power was without question an indispensable element in the development of capitalism; the latter would not have been possible without the controlled insertion of bodies into the machinery of production and the adjustment of the phenomena of population to economic processes. But this was not all it required; it also needed the growth of both these factors, their reinforcement as well as their availability and docility; it had to have methods of power capable of optimizing forces, aptitudes, and life in general without at the same time making them more difficult to govern. If the development of the great instruments of the state, as *institutions* of power, ensured the maintenance of production relations, the rudiments of anatomo- and biopolitics, created in the eighteenth century as *techniques* of power present at every level of the social body and utilized by very diverse institutions (the family and the army, schools and the police, individual medicine and the administration of collective bodies), operated in the sphere of economic processes, their development, and the forces working to sustain them. They also acted as factors of segregation and social hierarchization, exerting their influence on the respective forces of both these movements, guaranteeing relations of domination and effects of hegemony. The adjustment of the accumulation of men to that of capital, the joining of the growth of human groups to the expansion of productive forces and the differential allocation of profit, were made possible in part by the exercise of bio-power in its many forms and modes of application. The investment of the body, its valorization, and the distributive management of its forces were at the time indispensable.

One knows how many times the question has been raised concerning the role of an ascetic morality in the first formation of capitalism; but what occurred in the eighteenth century in some Western countries, an event bound up with the development of capitalism, was a different phenomenon having perhaps a wider impact than the new morality; this was nothing less than the entry of life into history, that is, the entry of phenomena peculiar to the life of the human species into the order of knowledge and power, into the sphere of political techniques. It is not a question of claiming that this was the moment when the first contact between life and history was brought about. On the contrary, the pressure exerted by the biological on the historical had remained very strong for thousands of years; epidemics and famine were the two great dramatic forms of this relationship that was always dominated by the menace of death. But through a circular process, the economic – and primarily agricultural – development of the eighteenth century, and an increase in productivity and resources even more rapid than the demographic growth it encouraged, allowed a measure of relief from these profound threats: despite some renewed outbreaks, the period of great ravages from starvation and plague had come to a close before the French Revolution; death was ceasing to torment life so directly. But at the same time, the development of the different fields of knowledge concerned with life in general, the improvement of agricultural techniques, and the observations and measures relative to man's life and survival contributed to this relaxation: a relative control over life averted some of the imminent risks of death. In the space for movement thus conquered, and broadening and organizing that space, methods of power and knowledge assumed responsibility for the life processes and undertook to control and modify them. Western man was gradually learning what it meant to be a living species in a living world, to have a body, conditions of existence, probabilities of life, an individual and collective welfare, forces that could be modified, and a space in which they could be distributed in an optimal manner. For the first time in history, no doubt, biological existence was reflected in political existence; the fact of living was no longer an inaccessible substrate that only emerged from time to time, amid the randomness of death and its fatality; part of it passed into knowledge's field of control and power's sphere of intervention. Power would no longer be dealing simply with legal subjects over whom the ultimate dominion was death, but with living beings, and the mastery it would be able to exercise over them would have to be applied at the level of life itself; it was the taking charge of life, more than the threat of death, that gave power its access even to the body. If one can apply the term *bio-history* to the pressures through which the movements of life and the processes of history interfere with one another, one would have to speak of *bio-power* to designate what brought life and its mechanisms into the realm of explicit calculations and made knowledge-power an agent of transformation of human life. It is not that life has been totally integrated into techniques that govern and administer it; it constantly escapes them. Outside the Western world, famine exists, on a greater scale than ever; and the biological risks confronting the species are perhaps greater, and certainly more serious, than before the birth of microbiology. But what might be called a society's "threshold of modernity" has been reached when the life of the species is wagered on its own political strategies. For millennia, man remained what he was for Aristotle: a living animal with the additional cap-

acity for a political existence; modern man is an animal whose politics places his existence as a living being in question. [...]

Another consequence of this development of bio-power was the growing importance assumed by the action of the norm, at the expense of the juridical system of the law. Law cannot help but be armed, and its arm, *par excellence*, is death; to those who transgress it, it replies, at least as a last resort, with that absolute menace. The law always refers to the sword. But a power whose task is to take charge of life needs continuous regulatory and corrective mechanisms. It is no longer a matter of bringing death into play in the field of sovereignty, but of distributing the living in the domain of value and utility. Such a power has to qualify, measure, appraise, and hierarchize, rather than display itself in its murderous splendor; it does not have to draw the line that separates the enemies of the sovereign from his obedient subjects; it effects distributions around the norm. I do not mean to say that the law fades into the background or that the institutions of justice tend to disappear, but rather that the law operates more and more as a norm, and that the judicial institution is increasingly incorporated into a continuum of apparatuses (medical, administrative, and so on) whose functions are for the most part regulatory. A normalizing society is the historical outcome of a technology of power centered on life. We have entered a phase of juridical regression in comparison with the pre-seventeenth-century societies we are acquainted with; we should not be deceived by all the Constitutions framed throughout the world since the French Revolution, the Codes written and revised, a whole continual and clamorous legislative activity: these were the forms that made an essentially normalizing power acceptable.

NOTES

1 Samuel von Pufendorf, *Le Droit de la nature* (French trans., 1734), p. 445.

2 "Just as a composite body can have properties not found in any of the simple bodies of which the mixture consists, so a moral body, by virtue of the very union of persons of which it is composed, can have certain rights which none of the individuals could expressly claim and whose exercise is the proper function of leaders alone." Pufendorf, *Le Droit de la nature*, p. 452.

8

The Gray Zone

Primo Levi

The network of human relationships inside the Lagers was not simple: it could not be reduced to the two blocs of victims and persecutors. Anyone who today reads (or writes) the history of the Lager reveals the tendency, indeed the need, to separate evil from good, to be able to take sides, to emulate Christ's gesture on Judgment Day: here the righteous, over there the reprobates. The young above all demand clarity, a sharp cut; their experience of the world being meager, they do not like ambiguity. In any case, their expectation reproduces exactly that of the newcomers to the Lagers, whether young or not; all of them, with the exception of those who had already gone through an analogous experience, expected to find a terrible but decipherable world, in conformity with that simple model which we atavistically carry within us – "we" inside and the enemy outside, separated by a sharply defined geographic frontier.

Instead, the arrival in the Lager was indeed a shock because of the surprise it entailed. The world into which one was precipitated was terrible, yes, but also indecipherable: it did not conform to any model; the enemy was all around but also inside, the "we" lost its limits, the contenders were not two, one could not discern a single frontier but rather many confused, perhaps innumerable frontiers, which stretched between each of us. One entered hoping at least for the solidarity of one's companions in misfortune, but the hoped for allies, except in special cases, were not there; there were instead a thousand sealed off monads, and between them a desperate covert and continuous struggle. This brusque revelation, which became manifest from the very first hours of imprisonment, often in the instant form of a concentric aggression on the part of those in whom one hoped to find future allies, was so harsh as to cause the immediate collapse of one's capacity to resist. For many it was lethal, indirectly or even directly: it is difficult to defend oneself against a blow for which one is not prepared.

Various aspects can be identified in this aggression. Remember that the concentration camp system even from its origins (which coincide with the rise to power of Nazism in Germany) had as its primary purpose shattering the adversaries' capacity to resist: for the camp management the new arrival was by definition an adversary, whatever the label attached to him might be, and he must immediately be demolished to make sure that he did not become an example or a germ of organized resistance. On this point the SS had very clear ideas, and it is from this viewpoint that the entire sinister ritual must be interpreted – varying from Lager to Lager, but basically similar – which accompanied the arrival: kicks and punches right away, often in the face; an orgy of orders screamed with true or simulated rage; complete nakedness after being stripped; the shaving off of all one's hair; the outfitting in rags. It is difficult to say whether all these details were devised by some expert or methodically perfected on the basis of experience, but they certainly were willed and not casual: it was all staged, as was quite obvious.

Nevertheless, the entry ritual, and the moral collapse it promoted, was abetted more or less consciously by the other components of the con-centration camp world: the simple prisoners and the privileged ones. Rarely was a newcomer received, I won't say as a friend but at least as a companion-in-misfortune; in the majority of cases, those with seniority (and seniority was acquired in three or four months; the changeover was swift!) showed irritation or even hostility. The "newcomer" (*Zugang*: one should note that in German this is an abstract, administrative term, meaning "access," "entry") was envied because he still seemed to have on him the smell of home, and it was an absurd envy, because in fact one suffered much more during the first days of imprisonment than later on, when habituation on one hand and experience on the other made it possible to construct oneself a shelter. He was derided and subjected to cruel pranks, as happens in all communities with "conscripts" and "rookies," as well as in the initiation ceremonies of primitive peoples: and there is no doubt that life in the Lager involved a regression, leading back precisely to primitive behavior.

It is probable that the hostility toward the *Zugang* was in substance motivated like all other forms of intolerance, that is, it consisted in an unconscious attempt to consolidate the "we" at the expense of the "they," to create, in short, that solidarity among the oppressed whose absence was the source of additional suffering, even though not perceived openly. Vying for prestige also came into play, a seemingly irrepressible need in our civilization: the despised crowd of seniors was prone to recognize in the new arrival a target on which to vent its humiliation, to find compensation at his expense, to build for itself and at his expense a figure of a lower rank on whom to discharge the burden of the offenses received from above.

As for the privileged prisoners, the situation was more complex, and also more important: in my opinion, it is in fact fundamental. It is naive, absurd, and historically false to believe that an infernal system such as National Socialism sanctifies its victims: on the contrary, it degrades them, it makes them resemble itself, and this all the more when they are available, blank, and lacking a political or moral armature. From many signs it would seem the time has come to explore the space which separates (and not only in Nazi Lagers) the victims from the persecutors, and to do so with a lighter hand, and with a less turbid spirit than has been done, for instance, in a number of films. Only a schematic rhetoric can claim that that space is empty: it never is, it is studded with obscene or pathetic figures (sometimes they possess both qualities simultaneously) whom it is indispensable to know if we want to know the human species, if we want to know how to defend our souls when a similar test should once more loom before us, or even if we only want to understand what takes place in a big industrial factory.

Privileged prisoners were a minority within the Lager population; nevertheless they represent a potent majority among survivors. In fact, even apart from the hard labor, the beatings, the cold, and the illnesses, the food ration was decisively insufficient for even the most frugal prisoner: the physiological reserves of the organism were consumed in two or three months, and death by hunger, or by diseases induced by hunger, was the prisoner's normal destiny, avoidable only with additional food. Obtaining that extra nourishment required a privilege – large or small, granted or conquered, astute or violent, licit or illicit – whatever it took to lift oneself above the norm.

Now, one mustn't forget that the greater part of the memories, spoken or written, of those who came back begin with the collision with the concentrationary reality and, simultaneously, the unforeseen and uncomprehended aggression on the part of a new and strange enemy, the functionary-prisoner, who instead of taking you by the hand, reassuring you, teaching you the way, throws himself at you, screaming in a language you do not understand, and strikes you in the face. He wants to tame you, extinguish any spark of dignity that he has lost and you perhaps still preserve. But trouble is in store for you if this dignity drives you to react. There is an unwritten but iron law, *Zurückschlagen*: answering blows with blows is an intolerable transgression that can only occur to the mind of a "newcomer," and anyone who commits it must be made an example. Other functionaries rush to the defense of the threatened order, and the culprit is beaten with rage and method until he's tamed or dead. Privilege, by definition, defends and protects privilege.

I remember now that the local Yiddish and Polish term to indicate privilege was *protekcja*, pronounced "protektsia," and is of obvious Italian and Latin origin. I was told the story of an Italian "newcomer," a Partisan, flung into a work Lager with the label "political prisoner" when he still had his full strength. He had been beaten when

forced to exercise this trade for months. It has been testified that a large amount of alcohol was put at the disposal of those wretches and that they were in a permanent state of complete debasement and prostration. One of them declared: "Doing this work, one either goes crazy the first day or gets accustomed to it." Another, though: "Certainly, I could have killed myself or got myself killed; but I wanted to survive, to avenge myself and bear witness. You mustn't think that we are monsters; we are the same as you, only much more unhappy."

Clearly what we know they said, and the innumerable other things they probably said but did not reach us, cannot be taken literally. One cannot expect from men who have known such extreme destitution a deposition in the juridical sense, but something that is at once a lament, a curse, an expiation, an attempt to justify and rehabilitate oneself: a liberating outburst rather than a Medusa-faced truth.

Conceiving and organizing the squads was National Socialism's most demonic crime. Behind the pragmatic aspect (to economize on able men, to impose on others the most atrocious tasks) other more subtle aspects can be perceived. This institution represented an attempt to shift onto others – specifically, the victims – the burden of guilt, so that they were deprived of even the solace of innocence. It is neither easy nor agreeable to dredge this abyss of viciousness, and yet I think it must be done, because what could be perpetrated yesterday could be attempted again tomorrow, could overwhelm us and our children. One is tempted to turn away with a grimace and close one's mind: this is a temptation one must resist. In fact, the existence of the squads had a meaning, a message: "We, the master race, are your destroyers, but you are no better than we are; if we so wish, and we do so wish, we can destroy not only your bodies but also your souls, just as we have destroyed ours."

Miklos Nyiszli, a Hungarian physician, was one of the very few survivors of the last Special Squad in Auschwitz. He was a renowned anatomical pathologist, expert in autopsies and the chief doctor of the Birkenau SS whose services Mengele – who died a few years ago, escaping justice – had secured; he had given him special treatment and considered him almost a colleague. Nyiszli was supposed to devote himself in particular to the study of twins: in fact, Birkenau was the only place in the world where it was possible to study the corpses of twins killed at the same moment. Alongside this particular task of his, to which, it should be said in passing, it does not appear he strenuously objected, Nyiszli was also the attending physician of the squad, with which he lived in close contact. Well, he recounts an episode that seems significant to me.

The SS, as I already said, carefully chose, from the Lagers or the arriving convoys, the candidates for the squads, and did not hesitate to eliminate on the spot anyone who refused or seemed unsuitable for those duties. The SS treated the newly engaged members with the same contempt and detachment that they were accustomed to show toward all prisoners and Jews in particular. It had been inculcated in them that these were despicable beings, enemies of Germany, and therefore not entitled to life; in the most favorable instance, they should be compelled to work until they died of exhaustion. But this is not how they behaved with the veterans of the squad: in them, they recognized to some extent colleagues, by now as inhuman as themselves, hitched to the same cart, bound together by the foul link of imposed complicity. So, Nyiszli tells how during a "work" pause he attended a soccer game between the SS and the SK (*Sonderkommando*), that is to say, between a group representing the SS on guard at the crematorium and a group representing the Special Squad. Other men of the SS and the rest of the squad are present at the game; they take sides, bet, applaud, urge the players on as if, rather than at the gates of hell, the game were taking place on the village green.

Nothing of this kind ever took place, nor would it have been conceivable, with other categories of prisoners; but with them, with the "crematorium ravens," the SS could enter the field on an equal footing, or almost. Behind this armistice one hears satanic laughter: it is consummated, we have succeeded, you no longer are the other race, the anti-race, the prime enemy of the millennial Reich; you are no longer the people who reject idols. We have embraced you, corrupted you, dragged you to the bottom with us. You are like us, you proud people: dirtied with your own blood, as we are. You too, like us and like Cain, have killed the brother. Come, we can play together.

Nyiszli describes another episode that deserves consideration. In the gas chamber have been jammed together and murdered the components of a recently arrived convoy, and the squad is performing its horrendous everyday work, sorting out the tangle of corpses, washing them with hoses, and transporting them to the crematorium, but on the floor they find a young woman who is still alive. The event is exceptional, unique; perhaps the human bodies formed a barrier around her, sequestered a pocket of air that remained breathable. The men are perplexed. Death is their trade at all hours, death is a habit because, precisely, "one either goes mad on the first day or becomes accustomed to it," but this woman is alive. They hide her, warm her, bring her beef broth, question her: the girl is sixteen years old, she cannot orient herself in space or time, does not know where she is, has gone through without understanding it the sequence of the sealed train, the brutal preliminary selection, the stripping, the entry into the chamber from which no one had ever come out alive. She has not understood, but she has seen; therefore she must die, and the men of the squad know it just as they know that they too must die for the same reason. But these slaves debased by alcohol and the daily slaughter are transformed; they no longer have before them the anonymous mass, the flood of frightened, stunned people coming off the boxcars: they have a person. [...]

Compassion and brutality can coexist in the same individual and in the same moment, despite all logic; and for all that, compassion itself eludes logic. There is no proportion between the pity we feel and the extent of the pain by which the pity is aroused: a single Anne Frank excites more emotion than the myriads who suffered as she did but whose image has remained in the shadows. Perhaps it is necessary that it can be so. If we had to and were able to suffer the sufferings of everyone, we could not live. Perhaps the dreadful gift of pity for the many is granted only to saints; to the members of the Special Squad and to all of us there remains in the best of cases only the sporadic pity addressed to the single individual, the *Mit-*

mensch, the co-man: the human being of flesh and blood standing before us, within the reach of our providentially myopic senses.

A doctor is called, and he revives the girl with an injection: yes, the gas has not had its effect, she will survive, but where and how? Just then Muhsfeld, one of the SS men attached to the death installations, arrives. The doctor calls him to one side and presents the case to him. Muhsfeld hesitates, then he decides: No, the girl must die. If she were older, it would be a different matter, she would have more sense, perhaps she could be convinced to keep quiet about what has happened to her. But she's only sixteen: she can't be trusted. And yet, he does not kill her with his own hands. He calls one of his underlings to eliminate her with a blow to the nape of the neck. Now, this man Muhsfeld was not a compassionate person; his daily ration of slaughter was studded with arbitrary and capricious acts, marked by his inventions of refined cruelty. He was tried in 1947, sentenced to death and hung in Krakow and this was right, but not even he was a monolith. Had he lived in a different environment and epoch, he probably would have behaved like any other common man. [...]

That single, immediately erased instant of pity is certainly not enough to absolve Muhsfeld. It is enough, however, to place him too, although at its extreme boundary, within the gray band, that zone of ambiguity which radiates out from regimes based on terror and obsequiousness.

It is not difficult to judge Muhsfeld, and I do not believe that the tribunal which sentenced him had any doubts. On the other hand, in contrast to this, our need and our ability to judge falters when confronted by the Special Squad. Questions immediately arise, convulsed questions for which one would be hard pressed to find an answer that reassures us about man's nature. Why did they accept that task? Why didn't they rebel? Why didn't they prefer death?

9

From *Eichmann in Jerusalem: A Report on the Banality of Evil*

Hannah Arendt

Judgment, Appeal, and Execution

Eichmann spent the last months of the war cooling his heels in Berlin, with nothing to do, cut by the other department heads in the R.S.H.A., who had lunch together every day in the building where he had his office but did not once ask him to join them. He kept himself busy with his defense installations, so as to be ready for "the last battle" for Berlin, and, as his only official duty, paid occasional visits to Theresienstadt, where he showed Red Cross delegates around. To them, of all people, he unburdened his soul about Himmler's new "humane line" in regard to the Jews, which included an avowed determination to have, "next time," concentration camps after "the English model." In April, 1945, Eichmann had the last of his rare interviews with Himmler, who ordered him to select "a hundred to two hundred prominent Jews in Theresienstadt," transport them to Austria, and install them in hotels, so that Himmler could use them as "hostages" in his forthcoming negotiations with Eisenhower. The absurdity of this commission seems not to have dawned upon Eichmann; he went, "with grief in my heart, as I had to desert my defense installations," but he never reached Theresienstadt, because all the roads were blocked by the approaching Russian armies. Instead, he ended up at Alt-Aussee, in Austria, where Kaltenbrunner had taken refuge. Kaltenbrunner had no interest in Himmler's "prominent Jews," and told Eichmann to organize a commando for partisan warfare in the Austrian mountains. Eichmann re-sponded with the greatest enthusiasm: "This was again something worth doing, a task I enjoyed." But just as he had collected some hundred more or less unfit men, most of whom had never seen a rifle, and had taken possession of an arsenal of abandoned weapons of all sorts, he received the latest Himmler order: "No fire is to be opened on English and Americans." This was the end. He sent his men home and gave a small strongbox containing paper money and gold coins to his trusted legal adviser, Regierungsrat Hunsche: "Because, I said to myself, he is a man from the higher civil services, he will be correct in the management of funds, he will put down his expenses ... for I still believed that accounts would be demanded some day."

With these words Eichmann had to conclude the autobiography he had spontaneously given the police examiner. It had taken only a few days, and filled no more than 315 of the 3,564 pages copied off the tape-recorder. He would like to have gone on, and he obviously did tell the rest of the story to the police, but the trial authorities, for various reasons, had decided not to admit any testimony covering the time after the close of the war. However, from affidavits given at Nuremberg, and, more important, from a much discussed indiscretion on the part of a former Israeli civil servant, Moshe Pearlman, whose book *The Capture of Adolf Eichmann* appeared in London four weeks before the trial opened, it is possible to complete the story; Mr. Pearlman's account was obviously based upon material from Bureau 06, the police office that was in charge of the preparations for the trial. (Mr. Pearlman's own version was that since he had retired from government service three weeks before Eichmann was kidnaped, he had written the book as a "private individual," which is not very convincing, because the Israeli police must have known of the impending capture several months before his retirement.) The book caused some embarrassment in Israel, not only because Mr. Pearlman had been able to divulge information about important prosecution documents prematurely and had stated that the trial authorities had already made up their minds about the untrustworthiness of Eichmann's testimony, but because a reliable account of how Eichmann was captured in Buenos Aires was of course the last thing they wanted to have published.

The story told by Mr. Pearlman was considerably less exciting than the various rumors upon which previous tales had been based. Eichmann had never been in the Near East or the Middle East, he had no connection with any Arab country, he had never returned to Germany from Argentina, he had never been to any other Latin American country, he had played no role in postwar Nazi activities or organizations. At the end of the war, he had tried to speak once more with Kaltenbrunner, who was still in Alt-Aussee, playing solitaire, but his former chief was in no mood to receive him, since "for this man he saw no chances any more." (Kaltenbrunner's own chances were not so very good either, he was hanged at Nuremberg.) Almost immediately thereafter, Eichmann was caught by American soldiers and put in a camp for S.S. men, where numerous interrogations failed to uncover his identity, although it was known to some of his fellow-prisoners. He was cautious and did not write to his family, but let them believe he was dead; his wife tried to obtain a death certificate, but failed when it was discovered that the only "eyewitness" to her husband's death was her brother-in-law. She had been left penniless, but Eichmann's family in Linz supported her and the three children.

In November, 1945, the trials of the major war criminals opened in Nuremberg, and Eichmann's name began to appear with uncomfortable regularity. In January, 1946, Wisliceny appeared as a witness for the prosecution and gave his damning evidence, whereupon Eichmann decided that he had better disappear. He escaped from the camp, with the help of the inmates, and went to the Lüneburger Heide, a heath about fifty miles south of Hamburg, where the brother of one of his fellow-prisoners provided him with work as a lumberjack. He stayed there, under the name of Otto Heninger, for four years, and he was probably bored to death. Early in 1950, he succeeded in establishing contact with ODESSA, a clandestine organization of S.S. veterans, and in May of that year he was passed through Austria to Italy, where a Franciscan priest, fully informed of his identity, equipped him with a refugee passport in the name of Richard Klement and sent him on to Buenos Aires. He arrived in mid-July and, without any difficulty, obtained identification papers and a work permit as Ricardo Klement, Catholic, a bachelor, stateless, aged 37 – seven years less than his real age.

He was still cautious, but he now wrote to his wife in his own handwriting and told her that "her children's uncle" was alive. He worked at a number of odd jobs – sales representative, laundry man, worker on a rabbit farm – all poorly paid, but in the summer of 1952 he had his wife and children join him. (Mrs. Eichmann obtained a German passport in Zurich, Switzerland, though she was a resident of Austria at the time, and under her real name, as a "divorcée" from a certain Eichmann. How this came about has remained a mystery, and the file containing her application has disappeared from the German consulate in Zurich.) Upon her arrival in Argentina, Eichmann got his first steady job, in the Mercedes-Benz factory in Suarez, a suburb of Buenos Aires, first as a mechanic and later as a foreman, and when a fourth son was born to him, he remarried his wife, supposedly under the name of Klement. This is not likely, however, for the infant was registered as Ricardo Francisco (presumably as a tribute to the Italian priest) Klement *Eichmann*, and this was only one of many hints that Eichmann dropped in regard to his identity as the years went by. It does seem to be true, however, that he told his children he was Adolf Eichmann's brother, though the children, being well acquainted with their grandparents and uncles in Linz, must have been rather dull to believe it; the oldest son, at least, who had been nine years old when he last saw his father, should have been able to recognize him seven years later in Argentina. Mrs. Eichmann's Argentine identity card, moreover, was never changed (it read "Veronika Liebl de Eichmann"), and in 1959, when Eichmann's stepmother died, and a year later, when his father died, the newspaper announcements in Linz carried Mrs. Eichmann's name among the survivors, contradicting all stories of divorce and remarriage. Early in 1960, a few months before his capture, Eichmann and his elder sons finished building a primitive brick house in one of the poor suburbs of Buenos Aires – no electricity, no running water – where the family settled down. They must have been very poor, and Eichmann must have led a dreary life, for which not even the children could compensate, for they showed "absolutely no interest in being educated and did not even try to develop their so-called talents."

Eichmann's only compensation consisted in talking endlessly with members of the large Nazi colony, to whom he readily admitted his identity. In 1955, this finally led to the interview with the Dutch journalist Willem S. Sassen, a former member of the Armed S.S. who had exchanged his Dutch nationality for a German passport during the war and had later been condemned to death *in absentia* in Belgium as a war criminal. Eichmann made copious notes for the interview, which was tape-recorded and then rewritten by Sassen, with considerable embellishments; the notes in Eichmann's own handwriting were discovered and they were admitted as evidence at his trial, though the statement as a whole was not. Sassen's version appeared in abbreviated form first in the German illustrated magazine *Der Stern*, in July, 1960, and then, in November and December, as a series of articles in *Life*. But Sassen, obviously with Eichmann's consent, had offered the story four years before to a *Time-Life* correspondent in Buenos Aires, and even if it is true that Eichmann's name was withheld, the content of the material could have left no doubt about the original source of the information. The truth of the matter is that Eichmann had made many efforts to break out of his anonymity, and it is rather strange that it took the Israeli Secret Services several years – until August, 1959 – to learn that Adolf Eichmann was living in Argentina under the name of Ricardo Klement. Israel has never divulged the source of her information, and today at least half a dozen persons claim they found Eichmann, while "well-informed circles" in Europe insist that it was the Russian Intelligence service that spilled the news. However that may have been, the puzzle is not how it was possible to discover Eichmann's hideout but, rather, how it was possible not to discover it earlier – provided, of course, that the Israelis had indeed pursued this

search through the years. Which, in view of the facts, seems doubtful.

No doubt, however, exists about the identity of the captors. All talk of private "avengers" was contradicted at the outset by Ben-Gurion himself, who on May 23, 1960, announced to Israel's wildly cheering Knesset that Eichmann had been "found by the Israeli Secret Service." Dr. Servatius, who tried strenuously and unsuccessfully both before the District Court and before the Court of Appeal to call Zvi Tohar, chief pilot of the El-Al plane that flew Eichmann out of the country, and Yad Shimoni, an official of the air line in Argentina, as witnesses, mentioned Ben-Gurion's statement; the Attorney General countered by saying that the Prime Minister had "admitted no more than that Eichmann was *found out* by the Secret Service," not that he also had been kidnaped by government agents. Well, in actual fact, it seems that it was the other way round: Secret Service men had not "found" him but only picked him up, after making a few preliminary tests to assure themselves that the information they had received was true. And even this was not done very expertly, for Eichmann had been well aware that he was being shadowed:

I told you that months ago, I believe, when I was asked if I had known that I was found out, and I could give you then precise reasons [that is, in the part of the police examination that was not released to the press]. . . . I learned that people in my neighborhood had made inquiries about real-estate purchases and so on and so forth for the establishment of a factory for sewing machines – a thing that was quite impossible, since there existed neither electricity nor water in that area. Furthermore, I was informed that these people were Jews from North America. I could easily have disappeared, but I did not do it, I just went on as usual, and let things catch up with me. I could have found employment without any difficulty, with my papers and references. But I did not want that.

There was more proof than was revealed in Jerusalem of his willingness to go to Israel and stand trial. Counsel for the defense, of course, had to stress the fact that, after all, the accused had been kidnaped and "brought to Israel in conflict with international law," because this enabled the defense to challenge the right of the court to prosecute him, and though neither the prosecution nor the judges ever admitted that the kidnaping had been an "act of state," they did not deny it either. They argued that the breach of international law concerned only the states of Argentina and Israel, not the rights of the defendant, and that this breach was "cured" through the joint declaration of the two governments, on August 3, 1960, that they "resolved to view as settled the incident which was caused in the wake of the action of citizens of Israel which violated the basic rights of the State of Argentina." The court decided that it did not matter whether these Israelis were government agents or private citizens. What neither the defense nor the court mentioned was that Argentina would not have waived her rights so obligingly had Eichmann been an Argentine citizen. He had lived there under an assumed name, thereby denying himself the right to government protection, at least as Ricardo Klement (born on May 23, 1913, at Bolzano – in Southern Tyrol – as his Argentine identity card stated), although he had declared himself of "German nationality." And he had never invoked the dubious right of asylum, which would not have helped him anyhow, since Argentina, although she has in fact offered asylum to many known Nazi criminals, had signed an International Convention declaring that the perpetrators of crimes against humanity "will not be deemed to be political criminals." All this did not make Eichmann stateless, it did not legally deprive him of his German nationality, but it gave the West German republic a welcome pretext for withholding the customary protection due its citizens abroad. In other words, and despite pages and pages of legal argument, based on so many precedents that one finally got the impression that kidnaping was among the most frequent modes of arrest, it was Eichmann's de facto statelessness, and nothing else, that enabled the Jerusalem court to sit in judgment on him. Eichmann, though no legal expert, should have been able to appreciate that, for he knew from his own career that one could do as one pleased only with stateless people; the Jews had had to lose their nationality before they could be exterminated. But he was in no mood to ponder such niceties, for if it was a fiction that he had come voluntarily to Israel to stand trial, it was true that he had made fewer difficulties than anybody had expected. In fact, he had made none.

On May 11, 1960, at six-thirty in the evening, when Eichmann alighted, as usual, from the bus that brought him home from his place of work, he was seized by three men and, in less than a minute, bundled into a waiting car, which took him to a previously rented house in a remote suburb of Buenos Aires. No drugs, no ropes, no handcuffs were used, and Eichmann immediately recognized that this was professional work, as no unnecessary violence had been applied; he was not hurt. Asked who he was, he instantly said: "*Ich bin Adolf Eichmann*," and, surprisingly, added: "I know I am in the hands of Israelis." (He later explained that he had read in some newspaper of Ben-Gurion's order that he be found and caught.) For eight days, while the Israelis were waiting for the El-Al plane that was to carry them and their prisoner to Israel, Eichmann was tied to a bed, which was the only aspect of the whole affair that he complained about, and on the second day of his captivity he was asked to state in writing that he had no objection to being tried by an Israeli court. The statement was, of course, already prepared, and all he was supposed to do was to copy it. To everybody's surprise, however, he insisted on writing his own text, for which, as can be seen from the following lines, he probably used the first sentences of the prepared statement:

I, the undersigned, Adolf Eichmann, hereby declare out of my own free will that since now my true identity has been revealed, I see clearly that it is useless to try and escape judgment any longer. I hereby express my readiness to travel to Israel to face a court of judgment, an authorized court of law. It is clear and understood that I shall be given legal advice [thus far, he probably copied], and I shall try to write down the facts of my last years of public activities in Germany, without any embellishments, in order that future generations will have a true picture. This declaration I declare out of my own free will, not for promises given and not because of threats. I wish to be at peace with myself at last. Since I cannot remember all the details, and since I seem to mix up facts, I request assistance by putting at my disposal documents and affidavits to help me in my effort to seek the truth." Signed: "Adolf Eichmann, Buenos Aires, May 1960."

(This document, though doubtless genuine, has one peculiarity: its date omits the day it was signed. The omission gives rise to the suspicion that the letter was written not in Argentina but in

Jerusalem, where Eichmann arrived on May 22. The letter was needed less for the trial, during which the prosecution did submit it as evidence, but without attaching much importance to it, than for Israel's first explanatory official note to the Argentine government, to which it was duly attached. Servatius, who asked Eichmann about the letter in court, did not mention the peculiarity of the date, and Eichmann could not very well mention it himself since, upon being asked a leading question by his lawyer, he confirmed, though somewhat reluctantly, that he had given the statement under duress, while tied to the bed in the Buenos Aires suburb. The prosecutor, who may have known better, did not cross-examine him on this point; clearly, the less said about this matter the better.) Mrs. Eichmann had notified the Argentine police of her husband's disappearance, but without revealing his identity, so no check of railway stations, highways, and airfields was made. The Israelis were lucky, they would never have been able to spirit Eichmann out of the country ten days after his capture if the police had been properly alerted.

Eichmann provided two reasons for his astounding cooperation with the trial authorities. (Even the judges who insisted that Eichmann was simply a liar had to admit that they knew no answer to the question: "Why did the accused confess before Superintendent Less to a number of incriminating details of which, on the face of it, there could be no proof but for his confession, in particular to his journeys to the East, where he saw the atrocities with his own eyes?") In Argentina, years before his capture, he had written how tired he was of his anonymity, and the more he read about himself, the more tired he must have become. His second explanation, given in Israel, was more dramatic: "About a year and a half ago [i.e., in the spring of 1959], I heard from an acquaintance who had just returned from a trip to Germany that a certain feeling of guilt had seized some sections of German youth . . . and the fact of this guilt complex was for me as much of a landmark as, let us say, the landing of the first man-bearing rocket on the moon. It became an essential point of my inner life, around which many thoughts crystallized. This was why I did not escape . . . when I knew the search commando was closing in on me. . . . After these conversations about the guilt feeling among young people in Germany, which made such a deep impression on me, I felt I no longer had the right to disappear. This is also why I offered, in a written statement, at the beginning of this examination . . . to hang myself in public. I wanted to do my part in lifting the burden of guilt from German youth, for these young people are, after all, innocent of the events, and of the acts of their fathers, during the last war" – which, incidentally, he was still calling, in another context, a "war forced upon the German Reich." Of course, all this was empty talk. What prevented him from returning to Germany of his own free will to give himself up? He was asked this question, and he replied that in his opinion German courts still lacked the "objectivity" needed for dealing with people like him. But if he did prefer to be tried by an Israeli court – as he somehow implied, and which was just barely possible – he could have spared the Israeli government much time and trouble. We have seen before that this kind of talk gave him feelings of elation, and indeed it kept him in something approaching good spirits throughout his stay in the Israeli prison. It even enabled him to look upon death with remarkable equanimity – "I know that the death sentence is in store for me," he declared at the beginning of the police examination.

There was some truth behind the empty talk, and the truth emerged quite clearly when the question of his defense was put to him. For obvious reasons, the Israeli government had decided to admit a foreign counselor, and on July 14, 1960, six weeks after the police examination had started, with Eichmann's explicit consent, he was informed that there were three possible counselors among whom he might choose, in arranging his defense – Dr. Robert Servatius, who was recommended by his family (Servatius had offered his services in a long-distance call to Eichmann's stepbrother in Linz), another German lawyer now residing in Chile, and an American law firm in New York, which had contacted the trial authorities. (Only Dr. Servatius' name was divulged.) There might, of course, be other possibilities, which Eichmann was entitled to explore, and he was told repeatedly that he could take his time. He did nothing of the sort, but said on the spur of the moment that he would like to retain Dr. Servatius, since he seemed to be an acquaintance of his stepbrother and, also, had defended other war criminals, and he insisted on signing the necessary papers immediately. Half an hour later, it occurred to him that the trial could assume "global dimensions," that it might become a "monster process," that there were several attorneys for the prosecution, and that Servatius alone would hardly be able "to digest all the material." He was reminded that Servatius, in a letter asking for power of attorney, had said that he "would lead a group of attorneys" (he never did), and the police officer added, "It must be assumed that Dr. Servatius won't appear alone. That would be a physical impossibility." But Dr. Servatius, as it turned out, appeared quite alone most of the time. The result of all this was that Eichmann became the chief assistant to his own defense counsel, and, quite apart from writing books "for future generations," worked very hard throughout the trial.

On June 29, 1961, ten weeks after the opening of the trial on April 11, the prosecution rested its case, and Dr. Servatius opened the case for the defense; on August 14, after 114 sessions, the main proceedings came to an end. The court then adjourned for four months, and reassembled on December 11 to pronounce judgment. For two days, divided into five sessions, the three judges read the 244 sections of the judgment. Dropping the prosecution's charge of "conspiracy," which would have made him a "chief war criminal," automatically responsible for everything which had to do with the Final Solution, they convicted Eichmann on all fifteen counts of the indictment, although he was acquitted on some particulars. "Together with others," he had committed crimes "against the Jewish people," that is, crimes against Jews *with intent to destroy the people*, on four counts: (1) by "causing the killing of millions of Jews"; (2) by placing "millions of Jews under conditions which were likely to lead to their physical destruction"; (3) by "causing serious bodily and mental harm" to them; and (4) by "directing that births be banned and pregnancies interrupted among Jewish women" in Theresienstadt. But they acquitted him of any such charges bearing on the period prior to August, 1941, when he was informed of the Führer's order; in his earlier activities, in Berlin, Vienna, and Prague, he had no intention "to destroy the Jewish people." These were the first four counts of the indictment. Counts 5 through 12 dealt with "crimes against humanity" – a strange concept in the Israeli law, inasmuch as it included both genocide if practiced against non-Jewish peoples (such as the Gypsies or the Poles) and all other crimes, including murder,

committed against either Jews or non-Jews, provided that these crimes were not committed with intent to destroy the people as a whole. Hence, everything Eichmann had done prior to the Führer's order and all his acts against non-Jews were lumped together as crimes against humanity, to which were added, once again, all his later crimes against Jews, since these were ordinary crimes as well. The result was that Count 5 convicted him of the same crimes enumerated in Counts 1 and 2, and that Count 6 convicted him of having "persecuted Jews on racial, religious, and political grounds"; Count 7 dealt with "the plunder of property... linked with the murder... of these Jews," and Count 8 summed up all these deeds again as "war crimes," since most of them had been committed during the war. Counts 9 through 12 dealt with crimes against non-Jews: Count 9 convicted him of the "expulsion of... hundreds of thousands of Poles from their homes," Count 10 of "the expulsion of fourteen thousand Slovenes" from Yugoslavia, Count 11 of the deportation of "scores of thousands of Gypsies" to Auschwitz. But the judgment held that "it has not been proved before us that the accused knew that the Gypsies were being transported to destruction" – which meant that no genocide charge except the "crime against the Jewish people" was brought. This was difficult to understand, for, apart from the fact that the extermination of Gypsies was common knowledge, Eichmann had admitted during the police examination that he knew of it: he had remembered vaguely that this had been an order from Himmler, that no "directives" had existed for Gypsies as they existed for Jews, and that there had been no "research" done on the "Gypsy problem" – "origins, customs, habits, organization... folklore... economy." His department had been commissioned to undertake the "evacuation" of thirty thousand Gypsies from Reich territory, and he could not remember the details very well, because there had been no intervention from any side; but that Gypsies, like Jews, were shipped off to be exterminated he had never doubted. He was guilty of their extermination in exactly the same way he was guilty of the extermination of the Jews. Count 12 concerned the deportation of ninety-three children from Lidice, the Czech village whose inhabitants had been massacred after the assassination of Heydrich; he was, however, rightly acquitted of the murder of these children. The last three counts charged him with membership in three of the four organizations that the Nuremberg Trials had classified as "criminal" – the S.S.; the Security Service, or S.D.; and the Secret State Police, or Gestapo. (The fourth such organization, the leadership corps of the National Socialist Party, was not mentioned, because Eichmann obviously had not been one of the Party leaders.) His membership in them prior to May, 1940, fell under the statute of limitations (twenty years) for minor offenses. (The Law of 1950 under which Eichmann was tried specifies that there is no statute of limitation for major offenses, and that the argument *res judicata* shall not avail – a person can be tried in Israel "even if he has already been tried abroad, whether before an international tribunal or a tribunal of a foreign state, for the same offense.") All crimes enumerated under Counts 1 through 12 carried the death penalty.

Eichmann, it will be remembered, had steadfastly insisted that he was guilty only of "aiding and abetting" in the commission of the crimes with which he was charged, that he himself had never committed an overt act. The judgment, to one's great relief, in a way recognized that the prosecution had not succeeded in proving him wrong on this point. For it was an important point; it touched upon the very essence of this crime, which was no ordinary crime, and the very nature of this criminal, who was no common criminal; by implication, it also took cognizance of the weird fact that in the death camps it was usually the inmates and the victims who had actually wielded "the fatal instrument with [their] own hands." What the judgment had to say on this point was more than correct, it was the truth: "Expressing his activities in terms of Section 23 of our Criminal Code Ordinance, we should say that they were mainly those of a person soliciting by giving counsel or advice to others and of one who enabled or aided others in [the criminal] act." But "in such an enormous and complicated crime as the one we are now considering, wherein many people participated, on various levels and in various modes of activity – the planners, the organizers, and those executing the deeds, according to their various ranks – there is not much point in using the ordinary concepts of counseling and soliciting to commit a crime. For these crimes were committed en masse, not only in regard to the number of victims, but also in regard to the numbers of those who perpetrated the crime, and the extent to which any one of the many criminals was close to or remote from the actual killer of the victim means nothing, as far as the measure of his responsibility is concerned. On the contrary, in general *the degree of responsibility increases as we draw further away from the man who uses the fatal instrument with his own hands* [my italics]."

What followed the reading of the judgment was routine. Once more, the prosecution rose to make a rather lengthy speech demanding the death penalty, which, in the absence of mitigating circumstances, was mandatory, and Dr. Servatius replied even more briefly than before: the accused had carried out "acts of state," what had happened to him might happen in future to anyone, the whole civilized world faced this problem, Eichmann was "a scapegoat," whom the present German government had abandoned to the court in Jerusalem, contrary to international law, in order to clear itself of responsibility. The competence of the court, never recognized by Dr. Servatius, could be construed only as trying the accused "in a representative capacity, as representing the legal powers vested in [a German court]" – as, indeed, one German state prosecutor had formulated the task of Jerusalem. Dr. Servatius had argued earlier that the court must acquit the defendant because, according to the Argentine statute of limitations, he had ceased to be liable to criminal proceedings against him on May 7, 1960, "a very short time before the abduction"; he now argued, in the same vein, that no death penalty could be pronounced because capital punishment had been abolished unconditionally in Germany.

Then came Eichmann's last statement: His hopes for justice were disappointed; the court had not believed him, though he had always done his best to tell the truth. The court did not understand him: he had never been a Jew-hater, and he had never willed the murder of human beings. His guilt came from his obedience, and obedience is praised as a virtue. His virtue had been abused by the Nazi leaders. But he was not one of the ruling clique, he was a victim, and only the leaders deserved punishment. (He did not go quite as far as many of the other low-ranking war criminals, who complained bitterly that they had been told never to worry about "responsibilities," and that they were now unable to call those responsible to account because these had "escaped and deserted" them – by committing suicide, or by having been hanged.) "I am not the monster I am made out to be," Eichmann said. "I am the victim of a fallacy." He did not use the word "scapegoat," but he confirmed what Servatius had said: it was his "profound conviction that [he] must suffer for the acts of others." After two more days, on Friday, December 15, 1961, at nine o'clock in the morning, the death sentence was pronounced.

Three months later, on March 22, 1962, review proceedings were opened before the Court of Appeal, Israel's Supreme Court, before five judges presided over by Itzhak Olshan. Mr. Hausner appeared again, with four assistants, for the prosecution, and Dr. Servatius, with none, for the defense. Counsel for the defense repeated all the old arguments against the competence of the Israeli court, and since all his efforts to persuade the West German government to start extradition proceedings had been in vain, he now demanded that Israel *offer* extradition. He had brought with him a new list of witnesses, but there was not a single one among them who could conceivably have produced anything resembling "new evidence." He had included in the list Dr. Hans Globke, whom Eichmann had never seen in his life and of whom he had probably heard for the first time in Jerusalem, and, even more startling, Dr. Chaim Weizmann, who had been dead for ten years. The *plaidoyer* was an incredible hodgepodge, full of errors (in one instance, the defense offered as new evidence the French translation of a document that had already been submitted by the prosecution, in two other cases it had simply misread the documents, and so on), its carelessness contrasted vividly with the rather careful introduction of certain remarks that were bound to be offensive to the court: gassing was again a "medical matter"; a Jewish court had no right to sit in judgment over the fate of the children from Lidice, since they were not Jewish; Israeli legal procedure ran counter to Continental procedure – to which Eichmann, because of his national origin, was entitled – in that it required the defendant to provide the evidence for his defense, and this the accused had been unable to do because neither witnesses nor defense documents were available in Israel. In short, the trial had been unfair, the judgment unjust.

The proceedings before the Court of Appeal lasted only a week, after which the court adjourned for two months. On May 29, 1962, the second judgment was read – somewhat less voluminous

than the first, but still 51 single-spaced legalsized pages. It ostensibly confirmed the District Court on all points, and to make this confirmation the judges would not have needed two months and 51 pages. The judgment of the Court of Appeal was actually a revision of the judgment of the lower court, although it did not say so. In conspicuous contrast to the original judgment, it was now found that "the appellant had received no 'superior orders' at all. He was his own superior, and he gave all orders in matters that concerned Jewish affairs"; he had, moreover, "eclipsed in importance all his superiors, including Müller." And, in reply to the obvious argument of the defense that the Jews would have been no better off had Eichmann never existed, the judges now stated that "the idea of the Final Solution would never have assumed the infernal forms of the flayed skin and tortured flesh of millions of Jews without the fanatical zeal and the unquenchable blood thirst of the appellant and his accomplices." Israel's Supreme Court had not only accepted the arguments of the prosecution, it had adopted its very language.

The same day, May 29, Itzhak Ben-Zvi, President of Israel, received Eichmann's plea for mercy, four handwritten pages, made "upon instructions of my counsel," together with letters from his wife and his family in Linz. The President also received hundreds of letters and telegrams from all over the world, pleading for clemency; outstanding among the senders were the Central Conference of American Rabbis, the representative body of Reform Judaism in this country, and a group of professors from the Hebrew University in Jerusalem, headed by Martin Buber, who had been opposed to the trial from the start, and who now tried to persuade Ben-Gurion to intervene for clemency. Mr. Ben-Zvi rejected all pleas for mercy on May 31, two days after the Supreme Court had delivered its judgment, and a few hours later on that same day – it was a Thursday – shortly before midnight, Eichmann was hanged, his body was cremated, and the ashes were scattered in the Mediterranean outside Israeli waters.

The speed with which the death sentence was carried out was extraordinary, even if one takes into account that Thursday night was the last possible occasion before the following Monday, since Friday, Saturday, and Sunday are all religious holidays for one or another of the three denominations in the country. The execution took place less than two hours after Eichmann was informed of the rejection of his plea for mercy; there had not even been time for a last meal. The explanation may well be found in two last-minute attempts Dr. Servatius made to save his client – an application to a court in West Germany to force the government to demand Eichmann's extradition, even now, and a threat to invoke Article 25 of the Convention for the Protection of Human Rights and Fundamental Freedoms. Neither Dr. Servatius nor his assistant was in Israel when Eichmann's plea was rejected, and the Israeli government probably wanted to close the case, which had been going on for two years, before the defense could even apply for a stay in the date of execution.

The death sentence had been expected, and there was hardly anyone to quarrel with it; but things were altogether different when it was learned that the Israelis had carried it out. The protests were short-lived, but they were widespread and they were voiced by people of influence and prestige. The most common argument was that Eichmann's deeds defied the possibility of human punishment, that it was pointless to impose the death sentence for crimes of such magnitude – which, of course, was true, in a sense, except that it could not conceivably mean that he who had murdered millions should for this very reason escape punishment. On a considerably lower level, the death sentence was called "unimaginative," and very imaginative alternatives were proposed forthwith – Eichmann "should have spent the rest of his life at hard labor in the arid stretches of the Negev, helping with his sweat to reclaim the Jewish homeland," a punishment he would probably not have survived for more than a single day, to say nothing of the fact that in Israel the desert of the south is hardly looked upon as a penal colony; or, in Madison Avenue style, Israel should have reached "divine heights," rising above "the understandable, legal, political, and even human considerations," by calling together "all those who took part in the capture, trial, and sentencing to a public ceremony, with Eichmann there in shackles, and with television cameras and radio to decorate them as the heroes of the century."

Martin Buber called the execution a "mistake of historical dimensions," as it might "serve to expiate the guilt felt by many young persons in Germany" – an argument that oddly echoed Eichmann's own ideas on the matter, though Buber hardly knew that he had wanted to hang himself in public in order to lift the burden of guilt from the shoulders of German youngsters. (It is strange that Buber, a man not only of eminence but of very great intelligence, should not see how spurious these much publicized guilt feelings necessarily are. It is quite gratifying to feel guilty if you haven't done anything wrong: how noble! Whereas it is rather hard and certainly depressing to admit guilt and to repent. The youth of Germany is surrounded, on all sides and in all walks of life, by men in positions of authority and in public office who are very guilty indeed but who *feel* nothing of the sort. The normal reaction to this state of affairs should be indignation, but indignation would be quite risky – not a danger to life and limb but definitely a handicap in a career. Those young German men and women who every once in a while – on the occasion of all the *Diary of Anne Frank* hubbub and of the Eichmann trial – treat us to hysterical outbreaks of guilt feelings are not staggering under the burden of the past, their fathers' guilt; rather, they are trying to escape from the pressure of very present and actual problems into a cheap sentimentality.) Professor Buber went on to say that he felt "no pity at all" for Eichmann, because he could feel pity "only for those whose actions I understand in my heart," and he stressed what he had said many years ago in Germany – that he had "only in a formal sense a common humanity with those who took part" in the acts of the Third Reich. This lofty attitude was, of course, more of a luxury than those who had to try Eichmann could afford, since the law presupposes precisely that we have a common humanity with those whom we accuse and judge and condemn. As far as I know, Buber was the only philosopher to go on public record on the subject of Eichmann's execution (shortly before the trial started, Karl Jaspers had given a radio interview in Basel, later published in *Der Monat*, in which he argued the case for an international tribunal); it was disappointing to find him dodging, on the highest possible level, the very problem Eichmann and his deeds had posed.

Least of all was heard from those who were against the death penalty on principle, unconditionally; their arguments would have remained valid, since they would not have needed to specify them for this particular case. They seem to have felt – rightly, I think – that this was not a very promising case on which to fight.

Adolf Eichmann went to the gallows with great dignity. He had asked for a bottle of red wine and had drunk half of it. He refused the help of the

Protestant minister, the Reverend William Hull, who offered to read the Bible with him: he had only two more hours to live, and therefore no "time to waste." He walked the fifty yards from his cell to the execution chamber calm and erect, with his hands bound behind him. When the guards tied his ankles and knees, he asked them to loosen the bonds so that he could stand straight. "I don't need that," he said when the black hood was offered him. He was in complete command of himself, nay, he was more: he was completely himself. Nothing could have demonstrated this more convincingly than the grotesque silliness of his last words. He began by stating emphatically that he was a *Gottgläubiger*, to express in common Nazi fashion that he was no Christian and did not believe in life after death. He then proceeded: "After a short while, gentlemen, *we shall all meet again*. Such is the fate of all men. Long live Germany, long live Argentina, long live Austria. *I shall not forget them*." In the face of death, he had found the cliché used in funeral oratory. Under the gallows, his memory played him the last trick; he was "elated" and he forgot that this was his own funeral.

It was as though in those last minutes he was summing up the lesson that this long course in human wickedness had taught us – the lesson of the fearsome, word-and-thought-defying *banality of evil*.

10

Initiation to Mass Murder:
The Józefów Massacre

Christopher R. Browning

It was probably on July 11 that Globocnik or someone on his staff contacted Major Trapp and informed him that Reserve Police Battalion 101 had the task of rounding up the 1,800 Jews in Józefów, a village about thirty kilometers slightly south and east of Biłgoraj. This time, however, most of the Jews were not to be relocated. Only the male Jews of working age were to be sent to one of Globocnik's camps in Lublin. The women, children, and elderly were simply to be shot on the spot.

Trapp recalled the units that were stationed in nearby towns. The battalion reassembled in Biłgoraj on July 12, with two exceptions: the Third Platoon of Third Company, including Captain Hoffmann, stationed in Zakrzów, as well as a few men of First Company already stationed in Józefów. Trapp met with First and Second Company commanders, Captain Wohlauf and Lieutenant Gnade, and informed them of the next day's task.[1] Trapp's adjutant, First Lieutenant Hagen, must have informed other officers of the battalion, for Lieutenant Heinz Buchmann learned from him the precise details of the pending action that evening.

Buchmann, then 38 years old, was the head of a family lumber business in Hamburg. He had joined the Nazi Party in May 1937. Drafted into the Order Police in 1939, he had served as a driver in Poland. In the summer of 1940 he applied for a discharge. Instead he was sent to officer training and commissioned as a reserve lieutenant in November 1941. He was given command of the First Platoon of First Company in 1942.

Upon learning of the imminent massacre, Buchmann made clear to Hagen that as a Hamburg businessman and reserve lieutenant, he "would in no case participate in such an action, in which defenseless women and children are shot." He asked for another assignment. Hagen arranged for Buchmann to be in charge of the escort for the male "work Jews" who were to be selected out and taken to Lublin.[2] His company captain, Wohlauf, was informed of Buchmann's assignment but not the reason for it.[3]

The men were not officially informed, other than that they would be awakened early in the morning for a major action involving the entire battalion. But some had at least a hint of what was to come. Captain Wohlauf told a group of his men that an "extremely interesting task" awaited them the next day.[4] Another man, who complained that he was being left behind to guard the barracks, was told by his company adjutant, "Be happy that you don't have to come. You'll see what happens."[5] Sergeant Heinrich Steinmetz warned his men of Third Platoon, Second Company, that "he didn't want to see any cowards."[6] Additional ammunition was given out.[7] One policeman reported that his unit was given whips, which led to rumors of a *Judenaktion*.[8] No one else, however, remembered whips.

Departing from Biłgoraj around 2:00 a.m., the truck convoy arrived in Józefów just as the sky was beginning to lighten. Trapp assembled the men in a half-circle and addressed them. After explaining the battalion's murderous assignment, he made his extraordinary offer: any of the older men who did not feel up to the task that lay before them could step out. Trapp paused, and after some moments one man from Third Company, Otto-Julius Schimke, stepped forward. Captain Hoffmann, who had arrived in Józefów directly from Zakrzów with the Third Platoon of Third Company and had not been part of the officers' meetings in Biłgoraj the day before, was furious that one of his men had been the first to break ranks. Hoffmann began to berate Schimke, but Trapp cut him off. After he had taken Schimke under his protection, some ten or twelve other men stepped forward as well. They turned in their rifles and were told to await a further assignment from the major.[9]

Trapp then summoned the company commanders and gave them their respective assignments. The orders were relayed by the first sergeant, Kammer, to First Company, and by Gnade and Hoffmann to Second and Third Companies. Two platoons of Third Company were to surround the village.[10] The men were explicitly ordered to shoot anyone trying to escape. The remaining men were to round up the Jews and take them to the marketplace. Those too sick or frail to walk to the marketplace, as well as infants and anyone offering resistance or attempting to hide, were to be shot on the spot. Thereafter, a few men of First Company were to escort the "work Jews" who had been selected at the marketplace, while the rest of First Company was to proceed to the forest to form the firing squads. The Jews were to be loaded onto the battalion trucks by Second Company and Third Platoon of Third Company and shuttled from the marketplace to the forest.[11]

After making the assignments, Trapp spent most of the day in town, either in a schoolroom converted into his headquarters, at the homes of the Polish mayor and the local priest, at the marketplace, or on the road to the forest.[12] But he did not go to the forest itself or witness the executions; his absence there was conspicuous. As one policeman bitterly commented, "Major Trapp was never there. Instead he remained in Józefów because he allegedly could not bear the sight. We men were upset about that and said we couldn't bear it either."[13]

Indeed, Trapp's distress was a secret to no one. At the marketplace one policeman remembered hearing Trapp say, "Oh, God, why did I have to be given these orders," as he put his hand on his heart.[14] Another policeman witnessed him at the schoolhouse. "Today I can still see exactly before my eyes Major Trapp there in the room pacing back and forth with his hands behind his back. He made a downcast impression and spoke to me. He said something like, 'Man, ... such jobs don't suit me. But orders are orders.'"[15] Another man remembered vividly "how Trapp, finally alone in our room, sat on a stool and wept bitterly. The tears really flowed."[16] Another also witnessed Trapp at his headquarters. "Major Trapp ran around excitedly and then suddenly stopped dead in front of me, stared, and asked if I agreed with this. I looked him straight in the eye and said, 'No, Herr Major!' He then began to run around again and wept like a child."[17] The doctor's aide encountered Trapp weeping on the path from the marketplace to the forest and asked if he could help. "He answered me only to the effect that everything was very terrible."[18] Concerning Józefów, Trapp later confided to his driver, "If this Jewish business is ever avenged on earth, then have mercy on us Germans."[19]

While Trapp complained of his orders and wept, his men proceeded to carry out the battalion's task. The noncommissioned officers divided some of their men into search teams of two, three, or four, and sent them into the Jewish section of Józefów. Other men were assigned as guards along the streets leading to the marketplace or at the marketplace itself. As the Jews were driven out of their houses and the immobile were shot, the air was filled with screams and gunfire. As one policeman noted, it was a small town and they could hear everything.[20] Many policemen admitted seeing the corpses of those who had been shot during the search, but only two admitted having shot.[21] Again, several policemen admitted having heard that all the patients in the Jewish "hospital" or "old people's home" had been shot on the spot, though no one admitted having actually seen the shooting or taken part.[22]

The witnesses were least agreed on the question of how the men initially reacted to the problem of shooting infants. Some claimed that along with the elderly and sick, infants were among those shot and left lying in the houses, doorways, and streets of the town.[23] Others, however, stressed quite specifically that in this initial action the men still shied from shooting infants during the search and clearing operation. One policeman was emphatic "that among the Jews shot in our section of town there were no infants or small children. I would like to say that almost tacitly everyone refrained from shooting infants and small children." In Józefów as later, he observed, "Even in the face of death the Jewish mothers did not separate from their children. Thus we tolerated the mothers taking their small children to the marketplace in Józefów."[24] Another policeman likewise noted "that tacitly the shooting of infants and small children was avoided by almost all the men involved. During the entire morning I was able to observe that when being taken away many women carried infants in their arms and led small children by the hand."[25] According to both witnesses, none of the officers intervened when infants were brought to the marketplace. Another policeman, however, recalled that after the clearing operation his unit (Third Platoon, Third Company) was reproached by Captain Hoffmann. "We had not proceeded energetically enough."[26]

As the roundup neared completion, the men of First Company were withdrawn from the search and given a quick lesson in the gruesome task that awaited them. They were instructed by the battalion doctor and the company's first sergeant. One musically inclined policeman who frequently played the violin on social evenings along with the doctor, who played a "wonderful accordion," recalled:

I believe that at this point all officers of the battalion were present, especially our battalion physician, Dr. Schoenfelder. He now had to explain to us precisely how we had to shoot in order to induce the immediate death of the victim. I remember exactly that for this demonstration he drew or outlined the contour of a human body, at least from the shoulders upward, and then indicated precisely the point on which the fixed bayonet was to be placed as an aiming guide.[27]

[. . .] When Trapp first made his offer early in the morning, the real nature of the action had just been announced and time to think and react had been very short. Only a dozen men had instinctively seized the moment to step out, turn in their rifles, and thus excuse themselves from the subsequent killing. For many the reality of what they were about to do, and particularly that they themselves might be chosen for the firing squad, had probably not sunk in. But when the men of First Company were summoned to the marketplace, instructed in giving a "neck shot," and sent to the woods to kill Jews, some of them tried to make up for the opportunity they had missed earlier. One policeman approached First Sergeant Kammer, whom he knew well. He confessed that the task was "repugnant" to him and asked for a different assignment. Kammer obliged, assigning him to guard duty on the edge of the forest, where he remained throughout the day.[28] Several other policemen who knew Kammer well were given guard duty along the truck route.[29] After shooting for some time, another group of policemen approached Kammer and said they could not continue. He released them from the firing squad and reassigned them to accompany the trucks.[30] Two policemen made the mistake of approaching Captain (and SS-Hauptsturmführer) Wohlauf instead of Kammer. They pleaded that they too were fathers with children and could not continue. Wohlauf curtly refused them, indicating that they could lie down alongside the victims. At the midday pause, however, Kammer relieved not only these two men but a number of other older men as well. They were sent back to the marketplace, accompanied by a noncommissioned officer who reported to Trapp. Trapp dismissed them from further duty and permitted them to return early to the barracks in Biłgoraj.[31]

Some policemen who did not request to be released from the firing squads sought other ways to evade. Noncommissioned officers armed with submachine guns had to be assigned to give so-called mercy shots "because both from excitement *as well as intentionally* [italics mine]" individual policemen "shot past" their victims.[32] Others had taken evasive action earlier. During the clearing operation some men of First Company hid in the Catholic priest's garden until they grew afraid that their absence would be noticed. Returning to the marketplace, they jumped aboard a truck that was going to pick up Jews from a nearby village, in order to have an excuse for their absence.[33] Others hung around the marketplace because they did not want to round up Jews during the search.[34] Still others spent as much time as possible searching the houses so as not to be present at the marketplace, where they feared being assigned to a firing squad.[35] A driver assigned to take Jews to the forest made only one trip before he asked to be relieved. "Presumably his nerves were not strong enough to drive more Jews to the shooting site," commented the man who took over his truck and his duties of chauffeuring Jews to their death.[36]

After the men of First Company departed for the woods, Second Company was left to complete the roundup and load Jews onto the trucks. When the first salvo was heard from the woods, a terrible cry swept the marketplace as the collected Jews realized their fate.[37] Thereafter, however, a quiet composure – indeed, in the words of German witnesses, an "unbelievable" and "astonishing" composure – settled over the Jews.[38]

If the victims were composed, the German officers grew increasingly agitated as it became clear that the pace of the executions was much too slow if they were to finish the job in one day. "Comments were repeatedly made, such as, 'It's not getting anywhere!' and 'It's not going fast enough!'"[39] Trapp reached a decision and gave new orders. Third Company was called in from its outposts around the village to take over close guard of the marketplace. The men of Lieutenant Gnade's Second Company were informed that they too must now go to the woods to join the shooters. Sergeant Steinmetz of Third Platoon once again gave his men the opportunity to report if they did not feel up to it. No one took up his offer.[40]

Lieutenant Gnade divided his company into two groups assigned to different sections of the woods. He then visited Wohlauf's First Company to witness a demonstration of the executions.[41] Meanwhile, Lieutenant Scheer and Sergeant Hergert took the First Platoon of Second Company, along with some men of Third Platoon, to a certain point in the woods. Scheer divided his men into four groups, assigned them each a shooting area, and sent them back to fetch the Jews they were to kill. Lieutenant Gnade arrived and heatedly argued with Scheer that the men were not being sent deep enough into the woods.[42] By the time each group had made two or three round trips to the collection point and carried out their executions, it was clear to Scheer that the process was too slow. He asked Hergert for advice. "I then made the proposal," Hergert recalled, "that it would suffice if the Jews were brought from the collection point to the place of execution by only two men of each group, while the other shooters of the execution commando would already have moved to the next shooting site. Furthermore, this shooting site was moved somewhat forward from execution to execution and thus always got closer to the collection point on the forest path. We then proceeded accordingly."[43] Hergert's suggestion speeded the killing process considerably.

In contrast to First Company, the men of Second Company received no instruction on how to carry out the shooting. Initially bayonets were not fixed as an aiming guide, and as Hergert noted, there was a "considerable number of missed shots" that "led to the unnecessary wounding of the victims." One of the policemen in Hergert's unit likewise noted the difficulty the men had in aiming properly. "At first we shot freehand. When one aimed too high, the entire skull exploded. As a consequence, brains and bones flew everywhere. Thus, we were instructed to place the bayonet point on the neck."[44] According to Hergert, however, using fixed bayonets as an aiming guide was no solution. "Through the point-blank shot that was thus required, the bullet struck the head of the victim at such a trajectory that often the entire skull or at least the entire rear skullcap was torn off, and blood, bone splinters, and brains sprayed everywhere and besmirched the shooters."[45]

Hergert was emphatic that no one in First Platoon was given the option of withdrawing beforehand. But once the executions began and men approached either him or Scheer because they could not shoot women and children, they were given other duties.[46] This was confirmed by one of his men. "During the execution word spread that anyone who could not take it any longer could report." He went on to note, "I myself took part in some ten shootings, in which I had to shoot men and women. I simply could not shoot at people anymore, which became apparent to my sergeant, Hergert, because at the end I repeatedly shot past. For this reason he relieved me. Other comrades were also relieved sooner or later, because they simply could no longer continue."[47]

Lieutenant Drucker's Second Platoon and the bulk of Sergeant Steinmetz's Third Platoon were assigned to yet another part of the forest. Like Scheer's men, they were divided into small groups of five to eight each rather than large groups of thirty-five to forty as in Wohlauf's First Company. The men were told to place the end of their carbines on the cervical vertebrae at the base of the neck, but here too the shooting was done initially without fixed bayonets as a guide.[48] The results were horrifying. "The shooters were gruesomely besmirched with blood, brains, and bone splinters. It hung on their clothing."[49]

When dividing his men into small groups of shooters, Drucker had kept about a third of them in reserve. Ultimately, everyone was to shoot, but the idea was to allow frequent relief and "cigarette breaks."[50] With the constant coming and going from the trucks, the wild terrain, and the frequent rotation, the men did not remain in fixed groups.[51] The confusion created the opportunity for work slowdown and evasion. Some men who hurried at their task shot far more Jews than others who delayed as much as they could.[52] After two rounds one policeman simply "slipped off" and stayed among the trucks on the edge of the forest.[53] Another managed to avoid taking his turn with the shooters altogether.

It was in no way the case that those who did not want to or could not carry out the shooting of human beings with their own hands could not keep themselves out of this task. No strict control was being carried out here. I therefore remained by the arriving trucks and kept myself busy at the arrival point. In any case I gave my activity such an appearance. It could not be avoided that one or another of my comrades noticed that I was not going to the executions to fire away at the victims. They showered me with remarks such as "shit-head" and "weakling" to express their disgust. But I suffered no consequences for my actions. I must mention here that I was not the only one who kept himself out of participating in the executions.[54]

By far the largest number of shooters at Józefów who were interrogated after the war came from the Third Platoon of Second Company. It is from them that we can perhaps get the best impression of the effect of the executions on the men and the dropout rate among them during the course of the action.

Hans Dettelmann, a 40-year-old barber, was assigned by Drucker to a firing squad. "It was still not possible for me to shoot the first victim at the first execution, and I wandered off and asked...Lieutenant Drucker to be relieved." Dettelmann told his lieutenant that he had a "very weak nature," and Drucker let him go.[55]

Walter Niehaus, a former Reemtsma cigarette sales representative, was paired with an elderly woman for the first round. "After I had shot the elderly woman, I went to Toni [Anton] Bentheim [his sergeant] and told him that I was not able to carry out further executions. I did not have to participate in the shooting anymore....my nerves were totally finished from this one shooting."[56]

For his first victim August Zorn was given a very old man. Zorn recalled that his elderly victim

could not or would not keep up with his countrymen, because he repeatedly fell and then simply lay there. I regularly had to lift him up and drag him forward. Thus, I only reached the execution site when my comrades had already shot their Jews. At the sight of his countrymen who had been shot, my Jew threw himself on the ground and remained lying there. I then cocked my carbine and shot him through the back of the head. Because I was already very upset from the cruel treatment of the Jews during the clearing of the town and was completely in turmoil, I shot too high. The entire back of the skull of my Jew was torn off and the brain exposed. Parts of the skull flew into Sergeant Steinmetz's face. This was grounds for me, after returning to the truck, to go to the first sergeant and ask for my release. I had become so sick that I simply couldn't anymore. I was then relieved by the first sergeant.[57]

Georg Kageler, a 37-year-old tailor, made it through the first round before encountering difficulty. "After I had carried out the first shooting and at the unloading point was allotted a mother with daughter as victims for the next shooting, I began a conversation with them and learned that they were Germans from Kassel, and I took the decision not to participate further in the executions. The entire business was now so repugnant to me that I returned to my platoon leader and told him that I was still sick and asked for my release." Kageler was sent to guard the marketplace.[58] Neither his pre-execution conversation with his victim nor his discovery that there were German Jews in Józefów was unique. Schimke, the man who had first stepped out, encountered a Jew from Hamburg in the marketplace, as did a second policeman.[59] Yet another policeman remembered that the first Jew he shot was a decorated World War I veteran from Bremen who begged in vain for mercy.[60]

Franz Kastenbaum, who during his official interrogation had denied remembering anything about the killing of Jews in Poland, suddenly appeared uninvited at the office of the Hamburg state prosecutor investigating Reserve Police Battalion 101. He told how he had been a member of a firing squad of seven or eight men that had taken its victims into the woods and shot them in the neck at point-blank range. This procedure had been repeated until the fourth victim.

The shooting of the men was so repugnant to me that I missed the fourth man. It was simply no longer possible for me to aim accurately. I suddenly felt nauseous and ran away from the shooting site. I have expressed myself incorrectly just now. It was not that I could no longer aim accurately, rather that the fourth time I intentionally missed. I then ran into the woods, vomited, and sat down against a tree. To make sure that no one was nearby, I called loudly into the woods, because I wanted to be alone. Today I can say that my nerves were totally finished. I think that I remained alone in the woods for some two to three hours.

Kastenbaum then returned to the edge of the woods and rode an empty truck back to the marketplace. He suffered no consequences; his absence had gone unnoticed because the firing squads had been all mixed up and randomly assigned. He had come to make this statement, he explained to the investigating attorney, because he had had no peace since attempting to conceal the shooting action.[61]

Most of those who found the shooting impossible to bear quit very early.[62] But not always. The men in one squad had already shot ten to twenty Jews each when they finally asked to be relieved. As one of them explained, "I especially asked to be relieved because the man next to me shot so impossibly. Apparently he always aimed his gun too high, producing terrible wounds in his victims. In many cases the entire backs of victims' heads were torn off, so that the brains sprayed all over. I simply couldn't watch it any longer."[63] At the unloading point, Sergeant Bentheim watched men emerge from the woods covered with blood and brains, morale shaken and nerves finished. Those who asked to be relieved he advised to "slink away" to the marketplace.[64] As a result, the number of policemen gathered on the marketplace grew constantly.[65]

As with First Company, alcohol was made available to the policemen under Drucker and Steinmetz who stayed in the forest and continued shooting.[66] As darkness approached at the end of a long summer day and the murderous task was still not finished, the shooting became even less organized and more hectic.[67] The forest was so full of dead bodies that it was difficult to find places to make the Jews lie down.[68] When darkness finally fell about 9:00 p.m. – some 17 hours after Reserve Police Battalion 101 had first arrived on the outskirts of Józefów – and the last Jews had been killed, the men returned to the marketplace and prepared to depart for Biłgoraj.[69] No plans had been made for the burial of the bodies, and the dead Jews were simply left lying in the woods. Neither clothing nor valuables had been officially collected, though at least some of the policemen had enriched themselves with watches, jewelry, and money taken from the victims.[70] The pile of luggage the Jews had been forced to leave at the marketplace was simply burned.[71] Before the policemen climbed into their trucks and left Józefów, a 10-year-old girl appeared, bleeding from the head. She was brought to Trapp, who took her in his arms and said, "You shall remain alive."[72]

When the men arrived at the barracks in Biłgoraj, they were depressed, angered, embittered, and shaken.[73] They ate little but drank heavily. Generous quantities of alcohol were provided, and many of the policemen got quite drunk. Major Trapp made the rounds, trying to console and reassure them, and again placing the responsibility on higher authorities.[74] But neither the drink nor Trapp's consolation could wash away the sense of shame and horror that pervaded the barracks. Trapp asked the men not to talk about it,[75] but they needed no encouragement in that direction. Those who had not been in the forest did not want to learn more.[76] Those who had been there likewise had no desire to speak, either then or later. By silent consensus within Reserve Police Battalion 101, the Józefów massacre was simply not discussed. "The entire matter was a taboo."[77] But repression during waking hours could not stop the nightmares. During the first night back from Józefów, one policeman awoke firing his gun into the ceiling of the barracks.[78]

Several days after Józefów the battalion, it would seem, narrowly missed participation in yet another massacre. Units of First and Second Company, under Trapp and Wohlauf, entered Alekzandrów – a so-called street village composed of houses strung out along the road twelve kilometers west of Józefów. A small number of Jews was rounded up, and both the policemen and the Jews feared that another massacre was imminent. After some hesitation, however, the action was broken off, and Trapp permitted the Jews to return to their houses. One policeman remembered vividly "how individual Jews fell on their knees before Trapp and tried to kiss his hands and feet. Trapp, however, did not permit this and turned away." The policemen returned to Biłgoraj with no explanation for the strange turn of events.[79] Then, on July 20, precisely one month after its departure from Hamburg and one week after the Józefów massacre, Reserve Police Battalion 101 left Biłgoraj for redeployment in the northern sector of the Lublin district.

NOTES

Editors' note: the author is citing from the archives of the Office of the State Prosecutor, Hamburg. HW refers to the file "Investigation and trial of Hoffman, Wohlauf and others, 141 Js 1957/62." G refers to the file "Investigation of G. and others, 141 Js 128/65."

1 As neither Trapp, his adjutant Hagen, nor Lieutenant Gnade survived to be interrogated in the 1960s, the only direct witness to this meeting was Captain Wohlauf. His versions were so numerous and self-serving, and crucial aspects of the rest of his testimony so overwhelmingly contradicted by other witnesses, that he simply cannot be relied on.
2 Heinz B., HW 819–20, 2437, 3355, 4414.
3 Julius Wohlauf, HW 4329–30.
4 Friedrich Bm., HW 2091.
5 Hans S., G 328.
6 Bruno D., HW 1874.
7 Alfred B., HW 440.
8 Rudolf B., HW 3692.
9 Otto-Julius S., 1953–4, 4576–9; August W., HW 2041–2, 3298, 4589. S. and W. were the only two witnesses who recalled Trapp's offer in precisely this way. Several others initially remembered a call for volunteers for the firing squad instead (Alfred B., HW 439–40; Franz G., HW 1189–90; Bruno G., HW 2020). Others, when questioned about the incident, either conceded the "possibility" that Trapp had made the offer (Anton B., HW 2693; Heinz B., HW 3356–7, 4415) or at least said they would not contest or deny it had happened. Trapp's stipulation about "older" men appears in S.'s testimony (HW 1953, 4578). W., who most explicitly confirmed S.'s testimony in other respects, did not mention this qualification and claimed that younger men stepped out as well. However, he does seem to have understood that Trapp made his offer to the older reservists. When asked to explain why he himself did not step out, he indicated that he was a relatively young volunteer, an "active" policeman – i.e., not a conscripted reservist (HW 2041–2, 4592). The greater precision and vivid detail of the S. and W. testimony and the subsequent behavior of the officers and noncoms of the battalion in accordance with Trapp's offer (i.e., those who belatedly asked out were released from firing squad

duty – something the officers and noncoms could never have done so consistently without the prior sanction of the commanding officer) have persuaded me that a much greater probability rests with their version than with any other.
10 It may well be that First and Second Platoons of Third Company had already been stationed in a cordon surrounding the village *before* Trapp's speech. None of the men from these two platoons remembered the speech, and one witness (Bruno G., HW 2020) testified that the two platoons were not present.
11 Heinrich S., HW 1563; Martin D., HW 1596; Paul H., HW 1648; Ernst N., HW 1685; Wilhelm K., HW 1767, 2300; Bruno G., HW 2019; August W., HW 2039; Wilhelm Gb., HW 2147; Heinrich B., HW 2596; Walter Z., HW 2618; Anton B., HW 2656; Ernst Hr., HW 2716; Joseph P., HW 2742; Kurt D., HW 2888; Otto I., HW 3521; Wolfgang H., HW 3565; August Z., G 275; Eduard S., G 639; Hellmut S., G 646; Karl S., G 657.
12 Georg G., HW 2182.
13 Hellmut S., G 647.
14 Friedrich E., HW 1356.
15 Bruno R., HW 1852.
16 Harry L., G 223.
17 Ernst G., G 383.
18 Hans Kl., G 363.
19 Oskar P., HW 1743.
20 Erwin G., HW 2503.
21 Georg K., HW 2633; Karl S., G 657.
22 Wilhelm K., HW 1769; Friedrich Bm., HW 2091; Ernst Hn., G 506. For other accounts of the search, see Max D., HW 1345–6; Alfred L., HW 1351; Friederick V., HW 1539; Friedrich B., HW 1579; Bruno D., HW 1875; Hermann W., HW 1947–8; Otto-Julius S., HW 1954; Bruno G., HW 2019; August W., HW 2040; Bruno R., HW 2084; Hans Kl., HW 2270; Walter Z., HW 2168–9; Anton B., HW 2687; Ernst Hr., HW 2716; Joseph P., HW 2742; August Z., G 275; Karl Z., G 318; Eduard S., G 640.
23 Friedrich B., HW 1579; Bruno G., HW 2019; August W., HW 2041.
24 Ernst Hr., HW 2716–17.
25 Walter Z., HW 2618. For confirming testimony, see Anton B., HW 2688; Joseph P., HW 2742.
26 Hermann W., HW 1948.
27 Ernst Hn., G 507. Two witnesses (Eduard S., G 642; Hellmut S., G 647) remembered the first sergeant but not the doctor.
28 Paul H., HW 1648–9.
29 Heinrich H., G 453.
30 Wilhelm I., HW 2237.
31 Friedrich Bm., HW 2092.
32 Hellmut S., G 647.
33 Heinrich Bl, HW 462.

34 Hermann W., HW 1948.
35 Alfred L., HW 1351.
36 Bruno R., HW 1852.
37 Erwin N., HW 1686.
38 Bruno D., HW 1870; Anton B., HW 4347; Wilhelm Gb., HW 4363; Paul M., G 202.
39 Ernst Hr., HW 2717.
40 Erwin G., HW 1640, 2505.
41 Friedrich Bm., HW 2092.
42 Wilhelm G., HW 2149.
43 Ernst Hr., HW 2718.
44 Wilhelm Gb., HW 2538.
45 Ernst Hr., HW 2719.
46 Ernst Hr., HW 2720.
47 Wilhelm Gb., HW 2539, 2149.
48 Erwin G., HW 1639–40, 2504; Alfred B., HW 2518.
49 Anton B., HW 4348. See also Max D., HW 2536.
50 Walter Z., HW 2619–20; Erwin G., HW 4345.
51 Heinrich S., HW 1567, 4364; Georg K., HW 2634.
52 Joseph P., HW 2743–5.
53 Paul M., G 206–7.
54 Gustav M., G 168.
55 Hans D., HW 1336, 3542.
56 Walter N., HW 3926, G 230.
57 August Z., G 277.
58 Georg K., HW 2634.
59 Otto-Julius S., HW 4579; Friederick V., HW 1540.
60 Rudolf B., HW 2434, 2951, 4357.
61 Franz K., HW 2483–6.
62 In addition to the above cases, another policeman who asked to be released when his nerves were finished after a few rounds was Bruno D., HW 1876, 2535, 4361.
63 Erwin G., HW 2505; confirmed by Rudolf K., HW 2646–7.
64 Anton B., HW 2691–3, 4348.
65 Willy R., HW 2085.
66 Alfred B., HW 440; Walter Z., HW 2621; Georg K., HW 2635; August Z., G 278.
67 Friedrich B., HW 1581.
68 Julius Wohlauf, HW 758.
69 Heinrich B., HW 2984.
70 Alfred B., HW 441.
71 August W., HW 2042.
72 Otto-Julius S., HW 1955.
73 Witness after witness used the terms *erschüttert, deprimiert, verbittert, niedergeschlagen, bedrückt, verstört, empört,* and *belastet* to describe the men's feelings that evening.
74 Friedrich Bm., HW 2093; Hellmut S., G 647.
75 Heinrich Br., HW 3050.
76 Wilhelm J., HW 1322.
77 Willy S., HW 2053. See also Wolfgang Hoffmann, HW 774–5; Johannes R., HW 1809; Bruno R., HW 2086.
78 Karl M., HW 2546, 2657.
79 Friedrich Bm., HW 2093–4. See also Karl G., HW 2194.

11

From *This Way for the Gas, Ladies and Gentlemen*

Tadeusz Borowski

All of us walk around naked. The delousing is finally over, and our striped suits are back from the tanks of Cyclone B solution, an efficient killer of lice in clothing and of men in gas chambers. Only the inmates in the blocks cut off from ours by the "Spanish goats"[1] still have nothing to wear. But all the same, all of us walk around naked: the heat is unbearable. The camp has been sealed off tight. Not a single prisoner, not one solitary louse, can sneak through the gate. The labor Kommandos have stopped working. All day, thousands of naked men shuffle up and down the roads, cluster around the squares, or lie against the walls and on top of the roofs. We have been sleeping on plain boards, since our mattresses and blankets are still being disinfected. From the rear blockhouses we have a view of the F.K.L. – *Frauen Konzentration Lager*; there too the delousing is in full swing. Twenty-eight thousand women have been stripped naked and driven out of the barracks. Now they swarm around the large yard between the block houses.

The heat rises, the hours are endless. We are without even our usual diversion: the wide roads leading to the crematoria are empty. For several days now, no new transports have come in. Part of "Canada" has been liquidated and detailed to a labor Kommando – one of the very toughest – at Harmenz. For there exists in the camp a special brand of justice based on envy: when the rich and mighty fall, their friends see to it that they fall to the very bottom. And Canada, our Canada, which smells not of maple forests but of French perfume, has amassed great fortunes in diamonds and currency from all over Europe.

Several of us sit on the top bunk, our legs dangling over the edge. We slice the neat loaves of crisp, crunchy bread. It is a bit coarse to the taste, the kind that stays fresh for days. Sent all the way from Warsaw – only a week ago my mother held this white loaf in her hands... dear Lord, dear Lord...

We unwrap the bacon, the onion, we open a can of evaporated milk. Henri, the fat Frenchman, dreams aloud of the French wine brought by the transports from Strasbourg, Paris, Marseille... Sweat streams down his body.

"Listen, *mon ami*, next time we go up on the loading ramp, I'll bring you real champagne. You haven't tried it before, eh?"

"No. But you'll never be able to smuggle it through the gate, so stop teasing. Why not try and 'organize' some shoes for me instead – you know, the perforated kind, with a double sole, and what about that shirt you promised me long ago?"

"*Patience, patience.* When the new transports come, I'll bring all you want. We'll be going on the ramp again!"

"And what if there aren't any more 'cremo' transports?" I say spitefully. "Can't you see how much easier life is becoming around here: no limit on packages, no more beatings? You even write letters home... One hears all kind of talk, and, dammit, they'll run out of people!"

"Stop talking nonsense." Henri's serious fat face moves rhythmically, his mouth is full of sardines. We have been friends for a long time, but I do not even know his last name. "Stop talking nonsense," he repeats, swallowing with effort. "They can't run out of people, or we'll starve to death in this blasted camp. All of us live on what they bring."

"All? We have our packages . . ."

"Sure, you and your friend, and ten other friends of yours. Some of you Poles get packages. But what about us, and the Jews, and the Russkis? And what if we had no food, no 'organization' from the transports, do you think you'd be eating those packages of yours in peace? We wouldn't let you!"

"You would, you'd starve to death like the Greeks. Around here, whoever has grub, has power."

"Anyway, you have enough, we have enough, so why argue?"

Right, why argue? They have enough, I have enough, we eat together and we sleep on the same bunks. Henri slices the bread, he makes a tomato salad. It tastes good with the commissary mustard.

Below us, naked, sweat-drenched men crowd the narrow barracks aisles or lie packed in eights and tens in the lower bunks. Their nude, withered bodies stink of sweat and excrement; their cheeks are hollow. Directly beneath me, in the bottom bunk, lies a rabbi. He has covered his head with a piece of rag torn off a blanket and reads from a Hebrew prayer book (there is no shortage of this type of literature at the camp), wailing loudly, monotonously.

"Can't somebody shut him up? He's been raving as if he'd caught God himself by the feet."

"I don't feel like moving. Let him rave. They'll take him to the oven that much sooner."

"Religion is the opium of the people," Henri, who is a Communist and a *rentier*, says sententiously. "If they didn't believe in God and eternal life, they'd have smashed the crematoria long ago."

"Why haven't you done it then?"

The question is rhetorical; the Frenchman ignores it.

"Idiot," he says simply, and stuffs a tomato in his mouth.

Just as we finish our snack, there is a sudden commotion at the door. The Muslims[3] scurry in fright to the safety of their bunks, a messenger runs into the Block Elder's shack. The Elder, his face solemn, steps out at once.

"Canada! *Antreten!* But fast! There's a transport coming!"

"Great God!" yells Henri, jumping off the bunk. He swallows the rest of his tomato, snatches his coat, screams "*Raus*" at the men below, and in a flash is at the door. We can hear a scramble in the other bunks. Canada is leaving for the ramp.

"Henri, the shoes!" I call after him.

"*Keine Angst!*" he shouts back, already outside.

I proceed to put away the food. I tie a piece of rope around the suitcase where the onions and the tomatoes from my father's garden in Warsaw mingle with Portuguese sardines, bacon from Lublin (that's from my brother), and authentic sweetmeats from Salonica. I tie it all up, pull on my trousers, and slide off the bunk.

"*Platz!*" I yell, pushing my way through the Greeks. They step aside. At the door I bump into Henri.

"*Was ist los?*"

"Want to come with us on the ramp?"

"Sure, why not?"

"Come along then, grab your coat! We're short of a few men. I've already told the Kapo," and he shoves me out of the barracks door.

We line up. Someone has marked down our numbers, someone up ahead yells, "March, march," and now we are running towards the gate, accompanied by the shouts of a multilingual throng that is already being pushed back to the barracks. Not everybody is lucky enough to be going on the ramp . . . We have almost reached the gate. *Links, zwei, drei, vier! Mützen ab!* Erect, arms stretched stiffly along our hips, we march past the gate briskly, smartly, almost gracefully. A sleepy S.S. man with a large pad in his hand checks us off, waving us ahead in groups of five.

"*Hundert!*" he calls after we have all passed.

"*Stimmt!*" comes a hoarse answer from out front.

We march fast, almost at a run. There are guards all around, young men with automatics. We pass camp II B, then some deserted barracks and a clump of unfamiliar green – apple and pear trees. We cross the circle of watch-towers and, running, burst on to the highway. We have arrived. Just a few more yards. There, surrounded by trees, is the ramp.

A cheerful little station, very much like any other provincial railway stop: a small square framed by tall chestnuts and paved with yellow gravel. Not far off, beside the road, squats a tiny wooden shed, uglier and more flimsy than the ugliest and flimsiest railway shack; farther along lie stacks of old rails, heaps of wooden beams, barracks parts, bricks, paving stones. This is where they load freight for Birkenau: supplies for the construction of the camp, and people for the gas chambers. Trucks drive around, load up lumber, cement, people – a regular daily routine.

And now the guards are being posted along the rails, across the beams, in the green shade of the Silesian chestnuts, to form a tight circle around the ramp. They wipe the sweat from their faces and sip out of their canteens. It is unbearably hot; the sun stands motionless at its zenith.

"Fall out!"

We sit down in the narrow streaks of shade along the stacked rails. The hungry Greeks (several of them managed to come along, God only knows how) rummage underneath the rails. One of them finds some pieces of mildewed bread, another a few half-rotten sardines. They eat.

"*Schweinedreck*," spits a young, tall guard with corn-colored hair and dreamy blue eyes. "For God's sake, any minute you'll have so much food to stuff down your guts, you'll bust!" He adjusts his gun, wipes his face with a handkerchief.

"Hey you, fatso!" His boot lightly touches Henri's shoulder. "*Pass mal auf*, want a drink?"

"Sure, but I haven't got any marks," replies the Frenchman with a professional air.

"*Schade*, too bad."

"Come, come, Herr Posten, isn't my word good enough any more? Haven't we done business before? How much?"

"One hundred. *Gemacht?*"

"*Gemacht*."

We drink the water, lukewarm and tasteless. It will be paid for by the people who have not yet arrived.

"Now you be careful," says Henri, turning to me. He tosses away the empty bottle. It strikes the rails and bursts into tiny fragments. "Don't take any money, they might be checking. Anyway, who the hell needs money? You've got enough to eat. Don't take suits, either, or they'll think you're planning to escape. Just get a shirt, silk only, with a collar. And a vest. And if you find something to drink, don't bother calling me. I know how to shift for myself, but you watch your step or they'll let you have it."

"Do they beat you up here?"

"Naturally. You've got to have eyes in your ass. *Arschaugen*."

Around us sit the Greeks, their jaws working greedily, like huge human insects. They munch on stale lumps of bread. They are restless, wondering what will happen next. The sight of the large beams and the stacks of rails has them worried. They dislike carrying heavy loads.

"*Was wir arbeiten?*" they ask.

"*Niks. Transport kommen, alles Krematorium, compris?*"

"*Alles verstehen*," they answer in crematorium Esperanto. All is well – they will not have to move the heavy rails or carry the beams.

In the meantime, the ramp has become increasingly alive with activity, increasingly noisy. The crews are being divided into those who will open and unload the arriving cattle cars and those who will be posted by the wooden steps. They receive instructions on how to proceed most efficiently. Motor cycles drive up, delivering S.S. officers, be-medalled, glittering with brass, beefy men with highly polished boots and shiny, brutal faces. Some have brought their briefcases, others hold thin, flexible whips. This gives them an air of military readiness and agility. They walk in and out of the commissary – for the miserable little shack by the road serves as their commissary, where in the summertime they drink mineral water, *Studentenquelle*, and where in winter they can warm up with a glass of hot wine. They greet each other in the state-approved way, raising an arm Roman fashion, then shake hands cordially, exchange warm smiles, discuss mail from home, their children, their families. Some stroll majestically on the ramp. The silver squares on their collars glitter, the gravel crunches under their boots, their bamboo whips snap impatiently.

We lie against the rails in the narrow streaks of shade, breathe unevenly, occasionally exchange a few words in our various tongues, and gaze listlessly at the majestic men in green uniforms, at the green trees, and at the church steeple of a distant village.

"The transport is coming," somebody says. We spring to our feet, all eyes turn in one direction. Around the bend, one after another, the cattle cars begin rolling in. The train backs into the station, a conductor leans out, waves his hand, blows a whistle. The locomotive whistles back with a shrieking noise, puffs, the train rolls slowly alongside the ramp. In the tiny barred windows appear pale, wilted, exhausted human faces, terror-stricken women with tangled hair, unshaven men.

They gaze at the station in silence. And then, suddenly, there is a stir inside the cars and a pounding against the wooden boards.

"Water! Air!" – weary, desperate cries.

Heads push through the windows, mouths gasp frantically for air. They draw a few breaths, then disappear; others come in their place, then also disappear. The cries and moans grow louder.

A man in a green uniform covered with more glitter than any of the others jerks his head impatiently, his lips twist in annoyance. He inhales deeply, then with a rapid gesture throws his cigarette away and signals to the guard. The guard removes the automatic from his shoulder, aims, sends a series of shots along the train. All is quiet now. Meanwhile, the trucks have arrived, steps are being drawn up, and the Canada men stand ready at their posts by the train doors. The S.S. officer with the briefcase raises his hand.

"Whoever takes gold, or anything at all besides food, will be shot for stealing Reich property. Understand? *Verstanden?*"

"*Jawohl!*" we answer eagerly.

"*Also los!* Begin!"

The bolts crack, the doors fall open. A wave of fresh air rushes inside the train. People... inhumanly crammed, buried under incredible heaps of luggage, suitcases, trunks, packages, crates, bundles of every description (everything that had been their past and was to start their future). Monstrously squeezed together, they have fainted from heat, suffocated, crushed one another. Now they push towards the opened doors, breathing like fish cast out on the sand.

"Attention! Out, and take your luggage with you! Take out everything. Pile all your stuff near the exits. Yes, your coats too. It is summer. March to the left. Understand?"

"Sir, what's going to happen to us?" They jump from the train on to the gravel, anxious, worn-out.

"Where are you people from?"

"Sosnowiec-Będzin. Sir, what's going to happen to us?" They repeat the question stubbornly, gazing into our tired eyes.

"I don't know, I don't understand Polish."

It is the camp law: people going to their death must be deceived to the very end. This is the only permissible form of charity. The heat is tremendous. The sun hangs directly over our heads, the white, hot sky quivers, the air vibrates, an occasional breeze feels like a sizzling blast from a furnace. Our lips are parched, the mouth fills with the salty taste of blood, the body is weak and heavy from lying in the sun. Water!

A huge, multicolored wave of people loaded down with luggage pours from the train like a blind, mad river trying to find a new bed. But before they have a chance to recover, before they can draw a breath of fresh air and look at the sky, bundles are snatched from their hands, coats ripped off their backs, their purses and umbrellas taken away.

"But please, sir, it's for the sun, I cannot..."

"*Verboten!*" one of us barks through clenched teeth. There is an S.S. man standing behind your back, calm, efficient, watchful.

"*Meine Herrschaften*, this way, ladies and gentlemen, try not to throw your things around, please. Show some goodwill," he says courteously, his restless hands playing with the slender whip.

"Of course, of course," they answer as they pass, and now they walk alongside the train somewhat more cheerfully. A woman reaches down quickly to pick up her handbag. The whip flies, the woman screams, stumbles, and falls under the feet of the surging crowd. Behind her, a child cries in a thin little voice "Mamele!" – a very small girl with tangled black curls.

The heaps grow. Suitcases, bundles, blankets, coats, handbags that open as they fall, spilling coins, gold, watches; mountains of bread pile up at the exits, heaps of marmalade, jams, masses of meat, sausages; sugar spills on the gravel. Trucks, loaded with people, start up with a deafening roar and drive off amidst the wailing and screaming of the women separated from their children, and the stupefied silence of the men left behind. They are the ones who had been ordered to step to the right – the healthy and the young who will go to the camp. In the end, they too will not escape death, but first they must work.

Trucks leave and return, without interruption, as on a monstrous conveyor belt. A Red Cross van drives back and forth, back and forth, incessantly: it transports the gas that will kill these people. The enormous cross on the hood, red as blood, seems to dissolve in the sun.

The Canada men at the trucks cannot stop for a single moment, even to catch their breath. They shove the people up the steps, pack them in tightly, sixty per truck, more or less. Near by stands a young, cleanshaven "gentleman", an S.S. officer with a notebook in his hand. For each departing truck he enters a mark; sixteen gone means one thousand people, more or less. The gentleman is calm, precise. No truck can leave without a signal from him, or a mark in his notebook: *Ordnung muss sein*. The marks swell into thousands, the thousands into whole transports, which afterwards we shall simply call "from Salonica," "from Strasbourg," "from Rotterdam." This one will be called "Sosnowiec-Będzin." The new prisoners from Sosnowiec-Będzin will receive serial numbers 131–2 – thousand, of course, though afterwards we shall simply say 131–2, for short.

The transports swell into weeks, months, years. When the war is over, they will count up the marks in their notebooks – all four and a half million of them. The bloodiest battle of the war, the greatest victory of the strong, united Germany. *Ein Reich, ein Volk, ein Führer* – and four crematoria.

The train has been emptied. A thin, pock-marked S.S. man peers inside, shakes his head in disgust and motions to our group, pointing his finger at the door.

"*Rein*. Clean it up!"

We climb inside. In the corners amid human excrement and abandoned wrist-watches lie squashed, trampled infants, naked little monsters with enormous heads and bloated bellies. We carry them out like chickens, holding several in each hand.

"Don't take them to the trucks, pass them on to the women," says the S.S. man, lighting a cigarette. His cigarette lighter is not working properly; he examines it carefully.

"Take them, for God's sake!" I explode as the women run from me in horror, covering their eyes.

The name of God sounds strangely pointless, since the women and the infants will go on the trucks, every one of them, without exception. We all know what this means, and we look at each other with hate and horror.

"What, you don't want to take them?" asks the pock-marked S.S. man with a note of surprise and reproach in his voice, and reaches for his revolver.

"You mustn't shoot, I'll carry them." A tall, gray-haired woman takes the little corpses out of my hands and for an instant gazes straight into my eyes.

"My poor boy," she whispers and smiles at me. Then she walks away, staggering along the path. I lean against the side of the train. I am terribly tired. Someone pulls at my sleeve.

"*En avant*, to the rails, come on!"

I look up, but the face swims before my eyes, dissolves, huge and transparent, melts into the motionless trees and the sea of people ... I blink rapidly: Henri.

"Listen, Henri, are we good people?"

"That's stupid. Why do you ask?"

"You see, my friend, you see, I don't know why, but I am furious, simply furious with these people – furious because I must be here because of them. I feel no pity. I am not sorry they're going to the gas chamber. Damn them all! I could throw myself at them, beat them with my fists. It must be pathological, I just can't understand ... "

"Ah, on the contrary, it is natural, predictable, calculated. The ramp exhausts you, you rebel – and the easiest way to relieve your hate is to turn against someone weaker. Why, I'd even call it healthy. It's simple logic, *compris?*" He props himself up comfortably against the heap of rails. "Look at the Greeks, they know how to make the best of it! They stuff their bellies with anything they find. One of them has just devoured a full jar of marmalade."

"Pigs! Tomorrow half of them will die of the shits."

"Pigs? You've been hungry."

"Pigs!" I repeat furiously. I close my eyes. The air is filled with ghastly cries, the earth trembles beneath me, I can feel sticky moisture on my eyelids. My throat is completely dry.

The morbid procession streams on and on – trucks growl like mad dogs. I shut my eyes tight, but I can still see corpses dragged from the train, trampled infants, cripples piled on top of the dead, wave after wave ... freight cars roll in, the heaps of clothing, suitcases and bundles grow, people climb out, look at the sun, take a few breaths, beg for water, get into the trucks, drive away. And again freight cars roll in, again people ... The scenes become confused in my mind – I am not sure if all of this is actually happening, or if I am dreaming. There is a humming inside my head; I feel that I must vomit.

Henri tugs at my arm.

"Don't sleep, we're off to load up the loot."

All the people are gone. In the distance, the last few trucks roll along the road in clouds of dust, the train has left, several S.S. officers promenade up and down the ramp. The silver glitters on their collars. Their boots shine, their red, beefy faces shine. Among them there is a woman – only now I realize she has been here all along – withered, flat-chested, bony, her thin, colorless hair pulled back and tied in a "Nordic" knot; her hands are in the pockets of her wide skirt. With a rat-like, resolute smile glued on her thin lips she sniffs around the corners of the ramp. She detests feminine beauty with the hatred of a woman who is herself repulsive, and knows it. Yes, I have seen her many times before and I know her well: she is the commandant of the F.K.L. She has come to look over the new crop of women, for some of them, instead of going on the trucks, will go on foot – to the concentration camp. There our boys, the barbers from Zauna, will shave their heads and will have a good laugh at their "outside world" modesty.

We proceed to load the loot. We lift huge trunks, heave them on to the trucks. There they are arranged in stacks, packed tightly. Occasionally somebody slashes one open with a knife, for pleasure or in search of vodka and perfume. One of the crates falls open; suits, shirts, books drop out on the ground . . . I pick up a small, heavy package. I unwrap it – gold, about two handfuls, bracelets, rings, brooches, diamonds . . .

"*Gib hier,*" an S.S. man says calmly, holding up his briefcase already full of gold and colourful foreign currency. He locks the case, hands it to an officer, takes another, an empty one, and stands by the next truck, waiting. The gold will go to the Reich.

It is hot, terribly hot. Our throats are dry, each word hurts. Anything for a sip of water! Faster, faster, so that it is over, so that we may rest. At last we are done, all the trucks have gone. Now we swiftly clean up the remaining dirt: there must be "no trace left of the *Schweinerei.*" But just as the last truck disappears behind the trees and we walk, finally, to rest in the shade, a shrill whistle sounds around the bend. Slowly, terribly slowly, a train rolls in, the engine whistles back with a deafening shriek. Again weary, pale faces at the windows, flat as though cut out of paper, with huge, feverishly burning eyes. Already trucks are pulling up, already the composed gentleman with the notebook is at his post, and the S.S. men emerge from the commissary carrying briefcases for the gold and money. We unseal the train doors.

It is impossible to control oneself any longer. Brutally we tear suitcases from their hands, impatiently pull off their coats. Go on, go on, vanish! They go, they vanish. Men, women, children. Some of them know.

Here is a woman – she walks quickly, but tries to appear calm. A small child with a pink cherub's face runs after her and, unable to keep up, stretches out his little arms and cries: "Mama! Mama!"

"Pick up your child, woman!"

"It's not mine, sir, not mine!" she shouts hysterically and runs on, covering her face with her hands. She wants to hide, she wants to reach those who will not ride the trucks, those who will go on foot, those who will stay alive. She is young, healthy, good-looking, she wants to live.

But the child runs after her, wailing loudly: "Mama, mama, don't leave me!"

"It's not mine, not mine, no!"

Andrei, a sailor from Sevastopol, grabs hold of her. His eyes are glassy from vodka and the heat. With one powerful blow he knocks her off her feet, then, as she falls, takes her by the hair and pulls her up again. His face twitches with rage.

"Ah, you bloody Jewess! So you're running from your own child! I'll show you, you whore!" His huge hand chokes her, he lifts her in the air and heaves her on to the truck like a heavy sack of grain.

"Here! And take this with you, bitch!" and he throws the child at her feet.

"*Gut gemacht*, good work. That's the way to deal with degenerate mothers," says the S.S. man standing at the foot of the truck. "*Gut, gut, Russki.*"

"Shut your mouth," growls Andrei through clenched teeth, and walks away. From under a pile of rags he pulls out a canteen, unscrews the cork, takes a few deep swallows, passes it to me. The strong vodka burns the throat. My head swims, my legs are shaky, again I feel like throwing up.

And suddenly, above the teeming crowd pushing forward like a river driven by an unseen power, a girl appears. She descends lightly from the train, hops on to the gravel, looks around inquiringly, as if somewhat surprised. Her soft, blonde hair has fallen on her shoulders in a torrent, she throws it back impatiently. With a natural gesture she runs her hands down her blouse, casually straightens her skirt. She stands like this for an instant, gazing at the crowd, then turns and with a gliding look examines our faces, as though searching for someone. Unknowingly, I continue to stare at her, until our eyes meet.

"Listen, tell me, where are they taking us?"

I look at her without saying a word. Here, standing before me, is a girl, a girl with enchanting blonde hair, with beautiful breasts, wearing a little cotton blouse, a girl with a wise, mature look in her eyes. Here she stands, gazing straight into my face, waiting. And over there is the gas chamber: communal death, disgusting and ugly. And over in the other direction is the concentration camp: the shaved head, the heavy Soviet trousers in sweltering heat, the sickening, stale odor of dirty, damp female bodies, the animal hunger, the inhuman labor, and later the same gas chamber, only an even more hideous, more terrible death...

Why did she bring it? I think to myself, noticing a lovely gold watch on her delicate wrist. They'll take it away from her anyway.

"Listen, tell me," she repeats.

I remain silent. Her lips tighten.

"I know," she says with a shade of proud contempt in her voice, tossing her head. She walks off resolutely in the direction of the trucks. Someone tries to stop her; she boldly pushes him aside and runs up the steps. In the distance I can only catch a glimpse of her blonde hair flying in the breeze.

I go back inside the train; I carry out dead infants; I unload luggage. I touch corpses, but I cannot overcome the mounting, uncontrollable terror. I try to escape from the corpses, but they are everywhere: lined up on the gravel, on the cement edge of the ramp, inside the cattle cars. Babies, hideous naked women, men twisted by convulsions. I run off as far as I can go, but immediately a whip slashes across my back. Out of the corner of my eye I see an S.S. man, swearing profusely. I stagger forward and run, lose myself in the Canada group. Now, at last, I can once more rest against the stack of rails. The sun has leaned low over the horizon and illuminates the ramp with a reddish glow; the shadows of the trees have become elongated, ghostlike. In the silence that settles over nature at this time of day, the human cries seem to rise all the way to the sky.

Only from this distance does one have a full view of the inferno on the teeming ramp. I see a pair of human beings who have fallen to the ground locked in a last desperate embrace. The man has dug his fingers into the woman's flesh and has caught her clothing with his teeth. She screams hysterically, swears, cries, until at last a large boot comes down over her throat and she is silent. They are pulled apart and dragged like

cattle to the truck. I see four Canada men lugging a corpse: a huge, swollen female corpse. Cursing, dripping wet from the strain, they kick out of their way some stray children who have been running all over the ramp, howling like dogs. The men pick them up by the collars, heads, arms, and toss them inside the trucks, on top of the heaps. The four men have trouble lifting the fat corpse on to the car, they call others for help, and all together they hoist up the mound of meat. Big, swollen, puffed-up corpses are being collected from all over the ramp; on top of them are piled the invalids, the smothered, the sick, the unconscious. The heap seethes, howls, groans. The driver starts the motor, the truck begins rolling.

"Halt! Halt!" an S.S. man yells after them. "Stop, damn you!"

They are dragging to the truck an old man wearing tails and a band around his arm. His head knocks against the gravel and pavement; he moans and wails in an uninterrupted monotone: "*Ich will mit dem Herrn Kommandanten sprechen* – I wish to speak with the commandant..." With senile stubbornness he keeps repeating these words all the way. Thrown on the truck, trampled by others, choked, he still wails: "*Ich will mit dem...*"

"Look here, old man!" a young S.S. man calls, laughing jovially. "In half an hour you'll be talking with the top commandant! Only don't forget to greet him with a *Heil Hitler!*"

Several other men are carrying a small girl with only one leg. They hold her by the arms and the one leg. Tears are running down her face and she whispers faintly: "Sir, it hurts, it hurts..." They throw her on the truck on top of the corpses. She will burn alive along with them.

The evening has come, cool and clear. The stars are out. We lie against the rails. It is incredibly quiet. Anemic bulbs hang from the top of the high lamp-posts; beyond the circle of light stretches an impenetrable darkness. Just one step, and a man could vanish for ever. But the guards are watching, their automatics ready.

"Did you get the shoes?" asks Henri.

"No."

"Why?"

"My God, man, I am finished, absolutely finished!"

"So soon? After only two transports? Just look at me, I...since Christmas, at least a million people have passed through my hands. The worst of all are the transports from around Paris – one is always bumping into friends."

"And what do you say to them?"

"That first they will have a bath, and later we'll meet at the camp. What would you say?"

I do not answer. We drink coffee with vodka; somebody opens a tin of cocoa and mixes it with sugar. We scoop it up by the handful, the cocoa sticks to the lips. Again coffee, again vodka.

"Henri, what are we waiting for?"

"There'll be another transport."

"I'm not going to unload it! I can't take any more."

"So, it's got you down? Canada is nice, eh?" Henri grins indulgently and disappears into the darkness. In a moment he is back again.

"All right. Just sit here quietly and don't let an S.S. man see you. I'll try to find you your shoes."

"Just leave me alone. Never mind the shoes." I want to sleep. It is very late.

Another whistle, another transport. Freight cars emerge out of the darkness, pass under the lamp-posts, and again vanish in the night. The ramp is small, but the circle of lights is smaller. The unloading will have to be done gradually. Somewhere the trucks are growling. They back up against the steps, black, ghostlike, their search-lights flash across the trees. *Wasser! Luft!* The same all over again, like a late showing of the same film: a volley of shots, the train falls silent. Only this time a little girl pushes herself halfway through the small window and, losing her balance, falls out on to the gravel. Stunned, she lies still for a moment, then stands up and begins walking around in a circle, faster and faster, waving her rigid arms in the air, breathing loudly and spasmodically, whining in a faint voice. Her mind has given way in the inferno inside the train. The whining is hard on the nerves: an S.S. man approaches calmly, his heavy boot strikes between her shoulders. She falls. Holding her down with his foot, he draws his revolver, fires once, then again. She remains face down, kicking the gravel with her feet, until she stiffens. They proceed to unseal the train.

I am back on the ramp, standing by the doors. A warm, sickening smell gushes from inside. The mountain of people filling the car almost halfway up to the ceiling is motionless, horribly tangled, but still steaming.

"*Ausladen!*" comes the command. An S.S. man steps out from the darkness. Across his chest hangs a portable searchlight. He throws a stream of light inside.

"Why are you standing about like sheep? Start unloading!" His whip flies and falls across our backs. I seize a corpse by the hand; the fingers close tightly around mine. I pull back with a shriek and stagger away. My heart pounds, jumps up to my throat. I can no longer control the nausea. Hunched under the train I begin to vomit. Then, like a drunk, I weave over to the stack of rails.

I lie against the cool, kind metal and dream about returning to the camp, about my bunk, on which there is no mattress, about sleep among comrades who are not going to the gas tonight. Suddenly I see the camp as a haven of peace. It is true, others may be dying, but one is somehow still alive, one has enough food, enough strength to work . . .

The lights on the ramp flicker with a spectral glow, the wave of people – feverish, agitated, stupefied people – flows on and on, endlessly. They think that now they will have to face a new life in the camp, and they prepare themselves emotionally for the hard struggle ahead. They do not know that in just a few moments they will die, that the gold, money, and diamonds which they have so prudently hidden in their clothing and on their bodies are now useless to them. Experienced professionals will probe into every recess of their flesh, will pull the gold from under the tongue and the diamonds from the uterus and the colon. They will rip out gold teeth. In tightly sealed crates they will ship them to Berlin.

The S.S. men's black figures move about, dignified, businesslike. The gentleman with the notebook puts down his final marks, rounds out the figures: fifteen thousand.

Many, very many, trucks have been driven to the crematoria today.

It is almost over. The dead are being cleared off the ramp and piled into the last truck. The Canada men, weighed down under a load of bread, marmalade and sugar, and smelling of perfume and fresh linen, line up to go. For several days the entire camp will live off this transport. For several days the entire camp will talk about "Sosnowiec-Będzin." "Sosnowiec-Będzin" was a good, rich transport.

The stars are already beginning to pale as we walk back to the camp. The sky grows translucent and opens high above our heads – it is getting light.

Great columns of smoke rise from the crematoria and merge up above into a huge black river which very slowly floats across the sky over Birkenau and disappears beyond the forests in the direction of Trzebinia. The "Sosnowiec-Będzin" transport is already burning.

We pass a heavily armed S.S. detachment on its way to change guard. The men march briskly, in step, shoulder to shoulder, one mass, one will.

"*Und morgen die ganze Welt . . .*" they sing at the top of their lungs.

"*Rechts ran!* To the right march!" snaps a command from up front. We move out of their way.

NOTES

1 Crossed wooden beams wrapped in barbed wire.

2 "Canada" designated wealth and well-being in the camp. More specifically, it referred to the members of the labor gang, or Kommando, who helped to unload the incoming transports of people destined for the gas chambers.

3 "Muslim" was the camp name for a prisoner who had been destroyed physically and spiritually, and who had neither the strength nor the will to go on living – a man ripe for the gas chamber.

12

From *Maus: A Survivor's Tale, II: And Here My Troubles Began*

Art Spiegelman

Part III

The Politics of Communal Violence

Plate 5: The Lynching of Lige Daniels (postcard), Center, Texas, August 3, 1920. [Published in *Without Sanctuary, Lynching Photography in America*, Santa Fe, NM: Twin Palms Publishers.]

13

From "Hellhounds"

Leon F. Litwack

On a Sunday afternoon, April 23, 1899, more than two thousand white Georgians, some of them arriving from Atlanta on a special excursion train, assembled near the town of Newman to witness the execution of Sam Hose, a black Georgian. The event assumed a familiar format. Like so many lynchings, this one became a public spectacle. As in most lynchings, the guilt of the victim had not been proven in a court of law. As in most lynchings, no member of the crowd wore a mask, nor did anyone attempt to conceal the names of the perpetrators; indeed, newspaper reporters noted the active participation of some of the region's most prominent citizens. And as in most lynchings, the white press and public expressed its solidarity in the name of white supremacy and ignored any information that contradicted the people's verdict.

Sam Hose worked for a planter, Alfred Cranford. He asked his employer for an advance in pay (some reported he had tried to collect wages already owed him) and for permission to visit his ill mother. The planter refused, precipitating a harsh exchange of words. On the following day, while Hose chopped wood, Cranford resumed the argument, this time drawing his pistol and threatening to kill Hose. In self-defense, Hose flung his ax, striking Cranford in the head and killing him instantly. Within two days, newspapers reported an altogether different version. Cranford had been eating dinner when Hose – "*a monster in human form*" – sneaked up on him, buried an ax in his skull, and after pillaging the house, dragged Mrs. Cranford into the room where her husband lay dying and raped her.

If versions of Cranford's death varied, the story of Sam Hose's fate did not. After stripping Hose of his clothes and chaining him to a tree, the self-appointed executioners stacked kerosene-soaked wood high around him. Before saturating Hose with oil and applying the torch, they cut off his ears, fingers, and genitals, and skinned his face. While some in the crowd plunged knives into the victim's flesh, others watched "*with unfeigning satisfaction*" (as one reporter noted) the contortions of Sam Hose's body as the flames rose, distorting his features, causing his eyes to bulge out of their sockets, and rupturing his veins. The only sounds that came from the victim's lips, even as his blood sizzled in the fire, were, "*Oh, my God! Oh, Jesus.*" Before Hose's body had even cooled, his heart and liver were removed and cut into several pieces and his bones were crushed into small particles. The crowd fought over these souvenirs. Shortly after the lynching, one of the participants reportedly left for the state capitol, hoping to deliver a slice of Sam Hose's heart to the governor of Georgia, who would call Sam Hose's deeds "*the most diabolical in the annals of crime.*"

The next morning, smoldering ashes and a blackened stake were all that remained. On the trunk of a tree near the scene, a placard read, "*We Must Protect Our Southern Women,*" and one prominent Georgia woman, Rebecca Felton, gave voice to that sentiment: "*The premeditated outrage on Mrs. Cranford was infinitely more intolerable than the murder of her husband.*" As for Hose, Felton claimed any "*true-hearted husband* or *father*" would have happily dispatched the "*beast,*" with no more concern than if he were shooting down a mad dog; indeed, "*The dog is more worthy of sympathy.*"

The leading newpaper in Atlanta urged its readers to "*keep the facts in mind*" when they judged the actions of the lynchers. "*The people of Georgia are orderly and conservative, the descendants of ancestors who have been trained in America for 150 years. They are a people intensely religious, homeloving and just. There is among them no foreign or lawless element.*" The newspaper then provided the "facts" of Hose's alleged offenses, rendering his fate that much more explicable. "*When the picture is printed of the ravisher in flames, go back and view that darker picture of Mrs. Cranford outraged in the blood of her murdered husband.*"

In a subsequent investigation, conducted by a white detective, Cranford's wife revealed that Hose had come to the house to pick up his wages and the two men had quarreled. When her husband went for his revolver, Hose, in self-defense, picked up and hurled the ax, which killed Cranford instantly. Hose then fled the scene. He never entered the house, she told the detective, nor did he assault her. Still another investigation, conducted by Ida B. Wells, a black journalist who had been driven from Memphis in 1892 for her "*incendiary*" editorials on lynching, reached the same conclusions. The results of neither investigation were of any apparent interest to the white press or presumably to the white public.[1]

Thousands of black men and women met the same fate. Varying only in degrees of torture and brutality, these execution rituals were acted out in every part of the South. Sometimes in small groups, sometimes in massive numbers, whites combined the roles of judge, jury, and executioner. Newspaper reporters dutifully reported the events under such lurid headlines as "COLORED MAN ROASTED ALIVE," describing in graphic detail the slow and methodical agony and death of the victim and devising a vocabulary that would befit the occasion. The public burning of a Negro would soon be known as a "*Negro Barbecue,*" reinforcing the perception of blacks as less than human.

The use of the camera to memorialize lynchings testified to their openness and to the self-righteousness that animated the participants. Not only did photographers capture the execution itself, but also the carnival-like atmosphere and the expectant mood of the crowd, as in the lynching of Thomas Brooks in Fayette Country, Tennessee, in 1915:

Hundreds of kodaks clicked all morning at the scene of the lynching. People in automobiles and carriages came from miles around to view the corpse dangling from the end of a rope. . . . Picture card photographers installed a portable printing plant at the bridge and reaped a harvest in selling postcards showing a photograph of the lynched Negro. Women and children were there by the score. At a number of country schools the day's routine was delayed until boy and girl pupils could get back from viewing the lynched man.[2]

During a lynching at Durant, Oklahoma, in 1911, the exuberant and proud lynchers bound their victim to some planks and posed around him while photographers recorded the scene. A black-owned newspaper in Topeka, Kansas, in printing the photograph, wanted every black newspaper to do likewise, so that "*the world may see and know what semi-barbarous America is doing.*" Many photographs of lynchings and burnings (such as the burning of Sam Hose) would reappear as popular picture postcards and trade cards to commemorate the event. A Unitarian minister in New York, John H. Holmes, opened his mail one day to find a postcard depicting a crowd in Alabama posing for a photographer next to the body of a black man dangling by a rope. Responding to the minister's recent condemnation of lynching, the person who sent the card wrote, "*This is the way we do them down here. The last lynching has not been put on card yet. Will put you on our regular mailing list. Expect one a month on the average.*"[3]

Some thirty years after emancipation, between 1890 and 1920, in response to perceptions of a New Negro born in freedom, undisciplined by slavery, and unschooled in proper racial etiquette, and in response to growing doubts that this new generation could be trusted to stay in its place without legal and extra-legal force, the white South denied blacks a political voice, imposed rigid patterns of racial segregation (Jim Crow), sustained an economic system – sharecropping and tenantry – that left little room for ambition or hope, refused blacks equal educational resources, and disseminated racial caricatures and pseudo-scientific theories that reinforced and comforted whites in their racist beliefs and practices.

The criminal justice system (the law, the courts, the legal profession) operated with ruthless efficiency in upholding the absolute power of whites to command the subordination and labor of blacks.

But even this overwhelming display of superiority did not afford white southerners the internal security they sought or relieve their fears of "uppity," "troublesome," ambitious, and independent-minded black men and women who had not yet learned the rituals of deference and submission. The quality of the racial violence that gripped the South made it distinctive in this nation's history. In the late nineteenth and early twentieth century, two or three black southerners were hanged, burned at the stake, or quietly murdered every week. In the 1890s, lynchings claimed an average of 139 lives each year, 75 percent of them black. The numbers declined in the following decades, but the percentage of black victims rose to 90 percent. Between 1882 and 1968, an estimated 4,742 blacks met their deaths at the hands of lynch mobs. As many if not more blacks were victims of legal lynchings (speedy trials and executions), private white violence, and "nigger hunts," murdered by a variety of means in isolated rural sections and dumped into rivers and creeks.

Even an accurate body count of black lynching victims could not possibly reveal how hate and fear transformed ordinary white men and women into mindless murderers and sadistic torturers, or the savagery that, with increasing regularity, characterized assaults on black men and women in the name of restraining their savagery and depravity. Nothing so dramatically or forcefully underscored the cheapness of black life in the South. The way one black Mississippian recalled white violence in the 1930s applied as accurately and even more pervasively to the late nineteenth and early twentieth centuries. "Back in those days, to kill a Negro wasn't nothing. It was like killing a chicken or killing a snake. The whites would say, 'Niggers jest supposed to die, ain't no damn good anyway – so jest go on an' kill 'em.'" Whatever their value as laborers, black people were clearly expendable and replaceable. "In those days it was 'Kill a mule, buy another. Kill a nigger, hire another,'" a black southerner remembered. "They had to have a license to kill anything but a nigger. We was always in season."[4]

The cheapness of black life reflected in turn the degree to which so many whites by the early twentieth century had come to think of black men and women as inherently and permanently inferior, as less than human, as little more than animals. "We Southern people don't care to equal ourselves with animals," a white Floridian told a northern critic. "The people of the South don't think any more of killing the black fellows than you would think of killing a flea ... and if I was to live 1,000 years that would be my opinion and every other Southern man." A former governor of Georgia, William J. Northen, after canvassing his state in the interest of law and order, found the same disregard for black life. "I was amazed to find scores and hundreds of men who believed the Negro to be a brute, without responsibility to God, and his slaughter nothing more than the killing of a dog."[5] [...]

The ordinary modes of execution and punishment no longer satisfied the emotional appetite of the crowd. To kill the victim was not enough; the execution became public theater, a participatory ritual of torture and death, a voyeuristic spectacle prolonged as long as possible (once for seven hours) for the benefit of the crowd. Newspapers on a number of occasions announced in advance the time and place of a lynching, special "excursion" trains transported spectators to the scene, employers sometimes released their workers to attend, parents sent notes to school asking teachers to excuse their children for the event, and entire families attended, the children hoisted on their parents' shoulders to miss none of the action and accompanying festivities. Returning from one such occasion, a 9-year-old white youth remained unsatisfied. "I have seen a man hanged," he told his mother; "now I wish I could see one burned."[6]

The story of a lynching, then, is more than the simple fact of a black man or woman hanged by the neck. It is the story of slow, methodical, sadistic, often highly inventive forms of torture and mutilation. If executed by fire, it is the red-hot poker applied to the eyes and genitals and the stench of burning flesh, as the body slowly roasts over the flames and the blood sizzles in the heat. If executed by hanging, it is the convulsive movement of the limbs. Whether by fire or rope, it is the dismemberment and distribution of severed bodily parts as favors and souvenirs to participants and the crowd: teeth, ears, toes, fingers, nails, kneecaps, bits of charred skin and bones. Such human trophies might reappear as watch fobs or be displayed conspicuously for public viewing. The severed knuckles of Sam Hose, for example, would be prominently displayed in the window of a grocery store in Atlanta.[7] [...]

The degree to which whites came to accept lynching as justifiable homicide was best revealed in how they learned to differentiate between *"good"* lynchings and *"bad"* lynchings. A newspaper reported the execution of Elmo Curl, at Mastadon, Mississippi, as *"a most orderly affair, conducted by the bankers, lawyers, farmers, and merchants of that county. The best people of the county, as good as there are anywhere, simply met there and hanged Curl without a sign of rowdyism. There was no drinking, no shooting, no yelling, and not even any loud talking."* What characterized a *"good"* lynching appeared to be the quick dispatch of the victim *"in a most orderly manner"* without prolonging his or her agony for the crowd's benefit. When a mob made up of *"prominent citizens,"* including a member of the South Carolina state legislature, lynched a black man near Charleston, the local newspaper thought it had been done in the *"most approved and up-to-date fashion."*[8]

No doubt the mob in Howard, Texas, thought itself orderly, even democratic in its ritualistic execution of a black man. Farmers in the surrounding neighborhood were notified to attend, and some two thousand spectators responded. The victim was given two hours for prayers, and the mob heeded his request to see his brother and sister before the execution. The question of how he should be executed was submitted to the crowd, and a majority voted for death by burning. [...]

Although some whites found lynchings unacceptable and barbaric, few of the perpetrators were ever brought to trial. Townspeople closed ranks to protect their own kind, thereby becoming partners in the crimes committed. Eyewitnesses refused to testify, and grand juries refused to bring indictments against easily identifiable mob participants. Even if they had, juries would have refused to convict, whatever the evidence. In the vast majority of reported lynchings, the courts, coroners' juries, or other official bodies chosen to investigate the murders concluded routinely that black victims had met their deaths *"at the hands of unknown parties,"* *"at the hands of persons unknown,"* or *"by persons unknown to the jury."* In an Alabama community, 110 whites examined for a jury that would judge members of a lynch mob were asked. *"If you were satisfied from the evidence beyond a reasonable doubt that the defendant took part with or abetted the mob in murdering a Negro, would you favour his conviction?"* Seventy-six answered no, and the remaining 34 would certainly have weighed very carefully the consequences of rendering a guilty verdict.[9]

Not only did distinguished public officials at all levels of government hesitate to condemn lynching, but some also chose to participate in lynch mobs. *"I led the mob which lynched Nelse Patton, and I am proud of it,"* a former US senator from Mississippi, William Van Amberg Sullivan, boasted in 1908. *"I directed every movement of the mob and I did everything I could to see that he was lynched."* In the public burning of John Hartfield in Jones County, Mississippi, the district attorney, who would later be elected to Congress, not only witnessed the burning but used the occasion for some electioneering and refused to bring charges against the mob leaders. [...]

When whites condemned lynching, they seemed less concerned over the black victims than over the very real possibility that white civilization itself was on trial. Even as whites could readily agree on the inferiority of blacks and the need to maintain white supremacy, some also perceived and expressed alarm over the destabilization of the social order and the descent of their region into anarchy and barbarism. *"The greater peril at this hour where outbreak and lawlessness are at the surface,"* a southern minister declared, *"is not that the negro will lose his skin, but that the Anglo-Saxon will lose his soul."* The mayor of Statesboro, Georgia, like some of the more conscientious public officials, expressed alarm over the breakdown of law and order, even as he confessed his helplessness in preventing lynchings. *"If our grand jury won't indict these lynchers, if our petit juries won't convict, and if our soldiers won't shoot, what are we coming to?"*[10] [...]

It took little time before a *"folk pornography"* emerged in the South, playing on themes from the past and adding some new dimensions.[11] To endorse lynching was to dwell on the sexual depravity of the black man, to raise the specter of the black beast seized by uncontrollable, savage, sexual passions that were inherent in the race. That is, the inhumanity, depravity, bestiality, and savagery practiced by white participants in lynchings would be justified in the name of humanity, morality, justice, civilization, and Christianity. And there was little reason to question the deep convictions on which whites acted; they came, in fact, to believe in their own rhetoric, much as the defenders of slavery had. The Negro as beast became a fundamental part of the white South's racial imagery, taking its place alongside the venerated and faithful Sambo retainer, and whites were perfectly capable of drawing on both to sustain their self-image. Blacks, after all, possessed a dual nature: they were docile and amiable when enslaved or severely repressed, but savage, lustful, and capable of murder and mayhem when free and uncontrolled – like those blacks who had grown up since the Civil War. This generation, a Memphis newspaper insisted, had "*lost in large measure the traditional and wholesome awe of the white race which kept the Negroes in subjection. . . . There is no longer a restraint upon the brute passion of the Negro.*"[12] [. . .]

White fears were based on the assumption that most lynchings stemmed from sexual assault. But in many cases, reports of sexual assault proved entirely baseless or upon closer examination revealed only that a black male had broken the rules of racial etiquette, had behaved in a manner construed as a racial insult, or had violated the bar on consensual interracial sex. What Walter White would call "*the Southern white woman's proneness to hysteria where Negroes are concerned,*" based on his investigation of scores of lynchings, created situations of imagined rather than actual sexual assaults in which both innocent white and black lives were lost in the name of preserving the sanctity of white womanhood.[13] The public's perception of lynching, fed by the media and improved means of communication, was invariably that a sexual crime by black men had precipitated it. "*Having created the Frankenstein monster (and it is no less terrifying because it is largely illusory),*" Walter White concluded, "*the lyncher lives in constant fear of his own creation.*"[14] [. . .]

Men lynch most readily, a southern critic observed, when the black victim has "*offended that intangible something called 'racial superiority.'*" That offense, in fact, with no suggestion of sexual impropriety, precipitated scores of brutal lynchings. "*When a nigger gets ideas,*" a federal official in Wilkinson County, Mississippi, declared, "*the best thing to do is to get him under ground as quick as possible.*" [. . .]

What had alarmed the white South during Reconstruction was not evidence of black failure but evidence of black success, evidence of black assertion, independence, and advancement, evidence of black men learning the uses of political power. The closer the black man got to the ballot box, one observer noted, the more he looked like a rapist.

NOTES

1 The account of the Hose lynching is based on the *Richmond Planet*, Oct. 14, 1899, which reprinted the extensive investigation conducted by a detective sent by Ida B. Wells, and on the *Savannah Tribune*, April 29, May 6, 13, 1899; *Atlanta Constitution*, April 14–25, 1899; *Atlanta Journal*, April 14, 1899; *New York Tribune*, April 24, 1899, *New York Times*, April 24, 25, 1899; *Boston Evening Transcript*, April 24, 1899; *Kissimmee Valley* (Florida) *Gazette*, April 28, 1899; *Springfield* (Massachusetts) *Weekly Republican*, April 28, 1899, in Ralph Ginzburg, *100 Years of Lynchings* (Baltimore, 1961, 1988), 10–21; Thomas D. Clark, *Southern Country Editor* (Indianapolis, 1948), 229–31; W. Fitzhugh Brundage, *Lynching in the New South: Georgia and Virginia, 1880–1930* (Urbana, 1993), 82–4; Donald L. Grant, *The Way It Was in the South: The Black Experience in Georgia* (New York, 1993), 162–4. Much of the press referred to him as Sam Holt. Only the *New York Times* (April 25, 1899) published the story of a lyncher procuring a slice of Hose's heart for the governor. Rebecca Felton's observation may be found in "How Should the Women and Girls in Country Districts Be Protected: A Symposium Secured by Mrs. Loulie M. Gordon," Rebecca Felton Papers, University of Georgia Library.

2 *Crisis* 10 (June 1915), 71.

3 *Topeka Plaindealer*, quoted in *Crisis*, Dec. 1911, 60; postcard in NAACP, Administrative File, Lynching, etc., 1885–1916, NAACP Papers, c371, Library of Congress; *Crisis*, Jan. 1912, 110.

4 Charles Evers, *Evers* (New York, 1971), 23; Neil R. McMillen, *Dark Journey: Black Mississippians in the Age of Jim Crow* (Urbana, Ill., 1989), 224.

5 *Crisis* 2 (May 1911), 32; *Crisis* 3 (Jan. 1912), 108.

6 Booker T. Washington to editor of *New Orleans Times-Democrat*, June 19, 1899, *Southern Workman*, 28 (Oct. 1899), 375.

7 For the reference to the Atlanta butcher shop, see W. E. B. DuBois, "My Evolving Program for Negro Freedom," in Rayford W. Logan, *What the Negro Wants* (Chapel Hill, 1944), 53.

8 J. Nelson Fraser, *America, Old and New: Impressions of Six Months in the States* (London, 1912), 277 N.

9 Ray Stannard Baker, *Following the Colour Line* (New York, 1908), 198.

10 Reverend John E. White, "The Need of a Southern Program on the Negro," *South Atlantic Quarterly* 6

(1907), 184–5; Baker, *Following the Colour Line*, 190.

11 Jacquelyn Dowd Hall, *Revolt against Chivalry: Jessie Daniel Ames and the Women's Campaign against Lynching* (New York, 1979), 150–1. The term "folk pornography" was used by Hall in her insightful chapter on lynching and rape.

12 *Memphis Daily Commercial*, May 17, 1892 quoted in Ida B. Wells, *Southern Horrors* (New York, 1892)

13 Walter White, *Rope and Faggot: A Biography of Judge Lynch* (New York, 1929), 57–8; *Crisis* 3 (Nov. 1911), 11. For instances in which both whites and blacks suffered from the hysteria over sexual assaults, see, for example, Edward L. Ayers, *Vengeance and Justice: Crime and Punishment in the 19th Century American South* (New York, 1984), 241–2.

14 NAACP. *Thirty Years of Lynching in the United States, 1889–1918* (New York, 1919), 36; White, *Rope and Faggot*, 56–7. See also Monroe N. Work (ed.), *Negro Year Book: An Annual Encyclopedia of the Negro, 1937–1938* (Tuskegee, Ala., 1937), 156–8.

14

From *Purity and Exile:* Violence, Memory, and National Cosmology among Hutu Refugees in Tanzania

Liisa H. Malkki

The Mythico-History

In virtually all aspects of contemporary social life in the Mishamo camp, the Hutu refugees made reference to a shared body of knowledge about their past in Burundi. Everyday events, processes, and relations in the camp were spontaneously and consistently interpreted and acted upon by evoking this collective past as a charter and blueprint. I had not come to this refugee camp to study history or historical consciousness, but it was unmistakable that history had seized center stage in everyday thought and social action in the camp.

Talk about history in Mishamo took the form of narratives of quite specific type. [...] Like the Bible stories and morality plays to which I have likened them, the refugees' historical narratives comprised a set of moral and cosmological ordering stories: stories which classify the world according to certain principles, thereby simultaneously creating it. [...]

The Hutu mythico-history represented an interlinked set of ordering stories which converged to make (or remake) a world. "Worldmaking," as Nelson Goodman says (1978: 7), is a process "on the one hand, of dividing wholes into parts and partitioning kinds into sub-species, analyzing complexes into component features, drawing distinctions; on the other hand, of composing wholes

and kinds out of parts and members and sub-classes, combining features into complexes, and making connections." The mythico-history was such a process of world making because it constructed categorical schemata and thematic configurations that were relevant and meaningful in confronting both the past in Burundi and the pragmatics of everyday life in the refugee camp in Tanzania. In both cases, the mythico-historical world making was an oppositional process; it was constructed in opposition to other versions of what was ostensibly the same world, or the same past. The oppositional process of construction also implied the creation of the collective past in distinction to other pasts, thereby *heroizing* the past of the Hutu as "a people" categorically distinct from others. [...]

Bodily traits, essential character, and contrasting forms of innate power

In the mythico-historical discourse, precise and lengthy descriptions of physical differences between Hutu and Tutsi abounded. It was clearly important that these differences be maintained and kept categorically unambiguous. The meticulously crafted maps of physical differences were superimposed in the mythico-history with analogous maps of what were seen as innate moral character differences. In this section I will briefly describe first, how physical difference was constructed and on what body parts the most significant difference was inscribed; second, how bodily differences were seen to express differences of "character traits" in Hutu and Tutsi, and how these differences of character and life-style were, in turn, seen to be legible from the body like symptoms; and finally, how physical difference was related to social and political inequality, the meaning of labor, and qualitatively different kinds of power.

The mythico-historical constructions of bodily differences between Hutu and Tutsi bore a remarkable resemblance to similar descriptions to be found in the colonial records of Burundi: "The Batutsi ... are of tall stature. Few are less than 1,80 m. They are in general of an extreme thinness, have a long head, a very aquiline nose, a fine mouth: such [types] among them recall in troubling fashion the type of the mummy of Ramses II" (Gahama 1983: 276). Further, "the race of the Batutsi is without doubt one of the most beautiful and most interesting of Equatorial Africa. In physique, the Mututsi is perfectly constituted. [... He] is a European under a black skin." The Hutu, on the other hand, were considered "negroes properly speaking," bearing the "negroid" characteristics: "round face, thick-lipped mouth, an astounding nose, squat stature" (Gahama 1983: 276). Even in recent years, among the whites in Tanzania who had had occasion to see (or to *think* that they had seen) both Hutu and Tutsi "types" and to hear the stereotypes recounted by other amateur naturalists, the same characterizations emerged. Thus, the Tutsi were supposed to be the tall, stately, thin people, and the Hutu the short, stockier, plain peasants. The fact that these distinctions were quite obviously heavily elaborated cultural constructs – ideal types confounded by the reality of physical diversity and variation – did not in the least detract from their power as classificatory tools, and trying to pin down their "objective" truth or falsity would be grossly missing their significance.

The fact to be explained is that the mythico-history reproduced these distinctions quite systematically, often in long lists, and accepted them as accurate descriptions. The highly conventionalized and stereotyped distinctions were replayed in detail: nose shape, color of tongue and gums, size of pupils, hair texture, prominence of ankle bones, protrusion of calves, lines on the palm of the hand were all markers of difference. It was also universally agreed that the Tutsi were more "beautiful" than the Hutu. In the mythico-history, as in the colonial record, the markers of bodily difference were closely linked with and superimposed on moral and social difference. It is here that the meaning of the bodily differences in the mythico-history became intelligible at another level. The maps of bodily difference were not drawn for any intrinsic interest they might possess, nor were the distinctions seen as mere facts of nature. Rather, while the components of the body maps were accepted without rebuttal, they were deployed in new configurations of meaning which were highly significant and central in the mythico-history. They became symptoms and proofs for claims reaching far beyond the body.

Body Maps

[... The] Tutsi are taller generally, [...] at the same time, thinner.... They are of a beautiful stature. They cannot do painful chores, for example, constructing houses in brick, in wood. [...] Their hair is not kinky, their eyes are a little round ... also, their noses are more or less long. Their faces are more or less long. [...] They are real drinkers of no matter what drink. [... The] Hutu: This is a vigorous man being long or short. He likes to work very much – painful jobs are play for him. He is not a drunkard, since he who loves painful work cannot drink much. The Tutsi did not know how to cultivate – up until today they have not learned [...]. The Tutsi are tall and light of build, and they are incapable of strenuous physical labor. They also have an aversion to hard work because they are lazy, and wish only to engage in the secret art of statecraft, administration, and chiefly duties. The whites of the Tutsis' eyes are brighter because they do not bend over hot, smoky fires.

Thus, the body maps were articulated with distinctions of supposedly innate character traits such as laziness, and, further, with life-style and work habits. One might say that something like a curious caste difference was being inscribed on the body. The mythico-historical use of the body as a surface for the elaboration of other social differences did not end here, however; several other layers of signification were produced in the mythico-history, as will soon become evident. [...]

The Death Trap of Tutsi Women's Beauty

They [the Tutsi], they are the herders. They do not have food. All that which they use for eating, that comes from us, the cultivators here [the speaker points to the base of the population pyramid that he has drawn in the sand]. All right, here, at the summit of the pyramid, there is a certain Tutsi. The better to get food, he flatters a Hutu, a cultivator. He says, "I give you my daughter, even two or three cows." Like this. Then the Hutu, since he sees a beautiful woman with a long nose and [who is] very tall also in stature – elegant, if you wish – and who squanders smiles.... This is the means of flattering the Hutu, the cultivator who has perhaps five tons of beans and two tons of maize. [...] She sees a Hutu cultivator, slave.... Then the Hutu has to augment his cultivating since he gets married [with the beautiful Tutsi woman]. Well then, instead of seeing that he is overburdening himself – yes, that he is putting too much on his shoulders – the Hutu now has to cultivate seven tons of beans. But the Tutsi is not yet satisfied. This Hutu directly begins to despise the other Hutu because he is flattered and he boasts [...] about his Tutsi wife! And his parents are proud. It was like this in the past. [...] [I]n the years [between] 1800 and 1920, up to '72, the Hutu parents would have been happy [about a Tutsi daughter-in-law] perhaps.[...] One cannot condemn them. They did not understand in those times. But! From 1950 to 1972, here it is the [Hutu] intellectuals who did this! This is why our revolution will take a long time. It was very bad what [the intellectuals] did because they understood. The intellectuals should have tried to help. [...] If ever these intellectuals return [from Europe], they will seek to get married with a Tutsi woman. I ask myself.... So that the Tutsi would not look at him badly, [the Hutu intellectual] has to take a Tutsi wife. Even the three Hutu ministers married with Tutsi women. So, the home of a Hutu minister is full of Tutsis – his wife and his servants. [...] Yes. He has to have Tutsi servants. If ever he were to have Hutu servants – he cannot. His servants have to be Tutsi. These are like spies. If ever he goes elsewhere during the night, [the servants] will know it. [... During] the genocides of '65, '69, and '72, the Tutsi – before killing the Hutu intellectuals – the Tutsi sought out the brothers-in-law of the Hutu who had married Tutsi women. That is to say that the brother-in-law is also Tutsi. They killed the Hutu husband and his children. So, why marry a Tutsi woman? I do not know – to show that he, too, that he has the power of marrying with this category.... Or to be able to pass the period of his life [in other words, to be able to live out his life without meeting with premature death]. [...]

The Concrete Enactment of the Body Maps and the Life/Death Axis

There are... symbols.... There are symbols for recognizing a Hutu. [...] Well... so, the first symbol was this: In the hand of the Hutu there was an "M." Like this, you see? [Informant shows the lines forming an "M" on his palm.] Between the hands of the Tutsi and the hands of the Hutu there is a difference. One had to show one's hand [to the Tutsi during the massacre]. Like this they were able to recognize him who was the Hutu. But there were also other symbols on which one based one's judgment]. [... T]he second symbol was this: The Tutsi do not have these bones... [Informant bends to pull up the leg of his trousers, and points to his ankle bones]. Do you see? These bones here. The Tutsi have a straight line here. The third symbol – a Tutsi has a straight line here. [Still standing, the narrator pulls up the leg of his trousers further to expose his calf muscle.] A completely straight line here, while the Hutu has a swollen calf, like this. [He points to his own calf.] The fourth thing, one observed above all the gums – [...] Yes, the gums. Especially the Tutsi have black gums. Exactly the majority of the Tutsi! Sometimes a few little red parts, but otherwise black. Altogether black gums.... One observed further the tongue. Their tongues are often black or blackish. For the Hutu, the gums and the tongue are always red or pink. Also, there are Hutu who have had the good fortune of having black gums and all the Tutsi symbols. Like this they have not been killed. There have been some mixtures of Hutu who have married Tutsi girls. [...] The fifth symbol was the language spoken – since the Tutsi do not speak like the Hutu. Their voice, their language.... They have a haughtiness in their language.... Example: For "you!" – do you understand? You! [...] So, for "you!" the Hutu says "sha!" The Tutsi says, "hya!" Or then the word for "goat": The Hutu says "impene." The Tutsi says "ihene." And other differences which differentiate the languages. It is a language which truly grates. With their pride! Arrogance![...] The sixth symbol, it is the fashion of walking – [...] If once a Hutu is walking, he walks – [The narrator gets up to demonstrate a brisk, energetic walk with arms swinging purposefully] – he walks vup! vup! vup! like this, fast. Whereas the Tutsi walks like he who has not eaten, who walks softly – like he who goes where he does not want to [go].... We arrive at the – seventh symbol, I think. Yes, the seventh: One looked precisely at the nose. The nose of the Tutsi is a big nose – pointy

– which goes in a straight line, a straight line, from the forehead to the pointed extremity of the nose. The nose is big – which has a straight line. It is a nose similar to [that] of a European, but I have made an observation: The Europeans have a curved line [at the base of the nose], like the Hutu. So, the eighth symbol. Let us go to the face. Almost always you find [the Tutsi] with shiny faces with slightly reddish eyes – when he is grown up. When he is still young, they are brilliant eyes! Clear! The eyes of the Hutu are not altogether red – at the same time, not altogether brilliant. An eye which is between white and red – when [the Hutu] are still little. For the Tutsi, this part – that which with you is blue – for the Tutsi that part is big, immense! He has the air of a timorous fellow! The rich Tutsi drink a very strong drink, so their eyes can become red. But the Hutu also have reddish eyes – here, they are adults. [The Hutu] have bizarre eyes, spoiled – with an old woman, tired eyes because of the smoke [from the cooking fires]. The Tutsi eyes are the eyes of a superior. You can determine that. Who has lived without working … one can see that. [...] The ninth symbol, this depends on the height. For the most part, the Tutsi are tall – but no rule without exception, as I have told you. There are also short Tutsi. There are also Hutu who are tall. When [the Tutsi soldiers] find him tall, it is the difficult problem whether he is Hutu or Tutsi. At this point, they utilized these other symbols. Looking at the hand, the legs, the calves … or then, walking. [...] Walking. They imposed: "Go get us that!" If he departed so fast, one knew that this is a Hutu. But: they did not kill him at this moment. They had to pass through all the other symbols.

Again, the body maps described here were far from being naturalistic descriptions of inert features for their own sake. Essentialist projects to determine the "objective" truth or falsity of these body maps would not address the most complex or important questions concerning, precisely, their power as cultural constructs inextricably encoded in other domains of social practice, and capable of being put to many uses. One use, or effect, of such maps is to help construct and imagine ethnic difference. [...] Through violence, bodies of individual persons become metamorphosed into *specimens* of the ethnic category for which they are supposed to stand. [...]

Necrographic Maps of Techniques for Destroying the Body

[... T]here were many manners of killing them.[...] With the sisters [nuns] – you are familiar

with bamboo? [...] They were split into two parts – of the length of 1.80 meters, 1.90 meters, or 2 meters, if you will. They were prepared with machetes, until the bamboo was pointed like a nail. So, a Hutu is placed on the ground. The bamboo is pushed from the anus to the head. It was like this that they did – to sisters, or padres – or to pastors. There are two other fashions. There are large nails, six centimeters, long, fat. It is planted with a hammer. The nail is placed on the head of a Hutu. Once hit, it begins to penetrate the head. Several techniques, several, several. Or, one can gather two thousand persons in a house – in a prison, let us say. There are some halls which are large. The house is locked. The men are left there for fifteen days without eating, without drinking. Then one opens. One finds cadavers. Not beaten, not anything. Dead. Or, [...] they were given an altogether weighty hammer – let us say, five kilograms. This was given to one Hutu among the Hutu seized. They were placed in a line. And then, the one who had received the hammer there received an order from the soldier to hit the hammer on the forehead of his friend, here. [The narrator motions splitting the forehead vertically in half]. They stay one behind the other [in the line]. I go with the hammer terminating one after the other. When I have terminated all of them, the soldier shoots me with a bullet. [...] Holes were made – trucks bringing cadavers, cadavers, cadavers. The cadavers were spilled into the hole. [In Gitega,] the katepila [Caterpillar bulldozers] were brought to make large trenches. [...] The trench was dug during the night. Very early in the morning, the Hutu seized were brought there. [An exact location is named and its geographic features described.] They were transported in trucks … perhaps twenty trucks. The people were arranged all around that trench and then the soldiers shot them. They fell in the hole. After, dust was put on top. The instrument which had dug the hole covered the cadavers. It is an instrument which moves on chains, which goes very slowly. It weighs a lot. This same instrument went on the filled hole [pressing down the earth] so that if by accident there is one still alive, he will not be able to climb out. Then the instruments and the soldiers left.

In giving such generalized, technical, subjectless, and detached accounts, informants seemed preoccupied with rendering practical facts and details as accurately as possible. Accounts of this kind appeared to be part of a process of precise documentation and historical recording for preservation; each detail was reflectively presented as essential and significant. The process of telling was often accompanied with body gestures which gave the accounts a hard visual commentary likewise demanding witness.

Another series of narratives draws attention more closely to the fact that the events described *were* atrocities which had been lived and witnessed by particular persons known to the narrator. The accounts seemed to converge upon a number of formulaic key themes even more strongly than did the "technical" descriptions.

The Mythico-history of Atrocity

The manners that the Tutsi employed – if, for example – yes, we are adults, well . . . for example: a pregnant woman (Hutu). There was a manner of cutting the stomach. Everything that was found in the interior was lifted out without cutting the cord. The cadaver of the mama, the cadaver of the baby, of the future, they rotted on the road. Not even burial. The mother was obliged to eat the finger of her baby. One cut the finger, and then one said to the mother: Eat! [. . .] Another . . . another case which I remember – They roped together a papa with his daughter, also in Bujumbura. They said: "Now you can party." They were thrown into the lake. [. . .] My older brother, he was roped, and then he was made to roll, slide on the asphalted road behind a car. [The Tutsis'] intention was to equalize the population, up until 50 percent. It was a plan. [My brother's] body was left in the forest. If it had been left on the road, the foreigners would have seen it, and they would have written about it. [. . .]

The girls in secondary schools, they killed each other. The Tutsi girls were given bamboos. They were made to kill by pushing the bamboo from below [from the vagina] to the mouth. It is a thing against the law of God. Our party would never do this. God must help us. [. . .] During the genocide, every Tutsi had to make an action [to kill]. In the hospitals, in the churches, . . . The Fathers had to kill each other, and to kill Hutu faithful. Even the sick were killed in the beds of the hospitals. The genocide lasted three months, from the twenty-ninth of April to the end of August. But the killing was started again in 1973, above all in Bukemba.

[In other cases,] a bonfire was lighted. Then the legs and the arms of the Hutu were tied. [Informant describes how the arms were tied in the back of the body, and the legs were fastened to the ground, so that a circle of captives around the fire was forced to bend backwards.] Then the fire, the heat, inflates the stomach, and the stomach is ruptured. You see, with the heat, much liquid develops in the stomach, and then the stomach is ruptured. For others, a barrel of water was heated, and the people were put into it. [. . .] For the pregnant women, the stomach was cut, and then the child who had been inside – one said to the mama: "Eat your child" – this embryo. One had to do it. And then, other women and children, they were put inside a house – like two hundred – and then the house was burned. Everything inside was burned. [. . .] Others utilized bamboos, pushing them from here [anus] until here [mouth].

Key themes of atrocity accounts

These passages suggest that there were certain body parts on which mutilation and destruction converged; and these body parts were also the points of thematic convergence in the narratives. While "techniques" or "manners" used were once again described in detail, it was the symbolic meaning of these events which was the more crucial aspect here. The sex of the body seems to have dictated the focal points for the infliction of violence on the body when the target was not a larger group. The mouth, the brain, and the head as a whole, as well as the anus, were focal areas on the bodies of men in particular. Women's bodies were said to have been destroyed largely through the vagina and the uterus. When the women captured were pregnant, the violence seems invariably to have focused on the womb and specifically on the link between mother and child. In the case of the school girls, the violence was initiated through the vagina. In the case of both men and women, the narratives suggest, a systematic connection was made between the vagina or anus and the head through the penetration of bamboo poles. The bamboo poles (themselves stereotypically emblems of Tutsi categorical identity) were sometimes specified to be 1.8 or 2 meters long. It is perhaps not coincidental that these lengths correspond to the stereotypic height of "a Tutsi." As reconstructed in the mythico-history, such connections did not appear haphazard or accidental. Rather, they seem to have operated through certain routinized symbolic schemes of nightmarish cruelty.

In the case of some informants, explicit links were made between these highly elaborated techniques of killing and their perceived symbolic or political intent. In other cases, the symbolic significance of the techniques was implicit in people's reflections on the "*causes*" of killing.

The disembowling of pregnant Hutu women was interpreted as an effort to destroy the procreative capability, the "new life," of the Hutu people. In several accounts, the unborn child or embryo was referred to, simply, as "the future." The penetration of the head through the anus, as well as other means of crushing the head, were seen as a decapitation of the intellect, and, on a more general level, as an effort to render the Hutu people powerless, politically impotent. (Reference was never made to any mutilation of the penis.) In particular, it was said that the intention was to squash the Hutus' efforts to gain higher education.

The anthropologist, upon hearing these accounts, predictably thinks of how in many societies, the linking of high and low, of the head with the anus or vagina, represents a profound form of defilement and humiliation, especially when these are linked through violent force. Similarly, the forcible penetration of the anus and vagina can only be seen as violent acts of humiliation and dehumanization. The implication of incest forced upon father and daughter by roping them together and forcing them to die in a sexualized position as they drown is likewise a cruel statement about their powerlessness to prevent either incest or death. How one dies is important here, as it is elsewhere in the world. And again, forcing a woman to eat the flesh of her own "flesh and blood," of her child, is imposing, not only cannibalism, but autophagy in the literal sense of devouring oneself. It represents a complete reversal of the "progress of nature" in which the mother's body nurtures, forms, and brings into the world "new life."

These accounts together documented a process of profound dehumanization of the Hutu as a people, of their objectification as something less than human and "natural." However, simultaneously, as these events and techniques were being described in the mythico-history by the refugees themselves, the dehumanizing gaze was necessarily turned against those who were considered to have produced and deployed the techniques of human destruction described. Thus, it was not specific individual perpetrators, but "the Tutsi" as a homogeneous category that had created the violence, perversity, and defilement. "They" are therefore seen as the source of the almost unimaginable evil and of the destruction of "the natural" as constituted in collective memory through the refugees' fifteen years of exile. The dehuman-ization of the Tutsi at this level acted as a culmination of earlier assertions in the mythico-history that the Tutsi did not belong to "the nation" in its pure, "natural" state. In narrative segments cited earlier, the Tutsi were cast as "the impostors from the north," "the foreigners," and further, as morally unworthy of membership in the nation because of their parasitism, thievery, and trickery. Here, then, the culmination of this reasoning was reached: Burundi as it is today is *not* and never can be a single harmonious nation, and the ruling Tutsi are the foreign, unnatural, evil element in it. They are not Bantu and not even human, *abantu*. In the mythico-history, the enemy of the "authentic nation" of Burundi is "the Tutsi."

This form of categorical enmity was powerfully constituted on many levels of the mythico-historical discourse. But in several cases the very persons who described the apocalypse in these categorizing, objectifying terms also gave accounts of how individual Tutsi played an instrumental role in their personal escape. The position of these accounts of individual Tutsi saviors in the mythico-history is not clearly articulated, but they could be interpreted as a way of accounting for one's own good fortune in being spared from death. Three such stories encountered also seemed to emphasize the role of random chance and luck in the escape from death. They did not seem to attenuate in the least the categorical distinction otherwise drawn between good and evil, Hutu and Tutsi – if anything, these exceptions seemed to strengthen the categories.

The form of the Hutu refugees' accounts of atrocity as a whole can, perhaps, be compared with the accounts of other victims of extreme violence – survivors of Nazi concentration camps, of the Armenian massacres, of the current civil war in Bosnia, and of many other tragedies. In most of these cases, it is relevant to ask how the accounts of atrocity come to assume thematic form, how they become formulaic. This is not a euphemistic way of charging survivors of atrocity with selective amnesia, or of denying the fact of their experiences. Rather, it is to ask when and how both the perpetration and the memory of violence may be formalized.

The first thing to be examined in the present case is the extent to which the techniques of cruelty actually used were already symbolically meaningful, already mythico-historical. Acts of cruelty and violence, after all, often take on conventions readily. They become stylized and mythologically meaningful even in their perpetration. One need only inspect reports from Amnesty International and other organizations whose main purpose is to document human-rights violations to begin to see that the conventionalization of torture, killing, and other forms of violence occurs not only routinely but in patterned forms in the contemporary world. Torture, in particular, is a highly symbolized form of violence. At this level, it can be said that historical actors mete out death and perpetrate violence mythically.

Yet the accounts presented here were more than simple recollection. Clearly, they had sprung first from lived fear and horror. But the accounts of atrocity, remembered and retold, themselves became acutely meaningful themes in the mythico-history. They had, in other words, an order – more precisely, they had been incorporated into the overarching moral order expressed in the mythico-history. The stories of atrocity thus stand as ordering stories at an extraordinary level. In this specific sense, the collective reconstruction and memory of violence may also be characterized as mythical.

Thus, acts of atrocity are not only enacted and perpetrated symbolically; they are also, after the fact, stylized or narratively constituted symbolically. To debate about which of these levels is more mythologized is perhaps not the most interesting or important question, however. It seems more essential to point out that in this case in particular, fatal cruelty does not lie outside of the social, nor is it unconnected to other arenas of social practice. The organization of the related set of panels seeks to make intelligible precisely the ways in which highly elaborated and extreme violence was linked up with such other practices as the inscription of differentiating schemata on human bodies, visions of the mixing of categories that "ought" to be kept distinct, and the structuring of totalizing inequality. For the massacre was seen in the mythico-history precisely as an apocalyptic culmination of such "dangerous" tendencies and processes which had been formative of Burundian society for decades and even centuries.

REFERENCES

Gahama, Joseph. 1983. *Le Burundi sous administration belge*. Paris: CRA, Karthala, ACCT.

Goodman, Nelson. 1978. *Ways of Worldmaking*. Indianapolis and Cambridge: Hackett.

15

From *We Wish To Inform You That Tomorrow We Will Be Killed With Our Families: Stories from Rwanda*

Philip Gourevitch

Back in 1987, a newspaper called *Kanguka* began appearing in Rwanda. *Kanguka* means "Wake Up," and the paper, edited by a Hutu from the south and backed by a prominent Tutsi business-man, was critical of the Habyarimana establish-ment. Its originality lay in presenting an analysis of Rwandan life based on economic rather than ethnic conflict. *Kanguka*'s courageous staff faced constant harassment, but the paper was a hit with the small public who could read it. So in early 1990, Madame Agathe Habyarimana secretly con-vened several leaders of the *akazu* with the idea of launching a rival publication. They didn't know the first thing about newspapers, but they were experts on human weakness – especially vanity and venality – and as their editor they hired a small-time hustler and big-time self-promoter named Hassan Ngeze, a former bus-fare collector who had established himself as an entrepreneur, selling newspapers and drinks outside a gas station in Gisenyi, and from that vantage point had turned himself into a humorous man-on-the-street corres-pondent for *Kanguka*.

The paper Ngeze produced, *Kangura* – "Wake It Up" – billed itself as "the voice that seeks to awake and guide the majority people." It began as little more than a lampoon of *Kanguka*, with an identical format that tricked readers into buying it. This ruse was helped along by the fact that just as *Kangura* appeared, the government

seized several numbers of *Kanguka*. But the paper's irreverent tone was a bit too much like its opposite's for the tastes of the *akazu*, and it annoyed Ngeze's sponsors that he devoted large portions of the first issues to photo-essays extol-ling his own virtues. In July of 1990, when Habyarimana's security force arrested the editor of *Kanguka* on charges of high treason, they made a show of balance by simultaneously jailing Has-san Ngeze for disturbing the public order. The ploy worked on several levels. Western human rights groups like Amnesty International issued joint appeals for the release of the two editors, bestowing on Ngeze an aura of antiestablishment martyrdom, when the truth was that he was a propagandist of the regime who had disappointed his patrons. At the same time, prison taught Ngeze that his welfare depended on his being a more diligent flunky, and he was an ambitious man who took the lesson to heart.

In October of 1990, as Rwanda's jails were being packed with alleged RPF accomplices, Ngeze was released to relaunch *Kangura*. (The editor of *Kanguka* remained conveniently locked away.) With the war as his backdrop, Ngeze struck a clever balance between his persona as a prison-accredited gadfly of the regime and his secret status as front man for the *akazu*. Even as he harangued Hutus to unite behind the President in the struggle against the Tutsi menace, he chided the President for failing to lead that struggle with sufficient vigilance. While government officials still felt publicly constrained by international pressure from speaking openly of ethnicity, Ngeze published what he claimed were RPF documents which purportedly "proved" that the rebel movement was part of an ancient Tutsi-supremacist conspiracy to subjugate Hutus in feudal bondage. He ran lists of prominent Tutsis and Hutu accomplices who had "infiltrated" public institutions, accused the government of betraying the revolution, and called for a rigorous campaign of national "self-defense" to protect the "gains" of 1959 and 1973. And he did all of this with his printing costs defrayed by government credit, giving away most of each print run to Rwanda's mayors to distribute free.

A host of new periodicals had appeared in Rwanda in 1990. All but *Kangura* served as voices of relative moderation, and all but *Kangura* are now largely forgotten. More than anybody else, Hassan Ngeze, the Hutu supremacist with the populist touch, plucked from obscurity by the President's wife to play the court jester, was writing the script for the coming Hutu crusade. It would be foolish to dispute his brilliance as a salesman of fear. When another paper ran a cartoon depicting Ngeze on a couch, being psychoanalyzed by "the democratic press" –

> Ngeze: I'm sick Doctor!!
> Doctor: Your sickness?!
> Ngeze: The Tutsis ... Tutsis ... Tutsis!!!!!!!

– Ngeze picked it up and ran it in *Kangura*. He was one of those creatures of destruction who turn everything hurled at them into their own weapon. He was funny and bold, and in one of the most repressed societies on earth, he presented the liberating example of a man who seemed to know no taboos. As a race theorist, Ngeze made John Hanning Speke look like what he was: an amateur. He was the original high-profile archetype of the Rwandan Hutu *génocidaire*, and his imitators and disciples were soon legion.

Although he was a practicing member of Rwanda's small Muslim community – the only religious community, according to one Christian leader, that "apparently behaved quite well, and as a group was not active in the genocide, even seeking to save Tutsi Muslims" – Ngeze's true religion was "Hutuness." His most famous article, published in December of 1990, was the credo of this newly crystallized faith: "The Hutu Ten Commandments." In a few swift strokes, Ngeze revived, revised, and reconciled the Hamitic myth and the rhetoric of the Hutu revolution to articulate a doctrine of militant Hutu purity. The first three commandments addressed the stubborn perception, constantly reinforced by the tastes of visiting white men and Hutus with status, that the beauty of Tutsi women surpasses that of Hutu women. According to Ngeze's protocols, all Tutsi women were Tutsi agents; Hutu men who married, befriended, or employed a Tutsi woman "as a secretary or concubine" were to be considered traitors, and Hutu women, for their part, were commanded to guard against the Tutsi-loving impulses of Hutu men. From sex, Ngeze moved on to matters of business, declaring every Tutsi dishonest – "his only aim is the supremacy of his ethnic group" – and any Hutu who had financial dealings with Tutsis an enemy of his people. The same held for political life; Hutus should control "all strategic positions, political, administrative, economic, military, and security." Hutus were further commanded to have "unity and solidarity" against "their common Tutsi enemy," to study and spread "the Hutu ideology" of the revolution of 1959, and to regard as a traitor any Hutu who "persecutes his brother Hutu" for studying or spreading this ideology.

"The Hutu Ten Commandments" were widely circulated and immensely popular. President Habyarimana championed their publication as proof of Rwanda's "freedom of the press." Community leaders across Rwanda regarded them as tantamount to law, and read them aloud at public meetings. The message was hardly unfamiliar, but with its whiff of holy war and its unforgiving warnings to lapsed Hutus, even Rwanda's most unsophisticated peasantry could not fail to grasp that it had hit an altogether new pitch of alarm. The eighth and most often quoted commandment said: "Hutus most stop having mercy on the Tutsis."

In December of 1990, the same month that Hassan Ngeze published "The Hutu Ten Commandments," *Kangura* also hailed President Mitterrand of France with a full-page portrait, captioned "A friend in need is a friend indeed." The salutation was apt. Fighting alongside Habyarimana's Forces Armées Rwandaises, hundreds of superbly equipped French paratroopers had kept the RPF from advancing beyond its first foothold in the northeast. Initially, Belgium and Zaire also sent troops to back up the FAR, but the Zaireans were so given to drinking, looting, and raping that Rwanda soon begged them to go home, and the Belgians withdrew of their own accord. The French remained, and their impact was such that after the first month of fighting Habyarimana pronounced the RPF defeated. In fact, the battered rebel forces merely retreated westward from the open grasslands of northeastern Rwanda to establish a new base on the jagged, rain-forested slopes of the Virunga volcanoes. There – cold, wet, and poorly supplied – the RPF suffered greater losses to pneumonia than to fighting, as they trained a steady trickle of new recruits into a fierce, and fiercely disciplined, guerrilla army that might have swiftly forced Habyarimana to the negotiating table, or brought him to outright defeat, had it not been for France.

A military agreement signed in 1975 between France and Rwanda expressly forbade the involvement of French troops in Rwandan combat, combat training, or police operations. But President Mitterrand liked Habyarimana, and Mitterrand's son Jean-Christophe, an arms dealer and sometime commissar of African affairs in the French Foreign Ministry, liked him too. (As military expenditures drained Rwanda's treasury and the war dragged on, an illegal drug trade developed in Rwanda; army officers set up marijuana plantations, and Jean-Christophe Mitterrand is widely rumored to have profited from the traffic.) France funneled huge shipments of armaments to Rwanda – right through the killings in 1994 – and throughout the early 1990s, French officers and troops served as Rwandan auxiliaries, directing everything from air traffic control and the interrogation of RPF prisoners to frontline combat.

In January of 1991, when the RPF took the key northwestern city of Ruhengeri, Habyarimana's home base, government troops backed by French paratroopers drove them out within 24 hours. A few months later, when the United States ambassador to Rwanda suggested that the Habyarimana government should abolish ethnic identity cards, the French ambassador quashed the initiative. Paris regarded Francophone Africa as "*chez nous*," a virtual extension of the motherland, and the fact that the RPF had emerged out of Anglophone Uganda inspired the ancient French tribal phobia of an Anglo-Saxon menace. Swaddled in this imperial security blanket, Habyarimana and his ruling clique were free to ignore the RPF for long stretches and to concentrate on their campaign against the unarmed "domestic enemy."

A few days after the RPF's overnight occupation of Ruhengeri, in January of 1991, Habyarimana's FAR faked an attack on one of its own military camps in the northwest. The RPF was blamed and, in retaliation, a local mayor organized massacres of the Bagogwe, a quasi-nomadic Tutsi subgroup that subsisted in extreme poverty; scores were killed, and the mayor had them buried deep in his own yard. More massacres followed; by the end of March hundreds of Tutsis in the northwest had been slaughtered.

"We were really terrorized in that period," Odette recalled. "We thought we were going to be massacred." In 1989, when she was fired from the hospital, Odette had been furious at the speed with which people she had trusted as friends turned away from her. A year later, she looked back on that time as the good old days. Like many Rwandan Tutsis, Odette first reacted to the war with indignation toward the refugee rebels for placing those who had stayed in the country in jeopardy. "We always thought those on the outside were well settled and better off," she told me. "We had come to see our situation here as normal. I used to tell my exiled cousins, 'Why come back? Stay there, you're much better off,' and they said, 'Odette, even you have adopted the discourse of Habyarimana.' The RPF had to make us aware that they suffered, living in exile, and we started to realize that we hadn't thought of these exiles for all this time. Ninety-nine percent of the Tutsis had no idea that the RPF would attack. But we began to discuss it, and realized these were our brothers coming and that the Hutus we'd lived with didn't regard us as equals. They rejected us."

When Odette and her husband, Jean-Baptiste, visited the wives of imprisoned Tutsis, Jean-Baptiste got a call from the Secretary-General of Intelligence, whom he considered a good friend. The intelligence chief's friendly advice was: "If you want to die, keep going to those people."

For those in jail, like Bonaventure Nyibizi, a staffer at the Kigali mission of the United States Agency for International Development, the expectation of death was even greater. "They were killing prisoners every night, and on October 26,

I was going to be killed," he told me. "But I had cigarettes. The guy came and said, 'I'm going to kill you,' and I gave him a cigarette, so he said, 'Well, we're killing people for nothing and I'm not going to kill you tonight.' People were dying every day from torture. They were taken out, and when they came back, they were beaten, bayoneted, and they were dying. I slept with dead people several nights. I think the initial plan was to kill everybody in prison, but the Red Cross started registering people, so it became difficult. The regime wanted to keep a good international image."

One of Bonaventure's best friends in prison was a businessman named Froduald Karamira. Bonaventure and Karamira both came from Gitarama, in the south, and both were Tutsi by birth. But early in life, Karamira had acquired Hutu identity papers, and he had benefited accordingly; in 1973, when Bonaventure was expelled from school because he was Tutsi, Karamira, who attended the same seminary, was left unmolested. "But the Habyarimana government didn't like the Hutus from Gitarama, and Karamira was rich, so they arrested him," Bonaventure explained. "He was a very nice person in prison, always trying to help people out, buying cigarettes, a place to sleep, blankets. When he got out of prison before me, my wife was pregnant with our first child, and he went straightaway to visit her. After March of 1991, when the government released all of us from prison, I saw him several times. He used to come to my house, or my office. And then one night" – Bonaventure snapped his fingers – "he changed completely. We couldn't talk anymore because I am Tutsi. This happened with so many people. They changed so quickly that you would say, 'Is this the same person?'"

In the summer of 1991, the much anticipated multiparty order had begun in Rwanda. Such a leap from totalitarianism to a political free market will be tumultuous even when it is undertaken by sincerely well-intentioned leaders, and in Rwanda the political opening was contrived in conspicuously bad faith. Most of the dozen parties that suddenly began scrapping for attention and influence were simply puppets of Habyarimana's MRND, created by the President and the *akazu* to sow confusion and make a mockery of the pluralist enterprise. Only one of the genuine opposition parties had a significant Tutsi membership; the rest were divided between committed reformers and Hutu extremists who swiftly transformed the

"democratic debate" into a wedge that further polarized the divided citizenry by presenting Rwandan politics as a simple question of Hutu self-defense. It was us against them – all of us against all of them: anybody who dared to suggest an alternative view was one of them and could prepare for the consequences. And it was Froduald Karamira, the convert to Hutuness, who gave this tidy proposition, and the cacophony of ideological discourse that crackled behind it, the enthusiastic name of Hutu Power.

"I don't know exactly what happened," Bonaventure told me. "People say that Habyarimana paid him tens of millions to change, and he did become the head of ElectroGaz" – the national utility company. "All I know is that he became one of the most important extremists, and that is not the way he was before. So much was changing so suddenly, and still it was hard to see – hard to believe – how much it was changing."

One day in January of 1992, soldiers visited Bonaventure's home in Kigali, while he and his wife were out. "They broke the doors," Bonaventure said. "They took everything, they tied up the house staff, and I had a son who was nine months old – they left grenades with him. He was there playing with a grenade in the living room, for three hours. Then somebody passed by and noticed, and fortunately my son was not killed."

So it went – an attack here, a massacre there – as the increasingly well-organized Hutu extremists stockpiled weapons, and Hutu youth militias were recruited and trained for "civil defense." First among these militias was the *interahamwe* – "those who attack together" – which had its genesis in soccer fan clubs sponsored by leaders of the MRND and the *akazu*. The economic collapse of the late 1980s had left tens of thousands of young men without any prospect of a job, wasting in idleness and its attendant resentments, and ripe for recruitment. The *interahamwe*, and the various copycat groups that were eventually subsumed into it, promoted genocide as a carnival romp. Hutu Power youth leaders, jetting around on motorbikes and sporting pop hairstyles, dark glasses, and flamboyantly colored pajama suits and robes, preached ethnic solidarity and civil defense to increasingly packed rallies, where alcohol usually flowed freely, giant banners splashed with hagiographic portraits of Habyarimana flapped in the breeze, and paramilitary drills were conducted like the latest hot dance moves. The President and his wife often turned out to be cheered at these spectacles, while in private the members of the *interahamwe* were organized into small neighborhood bands, drew up lists of Tutsis, and went on retreats to practice burning houses, tossing grenades, and hacking dummies up with machetes.

Play first turned to work for the *interahamwe* in early March of 1992, when the state-owned Radio Rwanda announced the "discovery" of a Tutsi plan to massacre Hutus. This was pure misinformation, but in preemptive "self-defense" militia members and villagers in the Bugesera region, south of Kigali, slaughtered three hundred Tutsis in three days. Similar killings occurred at the same time in Gisenyi, and in August, shortly after Habyarimana – under intense pressure from international donors – signed a cease-fire with the RPF, Tutsis were massacred in Kibuye. That October, the cease-fire was expanded to embrace plans for a new, transitional government that would include the RPF; one week later, Habyarimana delivered a speech dismissing the truce as "nothing but a scrap of paper."

Still, the foreign-aid money poured into Habyarimana's coffers, and weapons kept arriving – from France, from Egypt, from apartheid South Africa. Occasionally, when donors expressed concern about the killings of Tutsis, there were arrests, but releases followed swiftly; nobody was brought to trial, much less prosecuted for the massacres. To soothe foreign nerves, the government portrayed the killings as "spontaneous" and "popular" acts of "anger" or "self-protection." The villagers knew better: massacres were invariably preceded by political "consciousness-raising" meetings at which local leaders, usually with a higher officer of the provincial or national government at their side, described Tutsis as devils – horns, hoofs, tails, and all – and gave the order to kill them, according to the old revolutionary lingo, as a "work" assignment. The local authorities consistently profited from massacres, seizing slain Tutsis' land and possessions, and sometimes enjoying promotions if they showed special enthusiasm, and the civilian killers, too, were usually rewarded with petty spoils.

In retrospect, the massacres of the early 1990s can be seen as dress rehearsals for what proponents of Hutuness themselves called the "final solution" in 1994. Yet there was nothing inevitable about the horror. With the advent of multipartyism, the President had been compelled by popular pressure to make substantial concessions to reform-minded oppositionists, and it required a dogged uphill effort for Habyarimana's extremist entourage to prevent Rwanda from slipping toward moderation. Violence was the key to that effort. The *interahamwe* was bankrolled and supervised by a consortium of *akazu* leaders, who also ran their own death squads, with names like the Zero Network and the Bullets group. Madame Habyarimana's three brothers, along with a bevy of colonels and leaders of the northwestern business mafia, were founding members of these outfits, which first rolled into action alongside the *interahamwe* during the Bugesera massacre in March of 1992. But the most crucial innovation at Bugesera was the use of the national radio to prepare the ground for slaughter, and the ratcheting up of the suggestive message of us against them to the categorically compelling kill or be killed.

Genocide, after all, is an exercise in community building. A vigorous totalitarian order requires that the people be invested in the leaders' scheme, and while genocide may be the most perverse and ambitious means to this end, it is also the most comprehensive. In 1994, Rwanda was regarded in much of the rest of the world as the exemplary instance of the chaos and anarchy associated with collapsed states. In fact, the genocide was the product of order, authoritarianism, decades of modern political theorizing and indoctrination, and one of the most meticulously administered states in history. And strange as it may sound, the ideology – or what Rwandans call "the logic" – of genocide was promoted as a way not to create suffering but to alleviate it. The specter of an absolute menace that requires absolute eradication binds leader and people in a hermetic utopian embrace, and the individual – always an annoyance to totality – ceases to exist.

The mass of participants in the practice massacres of the early 1990s may have taken little pleasure in obediently murdering their neighbors. Still, few refused, and assertive resistance was extremely rare. Killing Tutsis was a political tradition in postcolonial Rwanda; it brought people together.

It has become a commonplace in the past fifty years to say that the industrialized killing of the Holocaust calls into question the notion of human progress, since art and science can lead straight through the famous gate – stamped with the words "Work Makes You Free" – to Auschwitz. Without all that technology, the argument goes, the Germans couldn't have killed all those Jews. Yet it was the Germans, not the machinery, who did the killing. Rwanda's Hutu Power leaders understood this perfectly. If you could swing the people who would swing the machetes, technological underdevelopment was no obstacle to genocide. The people were the weapon, and that meant everybody: the entire Hutu population had to kill the entire Tutsi population. In addition to ensuring obvious numerical advantages, this arrangement eliminated any questions of accountability which might arise. If everybody is implicated, then implication becomes meaningless. Implication in what? A Hutu who thought there was anything to be implicated in would have to be an accomplice of the enemy.

"We the people are obliged to take responsibility ourselves and wipe out this scum," explained Leon Mugesera, in November of 1992, during the same speech in which he urged Hutus to return the Tutsis to Ethiopia by way of the Nyabarongo River. Mugesera was a doctor, a vice president of the MRND, and a close friend and adviser of Habyarimana. His voice was the voice of power, and most Rwandans can still quote from his famous speech quite accurately; members of the *interabamwe* often recited favorite phrases as they went forth to kill. The law, Mugesera claimed, mandated death to "accomplices" of the "cockroaches," and he asked, "What are we waiting for to execute the sentence?" Members of opposition parties, he said, "have no right to live among us," and as a leader of "the Party" he invoked his duty to spread the alarm and to instruct the people to "defend themselves." As for the "cockroaches" themselves, he wondered, "What are we waiting for to decimate these families?" He called on those who had prospered under Habyarimana to "finance operations to eliminate these people." He spoke of 1959, saying it had been a terrible mistake to allow Tutsis to survive. "Destroy them," he said. "No matter what you do, do not let them get away," and he said, "Remember that the person whose life you save will certainly not save yours." He finished with the words "Drive them out. Long live President Habyarimana."

Mugesera had spoken in the name of the law, but it happened that the Minister of Justice at the time was a man named Stanislas Mbonampeka, who saw things differently. Mbonampeka was a man of parts: he was a well-to-do Hutu from the northwest, the owner of a half share in a toilet paper factory, and he was also an oppositionist, a lawyer and human rights advocate in the top ranks of the Liberal Party, the only opposition party with a sizable Tutsi membership. Mbonampeka studied Mugesera's speech and issued an arrest warrant against him for inciting hatred. Of course, Mugesera didn't go to jail – he went to the army for protection, then emigrated to Canada – and Mbonampeka was soon dismissed as Justice Minister. Mbonampeka saw which way the wind was blowing. By early 1993, all of Rwanda's newborn opposition parties had split into two factions – Power and anti-Power – and Mbonampeka went with Power. Before long, he could be heard on Radio Rwanda, warning the RPF: "Stop fighting this war if you do not want your supporters living inside Rwanda to be exterminated."

In the summer of 1995, I found Mbonampeka living in a drab little room at the Protestant Guest House in Goma, Zaire, about a mile from the Rwandan border. "In a war," he told me, "you can't be neutral. If you're not for your country, are you not for its attackers?" Mbonampeka was a large man with a calm and steady demeanor. He wore gold wire-rimmed spectacles, neatly pressed trousers, and a pink-and-white-striped shirt, and he had the absurd title of Minister of Justice in the Rwandan government in exile – a self-appointed body culled largely from officers of the regime that had presided over the genocide. Mbonampeka was not in that government in 1994, but he had operated informally as its agent, pleading the Hutu Power cause both at home and in Europe, and he regarded this as a normal career development.

"I said Mugesera must be arrested because he sets people against each other, which is illegal, and I also said that if the RPF continued to fight we must have civil defense," Mbonampeka told me. "These positions are consistent. In both cases I was for the defense of my country." And he added, "Personally, I don't believe in the genocide. This was not a conventional war. The enemies were everywhere. The Tutsis were not killed as Tutsis, only as sympathizers of the RPF."

I wondered if it had been difficult to distinguish the Tutsis with RPF sympathies from the rest. Mbonampeka said it wasn't. "There was no difference between the ethnic and the political," he told me. "Ninety-nine percent of Tutsis were pro-RPF."

Even senile grandmothers and infants? Even the fetuses ripped from the wombs of Tutsis, after radio announcers had reminded listeners to take special care to disembowel pregnant victims?

"Think about it," Mbonampeka said. "Let's say the Germans attack France, so France defends itself against Germany. They understand that all Germans are the enemy. The Germans kill women and children, so you do, too."

By regarding the genocide, even as he denied its existence, as an extension of the war between the RPF and the Habyarimana regime, Mbonampeka seemed to be arguing that the systematic state-sponsored extermination of an entire people is a provokable crime – the fault of the victims as well as the perpetrators. But although the genocide coincided with the war, its organization and implementation were quite distinct from the war effort. In fact, the mobilization for the final extermination campaign swung into full gear only when Hutu Power was confronted by the threat of peace.

On August 4, 1993, at a conference center in Arusha, Tanzania, President Habyarimana signed a peace agreement with the RPF, officially bringing the war to an end. The so-called Arusha Accords ensured a right of return for Rwanda's refugee diaspora, promised the integration of the two warring armies into a single national defense force, and established a blueprint for a Broad-Based Transitional Government, composed of representatives of all the national political parties, including the RPF. Habyarimana would remain President, pending elections, but his powers would be basically ceremonial. And, crucially, throughout the peace-implementation period a United Nations peacekeeping force would be deployed in Rwanda.

The RPF had never really expected to win its war on the battlefield; its objective had been to force a political settlement, and at Arusha it appeared to have done that. "You use war when there is no other means, and Arusha opened a means to come and struggle politically," Tito Ruteremara, one of the RPF leaders who negotiated the Accords, told me. "With Arusha we could go inside Rwanda, and if we had good ideas and a very nice organization, we'd make it. If we failed, it meant that our ideas were no good. The struggle wasn't ethnic, it was political, and Habyarimana feared us because we were strong. He had never wanted peace, because he saw that we could be politically successful."

For Habyarimana, it was true that the Arusha Accords amounted to a political suicide note. Hutu Power leaders cried treason, and charged that the President himself had become an "accomplice." Four days after the signing at Arusha, Radio Television Libres des Milles Collines, a new radio station funded by members and friends of the *akazu*, and devoted to genocidal propaganda, began broadcasting from Kigali. RTLM was a *Kangura* of the airwaves; its reach was virtually ubiquitous in radio-saturated Rwanda, and it became wildly popular with its mixture of rousing oratory and songs by such Hutu Power pop stars as Simon Bikindi, whose most famous number was probably "I Hate These Hutus" – a song of "good neighborliness":

*I hate these Hutus, these arrogant Hutus, braggarts,
    who scorn other Hutus, dear comrades . . .
I hate these Hutus, these de-Hutuized Hutus, who
    have disowned their identity, dear comrades.
I hate these Hutus, these Hutus who march blindly,
    like imbeciles,
this species of naive Hutus who are manipulated,
    and who tear themselves up, joining in a war
    whose cause they ignore.
I detest these Hutus who are brought to kill,
to kill, I swear to you,
and who kill the Hutus, dear comrades.
If I hate them, so much the better . . .*

And so on; it is a very long song.

"Anyone who thinks that the war is over as a result of the Arusha Accords is deceiving himself," Hassan Ngeze warned in *Kangura*, in January of 1994. Ngeze had railed against Arusha as a sellout from the start, and with the arrival of the blue-helmeted soldiers of the United Nations Assistance Mission in Rwanda at the end of 1993, he had a new target. UNAMIR, Ngeze proclaimed, was nothing but a tool "to help the RPF take power by force." But, he reminded his readers, the record showed that such peacekeepers were generally cowardly, inclined to "watching as spectators" when violence broke out. He predicted that there would be plenty to watch, and he explicitly warned UNAMIR to stay out of the way. "If the RPF has decided to kill us, then let's kill each other," he urged. "Let whatever is smoldering erupt. . . . At such a time, a lot of blood will be spilled."

Part IV

Why do People Kill?

Plate 6: On the Road from Tanzania to Kigali, Rwanda 1994. From *Migrations*, p. 170. Photo © Sebastião Salgado, Contact Press Images.

16

Behavioral Study of Obedience

Stanley Milgram

Obedience is as basic an element in the structure of social life as one can point to. Some system of authority is a requirement of all communal living, and it is only the man dwelling in isolation who is not forced to respond, through defiance or submission, to the commands of others. Obedience, as a determinant of behavior, is of particular relevance to our time. It has been reliably established that from 1933–45 millions of innocent persons were systematically slaughtered on command. Gas chambers were built, death camps were guarded, daily quotas of corpses were produced with the same efficiency as the manufacture of appliances. These inhumane policies may have originated in the mind of a single person, but they could only be carried out on a massive scale if a very large number of persons obeyed orders.

Obedience is the psychological mechanism that links individual action to political purpose. It is the dispositional cement that binds men to systems of authority. [...]

When you think of the long and gloomy history of man, you will find more hideous crimes have been committed in the name of obedience than have ever been committed in the name of rebellion. If you doubt that, read William Shirer's "Rise and Fall of the Third Reich." The German Officer Corps were brought up in the most rigorous code of obedience . . . in the name of obedience they were party to, and assisted in, the most wicked large scale actions in the history of the world.[1]

[...]

General Procedure

A procedure was devised which seems useful as a tool for studying obedience.[2] It consists of ordering a naive subject to administer electric shock to a victim. A stimulated shock generator is used, with 30 clearly marked voltage levels that range from 15 to 450 volts. The instrument bears verbal designations that range from Slight Shock to Danger: Severe Shock. The responses of the victim, who is a trained confederate of the experimenter, are standardized. The orders to administer shocks are given to the naive subject in the context of a "learning experiment" ostensibly set up to study the effects of punishment on memory. As the experiment proceeds the naive subject is commanded to administer increasingly more intense shocks to the victim, even to the point of reaching the level marked Danger: Severe Shock. Internal resistances become stronger, and at a certain point the subject refuses to go on with the experiment. Behavior prior to this rupture is considered "obedience," in that the subject complies with the commands of the experimenter. The point of rupture is the act of disobedience. A quantitative value is assigned to the subject's performance based on the maximum intensity shock he is willing to administer before he refuses to participate further. Thus for any particular subject and for any particular experimental condition the degree of obedience may be specified with a numerical value. The crux of the study is to systematically vary the factors believed to alter the degree of obedience to the experimental commands.

The technique allows important variables to be manipulated at several points in the experiment. One may vary aspects of the source of command, content and form of command, instrumentalities for its execution, target object, general social setting, etc. The problem, therefore, is not one of designing increasingly more numerous experimental conditions, but of selecting those that best illuminate the *process* of obedience from the sociopsychological standpoint. [. . .]

Procedure

One naive subject and one victim (an accomplice) performed in each experiment. A pretext had to be devised that would justify the administration of electric shock by the naive subject. This was effectively accomplished by the cover story. After a general introduction on the presumed relation between punishment and learning, subjects were told:

But actually, we know *very little* about the effect of punishment on learning, because almost no truly scientific studies have been made of it in human beings.

For instance, we don't know how *much* punishment is best for learning – and we don't know how much difference it makes as to who is giving the punishment, whether an adult learns best from a younger or an older person than himself – or many things of that sort.

So in this study we are bringing together a number of adults of different occupations and ages. And we're asking some of them to be teachers and some of them to be learners.

We want to find out just what effect different people have on each other as teachers and learners, and also what effect *punishment* will have on learning in this situation.

Therefore, I'm going to ask one of you to be the teacher here tonight and the other one to be the learner.

Does either of you have a preference?[. . .]

Shock generator. The instrument panel consists of 30 lever switches set in a horizontal line. Each switch is clearly labeled with a voltage designation that ranges from 15 to 450 volts. There is a 15-volt increment from one switch to the next going from left to right. In addition, the following verbal designations are clearly indicated for groups of four

switches going from left to right: Slight Shock, Moderate Shock, Strong Shock, Very Strong Shock, Intense Shock, Extreme Intensity Shock, Danger: Severe Shock. (Two switches after this last designation are simply marked XXX.)

Upon depressing a switch: a pilot light corresponding to each switch is illuminated in bright red; an electric buzzing is heard; an electric blue light, labeled "voltage energizer," flashes; the dial on the voltage meter swings to the right; various relay clicks are sounded.

The upper left-hand corner of the generator is labeled Shock Generator, Type ZLB, Dyson Instrument Company, Waltham, Mass. Output 15 Volts-450 Volts. [. . .]

Shock instructions. The subject is told to administer a shock to the learner each time he gives a wrong response. Moreover – and this is the key command – the subject is instructed to "move one level higher on the shock generator each time the learner flashes a wrong answer." He is also instructed to announce the voltage level before administering a shock. This serves to continually remind subjects of the increasing intensity of shocks administered to the learner. [. . .]

The experimenter instructs the subject to,

start from 15 volts and increase the shock level one step each time the learner gives a wrong answer.

Feedback from the victim. In all conditions the learner gives a predetermined set of responses to the word pair test, based on a schedule of approximately three wrong answers to one correct answer. In the present experimental condition no vocal response or other sign of protest is heard from the learner until Shock Level 300 is reached. When the 300-volt shock is administered, the learner pounds on the wall of the room in which he is bound to the electric chair. The pounding can be heard by the subject. From this point on, the learner's answers no longer appear on the four-way panel.

At this juncture, subjects ordinarily turn to the experimenter for guidance. The experimenter instructs the subject to treat the absence of a response as a wrong answer, and to shock the subject according to the usual schedule. He advises the subjects to allow 5–10 seconds before considering no response as a wrong answer, and to increase the shock level one step each time the learner fails to respond correctly. The learner's pounding is repeated after the 315-volt shock is administered; afterwards he is not heard from, nor do his answers reappear on the four-way signal box.

Experimenter feedback. At various points in the experiment the subject may turn to the experimenter for advice on whether he should continue to administer shocks. Or he may indicate that he does not wish to go on. It was important to standardize the experimenter's responses to these inquiries and reactions.

If the subject indicated his unwillingness to go on, the experimenter responded with a sequence of "prods," using as many as necessary to bring the subject into line.

Prod 1: Please continue, *or* Please go on.

Prod 2: The experiment requires that you continue.

Prod 3: It is absolutely essential that you continue.

Prod 4: You have no other choice, you *must* go on.

The prods were always made in sequence: Only if Prod I had been unsuccessful, could Prod 2 be used. If the subject refused to obey the experimenter after Prod 4, the experiment was terminated. The experimenter's tone of voice was at all times firm, but not impolite. The sequence was begun anew on each occasion that the subject balked or showed reluctance to follow orders.

Special prods. If the subject asked if the learner was liable to suffer permanent physical injury, the experimenter said:

Although the shocks may be painful, there is no permanent tissue damage, so please go on. [Followed by Prods 2, 3, and 4 if necessary.]

If the subject said that the learner did not want to go on, the experimenter replied:

Whether the learner likes it or not, you must go on until he has learned all the word pairs correctly. So please go on. [Followed by Prods 2, 3, and 4 if necessary.]

Measures

The primary measure for any subject is the maximum shock he administers before he refuses to go any further. In principle this may vary from 0 (for a subject who refuses to administer even the first shock) to 30 (for a subject who administers the highest shock on the generator). A subject who breaks off the experiment at any point prior to administering the thirtieth shock level is termed a *defiant* subject. One who complies with experimental commands fully, and proceeds to administer all shock levels commanded, is termed an *obedient* subject. [...]

Results

Result of Experiment I

With few exceptions subjects were convinced of the reality of the experimental situation, that they were administering shocks to another person, and the most potent shocks were extremely painful. In the post-experimental interview subjects were asked: "How painful to the learner were the last few shocks that you administered to him?" Subjects were instructed to indicate their answers on a printed 14-point scale ranging from "Not at all painful" to "Extremely painful." The modal response was 14 (Extremely painful) with the mean at 13.42.

Many subjects showed signs of nervousness in the experimental situation, and especially upon administering the more powerful shocks. In a large number of cases the degree of tension reached extremes that are rarely seen in sociopsychological laboratory studies. Subjects were observed to sweat, tremble, stutter, bite their lips, groan, and dig their fingernails into their flesh. These were characteristic rather than exceptional responses to the experiment.

One sign of tension was the regular occurrence of nervous laughing fits. Fourteen of the 40 subjects showed definite signs of nervous laughter and smiling. The laughter seemed entirely out of place, even bizarre. Full-blown, uncontrollable seizures were observed for 3 subjects. On one occasion we observed a seizure so violently convulsive that it was necessary to call a halt to the experiment. The subject, a 46-year-old encyclopedia salesman, was seriously embarrassed by his untoward and uncontrollable behavior. In the post-experimental interviews subjects took pains to point out that they were not sadistic types, and that the laughter did not mean they enjoyed shocking the victim. [...]

Upon command of the experimenter, each of the 40 subjects went beyond the expected breakoff point. No subject stopped prior to administering Shock Level 20. (At this level – 300 volts – the victim kicks on the wall and no longer provides answers to the teacher's multiple-choice questions.)

Of the 40 subjects, 5 refused to obey the experimental commands beyond the 300-volt level. Four more subjects administered one further shock, and then refused to go on. Two broke off at the 330-volt level, and 1 each at 345, 360, and 375 volts. Thus a total of 14 subjects defied the experimenter. It is instructive to reprint their remarks at the point of defiance, as transcribed from the tape recordings:

[0124] I think he's trying to communicate, he's knocking.... Well it's not fair to shock the guy...these are terrific volts. I don't think this is very humane.... Oh, I can't go on with this; no this isn't right. It's a hell of an experiment. The guy is suffering in there. No, I don't want to go on. This is crazy. [Subject refused to administer more shocks.]

[0123] He's banging in there. I'm gonna chicken out. I'd like to continue, but I can't do that to a man...I'm sorry I can't do that to a man. I'll hurt his heart. You take your check.... No really, I couldn't do it.

These subjects were frequently in a highly agitated and even angered state. Sometimes, verbal protest was at a minimum, and the subject simply got up from his chair in front of the shock generator, and indicated that he wished to leave the laboratory.

Of the 40 subjects, 26 obeyed the orders of the experimenter to the end, proceeding to punish the victim until they reached the most potent shock available on the shock generator. At that point, the experimenter called a halt to the session. (The maximum shock is labeled 450 volts, and is two steps beyond the designation: Danger: Severe Shock.) Although obedient subjects continued to administer shocks, they often did so under extreme stress. Some expressed reluctance to administer shocks beyond the 300-volt level, and displayed fears similar to those who defied the experimenter; yet they obeyed.

After the maximum shocks had been delivered, and the experimenter called a halt to the proceedings, many obedient subjects heaved sighs of relief, mopped their brows, rubbed their fingers over their eyes, or nervously fumbled cigarettes. Some shook their heads, apparently in regret. Some subjects had remained calm throughout the experiment; and displayed only minimal signs of tension from beginning to end.

Discussion

The experiment yielded two findings that were surprising. The first finding concerns the sheer strength of obedient tendencies manifested in this situation. Subjects have learned from childhood that it is a fundamental breach of moral conduct to hurt another person against his will. Yet, 26 subjects abandon this tenet in following the instructions of an authority who has no special powers to enforce his commands. To disobey would bring no material loss to the subject; no punishment would ensue. It is clear from the remarks and outward behavior of many participants that in punishing the victim they are often acting against their own values. Subjects often expressed deep disapproval of shocking a man in the face of his objections, and others denounced it as stupid and senseless. Yet the majority complied with the experimental commands. This outcome was surprising from two perspectives: first, from the standpoint of predictions made in the questionnaire described earlier. (Here, however, it is possible that the remoteness of the respondents from the actual situation, and the difficulty of conveying to them the concrete details of the experiment, could account for the serious underestimation of obedience.)

But the results were also unexpected to persons who observed the experiment in progress, through one-way mirrors. Observers often uttered expressions of disbelief upon seeing a subject administer more powerful shocks to the victim. These persons had a full acquaintance with the details of the situation, and yet systematically underestimated the amount of obedience that subjects would display.

The second unanticipated effect was the extraordinary tension generated by the procedures. One might suppose that a subject would simply break off or continue as his conscience dictated. Yet, this is very far from what happened. There were striking reactions of tension and emotional strain. One observer related:

I observed a mature and initially poised businessman enter the laboratory smiling and confident. Within 20 minutes he was reduced to a twitching, stuttering wreck, who was rapidly approaching a point of nervous collapse. He constantly pulled on his earlobe, and twisted his hands. At one point he pushed his fist into his forehead and muttered: "Oh God, let's stop it." And yet he continued to respond to every word of the experimenter, and obeyed to the end.

NOTES

1 C. P. Snow, "Either-or," *Progressive* (Feb. 1961), p. 24.
2 S. Milgram, "Dynamics of Obedience" (Washington: National Science Foundation, 25 Jan. 1961.) (Mimeo.)

17

Grief and a Headhunter's Rage

Renato Rosaldo

If you ask an older Ilongot man of northern Luzon, Philippines, why he cuts off human heads, his answer is brief, and one on which no anthropologist can readily elaborate: He says that rage, born of grief, impels him to kill his fellow human beings. He claims that he needs a place "to carry his anger." The act of severing and tossing away the victim's head enables him, he says, to vent and, he hopes, throw away the anger of his bereavement. Although the anthropologist's job is to make other cultures intelligible, more questions fail to reveal any further explanation of this man's pithy statement. To him, grief, rage, and headhunting go together in a self-evident manner. Either you understand it or you don't. And, in fact, for the longest time I simply did not.

In what follows, I want to talk about how to talk about the cultural force of emotions. The *emotional force* of a death, for example, derives less from an abstract brute fact than from a particular intimate relation's permanent rupture. It refers to the kinds of feelings one experiences on learning, for example, that the child just run over by a car is one's own and not a stranger's. Rather than speaking of death in general, one must consider the subject's position within a field of social relations in order to grasp one's emotional experience.

My effort to show the force of a simple statement taken literally goes against anthropology's classic norms, which prefer to explicate culture through the gradual thickening of symbolic webs of meaning. By and large, cultural analysts use not *force* but such terms as *thick description, multivocality, polysemy, richness,* and *texture.*

The notion of force, among other things, opens to question the common anthropological assumption that the greatest human import resides in the densest forest of symbols and that analytical detail, or "cultural depth," equals enhanced explanation of a culture, or "cultural elaboration." Do people always in fact describe most thickly what matters most to them?

The Rage in Ilongot Grief

Let me pause a moment to introduce the Ilongots, among whom my wife, Michelle Rosaldo, and I lived and conducted field research for 30 months (1967–9, 1974). They number about 3,500 and reside in an upland area some 90 miles northeast of Manila, Philippines.[1] They subsist by hunting deer and wild pig and by cultivating rain-fed gardens (swiddens) with rice, sweet potatoes, manioc, and vegetables. Their (bilateral) kin relations are reckoned through men and women. After marriage, parents and their married daughters live in the same or adjacent households. The largest unit within the society, a largely territorial descent group called the *bertan*, becomes manifest primarily in the context of feuding. For themselves, their neighbors, and their ethnographers, headhunting stands out as the Ilongots' most salient cultural practice.

When Ilongots told me, as they often did, how the rage in bereavement could impel men to headhunt, I brushed aside their one-line accounts as too simple, thin, opaque, implausible, stereotypical, or otherwise unsatisfying. Probably I naively equated grief with sadness. Certainly no personal experience allowed me to imagine the powerful rage Ilongots claimed to find in bereavement. My own inability to conceive the force of anger in grief led me to seek out another level of analysis that could provide a deeper explanation for older men's desire to headhunt.

Not until some 14 years after first recording the terse Ilongot statement about grief and a headhunter's rage did I begin to grasp its overwhelming force. For years I thought that more verbal elaboration (which was not forthcoming) or another analytical level (which remained elusive) could better explain older men's motives for headhunting. Only after being repositioned through a devastating loss of my own could I better grasp that Ilongot older men mean precisely what they say when they describe the anger in bereavement as the source of their desire to cut off human heads. Taken at face value and granted its full weight, their statement reveals much about what compels these older men to headhunt.

In my efforts to find a "deeper" explanation for headhunting, I explored exchange theory, perhaps because it had informed so many classic ethnographies. One day in 1974, I explained the anthropologist's exchange model to an older Ilongot man named Insan. What did he think, I asked, of the idea that headhunting resulted from the way that one death (the beheaded victim's) canceled another (the next of kin). He looked puzzled, so I went on to say that the victim of a beheading was exchanged for the death of one's own kin, thereby balancing the books, so to speak. Insan reflected a moment and replied that he imagined somebody could think such a thing (a safe bet, since I just had), but that he and other Ilongots did not think any such thing. Nor was there any indirect evidence for my exchange theory in ritual, boast, song, or casual conversation.

In retrospect, then, these efforts to impose exchange theory on one aspect of Ilongot behavior appear feeble. Suppose I had discovered what I sought? Although the notion of balancing the ledger does have a certain elegant coherence, one wonders how such bookish dogma could inspire any man to take another man's life at the risk of his own.

My life experience had not as yet provided the means to imagine the rage that can come with devastating loss. Nor could I, therefore, fully appreciate the acute problem of meaning that Ilongots faced in 1974. Shortly after Ferdinand Marcos declared martial law in 1972, rumors that firing squads had become the new punishment for headhunting reached the Ilongot hills. The men therefore decided to call a moratorium on taking heads. In past epochs, when headhunting had become impossible, Ilongots had allowed their rage to dissipate, as best it could, in the course of everyday life. In 1974, they had another option; they began to consider conversion to evangelical Christianity as a means of coping with their grief. Accepting the new religion, people said, implied abandoning their old ways, including headhunting. It also made coping with bereavement less agonizing because they could believe that the deceased had departed for a better world. No longer did they have to confront the awful finality of death.

The force of the dilemma faced by the Ilongots eluded me at the time. Even when I correctly recorded their statements about grieving and the need to throw away their anger, I simply did not grasp the weight of their words. In 1974, for example, while Michelle Rosaldo and I were living among the Ilongots, a six-month-old baby died, probably of pneumonia. That afternoon we visited the father and found him terribly stricken. "He was sobbing and staring through glazed and bloodshot eyes at the cotton blanket covering his baby."[2] The man suffered intensely, for this was the seventh child he had lost. Just a few years before, three of his children had died, one after the other, in a matter of days. At the time, the situation was murky as people present talked both about evangelical Christianity (the possible renunciation of taking heads) and their grudges against lowlanders (the contemplation of headhunting forays into the surrounding valleys).

Through subsequent days and weeks, the man's grief moved him in a way I had not anticipated. Shortly after the baby's death, the father converted to evangelical Christianity. Altogether too quick on the inference, I immediately concluded that the man believed that the new religion could somehow prevent further deaths in his family. When I spoke my mind to an Ilongot friend, he snapped at me, saying that "I had missed the point: what the man in fact sought in the new religion was not the denial of our inevitable deaths but a means of coping with his grief. With the advent of martial law, headhunting was out of the question as a means of venting his wrath and thereby lessening his grief. Were he to remain in his Ilongot way of life, the pain of his sorrow would simply be too much to bear."[3] My description from 1980 now seems so apt that I wonder how I could have written the words and nonetheless failed to appreciate the force of the grieving man's desire to vent his rage.

Another representative anecdote makes my failure to imagine the rage possible in Ilongot bereavement all the more remarkable. On this occasion, Michelle Rosaldo and I were urged by Ilongot friends to play the tape of a headhunting celebration we had witnessed some five years before. No sooner had we turned on the tape and heard the boast of a man who had died in the intervening years than did people abruptly tell us to shut off the recorder. Michelle Rosaldo reported on the tense conversation that ensued:

As Insan braced himself to speak, the room again became almost uncannily electric. Backs straightened and my anger turned to nervousness and something more like fear as I saw that Insan's eyes were red. Tukbaw, Renato's Ilongot "brother," then broke into what was a brittle silence, saying he could make things clear. He told us that it hurt to listen to a head-hunting celebration when people knew that there would never be another. As he put it: "The song pulls at us, drags our hearts, it makes us think of our dead uncle." And again: "It would be better if I had accepted God, but I still am an Ilongot at heart; and when I hear the song, my heart aches as it does when I must look upon unfinished bachelors whom I know that I will never lead to take a head." Then Wagat, Tukbaw's wife, said with her eyes that all my questions gave her pain, and told me: "Leave off now, isn't that enough? Even I, a woman, cannot stand the way it feels inside my heart."[4]

From my present position, it is evident that the tape recording of the dead man's boast evoked powerful feelings of bereavement, particularly rage and the impulse to headhunt. At the time I could only feel apprehensive and diffusely sense the force of the emotions experienced by Insan, Tukbaw, Wagat, and the others present.

The dilemma for the Ilongots grew out of a set of cultural practices that, when blocked, were agonizing to live with. The cessation of headhunting called for painful adjustments to other modes of coping with the rage they found in bereavement. One could compare their dilemma with the notion

that the failure to perform rituals can create anxiety.[5] In the Ilongot case, the cultural notion that throwing away a human head also casts away the anger creates a problem of meaning when the headhunting ritual cannot be performed. Indeed, Max Weber's classic problem of meaning in *The Protestant Ethic and the Spirit of Capitalism* is precisely of this kind.[6] On a logical plane, the Calvinist doctrine of predestination seems flawless: God has chosen the elect, but his decision can never be known by mortals. Among those whose ultimate concern is salvation, the doctrine of predestination is as easy to grasp conceptually as it is impossible to endure in everyday life (unless one happens to be a "religious virtuoso"). For Calvinists and Ilongots alike, the problem of meaning resides in practice, not theory. The dilemma for both groups involves the practical matter of how to live with one's beliefs, rather than the logical puzzlement produced by abstruse doctrine.

How I Found the Rage in Grief

One burden of this essay concerns the claim that it took some 14 years for me to grasp what Ilongots had told me about grief, rage, and headhunting. During all those years I was not yet in a position to comprehend the force of anger possible in bereavement, and now I am. Introducing myself into this account requires a certain hesitation both because of the discipline's taboo and because of its increasingly frequent violation by essays laced with trendy amalgams of continental philosophy and autobiographical snippets. [...]

All interpretations are provisional; they are made by positioned subjects who are prepared to know certain things and not others. Even when knowledgeable, sensitive, fluent in the language, and able to move easily in an alien cultural world, good ethnographers still have their limits, and their analyses always are incomplete. Thus, I began to fathom the force of what Ilongots had been telling me about their losses through my own loss, and not through any systematic preparation for field research.

My preparation for understanding serious loss began in 1970 with the death of my brother, shortly after his twenty-seventh birthday. By experiencing this ordeal with my mother and father, I gained a measure of insight into the trauma of a parent's losing a child. This insight informed my account, partially described earlier, of an Ilongot man's reactions to the death of his seventh child. At the same time, my bereavement was so much less than that of my parents that I could not then imagine the overwhelming force of rage possible in such grief. My former position is probably similar to that of many in the discipline. One should recognize that ethnographic knowledge tends to have the strengths and limitations given by the relative youth of fieldworkers who, for the most part, have not suffered serious losses and could have, for example, no personal knowledge of how devastating the loss of a long-term partner can be for the survivor.

In 1981 Michelle Rosaldo and I began field research among the Ifugaos of northern Luzon, Philippines. On October 11 of that year, she was walking along a trail with two Ifugao companions when she lost her footing and fell to her death some 65 feet down a sheer precipice into a swollen river below. Immediately on finding her body I became enraged. How could she abandon me? How could she have been so stupid as to fall? I tried to cry. I sobbed, but rage blocked the tears. Less than a month later I described this moment in my journal: "I felt like in a nightmare, the whole world around me expanding and contracting, visually and viscerally heaving. Going down I find a group of men, maybe seven or eight, standing still, silent, and I heave and sob, but no tears." An earlier experience, on the fourth anniversary of my brother's death, had taught me to recognize heaving sobs without tears as a form of anger. This anger, in a number of forms, has swept over me on many occasions since then, lasting hours and even days at a time. Such feelings can be aroused by rituals, but more often they emerge from unexpected reminders (not unlike the Ilongots' unnerving encounter with their dead uncle's voice on the tape recorder).

Lest there be any misunderstanding, bereavement should not be reduced to anger, neither for myself nor for anyone else. Powerful visceral emotional states swept over me, at times separately and at other times together. I experienced the deep cutting pain of sorrow almost beyond endurance, the cadaverous cold of realizing the finality of death, the trembling beginning in my abdomen and spreading through my body, the mournful keening that started without my willing, and frequent tearful sobbing. My present purpose of revising earlier understandings of Ilongot headhunting, and not a general view of bereavement, thus focuses on anger rather than on other emotions in grief.

Writings in English especially need to emphasize the rage in grief. Although grief therapists routinely encourage awareness of anger among the bereaved, upper-middle-class Anglo-American culture tends to ignore the rage devastating losses can bring. Paradoxically, this culture's conventional wisdom usually denies the anger in grief at the same time that therapists encourage members of the invisible community of the bereaved to talk in detail about how angry their losses make them feel. My brother's death in combination with what I learned about anger from Ilongots (for them, an emotional state more publicly celebrated than denied) allowed me immediately to recognize the experience of rage.[7]

Ilongot anger and my own overlap, rather like two circles, partially overlaid and partially separate. They are not identical. Alongside striking similarities, significant differences in tone, cultural form, and human consequences distinguish the "anger" animating our respective ways of grieving. My vivid fantasies, for example, about a life insurance agent who refused to recognize Michelle's death as job-related did not lead me to kill him, cut off his head, and celebrate afterward. In so speaking, I am illustrating the discipline's methodological caution against the reckless attribution of one's own categories and experiences to members of another culture. Such warnings against facile notions of universal human nature can, however, be carried too far and harden into the equally pernicious doctrine that, my own group aside, everything human is alien to me. One hopes to achieve a balance between recognizing wide-ranging human differences and the modest truism that any two human groups must have certain things in common.

Only a week before completing the initial draft of an earlier version of this introduction, I rediscovered my journal entry, written some six weeks after Michelle's death, in which I made a vow to myself about how I would return to writing anthropology, if I ever did so, "by writing Grief and a Headhunter's Rage..." My journal went on to reflect more broadly on death, rage, and headhunting by speaking of my "wish for the Ilongot solution; they are much more in touch with reality than Christians. So, I need a place to carry my anger – and can we say a solution of the imagination is better than theirs? And can we condemn them when we napalm villages? Is our rationale so much sounder than theirs?" All this was written in despair and rage.

Not until some 15 months after Michelle's death was I again able to begin writing anthropology. Writing the initial version of "Grief and a Headhunter's Rage" was in fact cathartic, though perhaps not in the way one would imagine. Rather than following after the completed composition, the catharsis occurred beforehand. When the initial version of this essay was most acutely on my mind, during the month before actually beginning to write, I felt diffusely depressed and ill with a fever. Then one day an almost literal fog lifted and words began to flow. It seemed less as if I were doing the writing than that the words were writing themselves through me. My use of personal experience serves as a vehicle for making the quality and intensity of the rage in Ilongot grief more readily accessible to readers than certain more detached modes of composition. [. . .]

Grief, Rage, and Ilongot Headhunting

When applied to Ilongot headhunting, the view of ritual as a storehouse of collective wisdom aligns headhunting with expiatory sacrifice. The raiders call the spirits of the potential victims, bid their ritual farewells, and seek favorable omens along the trail. Ilongot men vividly recall the hunger and deprivation they endure over the days and even weeks it takes to move cautiously toward the place where they set up an ambush and await the first person who happens along. Once the raiders kill their victim, they toss away the head rather than keep it as a trophy. In tossing away the head, they claim by analogy to cast away their life burdens, including the rage in their grief.

Before a raid, men describe their state of being by saying that the burdens of life have made them heavy and entangled, like a tree with vines clinging to it. They say that a successfully completed raid makes them feel light of step and ruddy in complexion. The collective energy of the celebration with its song, music, and dance reportedly gives the participants a sense of well-being. The expiatory ritual process involves cleansing and catharsis.

The analysis just sketched regards ritual as a timeless, self-contained process. Without denying the insight in this approach, its limits must also be considered. Imagine, for example, exorcism rituals described as if they were complete in themselves, rather than being linked with larger processes unfolding before and after the ritual period. Through what processes does the afflicted person recover or continue to be afflicted after the ritual? What are the social consequences of recovery or its absence? Failure to consider such questions diminishes the force of such afflictions and therapies for which the formal ritual is but a phase. Still other questions apply to differently positioned subjects, including the person afflicted, the healer, and the audience. In all cases, the problem involves the delineation of processes that occur before and after, as well as during, the ritual moment.

Let us call the notion of a self-contained sphere of deep cultural activity the *microcosmic view*, and an alternative view *ritual as a busy intersection*. In the latter case, ritual appears as a place where a number of distinct social processes intersect. The crossroads simply provides a space for distinct trajectories to traverse, rather than containing them in complete encapsulated form. From this perspective, Ilongot headhunting stands at the confluence of three analytically separable processes.

The first process concerns whether or not it is an opportune time to raid. Historical conditions determine the possibilities of raiding, which range from frequent to likely to unlikely to impossible. These conditions include American colonial efforts at pacification, the Great Depression, the Second World War, revolutionary movements in the surrounding lowlands, feuding among Ilongot groups, and the declaration of martial law in 1972. Ilongots use the analogy of hunting to speak of such historical vicissitudes. Much as Ilongot huntsmen say they cannot know when game will cross their path or whether their arrows will strike the target, so certain historical forces that condition their existence remain beyond their control. My book *Ilongot Headhunting, 1883–1974* explores the impact of historical factors on Ilongot headhunting.

Second, young men coming of age undergo a protracted period of personal turmoil during which they desire nothing so much as to take a head. During this troubled period, they seek a life partner and contemplate the traumatic dislocation of leaving their families of origin and entering their new wife's household as a stranger. Young men weep, sing, and burst out in anger because of their fierce desire to take a head and wear the coveted red hornbill earrings that adorn the ears of men who already have, as Ilongots say, arrived (*tabi*). Volatile, envious, passionate (at least according to their own cultural stereotype of the young unmarried man [*buintaw*]), they constantly lust to take a head. Michelle and I began fieldwork among the Ilongots only a year after abandoning our unmarried youths; hence our ready empathy with youthful turbulence. Her book on Ilongot notions of self explores the passionate anger of young men as they come of age.

Third, older men are differently positioned than their younger counterparts. Because they have already beheaded somebody, they can wear the red hornbill earrings so coveted by youths. Their desire to headhunt grows less from chronic adolescent turmoil than from more intermittent acute agonies of loss. After the death of somebody to whom they are closely attached, older men often inflict on themselves vows of abstinence, not to be lifted until the day they participate in a successful headhunting raid. These deaths can cover a range of instances from literal death, whether through natural causes or beheading, to social death where, for example, a man's wife runs off with another man. In all cases, the rage born of devastating loss animates the older men's desire to raid. This anger at abandonment is irreducible in that nothing at a deeper level explains it. Although certain analysts argue against the dreaded last analysis, the linkage of grief, rage, and headhunting has no other known explanation.

My earlier understandings of Ilongot headhunting missed the fuller significance of how older men experience loss and rage. Older men prove critical in this context because they, not the youths, set the processes of headhunting in motion. Their rage is intermittent, whereas that of youths is continuous. In the equation of headhunting, older men are the variable and younger men are the constant. Culturally speaking, older men are endowed with knowledge and stamina that their juniors have not yet attained, hence they care for (*saysay*) and lead (*bukur*) the younger men when they raid.

In a preliminary survey of the literature on headhunting, I found that the lifting of mourning pro-hibitions frequently occurs after taking a head. The notion that youthful anger and older men's rage lead them to take heads is more plausible than such commonly reported "explanations" of headhunting as the need to acquire mystical "soul stuff" or personal names.[8] Because the discipline correctly rejects stereotypes of the "bloodthirsty savage," it must investigate how headhunters create an intense desire to decapitate their fellow humans. The human sciences must explore the cultural force of emotions with a view to delineating the passions that animate certain forms of human conduct.

Summary

The ethnographer, as a positioned subject, grasps certain human phenomena better than others. He or she occupies a position or structural location and observes with a particular angle of vision. Consider, for example, how age, gender, being an outsider, and association with a neocolonial regime influence what the ethnographer learns. The notion of position also refers to how life experiences both enable and inhibit particular kinds of insight. In the case at hand, nothing in my own experience equipped me even to imagine the anger possible in bereavement until after Michelle Rosaldo's death in 1981. Only then was I in a position to grasp the force of what Ilongots had repeatedly told me about grief, rage, and headhunting. By the same token, so-called natives are also positioned subjects who have a distinctive mix of insight and blindness. Consider the structural positions of older versus younger Ilongot men, or the differing positions of chief mourners versus those less involved during a funeral. My discussion of anthropological writings on death often achieved its effects simply by shifting from the position of those least involved to that of the chief mourners.

Cultural depth does not always equal cultural elaboration. Think simply of the speaker who is filibustering. The language used can sound elaborate as it heaps word on word, but surely it is not deep. Depth should be separated from the presence or absence of elaboration. By the same token, one-line explanations can be vacuous or pithy. The concept of force calls attention to an enduring intensity in human conduct that can occur with or without the dense elaboration conventionally associated with cultural depth. Although relatively without elaboration in speech, song, or ritual, the rage of older Ilongot men who have suffered devastating losses proves enormously consequential in that, foremost among other things, it leads them to behead their fellow humans. Thus, the notion of force involves both affective intensity and significant consequences that unfold over a long period of time.

NOTES

1   The two ethnographies on the Ilongots are Michelle Rosaldo, *Knowledge and Passion: Ilongot Notions of Self and Social Life* (New York: Cambridge University Press, 1980), and Renato Rosaldo, *Ilongot Headhunting, 1883–1974: A Study in Society and History* (Stanford, CA: Stanford University Press, 1980).

2   R. Rosaldo, *Ilongot Headhunting, 1883–1974*, p. 286.

3   Ibid., p. 288.

4   M. Rosaldo, *Knowledge and Passion*, p. 33.

5   See A. R. Radcliffe-Brown, *Structure and Function in Primitive Society* (London: Cohen and West, Ltd.,

1952), pp. 133–52. For a broader debate on the "functions" of ritual, see the essays by Bronislaw Malinowski, A. R. Radcliffe-Brown, and George C. Homans, in *Reader in Comparative Religion: An Anthropological Approach* (4th ed.), ed. William A. Lessa and Evon Z. Vogt (New York: Harper and Row, 1979), pp. 37–62.

6   Max Weber, *The Protestant Ethic and the Spirit of Capitalism* (New York: Charles Scribner's Sons, 1958).

7   The Ilongot notion of anger (*liget*) is regarded as dangerous in its violent excesses, but also as life-enhancing in that, for example, it provides energy for work. See the extensive discussion in M. Rosaldo, *Knowledge and Passion*.

8   For a discussion of cultural motives for headhunting, see Robert McKinley, "Human and Proud of It! A Structural Treatment of Headhunting Rites and the Social Definition of Enemies," in *Studies in Borneo Societies: Social Process and Anthropological Explanation*, ed. G. Appell (DeKalb, IL: Center for Southeast Asian Studies, Northern Illinois University, 1976), pp. 92–126; Rodney Needham, "Skulls and Causality," *Man* 11 (1976): 71–88; Michelle Rosaldo, "Skulls and Causality," *Man* 12 (1977): 168–70.

18

Why Did You Kill?: The Cambodian Genocide and the Dark Side of Face and Honor

Alexander Laban Hinton

Why did you kill? From the first day I arrived in Cambodia to conduct ethnographic research, I had wanted to pose this question to a Khmer Rouge who had executed people during the genocidal Democratic Kampuchea regime (April 1975 to January 1979). When the Khmer Rouge – a radical group of Maoist-inspired Communist rebels – came to power after a bloody civil war in which 600,000 people died, they transformed Cambodian society into what some survivors now call "the prison without walls" (*kuk et chonhcheang*). The cities were evacuated; economic production and consumption were collectivized; books were confiscated and sometimes burned; Buddhism and other forms of religious worship were banned; freedom of speech, travel, residence, and occupational choice were dramatically curtailed; formal education largely disappeared; money, markets, and courts were abolished; and the family was subordinated to the Party Organization, *Ângkar*. Over one and a half million of Cambodia's 8 million inhabitants perished from disease, overwork, starvation, and outright execution under this genocidal regime (Kiernan 1996).

One of my fieldwork goals was to learn how perpetrators could participate in such mass violence. When I interviewed Khmer Rouge cadre and soldiers, however, they all denied killing people outside the context of the battlefield. Finally, in my last month in Cambodia, I arranged an interview with an ex-soldier who had worked at Tuol Sleng, the infamous Phnom Penh prison where at least 14,000 people were confined and then executed during Democratic Kampuchea (hereafter called "DK"), many after being tortured into giving a "confession." One person informed me that the man I was about to interview, whom I will call "Lohr," had once admitted to killing 400 people. Another individual, a surviving Tuol Sleng prisoner, told me that Lohr had in fact executed more than 2,000 men, women, and children. He said that Lohr "was savage like an animal in the forest. I didn't dare look at his face...we were terrified of him." Prior to the interview, I imagined that Lohr would exude evil from head to toe. Lohr was not what I had expected. He was a poor farmer, in his mid-to-late thirties, who greeted me with the broad smile and politeness that is characteristic of most Cambodians.

After we had exchanged pleasantries, I began asking him about his life as a Khmer Rouge soldier. Lohr denied being an interrogator or executioner at Tuol Sleng, but freely admitted to being a guard. In fact, he said he was later given responsibility for receiving new inmates and for transporting prisoners to a killing field located at Choeng Ek, a village just outside Phnom Penh. Lohr emphasized that he did not execute people; he simply transported the prisoners to Choeng Ek and checked off each person's name as he or she was taken away to be killed. The method of execution Lohr described was simple and brutal. One or two Khmer Rouge soldiers would lead a prisoner to a ditch in front of which he or she was ordered to kneel down. A guard would then strike the prisoner once on the back of the neck with an iron bar taken from the axle of an ox-cart. If the person did not die immediately, the soldier would hit him or her repeatedly until the victim fell into the mass grave, which later would be covered with dirt. Lohr said that while the terrified prisoners never tried to escape, they would often beg their executioner: "Please, don't kill me." Some prisoners screamed as they were killed; others went silently to their deaths.

As the interview continued, Lohr recounted how, in 1979, he was arrested and interrogated by district police of the new Vietnamese-backed government. Lohr thought he would surely be killed, so, when the police asked him how many people he had executed, he lied and said, "I am the killer, by myself, of 1,000 people." Lohr claimed he gave this false number in the hope that the police would kill him quickly. Surprisingly, the police just put Lohr in jail for a year and then released him. He returned to his native district in Southern Cambodia where he later married and had several children.

At this point I asked Lohr, "So, during the Pol Pot period you never killed anyone?" Lohr hesitated momentarily and then responded, "I did kill one or two people, but I did this so that others wouldn't accuse me of being unable to cut off my heart." While Lohr's comment that he had killed "one or two people" suggested to me that he had killed many others, I decided not to press him on the matter for fear he would stop giving detailed answers, a pattern I had encountered in other interviews. Instead, I asked Lohr to explain why he had killed the "one or two" prisoners. Lohr replied: "At the time, my boss was also present. . . . As we walked he asked me, 'Have you ever dared to kill one of them, Lohr?' I responded, 'I never have, elder brother.' So he said, 'Like your heart isn't cut off (*chett min dach khat*), go get that prisoner and try it once. Do it one time so I can see.'" Lohr told the soldier who was about to execute the prisoner to give him the iron bar and then "struck the prisoner so they could watch me. I hit him one time with the bar and he fell to the ground. Afterwards, I threw the bar aside and returned to the place where I marked off the names. When my boss asked me to do this, if I didn't do it [pause] . . . I couldn't refuse."

How do perpetrators like Lohr come to commit such genocidal acts? [. . .] This essay, based on 15 months of ethnographic fieldwork in Cambodia, illustrates how Cambodian cultural models related to face and honor, in combination with Communist Party ideology, came to serve as templates for genocide during DK. [. . .]

Hierarchy

Like other southeast Asian cultures, Cambodian society is extremely hierarchical. Relationships in Cambodia tend to be structured vertically in terms of power, status, and patronage. A person's place in the hierarchy is determined by a number of factors, including: age, sex, familial background, birth order, occupation, political position, influence, education, personal character, and financial benevolence. The notion that it is natural for people to be differentiated in the social hierarchy – what I will hereafter refer to as a cultural model of "natural inequality" – has an interesting twofold historical origin. On the one hand, Wolters has suggested that the early inhabitants of southeast Asia were often led by "big men" or "men of prowess" who were "attributed with an abnormal amount of personal and innate 'soul stuff,' which explained and distinguished their performance from that of others in their generation and especially among their own kinsmen" (1982: 6). This conception was then intensified by Hindu notions of potency, power, and hierarchical incorporation. On the other hand, the later introduction of Buddhism reinforced this notion of natural inequality since the Buddhist conception of merit and karma held that an individual's social status reflected the consequences of his or her past actions – hierarchical differences between people were thereby given a legitimizing moral basis (Kirsch 1981).

A consequence of this Cambodian moral order is that one must respect, honor, and obey one's social superiors, a cultural model reflected by the terms *korop* ("to respect, obey, honor," Headley 1977: 132) and, to a slightly lesser extent, *stap* ("to listen [to], to obey," Headley 1977: 1216). Children must thus *korop* and *stap* a parent, younger siblings an older sibling, a wife her husband, students their teachers, younger people an elder, little people a "big person" (*neak thum*), the "have nots" those who have (*neak mean*), prisoners a guard, subordinates their boss or patron, a private his or her officer, party members their political leader, and the populace the government. By extension, we can see that a journalist or editor is expected to respect a high-ranking politician who is his or her social superior (particularly in the case of Prince Ranariddh, who is of royal blood), a point to which I will later return.

Enculturation for this cultural model of obedience and respect begins at an early age. Parents often start teaching their children to greet politely (*sampeah, chumreap suor*) a visitor or elderly family member before the children can walk. Likewise, children are taught to call people by the appropriate pronoun. In contrast to English, the Khmer language is replete with hierarchical terms that differentiate people. When talking to monks or members of the royal family, for example, a speaker must employ a series of unique words that denotes their status. Cambodians thus use different terms when inviting the king, a monk, a guest or social superior, a peasant, a close friend, or a young child to "come eat" (i.e., *saoy, chhan, pisa, houp, nham, si*). Likewise, when Lohr, who was socially subordinate to me from a Cambodian perspective (since I was a "rich foreigner"), came to visit me, he called me "Sir" (*lok*) to acknowledge my status, while I called him "older brother" (*bâng*) to denote his older age. [...]

Status inequality is also embodied in a variety of nonverbal behaviors, one of the most common of which is "bending down" (*aon*) before a social superior. [...] One can see people *aon* in numerous contexts in Cambodia, from the classroom to the Royal Palace. Thus, when I greeted Lohr at my apartment before the interview, as he walked past me he bent down slightly, giving me the respect that he thought was due to someone of my status. As we will see below, both of us gained face by his doing so. The cultural model of a social subordinate giving honor, respect, and obedience to his or her social superior is reflected in a number of other nonverbal behaviors: a subordinate sits lower than a superior, a subordinate must not stare at a superior's face, a host rolls out a mat which allows a guest to sit in a slightly raised position, a subordinate allows his or her superior to walk first, a subordinate should not touch superiors and should get out of their way when they pass, and so on. Like linguistic registers, such hierarchical behaviors are internalized by Cambodians at an early age and are later performed regularly and often without much conscious reflection.

If a Cambodian's place in the social hierarchy is morally legitimized and determined by the factors I have mentioned, his or her position is not absolutely fixed. Though it is often difficult to do, one can enhance one's status in a variety of ways, such as by increasing one's wealth, knowledge, occupational level, political position, influence, and merit. Interestingly, this cultural model of "hierarchical mobility" has historical roots that are similar to those associated with the cultural model of natural inequality. Thus, while a "man of prowess" is regarded as naturally superior to his followers, anyone can potentially be invested with the large amount of "soul stuff" it takes to become such a leader. Likewise, although Buddhist doctrine holds that one's hierarchical position in life is largely determined by one's past actions, this status is not set at birth as it is, for example, in the Indian caste system (Cambodian royalty being the one exception). The merit that a person has accumulated in the past may suddenly result in a rise in status (Hanks 1962).

[...] Because Cambodians want to be respected and obeyed, they vigilantly protect and try to enhance their honor.

Maintaining Face and the Shield

The concept of Cambodian "face" (*mukh, mukh moat*) can be roughly defined as a sociocentric self-image that is based on the evaluations of others and shifts along an axis of honor and shame. The word *mukh* literally means "face, front" but has among its many connotations the notions of "place, position, rank, title" (Headley 1977:748). Face therefore reflects one's place in the social order, a position that is predicated on the extent to which others respect, honor, and obey you. [...] Lurking in the background of any public interaction is thus the fear of exposure and shame. [...]

In any given interaction, the extent to which one fears exposure and shame will depend upon a consideration of who is present, the degree of familiarity and social distance between them, and the type of social situation involved. The stereotype of Cambodians as "gentle" people is one that has most likely come from foreigners who interact with Cambodians in more formal situations in which politeness and smiles are the expected norm. Obviously, Cambodians, like people throughout the world, can be mean and violent in certain contexts, as the DK period and the murder of journalists illustrate. Thus, Lohr, who committed savage and murderous acts as a

Khmer Rouge soldier, acted extremely politely during an interview twenty years later, as is expected when one is meeting with a high-status individual whom one does not know well. Finally, individual variation in face-sensitivity also exists. While most people act in accordance with social expectations, some lack sensitivity to issues of honor and shame and therefore are said to have a "thick face" (*mukh kras*).

Given the strong cultural emphasis on avoiding shame, however, almost all Cambodians are extremely concerned with maintaining face. In fact, social interactions are structured in such a manner so as to buffer people from losing face. I will refer to this set of face-protecting norms and values as the cultural model of "the shield." One of the primary components of "the shield" is the expectation that people will act in accordance with preexisting rules of etiquette and respect. Therefore, as mentioned above, when two non-intimates interact in a formal situation (e.g., my meeting with Lohr), the subordinate person is expected to honor his or her social superior by employing the appropriate linguistic registers, assuming the proper body position and mannerisms, and generally acting in a polite and reverent manner. The subordinate person, in turn, receives honor by acting this way and by his or her superior's response. [...]

By enabling interactions to flow in a smooth and harmonious manner, the orderly performance of social roles and norms of etiquette helps Cambodians observe a fundamental social rule in Cambodia: mutual face-saving. People protect the face of others who, in turn, protect their own. Since one can lose face both by one's own performance and by one's treatment by others, this dimension of the shield adds predictability to social encounters – the knowledge that others will usually avoid any actions or words that might make one lose face.

In addition to being respectful and polite, Cambodian interactions are also often characterized by indirect speech, circumlocution, and the avoidance of conflict and/or sensitive topics. A person who wants to express displeasure (such feelings are frequently just kept to oneself) usually does so through slight changes in posture, facial expression, manner of eye contact, gestures, and tone of voice – shifts that are often almost imperceptible to a foreigner. [...]

This expectation of mutual face-saving created a problem when I interviewed former Khmer Rouge soldiers and cadre. To ask a person directly if he or she had executed people during the Khmer Rouge period would be rude, since the question would put the person in a situation in which he or she could lose a great deal of face. As a foreigner, I had a certain degree of latitude in this regard because of my assumed cultural ignorance. If I was able to slip in such a question, the interviewee would often engage in his or her own face-saving behavior by lying, shifting the topic, and/or withdrawing from the conversation. I generally found it more productive to ask ex-Khmer Rouge if they could guess why people executed others during DK. This type of indirection was culturally appropriate. During my interview with Lohr, we both observed the principle of mutual face-saving until the point at which I asked him if he had killed people. Since he was widely thought to have executed numerous people from Tuol Sleng, Lohr still attempted to avoid a loss of face by asserting he had given a false number to the police under duress and had actually only killed "one or two" people. [...]

Two further dimensions of face should be mentioned. One occurs when a person must respond to a challenge to his or her honor in order to save face; the other concerns situations in which a person interacts with others but does not feel constrained by face norms. Such "anomic behavior" (Lebra 1976) sometimes exists when a person ventures outside his or her known community and feels uninhibited. Anyone who has ever traveled along Cambodia's roads will be familiar with the reckless driving style that often results in the loss of life due to the implicit rule that whoever is bigger and more daring has the right-of-way. One newspaper reported how, after hitting a man with their armored personnel carrier, a group of soldiers simply moved his body over to the side of the road and continued onward (Moeun 1995: 17). Not coincidentally, this type of "heartless" behavior (Goffman 1967: 11) is also characteristic of situations in which a person acts as an anonymous member of a larger group. War is an obvious example, as soldiers are fighting against a generic sociopolitical enemy whom they are expected to kill without hesitation. Finally, if another person acts in a disrespectful manner that makes one lose face (and thus violates the principle of mutual face-saving), one will be more likely to disregard face norms when interacting with that person in the future. [...]

DK Ideology and Hierarchical Transformation

Cambodian society was radically transformed during DK: Buddhism was banned, the family unit undermined, socioeconomic activity communalized, and the political and administrative structure revamped (Chandler 1991; Jackson 1989; Ebihara 1990). Traditional forms of hierarchy were broken down during this process of radical change. In keeping with their goal of creating a peasant-based communist country, the Khmer Rouge claimed that DK was to be an egalitarian society and enacted a number of policies to achieve this end.

First, the Party attempted to suppress linguistic registers which connoted class, kinship, and status differences. While some of the old terms of address remained in use to differing extents in disparate areas, people most frequently called each other by the title "comrade friend" (*mitt*). Children were supposed to refer to their parents as "comrade" or "comrade mother/father." No one was permitted to use the word "Sir" (*lok*) anymore, as one man found when he used this appellation with a Khmer Rouge soldier: "'Don't call me sir, call me comrade,' said the fierce leader. 'No one is called sir after the revolution. We have been fighting to get rid of these words'" (May 1986: 111). Another soldier told the man that such words could not be used anywhere "as long as the High Revolutionary Committee exists" (May 1986: 121). Within this process of linguistic transformation, several terms associated with the urban areas – now regarded as the vile centers of capitalism, corruption, and class oppression – dropped out of usage. Thus, people most commonly used the rural (and, sometimes, urban colloquial) words for such activities as eating and sleeping (*houp* and *sâmrak* versus *nham* and *keng*).

The DK attack on the old hierarchy took place on several other fronts besides language. Many nonverbal behaviors connoting hierarchical difference, such as bending down and politely greeting others, were strongly discouraged during DK. By banning Buddhism, the Khmer Rouge also directly undermined the moral underpinnings of the belief system in "natural inequality." Status differences between men and woman (and the young and the old) were to be eliminated in the new egalitarian ethos. As one informant explained, "Previously women had been the heads of the household and had taken care of the children. During the Pol Pot period, however, this changed. Pol Pot taught that women had rights equal to those of men and thus should do the same work as men." To emphasize this gender equality, women were supposed to cut their hair short, perform strenuous labor on work teams, and dress in the same black garb as men. Finally, in order to do away with capitalism and eliminate the socioeconomic advantages of the wealthy, the Khmer Rouge evacuated the urban population into the countryside, eliminated currency, and communalized work, property, and dining.

Despite such steps to create an egalitarian society, DK nevertheless came to be dominated by new hierarchical elites (Chandler 1991; Kiernan 1996; Thion 1993): Khmer Rouge cadre and soldiers, the rural poor, and the young. Like Maoist China, DK favored peasants and the young because they were regarded as the groups that could most readily be molded into citizens of the new Communist society in which loyalty and obedience were to be given to the Party Organization. "In Maoist terms, these men and woman were 'poor and blank' pages on which a revolution could be inscribed" (Chandler 1991: 243).

Because they were impressionable and in the process of developing their identity (thus making them particularly sensitive about issues of face and honor), children, in particular, received a great deal of indoctrination aimed at socializing them into this Communist ethos. In Southwestern Cambodia, for example, teenagers returning from two-to-three week political training sessions supposedly "were fierce in their condemnation of 'old ways'; rejected parental authority; were passionate in their loyalty to the state and party; were critical and contemptuous of customs; and had a militant attitude" (Quinn 1976: 13). To foster the attainment of such a revolutionary consciousness, the Khmer Rouge attempted to undermine the bonds between parents and children by: linguistic changes, forced separations, difficult work schedules, children's groups, communalization, and antifamily propaganda. Lohr, who was just a teenager when he was indoctrinated into the army, remembers being told over and over: "Don't think about your mother and father, don't be attached to your siblings, just work hard to serve the state."

Like young people, the rural poor who had lived under Khmer Rouge rule during the civil war, often referred to as "old people" (*brâcheachon chas*) or "base people" (*brâcheachon moulâdthan*), were a favored group during DK. Given their traditional disempowerment and class grievances against the urban rich, many of these peasants strongly supported the Khmer Rouge, particularly in 1975 and 1976. By placing such people in positions of advantage and power, the Party received their loyalty and obedience in return. Rural life was idealized in the new, peasant-based, communist society. The cities were emptied; capitalist enterprises were forbidden; and everyone was expected to work, eat, sleep, and speak like a peasant. Because of their "pure" class background, "old people" were the first to be selected to positions of authority and generally enjoyed greater rights than the group at the bottom of the DK hierarchy – the urban evacuees (which included both city dwellers and peasants who had fled to the cities during the civil war), who were called "new people" (*brâcheachon tmey*) or "April 17 people" (*pouk dap brambel mesa*).

Given their suspect urban origins and their support for the Lon Nol regime during the civil war, "new people" were devalued by the Khmer Rouge. While both "old" and "new people" experienced great difficulty during DK, "new people" typically received less food, were allocated worse housing, were subject to more difficult relocation demands, and, perhaps most importantly, were given harsher punishments. With luck, an "old person" might get off with a warning if caught for a crime like stealing potatoes; a "new person" would almost always be killed for doing so. One DK village head told me that he was instructed by his immediate superior, Rom, that "if someone doesn't work hard, breaks a plow or harrow, or steals, he or she may be considered an enemy... in such cases, the guilt of an old person is low, but that of a new person heavy enough for them to be killed." Such comments reflected the Khmer Rouge attitude of distrust and scorn toward "new people." As one city evacuee explained, "To them... we weren't quite people. We were lower forms of life, because we were enemies. Killing us was like swatting flies, a way to get rid of undesirables" (Ngor 1987: 230).

Thus, even though the Khmer Rouge destroyed much of the old hierarchical system, status differences continued to be structured vertically in the Communist regime. A new hierarchy emerged in which the Party leadership was superior to cadre, cadre to "old people," and "old people" to "new people." Differences among the populace were morally legitimized by class as opposed to by merit and karma. The cultural model in which social subordinates gave honor, respect, and obedience (*korop* and *stap*) to their superiors remained operative at this time – the groups occupying the dominant position simply changed. Whereas the wealthy had previously been "bigger than" and "looked down upon" the poor, the situation was reversed in DK. A person's place in the hierarchy was now determined by such factors as his or her class background, political position, revolutionary activity, and loyalty to the Party.

Face in Democratic Kampuchea

Like hierarchy, cultural models associated with face continued to exist in DK. While Cambodian society had always been very public, life in DK was even more extreme in this regard. People were rarely alone due to long work hours in cooperative teams, communal dining, frequent public meetings, and spies who eavesdropped underneath houses at night. Parents even had to be careful about what they whispered to family members, since their children were exposed to Khmer Rouge propaganda that encouraged them to report on "traitors" of the revolution. Within this highly public atmosphere, people were constantly evaluated. The stakes in DK, however, were much higher than before. If a person failed to perform according to expectations, he or she would not just lose face, but would also quite possibly be put in prison or even executed. Positive evaluations, in turn, could result in procuring a better position, additional food, and/or some other advantage for one's family.

Given these dangers, it was imperative for people to keep up "the shield" at all times. Public meetings, for example, constituted a form of ideological face promotion in which people were expected to praise the revolution in an unqualified manner. In addition to singing revolutionary songs and reciting slogans, one "old person" told me that the assembly would listen to cadre "praise the kindness and power of the Revolutionary Organization through whose victory and leadership the construction of the country was progressing rapidly." People were expected to applaud enthusiastically and respond affirmatively to all that was said. If not, the Party and its officials would lose face and the offending person might be accused of being one of the "enemies" (*khmang, sâtrauw*) against whom the speakers spent a great deal of time haranguing. In general, both "new" and "old people" lived in constant fear of insulting their superiors and thus had to vigilantly maintain their "shield." One Banyan villager told me that when people encountered Phat, the head of the local subdistrict office, "We were really frightened, too scared to speak with her. We were afraid that if we said something wrong, she would notice and take us to be killed. She was really mean." Another threat to maintaining one's shield came from the newly instituted criticism sessions in which people would have to criticize themselves and/or endure being criticized by others without putting themselves in danger. Giving offense to a cadre like Phat or being singled out as an enemy in such meetings could mean a quick death.

While face work and the shield remained operative in many situations during DK, there was one context in which they did not – anomic interactions with a sociopolitical enemy. Previously, one encountered enemies in certain specified contexts such as war, law enforcement, and politics. In DK, this cultural model of violence against a sociopolitical enemy, which I have elsewhere called the "violent ethic" (Hinton 1996), was legitimized in everyday communal interactions by Khmer Rouge ideology focused around the metaphor of society being like an army at war (Marston 1994: 110).

Drawing in part on the ideology of Mao's Great Leap Forward, Khmer Rouge radio broadcasts, speeches, slogans, and revolutionary songs frequently referred to the "combative struggle" (*brâyut*) to "build and defend" (*kâsang neung karpear*) the country using military terminology (Carney 1989; Chandler 1991; Ponchaud 1978). This war was to be fought on two battlefields, the first of which was the economic "front lines" (*sâmârâphoum mukh*) on which the people, like soldiers, "launched offensives" (*veay sâmrok*). "The nation was still at war. We didn't just work, we 'struggled,' or else 'launched offensives.' We were to 'struggle to cultivate rice fields vigorously,' 'struggle to dig canals with great courage,' 'struggle to clear the forests' . . . to 'launch an offensive to plant strategic crops,' and 'launch an offensive to perform duty with revolutionary zeal'" (Ngor 1987: 197). Productive activity reflected this military metaphor, as "squads," "platoons," "companies," "battalions," and "divisions" of workers were sent to "struggle heroically" (*tâsou*) on the economic war front.

The second battlefield was national security. While the army fought against external enemies like Vietnam, the people were supposed to defend the country against internal foes who could sabotage the revolution. Party officials likened such enemies to a hidden "sickness" that still needed to be located and destroyed (Chandler, Kiernan, and Boua 1988; Ponchaud 1978). One cadre who underwent political training for three days at the district office recounted being repeatedly told to be on guard against agents of the CIA, KGB, and the Vietnamese who had infiltrated the country: "They asked us, 'Comrade, if your mother or father was such a traitor, would you dare to kill them? Could you cut off your feeling toward them?' None of us could say no. We had to answer that we would dare to do so without hesitation."

Lohr remembers receiving similar indoctrination. He said, "When I was in the army, they taught us to cut off our feeling from the enemy, even if it was our parents. At Tuol Sleng, they reinforced this training even more, telling us that we had to become detached and kill whoever had fault. Even if someone had been our friend before, we couldn't recognize them once they had become an enemy." Both local cadre and members of the general populace I interviewed frequently spoke about how they were told to defend the revolution against internal enemies. As one ex-Tuol Sleng prisoner explained, "That one word, 'enemy,' had great power. It could make a child stop recognizing his or her mother, father, and siblings. Upon hearing the word 'enemy,' everyone became nervous."

As a result of such Khmer Rouge ideology, the "violent ethic" became operative at the local level (Hinton 1996). People were supposed to be constantly on guard against enemies who might be working or eating beside them during the day. The Khmer Rouge used indoctrination to reinforce a cultural model of detachment, "cutting off one's feelings/heart" (*dach chett, dach khat, leng monosânhchetâna*), toward an enemy who, moments earlier, might have been a friend or family member. Once such a person was labeled an enemy, not only was it no longer necessary to feel constrained by face norms when interacting with him or her, but one was expected to treat this enemy in an anomic fashion.

This insight can help us understand the psychology of Khmer Rouge killers like Lohr. When Lohr told his superior that he had never killed anyone, the man questioned whether Lohr could "cut his heart off" from the enemy. Within the paranoid and distrustful atmosphere that pervaded DK, any questions about a person's loyalty to the Party could result in accusations that he or she was an enemy. If Lohr did not kill in this situation, he could have been accused of being a traitor – thus his statement that "I couldn't refuse." As Lohr explained, "I was afraid they would suspect me until they saw me kill with their own eyes, until they saw that I could cut off my heart [and kill]."

The Khmer Rouge attempted to manipulate this cultural model of legitimized, anomic violence against a sociopolitical enemy. Like the Nazis, they set up a bureaucratic system for executing people. Former village heads told me that they were required to maintain two ledgers that listed the names, ages, and former occupations of the people in their village. One was kept in the village; the other was given to the subdistrict office. In many parts of Cambodia, orders were passed down the Khmer Rouge line of command instructing village and district officials to round up those people on the lists who had suspect backgrounds (e.g., intellectuals, "new people," capitalists, former Lon Nol soldiers, police, and officials) and inform them they were to be "taken to a new village." These victims were then transported to extermination centers where they were killed *en masse* by Khmer Rouge who had been told they were killing the enemy. As one "old person" explained, "The executioners would be told, 'today you will destroy enemies that the Party has captured.' When they saw their victims arrive, they didn't think, 'oh, this person is gentle and honest' because the Party had told them that he or she was an enemy. Therefore, the person had to be killed."

Such anomic behavior against "the enemy" was also characteristic of local level executions. While there are certainly exceptions to the rule, life in areas run by cadre with local roots seems to have been generally much better than in places that were governed by strangers, particularly for "old people." In Region 41 of the Central Zone (part of what is now western Kompong Cham province), for example, the frequency of killings dramatically increased when cadre from southwestern Cambodia replaced officials who had ties to the area. The Khmer Rouge seem to have recognized this pattern and, to prevent internal enemies from escaping, tended to place cadre and soldiers without local

links in positions of power. Even if some of the cadre were locals, the ones who did the killings might come from the district office and be rotated periodically. One former cadre who worked with Rom told me that the executioners "killed in the area for fifteen days at most. They changed them for fear that if they worked in one place too long, they would develop attachments there. They executed people like we kill fish. Sometimes they would return laughing and happy. When they looked at their victims, they didn't think they were killing a fellow Khmer, just an enemy." Interestingly, such executions usually occurred at night and in the jungle, a place that is associated with the amoral, uncivilized, and disordered in Cambodian culture (Chandler 1982). In addition to providing secrecy, this "wild" anonymous setting was appropriate for the anomic behaviors that took place as people like Lohr executed enemies to whom face norms no longer applied.

Honor in Democratic Kampuchea

While most people were focused primarily on getting enough food and avoiding execution, the desire to achieve praise and honor nevertheless remained an important motivation during DK. As noted earlier, one's place and ability to rise within the new hierarchy depended upon such factors as: class background, youth, political connections and position, fulfillment of duty, loyalty to the Party, and revolutionary zeal. People continued to evaluate and compare themselves to others, but they did so on the basis of this new criteria of honor which favored the poor, rural "old people," and the young, as opposed to the rich, urbanites, and elders. In addition to giving one respect and authority, being "higher" than others could make the difference between life and death because "big people" had greater access to food and more security (assuming they were not purged and/or did not lose an offensive honor competition). Honor thus remained a scarce resource that was actively pursued by many people.

Perhaps the primary way of attaining honor during DK was to rise in political rank. Cadre like Boan, who arrested a Banyan villager named Vong for stealing potatoes, were viewed as having great honor. Vong said Boan "had honor since he was the village head and the people were scared of him. No one dared make trouble around him for fear he would have them taken away to be killed.

Boan could order us around as he pleased. We went hungry, while he ate his fill." Another Banyan villager stated that such Khmer Rouge cadre had honor "because we had to do whatever they said. They were the law and held total power over the populace. Everyone feared and honored them. The people didn't have much honor, we just thought about work and death." Thus, while circumstances had changed somewhat, people could still gain honor by rising in rank and being given the respect that was due to them. At meetings, people were supposed to praise the Party and therefore, by implication, its local representatives.

Given the advantages of elevating one's position in the DK hierarchy, it is not surprising that people continued to compete for honor. Within structured situations, one could gain praise and perhaps even be promoted for fulfilling one's duty and demonstrating loyalty to the Party. Khmer Rouge ideology, for example, glorified violence done in the name of the revolution (Chandler 1991; Jackson 1989). Blood sacrifice was a frequent theme in political speeches, revolutionary songs and slogans, and even the national anthem, which began with the following lines: "Blood red blood that covers towns and plains / Of Kampuchea, our motherland, / Sublime blood of workers and peasants, / Sublime blood of revolutionary men and women fighters! / The blood, changing into unrelenting hatred / And resolute struggle . . . " The Khmer Rouge exhorted people to defend the country by seeking out and destroying internal enemies, even if the traitor was a parent, spouse, or relative. One person told me a story about a female cadre who arrested her husband after discovering he had been stealing extra food. When the man asked his wife how she could execute her own husband, she replied, "I'm not killing my husband, I'm killing the enemy." My informant explained, "She had been brainwashed to love and be loyal to only the Party."

Influenced by doctrine asserting that violence against the enemy was a virtue, such Khmer Rouge cadre undoubtedly felt that they were fulfilling their duty to the revolution and gaining honor by killing people. Thus, one "new person" who lived in a harsh region of Battambang during DK explained that his cooperative leader, Chev, "killed to feel good about himself. If he purged enough enemies, he satisfied his conscience. He had done his duty to Angka . . . to the ever-smiling Chev, the act of killing was routine. Just part of the job. Not even worth a second thought" (Ngor 1987: 229). Similarly, while Lohr claimed to have had reservations about executing people, he admitted that he did so because it was his duty and "to demonstrate my loyalty to the Party."

Cambodia had always been a culture in which individuals were heavily invested in their roles, since maintaining and elevating one's status depended on performative competence. During DK, such "role commitment" (Lebra 1976: 85) was exaggerated through Khmer Rouge ideology, which encouraged the total renunciation of individualistic ties, behaviors, and ways of thinking (Ponchaud 1978: 114). Everything was to be subordinated to the collective good as defined by the Party. The metaphor of "building" (kâsang) this new mentality was prevalent in DK, as illustrated by slogans such as "Destroy the garden of the individual; build a united garden" (Marston 1994: 114). Those who thought too much about the past or persisted in holding counterrevolutionary attitudes were said to suffer from a "sick consciousness" (chheu sâtearum) and were often executed. In DK, people were supposed to love and be loyal only to the Party. The best way of demonstrating that one possessed this mentality was to perform one's duty in an enthusiastic, wholehearted, and unquestioning manner. Writing about the Japanese, DeVos (1973) has called this type of extreme commitment to and identification with one's duty "role narcissism." When we consider how Khmer Rouge doctrine glorified violence and "role narcissism," we can better understand how people like Lohr, Chev, Phat, Boan, and other cadre might have felt they were gaining honor and pleasing their superiors by killing people whom they regarded as the enemy.

It is also crucial to note that executions usually took place in front of a perpetrator's peers and/or superiors. Within this structured setting, the killers attempted to gain honor through the positive evaluations of others in a manner analogous to student exam competition and to Proh and Rel's work competition. Earlier I noted that during indoctrination sessions and political meetings, Khmer Rouge were repeatedly asked if they would "dare" (hean) to kill an enemy, even if the person was a parent, sibling, spouse, or relative. Such propaganda played upon a traditional cultural model of bravery (klahan) that is an important part of "Cambodian machismo" – the brave who dare gain face, cowards who do not dare are shamed. The Khmer Rouge used this ideology of bravery to facilitate killing. Those who killed were considered to have "defeated" and to be superior to those who did not dare. Proh explained that at extermination centers like Tuol Sleng, the executioners had to "act bravely like everyone else in the group. If just one person was not daring, he or she would be considered a coward, the most inferior person in the group, the one who had lost to the others and was looked down upon. Such people would lose face and honor, and their superior would stop trusting and giving power to them." Similarly, local level cadre like Phat, Chev, and Boan would compete to prove their loyalty to the party by daring to kill people. If they discovered and executed enough enemies, they would gain honor and perhaps even "defeat" their peers by being promoted.

While Lohr no doubt engaged in this type of structured honor competition in some contexts, the incident mentioned at the beginning of this essay is an example of defensive honor competition. By asking Lohr if he had "ever dared to kill" and questioning whether he could "cut off his heart," Lohr's superior was effectively challenging Lohr's honor and loyalty to the Party. If Lohr had tried to avoid killing the person, he would have lost face and perhaps even been subsequently labeled a traitor himself and put to death. Influenced by Khmer Rouge ideology that glorified violence, daring, and role narcissism, Lohr picked up the iron bar and killed "one or two" people. In doing so, Lohr defended his honor and demonstrated his loyalty, daring, and detachment from the enemy. Considering the paranoid ethos of DK, it seems likely that, like Lohr, Khmer Rouge cadre and soldiers throughout Cambodia were at times forced to defend their honor by killing people.

DK was also characterized by frequent attempts to seize power and authority (and thus honor) from others, or offensive honor competitions. For example, when the Southwest cadre arrived in Region 41, they immediately began to purge old cadre and replace their patronage networks with people loyal to themselves. One cadre who survived the purge told me, "The old and the new cadre were competing for authority. The Southwest faction wanted to seize total power so they would have the old cadre followed and carefully watched. If we said something wrong or made even a little mistake, the Southwest cadre would accuse us of being a traitor and have us arrested."

A great deal of tension also existed between the Southwest faction and local soldiers. One officer named Reap attempted to start a rebellion in Kompong Cham city after members of his faction had been jailed, and he realized that his power in the area was being usurped by the Southwest cadre. Reap was arrested and sent to Tuol Sleng. This tension continued with Reap's successor, Chuon. A leading Southwest cadre, Grandmother Yit, reported to the head of the Central Zone that Chuon had helped some "new people" escape and was "going against" him. Chuon denied the accusation and, unlike many Khmer Rouge against whom charges of treason were made, was believed by his superior. In fact, reporting on one's rivals was a common strategy in offensive honor competitions; it was encouraged by the DK regime and constitutes one of the reasons purges and paranoia were so rampant. As Proh explained, Khmer Rouge like "the Southwestern cadre would report to *Ângkar* that their rivals were traitors in the hope that *Ângkar* would drop or kill the accused individual. The Southwestern cadre would gain honor and be praised by *Ângkar* who might even raise their rank." When cadre won such honor competitions, they became even more powerful.

Conclusion: Culture and the Study of Genocide

Culture alone does not "cause" genocide; neither do historical events, sociopolitical transformations, or ideology. A complete understanding of genocide requires a nuanced analysis of how all of these factors interact to generate genocidal behaviors. [. . .]

As illustrated by the fact that these cultural models have not caused genocide in other historical periods, we must recognize that Cambodian culture is not "inherently" genocidal. In fact, culturally distinct models of face and honor exist in most societies, including the United States (Goffman 1967), though face and honor are particularly salient and highly elaborated in Cambodia. Such cultural knowledge only comes to serve as a template for mass violence within a certain context of historical and sociopolitical change. Thus, I noted how the Khmer Rouge initiated a number of sociopolitical transformations that revamped the structure of society. In addition to removing traditional constraints on violence, such changes had the effect of creating a new system of inequality in which certain groups (e.g., "new" people, rich "capitalists," the "enemy," old elites, and "traitors") were disempowered, devalued, and persecuted.

Sociopolitical transformations alone, however, do not necessarily entail genocide. Thus, despite radically transforming society, the Vietnamese Communist revolution did not lead to large-scale genocide (Newman 1978). To generate genocidal behaviors, sociopolitical changes must be accompanied by a violent ideology. In the case of DK, Khmer Rouge ideology glorified violence against the "enemy," promoted the persecution of "new people" and the continued waging of war on the local level, encouraged role narcissism, and invoked the doctrine of "cutting oneself off" from and daring to kill the enemy. Such ideology, in turn, was effective in motivating people to kill precisely because it drew upon preexisting cultural models that were highly salient to many Cambodians. A comprehensive explanation of genocide must therefore take account of how, within a given historical context, sociopolitical changes set up an environment in which mass murder may occur. For genocide to take place, though, these changes must be accompanied by a violent ideology that adapts traditional cultural knowledge to its lethal purposes. This is exactly what happened in Cambodia and, based on my preliminary investigations, in other countries such as Turkey, Rwanda, and Nazi Germany.

Before concluding, I would like briefly to reconsider Lohr's actions. Some people might wonder if Lohr, a soldier, was merely obeying the orders of his superior. As I have illustrated elsewhere (Hinton 1997a, 1997b), there is no doubt that Cambodian cultural models of obedience at times facilitated murderous acts. To reduce all killing to obedience, however, is a dramatic oversimplification of the situation. On the one hand, perpetrators often have a degree of choice about whether or not to participate in killings (Goldhagen 1996). On the other hand, human motivation is multiply determined. If Lohr had refused his superior's order, he might very well have been labeled a traitor and arrested. As I have demonstrated above, however, Lohr had other motives related to face and honor. Like many DK perpetrators, Lohr may also have believed Khmer Rouge propaganda that glorified the violent acts he carried out against "enemies" of the Revolution. As opposed to viewing the actions of such people in a unidimensional manner, we should see perpetrators as ne-gotiating their actions within fields of constraints and inducements that are operative under a violent regime. Individuals who commit murderous acts are usually not just coerced into doing so; they are often motivated by preexisting cultural models that are ideologically or individually adapted to the genocidal situation. The combination of cultural models theory and practice theory that I have used in this essay has made this insight possible and provides one framework for anthropologists to begin addressing the difficult issue of large-scale genocide.

REFERENCES

Carney, Timothy. 1989. "The Unexpected Revolution." In *Cambodia 1975–1978: Rendezvous with Death*, edited by Karl D. Jackson. Princeton: Princeton University Press.

Chandler, David P. 1982. "Songs at the Edge of the Forest: Perception of Order in Three Cambodian Texts." In *Moral Order and the Question of Change: Essays on Southeast Asian Thought*, eds. David K. Wyatt and Alexander Woodside. Monograph Series 24. New Haven, CT: Yale University Southeast Asia Studies.

——. 1991. *The Tragedy of Cambodian History: Politics, War and Revolution since 1945*. New Haven, CT: Yale University Press.

Chandler, David P., Ben Kiernan, and Chanthou Boua. 1988. *Pol Pot Plans the Future: Confidential Leadership Documents from Democratic Kampuchea, 1976–1977*. Monograph Series 33. New Haven, CT: Yale University Southeast Asia Studies.

DeVos, George A. 1973. *Socialization for Achievement: Essays on the Cultural Psychology of the Japanese*. Berkeley: University of California Press.

Ebrihara, May Mayko. 1990. "Revolution and Reformulation in Kampuchean Village Culture." In *The Cambodian Agony*, eds. David A. Ablin and Marlowe Hood. Armonk, NY: M. E. Sharpe.

Goffman, Erving. 1967. *Interaction Ritual: Essays on Face-to-Face Behavior*. New York: Pantheon Books.

Goldhagen, Daniel Jonah. 1996. *Hitler's Willing Executioners: Ordinary Germans and the Holocaust*. New York: Alfred A. Knopf.

Hanks, L. M. 1962. "Merit and Power in the Thai Social Order." *American Anthropologist* 64(6): 1247–61.

Headley, Robert K., Jr. 1977. *Cambodian-English Dictionary, volumes I and II*. Washington, DC: The Catholic University of America Press.

Hinton, Alexander Laban. 1996. "Agents of Death: Explaining the Cambodian Genocide in Terms of

Psychosocial Dissonance." *American Anthropologist* 98(4): 818–31.

——. 1997a. "Cambodia's Shadow: An Examination of the Cultural Origins of Genocide." Ph.D. diss., Department of Anthropology, Emory University.

——. 1997b. "Obedience, Culture, and the Cambodian Genocide." *International Network on Holocaust and Genocide* 12(1–2): 8–12.

Jackson, Karl D. 1989. "The Ideology of Total Revolution." In *Cambodia 1975–1978: Rendezvous with Death*, ed. Karl D. Jackson. Princeton: Princeton University Press.

Kiernan, Ben. 1986. "Kampuchea's Ethnic Chinese Under Pol Pot: A Case of Systematic Social Discrimination." *Journal of Contemporary Asia* 16(1): 18.

——. 1988. "Orphans of Genocide: The Cham Muslims of Kampuchea under Pol Pot." *Bulletin of Concerned Asian Scholars* 20(4): 2–33.

——. 1996. *The Pol Pot Regime: Race, Power, and Genocide in Cambodia under the Khmer Rouge, 1975–79*. New Haven, CT: Yale University Press.

Kirsch, A. Thomas. 1981. "The Thai Buddhist Quest for Merit." In *Clues to Thai Culture*. Bangkok: Central Thai Language Committee.

Lebra, Takie Sugiyama. 1976. *Japanese Patterns of Behavior.* Honolulu: University of Hawaii Press.

Marston, John. 1994. "Metaphors of the Khmer Rouge." In *Cambodian Culture since 1975: Homeland and Exile*, eds. May M. Ebihara, Carol A. Mortland, and Judy Ledgerwood. Ithaca: Cornell University Press.

Moeun Chhean Nariddh. 1995. "Police Blotter." *Phnom Penh Post* 4(3): 17.

Newman, Robert S. 1978. *Brahmin and Mandarin: A Comparison of the Cambodian and Vietnamese Revolutions.* Melbourne: Monash University Centre of Southeast Asian Studies.

Ngor, Haing. 1987. *A Cambodian Odyssey.* New York: Warner Books.

Ponchaud François. 1978. *Cambodia, Year Zero.* New York: Holt, Rinehart and Winston.

Quinn, Kenneth M. 1976. "Political Change in Wartime: The Khmer Krahom Revolution in Southern Cambodia, 1970–1974." *U.S. Naval War College Review* (Spring): 3–31.

Thion, Serge. 1993. *Watching Cambodia: Ten Paths to Enter the Cambodian Tangle.* Bangkok: White Lotus.

Wolters, O. W. 1982. *History, Culture, and Region in Southeast Asian Perspectives.* Singapore: Institute of Southeast Asian Studies.

Part V

The State Amok: State Violence and Dirty Wars

Plate 7: Jade Maiwan Avenue, Kabul, Afghanistan 1996. Photo © Sebastião Salgado, Contact Press Images.

19

Talking Terror

Michael Taussig

...and all the werewolves who exist in the darkness of history and keep alive that fear without which
there can be no rule.

> Horkheimer & Adorno, *Dialectic of Enlightenment*, "The Importance of the Body"

It was at a friend's place in Bogotá in late 1986 that I first met Roberto. My friend is a journalist and had told me she was worried about him. Amnesty International had gotten him a ticket out of the country, but he had not used it, and it was said that he was being shunned by his own political group as unstable. He was in his early thirties, an engineer, who in the very poor neighborhoods in the south of the city had, with a left-wing political group, been organizing meetings on silencing – on the repression of human rights. Together with another of the organizers he had been picked up from the meeting by the army at night, taken away, disappeared, and tortured – this in a country whose army totally denies its involvement in such activities. Thus, where the official voice can so strikingly contradict reality, and by means of such contradiction create fear, does Magical Realism move into its martial form. By a miracle he had not been killed when they put him in a bag, shot him through the head, and left him for dead in a public park. Like the disappeared that return alive in dreams, he had come back, if not to a dream, in the strict sense of the term, then certainly to an unreal life-state in which, being living testimony of what the army was doing, he was in constant fear of being killed and was forced into hiding

while the army mounted a campaign saying he was nothing more than a "vulgar kidnapper." They had taken his papers, without which he couldn't acquire a passport, and his lawyer was adamant that if he went to the DAS (the Security Police) to renew his papers he would never leave their offices alive. After one brief and accurate notice in the country's leading dailies, nothing more had appeared in the media. And while he was desperately afraid of being found, it was the media that, in his opinion, could keep him alive. He had to keep his name alive in the same public sphere that could kill him.

A week or so later I bumped into him in the street carrying the morning's newspaper. He told me he was going to live in Europe, or Canada, in a week. "Don't you know?" he asked. "I was disappeared. The army tortured me for two days then shot me but the bullet passed along the back of my neck." His children were with their mother in a place where there were a lot of people for protection. On hearing I was leaving for a trip west for a week or more with my wife and three children he impressed upon me: "Always make sure that if anything happens to you there will be publicity. Make sure there are journalists who know where you are going. Don't associate with anyone on the Left.

Just be a tourist." To my confusion he added: "Don't wear foreign clothes." He had a file on what he called "my case," and I said I would like to help.

Around five o'clock one afternoon he called without giving his name. "Do you know who is talking?" was his way of saying who he was. He wanted to meet at a busy supermarket and I went straight away. Approaching the meeting I began to feel nervous and scanned the cars for police spies. Everything started to look different, wrapped in the silent isolation of unknowable or ambiguous significance. He was spacing the pavement and I tried to make it look to anyone watching as if it was a delightful and unexpected encounter. He not quite so much. I said I had to buy bread. We entered the supermarket together with many women pushing one another in a ragged queue at the bread counter. I invited him to our place but he wanted to go to his so we walked there, in a roundabout way. There was a public phone on the corner and he asked if I wanted to call Rachel, which struck me as strange and I said I didn't.

He lived in a basement apartment which, to get into, you had to pass through two doors, one after the other, each with two locks. He was clean and neat in a light brown sports coat and open shirt. The corridor leading to the apartment was dark and damp and he took a long time to open the second door. I struggled to find a topic of conversation. We entered into a vault-like space with a thick corrugated milky-green plastic roof over a tiny dining place. The apartment had been the courtyard of a three-storied house. Further inside there was a neatly made dark blue covered double bed with a white clothes cupboard forming one wall. There were three pairs of shoes neatly laid out. It was a friend's apartment and he said he had to leave in two days. More and more the place gave me the feeling of a cage or of a laboratory, with us both keepers and kept, experimenters and subjects of someone's experiment.

He sat me down at the tiny table littered with newspaper cuttings and magazines, a half-empty bottle of *Aguardiente Cristal*, and the remains of a giant bottle of Coca-Cola. There was one upright chair. "What would you like?" he asked. "Whatever you've got," I answered. He moved about awkwardly, groping for something to do, I suppose, and put a cutting in front of me. Very tidily blue-inked on the margin it read *El Espectador* 12.IV.86. There were photos of two young men.

The one on the left was said to have been killed. The second was said to be Roberto, but he was unrecognizable to me without his beard, his mouth bashed wide, and two policemen watching him as he walked through a door. The article repeated what my journalist friend had told me about him being disappeared, and Roberto told me, in wonder, that the very park where the army disposed of him dead inside the bag was where ten years ago he had crash-landed in a plane in which all the passengers died except for him and one other.

As I read, trying to concentrate, I became aware not of being anxious – that would have been too direct, too honest a self-appraisal of what was going on – but of trying to repress wave after wave of foaming fear and thereby, somehow, merely through the awareness of the force of that repression, feeling in control instead of fearful. I remembered how only eleven days before, arriving at the airport at night after a year away from the country, we had been stopped abruptly out on the dark and isolated highway by men saying they were police. They went through our bags as if they were tearing them apart, saying they were looking for arms. Luckily there was a friend in a car behind with the lights on making it, I suppose, harder for them to screw us around and we were able, after showing them our papers from the local university, to resume our journey. "There are stories going around," a friend later told me, "of a certain general's bodyguard dressing up as airport police at night and hitting people up." Other people said it was because of a rumor that an important member of the M 19 guerrilla had flown in that day. Nobody could explain it, of course, but inexplicability is not the best thing to acknowledge in these situations of terror as usual as one fumbles with contradictory advice and rumors. In my notebook I had jotted down a short time later, having listened to many friends talking about "the situation" – "It all sounds so incredibly awful. And after two days I'm getting used to it." Roberto fussed around, poured a shot of *aguardiente* for me and fussed some more with copies of cuttings concerning his case. He couldn't find his keys, and I realized that you couldn't get out without them. Then we found them and he left without a word, the locks grating – all four of them – leaving me alone in the white cage whose door was reinforced on the inside by heavy gauge wire mesh, also painted white. I tried to read on, propelled by some dubious notion that this was being helpful, that this was what he clearly wanted me to do; to witness and to follow, in retrospect, the trajectory and ultimate disappearance of his case and hence his very being through the media trails of the public sphere while all the while there was a fluttering sensation which as soon as I was aware of it went away. It recurred, stronger. I felt I was being set up. I tried to read more but my eyes only flicked over the pages. Not a sound. A few minutes went by. I realized nobody knew where I was other than Roberto. Why hadn't I called Rachel? I looked up at the roof. It was only corrugated plastic. Almost transparent. Surely easy to break through? But then these places were built to be burglar-proof, and looking more closely it didn't seem that easy. But this was absurd. He'd be back soon. I was a miserable coward. I tried to read more of the cuttings. My eye was caught by random phrases, exacerbating the tension – as if all that horrific stuff scattered across the table in the feeble light of the Bogotá gloom filtered through the plastic was about what was about to happen to me. I had premonitions of how I would feel and to what desperate lengths I would go if I panicked. I didn't feel or allow myself to feel panicky at that stage. That was the most curious thing. I saw myself from afar, as it were, in another world, going crazy, not knowing what was happening, what was being plotted, what would happen next, unable to breathe. I looked again at the door with its tough wire. Immovable. It was raining hard. Every now and then a few drops fell through onto my head and neck. I turned back to the crumpled cuttings from the newspapers and the cheap Xerox copies of letters between institutions and government agencies and then, truly, waves of panic flooded over me absolutely unable to move waiting for the police to surge through the door. Any moment. Dark suits. Machine guns waving. Machismo ejaculated in the underground opera of the State. The handcuffs – *esposas*, in Spanish, also means wives – grinding into your wrists. Later, recounting what had happened to friends who lived all their life in Bogatá, I was made to realize that this fear was not without foundation since it is said to be not uncommon for victims of police or army brutality to become informers.

Then the door opened and in came Roberto with a small bottle of *aguardiente*. I was relieved but wanted to leave. The rain drummed down. Even the elements were against my leaving. He pulled up a stool by my side and poured a drink into two tiny olive-green plastic tumblers. "I'm not a drunk, Miguel," he said, and proceeded to tell me how he was tortured, how bad it was when they changed the handcuffs for rope, how he felt like drowning with the wet towel stuffed down his mouth, and what it was like being in the bag and shot but not killed. He leant his head forward almost onto my lap and guided my finger through the hair to the soft bulging wounds of irregularly dimpled flesh. "Like worshipers with Christ's wounds," murmured a friend days later to whom I was telling this.

"Surely the army knows you are here?" I asked. "No!" he replied, "I've learnt the skills of the urban guerrilla," and reaching for a blue writing pad he told me that he spent nearly all his time in the apartment and that he was writing about his case, trying, for instance, to win the attorney general over to his side and not believe in the campaign of defamation spread by the army. The attorney general had served as a judge in the small town in Antioquia where Roberto had been raised – malnourished from the start, he noted, in a large peasant family, and unable to walk until he was 21 months old after which, as a teenager, he had become a famous athlete. All this was in the letter to the attorney general.

He asked what I thought about his case and showed me more correspondence with Amnesty International. I mumbled about people I knew and ways of getting his story publicized, but I felt overwhelmed by the situation. Then he sprung it on me. "Could I stay in your apartment when you leave?" My heart sank. I so much wanted to help but to have him use the apartment would be to endanger a whole bunch of other people, beginning with Rachel and the three kids. I felt the most terrible coward, especially because my cowardice took the form of not being able to tell him that I thought his situation was too dangerous, for that would tear open the facade of normalcy that I at least felt we so badly needed in order to continue being and being together and that he needed to survive. In so many ways I too was an active agent in the war of silencing.

I feel terrible and less than human. I've become part of the process which makes him paranoid and a pariah. I am afraid of the powers real and imagined that have tortured and almost killed him. Even more I'm afraid and sickened by the inevitability of his paranoiac marginalization, people being suspicious of his miraculous escape, interpreting it as a sign of his possibly being a spy. And in the state of emergency which is not the exception but the rule, every possibility is a fact. Being victimized by the authorities doesn't stop with actual physical torture or the end to detention. In Roberto's "case" that's only the beginning. In a way he didn't come back to life at all. He's still disappeared, and only his case exists to haunt me in this endless night of terror's talk and terror's silence.

An hour later I was with my kids at the Moscow Circus, which was playing in a sports arena by one of the freeways ringing the inner city. It was unreal enough, but coming on top of the episode at Roberto's it was devastatingly so. The rain was pelting down outside in the pitch-black night onto the heads of thin-faced hungry people clamoring for attention selling candies and peanuts while, in their rough-cut woolen uniforms the police – perhaps the very ones that had participated in Roberto's disappearance – maintained order with their sad sullen faces as we moved inside into another world where joy and expectancy shone from people's faces, so far from the fears and suspicions outside. Here we were immersed in quickly shifting scenes of clowns, trapeze artists, balance, strength, tension, as the performers spun in their glittering costumes. The pink mobile flesh, firm and muscled, of the acrobats in their gold and silver tights made me think of my finger on Roberto's wounds. Laughter and wonder rippled through the crowd. But what I remember most of all was the beginning. In the shifting tube of light formed by the spotlight in the immense darkness of the arena, two Colombian clowns were arguing with one another and in the process beating up a life-sized female mannequin. They began to tear the mannequin to pieces and beat it onto the ground with fury as the crowd

laughed. Then the lights changed, music blared, and a disembodied voice came on:

"In 1986, this year of World Peace, we are proud to present..."

NOTES

This talk was given to the conference on "Talking Terrorism: Paradigms and Models in a Postmodern World," organized by the Institute of the Humanities of Stanford University, February, 1988.

REFERENCES

Benjamin, Walter. 1969. 'Theses on the Philosophy of History,' in *Illuminations*, ed. Hannah Arendt, pp. 253–64. Schocken: New York.

Bingham, Hiram. 1948. *Lost City of the Incas: The Story of Machu Picchu and its Builders*. New York: Duell, Sloan and Pearce.

Franco, Jean. 1986. 'Death Camp Confessions and Resistance to Violence in Latin America,' *Socialism and Democracy* 2: 5–17.

Hertz, Robert. 1960. 'A Contribution to the Study of the Collective Representation of Death,' in *Death and the Right Hand*. Aberdeen: Cohen and West [first published in 1907].

Mitchell, Stanley. 1973. 'Introduction,' in *Walter Benjamin: Understanding Brecht*. London: New Left Books.

Neruda, Pablo. 1966. *The Heights of Macchu Picchu*, tr. Nathaniel Tarn. New York: Farrar, Strauss, & Giroux.

——. 1976. *Memoirs*. New York: Farrar, Strauss, & Giroux.

O'Gorman, Edmundo. 1961. *The Invention of America*. Bloomington: Indiana University Press.

Vidal, Hernán. 1982. *Dar la vida por la vida: La Agrupacíon Chilena de Familiares de Detenidos y Desaparecidos (Ensayo de Antropología Simbólica)*. Minneapolis: Institute for the Study of Ideologies and Literature.

20

Bodies, Death, and Silence

Nancy Scheper-Hughes

I ground my discussion in the problem of the "disappeared," for the specter of missing, lost, disappeared, or otherwise out-of-place bodies and body parts haunts these pages even as it haunts the imaginations of the displaced people of the Alto do Cruzeiro in northeast Brazil who understand that their bodies, their lives, and their deaths are generally thought of as dispensable, as hardly worth counting at all. In this context even the most interpretive and qualitative of ethnographers becomes an obsessive counter, a folk demographer, her function that of the village clerk, the keeper of the records recording and numbering the anonymous dead and disappeared.

And yet short of a theological meditation on the passions of the soul, what meaning have these empty spaces, these missing and disappeared bodies? I hope to show the difference they make when the everyday, lived experience of a large number of threatened people is introduced into current debates on the state, the politics of fear, and the problem of the disappeared.

The Breakdown of Consensus

The multiple and contradictory social realities of Bom Jesus and its surrounds contribute to fleeting perceptions of the community as a ruthless, unstable, amoral place. There is a sense of almost desperate vitality and of chaos threatening to unleash itself, so that Bom Jesus sometimes feels like a place where almost anything can happen. If there are rules to discipline and govern public interactions, they appear to exist only in the negative,

to be violated, scoffed at. Only fools would obey a stop sign; never mind that the slow and fussy *solteirona* (old maid) of the Chaves family was knocked down by a speeding Fiat as she tried to cross the main *praça* of Bom Jesus on her way home from Mass. The obvious contradictions do at times rise to the surface and threaten a social consensus that is, at best, tentative and fragile. The guise of civility is rent by sudden explosions of violence, some apparently calculated, others merely reactive.

In 1986 the children of one of the wealthiest landowners in Bom Jesus were kidnapped in front of their home in broad daylight by masked *desperados* – angry "social bandits" from the interior of the state – who later demanded, and received, a huge ransom. The band of unemployed field hands then declared "war on the greedy *latifundiários*."

During the 1987 drought hungry rural workers throughout the *zona da mata* began looting stores, warehouses, and train depots, thereby forcing the governor of Pernambuco to send emergency rations to divert the looters. In an interview with the press the governor blamed the looting on the expulsion of rural workers from their *roçados*, which led to a "savage, violent, and disorderly urbanization" (Riding 1988: 1-A4), an "occupation and siege" mentality evidenced in the social geography of shantytown "invasions" and squatter camps throughout the state.

Several young men of the Alto do Cruzeiro, each of them black, young, and in trouble with the law for petty theft, drunkenness, vagrancy, glue sniffing, and other infractions, were seized from their homes just after Christmas in 1987 by unidentified men "in uniform" and were "disappeared." A few weeks later two of the bodies were found slashed, mutilated, and dumped between rows of sugarcane. The police arrived with graphic photos for family members. "How do you expect me to recognize *meu homem* [my man] in this picture?" Dona Elena screamed hysterically. Similar events were repeated in 1988 and 1989. Finally they came late one night for the teenage son of Black Irene, the boy everyone on the Alto knew affectionately as Nego De. The existence of paramilitary "death squads" with close ties to the local police force is suspected, but on this topic people are generally silent; if and when they do speak, it is in a rapid and complicated form of sign language. No one else wants to be marked.

In February 1987 Evandro Cavalcanti Filho, a young lawyer for the Pernambucan rural workers syndicate, representing 120 peasant families in dispute with local landowners in the area of Surubim, was shot dead in front of his wife and children on the patio of their home. One of the gunmen (a suspected informant) was shot and killed by military police.

One year later, in February 1988, a small group of *posseiros*, traditional squatters using the abandoned and marginal fields of a local plantation called the Engenho Patrimônio, a few miles outside of Bom Jesus, were ambushed by *capangas*, hired gunmen in the employ of the *senhor latifundiário*. The peasants were quietly tending their *roçados* when the gunmen opened fire without warning. One peasant was maimed; another, a 23-year-old father of a small family, was killed.

In 1989 rumors surfaced concerning the disappearance of street children, *meninos da rua* and *moleques*, several of whom lived in the open-air marketplace, took shelter at night in between the stalls and under canvas awnings, and helped themselves to bits of produce from crates and baskets. Even though many of the vendors were tolerant of the hungry street urchins, others enlisted the help of the local police in a local "pest control" campaign.

Throughout all, Bom Jesus da Mata continued to perceive itself as a quiet, peaceable interior town in the *zona da mata*, far from the violence and chaos of the large cities on the coast. As the initial excitement of each incident blew over, life resumed its normal course. The kidnappers were apprehended and the frightened children returned to their parents, but only a fraction of the ransom money was recovered. The sacking and looting of markets continued throughout the *zona da mata*, and a state of emergency was declared just before Holy Week in 1988, when suddenly the skies opened and torrential rains swept many Alto residents from their homes, which disappeared down rushing ravines of the shantytown. The *castigo* of drought was replaced by the *castigo* of floods. "Life is harsh. Man makes, but God destroys," said the *moradores* of the Alto do Cruzeiro philosophically.

The hired gunmen from the Engenho Patrimônio were arrested and then freed immediately on bail. The owner of the *engenho* was never cited or brought to trial. As of 1989 three ex-military police officers were in prison awaiting trial for the murder of Evandro Cavalcanti, but the special investigator appointed to the inquiry had resigned from the case, and another one had not been appointed. The disappearance of young black men continues on the Alto do Cruzeiro and in other poor *bairros* of Bom Jesus and is treated as a nonissue, not even thought worthy of a column in the mimeographed opposition newspaper of Bom Jesus. "Why should we criticize the 'execution' of *malandros* [good-for-nothings], rogues, and scoundrels?" asked a progressive lawyer of Bom Jesus and a frequent contributor to the alternative liberal newspaper. "The police have to be free to go about their business," said Mariazinha, the old woman who lived in a small room behind the church and who took care of the altar flowers. "The police know what they're doing. It's best to keep your mouth shut," she advised, zipping her lips to show me exactly what she meant.

Padre Agostino Leal shook his head sadly. "Is it possible that they murdered Nego De? What a shame! He was in reform. I trusted him. He even attended my Wednesday night Criminals' Circle." Then, after a pause, the good padre added ruefully, "I guess it was just too late for Nego De."

Violence and the Taken-for-Granted World

The tradition of the oppressed teaches us that the "state of emergency" in which we live is not the exception but the rule. We must attain to a conception of history that is in keeping with this insight.... One reason why Fascism has a chance is that in the name of progress its opponents treat it as a historical norm.

Walter Benjamin (cited in Taussig 1989: 64)

Writing about El Salvador in 1982, Joan Didion noted in her characteristically spartan prose that "the dead and pieces of the dead turn up everywhere, everyday, as taken-for-granted as in a nightmare or in a horror movie" (1982: 9). In *Salvador* there are walls of bodies; they are strewn across the landscape, and they pile up in open graves, in ditches, in public restrooms, in bus stations, along the sides of the road. "Vultures, of course, suggest the presence of a body. A knot of children on the street suggest the presence of a body" (9). Some bodies even turn up in a place called Puerto del Diablo, a well-known tourist site described in Didion's inflight magazine as a location "offering excellent subjects for color photography."

It is the anonymity and the routinization of it all that strikes the naive reader as so terrifying. Who are all these *desaparecidos* – the unknown and the "disappeared" – both the poor souls with plucked eyes and exposed, mutilated genitals lying in a ditch and those unidentifiable men in uniform standing over the ditches with guns in their hands? It is the contradiction of wartime crimes against ordinary peacetime citizens that is so appalling. Later we can expect the unraveling, the recriminations, the not-so-guilty confessions, the church-run commissions, the government-sponsored investigations, the arrests of tense and unyielding men in uniform, and finally the optimistic reports – Brazil, Argentina (later, perhaps even El Salvador) *nunca mais*. Quoth the raven, "*Nunca mais*." After the fall, after the aberration, we expect a return to the normative, to peacetime sobriety, to notions of civil society, human rights, the sanctity of the person (Mauss's *personne morale*), *habeas corpus*, and the unalienable rights to the ownership of one's body.

But here I intrude with a shadowy question. What if the disappearances, the piling up of civilians in common graves, the anonymity, and the routinization of violence and indifference were not, in fact, an aberration? What if the social spaces before and after such seemingly chaotic and inexplicable acts were filled with rumors and whisperings, with hints and allegations of what could happen, especially to those thought of by

agents of the social consensus as neither persons nor individuals? What if a climate of anxious, ontological insecurity about the rights to ownership of one's body was fostered by a studied, bureaucratic indifference to the lives and deaths of "marginals," criminals and other no-account people? What if the public routinization of daily mortifications and little abominations, piling up like so many corpses on the social landscape, provided the text and blueprint for what only appeared later to be aberrant, inexplicable, and extraordinary outbreaks of state violence against citizens?

In fact, the "extraordinary" outbreaks of state violence against citizens, as in Didion's *Salvador*, during the Argentine "Dirty War" (Suarez-Orozco 1987, 1990), in Guatemala up through the present day (Paul 1988; Green 1989), or in the harshest period following the Brazilian military coup of 1964 (Dassin 1986) entail the generalizing to recalcitrant members of the middle classes what is, in fact, normatively practiced in threats or open violence against the poor, marginal, and "disorderly" popular classes. For the popular classes every day is, as Taussig (1989) succinctly put it, "terror as usual." A state of emergency occurs when the violence that is normally contained to that social space suddenly explodes into open violence against the "less dangerous" social classes. What makes the outbreaks "extraordinary," then, is only that the violent tactics are turned against "respectable" citizens, those usually shielded from state, especially police, terrorism.

If, in the following ethnographic fragments, I seem to be taking an unduly harsh and critical view of the "state" of things in Brazil, let me hasten to say at the outset that I view this interpretation as generalizable to other bureaucratic states at a comparable level of political-economic "development" and in a different form to those characterized by a more "developed" stage of industrial capitalism such as our own. Violence is also "taken for granted" and routinized in parts of our police underworld operating through SWAT team attacks on suspected crack houses and crack dealers in inner-city neighborhoods. And state terrorism takes other forms as well. It is found in the cool jargon of nuclear weapons researchers, our own silent, yet deadly, technicians of practical knowledge. Carol Cohn (1987) penetrated this clean, closed world and returned with a chilling description of the way our nuclear scientists have created a soothing and normalizing discourse with which to discuss our government's capacity for blowing populations of bodies to smithereens. "Bio-power," indeed.

I share with Michel Foucault his suspiciousness of the state as a social formation that spawns what Franco Basaglia (1987a) called the official and legalized "institutions of violence." Yet Foucault (1979) believed that public spectacles of torture and execution had gone the way of the ancien régime. The use of torture by the state, associated with criminal proceedings, was abolished throughout the Western world in the eighteenth and nineteenth centuries, so that Victor Hugo could confidently announce in 1874 that "torture has ceased to exist" (Peters 1985: 6). In Foucault's analysis, the mutilated body as the icon of state repression and control gave way to the more aestheticized and spiritualized character of public discipline, regulation, and punishment. The retreat from the body allowed for new assaults on the mind and the moral character of citizens. The new objects of discipline and surveillance were the passions, will, thought, and desire.

In advanced industrialized societies and in modern, bureaucratic, and welfare states, the institutions of violence generally operate more covertly. A whole array of educational, social welfare, medical, psychiatric, and legal experts collaborate in the management and control of sentiments and practices that threaten the stability of the state and the fragile consensus on which it claims to base its legitimacy. We can call these institutions, agents, and practices the "softer" forms of social control, the gloved hand of the state. But even the most "advanced" state can resort to threats of violence or to open violence against "disorderly" citizens whenever the normal institutions for generating social consensus are weakening or changing. I think that this is the situation we are rapidly approaching today in the United States with respect to the general tolerance of violent police actions in our urban inner cities on behalf of combating the "drug war."

The Brazilian state has been thrown into considerable turmoil in recent years by the democratic "awakenings" of previously excluded and alienated populations to new forms of political praxis and mobilization in the proliferation of highly politicized shantytown associations, mothers clubs, squatters unions, rural workers defense leagues, and so on, many of these supported by the clergy

and hierarchy of the "new" Catholic church. The changing allegiance of the Catholic church, which, following the Latin American Bishops' Conference at Medellín withdrew much of its traditional support from the traditional landowning and industrial political-economic elite of Brazil, produced a crisis. Bishops and clergy throughout the country have in the last decade increasingly taken the side of peasants, squatters, Indians, and small landholders in disputes with *latifundários* and multinational companies, and they have publicly denounced the use of violence in extracting forced labor from plantation workers and in evicting peasants from their traditional holdings. In 1980 the Brazilian National Bishops' Conference released a statement that implicated not only landowners and hired *pistoleiros* in perpetrating the violence but also the state itself: "There is ample proof that such violence involves not only hired thugs and professional gunmen, but also the police, judges, and officers of the judiciary" (cited in Amnesty International 1988: 3). The result was a stepped-up campaign of police-initiated harassment culminating in the murder of priests and religious sisters associated with rural trade unions, land rights claims, and shantytown associations throughout Brazil.

Northeast Brazil is still at a transitional stage of state formation that contains many traditional and semifeudal structures, including its legacy of local political bosses (*coroneis*) spawned by an agrarian *latifundista* class of powerful plantation estate masters and their many dependents (see Lewin 1987). To this day most sugar plantation estates are protected by privately owned police forces or at least by hired *pistoleiros*. The web of political loyalties among the intermarried big houses and leading families of the interior leads directly to the governor and to the state legislature, which is still controlled by a traditional agrarian oligarchy. Consequently, civil police, appointed by local politicians, often collaborate with hired gunmen in the employ of the plantation estates owners and sometimes participate themselves in the operations of the "death squads," a widespread and pernicious form of police "moonlighting" in Brazil.

One could compare the semifeudal organization of contemporary Northeast Brazil with Anton Blok's (1974) description of the state and state terrorism in Sicily in the early decades of the twentieth century. In both cases state power is mediated through a class of landholding intermediaries and their hired guns: the *coroneis* and their *capangas* in the Brazilian case and the *gabelotti*, the wealthy leaseholders and landlords who supported the rural mafia, in the Sicilian case. The Sicilian mafia evolved in the late nineteenth and early twentieth centuries when the modern state superimposed itself on a marginal peasant society that was still feudal in its basic features. The mafia served as a kind of modus vivendi mediating the claims of the new state apparatus with traditional landowners and big men. Acts of graphic public violence underscored the authority of the traditional power elite and of the newly emergent state as well.

Similarly, northeast Brazil has not yet produced the range of modern social institutions, scientific ideologies, or specialized "technicians of practical knowledge" (a term first used by Sartre) to manage and individualize (and so contain) public expressions of dissent and discontent. The health and social welfare agencies, psychiatric clinics, occupational therapies, or varieties of counseling that help to bolster a wavering consent to the prevailing order of things are not yet completely in place. Clinical medicine in the interior of Brazil is fairly brutal and unsophisticated in its goals and techniques. In the interior of northeast Brazil there are only the police, a judiciary that has generally failed to prosecute cases of police brutality, the prison, the FEBEM federal reform schools for criminalized or simply marginalized youth, and the local death squads, all of them violent institutions.

There are three public security and law enforcement institutions in Brazil: the federal, civil, and military police. The federal police, under the jurisdiction of the Ministry of Justice, supervises immigration, protects the national frontiers, and investigates the black market and drug contraband in the country. Civil police are generally under the jurisdiction of the *município*, and the chief of police (*delegado de polícia*) is usually appointed by the mayor and is financially dependent on him and the town councilmen. In addition to the officially appointed civil police, a large number of ex-officio *vigias* (night watchmen) are nominated or tacitly approved by the chief of police. *Vigias* patrol virtually every *bairro* of Bom Jesus and are supported by weekly "dues" collected (or extracted) from each household on their beat. All *vigias* and most civil police have no formal training, and most are recruited from the poorer social classes. Often civil police and *vigias* are

difficult to distinguish from thugs and vigilantes. In addition to these is the military police, which, under the jurisdiction of both the army and the state, is responsible for maintaining public order and security. It is the military police that is usually called on to enforce, often with violence, the evictions of traditional squatters. Throughout the years of the dictatorship (1964–85), military police officers were heavily implicated in the disappearances, tortures, and deaths of suspected subversives in Bom Jesus as elsewhere in Brazil. The process of democratization has been painfully slow and has yet to challenge the local presence and the fearful psychological hold of the military police over the poorer populations (Amnesty International 1988, 1990). Consequently, poor *Nordestinos* have been living for many years with state violence and threats of violence. The alternative to "softer" forms of persuasion and control is direct attack on citizens: arrest and interrogation, imprisonment, disappearance, and, finally, torture, mutilation, and killing.

At certain levels of political-economic development – and the sugar plantation zone is one of these – violence and threats or fear of violence are sufficient to guarantee the "public order." In any case, violence is the only technique of public discipline available to a military government such as the one that ruled Brazil for twenty-one years and that still plays an important role in the state today. The military is not an educational, charitable, or social welfare institution; violence is intrinsic to its nature and logic. Violence is usually the only tactic the military has at its disposal to control citizens even during peacetime (see also Basaglia 1987b: 143–68).

One of the ways that modern military dictatorships have legitimized the use of violent acts against citizens is through the legal loophole of the *crimen exceptum* – that is, the "extraordinary crime" that warrants extraordinary and often cruel punishment. The concept may be extended to extraordinary situations warranting extraordinary measures to protect the state. And so, paradoxically, during an era of expansion and centralization in which the Brazilian state commands great strength and power to mobilize vast resources, state policy is nonetheless based on a concept of extreme vulnerability. The fear of subversive or simply of criminal activity can become obsessional (see Suarez-Orozco 1987 and Chapter 49), and torture may be used in an attempt to assert, as Elaine Scarry put it, the "incontestable reality" of a particular state's control over the population. "It is, of course," she continued, "precisely because the reality of power is so highly contestable, the regime so unstable, that torture is being used" (1985: 27). And so I have borrowed Franco Basaglia's notion of "peacetime crimes" as a way of addressing the routinization of violence in everyday aspects of contemporary *Nordestino* society.

What, then, is the rationale for turning a military, wartime arsenal against private citizens. What crimes have they committed (or do they threaten to commit)? What makes some citizens assume the character of "threats" or "dangers" to the state so as to make violence an acceptable form of social control, the legitimate "business" of the police? (Remember the words of Mariazinha, the religious spinster: "The police have to be free to go about their business.") The "dangerousness" of the poor and marginal classes derives directly from their condition of desperate want. Hunger and need always pose a threat to the artificial stability of the state. Following Basaglia (1987a: 122), we can say that the marginals of the Alto do Cruzeiro are guilty of "criminal needs."

In the specific instance of the *posseiros* (peasants who, by Brazilian law, acquire *legal* tenure in unused, though privately owned, plantation lands) who were ambushed by hired gunmen working for the owner of Engenho Patrimônio, the squatters were "executed" by criminals who were never brought to trial. The "crimes" of the poor, of the desperate – of the *posseiro* whose very way of life stands as a negation of "modern," bourgeois notions of property rights or of Nego De, whose petty thievery helped maintain his mother and siblings after the murder of his father – are understood as "race" crimes and as "naturally," rather than socially, produced. Nego De and other poor, young black men like him steal because it is thought to be in their "nature," "blood," or "race" to steal. They are *malandros*, and they are described in racist terms as *bichos da Africa*. Their crimes can be punished with impunity and without due process. *Posseiros*, with their precapitalist notions of "the commons," are viewed as dangerous retrogrades, and the gunmen contracted to kill them do so with the full, often explicit, understanding and tacit approval of the local police. Those few gunmen who are apprehended usually escape from jail with the help of local prison guards.

Meanwhile, the violent crimes of the wealthy classes are understood and forgiven as socially produced. Landowners must "protect" their patrimonies; politicians are "put into" totally corrupting situations. Lies and bribes are endemic to politics; they are part of the "game" of power. People are surprised to find an honest political leader or a fair and just employer. There is no such cultural and political immunity for the peasant squatters who occupy lands because they have no other way to survive or for Nego De, who was better able to sustain a large and desperate household by stealing than by "honest" work for one dollar a day in the cane fields. Although these are crimes of need, they are neither excused nor understood in social terms. Instead, they are seen as base, instinctual crimes that are natural to an "inferior" and "mulatto" population.

Increasingly today race and racial hatred have emerged as subliminal subtexts in the popular discourses that justify violent and illegal police actions in shantytown communities. Remnants of the older racial "harmony ideology" of *Nordestino* plantation society still render it "impolite" for the powerful and educated classes to comment in public on racial differences (while in private and behind closed doors racist discourse is rampant and particularly grotesque and virulent). But this same "polite" society can thereby fail to see, fail to recognize, that police persecution is now aimed at a specific segment and shade of the shantytown population. Even my radical black friend, João Mariano, was profoundly embarrassed when I raised the question of the racial nature of Alto disappearances at a study group formed by the small, literate, leftist intelligentsia of Bom Jesus, and the discussion was tabled.

Here we can begin to see the workings of a hegemonic discourse on criminality/deviance/marginality and on the "appropriateness" of police and state violence in which all segments of the population participate and to which they acquiesce, often contrary to their own class or race interests. How is this extraordinary consensus forged, and how is it maintained in the face of living (and dying) contradictions? Why is there so little expressed (or even submerged and seething) outrage against police and death squad terrorism in the shantytown? Why is there no strongly articulated human rights position among even the most progressive forces and parties of Bom Jesus?

What has made the people of the Alto so fearful of democratic and liberal reforms?

In an attempt to answer these questions my analysis proceeds in two directions: ideology and practice. The first, relying heavily on the writings of contemporary Brazilian social scientists, concerns the political ideology of democracy, the state, and citizenship in Brazil. The second, based on my observations of everyday life in Brazil, explores the mundane rituals and routines of humiliation and violence that assault the bodies and minds of the *moradores* as they go about the complicated business of trying to survive. Both tend to reinforce an acceptance of "terror as usual."

Citizenship and Justice in Brazil

Brazil's system of criminal justice is a "mixed system" containing elements of both the American and the European civil law tradition (Kant 1990). Contrary to the American system, there is no common-law tradition whereby precedents and jury verdicts can actually participate, in conjunction with the legislature, in making the law. And in addition to many modern, egalitarian, and individual rights protected by the Brazilian criminal justice system (such as the right to counsel and to *ampla defesa* – that is, the right to produce any possible evidence on equal footing with the prosecution), there are other, more traditional, and less liberal traditions. First among these is the tradition of progressing from a position of "systematic suspicion," rather than from an assumption of innocence, and, relatedly, the judge's "interrogation" of the accused relying on information produced by prior police investigations that are "inquisitorial" in nature. In the words of one police chief interviewed by Roberto de Lima Kant, police interrogations entail "a proceeding *against everything* and *everyone* to find out the *truth* of the facts" (1990: 6). Within this inquisitorial system, "torture becomes a legitimate – if unofficial – means of police investigation for obtaining information or a confession" (7). In all, "Brazilian criminal proceedings are organized to show a gradual, step by step, ritual of progressive incrimination and humiliation, the outcome of which must be either the confession or the acquittal. The legal proceedings are represented as a punishment in themselves" (22).

Within this political and legal context, one can understand the *moradores'* awesome fear of the judicial system and their reluctance to use the courts to redress even the most horrendous violations of their basic human rights. And, as Teresa Caldeira (1990) noted, the first stirrings of a new political discourse on "human rights," initiated by the progressive wing of the Catholic church and by leftist political parties in Brazil in the late 1970s and early 1980s and fueled in part by the international work of Amnesty International, was readily subverted by the Right. Powerful conservative forces in Brazil translated "human rights" into a profane discourse on special favors, dispensations, and privileges for criminals. Worse, the Brazilian Right played unfairly on the general population's fears of an escalating urban violence. These fears are particularly pronounced in poor, marginalized, and shantytown communities. And so, for example, following a 1989 presidential address broadcast on the radio and over loudspeakers in town announcing much-needed proposed prison reforms in Brazil, the immediate response of many residents of the Alto seemed paradoxical. Black Zulaide, for example, began to wail and wring her hands: "Now we are finished for sure," she kept repeating. "Even our president has turned against us. He wants to set all the criminals free so that they can kill and steal and rape us at will." It seemed to have escaped Black Zulaide that her own sons had at various times suffered at the hands of police at the local jail and that the prison reform act was meant to protect *her* class in particular. Nevertheless, Zulaide's fears had been fueled by the negative commentary of the police, following the broadcast, on the effects these criminal reforms would have on the people of Bom Jesus but especially on those living in "dangerous" *bairros* such as the Alto do Cruzeiro and needing the firm hand of the law to make life minimally "safe."

Similarly, Teresa Caldeira offered two illustrations of right-wing ideological warfare that equated the defense of human rights with the defense of special privileges for criminals. The first is from the "Manifesto of the Association of Police Chiefs" of the state of São Paulo, which was addressed to the general population of the city on October 4, 1985. The manifesto takes to task the reformist policies of the then-ruling central-leftist political coalition, the PMDB:

The situation today is one of total anxiety for you and total tranquility for those who kill, rob, and rape.

Your family is destroyed and your patrimony acquired with much sacrifice is being reduced.... How many crimes have occurred in your neighborhood, and how many criminals were found responsible for them?... The bandits are protected by so called human rights, something that the government considers that you, an honest and hard working citizen, do not deserve. (1990: 6)

Her second example is taken from an article published on September 11, 1983, in the largest daily newspaper of São Paulo, *A Folha de São Paulo*, written by an army colonel and the state secretary of public security:

The population's dissatisfaction with the police, including the demand for tougher practices... originates from the trumped up philosophy of "human rights" applied in favor of bandits and criminals. This philosophy gives preference to the marginal, protecting his "right" to go around armed, robbing, killing, and raping at will. (6)

Under the political ideology of favors and privileges, extended only to those who behave well, human rights cannot logically be extended to criminals and marginals, those who have broken, or who simply live outside, the law. When this negative conception of human rights is superimposed on a very narrow definition of "crime" that does not recognize the criminal and violent acts of the powerful and the elite, it is easy to see how everyday violence against the poor is routinized and defended, even by some of the poor themselves.

Mundane Surrealism

In Mario Vargas Llosa's novel *The Real Life of Alejandro Mayta*, the Peruvian narrator comments on the relations of imagination to politics and of literary fiction to history:

Information in this country has ceased to be objective and has become pure fantasy – in newspapers, radio, television, and in ordinary conversation. To report among us now means either to interpret reality according to our desires or fears, or to say simply what is convenient. It is an attempt to make up for our ignorance of what is going on – which in our heart of hearts we understand as irremediable and definitive. Since it is impossible to know what is really happening, we Peruvians lie, invent, dream, and take refuge in illusion. Because of these strange circum-

stances, Peruvian life, a life in which so few actually do read, has become literary. (1986: 246)

The magical realism of Latin American fiction has its counterparts in the mundane surrealism of ethnographic description, where it is also difficult to separate fact from fiction, rumor and fantasy from historical event, and the events of the imagination from the events of the everyday political drama. The blurring of fiction and reality creates a kind of mass hysteria and paranoia that can be seen as a new technique of social control in which everyone suspects and fears every other: a collective hostile gaze, a human panopticon (see Foucault 1979), is created. But when this expresses itself positively and a state of alarm or a state of emergency is produced, the shocks reveal the disorder in the order and call into question the "normality of the abnormal," which is finally shown for what it really is.

Peacetime Crimes

The peoples' death was as it had always been:
as if nobody had died, nothing,
as if those stones were falling
on the earth, or water on water....
Nobody hid this crime.
This crime was committed
in the middle of the Plaza.
                    Pablo Neruda (1991: 186–7)

What makes the political tactic of disappearance so nauseating – a tactic used strategically throughout Brazil during the military years (1964–85) against suspected subversives and "agitators" and now applied to a different and perhaps an even more terrifying context (i.e., against the shantytown poor and the economic marginals now thought of as a species of public enemy) – is that it does not occur in a vacuum. Rather, the disappearances occur as part of a larger context of wholly expectable, indeed even anticipated, behavior. Among the people of the Alto, disappearances form part of the backdrop of everyday life and confirm their worst fears and anxieties – that of losing themselves and their loved ones to the random forces and institutionalized violence of the state.

The practices of "everyday violence" constitute another sort of state "terror," one that operates in the ordinary, mundane world of the *moradores* both in the form of rumors and wild imaginings and in the daily enactments of various public rituals that bring the people of the Alto into contact with the state: in public clinics and hospitals, in the civil registry office, in the public morgue, and in the municipal cemetery. These scenes provide the larger context that makes the more exceptional and strategic, politically motivated disappearances not only allowable but also predictable and expected.

"You gringos," a Salvadorian peasant told an American visitor, "are always worried about violence done with machine guns and machetes. But there is another kind of violence that you should be aware of, too. I used to work on a hacienda. My job was to take care of the dueño's dogs. I gave them meat and bowls of milk, food that I couldn't give my own family. When the dogs were sick, I took them to the veterinarian. When my children were sick, the dueño gave me his sympathy, but no medicine as they died" (cited in Chomsky 1985: 6; also in Clements 1987: ix).

Similarly, the *moradores* of the Alto speak of bodies that are routinely violated and abused, mutilated and lost, disappeared into anonymous public spaces – hospitals and prisons but also morgues and the public cemetery. And they speak of themselves as the "anonymous," the "nobodies" of Bom Jesus da Mata. For if one is a "somebody," a *fildalgo* (a son of a person of influence), and a "person" in the aristocratic world of the plantation *casa grande*, and if one is an "individual" in the more open, competitive, and bourgeois world of the new market economy (the *rua*), then one is surely a nobody, a mere *fulano-de-tal* (a so-and-so) and João Pequeno (little guy) in the anonymous world of the sugarcane cutter (the *mata*).

Moradores refer, for example, to their collective invisibility, to the ways they are lost to the public census and to other state and municipal statistics. The otherwise carefully drafted municipal street map of Bom Jesus includes the Alto do Cruzeiro, but more than two-thirds of its tangle of congested, unpaved roads and paths are not included, leaving it a semiotic zero of more than 5,000 people in the midst of the bustling market town. CELPE, the state-owned power and light company, keeps track, of course, of those streets and houses that have access to electricity, but the names the company has assigned to identify the many intersecting *bicos*, *travessas*, and *ruas*

of the Alto do not conform to the names used among the *moradores* themselves. The usual right of the "colonizer" to name the space he has claimed is not extended to the marginal settlers of the Alto do Cruzeiro.

The people of the Alto are invisible and discounted in many other ways. Of no account in life, the people of the Alto are equally of no account in death. On average, more than half of all deaths in the *município* are of shantytown children under the age of five, the majority of them the victims of acute and chronic malnutrition. But one would have to read between the lines because the death of Alto children is so routine and so inconsequential that for more than three-fourths of recorded deaths, the cause of death is left blank on the death certificates and in the ledger books of the municipal civil registry office. In a highly bureaucratic society in which triplicates of every form are required for the most banal of events (registering a car, for example), the registration of child death is informal, and anyone may serve as a witness. Their deaths, like their lives, are quite invisible, and we may as well speak of their bodies, too, as having been disappeared.

The various mundane and everyday tactics of disappearance are practiced perversely and strategically against people who view their world and express their own political goals in terms of bodily idioms and metaphors. The people of the Alto inhabit a world with a comfortable human shape, a world that is intimately embodied. The *moradores* of the Alto "think" the world with their bodies within a somatic culture. At their base community meetings the people of the Alto say to each other with conviction and with feeling, "Every man should be the *dono* [owner] of his own body." Not only their politics but their spirituality can be described as "embodied" in a popular Catholicism, with its many expressions of the carnal and of physical union with Jesus, with His mother Mary, and with the multitude of saints, more than enough for every day of the year and to guide every human purpose. There is a saint for every locale, for every activity, and for every part of the body. And the body parts of the saints, splintered into the tiniest relics, are guarded and venerated as sacred objects.

Embodiment does not end with death for the people of the Alto. Death is itself no stranger to people who handle a corpse with confidence, if not with ease. ("When you die, Dona Nancí," little

Zefinha used to say affectionately, "I'm going to be the first to eat your big legs," the highest compliment she could think of to pay me.) On the death of a loved one, a local photographer will often be called to take a photo of the adult or child in her or his coffin. That same photo will be retouched to erase the most apparent signs of death, and it will become the formal portrait that is hung proudly on the wall. The deceased continue to appear in visions, dreams, and apparitions through which they make their demands for simple pleasures and creature comforts explicit. As wretched *almas penadas*, "restless souls" from purgatory, the dead may request food and drink or a pair of shoes or stockings to cover feet that are cold and blistered from endless wandering. Because the people of the Alto imagine their own souls to have a human shape, they will bury an amputated foot in a tiny coffin in the local cemetery so that later it can be reunited with its owner, who can then face his Master whole and standing "on his own two feet."

Against these compelling images of bodily autonomy and certitude is the reality of bodies that are simultaneously discounted and preyed on and sometimes mutilated and dismembered. And so the people of the Alto come to imagine that there is nothing so bad, so terrible that it cannot happen to them, to their bodies, because of sickness (*por culpa de doença*), because of doctors (*por culpa dos médicos*), because of politics and power (*por culpa de política*), or because of the state and its unwieldy, hostile bureaucracy (*por culpa da burocracia*).

I am not going so far as to suggest that the fears of mutilation and of misplacement of the body are not shared with other social classes of Brazil, which also "privilege" the body in a culture that prides itself on its heightened expressions and pleasures of the sensual. What is, however, specific to the "marginal" classes of the Alto do Cruzeiro is a self-conscious sort of thinking with and through the body, a "remembering" of the body and of one's "rights" in it and to it. The affluent social classes take for granted these rights to bodily integrity and autonomy to the extent that they "go without saying." The police oppressors know their victims all too well, well enough to mutilate, castrate, make disappear, misplace, or otherwise lose the bodies of the poor, to actualize their very worst fears. It is the sharing of symbols between the torturer and the tortured that makes the terror so

effective (see Scarry 1985: 38–45 and Chapter 46; Suarez-Orozco 1987 and Chapter 49).

The unquestionability of the body was, for Wittgenstein, where all knowledge and certainty began. "If you do know that here is one hand," he began his last book, *On Certainty*, "we'll grant you all the rest" (1969: 2e). And yet Wittgenstein himself, writing this book while he was working with patients hospitalized during the war, was forced to reflect on the circumstances that might take away the certainty of the body. Here, in the context of *Nordestino* life, I am exploring another set of circumstances that have given a great many people grounds to lose their sense of bodily certitude to terrible bouts of existential doubt – "My God, my God, what ever will become of us?" – the fear of being made to vanish, to disappear without a trace.

It is reminiscent of the situation described by Taussig with reference to a similar political situation in Colombia: "I am referring to a state of doubleness of social being in which one moves in bursts between somehow accepting the situation as normal, only to be thrown into a panic or shocked into disorientation by an event, a rumor, a sight, something said, or not said – something even while it requires the normal in order to make its impact, destroys it" (1989: 8; see also Chapter 19). The intolerableness of the situation is increased by its ambiguity. Consciousness moves in and out of an acceptance of the state of things as normal and expectable – violence as taken for granted and sudden ruptures whereby one is suddenly thrown into a state of shock (*susto, pasmo, nervios*) – that is endemic, a graphic body metaphor secretly expressing and publicizing the reality of the untenable situation. There are nervous, anxious whisperings, suggestions, hints. Strange rumors surface.

REFERENCES

Amnesty International. 1988. "Brazil: Killing with Impunity." Briefing, Sept. New York: Amnesty International.
——. 1990. "Brazil: Torture and Extrajudicial Execution in Urban Brazil." Briefing, June. New York: Amnesty International.
Basaglia, Franco. 1987a. "Institutions of Violence" and "The Disease and Its Double." In *Psychiatry Inside Out: Selected Writings of Franco Basaglia*, eds.

Nancy Scheper-Hughes and Anne M. Lovell, 59–86, 101–34. New York: Columbia University Press.

——. 1987b. "Peacetime Crimes: Technicians of Practical Knowledge." In *Psychiatry Inside Out: Selected Writings of Franco Basaglia*, eds. Nancy Scheper-Hughes and Anne M. Lovell, 143–68. New York: Columbia University Press.

Blok, Anton. 1974. *The Mafia of a Sicilian Village, 1860–1960*. Oxford: Blackwell.

Caldeira, Teresa Pires do Rio. 1990. "The Experience of Violence: Order, Disorder, and Social Discrimination in Brazil." Berkeley: Department of Anthropology, University of California. Manuscript.

Chomsky, Noam. 1985. *Turning the Tide: United States Intervention in Central America and the Struggle for Peace*. Boston: South End.

Clements, Charles. 1987. Introduction, p. ix. *A Peasant of El Salvador* by Peter Gould and Stephen Stearns. Brattleboro, VT: Whetstone Books.

Cohn, Carol. 1987. "Sex and Death in the Rational World of Defense Intellectuals." *Signs* 12(4): 687–718.

Dassin, Joan, ed. 1986. *Torture in Brazil: A Report by the Archdiocese of São Paulo*. New York: Random House. (Translation of 1985. *Brasil: Nunca Mais*. Petrópolis: Vozes.)

Didion, Joan. 1982. *Salvador*. New York: Pocket Books.

Foucault, Michel. 1979. *Discipline and Punish*. New York: Vintage/Random House.

Green, Linda. 1989. "The Realities of Survival: Mayan Widows and Development Aid in Rural Guatemala." Paper presented at the meeting of the American Anthropological Association, Washington, DC, Nov. 15.

Kant, Roberto de Lima. 1990. "Criminal Justice: A Comparative Approach, Brazil and the United States." Notre Dame, IN: Kellogg Institute, University of Notre Dame. Manuscript.

Lewin, Linda. 1987. *Politics and Parentela in Paraíba*. Princeton, NJ: Princeton University Press.

Llosa, Mario Vargas. 1986. *The Real Life of Alejandro Mayta*. New York: Vintage.

Neruda, Pablo. 1991. *Canto General*. Berkeley and Los Angeles: University of California Press. (Translation of 1976. *Canto General*. Caracas: Biblioteca Ayacucho.)

Paul, Benjamin. 1988. "The Operation of a Death Squad in a Lake Atitlan Community." In *Harvest of Violence: The Mayan Indians and the Guatemalan Crisis*, ed. Robert M. Carmack, 119–55. Norman: University of Oklahoma Press.

Peters, Edward. 1985. *Torture*. Oxford: Blackwell.

Riding, Alan. 1988. "In Brazil's Northeast Misery Molded by Man and Nature." *New York Times*, May 3, 1, A-4.

Sartre, Jean-Paul. 1956. *Being and Nothingness*. London: Methuen.

Scarry, Elaine. 1985. *The Body in Pain: The Making and Unmaking of the World*. New York: Oxford University Press.

Suarez-Orozco, Marcelo. 1987. "The Treatment of Children in the 'Dirty War': Ideology, State Terrorism, and the Abuse of Children in Argentina." In *Child Survival: Anthropological Approaches to the Treatment and Maltreatment of Children*, ed. Nancy Scheper-Hughes, 227–46. Dordrecht: Reidel.

——. 1990. "Speaking of the Unspeakable: Toward a Psychosocial Understanding of Responses to Terror." *Ethos* 18(3): 353–83.

Taussig, Michael. 1989. "Terror as Usual." *Social Text* (Fall–Winter): 3–20.

Wittgenstein, Ludwig. 1969. *On Certainty*. New York: Harper and Row.

21

Living in a State of Fear

Linda Green

How does one become socialized to terror? Does it imply conformity or acquiescence to the status quo, as a friend suggested? While it is true that with repetitiveness and familiarity people learn to accommodate themselves to terror and fear, low-intensity panic remains in the shadow of waking consciousness. One cannot live in a constant state of alertness, and so the chaos one feels becomes diffused throughout the body. It surfaces frequently in dreams and chronic illnesses. In the morning, my neighbors and friends would sometimes speak of their fears during the night, of being unable to sleep or being awakened by footsteps or voices, of nightmares of recurring death and violence. After six months of living in Xe'caj [Guatemala], I too started having my own dreams of death, disappearances, and torture. Whisperings, innuendoes, rumors of death lists circulating would put everyone on edge. One day a friend, Tomas, from Xe'caj, came to my house feeling very anxious. He explained, holding back his tears, that he had heard his name was on the newest death list at the military encampment. As Scheper-Hughes (1992: 223; and Chapter 20) has noted in the Brazilian context, "the intolerableness of the[se] situation[s] is increased by its ambiguity." A month later, two soldiers were killed one Sunday afternoon in a surprise guerrilla attack a kilometer from my house. That evening, several women from the village came to visit, emotionally distraught; they worried that la violencia, which had been stalking them, had at last returned. As doña Alejandra said, violence is like fire: it can flare up suddenly and burn you.

The people in Xe'caj live under constant surveillance. The local *destacamento* (military encampment) looms large in the pueblo, situated on a nearby hillside above town. From there everyone's movements come under close scrutiny. The town is laid out in the colonial quadrangle pattern common throughout the altiplano. The town square, as well as all the roads leading to the surrounding countryside, is visible from above. To an untrained eye, the encampment is not obvious from below. The camouflaged buildings fade into the hillside, but once one has looked down from there it is impossible to forget that those who live below do so in a fishbowl. Military commissioners, civil patrollers, and *orejas* (spies) are responsible for most of this scrutiny. These local men are often former soldiers and willingly report to the army any suspicious activities of their neighbors.

The impact of the civil patrols (PACs) at the local level has been profound. One of the structural effects of the PACs in Xe'caj has been the subordination of village political authority to the local army commander. When I arrived in Xe'caj, I went to the *alcalde* (mayor) first to introduce myself and ask for his permission to work in the township and surrounding villages. But midway through my explanation he cut me off abruptly, explaining impatiently that if I hoped to work there I really needed the explicit permission of the commandante at the army garrison. The civil patrols guard the entrances and exits to the villages in Xe'caj, he said. Without permission from the army, the civil patrols would not allow me to enter. My presence as a stranger and foreigner produced suspicions. "Why do you want to live and work here with us? Why do you want to talk to the widows? For whom do you work?" the alcalde asked. The local army officers told me it was a free country and that I could do as I pleased, provided I had *their* permission.

One of the ways terror becomes defused is through subtle messages, much as Carol Cohn (1987 and Chapter 45) describes in her unsettling account of the use of language by nuclear scientists to sanitize their involvement in the production of nuclear weaponry. In Guatemala language and symbols are utilized to normalize a continual army presence. From time to time, army troops would arrive in an aldea obliging the villagers to assemble for a community meeting. The message was more or less the same each time I witnessed these gatherings. The commandante would begin by telling the people that the army was their friend, that the soldiers were there to protect them against subversion, against the communists hiding out in the mountains. At the same time, he would admonish them that if they did not cooperate, Guatemala could become like Nicaragua, El Salvador, or Cuba. Subtieniente Rodriguez explained to me during one such meeting that the army was preserving peace and democracy in Guatemala through military control of the entire country. Ignacio Martin-Baro (1989) has characterized social perceptions reduced to rigid and simplistic schemes as "official lies," where social knowledge is cast in dichotomous terms, black or white, good or bad, friend or enemy, without the nuances and complexities of lived experience.

Guatemalan soldiers at times arrived in villages accompanied by US National Guard doctors or dentists who would hold clinics for a few days. This was part of a larger strategy developed under the Kennedy doctrine of Alliance for Progress in which civic actions are part of counterinsurgency strategies. Yet mixing so-called benevolent help with military actions does not negate the essential fact that violence is intrinsic to the military's nature and logic. Coercion is the mechanism that the military uses to control citizens even in the absence of war (Scheper-Hughes 1992: 224; and Chapter 20).

I was with a group of widows and young orphaned girls one afternoon watching a soap opera on television. It was in mid-June, a week or so before Army Day. During one of the commercial breaks, a series of images of Kaibiles appeared on the screen; they were dressed for combat with painted faces, clenching their rifles while running through the mountains. Each time a new frame appeared there was an audible gasp in the room. The last image was of soldiers emerging from behind corn stalks while the narrator said, "The army is ready to do whatever is necessary to defend the country." One young girl turned to me and said, "Si pues, siempre estan lista que se matan la gente" (well, yes, they are always ready to kill the people).

The use of camouflage cloth for clothing and small items sold at the market is a subtle and insidious militarization of daily life. Wallets, key chains, belts, caps, and toy helicopters made in Taiwan are disconcerting in this context. As these seemingly mundane objects circulate, they normalize the extent to which civilian and the military life have commingled in the altiplano. Young men who have returned to villages from military service often wear army boots, t-shirts denoting in which military zone they had been stationed, and their dog tags. The boots themselves are significant. The women would say they knew who it was that kidnapped or killed their family members, even if dressed in civilian clothes, because the men were wearing army boots.

When my neighbor's cousin on leave from the army came for a visit, the young boys brought him over to my house so they could show off his photo album. As the young soldier stood in the background shyly, Eduardo and Luisito pointed enthusiastically to a photograph of their cousin leaning on a tank with his automatic rifle in hand and a bandolier of bullets slung over his shoulder; in another he was throwing a hand grenade. Yet these same boys told me, many months after I had moved into my house and we had become friends, that when I first arrived they were afraid I might kill them. And doña Sofia, Eduardo's mother, was shocked to learn that I didn't carry a gun.

In El Salvador, Martin-Baro (1989) analyzed the subjective internalization of war and militarization among a group of 203 children in an effort to understand to what extent they have assimilated the efficacy of violence in solving personal and social problems. While generalizations cannot easily be drawn from the study, Martin-Baro found that the majority of the children interviewed stated that the best way to end the war and attain peace was to eliminate the enemy through violent means (whether this was understood as the Salvadoran army or the FMLN [Farbundo Martí National Liberation Front]). Martin-Baro has referred to this tendency to internalize violence as the "militarization of the mind" (1990).

The presence of soldiers and ex-soldiers in these communities is illustrative of lived contradictions in the altiplano and provides another example of how the routinization of terror functions. The foot soldiers of the army are almost exclusively young rural Mayas, many still boys, only fourteen or fifteen years old, rounded up on army sweeps through rural towns. The recruiters arrive in two-ton trucks grabbing all young men in sight, usually on festival or market days when large numbers of people have gathered together in the center of the pueblo. One morning at dawn I witnessed four such loaded trucks driving from one of the towns of Xe'caj, soldiers standing in each corner of the truck with rifles pointed outward. The soon-to-be foot soldiers were packed in like cattle. Little is known about the training these young soldiers receive, but anecdotal data from some who were willing to talk suggests that the training is designed to break down their sense of personal dignity and respect for other human beings. As one young man described it to me, "Soldiers are trained to kill and nothing more" (see Forester 1992; Sanford 1993). Another said he learned to hate everyone, including himself.

The soldiers who pass through the villages on recognizance and take up sentry duty in the pueblos are Mayas, while the officers, who cannot speak the local language, are ladinos from other regions of the country. A second lieutenant explained to me that army policy dictates that the foot soldiers and the commanders of the local garrisons change assignments every three months to prevent soldiers from getting to know the people and the commandantes from getting bored. A small but significant number of men in Xe'caj have served in the army. Many young men return to their natal villages after they are released from military duty. Yet their reintegration into the community is often difficult. As one villager noted, "They leave as Indians, but they don't come back Indian." During their service in the army, some of these soldiers have been forced to kill and maim. Set adrift, these young men often go on to become

the local military commissioners, heads of the civil patrol, or paid informers for the army. Many are demoralized, frequently drinking and turning violent. Others marry and settle in their villages to resume their lives as best they can. Padre Juan, a local Catholic priest at the time of my fieldwork, said that many ex-soldiers in Xe'caj would get drunk before going to confession, where they intermittently sobbed as they related to him in brutal detail what they had done and seen while in the army.

The Structure of Fear

[. . .] Terror is the taproot of Guatemala's past and stalks its present. When speaking of la violencia of the 1980s, I was struck by how frequently people used the metaphor of conquest to describe it. "Lo mismo cuando se mato a Tecum Uman" (it is the same when they killed Tecum Uman), doña Marta said when describing the recent whirlwind of death, alluding to the Maya-K'iche hero who died valiantly in battle against the Spanish. Although references to the Spanish conquest became more commonplace on the cusp of the quincentenary in 1992, in 1988 and early 1989 rural constructions of local experiences in terms of the invasion were striking, haunting, as if a collective memory had been passed generation to generation. In this way, history engaged through memory becomes a social force comprising "both group membership and individual identity out of a dynamically chosen selection of memories and the constant reshaping, reinvention, and reinforcement of those memories as members contest and create the boundaries and links among themselves" (Boyarin 1994: 26).

George Lovell (1992: epilogue 34) has compared some of the occupation strategies of the Spanish Crown with those of the modern Guatemalan state and concludes that "the policy remains the same: to dismantle existing forms of community organization, to drive a wedge between people and place; to force families to live not where they wish but where they are told, in nucleated centers where movements are scrutinized, routines disrupted, attitudes and behavior modified." Franciscan documents from the sixteenth century describe the disorder resulting from a local judge's order to burn down towns when Indians refused to comply with official degrees. Lovell writes (1992: 35): "Chaos ensued. Roads and trails were strewn with poor Indian women, tied as prisoners, carrying children on their backs, left to fend for themselves." Five hundred years later, publications by anthropologists (Carmack 1988; Manz 1988; Falla 1983, 1992) and numerous international human rights groups (America's Watch, Amnesty International reports throughout the 1980s) recount violations of a similar magnitude. Fear has been the motor of oppression in Guatemala. [...]

Despite this hideous record of documented human rights abuses, the United Nations Commission on Human Rights decided in 1992 to downplay Guatemala's record for the fifth consecutive year, placing it in the "advisory" rather than "violations" category. Yet inside the country, repression continued unchecked. Repression is used selectively: to threaten, intimidate, disappear, or kill one or two labor leaders, students, or campesinos is to paralyze everyone else with fear. If one crosses the arbitrary line, the consequences are well known; the problem is that one cannot be sure where the line is, nor when one has crossed it, until it is too late.

After several months of searching for a field site, I settled on Xe'caj because although it had seen much bloodshed and repression during the early 1980s, la situacion was reportedly *tranquila* (calm) in 1988. The terror and fear that pervaded daily life were not immediately perceptible to me. Military checkpoints, the army garrison, and civil patrols were clearly visible, yet daily life appeared normal. The guerrilla war, which reached a climax in the early 1980s, had ended at least in theory if not in practice. Although guerrilla troops moved throughout the area, clashes between them and the army were limited. The war had reached a stalemate. While the army claimed victory, the guerrillas refused to admit defeat. The battlefield was quiescent, yet political repression continued. Scorched-earth tactics, massacres, and large population displacements had halted, but they were replaced by selective repression, militarization of daily life, and relentless economic insecurity. Army General Alejandro Gramajo's now infamous inversion of Clausewitz – "politics as a continuation of war" – was clearly accurate. The counterinsurgency war had transformed everyday life in the altiplano into a permanent state of repression, fortified by economic arrangements that led to increasing poverty, hunger, and misery (Smith 1990b).

Silence and Secrecy

The dual lessons of silence and secrecy were for me the most enlightening and disturbing. Silence about the present situation when talking with strangers is a survival strategy that Mayas have long utilized. Their overstated politeness toward ladino society and seeming obliviousness to the jeers and insults hurled at them, their servility in the face of overt racism, make it seem as though Mayas have accepted their subservient role in Guatemalan society. Apparent Mayan obsequiousness has served as a shield to provide distance and has also been a powerful shaper of Mayan practice. When Sophia disclosed to a journalist friend of mine from El Salvador her thoughts about guerrilla incursions today, her family castigated her roundly for speaking, warning her that what she said could be twisted and used against her and the family. Alan Feldman (1991: 11), writing about Northern Ireland, notes that secrecy is "an assertion of identity and symbolic capital pushed to the margins. Subaltern groups construct their own margins as fragile insulators from the center."

When asked about the present situation, the usual response from almost everyone was "pues, tranquila" (calm, peaceful), but it was a fragile calm. Later, as I got to know people, when something visible broke through the facade of order and forced propaganda speeches – for example, when a soldier was killed and another seriously injured in an ambush in Xe'caj – people would whisper of their fears of a return to la violencia. In fact, the unspoken but implied conclusion to the statement "pues, tranquila" is "ahorita, pero manana saber?" (for now, but who knows about tomorrow?). When I asked the head of a small (self-sufficient) development project that was organizing locally if he was bothered by the army, he said he was not. The army came by every couple of months and searched houses or looked at his records, but he considered this "tranquila."

Silence can operate as a survival strategy, yet silencing is a powerful mechanism of control enforced through fear. While I talked with the women, at times our attention would be distracted momentarily by a military plane or helicopter flying close and low. We would all lift our heads, watching until it passed out of sight yet withholding comment. Sometimes, if we were inside a house we might all step out to the patio to look skyward. Silence. Only once was the silence broken. On that day, doña Tomasa asked rhetorically, after the helicopters had passed overhead, why my government sent bombs to kill people. On another occasion, at Christmas Eve mass in 1989, 25 soldiers entered the church suddenly, soon after the service had begun. They occupied three middle pews on the men's side, never taking their hands off their rifles, only to leave abruptly after the sermon. Silence. The silences in these cases do not erase individual memories of terror but create more fear and uncertainty by driving a wedge of paranoia between people. Terror's effects are not only psychological and individual but social and collective as well. Silence imposed through terror has become the idiom of social consensus in the altiplano, as Suarez-Orozco (1990) has noted in the Argentine context.

A number of development projects in Xe'caj work with women and children who have been severely affected by the violence. Most do not address the reality in which people live. These projects provide a modicum of economic aid but without acknowledging the context of fear and terror that pervade Xe'caj. When a Vision Mundial (World Vision) administrator explained the project's multitiered approach to development, he spoke proudly of the group's emphasis on assisting the whole person, materially, emotionally, and spiritually. When I asked him how the project was confronting the emotional trauma of war and repression in which the widows live, he admitted obliquely that it did not. To do so, of course, would put the project workers and the women at jeopardy. Yet not to address the situation perpetuates the official lies. Development aid, by constituting itself as apolitical, serves to legitimate the status quo (Uvin 1998), which in the case of Guatemala has deadly consequences.

On Breaking the Silence

Despite the fear and terror engendered by relentless human rights violations and deeply entrenched impunity, hope existed during this period. With the appointment in 1983 of Archbishop Prospero Penados del Barrio, the Guatemalan Catholic Church had become more outspoken in its advocacy of peace and social justice. The Guatemalan Bishops' Conference, in particular, issued a number of pastoral letters that have become important sources of social criticism in the country; the 1988 "Cry for Land," for example, was an extraordinarily articulate commentary on one of the country's fundamental structures of inequality. In 1990 the Archdiocese of Guatemala opened a human rights office to provide legal assistance to victims of human rights abuses and to report violations to national and international institutions. And more recently, in 1994, the archdiocesan office began the Interdiocesan Recuperation of the Historic Memory Project (REHMI). The goal of the project was to collect individual stories of repression to document as precisely as possible under the present circumstances the extent of the violence that had taken place. The project began collecting testimony in 1995 from thousands of mostly indigenous people in rural communities whose stories would have likely not been heard by the formal Truth Commission created under the tenets of the peace accords. The official report was published in April 1998. Perhaps what is most remarkable about the project is the use of Mayan promoters to gather the testimonies, often in Mayan languages, throughout the regions most affected by the violence. As such, the project had the potential of rebuilding people's ties to one another through "recuperating memory" and breaking the silence, a necessary component of ongoing repression and impunity. In effect, the project laid the groundwork for ongoing political struggles between the state and the victims and survivors over the interpretations of the history of the war. Its findings may effectively serve as a counterpoint to the Amnesty Law and Truth Commission created by the peace accords.

Collective responses to the silence imposed through terror began in 1984 when two dozen people, mostly women, formed the human rights organization called the GAM (Grupo de Apoyo Mutuo). Its members are relatives of some of the estimated 42,000 people who have disappeared in Guatemala over the past three decades. Modeled after the Mothers of Plaza de Mayo in Argentina (Agoson 1987), this small group of courageous women and men decided to break the silence. They went to government offices to demand that the authorities investigate the crimes against their families. As they marched in silence every Friday in front of the national palace with placards bearing the photos of those who had disappeared, they ruptured the official silence, bearing testimony with their own bodies to those who have vanished.

In 1990 Roberto Lemus, a Guatemalan judge in the district court of Santa Cruz del Quiche, began accepting petitions from local people to exhume sites in the villages where people claimed clandestine graves were located. Family members said they knew where their loved ones had been buried after having been killed by security forces. While other judges in the area had previously allowed the exhumations, this was the first time they were performed with the intention of gathering physical evidence for verbal testimonies of survivors in order to corroborate reports against those responsible. (Judge Lemus was eventually forced to seek political exile.) During the same period, the eminent forensic anthropologist Dr. Clyde Snow assembled and trained a Guatemalan Forensic Anthropology Team with assistance from the Argentine Forensic Anthropology Team. There are estimated to be hundreds, perhaps thousands, of clandestine cemeteries throughout the altiplano. These cemeteries and mass graves are the *secreto a voces*: something everyone knows about but does not dare to discuss publicly.

In Xe'caj, people would point out such sites to me. On several occasions, when I was walking with them in the mountains, women took me to the places where they knew their husbands were buried and said, "Mira, el esta alli" (Look, he is over there). Others claimed that there are at least three mass graves in Xe'caj itself. The act of unearthing the bones of family members allows individuals to reconcile themselves to the past openly, to acknowledge at last the culpability for the death of their loved ones, and to lay them to rest. Such unearthing is, at the same time, a most powerful statement against impunity because it reveals the magnitude of the political repression that has taken place. These are not solely the work of individuals with individual consequences; they are public crimes that have deeply penetrated the social body and contest the legitimacy of the body politic.

Thus, as has been the case in Uruguay, Chile, Argentina, Brazil, and El Salvador (Weschler 1990), the dual issues of impunity and accountability are obstacles in the way of peace and social justice in Guatemala. As such, amnesty becomes both a political and an ethical problem, with not only individual but social dimensions. Ramiro de Leon Carpio, the Guatemalan human rights ombudsman (who later served as Guatemalan president between 1993 and 1995) suggested that to

forgive and forget is the only way democracy will be achieved in Guatemala. In a newspaper interview in 1991, he said: "The ideal would be that we uncover the truth, to make it public and to punish those responsible, but I believe that is impossible. . . . We have to be realistic" (*La Hora* 1991).

Certainly, the idea of political expediency has a measure of validity to it. The problem, however, turns on "whether pardon and renunciation are going to be established on a foundation of truth and justice or on lies and continued injustice" (Martin-Baro 1990: 7). Hannah Arendt has argued against forgiveness without accountability, because it undermines the formation of democracy by obviating any hope of justice and makes its pursuit pointless (1973). Further, while recognizing that forgiveness is an essential element for freedom, Arendt contends that "the alternative to forgiveness, but by no means its opposite, is punishment, and both have in common that they attempt to put an end to something that without interference could go on endlessly" (Arendt 1958: 241). The military's self-imposed amnesty, which has become the vogue throughout Latin America in recent years, forecloses the very possibility of forgiveness. Without a settling of accounts, democratic rule will remain elusive in Guatemala as has been the case elsewhere in Latin America. Social reparation is a necessary requisite to healing the body politic.

Living in a State of Fear

During the first weeks we lived in Xe'caj, Sophia and I drove to several villages in the region talking with women – widows – in small groups, asking them if they might be willing to meet with us weekly over the next year or so. At first many people thought we might be representing a development project and therefore distributing material aid. When this proved not to be the case, some women lost interest, but others agreed to participate. During the second week, we drove out to Ri Bay, a small village that sits in a wide U-shaped valley several thousand meters lower in altitude than Xe'caj and most of the surrounding hamlets. The only access is a one-lane dirt road that cuts across several ridges in a series of switchbacks before beginning the long, slow descent into the valley.

Fortunately for me, there was little traffic on these back roads. Bus service was suspended during the height of the violence in the early 1980s, and by the early 1990s it was virtually nonexistent, although a few buses did provide transport to villagers on market day. The biggest obstacle to driving is the possibility of meeting head on logging trucks carrying rounds of oak and cedar for export. With their heavy loads, it is impossible for them to maneuver, and so I would invariably have to back up- or downhill until I found a turnout wide enough to allow the truck to pass. Yet the most frightening experience was rounding a curve and suddenly encountering a military patrol.

On this day in February 1989 it was foggy and misty, and a cold wind was blowing. Although the air temperature was in the fifties (degrees Fahrenheit), the chill penetrated to the bone. "El expreso de Alaska," Sophia laughed, wrapping her shawl more tightly around her. Heading north, we caught glimpses of the dark ridges of the Sierra de Cuchumatanes brooding in the distance. The scenery was breathtaking. Every conceivable hue of green was present – pine, cedar, ash, oak, bromeliades, and the wide lush leaves of banana trees – and mingled with brilliant purple bougainvillea and ivory calla lilies that lined the roadway. The hills, the softness of the sky, and the outline of trees created an unforgettable image. This was the Guatemala of eternal spring.

On each side of the road, houses were perched on the slopes, surrounded by the milpas, which lay fallow after the harvest in late January, only the dried stalks left half-standing, leaning this way and that. In the altiplano several houses made from a mix of cane or corn stalks, adobe, and wood are usually clustered together. The red tile roofs seen further west have all but disappeared from Xe'caj. Most people now use tin roofs (*lamina*), even though they make houses more oppressively warm in the hot dry season and colder when it is damp and rainy. The department of Chimaltenango was one of the hardest hit by the 1976 earthquake in which nationwide more than 75,000 people died and one million were left homeless. Many people were crushed under the weight of the tiles as roofs caved in on them. Today, half-burned houses stand as testimony to the scorched-earth campaign, while civil patrollers take up their posts nearby with rifles in hand.

Although we frequently saw people on foot, most women and children ran to hide when they saw us coming in the truck. Months passed before women and children walking along the road would accept a ride with me. And even then, many did so reluctantly. Most would ask Sophia in Kaqchikel if it were true that I wanted to steal their children and that gringos ate children.

On this particular day, Sophia and I drove as far as we could and then left my pickup at the top of the hill when the road became impassable. Walking the last four miles down to the village, we met local men repairing large ruts in the road where the heavy September rains had washed away the soil. Soil in this area is sandy and unstable. Most of the trees on the ridge above the road had been clear-cut, and the erosion was quite pronounced. The men were putting in culverts and filling in the deep crevasses that dissected the road; their only tools were shovels and pickaxes. Although the pay was only US$1.50 per day, it was desirable work, one of the few opportunities to earn cash close to home rather than away on the coastal plantations.

As we descended to the lower elevations, Sophia and I mused over the fact that there were only seven widows in Ri Bay, a village of 300 people. In the several other villages where we had visited women, there were 30 to 40 widows, or about 15 to 20 percent of the current population. Perhaps there had not been much violence in Ri Bay, I suggested. It was one of the notable features of the military campaign known as scorched earth that neighboring villages fared quite differently. One might be destroyed and another left untouched, depending on the army's perceived understanding of guerrilla support. The military's campaign of terror had happened in two phases. Army strategy began with selective repression against community leaders not only to garner information but also to spread fear. The second phase of the counterinsurgency plan included cutting off rural areas from the city. This began with sweeping operations that fanned out from the city first westward to the department of Chimaltenango and then south to Quiche and later further north and westward (see Falla 1992). The massacres and brutality seemed to occur according to some deliberate plan, despite the disorder and panic they provoked: while some villages were left unscathed, others were completely razed. For example, according to an eyewitness of the massacre in the village of Los Angelas, Ixcan, on March 23, 1982, the soldiers had a list of pueblos and villages that were to be targeted (Falla 1992). And in numerous testimonies of survivors, the army more often than not launched its so-called reprisals against the guerrillas by brutally killing the population at large.

Sophia and I found Marcelina, Eufemia, and a third younger woman sitting in front of the school where we had agreed to meet. We greeted the women and sat down in the sun that was just breaking through the clouds. The women had brought several bottles of Pepsi for us to share. I asked doña Marcelina, a small thin woman with an intelligent face, why there were so few widows in Ri Bay and held my breath waiting for the hoped-for answer: that the violence there had been much less. She replied that it was because so many people had been killed, not just men but whole families, old people, children, and women. The village was deserted for several years, its inhabitants had fled to the mountains, the pueblo, or the city. Many people never returned, whether because they were dead or merely displaced, no one knew for sure.

This was the third village we had visited, and each time it was the same. The women, without prompting, took turns recounting their stories of horror. Using vivid detail, they would tell of the events surrounding the deaths or disappearances of their husbands, fathers, sons, brothers as if they had happened the previous week or month rather than six or eight years before. And the women – Marcelina, Eufemia, Juana, Martina, Alejandra, Elena – continued to tell me their stories over and over during the time I lived among them. Why? At first as strangers, and then later as friends, why were these women repeatedly recounting their Kafkaesque tales to me? What did they gain by the telling? What was the relationship between silence and testimony? As Suarez-Orozco has noted, "Testimony [is] a ritual of both healing and a condemnation of injustice. . . . The concept of testimony contains both connotations of something subjective and private and something objective, juridical and political" (1992: 367; and Chapter 49). The public areas used to thwart surveillance were transformed into a liminal space that was both private and public during the recounting.

In each of the villages where I met with women, the routine was always the same in the beginning. We would meet in groups of three or four in front of the village health post, the school, or the church,

always in a public space. It would be three months or more before anyone invited me into her home or spoke with me privately and individually. Above all else, they did not want the gringa to be seen coming to their houses. Under the scrutiny of surveillance, the women were afraid of what others in the village might say about them and me. And when I did start going to people's homes, rumors did spread. The reports themselves seemed innocuous to me – that I was helping the widows or that I was writing a book about women – yet the repercussions were potentially dangerous.

During one particularly tense period, my visits caused an uproar. One day when I arrived to visit with Juana and Martina, I found them both very anxious and agitated. When I asked what was going on, they said that the military commissioner was looking for me, that people were saying I was helping the widows and talking against others in the community. "There are deep divisions within the community. People don't trust one another," explained Juana. "Families are divided, and not everyone thinks alike," Martina added.

When I said that I would go look for don Martin, the military commissioner, they became very upset. "He said that he would take you to the garrison; please don't go, Linda. We know people who went into the garrison and were never seen again." "But I have done nothing wrong," I said. "I must talk with them, find out what is wrong." I worried that my presence might reflect negatively on the women. So I went. Sophia insisted on accompanying me, dismissing my concerns for her well-being by saying, "Si nos matan es el problema de ellos" (if they kill us, it will be their problem). Fortunately for us, the commissioner wasn't home, so I left a message with his wife.

The next day I decided to go to the destacamento alone. The trek uphill to the garrison was a grueling walk, or so it seemed to me. The last 100 yards were the most demanding emotionally. Rounding the bend, I saw several soldiers sitting in a small guardhouse, a machine gun perched on a three-foot stanchion pointed downward and directly at me. Franz Kafka's *The Trial* flashed through my mind, with its protagonist Joseph K., accused of a crime against which he had to defend himself but about which he could get no information. "I didn't do anything wrong. I must not look guilty," I repeated this mantra to myself over and over. I had to calm myself. Finally, stomach churning and nerves frayed, I arrived, breathless and terrified. Ultimately, I knew, I could be found guilty merely because I was against the system of violence, terror, and oppression that surrounded me. I asked to speak to the commandante, and he received me outside the gates. This struck me as unusual and increased my agitation, as on every other occasion when I had been to the garrison – to greet each new commandante and to renew my permission papers to continue my work – I had been invited into the compound. The commandante said he knew nothing about why I was being harassed by the military commissioner and the civil patrol in Be'cal, and he assured me that I could continue with my work and that he personally would look into the situation. A few days later, the commandante and several soldiers arrived in the village, called a communitywide meeting, and instructed everyone to cooperate with the gringa who was doing a study.

When the matter had been settled, some of the women explained their concerns to me. They told stories of how widows from outlying villages who had fled to the relative safety of Xe'caj after their husbands had been killed or kidnapped had been forced to bring food and firewood to the soldiers at the garrison and then were raped and humiliated at gunpoint. As one story goes, a brave woman with a baby on her back went to the garrison demanding to see her husband. The soldiers claimed he was not there, but she knew they were lying because his dog was standing outside the gates and the dog never left his side. Either they still had him, or they had already killed him. She demanded to know which and told them to go ahead and kill her and the baby because she had nothing more to lose. Today she is a widow.

The stories continued. In the hour before dawn on a March day in 1981, doña Marcelina recounted, she had arisen early to warm tortillas for her husband's breakfast before he left to work in the milpa. He was going to burn and clean it in preparation for planting soon after the first rains in early May. He had been gone only an hour when neighbors came running to tell her that her husband was lying in the road, shot. When Marcelina reached him, he was already dead. With the help of neighbors, she took the body home to prepare it for burial. Marcelina considers herself lucky because at least she was able to bury him herself, unlike so many women whose husbands were dis-

appeared. The disappeared are among what Robert Hertz (1960) has called the "unquiet dead," referring to those who have died violent or unnatural deaths. Hertz has argued that funeral rituals are a way of strengthening the social bond. The Mayas believe that without proper burial souls linger in the liminal space between earth and the afterlife, condemned in time between death and the final obsequies. And yet these wandering souls may act as intermediaries between nature and the living, buffering as well as enhancing memories through the imagery of their violent history.

Sitting next to Marcelina was her daughter, Elena, also a widow. Elena took Marcelina's nod as a sign to begin. In a quiet voice, she said that she was 17 when her husband was killed on the patio of her house while her two children, Marcelina, and her sister stood by helpless and in horror. It was August 1981, five months after her father had been killed. Soldiers arrived before dawn, pulled Elena's husband out of bed, and dragged him outside, where they punched and kicked him until he was unconscious and then hacked him to death with machetes.

Just as Eufemia was beginning to recall the night her husband was kidnapped, a man carrying a load of wood stopped on the path about 50 feet away to ask who I was and why I was in the village. Don Pedro was the military commissioner in the community. I introduced myself and showed him my permission papers from the commandante of the local garrison. After looking at my papers, Pedro told me I was free to visit the community but advised me to introduce myself to the head of the civil patrol as well.

Eufemia anxiously resumed her story. Her husband had been disappeared by soldiers one night in early 1982. Several days later she had gone to the municipio to register his death, and the authorities told her that if he was missing he was not considered dead. Some weeks later, she did find his mutilated body, but she did not return to register his death until several years later. She was then told that she now owed a fine of Q100 because of the lateness of her report. Eufemia planned to leave in a few weeks to pick coffee on a piedmont plantation to earn the money. She also wanted to secure legal title to her small parcel of land and the house, which her husband had bought in 1981 but for which he never received official papers. This village had been a finca de mozos. The owner of

the coffee plantation also held land in the highlands that he rented to the campesinos in return for
the labor during the harvest.

Las Guardiaespaldas (The Bodyguards)

After the disconcerting visit to the commandante
at the destacamento, I had walked away somewhat
wobbly legged to sit on the bench outside the alcalde's office to wait for a bus to return to one of
the other pueblos in Xe'caj. As I sat there reading,
occasionally glancing up to watch the children
playing at recess, I suddenly noticed Commandante Lopez walking across the square toward
me, dressed in his Kaibil uniform; next to him
was a slightly taller man also dressed in a special
forces uniform but, instead of the maroon beret of
the Kaibiles, wearing the black beret of the para-
chute forces. Closely surrounding the two were
their bodyguards, their M-16s at the ready.
Neither of the two officers had guns, but each had
a long sheathed knife hanging off his belt. They
walked slowly and deliberately toward me. I took
a deep breath and waited. Commandante Lopez
introduced the other to me as an officer from
the *Zona Militar* 320 (military base 320) in Chimaltenango who also wanted to meet me. This
fellow sat down on the bench next to me and
began to speak in English. When I asked where he
had learned to speak English so well, he told me he
had spent some time in North Carolina and Georgia. After asking very detailed questions about
what I was doing in the region and for whom
I was working, they left as abruptly as they had
arrived.

Later, on the ride home, a very old man who
had lost both eyes boarded the bus. Wearing a
tattered but clean traje, he was being led by
a young boy in patched clothing, his grandson,
I presumed. They were obviously poorer than
most. As I sat there wondering about their story,
in my mind's eye I contrasted the two images: the
commandantes with their bodyguards walking
toward me in the square, self-assured in their perfectly pressed combat uniforms, their bodies
straight and tall, and this old man with his empty
sockets, hunched over and smiling, being led ten-
derly by his grandson. As one pair of bodies
echoed stories of privilege and discipline, the
other spoke of suffering and dignity. Each in its
own way embodied a representation of Guatemala's reality.

REFERENCES

Agoson, Marjorie. 1987. "A Visit to the Mothers of the
Plaza de Mayo." *Human Rights Quarterly* 9: 426–35.

Arendt, Hannah. 1958. *The Human Condition*. Chicago:
University of Chicago Press.

Boyarin, Jonathan, ed. 1994. *Remapping Memory: The
Politics of Time and Space*. Minneapolis: University of
Minnesota Press.

Carmack, Robert, ed. 1988. *Harvest of Violence: The
Mayan Indians and the Guatemalan Crisis*. Norman:
University of Oklahoma Press.

Cohn, Carol. 1987. "Sex and Death in the Rational
World of Defense Intellectuals." *Signs* 12(4): 687–718.

Falla, Ricardo. 1983. "The Massacre at the Rural Estate
of San Francisco," July 1982. *Cultural Survival Quarterly* 7(1): 37–42.

———. 1992. *Masacres de la Selva, Ixcan, Guatemala,
1975–1982*. Guatemala: Universidad de San Carlos
de Guatemala.

Feldman, Alan. 1991. *Formations of Violence: The Narrative of the Body and Political Terror in Northern
Ireland*. Chicago: University of Chicago Press.

Forester, Cindy. 1992. "A Conscript's Testimony: Inside
the Guatemalan Army." *Report on Guatemala* 13(2):
6, 14.

Hertz, Robert. 1960. "Contribution to the Study of the
Collective Representation of Death." *In Death and the
Right Hand*, pp. 29–88. London: Cohen and West.

Lovell, W. George. 1992. *Conquest and Survival in Colonial Guatemala*. Kingston, Ont.: Queens University
Press.

Manz, Beatriz. 1988. *Refugees of a Hidden War: The
Aftermath of Counterinsurgency in Guatemala*.
Albany: State University of New York Press.

Martin-Baro, Ignacio. 1989. "La institucionalizacion de
la guerra." Conferencia prenunciada en el XXII Con-
greso International Psicologia. Buenos Aires, June
25–30.

———. 1990. "La violencia en Centroamerica: Una vision
psicosocial." *Revista de Psicologia de El Salvador*
9(35): 123–46.

Sanford, Victoria. 1993. "Victim as Victimizer: Indigenous Childhood and Adolescence in Guatemala's Culture of Terror." Master's thesis, San Francisco State
University.

Scheper-Hughes, Nancy. 1992. *Death Without Weeping:
The Violence of Everyday Life in Brazil*. Berkeley:
University of California Press.

Suarez-Orozco, Marcelo. 1990. "Speaking of the Unspeakable: Toward a Psycho-Social Understanding of
Responses to Terror." *Ethos* 18(3): 353–83.

Uvin, Peter. 1998. *Aiding Violence: The Development
Enterprise in Rwanda*. West Hartford, CT: Kumarian.

Weschler, Lawrence. 1990. *A Miracle, a Universe: Settling Accounts with Torturers*. New York: Penguin.

22

Killing Priests, Nuns, Women, Children

Jean Franco

The murder of three American nuns in El Salvador in December 1980, the murder of priests in Brazil and Argentina, the torture of pregnant women in Uruguay, the farming out of "terrorists'" children to military families in the southern cone, the admonitory raping of women in front of their families in several Latin American countries, the Mexican army's attack on unarmed male and female students in Tlatelolco in 1968, the recent kidnapping in broad daylight of a well-known writer, university teacher, and feminist, Alaíde Foppa, in Guatemala, the dislodging of Indian communities from traditional lands, plus countless other incidents, all appear more and more to be the well-thought-out atrocities of a concerted offensive. It is part of a war that has pitted unequal forces against one another – on the one hand, the overarmed military who have become instruments of the latest stage of capitalist development and, on the other, not only the left but also certain traditional institutions, the Indian community, the family, and the Church (which still provide sanctuary and refuge for resistance). These institutions owe their effectiveness as refuges to historically based moral rights and traditions, rather like the immunities which (before the recent attack on the Spanish embassy in Guatemala) had accrued to diplomatic space. Homes were, of course, never immune from entry and search, but until recently, it was generally males who were rounded up and taken away, often leaving women to carry on and even transmit resistance from one generation to another. Families thus inherited opposition as others inherited positions in the government and bureaucracy.

But what is now at stake is the assault on such formerly immune territories. The attack on the Cathedral in El Salvador in 1980 and the assassination of Archbishop Romero, for instance, showed how little the Church could now claim to be a sanctuary. The resettlement of Indians in Guatemala, of working-class families from militant sectors of Buenos Aires, the destruction of the immunity formerly accorded to wives, mothers, children, nuns, and priests have all taken away every immune space. This assault is not as incompatible as it might at first seem with the military government's organization of its discourse around the sanctity of Church and family. Indeed these convenient abstractions, which once referred to well-defined physical spaces, have subtly shifted their range of meaning. Thus, for instance, the "saucepan" demonstrations of Chilean women during the last months of the Allende regime plainly indicated the emergence of the family as consumer in a society which, under Pinochet, was to acquire its symbolic monument – the spiral-shaped tower of the new labyrinthine shopping centre. The Church, once clearly identified as the Catholic Church, and the parish as its territory, has now been replaced by a rather more flexible notion of religion. The conversion of massive sectors of the population all over Latin America to one form or another of Protestantism, the endorsement by Rios Montt, when President of Guatemala, of born-again Christianity, and the active encouragement, in other countries, of fundamentalist sects, all indicate a profound transformation which, until recently, had gone almost unnoticed. Radio and television now promote a serialized and privatized religious experience which no longer needs to be anchored in the physical reality of the parish and in the continuity of family life.

This process can be described as "deterritorialization," although I use this term in a sense rather different from that used by Deleuze and Guattari. In their view (see Gilles Deleuze and Félix Guattari, *Anti-Oedipus: Capitalism and Schizophrenia*, New York, 1977), primitive society (the social machine) does not distinguish between the family and the rest of the social and political field, all of which are inscribed on the socius (that is, the social machine that distinguishes people according to status and affiliations). In the primitive tribe, the socius is the mother earth. What Deleuze and Guattari describe is a process of abstraction which takes place with the emergence of the despotic state that now inscribes people according to their residence, and in doing so "divides the earth as an object and subjects men to a new imperial inscription, in other words to the abstract unity of the State." This they call "pseudo-territoriality," and see it as the substitution of abstract signs (e.g. money) for the signs of the earth and a privatization of the earth itself (as state or private property). Advanced capitalism carries this abstraction much further, recoding persons and making repression into self-repression, exercised not only in the workplace and the streets but within the family, the one place under capitalism where desire can be coded and territorialized (as with Oedipus).

What seems unsatisfactory in Deleuze and Guattari's description of the family is that even though, reading these authors, we may recognize the family's restrictive and repressive qualities, we do not recognize the family's power as a space of refuge and shelter. What seduces us about the home (and what seduces some people about the convent) is that it is a refuge, a place for turning one's back on the world. Max Horkheimer saw (albeit in an idealized fashion) that the family could nourish subjectivities that were alien to capitalism. (Thomas Mann's *Buddenbrooks* is a good example of the subversive effects of the mother inculcating into her son all that will make him incapable of reproducing the work ethic.) In Latin America, this sense of refuge and the sacredness that attaches to certain figures like the mother, the virgin, the nun, and the priest acquire even greater significance, both because the Church and the home retained a traditional topography and

traditional practices over a very long period, and also because during periods when the state was relatively weak these institutions were the only functioning social organizations. They were states within the state, or even counterstates, since there are certain parishes and certain families which have nourished traditions of resistance to the state and hold on to concepts of "moral right" (E. P. Thompson's term), which account for their opposition to "modernization" (i.e. integration into capitalism). This is not to say that the patriarchal and hierarchical family, whose priority was the reproduction of the social order, has not rooted itself in Latin American soil. But the family has been a powerful rival to the state, somehow more real, often the source of a maternal power which is by no means to be despised, particularly when, as in contemporary Latin America, the disappearance of political spaces has turned the family (and the mother, in particular) into a major institution of resistance.

It is only by recognizing the traditional power of the family and the Church and the association of this power with a particular space (the home, the Church building) that we can begin to understand the significance of recent events in Latin America. Beginning in the fifties and early sixties, "development" brought new sectors of the population, including women, into the labour force. The expansion of transnational companies into Latin America depended on the pool of cheap labour formed from the uprooted peasantry and the ever-growing sector of urban underclasses. The smooth functioning of this new industrial revolution was imperilled by the guerrilla movements and movements of national liberation which, in turn, confronted the counterinsurgency campaigns of the sixties that "modernized" the armies of Latin America, making them pioneers in the newest of torture methods and inventive masters of the art of "disappearance." It is this counterinsurgency movement which has destroyed both the notion of sacred space and the immunity which, in theory if not in practice, belonged to nuns, priests, women and children.

Though women have never enjoyed complete immunity from state terror – indeed rape has been the casually employed resource of forces of law and order since the Conquest – the rapidity with which the new governments have been able to take immunity away from the traditional institutions of Church and family calls for explanation.

Such an explanation would involve understanding not only the particular incidents mentioned at the beginning of this essay, but the profound consequences of destroying what Bachelard, in *The Poetics of Space*, called the "images of felicitous spaces," or topophilia. Bachelard's investigations "seek to determine the human value of the sorts of space that may be grasped, that may be defended against adverse forces, the space we love. For diverse reasons, and with the differences entailed by poetic shadings, this is eulogized space. Attached to its protective value, which can be a positive one, are also imagined values, which soon become dominant." In this essay, I want to give these felicitous spaces a more concrete and historical existence than Bachelard's phenomenology allows, for only in this way can we understand the really extraordinary sacrilege that we are now witnessing.

Although it is impossible to separate the literary from the social, literature is a good place to begin to understand this Latin American imaginary with its clearly demarcated spaces. In common with Mediterranean countries, public space in Latin America was strictly separated from the private space of the house (brothel), home, and convent, that is, spaces which were clearly marked as "feminine." These spaces gave women a certain territorial but restricted power base and at the same time offered the "felicitous" spaces for the repose of the warrior. [. . .]

The very structure of the Hispanic house emphasized that it was a private world, shut off from public activity. It was traditionally constructed around two or more patios, the windows onto the street being shuttered or barred. Inside, the patios with their plants and singing birds represented an oasis, a domestic replica of the perfumed garden. Respectable women only emerged from the house when accompanied and when necessary. Their lives were almost as enclosed as those of their counterparts, the brothel whore and the nun. In the fifties, I lived in such a house where windows onto the outside were felt to mark the beginning of danger as indeed, after curfew, they did. A prison yes, but one that could easily be idealized as a sanctuary given the violence of political life.

The convent was also a sanctuary of sorts, one that gathered into itself the old, the homeless, and the dedicated to God. In José Donoso's novel *The Obscene Bird of Night*, the convent has become an extended building housing the archaic, the mythic and the hallucinating desires which are outlawed from the rest of society. It is this aspect of the Hispanic imaginary which Buñuel's films also capture. Archaic in topography, its huge, empty, decrepit rooms not only sealed it off entirely from the outside world but made it into a taboo territory, the violation of which tempted and terrorized the male imagination.

Finally there was the brothel, the house whose topography mimed that of the convent, with its small cell-like rooms and which, as described by Mario Vargas Llosa in his novel *The Green House*, was another version of the oasis. As the convent gathered to itself the women who were no longer sexual objects, the green house offered them as the common receptacles of a male seed absolved from the strict social rules that governed reproduction.

Blacks, mulattoes, mixtures of all kinds, drunks, somnolent or frightened half-breeds, skinny Chinese, old men, small groups of young Spaniards and Italians walking through the patios out of curiosity. They walked to and fro passing the open doors of the bedrooms, stopping to look in from time to time. The prostitutes, dressed in cotton dresses were seated at the back of the rooms on low boxes. Most of them sat with their legs apart showing their sex, the "fox" which was sometimes shaved and sometimes not. (José María Arguedas, *The Fox Above and the Fox Below*)

In describing these spaces, I am not describing categories of women but an imaginary topography in which the "feminine" was rigidly compartmentalized and assigned particular territories. Individual women constantly transgressed these boundaries but the territories themselves were loaded with significance and so inextricably bound to the sacred that they were often taken for spaces of immunity. With the increase in state terrorism in the sixties, mothers used this traditional immunity to protest, abandoning the shelter of homes for the public square, taking charge of the dead and the disappeared and the prisoners whose existence no one else wished to acknowledge. With the seizure of power by the military, the dismantling of political parties and trade unions, this activity acquired a special importance. Homes became hiding places, bomb factories, escape hatches, people's prisons. From the signifier of passivity and peace, "mother" became a signifier of resistance. Nothing illustrates this in more dramatic fashion than an article by Rodolfo Walsh (an Argentine writer who would himself "disappear" shortly after writing this piece). His daughter, who was the mother of a small child and whose lover had already disappeared, was one of a group of *montoneros* killed in the army attack on a house, an attack which deployed 150 men, tanks and helicopters. A soldier who had participated in this battle described the girl's final moments.

The battle lasted more than an hour and a half. A man and woman were shooting from upstairs. The girl caught our attention because every time she fired and we dodged out of the way, she laughed. All at once there was silence. The girl let go of the machine gun, stood up on the parapet and opened her arms. We stopped firing without being ordered to and we could see her quite well. She was skinny, with short hair and she was wearing a nightdress. She began to talk to us calmly but clearly. I don't remember everything she said, but I remember the last sentence. In fact, I could not sleep for thinking of it. "You are not killing us," she said, "we choose to die." Then she and the man put pistols to their foreheads and killed themselves in front of us.

When the army took over the house, they found a little girl sitting unharmed on the bed and five dead bodies.

The significance of such an event goes far beyond the rights and wrongs of local politics. Like the murder of the nuns in El Salvador and the kidnapping and killing of Alaíde Foppa in Guatemala, it is a cataclysmic event which makes it impossible to think of the Utopian in terms of space or of the feminine in the traditional sense. Most disconcerting of all, the destruction of these Utopian spaces has been conducted not by the left but by the right-wing military who have nothing left to offer but the unattainable commodity (unattainable, that is, for all but the army and the technocrats). It is true that the military of some southern-cone countries are now in (temporary?)

eclipse, but the smell of the cadaver will not be dispelled by the commodity culture, a debt-ridden economy and the forms of restored political democracy.

It is some time since Herbert Marcuse drew attention to the terrors of a desublimated world, one in which such spaces and sanctuaries had been wiped out. His analysis and that of Horkheimer can be seen as overburdened with nostalgia for that *gemütlich* interior of European bourgeois family life in which all the children played instruments in a string quartet. But even if we can no longer accept the now challenged Freudian language of his analysis, he undoubtedly deserves credit for monitoring the first signals from an empty space once occupied by archaic but powerful figures. Feminist criticism based on the critique of patriarchy and the traffic in women has rightly shed no tears for this liquidation of mother figures whose power was also servitude. Yet such criticism has perhaps underestimated the oppositional potentialities of these female territories whose importance as the *only* sanctuaries became obvious at the moment of their disappearance.

This is, however, an essay without a conclusion. I wrote it, thinking of an old friend of mine, Alaíde Foppa, who in 1954 provided sanctuary for those of us left behind in Guatemala and trying to get out after the Castillo Armas coup. I have a vivid memory of her reciting a poem about her five children "like the five fingers of her hand." Today there are only three children left. During the 1960s and 1970s, Alaíde became the driving force behind the feminist movement in Mexico. She was used to going back home once a year to Guatemala to visit her mother. In 1980 she did not come back. A Guatemalan newspaper reported that her whereabouts and that of her chauffeur were "unknown." To this day, Alaíde "continues disappeared" in the words of the newspaper, like many other men, women, priests, nuns, and children in Latin America who no longer occupy space but who have a place.

23

The Fear of Indifference: Combatants' Anxieties about the Political Identity of Civilians during Argentina's Dirty War

Antonius Robben

Armed combatants, locked in violent dispute, expect civilians to take a stand on their conflict. They want people to be forthright about their political sympathies, and declare who has truth, justice, and morality on their side. As is the case in all major outbreaks of violence, so too in Argentina during the 1970s, each party believed that its use of violence was justified. The commanders of the armed forces and the guerrilla organizations considered it immoral *not* to choose sides. Each party tried to draw the Argentine people into its camp and persuade them that the use of violence was of historical necessity. This public discourse was so predominant that it concealed the deep anxiety which hesitant civilians provoked among the disputants of power.

Much has been written about state terror and cultures of fear in Latin America, but next to nothing has appeared about the fears and anxieties of the protagonists of violence themselves. These fears and anxieties, however, are dwarfed in comparison to the immeasurably greater suffering of the civilian victims of state terror. Nevertheless, such sentiments among the victimizers deserve to be studied, because an analysis of the complex and ambiguous relation between combating forces and a civilian population will add another dimension to our understanding of Latin American societies of fear.

Seemingly indifferent civilians provoked contempt and anxiety, as well as fear and uneasy feelings, among the government forces and revolutionary guerrilla forces in Argentina during their conflict in the 1970s. This fear was not a fear of terror – of which, in different degrees, they were its masters – but a fear of defeat, fed by an anxiety over the large number of uncommitted civilians. The Argentine protagonists were troubled by people who refused to rally actively behind either party. These uncommitted civilians fell outside the social categories that had been established with so much bloodshed. They undermined the structure of enmity that characterized a violent conflict presented as an historical inevitability. Their aloofness, it was felt by the protagonists, could result in a defeat by default. Such civilians were the inversion of the men of action, the military and the revolutionary; those who took their own fate and that of others in their hands. I shall use Derrida's neology *undecidable* to describe those civilians.[1] I prefer the term undecidable to the term indecisive, because undecidability does not necessarily imply indecisiveness, passiveness, or even paralysis. Undecidability can also be motivated by an active moral stance against violence. The majority of the Argentine people may be characterized as uncommitted undecidables. The Argentine human rights activists who actively opposed the violence of the military and guerrilla forces represent the involved undecidables.

The Emergence of Political Violence in Argentina

"War," so writes Elaine Scarry, is "a huge structure for the derealization of cultural constructs and, simultaneously, for their eventual reconstitution. The purpose of the war is to designate as an outcome which of the two competing cultural constructs will by both sides be allowed to become real."[2] The revolution which the Argentine *guerrilleros* tried to achieve in the 1970s, and the cultural and political institutions which the military were defending, were conflicting cultural constructs.[3] Theirs was not a contest about power but a contest about the space of culture, about the cultural confines and conditions within which the Argentine people could lead their lives. These lives were manifested in social institutions, conventions and mores, beliefs, symbols and meanings. In the words of General Díaz Bessone: "I insist that war becomes inevitable when values are diametrically opposed. There is no other way. They cannot coexist. That's why war intervenes, because the values are contrary... Subversion means the changing of values, the changing of a national culture. Culture is not just sculpture and painting. No, no. Culture is everything."[4] The Argentine military officers and revolutionaries risked their lives to impose a particular cultural construct on society. Victory could be achieved only at the cost of great sacrifice, because both parties were convinced that the political ills of Argentina were deep-seated.

Political opposition as enmity can be traced back in Argentina to the first half of the nineteenth century, when civil wars plagued a country that at the same time was fighting a war of independence from Spain. Regional *caudillos* disputed the hegemony of the postcolonial elite in Buenos Aires, and violent conflicts about the terms of government and political representation were waged for decades between federalists and centralists. Argentina was to suffer several more outbreaks of violence during the twentieth century in the form of *coups d'état* and bloodily repressed labor strikes and student demonstrations. The political violence reached an unprecedented level during the 1970s, a period which is comparable only to the civil wars of the nineteenth century. Political tensions that had been mounting since the overthrow of the populist president Juan Domingo Perón in a military coup in 1955, gestated into stark enmity during the 1960s as military dictators tightened their grip on the working class and the student body. This political conflict erupted into open violence during the 1970s.

Following the overthrow of Perón, there was a groundswell of political dissatisfaction in Argentina.[5] The continued frustration among the working class at the proscription of the Peronist movement, and the emergence of a class-conscious younger generation that desired political participation, coalesced between 1969 and 1973 into an unstoppable force of opposition to the then ruling military government. Labor unions organized massive strikes. Peronist youth organizations held street demonstrations, and a handful of small paramilitary groups, under the encouragement of Perón, bombed large foreign-owned corporations and would for several hours take control of small towns to create a general sense of insecurity in the country. This popular mobilization was effective. By late 1972 the military government negotiated with Perón about the cession of power through free elections in March 1973.

Several Marxist groups rode the wave of the Peronist protest with success, and managed to attract a small but highly motivated following. They believed that the revolutionary consciousness of the popular masses had reached a decisive level. The People's Revolutionary Army (ERP) – the military branch of the Workers Revolutionary Party (PRT) – emerged from the early 1970s as the most important guerrilla organization.[6] This organization continued with its armed attacks, even after the dictatorship in 1973 made place for a democratic Peronist government. The commanders were convinced that a popular insurrection was within reach, although they knew that it might still take years before a final victory could be achieved. The Marxist organizations based this optimism on what they believed to be an objective and scientific assessment of the political forces in Argentina.[7] The former ERP member, Pedro Cazes Camarero, explained this political scenario two decades later as follows:

What happens is that in addition to this [assessment] we believed in a dialectic of power accumulation. This dialectic of power accumulation occurred partly because the fight against the enemy would tend to strengthen instead of weaken us. Even though we would receive some blows, we would produce a visible political effect that would tend to polarize the political forces around our own force.[8]

This belief in the inevitability of a dialectical political process and the certainty of a revolutionary outcome was communicated to the armed forces and the Argentine people: "We must attack the enemy army at once, now, always, until it is destroyed, in order to have a real, popular, workers' government."[9] [...]

The Structure of Enmity in the 1970s

The Argentine armed forces and the revolutionary organizations have been portrayed by some political analysts and actors as two demons who were involved in a voracious dialectic of mutual destruction entirely disengaged from the wider political and historical context.[10] The human rights activist Graciela Fernández Meijide makes the following observation:

In this society they always try to divide things into two, into two positions. Thus, you have the theory of the two demons, the two pavements (veredas), and the two parties (bandas). This is for me all very Manichaean, totally Manichaean, and it doesn't help at all the development of a third position which would certainly comprise the majority of Argentines.[11]

Fernández Meijide points at the Manichaean aspect of Argentine culture, which continues to create new conflicts and oppositions without resolving previous ones. For this reason, it would be a simplification to characterize the complex political situation in Argentina during the 1970s as only an armed conflict between the military and the revolutionaries. The Argentine revolutionary organizations were certainly not the equivalent of the Italian Red Brigades or the German Red Army Faction which operated in a political vacuum, far from the concerns of the Italian and German working class. Rather the Argentine revolutionaries operated in a general climate of popular commotion. "The violence from above generates the violence from below," was a popular slogan at the time. Tensions took place in factories, universities, parishes, army barracks and on the streets of the major industrial cities. The military denounced

communist agitation and foreign infiltration, while the revolutionary organizations pointed at the exploitation of the working class by imperialist world powers and the national bourgeoisie as the causes of violence. These broad denunciations comprised the threat perception to the cultural constructs that each party tried to impose with violence on Argentine society. An analysis of the public discourse shows that the threat perception remained the same during the 1970s – communism versus capitalist imperialism – but that the operational target changed from year to year according to shifting political forces.[12] [...]

This division into two hostile camps characterizes most armed conflicts, according to Scarry: "[The] participants enter into a structure that is a self-cancelling duality. They enter into a formal duality, but one understood by all to be temporary and intolerable."[13] Each party tries to out-injure its opponent, so that the victorious can impose their conditions on the defeated. Hostile parties should not be defined narrowly in terms of commanders and combatants, but each side tries to draw the rest of society into the conflict. The physical, political and ideological support of the great mass of people – many of whom would prefer simply to carry on with their lives – can be decisive for the final victory. Nobody remains untouched by the violence, as even those who succeed in avoiding any active incorporation can become victims. Societies that fracture along hostile rifts, as was the case in Argentina during the 1970s, deny all grounds for neutrality.

The guerrilla organizations regarded an enemy-foe division in Argentine society as the inevitable outcome of their revolutionary struggle. There was no legitimate middle ground between the two opposed parties: "The sharpening of the repression and the beginning of a generalized civil war will polarize the camps and eliminate intermediary positions."[14] Political violence was intended to accelerate the polarization of Argentine society. The armed forces also believed that the violent confrontation was unavoidable.

Important as Scarry's definition of war as a self-canceling duality is in understanding the clash of opposing cultural constructs, this structure of enmity is a construct in itself. This social construction of enmity becomes visible in the anxieties about the presence of undecidables. Undecidables challenge existing and utopian cultural constructs by adhering to none, and undermine the inevitability of the structure of enmity. The many Argentines who did not want to become involved in the incipient civil war that was waged during the 1970s worried the parties in conflict considerably.

Enemy, Friend, and Indifferent

The Argentine guerrilla organizations viewed the human rights organizations with ambiguity. They were praised for bringing the human and civil rights violations of the government forces to public attention, but were regarded privately as bourgeois institutions that failed to see the need for justified revolutionary violence. For instance, the journalist-writer Osvaldo Bayer called fellow-intellectuals to account. Bayer argued that the military were successful in their harsh repression because most Argentines applauded them with enthusiasm, guarded an accessory silence, or waged a "constructive" opposition by maintaining a dialogue with the dictatorship. He denounced the "neutralist line" of certain politicians and intellectuals who declared that they were "against violence from whatever brand" and were eager to show that they were free from "subversive or communist ideas."[15] Former president Raúl Alfonsín and the writer Ernesto Sábato were mentioned as notable examples of those despicable neutrals. The voices of moderation and dialogue who wished to bring the hostilities to a halt could, apparently, not be tolerated by the parties in conflict.

The official government discourse also departed from a belief in an inevitable polarization of Argentine society. Whereas in 1975 the armed combatants were still targeted as the principal enemy, in 1976 the military began to include so-called ideologues and sympathizers. General Vilas, who had left Tucumán and was stationed in the Patagonian province of Bahia Blanca, declared in August 1976: "The fight against subversion . . . has been carried on until now against the visible head, the subversive delinquent, but not against the ideologue who generates, forms, and molds this new class of delinquents."[16]

The targets were now to be found at both the armed and the ideological fronts. Military doctrine, which was influenced considerably by the counter-insurgency practices of the French during the wars of independence in Algeria and Indo-China, taught the Argentine military that guerrilla warfare was always waged on these two fronts. A 1967 text stated that "Although it is true that the

objective of the subversion is the mind of man, it is no less true that for its conquest it uses both weapons and ideas. As a consequence, there are two camps in which the subversion develops itself: the mental battle and the armed battle."[17] The military were aware that this much more inclusive enemy definition implied a considerable adjustment of public opinion which still viewed war as the confrontation of two regular armies. Members of the military junta emphasized over and again during 1976, 1977, and 1978 that "not only he who attacks with a bomb, a gun, or carries out a kidnapping is an aggressor, but also he who on the level of ideas wants to change our way of life."[18] By 1977, ideologues were said to be even more dangerous than combatants: "I am much more concerned about an ideologue than a combatant; the combatant is dangerous because he is destructive, because his bomb may end many lives. But the ideologue is the one who poisons, who robs children, who destroys the family, and who may create chaos."[19]

Who were considered ideologues and who sympathizers? Did they mean the political strategists of the guerrilla organizations or the editors of clandestine papers such as *El Combatiente, Estrella Roja*, or *Evita Montonera* who, with their vitriolic pens, tried to incite the Argentine people to a popular uprising? Jaime Swart, a minister of the Buenos Aires provincial government, specified that the ideologues were "politicians, priests, journalists, and professors from all levels of education."[20] Everyone who was involved in any sort of political activism, everyone who called publicly for social justice and respect for civil and human rights, could be branded as an ideologue. Sympathizers were all those who felt some affinity for the utopian ideals of the revolutionary left. An overwhelming majority of the 10,000–30,000 "disappeared" of the years of repression were labeled as ideologues and sympathizers, many of whom never brandished a weapon or participated in any armed assault. The military regarded them as dangerous because they were considered responsible for spreading subversive ideas, distributing illegal pamphlets, providing shelter and assistance to *guerrilleros*, or were believed to pertain to the large pool of people from which the guerrilla organizations drew their recruits.

All those who did not openly profess to be on the side of the military were regarded as supporting the enemy: "The enemy are not only the terrorists, but the enemies of the Republic are also the impatient, those who place sectorial interests above the country, the frightened, and the indifferent."[21] This incorporation of the entire Argentine nation into the conflict went even so far that General Ibérico Saint-Jean, the governor of the province of Buenos Aires, declared in May 1976: "First we will kill all the subversives: then we will kill their collaborators; then...their sympathizers, then...those who remain indifferent; and finally we will kill the timid."[22]

This lumping together of the indifferent, the frightened, and the timid with enemy combatants, ideologues, and collaborators was a brutal attempt to impose the structure of enmity on a large segment of Argentine society that fell outside the self-canceling duality. In the eyes of the combatants, the indifferent refused to commit themselves to the armed contest, while the frightened and timid were fleeing from the open hostility to a self-absorbed private world. The indifferent, the timid, and the frightened did not constitute a miliary or political threat but a conceptual and moral threat, a threat to the oppositional meaning of enmity and the partisan morality it entailed. They showed that the violence was not inevitable, but a product of human choice and making. Whereas the enemy became defined and definable through political violence, the indifferent escaped the logic of difference and became unclassifiable. They had become, in Douglas's terms, "anomalies" and, in Derrida's terminology, "undecidables" who undermined the taken for granted opposition of enemy and friend.[23] Bauman observes in this connection:

They are that "third element" which should not be. The true hybrids, the monsters: not just unclassified, but unclassifiable. They therefore do not question this one [friend–foe] opposition here and now: they question oppositions as such, the very principle of the opposition, the plausibility of dichotomy it suggests. They unmask the brittle artificiality of division – they destroy the world.[24]

The indifferent undermined through their aloofness a duality that had been proclaimed as fundamental to society and, even more threatening, undermined the moral hierarchy of good versus evil that was implied by the opposition of enemy and friend.

Derrida argues that dichotomies, such as life and death, good and evil, culture and nature, soul and body, male and female, speech and writing,

master and servant, and inside and outside, are all hierarchized cultural constructions in which the former pole is treated as being superior to the latter. Against these dichotomies, Derrida places so-called undecidables with contradictory meanings whose signified meanings can be derived only from their syntactical relations. Undecidables have "false" properties that resist their inclusion in binary oppositions, yet without constituting a separate third term. Instead, they disorganize these dichotomies by inhabiting them.[25] [...]

Undecidables and the Uncanny

By considering undecidables as enemies of Argentine society, it became increasingly difficult for the warring parties during the mid-1970s to tell friend from foe, and even to discover whether their own bellicose selves had not become subverted. The enemy had become so diffuse that the Argentine armed forces became uncertain about their own identity, and began to define themselves through the contours of their opponent. Oneself was everything that the enemy was not. Brigadier-General Agosti proclaimed in 1978: "Now we recognize our enemies. We know how they act and we know their objectives. We have proven that they are fundamentally different from us, some in their behavior, others conceptually and ideologically. When we have doubts about our own identity, we can find it by analyzing the identity of our enemy."[26] The enemy had advanced to the perimeters of the self. The enemy was not just the one who attacked or subverted society, the one who infiltrated and poisoned one's family, but the enemy was the negation of the self. A self which could only be protected from total collapse by making a united stand. The people had to become a standing force against the subversion in which "every citizen [is] dressed, in the inmost of his heart, in the combat uniform that the gravity of the hour demands from us all."[27]

The Marxist revolutionary organizations also began to have doubts about their identity as the conflict progressed and the number of casualties increased. The losses were attributed to a faltering loyalty, ideological purity, and the suspicious class background of members and leaders. The Marxist PRT-ERP promoted members of undisputable working-class origins to commanding positions. Identity became defined as a self shaped by working-class parents and matured through revolutionary struggle.

The Peronist Montoneros were equally concerned about their identity. They tried to instill its members with a revolutionary spirit, and instituted tribunals to enforce the political doctrine. One notable case is the fate of Tulio Valenzuela, a Montonero officer who was captured by the Argentine army in 1978. In order to save the lives of his wife and himself, he pretended to go along with a plan to assassinate Mario Firmenich, the First Commander of the Montoneros. Valenzuela was to lead an infiltrator to Firmenich's hideout in Mexico. Once in Mexico, Valenzuela escaped from his captors, warned Firmenich about the plot, and prevented the liquidation. But the Montonero commanders wondered about Valenzuela. Who is he? Is he a loyal member who against all odds thwarted the decapitation of the movement or is he a turncoat? On whose side does he stand? Valenzuela was court-martialed and convicted of treason. He was not executed, because of obvious extenuating circumstances, but degraded to second lieutenant and ordered to provide self-criticism. Valenzuela criticized himself for his arrogance in believing that he could singlehandedly combat the enemy from within, for violating the revolutionary doctrine, and for trying to reconcile his personal interests with the interests of the revolutionary movement. Demonstrating his loyalty to the guerrilla organization in a near-suicidal mission, he entered Argentina with false documents to continue the resistance against the dictatorship. Soon, he was caught and killed.[28]

In the eyes of the military and the guerrilla, society had to be placed ahead of the self if both were to survive. A self could be protected from total collapse only if society would make a united stand, either on the left or on the right. Every man and woman had to be mobilized in this war and be incorporated in the national forces of defence or, according to the guerrilla leaders, into a popular militia. If such national union could be achieved by either party, then the opponent would be facing an invincible force.

The discourse of enmity was a narrative about difference. This narrative emerged from opposed cultural conceptions about self and society, from opposed conceptions about how to organize Argentina, its political institutions, and national identity. Violence became the idiom to achieve the society which both parties, in their messianism and utopianism, believed the Argentine people intensely desired. This narrative had to be sustained during the armed contest, not only to justify the use of force, but also to impel the parties to action, sharpen their political views, and maintain the desire to kill fellow human beings defined as the negation of one's own existence.

NOTES

1 See Derrida, *Disseminations*; Derrida, *Positions*.
2 See Scarry, *The Body in Pain*, p. 137.
3 The political violence of the 1970s or, more narrowly, the military rule of Argentina between 1976 and 1983, has been described with a confusing array of names that each betray different imputed causes, conditions, and consequences. The military have used terms such as dirty war, antirevolutionary war, fight against the subversion, and the Process of National Reorganization. Human rights groups talk about state terror, repression, and military dictatorship. Former revolutionary organizations employ terms used by human rights groups, but also talk about civil war, war of liberation, and anti-imperialist struggle. Whether the violence of the 1970s is described with the term antirevolutionary war, civil war, or state terror is important for these groups because each designation implies a different moral and historical judgment that may turn patriots into oppressors, victims into ideologues, and heroes into subversives.
4 Author's interview with General Díaz Bessone on 12 June 1989.
5 See Crassweller, *Perón and the Enigmas*; James, *Resistence and Integration*; Munck, *Argentina*; Page, *Perón: A Biography*.
6 See Mattini, *Hombres y mujeres*; Santucho, *Los ultimos Guevaristas*; Seoane, *Todo o nada*.
7 Hannah Arendt's critique of ideology (Arendt, *Origins of Totalitarianism*, p. 469) applies here as much to the revolutionaries as to the military leaders who justified the 1976 *coup d'état* as a new beginning: "Ideologies pretend to know the mysteries of the whole historical process – the secrets of the past, the intricacies of the future – because of the logic inherent in their respective ideas. Ideologies are never interested in the miracle of being. They are historical, concerned with becoming and perishing, with the rise and fall of cultures, even if they try to explain history by some 'law of nature.'"
8 Author's interview with former ERP member Pedro Cazes Camarero, on 29 May 1991.
9 *El Combatiente* 6(93), 1973: 4.
10 See Schiller et al., *Hubo dos terrorismos?*

11   Author's interview with Graciela Fernández Meijide on 16 May 1990.
12   Perelli, "Military's Perception," confuses threat perception with enemy definition in an otherwise interesting article about the military as political actors. Pion-Berlin (*Ideology*, pp. 5–7) argues that the Argentine military's violent response to the counterinsurgency was not based on an objective assessment of the real threat, but on preconceived notions about a supposed threat.
13   Scarry, *The Body in Pain*, p. 87.
14   *El Combatiente* 9(221), 1976: 11.
15   Bayer, "Pequeño recordatório," pp. 203, 208.
16   *La Nación*, 5 Aug. 1976.
17   Masi, "Lucha contra la subversión," p. 38.
18   General Videla, quoted in *La Nación*, 18 Dec. 1977.
19   General Chasseing, quoted in *La Nación*, 19 Sept. 1978.
20   Quoted in *La Nación*, 12 Dec. 1976.
21   Admiral Massera, quoted in *La Nación*, 4 Dec. 1976.
22   General Ibérico Saint-Jean, quoted in Simpson and Bennett, *The Disappeared*, p. 66.
23   See Douglas, *Purity and Danger*; Derrida, *Disseminations*.
24   Bauman, "Modernity and Ambivalence," pp. 148–9.
25   See Derrida, *Disseminations*, pp. 97, 221, Derrida, *Positions*, p. 43.
26   Agosti, *Discursos*, pp. 66–8.
27   Admiral Massera, quoted in *La Nación*, 4 March 1977.
28   See Bonasso, *Recuerdo de la muerte*, pp. 185–99, 217–27; Gasparini, *Montoneros*, pp. 219–20.

REFERENCES

Agosti, Orlando Ramón, *Discursos del Comandante en Jefe de la Fuerza Aerea Argentina Brigadier General Orlando Ramón Agosti*. Author's edition, 1978.
Arendt, Hannah. *The Origins of Totalitarianism*. Cleveland, OH: Meridian Books, 1968 [1951].
Bauman, Zygmunt, "Modernity and Ambivalence," in Mike Featherstone (ed.), *Global Culture: Nationalism, Globalization, and Modernity*. London: Sage, 1990, pp. 143–69.
Bayer, Osvaldo, "Pequeño recordatório para un país sin memória," in Saúl Sosnowski (ed.), *Represión y recon-strucción de una cultura: el caso Argentino*. Buenos Aires: EUDEBA, 1988, pp. 203–27.
Bonasso, Miguel, *Recuerdo de la muerte*. Mexico: Ediciones Era, 1984.
Crassweller, Robert D., *Perón and the Enigmas of Argentina*. New York: W. W. Norton, 1987.
Derrida, Jacques, *Positions*. Chicago: University of Chicago Press, 1981.
—— *Disseminations*. London: Athlone Press, 1981.
Douglas, Mary, *Purity and Danger: An Analysis of Concepts of Pollution and Taboo*. London: Penguin, 1970.
Gasparini, Juan, *Montoneros: Final de cuentas*. Buenos Aires: Puntosur, 1988.
James, Daniel, *Resistance and Integration: Peronism and the Argentine Working Class, 1946–1976*. Cambridge: Cambridge University Press, 1988.
Masi, Juan José, "Lucha contra la subversión," *Revista de la Escuela Superior de Guerra* 45(373), 1967: 36–90.
Mattini, Luis, *Hombres y mujeres del PRT-ERP*. Buenos Aires: Editorial Contrapunto, 1990.
Munck, Ronaldo, *Argentina: From Anarchism to Peronism. Workers, Unions and Politics, 1855–1985*. London: Zed, 1987.
Page, Joseph A., *Perón: A Biography*. New York: Random House, 1983.
Perelli, Carina, "The Military's Perception of Threat in the Southern Cone of South America," in Louis W. Goodman, Johanna S. R. Mendelson, and Juan Rial (eds.), *The Military and Democracy: The Future of Civil–Military Relations in Latin America*. Lexington, MA and Toronto: Lexington Books, 1990, pp. 93–105.
Pion-Berlin, David, *The Ideology of State Terror: Economic Doctrine and Political Repression in Argentina and Peru*. Boulder, CO: Lynne Rienner, 1989.
Santucho, Julio, *Los últimos Guevaristas: Surgimiento y eclipse del Ejercito Revolucionario del Pueblo*. Buenos Aires: Puntosur, 1988.
Scarry, Elaine, *The Body in Pain: The Making and Unmaking of the World*. Oxford and New York: Oxford University Press, 1985.
Schiller, Herman, et al., *Hubo dos terrorismos?* Buenos Aires: Ediciones Reencuentro, 1986.
Seoane, María, *Todo o nada*. Buenos Aires: Planeta, 1991.
Simpson, John and Jana Bennett, *The Disappeared and the Mothers of the Plaza*. New York: St Martin's Press, 1985.

24

On Cultural Anesthesia: From *Desert Storm to Rodney King*

Allen Feldman

We lost any sense of seasons of the year, and we lost any sense of the future. I don't know when the spring was finished, and I don't know when the summer started. There are only two seasons now. There is a war season, and somewhere in the world there is a peace season.

Resident of besieged Sarajevo[1]

Cultural anesthesia is my gloss of Adorno's (1973) insight that, in a post-Holocaust and late capitalist modernity, the quantitative and qualitative dissemination of objectification *increases* the social capacity to inflict pain upon the Other[2] – and I would add – to render the Other's pain inadmissible to public discourse and culture.[3] It is upon this insight that a political anthropology of the senses in modernity can be elaborated. This formula implies that the communicative and semantic legitimacy of sensory capacities, and their ability to achieve collective representation in public culture, is unevenly distributed within systems of economic, racial, ethnic, gender, sexual, and cultural domination.[4] Adorno's point about modernity's pain can be linked to the respective theses of Lukács (1971), Foucault (1978), Jameson (1981), Corbin (1986), Taussig (1992), and Feldman (1995) that the construction of the modern political subject entailed the stratification and specialization of the senses, and the consequent repression of manifold perceptual dispositions (see Seremetakis 1993).[5] As a driving force in this historical dynamic, the mass media's depiction of the agents and objects of violence is crucial to the modernizing embodiment of those political subjects who occupy both sides of the screen of public representation. This is all the more pertinent when

the very embodied character of violence is evaded, ignored, or rewritten for collective reception.

Like other institutions (industrial, penological, psychiatric, and medical), the mass production of facts, *and of facticity itself*, are based on techniques and disciplines that, in the case of the media, materially mold a subject and culture of perception. The mass media has universalizing capacities that promote and inculcate sensory specializations and hierarchical rankings such as the priority of visual realism and the often commented on gendered or racial gaze. Like the normative optics of gender and race, objective realism, the depictive grammar of the mass media, should not be perceived as an ahistorical given; it is an apparatus of internal and external perceptual colonization that disseminates and legitimizes particular sensorial dispositions over others within and beyond our public culture.

In the 19th century, "realism" was associated with modes of narration and visualization that presumed an omniscient observer detached from and external to the scenography being presented. It was linked to formal pictorial perspectivism and narrative linearity with all its assumptions about causality, space, and time. Yet during this period, cultural and scientific attention gradually detached itself from exclusive concentration on the scene observed in order to dissect and depict the act of observation itself (Crary 1991). The perceiving subject could no longer remain external once perception became one object among others of realist representation. The scientific objectification of perception dovetailed with the commodification of perception by such forces as new media technologies, the manufacture and consumption of reproducible mass articles and experiences, advertising, new leisure practices, the acceleration of time, and the implosions of urban space – all of which involved the remolding of everyday sensory orientations.

In the 1930s, Ernst Bloch, redefined "realism" as *the cult of the immediately ascertainable fact*, thereby pointedly linking it to norms of rapid and easy consumer satisfaction (see Bloch 1990). More recently, David Harvey's (1989) spatial analyses implicitly show the historical connection between the mass production/consumption of facticity and the apparent increase in perceptual mobility that accompanies the space/time compression characteristic of late modernity. Space/time compression can be defined as the implosion of perceptual simultaneity – the abutment of persons, things, and events from a plurality of locales, chronologies, and levels of experience once discrete and separate. Harvey attributes this not only to technological advances, but also to the accelerated circulation and increasingly efficient distribution of commodities, and to the permeation of exchange values in which new objects, spaces, and activities become commodifiable and measurable and, thus, interchangeable with each other. When previously uncommodified things, activities, and spaces become interchangeable and substitutable and carry mobile valuations, they take on new temporal and spatial coordinates for human perception (Feldman 1991c).

The economic and psychic binding of perceptual command to consumer satisfaction, discernment, and skills generates a pseudo-mastery over "the real" through the experience and manipulation of simultaneity. The media's mass production and commodification of visual and audio facticity both creates and depends upon a perceptual apparatus of holistic realism. Here the ingestion of totality, perceptual holism – the personal capacity to encompass things through prosthetics – becomes a valued commodity in itself. The holistic apparatus frequently jettisons the indigestible depth experience of particular sensory alterities. This is the case when sensory difference conflicts with the myth of

immediate and totalizing perceptual command by resisting norms of accelerated consumption and the easy disposability of things (Seremetakis 1993, 1994). These complex interactions of perception, space, time, facticity, consumption, and material culture pose an eminently modernist dilemma: *that the perception of history is irrevocably tied to the history of sensory perception.*[6]

* * *

Cultural anesthesia is a reflexive passageway into historical consciousness and representation, as Alain Corbin (1986) pointed out when he complained that Western history, as written, has no odor. In the mass media, perceptual holism and cultural anesthesia converge and take many forms. Generalities of bodies – dead, wounded, starving, diseased, and homeless – are pressed against the television screen as mass articles. In their pervasive depersonalization, this anonymous corporeality functions as an allegory of the elephantine, "archaic," and violent histories of external and internal subalterns. The panopticism of documentary television, like its penological predecessor (Foucault 1978),[7] creates a new cellular intervention that captures and confines disordered and disordering categories of bodies. Staged, mounted, framed, and flattened by a distilling electronic sieve, these icons of the static become moral inversions of the progressively malleable bodies of the ideal American viewer, whose public body is sensualized and mythicized by the orchestration of commercial messages on cosmetics, exercise, automobiles, fashion, dieting, recreation, and travel. This visual polarity between the reformable bodies of the observer and the determined, deformed, and reduced bodies of the observed disseminates for the viewing public a cultural scenario first identified by Hegel's master/slave dialectic: that relations of domination are spatially marked by the increase of perceptual (and thus social) distance from the body of the Other. In turn, this body is essentialized by material constraints that deny it recognizable sentience and historical possibility (Kojéve 1969).[8]

But cultural anesthesia can also disembody subjects, which is what occurred in crucial segments of the televising of Operation Desert Storm. Here the media both pre-empted and merged with the American military arsenal through the video erasure of "Arab" bodies. In order to fuse perceptual dominance with topographic conquest enemy,

Oriental bodies were electronically "disappeared" like the troublemakers in Joseph Heller's novel *Catch 22* (1961); Iraqis were magically transmuted into infinitesimal grains of sand that threatened the American war machine. Here the body vanished was a priori the body vanquished. And a mass war against the built environment was mystified as a crusade against the desert as Orientalist topography.

The eulogized smartbombs were prosthetic devices that extended our participant observation in the video occlusion of absented Iraqi bodies. What were these celebrated mechanisms but airborne televisions, visualizing automata, that were hurled down upon the enemy creating his conditions of (non)visibility? Their broadcast images functioned as electronic simulacra that were injected into the collective nervous system of the audience as antibodies that inured the viewer from realizing the human-material consequences of the war. Visual mastery of the campaign pushed all other sensory dimensions outside the perceptual terms of reference. Culturally biased narrations, abetted by information technology historically molded to normative concepts of sensory truth, precluded any scream of pain, any stench of corpse from visiting the American living room.

The spectatorship cultivated by the televising of Desert Storm cannot be reduced to voyeurism as some have suggested (see Stam 1991), for perceptual entanglement with the video simulation of the war was crucial to the manufacturing of consent and, thus, politically and instrumentally implicated the viewing public in the action of violence. When a voyeur acts through a surrogate, it is to avoid material complicity, not to share in it. Yet in Desert Storm, the perceptual tools of the media exploited and elaborated the post-Vietnam political fantasy of American reempowerment. This metanarrative blurred the effective and moral distance between viewing and acting, thereby engendering material complicity on the part of the ideal electronic spectator. Here sensory selection was a productive apparatus fashioning mutual political agency (and not passivity) between those who acted by looking and those whose acts of death were cinematized. Civilian television observation was continuous with the military optics of the fighter pilot and bombardier who were dependent on analogous prosthetic technology and who killed at a distance with the sensory impunity and omniscient vision of the living-room

spectator. The combat crews who played with aggressive drives by watching pornographic videos prior to flying missions demonstrated the uniform sensorium between viewing and violence as they up-shifted from one virtual reality to another.

* * *

It didn't make any sense to me, I couldn't see why they were doing what they were doing.... He moved, they hit him.... I was trying to look at and view what they were looking at.... Evidently they saw something I didn't see. [Los Angeles Police Department Officer Theodore Briseno on the arrest of Rodney Glen King][9]

Less than two months into Operation Desert Storm, the effaced body of the Other reappeared close at hand with the televised beating of Rodney King. Originally visualized outside the prescribed circuits of fact production, this black body broke through the nets of anesthesia. Its shock effect derived not only from long-standing racial scars, but also from the concurrent myth being played out with Desert Storm. The media campaign in the desert succeeded in sterilizing the post-Vietnam violence of the state, but the images of King's beating showed the state making pain. The immediate shock of the televised beating originated in unprogrammed sensory substitution. Even the viewer insulated by race and class could experience the involuntary projection of his or her body to that point of the trajectory marked by the swinging police batons as they came down upon the collective retina that was suddenly rendered tactile. The spectacle of state-manufactured trauma interdicted the visual myth of sanitary violence. King's beating was the skeletal X-ray image flashed upon the technologized surface of state rationality. Desert Storm and the beating of Rodney King evolved into two irreconcilable national narratives. Desert Storm celebrated a triumphalist sense of an ending, while King's beating laid bare another layer of wounding encounters: unfinished history as mise-en-scène – bound to return in the near future despite all attempts to change channels.[10] Two antagonistic icons of national experience impinged on the public screen of electronic consciousness without resolution, without one set of images offering a coherent account of the other.

It is no coincidence that, a year later, the dominant tropes of Operation Desert Storm seemed to work their way into the juridical reconstruction of

King's beating. The trial of the Los Angeles police officers rescripted King's video. This reconstruction successfully returned the violence inflicted upon King to the protective corridors of state rationality. The legal restitution of state violence drew upon the depth structures of neocolonial racial logic that had worked so well in the Desert Storm propaganda: qualification of the body of the Other by geography, disembodiment of the Other's pain, and facilitation of cultural anesthesia for all those who could be rendered directly or indirectly accountable for the pain of the Other.

The actual beating of Rodney King and its subsequent jural reconstruction mobilized a series of spaces within which King's body could be processed as a racial, a disciplinary, and a legal object. Through this metonymy of spaces, explicit and inferred, King achieved a dynamic visibility within which the video of the beating was only a trailer.

Twenty minutes prior to King's car's being stopped by the police, Officer Powell[11] tapped that infamous statement into his communication unit concerning a recent case: "Sounds almost as exciting as our last call, it was right out of 'Gorillas in the Mist'" (Courtroom Television Network 1992). He was referring to a domestic quarrel involving an African-American family, though he later denied any racial connotation to the remark. In gravitating to this image, the media and the prosecution missed its deeper significance by artificially detaching the racist imagery of Powell's remark from the everyday exercise of state power. Beyond and below state formalism, legal codes, and official police procedures, there lies a symbolic logic of the state, animated by empowering micropractices of depersonalization, that is, readily fed by and articulated with culturally in-place racist archetypes.

The phrase "Gorillas in the Mist" in this instance, clearly evokes the jungle, the wilderness, the frontier – outside spaces opposed to a civilizational interior. These are presocial, naturalized terrain from which the sanctioned enforcer extracts the disciplinary subject as so-much raw material to be reworked by the state.[12] Likewise, the mythic antisocietal zones from which the disciplinary subject is obtained, mark the latter's embodiment as presocial through the stigma of animality. The bodily alterity of the suspect-as-animal predetermines the material character and physical locus of police action on their captive.

Bestial imagery continued to leak into subsequent characterizations of King made by defense witnesses and the accused. King was referred to as "bear-like" (Riley 1992a) and as "getting on his haunches" by Officer Powell in testimony (Courtroom Television Network 1992).[13]

Animal imagery may have informed Officer Powell's project of both taming and caging King within a prescribed spatial perimeter, a practice that has both penal and racial overtones. He made the following statements during his examination by his attorneys and the prosecution:

I yelled at him [King] to get down on the ground, to lay down on the ground.... He repeated the motion again, getting up again.... I stopped and evaluated whether he was going to lie there on the ground or whether he was going to get up again.... It was a continuing series of him getting back up on his arms, pushing up, sometimes raising to his knees, sometimes getting on his haunches. I commanded him to get down on the ground, and when he wouldn't go for it, I hit him in the arms and tried to knock him back down. [Courtroom Television Network 1992]

At one point, the prosecutor asked: "What was the reason for hitting him?" Powell replied:

——I didn't want him to get back up.
——What were you striking at?
——I was striking at his arms.... I was trying to knock him down from the push up position, back down onto the ground where he would be in a safer position.... I was scared because he was being told to lie down on the ground; he was getting hit with the baton several times; and he continued to get back up.... I was looking up for something else to keep him down on the ground. [Courtroom Television Network 1992]

It took Officer Powell 46 blows with his baton to incarcerate King into the spatial corridor he called "the ground." Officer Powell's geographical perception moved from "jungle" to "the ground," a provisional and surrogate territory of the state, while King, through violence, was shifted from animality to a subject in compliance. Sergeant Charles Duke, the defense's police procedures expert, described this compliance as viewed from the video:

[W]hen he was in a flat position, where his feet were not cocked, where they were straight up and down, and where his hands were above his head or at his side, he was not hit. [Courtroom Television Network 1992]

Sergeant Stacey Koon, the presiding officer at the scene of King's beating, also testified to the meaning of this posture and added that at this point King's bodily response *and directed speech* to the officers beating him signaled the final level of compliance. The successful confinement of King – the symmetry of a body lying at attention with the face in the dirt – *and* the acquisition of linguistic reciprocity marked the neutering of the animalized body and its internalization of the will of the state. A "gorilla in the mist," a black "bear" that insisted on rising on its "haunches," was turned by violence into a speaking subject. Official LAPD procedures underwrite this civilizing sequence. Police department directives on the use of violence while performing an arrest locate the subject capable of discourse at the lowest end of the scale of noncompliance and physical intervention. The subject in *logos* is the subject in law. The further removed the arrestee is from language, the closer the suspect is to the body and, thus, closer to escalating violence by the state. It is my suggestion that, for the police who beat him, this violent passage of King from animality and the body to language and compliance intimately involved judgments concerning his capacity to sense and to remember pain.

Rodney King had to be taken to a hospital after his beating. Medical attendants assisting at his treatment testified to the following statements made by Officer Powell (and denied by him) to King, who worked at a sports stadium:

We played a little hardball tonight. Do you *remember* who was playing? . . . We won and you lost. [Riley 1992a: 30, emphasis added]

It is a moment of reflection and summation after the act. King's wounds are being tended at the instruction of the man who beat him. The author of violence, grown intimate after his labors, inquires whether his prisoner can recollect what has passed between them, and whether he recognizes the social relation they have entered. This inquiry presumes King's participation in common cultural ground; a mutuality that exists for Officer Powell only after the beating. Baseball, as a ludic metaphor of male dominance, converts batons into bats. King's recognition of this conversion, the admission of a shared culture of sport, more than being another

stage in his socialization, would normalize the violence inflicted on him, thus, placing Powell's acts within the realm of the acceptable.

It is through this dialogue of recognition that the agent of violence retrieves what he has authored through his acts. What is expected to answer him is his creation, his violence, and his body doubled by the logos and submission of the subaltern. Powell's hospital discourse is too deeply anchored in the narratology of torture to have been fabricated (see Feldman 1991a). Artifice follows political life here. In the second volume of Paul Scott's *Raj Quartet* (1978), an analogous encounter takes place between a white English policeman and his Indian prisoner he has just finished beating. The victim, Hari Kumar, describes "the situation" – the creation and acknowledgement of dominance through torture – to an ex post facto government investigation:

——What in fact was this situation? . . .
——It was a situation of enactment.
——These ideas of what you call the situation were the DSP's [District Superintendent of Police] not your own?
——Yes he wanted them to be clear to me. . . . Otherwise the enactment would be incomplete. . . . The ideas without the enactment lose their significance. He said if people would enact a situation they would understand its significance. . . . He said that up until then our relationship had only been symbolic. It had to become real. . . . He said . . . [it] wasn't enough to say he was English and I was Indian, that he was ruler and I was one of the ruled. We had to find out what it meant . . . the contempt on his side and the fear on mine. . . . He said . . . we had to enact the situation as it really was, and in a way that would mean neither of us ever *forgetting* [Scott 1978:298–9, emphasis added]

In his own "situation of enactment," Powell confirms the socializing function of his graphic usage of King's body. Through violence, King, like Hari Kumar, is meant to acquire *memory*; a history of who "won" and who "lost." King is asked to recollect hierarchy, its origin, and his position in it. He is progressively shifted from the jungle to the liminality of his beating ground only to come home to a baseball diamond, a preeminent terrain of American normalization (where he is subjected to hardball or becomes one). These qualifying spaces, jungle, ground, baseball field, and their various personae, gorillas, bear, and hardball, trace the incremental objectification of King and the gradated effacement of his subject-hood *and his pain*. King's pain achieves presence only at the end of this progression and solely as an artifact of power; his pain is the affective presence of the state within his body and person.

This is why Officer Powell speaks to King about baseball, memory, and hierarchy at precisely the moment that his victim is receiving medical attention. Police violence assaulted King's body, and police-ordered medical treatment attempts to redress the effaced sensory integrity of that body, thereby crediting the now socialized King with somatic capacities denied to him during the beating (see below). It is at this juncture that Powell asks King to remember through the senses, through the vehicle of recalled pain. Removal and manipulative restoration of the senses facilitates the state's coercive construction of personal memory and identity (see Feldman 1991a: 128–38). Hari Kumar, in Scott's novel, identifies the attempted restitution of sensory integrity by his aggressor as the last act of political degradation: "the offer of charity. He gave me water. He bathed the lacerations" (Scott 1978: 299).

* * *

The final territorialization of King's body took place at court. Isolated frames of the video were time coded by the prosecution and freeze framed and grid mapped by the defense as if the event were an archaeological site. This reorganization of the video's surface resembled the video grids superimposed upon their targets by the smart bombs of Desert Storm. In the Simi Valley courtroom, fragments of action and isolated body parts achieved visibility as material evidence through analogous optical framing. The grid mapping detached King's limbs from each other in a division of labor that sorted out pertinent parts and actions from inadmissible and irrelevant residues. Visual dissection of King's body provided the defense argument with crucial perceptual fictions that were culturally mediated as objective and real. Thus, cinematized time informed the following typical analysis of King's videotaped postures by Sergeant Duke, the defense's police procedures expert: "It would be a perception that position 336:06 [time code] to be [*sic*] an aggressive position" (Courtroom Television Network 1992). This discourse was possible because of the colonization of King's body by the virtual temporalities of slow motion, fast forward,

and freeze frame. With cinematic artifice, King's body was montaged into a purely electronic entity with no inwardness or tangibility. His body became a surface susceptible to endless reediting and rearrangement, as it suited both the prosecution and the defense. Further, by automatically admitting such cinematic fictions and grammars as *material evidence* and as objective data, the court also collapsed the perceptual and temporal divergence between watching edited video fragments and the in-situ intent and subjectivity of the participants during the action of violence. In this variant of visual realism, the equivalent of a refiguring pictorial perspectivism was created by foregrounding selected body parts and actions and backgrounding others. The narration of authoritative witnesses fabricated, in the present, the formal point of view of the spectator.

These fabrications provided the prosecution, the defense, and the jury with an extraordinary prosthetic penetration to the same extent that the subjective and sensorial side of violence undergone by King was eviscerated. The agency of the participants in the trial was based on sensory privileges that were denied to King from beating to verdict (King never testified in court). As the accused policemen accounted for their actions that night, they re-viewed and re-cast their violence through the pseudo-exactitude of the technologized eye, thereby flattening the chasm between enactment and testimony (as reenactment). The reediting of the video juxtaposed temporally and spatially distanced acts, creating a perceptual apparatus of holistic space-time compression that extended to, and empowered, the courtroom vision and discourse of the defendants. By such means, the defense was able to convert the video into a time-motion study in police efficiency.[14] In his "expert" testimony, Sergeant Duke exploited the camera's eye to rationalize the defendants' violence and to exaggerate their visual capacities in the midst of their delivery of over 100 blows to King. Sergeant Duke simply invented a semiotics of King's imminent aggression and indicted the victim through the mindless autonomy of his beaten limbs:

The suspect has the hand flat on the ground. The arm appears to be cocked. His left leg appears to be bent, coming up in a kneeling position; it appears to be in a rocking position with the other arm flat on the ground in a pushing position. [Courtroom Television Network 1992]

When asked by the prosecution if he considered King to be an animal, Officer Powell replied that King "was acting like one . . . because of his uncontrollable behavior" (Courtroom Television Network 1992). In other words, King was bestial to the extent that he could not feel and therefore could resist the baton blows. Animalistic anesthesia to pain provided a negative aura that retroactively established the sensitized and almost humanistic application of "reasonable violence" by the police. The police and King were distributed along a graded sensory scale. It is the fictionalized visual acuity of the police in assessing the impact of their own violence after the fact that separates them, in a Cartesian fashion, from their own bodies and actions, and which becomes a contributing factor in the jury's verdict. However, King could not be reasonable or lawful, for the police and the jury, because he was submerged in a resistant body, without senses and without corresponding judgment. Confronting his alleged insensate resistance, the police endowed King with affectivity by exploring the levels of pain that could finally register the will of the state on his body.

Narcosis was the final ingredient in the racial stew used to make King's anesthesia. The defendants testified to their certainty that King was under the influence of "PCP" at the time of his arrest. Yet, no physical collaboration was ever provided for this assertion, despite King's medical examination. The powerful combination of racial innuendo and cinematic dismemberment forged the complicity of the jury in the subtraction of King's senses. As one jury member declaimed after the trial:

I am thoroughly convinced as the others I believe, that Mr. King was in full control of the whole situation at all times. *He was not writhing in pain.* He was moving to get away from the officers and he gave every indication that he was under PCP. [Riley 1992b: 116, emphasis added]

King was drugged yet in control. He felt no pain because he was drugged, but he was trying to escape through the massive cordon of police that surrounded him with baton blows that he could not feel. The reciprocal cancellation of these assertions could only be evaded through the alliance of subtextual racist stereotypes and an equally fictitious and decontextualizing micrological optic. Such statements by members of the jury attest to the probity that informed the verdict. Another jury member was able to deliver an auteur theory of the Rodney King movie: "King was directing all the action. . . . [He] was choosing the moment when he wanted to be handcuffed" (Riley 1992b: 116). King, drugged and knocked prostrate to the ground from which he tries to crawl upward, presides over the violence to such an extent that it becomes self-inflicted and self-authored.

The defendant's testimony (with the exception of Briseno) smuggled the authorial site of violence from the police and planted it on the victim. This was *embodiment by directed mimesis* and a classic Lacanian "mirror relation" in which an imagined and specular Other is endowed with ideological attributes by the originating and dissimulating subject who provides the raw material of the refraction, thereby covertly restaging itself in that Other (Lacan 1977). Through racist transcription, the aggression originating in the model (the police) became the qualifying somatic attribute of the copy (King). In transferring the origins of their violence to King, the police inhabit and possess his body in an imaginary relation where the black body becomes protective camouflage for state aggression. Police violence was a *reenactment* of the intrinsic violence "known" to already inhabit King's person. By this mimetic logic, King was the magnetized pole attracting, soliciting, and, therefore, animating the bodies of the police.

The conversion of King from the terminus to the source of aggression was enabled by a series of iconic displacements that embodied him in tandem with the disembodiment of police violence. Blackness, bestiality, narcosis, and anesthesia created both the specularization and the racial density of King's body. King, once invested with these mythemes, functioned like a neocolonial mirror that radiated an autonomous racial miasma that prejustified state violence. Stretched out on the rack of distorted cinematic time and space, King's body could be described by Sergeant Duke as "a *spectrum* of aggressive movements" (Courtroom Television Network 1992, emphasis added). In the logic of the colonial mirror (Taussig 1987, 1992), the body to be colonized is defaced by myth and violence in order to turn it into an empty vessel that can serve as repository for the cultural armature and demonology of the colonizer (Feldman 1991b, 1995). By fashioning the murky density of the Other, the colonial regime succeeds in dematerializing and purifying its own violence in a crucial hegemonic transposition. The colonized mirror creature, though specular, becomes "real" and laden with a negative material gravity in an *exchange* where the violence of the colonizer becomes spiritualized – that is, made rational and lawful. The *dematerialization* of state violence by perceptual technologies contributed to the legitimacy of Operation Desert Storm and was also an important dynamic in the Simi Valley courtroom, as indicated by one juror who stated, "They [the jury] didn't think much damage had been done to King as they looked at the photos [that displayed his bruises]" (Riley 1992b: 5).

* * *

Three little girls were playing tag in the living room, a small white dog was barking happily and Sgt. Stacy Koon was rolling around on the rug, demonstrating the actions of the man who was beaten, Rodney G. King.... The large screen television set dominates his living room, and Sergeant Koon cannot seem to stay away from it.... "There's 82 seconds of use-of-force on this tape, and there's 30 frames per second," he said. "There's like 2,500 frames on this tape and I've looked at every single one of them not once but a buzillion times and the more I look at the tape the more I see in it.... When I started playing this tape and I started blowing it up to 10 inches like I'd blow it up on this wall ... fill up the whole wall ... and all of a sudden, this thing came to life! ... You blow it up to full size for people, or even half size, if you make Rodney King four feet tall in that picture as opposed to three inches, boy you see a whole bunch of stuff ... He's like a bobo doll.... Ever hit one? Comes back and forth, back and forth. [Mydans 1993: A14]

In this startling interview with Koon, he appears to be taken over by, and obsessed with, the video. Through such reenactments as described above, he creates a physically mimetic bond with King's iconic body. Here, Koon uses his own body to perform King's. It is my suggestion that this ex post facto mimicry not only reflects and extends racial fictions and other constructions in Koon's courtroom testimony, but also echoes the actual police violence that, with each baton blow, simulated and inflicted a mythic black-bestial body on King's. When Sergeant Stacey Koon rolls around on his living room floor imitating, without sensory pain or shock, the man he has beaten, he merely plays the black body that was always his own. This play before the television screen, so reminiscent of the child's improvisations before the Lacanian mirror icon, testifies to that inversion in the (neo)-

colonial mirror relation when the possessor becomes the possessed and the author his creation (see Lacan 1977; Taussig 1987). Mimetic possession extends also to the somatic/technological interface. Sergeant Koon's quasi-visceral replay of that night is also a human mimicry of the video's capacity for flashback, fast forward, and freeze frame. Sergeant Koon's body and memory have now become the screen upon which the video is played and replayed "back and forth" like a "bobo doll." [...]

* * *

When normative institutional procedures, practices, and depictions achieve literality and truth through the denial of their own material consequences and other people's sensory inscription, hegemony is created, and forms of political consent are elicited that bar the Other from being present at the tribunal of historical actuality. Rather than being withdrawn by state monopoly, as Norbert Elias (1982) asserted, the violence of the state can invisibly merge with vernacular experience. Sensory colonization brought about by the articulation of state culture, the media, and the perceptual mythologies (racial, ethnic, and gendered) of modernity, interdicts the structure of the everyday as a semiautonomous zone of historical possibility and life chances. State, legal, and media rationality, separately or combined, can erect a *cordon sanitaire* around "acceptable" or "reasonable" chronic violence to the same extent that they successfully infiltrate social perception to neuter collective trauma, subtract or silence victims, and install public zones of perceptual amnesia that privatize and incarcerate historical memory. [...]

Rodney King was the absent, the invisible man at the trial that exposed his body to the exhaustive optics of advanced technology and racial conclusion. This established his sensory kinship with the Iraqis, whose deaths were electronically deleted from the American conscience. King not only disappeared, but also was replaced by a surrogate, a stand-in, through the mirror dynamics of racist and cinematic fetishism. The defendants and their counsel transformed the Simi Valley courtroom into a transvestite minstrel theater, where whites armed with special effects and archetypal narratives, donned black face, wore blacks masks, mimed a black body and staged a shadow play of domination and law.[15]

NOTES

1   As heard by the author on National Public Radio's "All Things Considered" on July 15, 1992.

2   In recent anthropological discourse, the term "Other" has been assumed to apply solely to a member of another discrete culture or subculture. But in Hegelian, existentialist, and Lacanian theory, the term denotes relational social forms within the same society without excluding its cross-cultural application. The use of the term in this article is not meant to imply some essentialistic, fixed, homogeneous, or ahistorical condition of an ethnic, religious, or gendered group. The Other is a plural relation and not a monadic entity. This relation emerges from situated practices of domination and social violence. The term is not meant to imply a uniform category, insofar as uniformity itself can be an element of the apparatus of domination, nor is the condition of Otherhood confined to complimentary binary oppositions. It may be thought of as analogous to Robert Hertz's notion of the "left hand" or side – that which can never be definitively named. It is the heterogeneity and instability that marks the limits of monological power as much as it stands for the political aggression of certain acts of naming.

3   Though, in certain instances, pain itself can be objectified or aestheticised and rendered an object of cultural consumption in which subjective noncommodifiable and/or nonaesthetic dimensions would still be excluded.

4   See Williams (1991: 57–58) on the connection between race and sensory inadmissibility in truth-claiming situations.

5   Fabian (1983), Stoller (1989), Tyler (1987), and Seremetakis (1991, 1993, 1994) have presented significant discussions of the impact of sensory specialization and stratification on ethnographic perception. The relationship between state violence and sensory manipulation is analyzed in Feldman (1991a: 123–37).

6   The concept of historical perception used here is, of course, not limited to textual or even linguistic genres, forms, and practices. It also implies that historical perception is always a re-perception.

7   Foucault's (1978) well-known model of penological visual domination and training, inspired by Bentham's panopticon, frequently refers to the perceptual contributions of proscenium staging and back lighting to cellular surveillance.

8   Kojéve (1969) demarcates the Hegelian master from the slave or bondsman in terms of the former's exclusive engagement with consumption and the latter's immersion in labor. This implies normative sensualization of the master's body and punitive desensualization of the slave's body through alienated labor.

9   From "The Rodney King Case: What the Jury Saw in California versus Powell" (Courtroom Television Network 1992). This and all other citations of Courtroom Television Network are my transcriptions of the commercially released videotape. All ellipses reflect my editing of the transcripts.

10 Much of this unfinished history tends to find expression in violent reenactments of the initiation, ritualized entry, or processing of racial Others by the dominant institutions of white society.

11 LAPD vehicles use a keyboard communications system.

12 Harvey (1989) refers to the reciprocal defining powers of marking certain urban zones as defiling and transgressive, as does Williams (1991). This wilderness imagery, which obscures the particularities of community context, from which racial others are subtracted, may well be a devolved variation of what Patterson (1982) identifies as "natal alienation." Natal alienation encompasses the renaming, branding, and degradation practices in enslavement scenarios and may still be a symbolic moment in the "Americanization" of racial others, including African-Americans.

13 See Feldman (1991a: 81–4) and Taussig (1987) on the political relation between animal imagery and violence.

14 There is a strong analogy between this re-editing of the video and Lukács's (1971) description of the bifurcation of the body of the assembly-line worker into productive, commodifiable parts and actions and unproductive, economically devalued and "irrational" gestures. From this vantage point, the link between the defense's version of the video and the freeze-frame, time-motion photography of Fordist theoreticians is clear. The defense's discourse on reasonable police violence is the indirect heir of labor efficiency performance analysis (see Rabinbach 1990).

15 Frantz Fanon (1986), in *Black Skin, White Masks*, identified transvestitism as an essential element of the consciousness of the colonized. I am suggesting that it is crucial to the political prosthetics of the colonizer once the ideological and hegemonic power of the colonial mirror relation is considered.

REFERENCES

Adorno, Theodor. 1973. *Negative Dialectics*. E. B. Ashton, trans. New York: Continuum.

Bloch, Ernst. 1990. *Heritage of Our Times*. N. Plaice and S. Plaice, trans. Cambridge: MIT Press.

Corbin, Alain. 1986. *The Foul and the Fragrant: Odor and the French Social Imagination*. M. Kochan, R.

Porter, and C. Pendergast, trans. Cambridge: Harvard University Press.

Courtroom Television Network. 1992. *"The Rodney King Case," What the Jury Saw in California versus Powell*. New York: Courtroom Television Network.

Crary, Jonathan. 1991. *Techniques of the Observer: On Vision and Modernity in the Nineteenth Century*. Cambridge: MIT Press.

Elias, Norbert. 1982. *State Formation and Civilization*. Edmund Jephcott, trans. Oxford: Blackwell.

Fanon, Frantz. 1986. *Black Skin, White Masks*. Charles Lam Markman, trans. London: Pluto Press.

Feldman, Allen. 1991a. *Formations of Violence: The Narrative of the Body and Political Terror in Northern Ireland*. Chicago: The University of Chicago Press.

——. 1991b. Collage and History: Max Ernst, Ernst Bloch, Walter Benjamin and the Ethnography of Everyday Life. Author's collection, unpublished manuscript.

——. 1991c. The Automaton, the Body and the Commodity Form: Sensory Hierarchies and Mimetic Others in Modernity. Paper presented at the Annual Meeting of the American Anthropological Association, Chicago.

——. 1995. *Towards a Political Anthropology of the Body: A Theoretical and Cultural History*. Boulder, CO: Westview Press.

Foucault, Michel. 1978. The Eye of Power. *Semiotext* 3(2): 6–9.

Harvey, David. 1989. *The Condition of Postmodernity: An Enquiry into the Origins of Cultural Change*. Oxford: Blackwell.

Heller Joseph. 1961. *Catch 22*. New York: Modern Library.

Kojéve, Alexandre. 1969. *Introduction to the Reading of Hegel: Lectures in the Phenomenology of the Spirit*. Ithaca: Cornell University Press.

Jameson, Federic. 1981. *The Political Unconscious: Narrative as a Socially Symbolic Act*. Ithaca: Cornell University Press.

Lacan, Jacques. 1977. *Ecrits: A Selection*. New York: W. W. Norton.

Lukács, Georg. 1971. *History and Class Consciousness: Studies in Marxist Dialectics*. Rodney Livingstone, trans. Cambridge: MIT Press.

Mydans, Seth. 1993. Their Lives Consumed, Officers Await 2d Trial. New York Times, February 2: A14.

Patterson, Orlando. 1982. *Slavery and Social Death: A Comparative Study*. Cambridge: Harvard University Press.

Rabinbach, Anson. 1990. *The Human Motor: Energy, Fatigue and the Origins of Modernity*. New York: Basic Books.

Riley, John. 1992a. The King Trial: What the Judge and the Jury Saw and Heard that the Public Didn't. New York Newsday, May 13: 17, 30.

——. 1992b. The King Trial: The Judge and the Jury. New York Newsday, May 14: 5, 116.

Scott, Paul. 1978. *The Day of the Scorpion*. New York: Avon Books.

Seremetakis, C. Nadia. 1993. The Memory of the Senses: Historical Perception, Commensal Exchange and Modernity. *Visual Anthropology Review* 9(1): 2–18.

——. 1994. *The Senses Still: Memory and Perception as Material Culture in Modernity*. Boulder, CO: Westview Press.

Stam, Robert. 1991. Mobilizing Fictions: The Gulf War, the Media and the Recruitment of the Spectator. *Public Culture* 4(2): 25–37.

Taussig, Michael. 1987. *Shamanism, Colonialism and the Wild Man: A Study in Terror and Healing*. Chicago: University of Chicago Press.

——. 1992. *Mimesis and Alterity: A Particular History of the Senses*. New York: Routledge.

Tyler, Stephen. 1987. *The Unspeakable: Discourse, Dialogue and Rhetoric in the Postmodern World*. Madison: University of Wisconsin Press.

Williams, Patricia J. 1991. *The Alchemy of Race and Rights*. Cambridge: Harvard University Press.

25

The New War Against Terror: Responding to 9/11

Noam Chomsky

During [the past] 200 years, we, the United States expelled or mostly exterminated the indigenous population, that's many millions of people, conquered half of Mexico, carried out depredations all over the region, Caribbean and Central America, sometimes beyond, conquered Hawaii and the Philippines, killing several 100,000 Filipinos in the process. Since the Second World War, it has extended its reach around the world in ways I don't have to describe. But it was always killing someone else, the fighting was somewhere else, it was others who were getting slaughtered. Not here. Not the national territory.

In the case of Europe, the change is even more dramatic because its history is even more horrendous than ours. We are an offshoot of Europe, basically. For hundreds of years, Europe has been casually slaughtering people all over the world. That's how they conquered the world, not by handing out candy to babies. During this period, Europe did suffer murderous wars, but that was European killers murdering one another. The main sport of Europe for hundreds of years was slaughtering one another. The only reason that it came to an end in 1945, was ... it had nothing to do with Democracy or not making war with each other and other fashionable notions. It had to do with the fact that everyone understood that the next time they play the game it was going to be the end for the world. Because the Europeans, including us, had developed such massive weapons of destruction that that game just has to be over. And it goes back hundreds of years. In the seventeenth century, about probably 40 percent of the entire population of Germany was wiped out in one war.

But during this whole bloody murderous period, it was Europeans slaughtering each other, and Europeans slaughtering people elsewhere. The Congo didn't attack Belgium, India didn't attack England, Algeria didn't attack France. It's uniform. There are again small exceptions, but pretty small in scale, certainly invisible in the scale of what Europe and us were doing to the rest of the world. This is the first change. The first time that the guns have been pointed the other way. And in my opinion that's probably why you see such different reactions on the two sides of the Irish Sea which I have noticed, incidentally, in many interviews on both sides, national radio on both sides. The world looks very different depending on whether you are holding the lash or whether you are being whipped by it for hundreds of years, very different. So I think the shock and surprise in Europe and its offshoots, like here, is very understandable. It is a historic event but regrettably not in scale, in something else and a reason why the rest of the world ... most of the rest of the world looks at it quite differently. Not lacking sympathy for the victims of the atrocity or being horrified by them, that's almost uniform, but viewing it from a different perspective. Something we might want to understand.

What is the War Against Terrorism?

The war against terrorism has been described in high places as a struggle against a plague, a cancer which is spread by barbarians, by "depraved opponents of civilization itself." That's a feeling that I share. The words I'm quoting, however, happen to be from 20 years ago. Those are... that's President Reagan and his Secretary of State. The Reagan administration came into office 20 years ago declaring that the war against international terrorism would be the core of our foreign policy... describing it in terms of the kind I just mentioned and others. And it was the core of our foreign policy. The Reagan administration responded to this plague spread by depraved opponents of civilization itself by creating an extraordinary international terrorist network, totally unprecedented in scale, which carried out massive atrocities all over the world, primarily... well, partly nearby, but not only there. I won't run through the record, you're all educated people, so I'm sure you learned about it in High School.

Reagan–US War Against Nicaragua

But I'll just mention one case which is totally uncontroversial, so we might as well not argue about it, by no means the most extreme but uncontroversial. It's uncontroversial because of the judgments of the highest international authorities the International Court of Justice, the World Court, and the UN Security Council. So this one is uncontroversial, at least among people who have some minimal concern for international law, human rights, justice and other things like that. And now I'll leave you an exercise. You can estimate the size of that category by simply asking how often this uncontroversial case has been mentioned in the commentary of the last month. And it's a particularly relevant one, not only because it is uncontroversial, but because it does offer a precedent as to how a law abiding state would respond to... did respond in fact to international terrorism, which is uncontroversial. And was even more extreme than the events of September 11th. I'm talking about the Reagan–US war against Nicaragua which left tens of thousands of people dead, the country ruined, perhaps beyond recovery.

Nicaragua's Response

Nicaragua did respond. They didn't respond by setting off bombs in Washington. They responded by taking it to the World Court, presenting a case,

they had no problem putting together evidence. The World Court accepted their case, ruled in their favor, ordered the... condemned what they called the "unlawful use of force," which is another word for international terrorism, by the United States, ordered the United States to terminate the crime and to pay massive reparations. The United States, of course, dismissed the court judgment with total contempt and announced that it would not accept the jurisdiction of the court henceforth. Then Nicaragua then went to the UN Security Council which considered a resolution calling on all states to observe international law. No one was mentioned but everyone understood. The United States vetoed the resolution. It now stands as the only state on record which has both been condemned by the World Court for international terrorism and has vetoed a Security Council resolution calling on states to observe international law. Nicaragua then went to the General Assembly where there is technically no veto but a negative US vote amounts to a veto. It passed a similar resolution with only the United States, Israel, and El Salvador opposed. The following year again, this time the United States could only rally Israel to the cause, so 2 votes opposed to observing international law. At that point, Nicaragua couldn't do anything lawful. It tried all the measures. They don't work in a world that is ruled by force.

This case is uncontroversial but it's by no means the most extreme. We gain a lot of insight into our own culture and society and what's happening now by asking "how much we know about all this? How much we talk about it? How much you learn about it in school? How much it's all over the front pages?" And this is only the beginning. The United States responded to the World Court and the Security Council by immediately escalating the war very quickly, that was a bipartisan decision incidentally. The terms of the war were also changed. For the first time there were official orders given... official orders to the terrorist army to attack what are called "soft targets," meaning undefended civilian targets, and to keep away from the Nicaraguan army. They were able to do that because the United States had total control of the air over Nicaragua and the mercenary army was supplied with advanced communication equipment, it wasn't a guerilla army in the normal sense and could get instructions about the disposition of the Nicaraguan army forces so they could attack agricultural collectives, health clinics, and so on ... soft targets with impunity. Those were the official orders.

What was the Reaction Here?

What was the reaction? It was known. There was a reaction to it. The policy was regarded as sensible by left liberal opinion. So Michael Kinsley who represents the left in mainstream discussion, wrote an article in which he said that we shouldn't be too quick to criticize this policy as Human Rights Watch had just done. He said a "sensible policy" must "meet the test of cost benefit analysis" – that is, I'm quoting now, that is the analysis of "the amount of blood and misery that will be poured in, and the likelihood that democracy will emerge at the other end." Democracy as the US understands the term, which is graphically illustrated in the surrounding countries. Notice that it is axiomatic that the United States, US elites, have the right to conduct the analysis and to pursue the project if it passes their tests. And it did pass their tests. It worked. When Nicaragua finally succumbed to superpower assault, commentators openly and cheerfully lauded the success of the methods that were adopted and described them accurately. So I'll quote Time Magazine just to pick one. They lauded the success of the methods adopted: "to wreck the economy and prosecute a long and deadly proxy war until the exhausted natives overthrow the unwanted government themselves," with a cost to us that is "minimal," and leaving the victims "with wrecked bridges, sabotaged power stations, and ruined farms," and thus providing the US candidate with a "winning issue": "ending the impoverishment of the people of Nicaragua." *The New York Times* had a headline saying "Americans United in Joy" at this outcome.

Terrorism Works – Terrorism is Not the Weapon of the Weak

That is the culture in which we live and it reveals several facts. One is the fact that terrorism works. It doesn't fail. It works. Violence usually works. That's world history. Secondly, it's a very serious analytic error to say, as is commonly done, that terrorism is the weapon of the weak. Like other means of violence, it's primarily a weapon of the strong, overwhelmingly, in fact. It is held to be a

weapon of the weak because the strong also control the doctrinal systems and their terror doesn't count as terror. Now that's close to universal. I can't think of a historical exception, even the worst mass murderers view the world that way. So pick the Nazis. They weren't carrying out terror in occupied Europe. They were protecting the local population from the terrorisms of the partisans. And like other resistance movements, there was terrorism. The Nazis were carrying out counter-terror. Furthermore, the United States essentially agreed with that. After the war, the US army did extensive studies of Nazi counter-terror operations in Europe. First I should say that the US picked them up and began carrying them out itself, often against the same targets, the former resistance. But the military also studied the Nazi methods published interesting studies, sometimes critical of them because they were inefficiently carried out, so a critical analysis, you didn't do this right, you did that right, but those methods with the advice of Wermacht officers who were brought over here became the manuals of counter insurgency, of counter terror, of low intensity conflict, as it is called, and are the manuals, and are the procedures that are being used. So it's not just that the Nazis did it. It's that it was regarded as the right thing to do by the leaders of western civilization, that is us, who then proceeded to do it themselves. Terrorism is not the weapon of the weak. It is the weapon of those who are against "us" whoever "us" happens to be.

How We Regard Terrorism

[...] The power of American propaganda and doctrine is so strong that even among the victims it's barely known. I mean, when you talk about this to people in Argentina, you have to remind them. Oh, yeah, that happened, we forgot about it. It's deeply suppressed. The sheer consequences of the monopoly of violence can be very powerful in ideological and other terms. [...]

[...] During the Reagan years alone, South African attacks, backed by the United States and Britain, US/UK-backed South African attacks against the neighboring countries killed about a million and a half people and left 60 billion dollars in damage and countries destroyed. And if we go around the world, we can add more examples. [...]

Haiti, Guatemala, and Nicaragua

Nicaragua has now become the second poorest country in the hemisphere. What's the poorest country? Well that's of course Haiti, which also happens to be the victim of most US intervention in the twentieth century by a long shot. We left it totally devastated. It's the poorest country. Nicaragua is second ranked in degree of US intervention in the twentieth century. It is the second poorest. Actually, it is vying with Guatemala. They interchange every year or two as to who's the second poorest. And they also vie as to who is the leading target of US military intervention. We're supposed to think that all of this is some sort of accident. That is has nothing to do with anything that happened in history. Maybe.

Colombia and Turkey

The worst human rights violator in the 1990s is Colombia, by a long shot. It's also the, by far, the leading recipient of US military aid in the 1990s maintaining the terror and human rights violations. In 1999, Colombia replaced Turkey as the leading recipient of US arms worldwide, that is excluding Israel and Egypt which are a separate category. And that tells us a lot more about the war on terror right now, in fact.

Why was Turkey getting such a huge flow of US arms? Well if you take a look at the flow of US arms to Turkey, Turkey always got a lot of US arms. It's strategically placed, a member of NATO, and so on. But the arms flow to Turkey went up very sharply in 1984. It didn't have anything to do with the cold war. I mean Russia was collapsing. And it stayed high from 1984 to 1999 when it reduced and it was replaced in the lead by Colombia. What happened from 1984 to 1999? Well, in 1984, [Turkey] launched a major terrorist war against Kurds in southeastern Turkey. And that's when US aid went up, military aid. And this was not pistols. This was jet planes, tanks, military training, and so on. And it stayed high as the atrocities escalated through the 1990s. Aid followed it. The peak year was 1997. In 1997, US military aid to Turkey was more than in the entire period 1950 to 1983, that is the cold war period, which is an indication of how much the cold war has affected policy. And the results were awesome. This led to 2–3 million refugees. Some of the worst ethnic cleansing of the late 1990s. Tens of thousands of people killed, 3,500 towns and villages destroyed, way more than Kosovo, even under NATO bombs. And the United States was providing 80 percent of the arms, increasing as the atrocities increased, peaking in 1997. It declined in 1999 because, once again, terror worked as it usually does when carried out by its major agents, mainly the powerful. So by 1999, Turkish terror, called of course counter-terror, but as I said, that's universal, it worked. Therefore Turkey was replaced by Colombia which had not yet succeeded in its terrorist war. And therefore had to move into first place as recipient of US arms.

Self-congratulation on the Part of Western Intellectuals

Well, what makes this all particularly striking is that all of this was taking place right in the midst of a huge flood of self-congratulation on the part of Western intellectuals which probably has no counterpart in history. I mean you all remember it. It was just a couple years ago. Massive self-adulation about how for the first time in history we are so magnificent; that we are standing up for principles and values; dedicated to ending inhumanity everywhere in the new era of this-and-that, and so-on-and-so-forth. And we certainly can't tolerate atrocities right near the borders of NATO. That was repeated over and over. Only within the borders of NATO where we can not only can tolerate much worse atrocities but contribute to them. Another insight into Western civilization and our own, is how often was this brought up? Try to look. I won't repeat it. But it's instructive. It's a pretty impressive feat for a propaganda system to carry this off in a free society. It's pretty amazing. I don't think you could do this in a totalitarian state. [. . .]

What is Terrorism?

[. . .] A brief statement taken from a US army manual, is fair enough, is that terror is the calculated use of violence or the threat of violence to attain political or religious ideological goals through intimidation, coercion, or instilling fear. That's terrorism. That's a fair enough definition. [. . .]

[But] if you use the official definition of terrorism in the comprehensive treaty you are going to get completely the wrong results. So that can't be done. In fact, it is even worse than that. If you take a look at the definition of Low Intensity Warfare which is official US policy you find that it is a very close paraphrase of what I just read. In fact, Low Intensity Conflict is just another name for terrorism. That's why all countries, as far as I know, call whatever horrendous acts they are carrying out, counter-terrorism. We happen to call it Counter Insurgency of Low Intensity Conflict. [...]

Why did the United States and Israel Vote Against a Major Resolution Condemning Terrorism?

There are some other problems. Some of them came up in December 1987, at the peak of the first war on terrorism, that's when the furor over the plague was peaking. The United Nations General Assembly passed a very strong resolution against terrorism, condemning the plague in the strongest terms, calling on every state to fight against it in every possible way. It passed unanimously. One country, Honduras, abstained. Two votes against; the usual two, United States and Israel. Why should the United States and Israel vote against a major resolution condemning terrorism in the strongest terms, in fact pretty much the terms that the Reagan administration was using? Well, there is a reason. There is one paragraph in that long resolution which says that nothing in this resolution infringes on the rights of people struggling against racist and colonialist regimes or foreign military occupation to continue with their resistance with the assistance of others, other states, states outside in their just cause. Well, the United States and Israel can't accept that. The main reason that they couldn't at the time was because of South Africa. South Africa was an ally, officially called an ally. There was a terrorist force in South Africa. It was called the African National Congress. They were a terrorist force officially. South Africa in contrast was an ally and we certainly couldn't support actions by a terrorist group struggling against a racist regime. That would be impossible.

And of course there is another one. Namely the Israeli occupied territories, now going into its thirty-fifth year. Supported primarily by the United States in blocking a diplomatic settlement for 30 years now, still is. And you can't have that. There is another one at the time. Israel was occupying southern Lebanon and was being combated by what the US calls a terrorist force, Hizbullah, which in fact succeeded in driving Israel out of Lebanon. And we can't allow anyone to struggle against a military occupation when it is one that we support so therefore the US and Israel had to vote against the major UN resolution on terrorism. And I mentioned before that a US vote against... is essentially a veto. Which is only half the story. It also vetoes it from history. So none of this was ever reported and none of it appeared in the annals of terrorism. If you look at the scholarly work on terrorism and so on, nothing that I just mentioned appears. The reason is that it has got the wrong people holding the guns. You have to carefully hone the definitions and the scholarship and so on so that you come out with the right conclusions; otherwise it is not respectable scholarship and honorable journalism. Well, these are some of the problems that are hampering the effort to develop a comprehensive treaty against terrorism. Maybe we should have an academic conference or something to try to see if we can figure out a way of defining terrorism so that it comes out with just the right answers, not the wrong answers. That won't be easy.

What are the Origins of the September 11 Crime?

Here we have to make a distinction between 2 categories which shouldn't be run together. One is the actual agents of the crime, the other is kind of a reservoir of at least sympathy, sometimes support that they appeal to even among people who very much oppose the criminals and the actions. And those are 2 different things.

Category 1: The Likely Perpetrators

[...] Well, where do they come from? We know all about that. Nobody knows about that better than the CIA because it helped organize them and it nurtured them for a long time. They were brought together in the 1980s actually by the CIA and its associates elsewhere: Pakistan, Britain, France, Saudi Arabia, Egypt, China was involved, they may have been involved a little bit earlier, maybe by 1978. The idea was to try to harass the Russians, the common enemy. According to President Carter's National Security Advisor, Zbigniew Brzezinski, the US got involved in mid-1979. Do you remember, just to put the dates right, that Russia invaded Afghanistan in December 1979. Ok. According to Brzezinski, the US support for the mojahedin fighting against the government began 6 months earlier. He is very proud of that. He says we drew the Russians into, in his words, an Afghan trap, by supporting the mojahedin, getting them to invade, getting them into the trap. Now then we could develop this terrific mercenary army. Not a small one, maybe 100,000 men or so bringing together the best killers they could find, who were radical Islamist fanatics from around North Africa, Saudi Arabia...anywhere they could find them. They were often called the Afghanis but many of them, like bin Laden, were not Afghans. They were brought by the CIA and its friends from elsewhere. Whether Brzezinski is telling the truth or not, I don't know. He may have been bragging, he is apparently very proud of it, knowing the consequences incidentally. But maybe it's true. We'll know someday if the documents are ever released. Anyway, that's his perception. By January 1980 it is not even in doubt that the US was organizing the Afghanis and this massive military force to try to cause the Russians maximal trouble. It was a legitimate thing for the Afghans to fight the Russian invasion. But the US intervention was not helping the Afghans. In fact, it helped destroy the country and much more. The Afghanis, so called, had their own...it did force the Russians to withdraw, finally. Although many analysts believe that it probably delayed their withdrawal because they were trying to get out of it. Anyway, whatever, they did withdraw.

Meanwhile, the terrorist forces that the CIA was organizing, arming, and training were pursuing their own agenda, right away. It was no secret. One of the first acts was in 1981 when they assassinated the President of Egypt, who was one of the most enthusiastic of their creators. In 1983, one suicide bomber, who may or may not have been connected, it's pretty shadowy, nobody knows. But one suicide bomber drove the US army-military out of Lebanon. And it continued. They have their own agenda. The US was happy to mobilize them to fight its cause but meanwhile they are doing their own thing. They were very clear about it. After 1989, when the Russians had withdrawn, they simply turned elsewhere. Since then they have been fighting in Chechnya, western China, Bosnia, Kashmir, southeast Asia, North Africa, all over the place.

They Are Telling Us What They Think

They are telling us just what they think. The United States wants to silence the one free television channel in the Arab world because it's broadcasting a whole range of things from Powell over to Osama bin Laden. So the US is now joining the repressive regimes of the Arab world that try to shut it up. But if you listen to it, if you listen to what bin Laden says, it's worth it. [...] Their prime enemy is what they call the corrupt and oppressive authoritarian brutal regimes of the Arab world and when they say that they get quite a resonance in the region. They also want to defend and they want to replace them by properly Islamist governments. That's where they lose the people of the region. But up till then, they are with them. From their point of view, even Saudi Arabia, the most extreme fundamentalist state in the world, I suppose, short of the Taliban, which is an offshoot, even that's not Islamist enough for them. Ok, at that point, they get very little support, but up until that point they get plenty of support. Also they want to defend Muslims elsewhere. They hate the Russians like poison, but as soon as the Russians pulled out of Afghanistan, they stopped carrying out terrorist acts in Russia as they had been doing with CIA backing before that within Russia, not just in Afghanistan. They did move over to Chechnya. But there they are defending Muslims against a Russian invasion. Same with all the other places I mentioned. From their point of view, they are defending the Muslims against the infidels. And they are very clear about it and that is what they have been doing. [...]

What are the Policy Options?

Well, there are a number. A narrow policy option from the beginning was to follow the advice of really far out radicals like the Pope. The Vatican immediately said look it's a horrible terrorist crime. In the case of crime, you try to find the perpetrators, you bring them to justice, you try them. You don't kill innocent civilians. Like if somebody robs my house and I think the guy who did it is probably in the neighborhood across the street, I don't go out with an assault rifle and kill everyone in that neighborhood. That's not the way you deal with crime, whether it's a small crime like this one or really massive one like the US terrorist war against Nicaragua. [...]

IRA Bombs in London

When the IRA set off bombs in London, which is pretty serious business, Britain could have, apart from the fact that it was unfeasible, let's put that aside, one possible response would have been to destroy Boston which is the source of most of the financing. And of course to wipe out West Belfast. Well, you know, quite apart from the feasibility, it would have been criminal idiocy. The way to deal with it was pretty much what they did. You know, find the perpetrators; bring them to trial; and look for the reasons. Because these things don't come out of nowhere. They come from something. Whether it is a crime in the streets or a monstrous terrorist crime or anything else. There's reasons. And usually if you look at the reasons, some of them are legitimate and ought to be addressed, independently of the crime, they ought to be addressed because they are legitimate. And that's the way to deal with it. There are many such examples. [...]

Leaderless Resistance

You know, it could be that the people who did it, killed themselves. Nobody knows this better than the CIA. These are decentralized, nonhierarchic networks. They follow a principle that is called Leaderless Resistance. That's the principle that has been developed by the Christian Right terrorists in the United States. It's called Leaderless Resistance. You have small groups that do things. They don't talk to anybody else. There is a kind of general background of assumptions and then you do it. Actually people in the anti war movement are very familiar with it. We used to call it affinity groups. If you assume correctly that whatever group you are in is being penetrated by the FBI, when something serious is happening, you don't do it in a meeting. You do it with some people you know and trust, an affinity group and then it doesn't get penetrated. That's one of the reasons why the FBI has never been able to figure out what's going on in any of the popular movements. And other intelligence agencies are the same. They can't. That's leaderless resistance or affinity groups, and decentralized networks are extremely hard to penetrate. And it's quite possible that they just don't know. When Osama bin Laden claims he wasn't involved, that's entirely possible. In fact, it's pretty hard to imagine how a guy in a cave in Afghanistan, who doesn't even have a radio or a telephone could have planned a highly sophisticated operation like that. Chances are it's part of the background. You know, like other leaderless resistance terrorist groups. Which means it's going to be extremely difficult to find evidence. [...]

Conclusion

It's hard to find many rays of light in the last couple of weeks but one of them is that there is an increased openness. Lots of issues are now open for discussion, even in elite circles, certainly among the general public. [...] There is much more openness and willingness to think about things that were under the rug and so on. These are opportunities and they should be used, at least by people who accept the goal of trying to reduce the level of violence and terror, including potential threats that are extremely severe and could make even September 11th pale into insignificance.

26

Violence Foretold: Reflections on 9/11

Nancy Scheper-Hughes

As [Immanuel] Levinas writes, "Morality does not belong to culture: [it] enables one to judge it."

We are still in a state of shock and raw grief in the wake of September 11, the events of which were to a certain extent overdetermined, even predictable, had "we" been more alert and attentive to the way that we – the passive beneficiaries of global affluence – are perceived from below, not in the hierarchical sense, but in the "view from the barrio," from the refugee camp, from the *favela*, from the inner city, and from the shantytowns and squatter camps where most of the world's populations live. (At any rate, we like to *think* these events were predictable, for who wants to face the possibility of an utterly random and chaotic world?)

In the days and weeks following the attacks of September 11 that have so challenged our sense of rootedness, our basic ontological security in the world, I found myself returning to a few key texts: Gabriel Marquez's *Chronicle of a Death Foretold* – how could we not have read the signs? Hannah Arendt's *The Human Condition* and *Eichmann in Jerusalem*, with its thesis on the utter banality of evil; Eichmann seems so ordinary, so perfectly normal, a hard-working bureaucrat doing his best to rise up in the ranks of his institution. And W. B. Yeats's poem "Second Coming":

Things fall apart; the centre cannot hold;
Mere anarchy is loosed upon the world,
The blood dimmed tide is loosed, and everywhere
The ceremony of innocence is drowned;
The best lack all conviction, while the worst

Are full of passionate intensity.

Vincent Crapanzano's anthropological monograph, *Waiting*, had particular salience, with its portrait of ostrich-like South African whites buried in the inane riduculosa of everyday bourgeois life, hoping, wishing, *waiting* for the future, which (and *not only* in South Africa) is a black and brown future, to go away and pass them by.

Finally, I returned to René Girard's writings on sacrificial violence and the uses of the surrogate victim, the one whose death helps to resolve terrible, unbearable conflicts, difficulties, and collective anxieties. In the most recent instance, the sacrificial violence and victimhood were shared not only by the thousands of victims and survivors of the World Trade Center and Pentagon attacks but equally by the young terrorists (and their family members), whose lives were held hostage by their religious convictions and who were readily, even eagerly, offered up, given up – *sacrificed*, that is – by their own religious and political leaders.

Individually and collectively, we grasp at straws, searching for meaning. At times of crisis and at moments of intense suffering people everywhere demand an answer to the existential question: "Why me, oh God? Why me? Why me of all people? Why now?" The quest for meaning may be posed to vindicate an indifferent God, to quell self-doubt, or to shore up a fragile faith in an orderly and just world.

At the same time, following a national emergency, an epidemic, a natural disaster, or a political attack, whenever tragedy hits an entire collectivity, the "Why me?" question often becomes the "Why *not* me?" "Why was I (of all people) spared?" as survivors try to find some logic, some coherence, some purpose even behind their exemption, their saving grace. The one thing humans seem unable to accept is the idea that the world may be utterly deficient in meaning.

I would argue that the attacks of September 11 are part of a continuum of violence that starts in ostensibly mundane ways and proceeds all the way to genocide. Everyday violence – normally directed against the least powerful and most dependent members of society, the homeless mad, the heroin addict, the common thief, the illegal immigrant, the welfare mother, the very young, or the very old – is so deeply inscribed in our ordinary, unexamined ways of life that no one is exempt, least of all the "critical and militant" anthropologist who from time to time has had to pause to consider her own "bystander" status as an anthropologist recording the misery of chronic hunger, child death, and the extermination of street kids in Brazil, on the one hand, and the woefully reduced status of her dear parents consigned to the "care" of a nursing home in Baltimore, on the other. Obviously, social and political criticism must extend to self-criticism, to illuminating how ordinary, everyday ways of thinking, loving, and being in the world are implicated in the violence that we are trying to understand and to combat. The demons have not fled – we have faced the terrorist . . . and she is also ourselves.

All forms of violence are sustained by the passively averted gaze. The critical lens moves in and out, intentionally juxtaposing the different levels of violence – macro and micro, economic, epistemic, and the deeply personal and subjective. Mass violence is part of a continuum; it is socially incremental and often experienced by perpetrators, collaborators, bystanders, and even by victims themselves, as ordinary, routine, even justified.

The preparation for mass killing is found in social sentiments and in institutions ranging from the family to schools, churches, hospitals, and the military. The early "warning signs" include an evolving social consensus toward the devaluation of certain forms of human life; a refusal of social support and humane care to vulnerable and stigmatized social groups identified as "social parasites"; the militarization of everyday life (e.g., the growth of prisons, the unreflective acceptance of capital punishment, and proliferation of heightened technologies of personal security, including the house gun and gated communities); increasing social polarization, fear, and moral panics (such as the perceptions of the underclass, street children, or certain racial or ethnic groups as dangerous and socially polluting public enemies); and, finally, reversed feelings of victimization, as dominant social groups and social classes demand strong policing to put despised subordinate or marginal groups in their proper place.

Once recognized, how can the violence continuum be interrupted? Minimally, it requires a powerful social ethic to challenge the belief (one that may even be hidden to the conscious self) that certain despised or "alien" populations are better off dead or having never been born at all. I have found useful Immanuel Levinas's notion of the "primacy of the ethical," which suggests certain culturally transcendent, transparent, and essential first principles. Anthropologists have traditionally understood morality as contingent on, and embedded within, specific cultural assumptions about human life. But there is another philosophical and theological position that posits "the ethical" as existing *prior to* culture. Some events, such as genocide and mass violence, are not amenable to a relativizing discourse. As Levinas writes, "Morality does not belong to culture: [it] enables one to judge it."

The demand for mutual responsibility and accountability to "the other" – the ethical, as I define it – is *pre*cultural to the extent that our existence as uniquely social beings presupposes the presence of the other. "Basic strangeness," the profound shock of misrecognition reported by some mothers in their first encounters with a newborn, is perhaps the prototype of all dangerously alienated "self-other" relations, including those leading to genocide and other forms of mass violence (see Chapter 33). Ultimately, as every new mother knows, for fragile life to grow and prosper, "basic strangeness" must eventually be overcome by "basic love." The primacy of the ethical demands a radical de-estrangement, and deracialization, a surrender of one's attachments and loyalties to old nations, old religions, old races, old social classes, and old entitlements. Martin Buber's formulation of I–Thou over I–It relations certainly comes to mind.

Above all, it is essential that we all exercise a defensive hypervigilance and hypersensitivity to all the mundane, normative, and permitted acts of violence that are directed against certain "classes" of disqualified humans. Perhaps a collective self-mobilization for constant shock and hyperarousal about the little violences of everyday life is one ethical response to Walter Benjamin's view of late modern history as a chronic "state of emergency."

READINGS

Many authors have explored the phenomena of violence and suffering in society and culture. Among the works directly related to this essay are Hannah Arendt's *The Human Condition* (Chicago: University of Chicago Press, 1958), *Eichmann in Jerusalem: A Report on the Banality of Evil* (New York: Vintage, 1963), and *On Violence* (New York: Harcourt, Brace, 1969), the last of which deals at length with politically motivated violence. For more on the assignment of blame and its role in violence, see René Girard, "Generative Scapegoating," in *Violent Origins: Ritual Killing and Cultural Formation*, edited by R. Hamerton-Kelly (Palo Alto, CA: Stanford University Press, 1987). The work of Immanuel Levinas is well represented by "Useless Suffering," in *Face to Face with Levinas*, edited by Richard Cohn (Albany: State University of New York Press, 1986). A "literary" perspective can be found in Gabriel Garcia Marquez, *Chronicle of a Death Foretold* (New York: Alfred Knopf, 1982).

Part VI

Violence and Political Resistance

Plate 8: Squatters on the Cuiabá Plantation in the Xingó sertão, State of Sergipe, Brazil 1996. Photo © Sebastião Salgado, Contact Press Images.

27

Preface to Frantz Fanon's
Wretched of the Earth

Jean-Paul Sartre

In the colonies the truth stood naked, but the citizens of the mother country preferred it with clothes on: the native had to love them, something in the way mothers are loved. The European elite undertook to manufacture a native elite. They picked out promising adolescents; they branded them, as with a red-hot iron, with the principles of Western culture; they stuffed their mouths full with high-sounding phrases, grand glutinous words that stuck to the teeth. After a short stay in the mother country they were sent home, whitewashed. [...]

It came to an end; the mouths opened by themselves; the yellow and black voices still spoke of our humanism but only to reproach us with our inhumanity. We listened without displeasure to these polite statements of resentment, at first with proud amazement. What? They are able to talk by themselves? Just look at what we have made of them! We did not doubt but that they would accept our ideals, since they accused us of not being faithful to them. Then, indeed, Europe could believe in her mission; she had hellenized the Asians; she had created a new breed, the Greco-Latin Negroes. We might add, quite between ourselves, as men of the world: "After all, let them bawl their heads off, it relieves their feelings; dogs that bark don't bite."

A new generation came on the scene, which changed the issue. With unbelievable patience, its writers and poets tried to explain to us that our values and the true facts of their lives did not hang together, and that they could neither reject them completely nor yet assimilate them. By and large, what they were saying was this: "You are making us into monstrosities; your humanism claims we are at one with the rest of humanity but your racist methods set us apart." Very much at our ease, we listened to them all; colonial administrators are not paid to read Hegel, and for that matter they do not read much of him, but they do not need a philosopher to tell them that uneasy consciences are caught up in their own contradictions. They will not get anywhere; so, let us perpetuate their discomfort; nothing will come of it but talk. If they were, the experts told us, asking for anything at all precise in their wailing, it would be integration. Of course, there is no question of granting that; the system, which depends on overexploitation, as you know, would be ruined. But it's enough to hold the carrot in front of their noses, they'll gallop all right. As to a revolt, we need not worry at all; what native in his senses would go off to massacre the fair sons of Europe simply to become European as they are? In short, we encouraged these disconsolate spirits and thought it not a bad idea for once to award the Prix Goncourt to a Negro. That was before '39.

1961. Listen: "Let us waste no time in sterile litanies and nauseating mimicry. Leave this Europe where they are never done talking of Man, yet murder men everywhere they find them, at the corner of every one of their own streets, in all the corners of the globe. For centuries they have stifled almost the whole of humanity in the name of a so-called spiritual experience." The tone is new. Who dares to speak thus? It is an African, a man from the Third World, an ex-"native." He adds: "Europe now lives at such a mad, reckless pace that she is running headlong into the abyss; we would do well to keep away from it." In other words, she's done for. A truth which is not pleasant to state but of which we are all convinced, are we not, fellow-Europeans, in the marrow of our bones? [...]

The black Goncourts and the yellow Nobels are finished; the days of colonized laureates are over. An ex-native, French-speaking, bends that language to new requirements, makes use of it, and speaks to the colonized only: "Natives of all underdeveloped countries, unite!" What a downfall! For the fathers, we alone were the speakers; the sons no longer even consider us as valid intermediaries: we are the objects of their speeches. Of course, Fanon mentions in passing our well-known crimes: Sétif, Hanoi, Madagascar: but he does not waste his time in condemning them; he uses them. If he demonstrates the tactics of colonialism, the complex play of relations which unite and oppose the colonists to the people of the mother country, it is for his brothers; his aim is to teach them to beat us at our own game. [...]

The settler has only recourse of one thing: brute force, when he can command it; the native has only one choice, between servitude or supremacy. What does Fanon care whether you read his work or not? It is to his brothers that he denounces our old tricks, and he is sure we have no more up our sleeves. It is to them he says: "Europe has laid her hands on our continents, and we must slash at her fingers till she lets go. It's a good moment; nothing can happen at Bizerta, at Elizabethville or in the Algerian bled that the whole world does not hear about. The rival blocs take opposite sides, and hold each other in check; let us take advantage of this paralysis, let us burst into history, forcing it by our invasion into universality for the first time. Let us start fighting; and if we've no other arms, the waiting knife's enough." [...]

Fanon explains you to his brothers and shows them the mechanism by which we are estranged from ourselves; take advantage of this, and get to know yourselves seen in the light of truth, objectively. Our victims know us by their scars and by their chains, and it is this that makes their evidence irrefutable. It is enough that they show us what we have made of them for us to realize what we have made of ourselves. But is it any use? Yes, for Europe is at death's door. But, you will say, we live in the mother country, and we disapprove of her excesses. It is true, you are not settlers, but you are no better. For the pioneers belonged to you;

you sent them overseas, and it was you they enriched. You warned them that if they shed too much blood you would disown them, or say you did, in something of the same way as any state maintains abroad a mob of agitators, *agents provocateurs*, and spies whom it disowns when they are caught. You, who are so liberal and so humane, who have such an exaggerated adoration of culture that it verges on affectation, you pretend to forget that you own colonies and that in them men are massacred in your name. Fanon reveals to his comrades – above all to some of them who are rather too Westernized – the solidarity of the people of the mother country and of their representatives in the colonies. Have the courage to read this [Fanon's] book, for in the first place it will make you ashamed, and shame, as Marx said, is a revolutionary sentiment. You see, I, too, am incapable of ridding myself of subjective illusions; I, too, say to you: "All is lost, unless ... " As a European, I steal the enemy's book, and out of it I fashion a remedy for Europe. Make the most of it. [...]

During the last century, the middle classes looked on the workers as covetous creatures, made lawless by their greedy desires; but they took care to include these great brutes in our own species, or at least they considered that they were free men – that is to say, free to sell their labor. In France, as in England, humanism claimed to be universal. [...]

Our soldiers overseas, rejecting the universalism of the mother country, apply the "numerus clausus" to the human race: since none may enslave, rob, or kill his fellow man without committing a crime, they lay down the principle that the native is not one of our fellow men. Our striking power has been given the mission of changing this abstract certainty into reality: the order is given to reduce the inhabitants of the annexed country to the level of superior monkeys in order to justify the settler's treatment of them as beasts of burden. Violence in the colonies does not only have for its aim the keeping of these enslaved men at arm's length; it seeks to dehumanize them. Everything will be done to wipe out their traditions, to substitute our language for theirs and to destroy their culture without giving them ours. Sheer physical fatigue will stupefy them. Starved and ill, if they have any spirit left, fear will finish the job; guns are leveled at the peasant; civilians come to take over his land and force him by dint of flogging to till the land for them. If he shows fight, the soldiers fire and he's a dead man; if he gives in, he degrades himself and he is no longer a man at all; shame and fear will split up his character and make his inmost self fall to pieces. The business is conducted with flying colors and by experts; the "psychological services" weren't established yesterday; nor was brainwashing. And yet, in spite of all these efforts, their ends are nowhere achieved: neither in the Congo, where Negroes' hands were cut off, nor in Angola, where until very recently malcontents' lips were pierced in order to shut them with padlocks. I do not say that it is impossible to change a man into an animal: I simply say that you won't get there without weakening him considerably. Blows will never suffice; you have to push the starvation further, and that's the trouble with slavery.

For when you domesticate a member of our own species, you reduce his output, and however little you may give him, a farmyard man finishes by costing more than he brings in. For this reason the settlers are obliged to stop the breaking-in halfway; the result, neither man nor animal, is the native. Beaten, undernourished, ill, terrified – but only up to a certain point – he has, whether he's black, yellow, or white, always the same traits of character: he's a sly-boots, a lazybones, and a thief, who lives on nothing, and who understands only violence.

Poor settler; here is his contradiction naked, shorn of its trappings. He ought to kill those he plunders, as they say djinns do. Now, this is not possible, because he must exploit them as well. Because he can't carry massacre on to genocide, and slavery to animal-like degradation, he loses control, the machine goes into reverse, and a relentless logic leads him on to decolonization.

But it does not happen immediately. At first the European's reign continues. He has already lost the battle, but this is not obvious; he does not yet know that the natives are only half native; to hear him talk, it would seem that he ill-treats them in order to destroy or to repress the evil that they have rooted in them; and after three generations their pernicious instincts will reappear no more. What instincts does he mean? The instincts that urge slaves on to massacre their master? Can he not here recognize his own cruelty turned against himself? In the savagery of these oppressed peasants, does he not find his own settler's savagery, which they have absorbed through every pore and for which there is no cure? The

reason is simple; this imperious being, crazed by his absolute power and by the fear of losing it, no longer remembers clearly that he was once a man; he takes himself for a horsewhip or a gun; he has come to believe that the domestication of the "inferior races" will come about by the conditioning of their reflexes. But in this he leaves out of account the human memory and the ineffaceable marks left upon it; and then, above all there is something which perhaps he has never known: we only become what we are by the radical and deep-seated refusal of that which others have made of us. Three generations did we say? Hardly has the second generation opened their eyes than from then on they've seen their fathers being flogged. In psychiatric terms, they are "traumatized" for life. But these constantly renewed aggressions, far from bringing them to submission, thrust them into an unbearable contradiction which the European will pay for sooner or later. After that, when it is their turn to be broken in, when they are taught what shame and hunger and pain are, all that is stirred up in them is a volcanic fury whose force is equal to that of the pressure put upon them. You said they understand nothing but violence? Of course; first, the only violence is the settler's; but soon they will make it their own; that is to say, the same violence is thrown back upon us as when our reflection comes forward to meet us when we go toward a mirror.

Make no mistake about it; by this mad fury, by this bitterness and spleen, by their ever-present desire to kill us, by the permanent tensing of powerful muscles which are afraid to relax, they have become men: men *because of* the settler, who wants to make beasts of burden of them – because of him, and against him. Hatred, blind hatred which is as yet an abstraction, is their only wealth; the Master calls it forth because he seeks to reduce them to animals, but he fails to break it down because his interests stop him halfway. Thus the "half natives" are still humans, through the power and the weakness of the oppressor which is transformed within them into a stubborn refusal of the animal condition. We realize what follows; they're lazy: of course – it's a form of sabotage. They're sly and thieving; just imagine! But their petty thefts mark the beginning of a resistance which is still unorganized. That is not enough; there are those among them who assert themselves by throwing themselves barehanded against the guns; these are their heroes. Others make men of themselves by murdering Europeans, and these are shot down; brigands or martyrs, their agony exalts the terrified masses.

Yes, terrified; at this fresh stage, colonial aggression turns inward in a current of terror among the natives. By this I do not only mean the fear that they experience when faced with our inexhaustible means of repression but also that which their own fury produces in them. They are cornered between our guns pointed at them and those terrifying compulsions, those desires for murder which spring from the depth of their spirits and which they do not always recognize; for at first it is not *their* violence, it is ours, which turns back on itself and rends them; and the first action of these oppressed creatures is to bury deep down that hidden anger which their and our moralities condemn and which is however only the last refuge of their humanity. Read Fanon: you will learn how, in the period of their helplessness, their mad impulse to murder is the expression of the natives' collective unconscious.

If this suppressed fury fails to find an outlet, it turns in a vacuum and devastates the oppressed creatures themselves. In order to free themselves they even massacre each other. The different tribes fight between themselves since they cannot face the real enemy – and you can count on colonial policy to keep up their rivalries; the man who raises his knife against his brother thinks that he has destroyed once and for all the detested image of their common degradation, even though these expiatory victims don't quench their thirst for blood. They can only stop themselves from marching against the machine-guns by doing our work for us; of their own accord they will speed up the dehumanization that they reject. Under the amused eye of the settler, they will take the greatest precautions against their own kind by setting up supernatural barriers, at times reviving old and terrible myths, at others binding themselves by scrupulous rites. It is in this way that an obsessed person flees from his deepest needs – by binding himself to certain observances which require his attention at every turn. They dance; that keeps them busy; it relaxes their painfully contracted muscles; and then the dance mimes secretly, often without their knowing, the refusal they cannot utter and the murders they dare not commit. In certain districts they make use of that last resort – possession by spirits. Formerly this was a religious experience in all its simplicity, a certain communion of the faithful with sacred

things; now they make of it a weapon against humiliation and despair; Mumbo-Jumbo and all the idols of the tribe come down among them, rule over their violence and waste it in trances until it is exhausted. At the same time these high-placed personages protect them; in other words the colonized people protect themselves against colonial estrangement by going one better in religious estrangement, with the unique result that finally they add the two estrangements together and each reinforces the other. Thus in certain psychoses the hallucinated person, tired of always being insulted by his demon; one fine day starts hearing the voice of an angel who pays him compliments; but the jeers don't stop for all that; only from then on, they alternate with congratulations. This is a defense, but it is also the end of the story; the self is disassociated, and the patient heads for madness. Let us add, for certain other carefully selected unfortunates, that other witchery of which I have already spoken: Western culture. If I were them, you may say, I'd prefer my Mumbo-Jumbo to their Acropolis. Very good: you've grasped the situation. But not altogether, because you *aren't* them – or not yet. Otherwise you would know that they can't choose; they must have both. Two worlds: that makes two bewitchings; they dance all night and at dawn they crowd into the churches to hear mass; each day the split widens. Our enemy betrays his brothers and becomes our accomplice; his brothers do the same thing. The status of "native" is a nervous condition introduced and maintained by the settler among colonized people *with their consent*.

Laying claim to and denying the human condition at the same time: the contradiction is explosive. For that matter it does explode, you know as well as I do; and we are living at the moment when the match is put to the fuse. When the rising birth rate brings wider famine in its wake, when these newcomers have life to fear rather more than death, the torrent of violence sweeps away all barriers. In Algeria and Angola, Europeans are massacred at sight. It is the moment of the boomerang; it is the third phase of violence; it comes back on us, it strikes us, and we do not realize any more than we did the other times that it's we who have launched it. The "liberals" are stupefied; they admit that we were not polite enough to the natives, that it would have been wiser and fairer to allow them certain rights in so far as this was possible; they ask nothing better than to admit them in batches and without sponsors to that very exclusive club, our species; and now this barbarous, mad outburst doesn't spare them any more than the bad settlers. The Left at home is embarrassed; they know the true situation of the natives, the merciless oppression they are submitted to; they do not condemn their revolt, knowing full well that we have done everything to provoke it. But all the same, they think to themselves, there *are* limits; these guerrillas should be bent on showing that they are chivalrous; that would be the best way of showing they are men. Sometimes the Left scolds them . . . "You're going too far; we won't support you any more." The natives don't give a damn about their support; for all the good it does them they might as well stuff it up their backsides. Once their war began, they saw this hard truth: that every single one of us has made his bit, has got something out of them; they don't need to call anyone to witness; they'll grant favored treatment to no one.

There is one duty to be done, one end to achieve: to thrust out colonialism by *every* means in their power. The more farseeing among us will be, in the last resort, ready to admit this duty and this end; but we cannot help seeing in this ordeal by force the altogether inhuman means that these less-than-men make use of to win the concession of a charter of humanity. Accord it to them at once, then, and let them endeavor by peaceful undertakings to deserve it. Our worthiest souls contain racial prejudice.

They would do well to read Fanon; for he shows clearly that this irrepressible violence is neither sound and fury, nor the resurrection of savage instincts, nor even the effect of resentment: it is man recreating himself. I think we understood this truth at one time, but we have forgotten it – that no gentleness can efface the marks of violence; only violence itself can destroy them. The native cures himself of colonial neurosis by thrusting out the settler through force of arms. When his rage boils over, he rediscovers his lost innocence and he comes to know himself in that he himself creates his self. Far removed from his war, we consider it as a triumph of barbarism; but of its own volition it achieves, slowly but surely, the emancipation of the rebel, for bit by bit it destroys in him and around him the colonial gloom. Once begun, it is a war that gives no quarter. You may fear or be feared; that is to say, abandon yourself to the disassociations of a sham existence or conquer your birthright of unity. When the peasant takes a gun in his hands, the old myths grow dim and the

prohibitions are one by one forgotten. The rebel's weapon is the proof of his humanity. For in the first days of the revolt you must kill: to shoot down a European is to kill two birds with one stone, to destroy an oppressor and the man he oppresses at the same time: there remain a dead man, and a free man; the survivor, for the first time, feels a *national* soil under his foot. At this moment the Nation does not shrink from him; wherever he goes, wherever he may be, she is; she follows, and is never lost to view, for she is one with his liberty. But, after the first surprise, the colonial army strikes; and then all must unite or be slaughtered. Tribal dissensions weaken and tend to disappear; in the first place because they endanger the revolution, but for the more profound reason that they served no other purpose before than to divert violence against false foes. When they remain – as in the Congo – it's because they are kept up by the agents of colonialism. The Nation marches forward; for each of her children she is to be found wherever his brothers are fighting. Their feeling for each other is the reverse of the hatred they feel for you; they are brothers inasmuch as each of them has killed and may at any moment have to kill again. Fanon shows his readers the limits of "spontaneity" and the need for and dangers of "organization." But however great may be the task at each turning of the way the revolutionary consciousness deepens. The last complexes flee away; no one need come to us talking of the "dependency" complex of an ALN soldier.[1]

With his blinkers off, the peasant takes account of his real needs; before they were enough to kill him, but he tried to ignore them; now he sees them as infinitely great requirements. In this violence which springs from the people, which enables them to hold out for five years – for eight years as the Algerians have done – the military, political, and social necessities cannot be separated. The war, by merely setting the question of command and responsibility, institutes new structures which will become the first institutions of peace. Here, then, is man even now established in new traditions, the future children of a horrible present; here then we see him legitimized by a law which will be born or is born each day under fire: once the last settler is killed, shipped home, or assimilated, the minority breed disappears, to be replaced by socialism. And that's not enough; the rebel does not stop there; for you can be quite sure that he is not risking his skin to find himself at the level of a former inhabitant of the old mother country. Look how patient he is! Perhaps he dreams of another Dien Bien Phu,[2] but don't think he's really counting on it; he's a beggar fighting, in his poverty, against rich men powerfully armed. While he is waiting for decisive victories, or even without expecting them at all, he tires out his adversaries until they are sick of him.

It will not be without fearful losses; the colonial army becomes ferocious; the country is marked out, there are mopping-up operations, transfers of population, reprisal expeditions, and they massacre women and children. He knows this; this new man begins his life as a man at the end of it; he considers himself as a potential corpse. He will be killed; not only does he accept this risk, he's sure of it. This potential dead man has lost his wife and his children; he has seen so many dying men that he prefers victory to survival; others, not he, will have the fruits of victory; he is too weary of it all. But this weariness of the heart is the root of an unbelievable courage. We find our humanity on this side of death and despair; he finds it beyond torture and death. We have sown the wind; he is the whirlwind. The child of violence, at every moment he draws from it his humanity. We were men at his expense, he makes himself man at ours: a different man; of higher quality. [...]

We in Europe too are being decolonized: that is to say that the settler which is in every one of us is being savagely rooted out. Let us look at ourselves, if we can bear to, and see what is becoming of us. First, we must face that unexpected revelation, the striptease of our humanism. There you can see it. quite naked. and it's not a pretty sight. It was nothing but an ideology of lies, a perfect justification for pillage; its honeyed words, its affectation of sensibility were only alibis for our aggressions. A fine sight they are too, the believers in non-violence, saying that they are neither executioners nor victims. Very well then; if you're not victims when the government which you've voted for, when the army in which your younger brothers are serving without hesitation or remorse have undertaken race murder, you are, without a shadow of doubt, executioners. And if you choose to be victims and to risk being put in prison for a day or two, you are simply choosing to pull your irons out of the fire. But you will not be able to pull them out; they'll have to stay there till the end. Try to understand this at any rate: if violence began this very evening and if exploitation and

oppression had never existed on the earth, perhaps the slogans of non-violence might end the quarrel. But if the whole regime, even your non-violent ideas, are conditioned by a thousand-year-old oppression, your passivity serves only to place you in the ranks of the oppressors.

You know well enough that we are exploiters. You know too that we have laid hands on first the gold and metals, then the petroleum of the "new continents," and that we have brought them back to the old countries. This was not without excellent results, as witness our palaces, our cathedrals, and our great industrial cities; and then when there was the threat of a slump, the colonial markets were there to soften the blow or to divert it. Crammed with riches, Europe accorded the human status *de jure* to its inhabitants. With us, to be a man is to be an accomplice of colonialism, since all of us without exception have profited by colonial exploitation. This fat, pale continent ends by falling into what Fanon rightly calls narcissism. Cocteau became irritated with Paris – "that city which talks about itself the whole time." Is Europe any different? And that super-European monstrosity, North America? Chatter, Chatter: liberty, equality, fraternity, love, honor, patriotism, and what have you. All this did not prevent us from making anti-racial speeches about dirty niggers, dirty Jews, and dirty Arabs. High-minded people, liberal or just softhearted, protest that they were shocked by such inconsistency; but they were either mistaken or dishonest, for with us there is nothing more consistent than a racist humanism since the European has only been able to become a man through creating slaves and monsters. While there was a native population somewhere this imposture was not shown up; in the notion of the human race we found an abstract assumption of universality which served as cover for the most realistic practices. [...]

Violence has changed its direction. When we were victorious we practiced it without its seeming to alter us; it broke down the others, but for us men our humanism remained intact. United by their profits, the peoples of the mother countries baptized their commonwealth of crimes, calling them fraternity and love; today violence, blocked everywhere, comes back on us through our soldiers, comes inside and takes possession of us. Involution starts; the native recreates himself, and we, settlers and Europeans, ultras and liberals, we break up. Rage and fear are already blatant; they show themselves openly in the nigger-hunts in Algiers. Now, which side are the savages on? Where is barbarism? Nothing is missing, not even the tom-toms; the motorhorns beat out "Al-gér-ie fran-çaise" while the Europeans burn Moslems alive. Fanon reminds us that not so very long ago, a congress of psychiatrists was distressed by the criminal propensities of the native population. "Those people kill each other," they said, "that isn't normal. The Algerian's cortex must be under-developed." In central Africa, others have estab-lished that "the African makes very little use of his frontal lobes." These learned men would do well today to follow up their investigations in Europe, and particularly with regard to the French. For we, too, during the last few years, must be victims of "frontal sluggishness" since our patriots do quite a bit of assassinating of their fellow-countrymen, and if they're not at home, they blow up their house and their *concierge*. This is only a beginning; civil war is forecast for the autumn, or for the spring of next year. Yet our lobes seem to be in perfect condition; is it not rather the case that, since we cannot crush the natives, violence comes back on its tracks, accumulates in the very depths of our nature and seeks a way out? The union of the Algerian people causes the disunion of the French people; throughout the whole territory of the ex-mother-country, the tribes are dancing their war dances. The terror has left Africa, and is set-tling here; for quite obviously there are certain furious beings who want to make us pay with our own blood for the shame of having been beaten by the native. [...]

It would be better for you to be a native at the uttermost depths of his misery than to be a former settler. It is not right for a police official to be obliged to torture for ten hours a day; at that rate, his nerves will fall to bits, unless the torturers are forbidden in their own interests to work over-time. When it is desirable that the morality of the nation and the army should be protected by the rigors of the law, it is not right that the former should systematically demoralize the latter, nor that a country with a Republican tradition should confide hundreds and thousands of its young folk to the care of putschist officers. It is not right, my fellow-country-men, you who know very well all the crimes committed in our name, it's not at all right that you do not breathe a word about them to anyone, not even to your own soul, for fear of having to stand in judgment of yourself. I am willing to believe that at the beginning you did not realize what was happening; later, you doubted whether such things could be true; but now you know, and still you hold your tongues. Eight years of silence; what degradation! And your silence is all to no avail; today, the blinding sun of torture is at its zenith; it lights up the whole coun-try. Under that merciless glare, there is not a laugh that does not ring false, not a face that is not painted to hide fear or anger, not a single action that does not betray our disgust, and our compli-city. It is enough today for two French people to meet together for there to be a dead man between them. One dead man did I say? In other days France was the name of a country. We should take care that in 1961 it does not become the name of a nervous disease.

Will we recover? Yes. For violence, like Achilles' lance, can heal the wounds that it has inflicted. Today, we are bound hand and foot, humiliated and sick with fear; we cannot fall lower. [...] This is the end of the dialectic; you condemn this war but do not yet dare to declare yourselves to be on the side of the Algerian fighters; never fear, you can count on the settlers and the hired soldiers; they'll make you take the plunge. Then, perhaps, when your back is to the wall, you will let loose at last that new violence which is raised up in you by old, oft-repeated crimes. But, as they say, that's another story: the history of mankind. The time is drawing near, I am sure, when we will join the ranks of those who make it.

NOTES

1   National Army of Liberation in Algeria. – *Trans.*
2   The French army's drastic defeat at Dien Bien Phu ended the war in Indo-China. – *Trans.*

28

From *On Violence*

Hannah Arendt

I propose to raise the question of violence in the political realm. This is not easy; what Sorel remarked sixty years ago, "The problems of violence still remain very obscure,"[1] is as true today as it was then. I mentioned the general reluctance to deal with violence as a phenomenon in its own right, and I must now qualify this statement. If we turn to discussions of the phenomenon of power, we soon find that there exists a consensus among political theorists from Left to Right to the effect that violence is nothing more than the most flagrant manifestation of power. "All politics is a struggle for power; the ultimate kind of power is violence," said C. Wright Mills, echoing, as it were, Max Weber's definition of the state as "the rule of men over men based on the means of legitimate, that is allegedly legitimate, violence."[2] The consensus is very strange; for to equate political power with "the organization of violence" makes sense only if one follows Marx's estimate of the state as an instrument of oppression in the hands of the ruling class. Let us therefore turn to authors who do not believe that the body politic and its laws and institutions are merely coercive superstructures, secondary manifestations of some underlying forces. Let us turn, for instance, to Bertrand de Jouvenel, whose book *Power* is perhaps the most prestigious and, anyway, the most interesting recent treatise on the subject. "To him," he writes, "who contemplates the unfolding of the ages war presents itself as an activity of States *which pertains to their essence*."[3] This may prompt us to ask whether the end of warfare, then, would mean the end of

states. Would the disappearance of violence in relationships between states spell the end of power?

The answer, it seems, will depend on what we understand by power. And power, it turns out, is an instrument of rule, while rule, we are told, owes its existence to "the instinct of domination."[4] We are immediately reminded of what Sartre said about violence when we read in Jouvenel that "a man feels himself more of a man when he is imposing himself and making others the instruments of his will," which gives him "incomparable pleasure."[5] "Power," said Voltaire, "consists in making others act as I choose"; it is present wherever I have the chance "to assert my own will against the resistance" of others, said Max Weber, reminding us of Clausewitz's definition of war as "an act of violence to compel the opponent to do as we wish." The word, we are told by Strausz-Hupé, signifies "the power of man over man."[6] To go back to Jouvenel: "To command and to be obeyed: without that, there is no Power – with it no other attribute is needed for it to be.... The thing without which it cannot be: that essence is command." If the essence of power is the effectiveness of command, then there is no greater power than that which grows out of the barrel of a gun, and it would be difficult to say in "which way the order given by a policeman is different from that given by a gunman." (I am quoting from the important book *The Notion of the State*, by Alexander Passerin d'Entrèves, the only author I know who is aware of the importance of distinguishing between violence and power. "We have to decide whether and in what sense 'power' can be distinguished from 'force', to ascertain how the fact of using force according to law changes the quality of force itself and presents us with an entirely different picture of human relations," since "force, by the very fact of being qualified, ceases to be force." But even this distinction, by far the most sophisticated and thoughtful one in the literature, does not go to the root of the matter. Power in Passerin d'Entrèves's understanding is "qualified" or "institutionalized force." In other words, while the authors quoted above define violence as the most flagrant manifestation of power, Passerin d'Entrèves defines power as a kind of mitigated violence. In the final analysis, it comes to the same.)[7] Should everybody from Right to Left, from Bertrand de Jouvenel to Mao Tse-tung agree on so basic a point in political philosophy as the nature of power?

In terms of our traditions of political thought, these definitions have much to recommend them. Not only do they derive from the old notion of absolute power that accompanied the rise of the sovereign European nation-state, whose earliest and still greatest spokesmen were Jean Bodin, in sixteenth-century France, and Thomas Hobbes, in seventeenth-century England; they also coincide with the terms used since Greek antiquity to define the forms of government as the rule of man over man – of one or the few in monarchy and oligarchy, of the best or the many in aristocracy and democracy. Today we ought to add the latest and perhaps most formidable form of such dominion: bureaucracy or the rule of an intricate system of bureaus in which no men, neither one nor the best, neither the few nor the many, can be held responsible, and which could be properly called rule by Nobody. (If, in accord with traditional political thought, we identify tyranny as government that is not held to give account of itself, rule by Nobody is clearly the most tyrannical of all, since there is no one left who could even be asked to answer for what is being done. It is this state of affairs, making it impossible to localize responsibility and to identify the enemy, that is among the most potent causes of the current world-wide rebellious unrest, its chaotic nature, and its dangerous tendency to get out of control and to run amuck.)

Moreover, this ancient vocabulary was strangely confirmed and fortified by the addition of the Hebrew-Christian tradition and its "imperative conception of law." This concept was not invented by the "political realists" but was, rather, the result of a much earlier, almost automatic generalization of God's "Commandments," according to which "the simple relation of command and obedience" indeed sufficed to identify the essence of law.[8] Finally, more modern scientific and philosophical convictions concerning man's nature have further strengthened these legal and political traditions. The many recent discoveries of an inborn instinct of domination and an innate aggressiveness in the human animal were preceded by very similar philosophic statements. According to John Stuart Mill, "the first lesson of civilization [is] that of obedience," and he speaks of "the two states of the inclinations . . . one the desire to exercise power over others; the other . . . disinclination to have power exercised over themselves."[9] If we would trust our own experiences in these matters, we should know that the instinct of submission, an ardent desire to obey and be ruled by some strong man, is at least as prominent in human psychology as the will to power, and, politically, perhaps more relevant. The old adage "How fit he is to sway / That can so well obey," some version of which seems to have been known to all centuries and all nations,[10] may point to a psychological truth: namely, that the will to power and the will to submission are interconnected. "Ready submission to tyranny," to use Mill once more, is by no means always caused by "extreme passiveness." Conversely, a strong disinclination to obey is often accompanied by an equally strong disinclination to dominate and command. Historically speaking, the ancient institution of slave economy would be inexplicable on the grounds of Mill's psychology. Its express purpose was to liberate citizens from the burden of household affairs and to permit them to enter the public life of the community, where all were equals; if it were true that nothing is sweeter than to give commands and to rule others, the master would never have left his household.

However, there exists another tradition and another vocabulary no less old and time-honored. When the Athenian city-state called its constitution an isonomy, or the Romans spoke of the *civitas* as their form of government, they had in mind a concept of power and law whose essence did not rely on the command-obedience relationship and which did not identify power and rule or law and command. It was to these examples that the men of the eighteenth-century revolutions turned when they ransacked the archives of antiquity and constituted a form of government, a republic, where the rule of law, resting on the power of the people, would put an end to the rule of man over man, which they thought was a "government fit for slaves." They too, unhappily, still talked about obedience – obedience to laws instead of men; but what they actually meant was support of the laws to which the citizenry had given its consent. Such support is never unquestioning, and as far as reliability is concerned it cannot match the indeed "unquestioning obedience" that an act of violence can exact – the obedience every criminal can count on when he snatches my pocketbook with the help of a knife or robs a bank with the help of a gun. It is the people's support that lends power to the institutions of a country, and this support is but the continuation of the consent that brought the laws into existence to begin with. Under conditions of representative government the people are supposed to rule those who govern them. All political institutions are manifestations and materializations of power; they petrify and decay as soon as the living power of the people ceases to uphold them. This is what Madison meant when he said "all governments rest on opinion," a word no less true for the various forms of monarchy than for democracies. ("To suppose that majority rule functions only in democracy is a fantastic illusion," as Jouvenel points out: "The king, who is but one solitary individual, stands far more in need of the general support of Society than any other form of government."[11] Even the tyrant, the One who rules against all, needs helpers in the business of violence, though their number may be rather restricted.) However, the strength of opinion, that is, the power of the government, depends on numbers; it is "in proportion to the number with which it is associated,"[12] and tyranny, as Montesquieu discovered, is therefore the most violent and least powerful of forms of government. Indeed one of the most obvious distinctions between power and violence is that power always stands in need of numbers, whereas violence up to a point can manage without them because it relies on implements. A legally unrestricted majority rule, that is, a democracy without a constitution, can be very formidable in the suppression of the rights of minorities and very effective in the suffocation of dissent without any use of violence. But that does not mean that violence and power are the same.

The extreme form of power is All against One, the extreme form of violence is One against All.

And this latter is never possible without instruments. To claim, as is often done, that a tiny unarmed minority has successfully, by means of violence – shouting, kicking up a row, et cetera – disrupted large lecture classes whose overwhelming majority had voted for normal instruction procedures is therefore very misleading. (In a recent case at some German university there was even one lonely "dissenter" among several hundred students who could claim such a strange victory.) What actually happens in such cases is something much more serious: the majority clearly refuses to use its power and overpower the disrupters; the academic processes break down because no one is willing to raise more than a voting finger for the *status quo*. What the universities are up against is the "immense negative unity" of which Stephen Spender speaks in another context. All of which proves only that a minority can have a much greater potential power than one would expect by counting noses in public-opinion polls. The merely onlooking majority, amused by the spectacle of a shouting match between student and professor, is in fact already the latent ally of the minority. (One need only imagine what would have happened had one or a few unarmed Jews in pre-Hitler Germany tried to disrupt the lecture of an anti-Semitic professor in order to understand the absurdity of the talk about the small "minorities of militants.")

It is, I think, a rather sad reflection on the present state of political science that our terminology does not distinguish among such key words as "power," "strength," "force," "authority," and, finally, "violence" – all of which refer to distinct, different phenomena and would hardly exist unless they did. (In the words of d'Entrèves, "might, power, authority: these are all words to whose exact implications no great weight is attached in current speech; even the greatest thinkers sometimes use them at random. Yet it is fair to presume that they refer to different properties, and their meaning should therefore be carefully assessed and examined. . . . The correct use of these words is a question not only of logical grammar, but of historical perspective.")[13] To use them as synonyms not only indicates a certain deafness to linguistic meanings, which would be serious enough, but it has also resulted in a kind of blindness to the realities they correspond to. In such a situation it is always tempting to introduce new definitions, but – though I shall briefly yield to temptation – what is involved is not simply a matter of careless speech. Behind the apparent confusion is a firm conviction in whose light all distinctions would be, at best, of minor importance: the conviction that the most crucial political issue is, and always has been, the question of Who rules Whom? Power, strength, force, authority, violence – these are but words to indicate the means by which man rules over man; they are held to be synonyms because they have the same function. It is only after one ceases to reduce public affairs to the business of dominion that the original data in the realm of human affairs will appear, or, rather, reappear, in their authentic diversity.

These data, in our context, may be enumerated as follows:

Power corresponds to the human ability not just to act but to act in concert. Power is never the property of an individual; it belongs to a group and remains in existence only so long as the group keeps together. When we say of somebody that he is "in power" we actually refer to his being empowered by a certain number of people to act in their name. The moment the group, from which the power originated to begin with (*potestas in populo*, without a people or group there is no power), disappears, "his power" also vanishes. In current usage, when we speak of a "powerful man" or a "powerful personality," we already use the word "power" metaphorically; what we refer to without metaphor is "strength."

Strength unequivocally designates something in the singular, an individual entity; it is the property inherent in an object or person and belongs to its character, which may prove itself in relation to other things or persons, but is essentially independent of them. The strength of even the strongest individual can always be overpowered by the many, who often will combine for no other purpose than to ruin strength precisely because of its peculiar independence. The almost instinctive hostility of the many toward the one has always, from Plato to Nietzsche, been ascribed to resentment, to the envy of the weak for the strong, but this psychological interpretation misses the point. It is in the nature of a group and its power to turn against independence, the property of individual strength.

Force, which we often use in daily speech as a synonym for violence, especially if violence serves as a means of coercion, should be reserved, in terminological language, for the "forces of

nature" or the "force of circumstances" (*la force des choses*), that is, to indicate the energy released by physical or social movements.

Authority relating to the most elusive of these phenomena and therefore, as a term, most frequently abused, can be vested in persons – there is such a thing as personal authority, as, for instance, in the relation between parent and child, between teacher and pupil – or it can be vested in offices, as, for instance, in the Roman senate (*auctoritas in senatu*) or in the hierarchical offices of the Church (a priest can grant valid absolution even though he is drunk). Its hallmark is unquestioning recognition by those who are asked to obey; neither coercion nor persuasion is needed. (A father can lose his authority either by beating his child or by starting to argue with him, that is, either by behaving to him like a tyrant or by treating him as an equal.) To remain in authority requires respect for the person or the office. The greatest enemy of authority, therefore, is contempt, and the surest way to undermine it is laughter.

Violence, finally, as I have said, is distinguished by its instrumental character. Phenomenologically, it is close to strength, since the implements of violence, like all other tools, are designed and used for the purpose of multiplying natural strength until, in the last stage of their development, they can substitute for it. [. . .]

It is particularly tempting to think of power in terms of command and obedience, and hence to equate power with violence, in a discussion of what actually is only one of power's special cases – namely, the power of government. Since in foreign relations as well as domestic affairs violence appears as a last resort to keep the power structure intact against individual challengers – the foreign enemy, the native criminal – it looks indeed as though violence were the prerequisite of power and power nothing but a façade, the velvet glove which either conceals the iron hand or will turn out to belong to a paper tiger. On closer inspection, though, this notion loses much of its plausibility. For our purpose, the gap between theory and reality is perhaps best illustrated by the phenomenon of revolution.

Since the beginning of the century theoreticians of revolution have told us that the chances of revolution have significantly decreased in proportion to the increased destructive capacities of weapons at the unique disposition of governments.

The history of the last seventy years, with its extraordinary record of successful and unsuccessful revolutions, tells a different story. Were people mad who even tried against such overwhelming odds? And, leaving out instances of full success, how can even a temporary success be explained? The fact is that the gap between state-owned means of violence and what people can muster by themselves – from beer bottles to Molotov cocktails and guns – has always been so enormous that technical improvements make hardly any difference. Textbook instructions on "how to make a revolution" in a step-by-step progression from dissent to conspiracy, from resistance to armed uprising, are all based on the mistaken notion that revolutions are "made." In a contest of violence against violence the superiority of the government has always been absolute; but this superiority lasts only as long as the power structure of the government is intact – that is, as long as commands are obeyed and the army or police forces are prepared to use their weapons. When this is no longer the case, the situation changes abruptly. Not only is the rebellion not put down, but the arms themselves change hands – sometimes, as in the Hungarian revolution, within a few hours. (We should know about such things after all these years of futile fighting in Vietnam, where for a long time, before getting massive Russian aid, the National Liberation Front fought us with weapons that were made in the United States.) Only after this has happened, when the disintegration of the government in power has permitted the rebels to arm themselves, can one speak of an "armed uprising," which often does not take place at all or occurs when it is no longer necessary. Where commands are no longer obeyed, the means of violence are of no use; and the question of this obedience is not decided by the command–obedience relation but by opinion, and, of course, by the number of those who share it. Everything depends on the power behind the violence. The sudden dramatic breakdown of power that ushers in revolutions reveals in a flash how civil obedience – to laws, to rulers, to institutions – is but the outward manifestation of support and consent.

Where power has disintegrated, revolutions are possible but not necessary. We know of many instances when utterly impotent regimes were permitted to continue in existence for long periods of time – either because there was no one to test their strength and reveal their weakness or because they

were lucky enough not to be engaged in war and suffer defeat. Disintegration often becomes manifest only in direct confrontation; and even then, when power is already in the street, some group of men prepared for such an eventuality is needed to pick it up and assume responsibility. We have recently witnessed how it did not take more than the relatively harmless, essentially nonviolent French students' rebellion to reveal the vulnerability of the whole political system, which rapidly disintegrated before the astonished eyes of the young rebels. Unknowingly they had tested it; they intended only to challenge the ossified university system, and down came the system of governmental power, together with that of the huge party bureaucracies – *"une sorte de désintégration de toutes les hiérarchies."* It was a textbook case of a revolutionary situation that did not develop into a revolution because there was nobody, least of all the students, prepared to seize power and the responsibility that goes with it. Nobody except, of course, de Gaulle. Nothing was more characteristic of the seriousness of the situation than his appeal to the army, his journey to see Massu and the generals in Germany, a walk to Canossa, if there ever was one, in view of what had happened only a few years before. But what he sought and received was support, not obedience, and the means were not commands but concessions. If commands had been enough, he would never have had to leave Paris.

No government exclusively based on the means of violence has ever existed. Even the totalitarian ruler, whose chief instrument of rule is torture, needs a power basis – the secret police and its net of informers. Only the development of robot soldiers, which, as previously mentioned, would eliminate the human factor completely and, conceivably, permit one man with a push button to destroy whomever he pleased, could change this fundamental ascendancy of power over violence. Even the most despotic domination we know of, the rule of master over slaves, who always outnumbered him, did not rest on superior means of coercion as such, but on a superior organization of power – that is, on the organized solidarity of the masters. Single men without others to support them never have enough power to use violence successfully. Hence, in domestic affairs, violence functions as the last resort of power against criminals or rebels – that is, against single individuals who, as it were, refuse to be overpowered by the consensus of the majority. And as for actual warfare, we have seen in Vietnam how an enormous superiority in the means of violence can become helpless if confronted with an ill-equipped but well-organized opponent who is much more powerful. This lesson, to be sure, was there to be learned from the history of guerrilla warfare, which is at least as old as the defeat in Spain of Napoleon's still-unvanquished army.

To switch for a moment to conceptual language: Power is indeed of the essence of all government, but violence is not. Violence is by nature instrumental; like all means, it always stands in need of guidance and justification through the end it pursues. And what needs justification by something else cannot be the essence of anything. The end of war – end taken in its twofold meaning – is peace or victory; but to the question And what is the end of peace? there is no answer. Peace is an absolute, even though in recorded history periods of warfare have nearly always outlasted periods of peace. Power is in the same category; it is, as they say, "an end in itself." (This, of course, is not to deny that governments pursue policies and employ their power to achieve prescribed goals. But the power structure itself precedes and outlasts all aims, so that power, far from being the means to an end, is actually the very condition enabling a group of people to think and act in terms of the means-end category.) And since government is essentially organized and institutionalized power, the current question What is the end of government? does not make much sense either. The answer will be either question-begging – to enable men to live together – or dangerously utopian – to promote happiness or to realize a classless society or some other nonpolitical ideal, which if tried out in earnest cannot but end in some kind of tyranny.

Power needs no justification, being inherent in the very existence of political communities; what it does need is legitimacy. The common treatment of these two words as synonyms is no less misleading and confusing than the current equation of obedience and support. Power springs up whenever people get together and act in concert, but it derives its legitimacy from the initial getting together rather than from any action that then may follow. Legitimacy, when challenged, bases itself on an appeal to the past, while justification relates to an end that lies in the future. Violence can be justifiable, but it never will be legitimate. Its justification loses in plausibility the farther its intended

end recedes into the future. No one questions the use of violence in self-defense, because the danger is not only clear but also present, and the end justifying the means is immediate.

Power and violence, though they are distinct phenomena, usually appear together. Wherever they are combined, power, we have found, is the primary and predominant factor. The situation, however, is entirely different when we deal with them in their pure states – as, for instance, with foreign invasion and occupation. We saw that the current equation of violence with power rests on government's being understood as domination of man over man by means of violence. If a foreign conqueror is confronted by an impotent government and by a nation unused to the exercise of political power, it is easy for him to achieve such domination. In all other cases the difficulties are great indeed, and the occupying invader will try immediately to establish Quisling governments, that is, to find a native power base to support his dominion. The head-on clash between Russian tanks and the entirely nonviolent resistance of the Czechoslovak people is a textbook case of a confrontation between violence and power in their pure states. But while domination in such an instance is difficult to achieve, it is not impossible. Violence, we must remember, does not depend on numbers or opinions, but on implements, and the implements of violence, as I mentioned before, like all other tools, increase and multiply human strength. Those who oppose violence with mere power will soon find that they are confronted not by men but by men's artifacts, whose inhumanity and destructive effectiveness increase in proportion to the distance separating the opponents. Violence can always destroy power; out of the barrel of a gun grows the most effective command, resulting in the most instant and perfect obedience. What never can grow out of it is power.

In a head-on clash between violence and power, the outcome is hardly in doubt. If Gandhi's enormously powerful and successful strategy of nonviolent resistance had met with a different enemy – Stalin's Russia, Hitler's Germany, even prewar Japan, instead of England – the outcome would not have been decolonization, but massacre and submission. However, England in India and France in Algeria had good reasons for their restraint. Rule by sheer violence comes into play where power is being lost; it is precisely the shrinking power of the Russian government, internally and externally, that became manifest in its "solution" of the Czechoslovak problem – just as it was the shrinking power of European imperialism that became manifest in the alternative between decolonization and massacre. To substitute violence for power can bring victory, but the price is very high; for it is not only paid by the vanquished, it is also paid by the victor in terms of his own power. This is especially true when the victor happens to enjoy domestically the blessings of constitutional government. Henry Steele Commager is entirely right: "If we subvert world order and destroy world peace we must inevitably subvert and destroy our own political institutions first."[14] The much-feared boomerang effect of the "government of subject races" (Lord Cromer) on the home government during the imperialist era meant that rule by violence in faraway lands would end by affecting the government of England, that the last "subject race" would be the English themselves. The recent gas attack on the campus at Berkeley, where not just tear gas but also another gas, "outlawed by the Geneva Convention and used by the Army to flush out guerrillas in Vietnam," was laid down while gas-masked Guardsmen stopped anybody and everybody "from fleeing the gassed area," is an excellent example of this "backlash" phenomenon. It has often been said that impotence breeds violence, and psychologically this is quite true, at least of persons possessing natural strength, moral or physical. Politically speaking, the point is that loss of power becomes a temptation to substitute violence for power – in 1968 during the Democratic convention in Chicago we could watch this process on television – and that violence itself results in impotence. Where violence is no longer backed and restrained by power, the well-known reversal in reckoning with means and ends has taken place. The means, the means of destruction, now determine the end – with the consequence that the end will be the destruction of all power.

Nowhere is the self-defeating factor in the victory of violence over power more evident than in the use of terror to maintain domination, about whose weird successes and eventual failures we know perhaps more than any generation before us. Terror is not the same as violence; it is, rather, the form of government that comes into being when violence, having destroyed all power, does not abdicate but, on the contrary, remains in full control. It has often been noticed that the effectiveness of terror depends almost entirely on the degree of social atomization. Every kind of organized opposition must disappear before the full force of terror can be let loose. This atomization – an outrageously pale, academic word for the horror it implies – is maintained and intensified through the ubiquity of the informer, who can be literally omnipresent because he no longer is merely a professional agent in the pay of the police but potentially every person one comes into contact with. How such a fully developed police state is established and how it works – or, rather, how nothing works where it holds sway – can now be learned in Aleksandr I. Solzhenitsyn's *The First Circle*, which will probably remain one of the masterpieces of twentieth-century literature and certainly contains the best documentation on Stalin's regime in existence. The decisive difference between totalitarian domination, based on terror, and tyrannies and dictatorships, established by violence, is that the former turns not only against its enemies but against its friends and supporters as well, being afraid of all power, even the power of its friends. The climax of terror is reached when the police state begins to devour its own children, when yesterday's executioner becomes today's victim. And this is also the moment when power disappears entirely. There exist now a great many plausible explanations for the de-Stalinization of Russia – none, I believe, so compelling as the realization by the Stalinist functionaries themselves that a continuation of the regime would lead, not to an insurrection, against which terror is indeed the best safeguard, but to paralysis of the whole country.

To sum up: politically speaking, it is insufficient to say that power and violence are not the same. Power and violence are opposites; where the one rules absolutely, the other is absent. Violence appears where power is in jeopardy, but left to its own course it ends in power's disappearance. This implies that it is not correct to think of the opposite of violence as nonviolence; to speak of nonviolent power is actually redundant. Violence can destroy power; it is utterly incapable of creating it. Hegel's and Marx's great trust in the dialectial "power of negation," by virtue of which opposites do not destroy but smoothly develop into each other because contradictions promote and do not paralyze development, rests on a much older philosophical prejudice: that evil is no more than a privative *modus* of the good, that good can come out of evil; that, in short, evil is but a temporary manifestation of a still-hidden good. Such time-honored opinions have become dangerous. They are shared by many who have never heard of Hegel or Marx, for the simple reason that they inspire hope and dispel fear – a treacherous hope used to dispel legitimate fear. By this, I do not mean to equate violence with evil; I only want to stress that violence cannot be derived from its opposite, which is power, and that in order to understand it for what it is, we shall have to examine its roots and nature.

NOTES

1 Georges Sorel, *Reflections on Violence*, "Introduction to the First Publication" (1906), New York, 1961, p. 60.

2 *The Power Elite*, New York, 1956, p. 171; Max Weber in the first paragraphs of *Politics as a Vocation* (1921). Weber seems to have been aware of his agreement with the Left. He quotes in the context Trotsky's remark in Brest-Litovsk, "Every state is based on violence," and adds, "This is indeed true."

3 *Power: The Natural History of Its Growth* (1945), London, 1952, p. 122.

4 Ibid., p. 93.

5 Ibid., p. 110.

6 See Karl von Clausewitz, *On War* (1832), New York, 1943, ch. 1; Robert Strausz-Hupé, *Power and Community*, New York, 1956, p. 4.

7 *The Notion of the State, An Introduction to Political Theory*, Oxford, 1967, pp. 64, 70, and 105.

8 Ibid., p. 129.

9 *Considerations on Representative Government* (1861), Liberal Arts Library, pp. 59 and 65.

10 John M. Wallace, *Destiny His Choice: The Loyalism of Andrew Marvell*, Cambridge, 1968, pp. 88–9. I owe this reference to the kind attention of Gregory Des Jardins.

11 Op. cit., p. 98.

12 *The Federalist*, no. 49.

13 Op. cit., p. 7. Cf. also p. 171, where, discussing the exact meaning of the words "nation" and "nationality," he rightly insists that "the only competent guides in the jungle of so many different meanings are the linguists and the historians. It is to them that we must turn for help." And in distinguishing authority and power, he turns to Cicero's *potestas in populo, auctoritas in senatu.*

14 "Can We Limit Presidential Power?" in *The New Republic*, April 6, 1968.

29

Dirty Protest: Symbolic Overdetermination and Gender in Northern Ireland Ethnic Violence

Begoña Aretxaga

Introduction

From 1978 to 1981 IRA and Irish National Liberation Army (INLA) male prisoners in Northern Ireland undertook an extraordinary form of protest against prison authorities and the British government. They refused to leave their cells either to wash or to use the toilets, living instead in the midst of their own dirt and body waste. In 1980 they were joined by their female comrades, thus adding menstrual blood to the horrendous excretal imagery of the protest. Unlike the hunger strike on which the prisoners would embark in 1981, the Dirty Protest had no precedent in the existing political culture. This action, which resonated with notions of savagery, irrationality, and madness, was shocking and largely incomprehensible to the public in Ireland and Britain. Not only did relatives and supporters of the prisoners admit this popular incomprehensibility, but the main newspapers treated the protest as "a bizarre and foul exercise," to use the not uncommon words of the English *Times*. The striking form of this political action, coupled on the one hand with the strong emotional reactions that it provoked and on the other with its genderized character, makes the Dirty Protest a particularly suitable case for the exploration of how subjectivity, gender, and power are articulated in situations of heightened political violence.

Bodily violence has been extensively theorized as a disciplinary mechanism (Asad 1983; Feldman 1991; Foucault 1979; Scarry 1985). In *Discipline and Punish* Foucault powerfully analyzed punishment as a political technology of the body aimed at the production of submissive subjects. In the modern prison discipline and punishment are directed at the subjective transformation of individuals from dangerous criminals to docile citizens. In Foucault's analysis the body ceases to be the repository of signs to become the material through which subjectivities are molded (1979: 23). What Foucault has not addressed are the points at which the technology of normalization breaks down, the moments in which rational disciplines of the body fail to produce docile subjects, either because the subjects refuse to be normalized, even at the cost of death, or because the exercise of punishment indulges in an excess that betrays its rational aims, becoming a drama of its own rather than merely a political tactic, as recent work has well shown (Graziano 1992; Obeyesekere 1992; Suarez-Orozco 1992; Taussig 1987). [...]

The Dirty Protest is a good case for an approach that combines a Foucaudian critique of power with an interpretative anthropology sensitive to the "deep play" of subjectivity. To develop this analysis I conceptualized the feces and menstrual blood that characterized the Dirty Protest not as artifacts but as overdetermined primordial symbols. I do not mean by *primordial* an onto-logical essence. I use *primordial symbols* here for lack of a better word to refer to those symbols that resort to physiological material of great psychological significance and that are elaborated in one form or another in all cultures.[...] I mean over-determination in the Freudian sense of the term, as the condensation of different strands of meaning, none of which are in themselves necessarily determinant. [...] The prisoners' excreta and menstrual blood tap into the interconnected domains of prison violence, colonial history, unconscious motivation, and gender discourses.

Resisting Normalization

With the escalation of the political crisis that followed the riots of 1969 in Northern Ireland, large numbers of people in the working class Catholic communities of Belfast were arrested. Most of them were accused of crimes against the state, a general label that included a wide variety of actions ranging from the wearing of combat jackets to participation in demonstrations to the use of firearms. After a hunger strike in 1972, the British government agreed to give the prisoners "special category" status, regarding them as de facto political prisoners. These included members of Irish paramilitary organizations, both Republican and Loyalists.[1]

In 1976 the British government, as part of a more general counterinsurgency operation, withdrew "special category" status from Republican and Loyalist prisoners, who were then to be considered and treated as ODCs (Ordinary Decent Criminals), in British legal parlance. This entailed the use of prison uniforms instead of personal clothes and the cancellation of rights of association, internal organization, and free disposal of time. Republican prisoners resisted government regulations by refusing to wear the prison uniforms. Since other clothes were lacking, the prisoners covered themselves with blankets. The prison administration penalized their insubordination with an array of disciplinary measures: 24-hour cell confinement, inadequate food, lack of exercise and intellectual stimulation, curtailment of visits, frequent beatings, and recurrent body and cell searches. The prisoners (three-quarters of whom were between the ages of 17 and 21) left their cells only for trips to the toilet, weekly showers, Sunday mass, and monthly visits. Physio-logical necessities such as food and excretory functions became a focus of humiliating practices. The already inadequate diet was frequently spoiled with defiling substances such as spit, urine, roaches, or maggots. Access to the toilet was controlled by the permission of guards who would delay or deny it at will. After a year of this situation the prison administration forbade wearing blankets outside the cells. Prisoners had to leave their cells naked on their way to toilets and showers. Harassment increased at these times, leaving prisoners especially vulnerable to beatings, guards' mockery and sexual insults, as well as the hated body searches. These were described to me by an IRA ex-prisoner:

They made you squat on the floor on your haunches. You wouldn't do that so they beat you, they sat over you and probed your back passage, and then with the same finger some would search your mouth, your nose, your hair, your beard, every part of your body, there was nothing private about your body.

According to prisoners, it was the increased harassment and heightened violence accompanying the use of toilets that sparked the Dirty Protest in 1978. In a coordinated action, prisoners refused to leave their cells except to go to mass and visits. At first they emptied the chamber pots through windows and peepholes of the doors. When the guards boarded them up prisoners began to dispose of feces by leaving them in a corner of their cells. This, however, allowed the guards to mess the mattresses and blankets of prisoners with the feces during cell searches. Finally, prisoners began to smear their excreta on the walls of their cells.

In 1980 the Republican women in Armagh prison joined their male comrades in the Dirty Protest. They had also been resisting the change of status from political prisoners to criminals since 1976 by refusing to do mandatory prison work and were also enduring similar disciplinary measures. But in contrast to the male prisoners in Long-Kesh, Republican women were allowed to use their own clothes – as were all female prisoners in Britain. Although harassment and tension had been rising inside the jail, what prompted women into the Dirty Protest was not humiliation accompanying use of the toilets but an assault by male officers – the second of its kind – followed by two days' lock-up in their cells. What justified this assault was the search of "subversive garments." If in Long-Kesh male prisoners spurned the prison uniform to assert their political identity, in a similar metonymic move Armagh women used their clothes to improvise IRA uniforms. It was in search of those small pieces of apparel – berets, black skirts; trivial in themselves yet full of significance in the encoded world of the prison – that military men in full riot gear entered the cells of IRA prisoners on February 7, 1980, kicking and punching the women. The following quote from a report smuggled out of jail by one of the prisoners illustrates the sexual overtones of the assault:

At around 3:45pm on Thursday Feb. 7th, numerous male and female screws [guards] invaded my cell in order to get me down to the governor. They charged in full riot gear equipped with shields. I sat unprotected but aware of what was going to happen as I had heard my comrades screaming in pain. I was suddenly pinned to the bed by a shield and the weight of a male screw on top of me. Then my shoes were dragged off my feet. I was bodily assaulted, thumped, trailed and kicked. I was then trailed out of my cell, and during the course of my being dragged and hauled from the wing both my breasts were exposed to the jeering and mocking eyes of all the screws, there must have been about twenty of them. While being carried, I was also abused with punches to the back of my head and my stomach. I was eventually carried into the governor, my breasts were still exposed. While I was held by the screws the governor carried out the adjudication, and I was then trailed back and thrown into a cell.[2]

Sexual harassment by state forces has been a systematic complaint during the last 20 years that reappears in informal conversations with women as well as in their narratives of encounters with security forces. For the prisoners, the assault was as much a political attempt to discipline through punishment as a humiliating assertion of male dominance. Moreover, at the time of the assault, there was a lot of pain, grief, and anger among women prisoners. In addition to health problems and increasing petty harassment, a high percentage of women lost close relatives in shootings by Loyalist paramilitaries or British army during their time in jail. The devastating emotions of mourning were repressed to preserve collective morale and inner strength as well as to avoid special targeting from guards. The assault and enforced locked up in the cells provoked a strong response. Shortly after the beginning of the protest, Mairead Farrell,

leader of the women prisoners, described their situation in a letter smuggled out of jail:

The stench of urine and excrement clings to the cells and our bodies. No longer can we empty the pots of urine and excrement out the window, as the male screws [guards] have boarded them up. Little light or air penetrates the thick boarding. The electric light has to be kept constantly on in the cells; the other option is to sit in the dark. Regardless of day or night, the cells are dark. Now we can't even see out the window; our only view is the wall of excreta. The spy holes are locked so they can only be open by the screws to look in. Sanitary towels are thrown into us without wrapping. We are not permitted paper bags or such like so they lie in the dirt until used. For twenty-three hours a day we lie in these cells.[3]

The Dirty Protest was by any standard of political culture, and certainly by that of Ireland, an unusual political action. [...] It was as incomprehensible to the general public as it was to prison officers and government administration. In the Catholic communities, massive support for the prisoners was not reached, for instance, until the end of the Dirty Protest and the beginning of the hunger strike. The Dirty Protest provoked an inexpressible horror and a rising spiral of violence inside and outside the jails. If the men's Dirty Protest was incomprehensible, the women's was unthinkable, generating in many men, even among the ranks of supporting Republicans, reactions of denial. It was no doubt a form of warfare, a violent contest of power, as Feldman (1991) has noted. But why this form and not another?

Humiliation and Violence: The Deep Play of Subjectivity

[...] The disciplines and ritual punishments enacted in jail were deliberately aimed at socializing the prisoners into the new social order of the prison. To that end the identity of the prisoner as a political militant had to be destroyed. The random beatings, scarce diet, constant visibility, body searches, and denial of control over their excretory functions were directed at defeating the will of autonomous individuals and transforming them into dependent infantilized subjects through physical pain and humiliating practices. This divestment of individual identity is, in more or less drastic forms, characteristic of what Goffman

(1959) called "total institutions." Once the power battle was displaced to the psychological arena of childhood and the prisoners were left in a state of absolute powerlessness with nothing but their bodies to resist institutional assault, they resorted to the primordial mechanism of feces, at once a weapon and a symbol of utter rejection. Thus, an ex-prison officer admitted to anthropologist Allen Feldman that "[h]umiliation was a big weapon. Prisoners were constantly propelled into an infantile role. You could see the Dirty Protest as virtually resistance to toilet training in a bizarre way" (Feldman 1991: 192). That is to say, the Dirty Protest can be interpreted as simultaneously literal and symbolic resistance to prison socialization and the accompanying moral system that legitimized it. Feldman has suggested that the prisoners carried out this resistance by utilizing the excretory function as a detached weapon (1991: 178). The use of excreta as a weapon of resistance was not, however, the only bodily weapon available to the prisoners. The hunger strike, to which the prisoners resorted later on, was a more likely and socially understandable form of political resistance. Neither was the Dirty Protest very effective in attracting international sympathy. Amnesty International, for example, concluded upon examination of the case that the prisoners' conditions were self-inflicted.[4] Any socialization process implies an emotional dynamic that Feldman does not analyze. After a year of close contact an IRA ex-prisoner man openly admitted the turmoil of emotions provoked by our lengthy conversation on the Dirty Protest:

I feel funny now, my emotions are mixed. You suffer a lot in jail, some people more than others. Some people remember the good things about jail, the laughs. You don't want to remember the times you felt like crying. . . . It was just strange. You are on your own, you worry sick no matter how much you laugh or share, you have irrational fears. People cry in jail. A lot of strange things happen to you.

I would like to suggest that far from being a detached weapon, the Dirty Protest entailed a deep personal involvement, a process that was tremendously painful psychologically and physically.

Physical pain, insufficient diet, and constant humiliation evoked in the prisoners, in acute and extreme form, the vulnerability and powerlessness of childhood. The sense of permanent physical insecurity produced, as is frequently the case in these situations, anxieties about disfigurement (Goffman 1959: 21; Scarry 1985: 40–1). Fantasies of dismemberment, dislocation, and mutilation accompanied any venture outside the cells and were particularly present during body searches, forced baths, and wing shifts.[6] In a personal interview, an IRA ex-prisoner recalled the terror experienced at being suspended in the air held spread eagle by four officers who were pulling his arms and legs during a body search while another inspected his anus: "It was very, very frightening because there were times when you thought you were going to tear apart." Forced baths entailed heavy scrubbing with rough brushes that left the body bruised and scarred. They also involved forced shaving of beard and hair with the frequent result of skin cuts. Not only physical pain but the images of mutilation triggered by the hostility of warders made the baths terrifying experiences:

They used scrubbing brushes to wash you. The whole thing was very violent, a terrifying experience. After they finished they dragged me to the zinc and one cut my head with a razor and they cut my head in a whole lot of places while all the time they were making fun of me. Then they threw me to the floor, spread eagle. I had massive dark bruises all over my ribs and they painted them with a white stuff, I don't know what it was and they painted my face too.

The terror was augmented by the association of cleaning and death in other contexts. For example, another ex-prisoner of the same affiliation commented, apropos of the situation: "It just reminded me of the Jews in the concentration camps because every man in the [visiting] room was bald and we were all very thin and frightened" (see also Feldman 1991).

The prison dynamic of punishment and humiliation fueled feelings of hate and anger that threatened to overcome the psychological integrity of the prisoners. The following quotes from two prisoners interviewed by Feldman illustrate best the force of these feelings:

I hated the screws [prison officers]. I used to live for the day that I got out. I would have taken three day before a killed a screw. I was wrapped up in the hatred thing, and it wasn't political motivation at all. [1991: 196–7]

The hate, I found out what hatred was. I used to talk about hate on the outside, but it was superstitious, it was depersonalized. There were wee people you didn't like. But it was in jail that I came face to face with the naked hatred. It frighten the life out of me when I seen it for what it was. When you thought of getting your own back on the screw, how much you would enjoy it, it really frighten you. You just blacked those thoughts out of your mind. At the end of the day I knew I was smarter than the screws. But I knew the road of black hatred. I just got a glimpse of it. It scared the balls clean out of me. [1991: 197]

The Dirty Protest was simultaneously a sign of rejection and an instrument of power, but one that constituted also the symbolic articulation of dangerous feelings that could not be expressed in other forms without risking madness or serious physical injury. The feces constituted not so much the instrument of a mimetic violence, as Feldman has suggested, but the crystallization of a conflict between the desire of mimetic violence against prison officers and the need for restraint to preserve some physical and psychological integrity. In this sense, the feces appear as a compromise formation, a symptom in the Freudian sense of the term. However, unlike the hysterical symptom, the Dirty Protest had conscious meaning and political intentionality for the prisoners. Its significance was elaborated by them in the idiom of Republican resistance, which is part of Northern Ireland's nationalist culture. The prisoners' political beliefs arise out of a shared social experience of the working-class ghettos and are essential to the protest in that they provide its rationale and moral legitimation, as the ethnographies of Burton (1978) and Sluka (1989) have well shown. In other words, the prisoners knew why they were smearing their cells with excrement and under which conditions they would cease to do so. They were also aware that their political language made sense to an audience outside the jail, even when their action remained largely uncomprehended. Thus, if we consider the Dirty Protest as an emotionally loaded compromise formation meaningful to the actors yet not to the larger society, we can read it as a symptom of profound alienation midway between the elusive hysterical symptom and the graspable cultural symbol. [. . .]

The prison experience since 1976 evoked for Republicans in extreme form the historical experience of neglect and the desire for social recognition that characterized the lives of working-class Catholics in Northern Ireland. The claim to political status was so important to them precisely because it implied a deep existential recognition, the acknowledgment that one's being-in-the-world mattered. Recognition can only come from an "other." At the closest level the significant "other" was represented by the Loyalist guards with whom prisoners interacted daily. Although in terms of profession the guards occupied the lower ranks of the social structure, as Protestants they occupied a position of social superiority vis-à-vis Catholics. Thus, the relation between prisoners and guards was mediated by a relation of social inequality larger and historically more significant than that existing in the prison universe. At a more removed level, however, the position of the "other" was occupied by the British government, which became the embodiment of the "Law of the Father." Britain became the absent presence whose law threatened to erase the prisoners by eliminating their political identity. The desire of recognition from Britain was implicit in the prisoners' and supporters' representation of the protest as a battle between Ireland and Britain. The prison disciplines, with their uniformity, the substitution of names for numbers, and extreme forms of humiliation, constituted an ultimate form of erasure.

If existential recognition was essential to the prisoners – literally a matter of life and death – the Dirty Protest must be understood as a violent attempt to force such recognition without succumbing to physical elimination, which could ultimately happen – as it did happen in 1981 – with a hunger strike. In this context, which links prison power relations with larger social-political arenas, the feces of the Dirty Protest tap into a whole new domain of meaning. They are not just a symbolic and material weapon against the prison regime, and a symptom of the alienation of the prisoners qua prisoners, but also a social symptom that must be understood in historical perspective. [. . .]

In the case of the Dirty Protest what we have is the reelaboration of Anglo-Irish history. The excreta on the walls of the cells made visible the hidden history of prison violence; furthermore, it appeared to the world as *a* record of Irish history. The Catholic Primate of Ireland, Archbishop Tomas O'Fiaich, upon visiting the Long-Kesh jail, declared publicly that the situation of the prisoners was inhuman. He denounced the inflexibility of the British government that was violating the personal dignity of the prisoners and voiced concern about beatings and ill-treatment of the prisoners (*Times* and *Guardian*, August 2, 1978). Archbishop O'Fiaich's press declaration unleashed a polemic storm. The British government emphatically denied any liability for the protest as well as any mistreatment of the prisoners: "These criminals are totally responsible for the situation in which they find themselves.... There is no truth in those allegations [of mistreatment]" (*Times*, August 2, 1978). While unionist and conservative parties accused O'Fiaich of IRA sympathy (*Times*, August 3, 1978), Nationalist parties supported the Arbishop's concern. The Presbyterian church, on the other hand, attacked O'Fiaich for his "grave moral confusion" (*Guardian* and *Times*, August 5, 1978). The prison violence came to occupy an important place in public political discussions in Ireland and England, attracting also the attention of the international media. The connection between prison and colonial violence was drawn during the years of the Dirty Protest not only by the prisoners and their Republican supporters. The *Washington Post* compared the inflexibility of the British government with the "iron-fisted rule of Oliver Cromwell" (quoted in the *Times*, November 22, 1978). Even the European Court of Human Rights, while ruling that the prisoners were not entitled to political status, expressed its concern "at the inflexible approach of the State authorities which has been concerned more to punish offenders against prison discipline than to explore ways of resolving such a serious deadlock" (European Law Centre 1981: 201).

The rigidity of the British government, which held onto the banner of "The Law" with an intransigence highly evocative of paternal authority, as well as the refusal by prison officers to acknowledge any responsibility in the emergence of the Dirty Protest, echoed the historical denial of British responsibility in the dynamics of violence in Ireland.

Historical amnesia, though common enough, is never trivial or accidental (De Certeau 1988). Such emphatic negation of any relation to the dirty prisoners, coupled with the inability to end the protest, reveals perhaps a stumbling block in the history of Britain and Ireland that remains to be explained. In this context the power of feces as a symptom of the political (dis)order of Northern Ireland may lie not so much in what it signified, but precisely in that which resisted symbolization: its capacity to tap into unconscious fears, desires, and fantasies that had come to form part of ethnic violence in Ireland through a colonial discourse of dirtiness. This discourse provided yet another arena, or another field of power, if you will, in which the Dirty Protest acquired a new set of cultural resonances appearing as a materialization of the buried "shit" of British colonization, a demetaphorization of the "savage, dirty Irish."

Excrement and the Fiction of Civilization

Dirtiness has been a metaphor of barbarism in British anti-Irish discourse for centuries. From Elizabethan writings to Victorian accounts of Ireland there have been recurrent descriptions of the dirtiness, misery, and primitiveness of the country and its people. "Irish" and "primitive" soon implicated each other, and the image of the dirty, primitive Irish became familiar to the English imagination through jokes, cartoons, and other popular forms of representation. Such images have proliferated at times of political turmoil in Ireland, with the Irish frequently depicted with simian or pig-like features (Curtis 1971; Darby 1983). After the partition of Ireland, "dirty" continued to be a favorite epithet to debase Catholics in Northern Ireland. My Nationalist informants were acutely aware of the operativity of this discourse, and many, like this middle-aged woman, recalled growing up hearing that they were dirty: "You would hear people saying that Catholics were dirty, and live like rats, and had too many children...and you suddenly realized that was you and your family."

The investment of excrement and dirt with intense feelings of disgust, which are then associated with aggression and fear of racial contamination, is well known and need not be underscored here. Notions of dirt and purity are crucial, as Mary Douglas (1966) noted, in organizing ideas of savagery and civilization and highly significant in establishing social boundaries and cultural differentiations. For many people in England and Ireland the prisoners living amid their own excreta constituted the image par excellence of the uncivilized, the erasure of categorical distinctions that structure human society, the regression to a pre-social state, with its concomitant power of pollution and contagion. In the women's prison of Armagh officers wore masks, insulating suits, and rubber boots that shielded them from the polluting conditions of the prisoners' wing. Prisoners noted that the guards did not like to touch anything belonging to the prisoners even though they used gloves. Prison officers felt defiled coming in contact with the prisoners. As the women looked increasingly dirty, the guards tried to counteract defilement by increasing their care in making themselves up and having their hair done. Similarly, in Long-Kesh physical contact with the prisoners was abhorrent for guards.

The images of the prisoners surrounded by excreta seemed to reinforce stereotypes of Irish barbarism, yet the inability of government and administrators to handle the situation reveals other effects. Thus, I would argue that the fantasies of savagery projected onto Catholics were appropriated, literalized, and enacted by the prisoners. This materialization inevitably confronted the officers in an inescapable physical form with their own aggressive fantasies, which produced shock, horror, and the futile attempt to erase them by increasing violence, forced baths, and periodic steam cleaning of cells – acts of cleansing that, like the dirtying of the prisoners, were both literal and symbolic (Feldman 1991: 185). The "Dirty Irish" had became *really* shitty. In so doing they were transforming the closed universe of prison into an overflowing cloaca, exposing in the process a Boschian vision of the world, a scathing critique of Britain and, by association, of civilization. One cannot help but find a parallel of this critique in the writings of that polemic Irishman, Jonathan Swift. [. . .]

The guards' rising brutality reproduced on the incarcerated bodies the same barbarity attributed to the prisoners. Such mimesis seems inherent to the colonial production of reality, which frequently uses the fiction of the savage (or the terrorist) to create a culture of terror (Bhaba 1984; Taussig 1987). In Northern Ireland the fiction of criminality of Republican prisoners ultimately exposed and reproduced the savagery of state policies. Inside Long-Kesh positions had been reversed: from objects of a defiling power, the prisoners had come to be the subjects that controlled it (Feldman 1991). Yet the prisoners were inescapably locked in a political impasse characterized by a vicious cycle of projection-reflection that spilled the violence from the prison onto the wider society. While the men's Dirty Protest was locked in its own violence, the women's provoked a movement of social transformation. The impulse of such transformation came from the articulation

of menstrual blood as a symbol of sexual difference with ongoing feminist discourse.

Dirt and Blood: The Meaning of Sexual Difference

Inside the walls of Armagh prison filthiness was tainted with menstrual blood. An additional set of meanings resonated there. [. . .]

What can make 30 dirty women more revolting than 400 dirty men if not the exposure of menstrual blood – an element that cannot contribute much to the fetid odors of urine and feces but can turn the stomach. [. . .]

Women did not belong to prison in popular consciousness, even though they had participated in armed operations and had been imprisoned in rising numbers since 1972. Most Nationalists perceived women's presence in jail as a product of an idealistic youth and the freedom from family commitments. Through the course of my fieldwork, some women ex-prisoners acknowledged that Republican men still assumed that after marriage women would abandon political activities that entail a risk of death or imprisonment. Although this frequently happens it is by no means always the case. On the other hand, the image of male prisoners did not have an age reference. Although the majority of male prisoners were young, it was not rare for them to be married and have children. In contrast to male prisoners, female prisoners were permanently thought of as girls. Their cultural space was in this sense liminal. Neither men nor completely women, they were perceived at a general social level as gender neutral.

Women prisoners did not consider gender a significant element of differentiation either. Female members of the IRA had fought to be part of this organization rather than part of its feminine counterpart, Cumman na mBan. Thus, they had consciously rejected gender as a differential factor in political militancy. To prove that gender was irrelevant to military performance in a male organization de facto entailed downplaying women's difference and interiorizing men's standards. At the level of consciousness gender difference was at the beginning of the Dirty Protest completely accidental to its meaning. From the point of view of Armagh women their Dirty Protest was not different from that of the men's: it was same struggle undertaken by equal comrades for political recognition. The emphatic reassertion of the sameness of prisoners' identity regardless of gender must be understood as an attempt to counteract the overshadowing of women prisoners under the focus of attention given to male prisoners. Such an eclipse was partly a consequence of the fact that women were not required to use prison uniforms and thus were not subjected to the dramatic conditions that the men were. That fact asserted from the start a gender difference that worked against their political visibility. At this level the Dirty Protest was for Armagh women an attempt to erase that gender difference introduced by the penal institution and to thus reassert their political visibility. Yet, unintentionally, the menstrual blood brought to the surface the contradictions involved in this process, shifting the meaning of the protest. It objectified a difference that women had carefully obliterated in other dimensions of their political life. That is, while their political identity as members of the IRA entailed at one level a cultural desexualization, and the Dirty Protest a personal defeminization, at a deeper level the exposure of menstrual blood subverted this process by radically transforming the asexual bodies of "girls" into the sexualized bodies of women. In so doing, the menstrual blood became a symbol through which gender identity was reflected upon, bringing to the surface what had been otherwise erased.

Menstruation as an elemental sign of womanhood also marks women's social vulnerability. At the level of representation it is a metonym linking sex and motherhood, a sign of the dangerously uncontrolled nature of women's flesh in Catholic ideology from which only the mother of god escaped (Warner 1983); a tabooed and polluting substance that must be hidden from discourse as it is from sight. In the context of arrest it is a sabotage of the body. The meaning of this sabotage has been forcefully expressed by Northern Ireland writer and Republican ex-prisoner Brenda Murphy in a short story entitled "A Curse." An arrested young woman gets her period in between interrogation shifts and is forced to talk about it to a male officer:

"I've taken my period" she said simply. "I need some sanitary napkins and a wash." He looked at her with disgust. "Have you no shame? I've been married twenty years and my wife wouldn't mention things like that." What is the color of shame? All she could see was red as it trickled down her legs. [1989: 226–7]

[. . .] The shocking character of the imagery that the words of released prisoners evoked was recalled to me by Mary, a middle-aged Republican woman:

I remember one rally in which a girl released from Armagh spoke about what it was for them during their periods. It was very hard for her to talk about menstruation, to say that even during that time they could not get a change of clothes, could not get washed. And some people, including Republican men, were saying "How can she talk about that?" They did not want to hear that women were being mistreated in Armagh jail during their menstruation. And so, the Republican movement did not talk about it. They only talked about the men, but they did not want to hear about girls. Some people just could not cope with that.

What the Nationalist community did not understand and could not cope with was *women's* pain. Not a mother's suffering, which ultimately roused the emotions of Nationalist people in support of the prisoners. Nor the suffering of incarcerated young men, whose image, naked and beaten, resembled that of Jesus Christ. Unintentionally, the women prisoners in Armagh brought to the fore a different kind of suffering, one systematically obscured in social life and in cultural constructions, devalued in Catholic religion and Nationalist ideologies: that women's pain of which menstruation is a sign and a symbol.

If the men's Dirty Protest represented the rejection of the civilizing mission of British colonialism, the Armagh women permeated that rejection with gender politics. At one level it encapsulated the negation of dominant models of femininity embedded in the idealized asexual Catholic mother and elaborated in Nationalist discourse around the image of Mother Ireland. This model provokes high ambivalence in many Nationalist women for whom motherhood is at once a source of comfort and support and a restrictive social role. On the other hand, the women's Dirty Protest represented also a rejection of male violence fused, as noted below, with political dominance in colonial discourse and practice. In the prison context the visibility of menstrual blood can be read as a curse redirected from the bodies of women to the male "body politic" of colonialism.

Conclusion

[...] I regard gender not just as a dimension of violence but as an intrinsic component of it, crucial to the understanding of its meanings, deployments, and ends. My analysis suggests that political violence performed on and from the body cannot escape the meaning of sexual difference. Despite the shared political consciousness and goals of men and women prisoners, their protests had different significance. While the men's protest was articulated through an intense dynamic of violence, the women's protest was crystallized around the meaning of sexual difference. Armagh women provoked, albeit unintentionally, a reformulation of feminine subjectivity. Inasmuch as sexual difference is, in Ireland as everywhere else, inseparable from class, ethnic, and even political positions, such reformulation in turn sparked a transformation of dominant discourses of feminism and nationalism.

I have suggested in this article that ethnic and political violence predicated on the bodies of women cannot be considered as an addendum to violence performed on men's bodies. As I have shown, it might have disparate meanings and effects that are crucial to both the construction of sexual difference and the construction of ethnic identity.

NOTES

1 Republicans favor Irish reunification and independence from Britain; they include IRA and INLA. Loyalists are pro-British and radically opposed to Irish reunification.
2 *Republican News*, February 16, 1980; McCafferty 1981; Women against Imperialism 1980. The sexual overtones of the assault were confirmed by personal interview.
3 *Republican News*, February 23, 1980; Report by Women against Imperialism, April 9, 1980, p. 27.
4 Amnesty International Report on Long-Kesh 1977.

REFERENCES

Asad, Talal. 1983. Notes on Body Pain and Truth in Medieval Christian Ritual. *Economy and Society* 12:1.

Bhabha, Homi. 1984. Of Mimicry and Man: The Ambivalence of Colonial Discourse. *October* 28: 123–33.

Burton, Frank. 1978. *The Politics of Legitimacy: Struggles in a Belfast Community.* London: Routledge & Kegan Paul.

Curtis, L. Perry. 1971. *Apes and Angels.* Washington, DC.

Darby, John. 1983. *Dressed To Kill: Cartoonists and the Northern Ireland Conflict.* Belfast: Appletree.

De Certeau, Michel. 1988. *The Writing of History.* New York: Columbia University Press.

Douglas, Mary. 1966. *Purity and Danger: An Analysis of the Concepts of Pollution and Taboo.* London: Routledge & Kegan Paul.

European Law Centre. 1981. European Human Rights Reports, Part 10.

Feldman, Allen. 1991. *Formations of Violence: The Narrative of the Body and Political Terror in Northern Ireland.* Chicago: University of Chicago Press.

Foucault, Michel. 1979. *Discipline and Punish: The Birth of the Prison.* New York: Vintage Books.

Goffman, Erving. 1959. *Asylums: Essays on the Social Situation of Mental Patients and Other Inmates.* New York: Anchor Books.

Graziano, Frank. 1992. *Divine Violence: Spectacle, Psychosexuality and Radical Christianity in the Argentine Dirty War.* Boulder, CO: Westview Press.

Obeyesekere, Gananath. 1992. *The Apotheosis of Captain Cook: European Myth Making in the Pacific.* Princeton: Princeton University Press.

Scarry, Elaine. 1985. *The Body in Pain: The Making and Unmaking of the World.* New York: Oxford University Press.

Sluka, Jeffrey. 1989. *Hearts and Minds, Water and Fish: Support for the INLA in a Northern Irish Ghetto.* Greenwich, CT: AI Press.

Suarez-Orozco, Marcelo. 1992. Dirty War and Post Dirty War in Argentina. *In The Paths of Domination Resistance and Terror.* C. Nordstrom and J. A. Martin, eds. Berkeley: California University Press, pp. 219–60.

Taussig, Michael. 1987. *Shamanism, Colonialism and the Wild Man.* Chicago: University of Chicago Press.

Warner, Marina. 1983. *Alone of All Her Sex: The Myth and the Cult of the Virgin Mary.* New York: Vintage.

30

Who's the Killer? Popular Justice and Human Rights in a South African Squatter Camp

Nancy Scheper-Hughes

Writing Violence

As a critical medical anthropologist, my terrain is the "body," which, like the vexed designation "coloured,"[1] requires a standing set of quotation marks to indicate the body's contested status as both bio-existentially "given" (the source of all certitude, as Wittgenstein [1969] saw it) and just as surely "made up" (and the source of all doubt). My specific set of concerns, derived from an early and indelible reading of Foucault, is the "everyday violence," the little routines and enactments of violence practiced normatively on vulnerable bodies in families, schools, hospitals, medical clinics, in various administrative and bureaucratic settings (from mayor's office and public registry office to the public morgue and the graveyard) – all of which, in Franco Basaglia's (1986) sense of the term, are "institutions of violence." [. . .]

Here I will briefly contrast two well-publicized incidents of township violence attributed to "wild," asocial youth with a contrasting backstage "incident" of an averted triple necklacing that occurred in the "Chris Hani" squatter camp. These events transpired in the course of my ongoing fieldwork on the political transition in Franschhoek, the *verkrampte* (right-wing, conservative) farm community known to some as "Wyndahl," the site of Vincent Crapanzano's (1985) study of the "whites of South Africa" in his controversial book, *Waiting*.

Dry White Season

At a special showing of the once-banned anti-apartheid film, *A Dry White Season*, at the Baxter Theater at UCT (University of Cape Town) last August [1994], I was unprepared for a spontaneous audience reaction: some muted but audible boos and hisses accompanied the scene of the 1976 Soweto school children's uprising against forced instruction in Afrikaans. "Why would a liberal audience of Capetonians react so negatively to the scene of Black township youth defending their rights?" I asked a new colleague the next day. I had just recently arrived in South Africa and, still suffering from the dislocation, I desperately needed a running interpretation of the subtexts of everyday life. "I suppose some people are sick and tired of violent school children on rampage," she replied in her elliptical way. The answer surprised me and I tucked it away in a field note.

Before the month was out, I too had seen my fill of newspaper and TV media images of local township school children burning textbooks, *toyitoying*[3] while chanting for death to the "settlers," and "torching" the cars of suspected government "agents" – meaning almost any non-Blacks to enter the townships during the ANC-initiated teachers' strike called "Operation Barcelona." The strike took its name from the 1992 Olympic Games in Barcelona and the torches carried by the lead runners. In the townships, torches were also a symbol of liberty. However, they were used more ominously to keep out suspected "settlers," whose cars could be overturned, and to "burn out" suspected collaborators and other "bad eggs" in the township by torching their shacks or setting their bodies on fire with "necklaces" of gasoline-filled tires wrapped around their necks. At least that is what we read, almost daily. [...]

Body Counts

By this time I was carefully documenting the "everyday violence" of township life, especially for young people. Most violent deaths in the Black townships are recorded only as body counts. Meanwhile, white deaths "count" (in news reports of the victims of the St. James and Heidleberg pub "massacres," the victims have names, personalities, histories, and grieving family members); the Black victims of township violence are merely counted. The following minor headlines from Cape Town newspapers are illustrative: "Another 40 *bodies* found on the East Rand"; "Dozen *Bodies* Removed from Guguletu in Weekend Casualties"; "The *charred bodies* of seven people, including a 50-year-old woman and her teenage daughter, were found in Thokoza hostel and Katlehong on Friday...The burned *bodies* of two young men were found at the Mandela squatter camp in Thokoza and another body at Katlehong railway station" (*Cape Times*, Sept. 1993). Finally, "*Charred bodies* of two witches found in Nyanga" (*Argus*, Jan. 21, 1994). The women accused of witchcraft had been bound together with rope and were "badly burnt." In the above article, Police Colonel Dowd strongly condemned black-on-black violence and the operation of kangaroo courts. "We hope," he is quoted as saying sanctimoniously, "that this is not the beginning of a resurgence of this horrific practice."

Stop the Senseless Violence

Though horrible, these remained "distant" images, for nearby Black townships turned into increasingly hostile "no-go zones" for non-Blacks, comrades or not in the struggle. (We learned our own lesson when our car was angrily chased away by trash pickers at a muddy entrance to New Cross-roads squatter camp in a failed attempt to attend an Ecumenical peace service announced at St. George's Cathedral.) Yet the circle closed when on August 25, 1993, Fulbright scholar Amy Biehl was dragged from her car in Guguletu township and, like St. Stephen, was stoned to death by angry youth who were shouting "Death to the Settler!" I began to internalize the sensationalist media images descrying a "lost generation" of destructive, deranged, and demonized African youth. While stones continued to shower down on her car, the already wounded Amy crawled out and, still smiling, approached the angry youth and identified herself as a friend, a comrade. The crowd of about 20 youth nonetheless ran after her and threw more stones. Then one of them came forward to stab her in the back, head, and face until she fell to the ground. Another boy then stole her purse.

Biehl's death represented a journalistic watershed and South African political leaders of all stripes began to worry that township youth were totally out of control. At the memorial service held the next day at the University of the Western Cape, Amy's mentor and feminist activist, Rhoda Kadalie, spoke tearfully of Amy's death at the hands of the "young monsters" created and set loose by the apartheid machine: "Now they are afoot in the land and no one can stop them. They are eating us and eating each other..." Following the memorial service, representatives of the ANC Women's League called for "white" and "coloured" women to join a spontaneous march into Guguletu to "take back the township" from the young "criminal elements" who were holding people hostage to chaotic violence and to make the community safe for people of all colors.

I hurriedly (and without thinking) picked up an ANC poster reading "Stop the Senseless Violence" and joined the march, which moved from the Shoprite supermarket, over the bridge, and through the squatter camp across the highway leading into "Gugs." Less than 24 hours after Amy was "extra-judicially executed," I anxiously *toyi-toyied* past hostile young men, all the while trying to second guess people's reactions to the thoughtless, senseless words for which I was now a poster girl. Did "senseless violence" imply that the police were "sensible" in their attacks and raids on Black townships? Was "senseless violence" a racist code for irrational Black violence, as opposed to rational, sensible white violence? What could "take back the township" mean in this beleaguered place? "Gugs" was not a friendly place and not one person from the township joined our pathetic little protest march. It was only half a kilometer from the main road to the ENGEN gas station, where in full view of a row of neat cement block houses, Amy had been attacked in broad daylight for the error of carrying her comrades home. Why didn't anyone stop the attack? Did this section of the township "belong" to the Pan African Congress (PAC) and was Amy's murder a declaration of war against the ANC? Was the attack less than senseless and apolitical after all? Is this what political resistance looks like when it is up in your face? Or was it just Amy's big, smiling white "settler" face that got in the way? I left the march determined to find out more about Amy's alleged attackers.

"The Coming of the Barbarians"

A significant concern about South African township youth expressed in the white South African press and also circulated among social scientists (e.g., du Toit 1994; Kleinman and Desjarlais 1993) relates to the emergence of acts of violence in which overtly criminal acts are disguised as political or even revolutionary acts. These reports argue that recent township violence – including the anonymous "charred bodies," the more publicized deaths of Amy Biehl, the St. James Massacre in July 1993, and the Heidleberg Pub Massacre on New Year's Eve – is perpetrated by gangs of youth who may have once participated in political struggle, but have since become involved in, or addicted to, violence for the sake of violence alone. Thus, the "new wave" of township violence is referred to as "senseless," "wild," "asocial," and "apolitical." With instrumental and political motives broadly discounted (see Arendt 1970 for an alternative perspective), we are left in the dark staring at an autonomous, self-perpetuating, sociobiological violence "machine," fueled by a primordial "will to destroy" (Kleinman and Desjarlais 1993).

A related perception was articulated by some white middle-class "survivors" (collectively, the members of the congregation) of the St. James Massacre of July 1993, whom I interviewed shortly after the church attack attributed to PAC youth. The St. James survivors tended to discount any possible political motives on the part of their attackers. They insisted that their church and its almost completely white and suburban congregation were *nonpolitical* and *nonracial*, making any selective "political" attack on them seem all the more random, chaotic, and "senseless." A few of those interviewed referred to the people who exploded into their Sunday service as "savages." The more forgiving among them said that their attackers were misguided township youth who were "bought" or otherwise "used," or who "did not know what they were doing," had been "duped" by malicious (white) outsiders (the "Third Force") using them for their own nefarious, but motivated and instrumental political ends. (White people have political *goals*; Black youth have "inarticulate" *needs*?)

The media images are particularly brutal and archetypal: the play of shadows on the wall as "witches" and suspected "collaborators" are burned alive; the brutality of people's courts ("kangaroo courts") that demand floggings and amputations – an eye for an eye, a hand for a hand, or in one story, even a breast for a breast; and the grossly racist police identity-kit portrait of the alleged "Station Strangler" that was repeatedly published on the front pages of the Cape Town newspapers and that preyed on "coloured" people's fears of young Black men. Delirium, dance, death, and rebellion are the images and representations that describe one sector of South African society as utterly "lost," a perception once even echoed by President Mandela, who in a recent speech lamented the transformation of the proud "Young Lions" of previous decades into the young anarchists of today:

The youth in the townships have had over the decades a visible enemy, the government. Now that enemy is no longer visible because of the [political] transformation that is taking place. Their enemy is now you and me – people who drive a car and have a house.

White Justice: The Amy Biehl Trial

Of the seven youths originally identified and detained for questioning in the Biehl murder case, three young men finally stood trial in the municipal Supreme Court of Cape Town: Mongezi Manquina, "Easy" Nofemela, and Vusumzi Ntamo. For Amy's single death, there was a "royal" dispensation: three judges – a "President Judge" flanked by two assessors, one white, one Black. Judge Friedman was addressed reverently as "My Lord" by defense and state lawyers. The robes were red and the court room was rich in polished hardwood benches and pews. The lawyers for the state were white Afrikaners; the lawyers for the defense were Black and of radical political backgrounds. The trial moved at a snail's pace, focusing on the defense accusations of forced confessions.

As we climbed the steps of the Supreme Court for the first of many days observing the courtroom proceedings, we were accosted by a few dozen APLA and PAC-affiliated youth chanting and *toyi-toying*. They marched in formation, aimed imaginary firearms at the court house, and jumped in front of cars. A sizable contingent of police in camouflage uniforms, arrayed for urban battle, did nothing to check the provocative behavior of the "wild" youth, some of whom were as young as 9 or 10 years. In between revolutionary marches and dances, the younger boys knocked about a slightly deflated soccer ball.

During the first stages of the trial as witnesses came forward to describe in horrible detail Amy Biehl's final agony, her pleadings and moans while being stoned and stabbed, the young PAC supporters who packed the court's upper gallery laughed and cheered. Judge Friedman, revolted by their outburst, cleared the courtroom. "Why did the boys laugh?" I was asked repeatedly on a return visit to the US in November of 1993. I was more impressed by what was left out of the reports, the reaction of Nofemela (defendant no. 2), who whipped around to correct the festive spirit in the gallery: "*What's wrong with you?*" Nofemela said in disgust. "Why don't you all get out of here!"

"But why *did* the youth laugh?" I asked Nona Goso, the elegant and soft-spoken lawyer for the defense.

"The laughter was not acceptable to me, nor to anyone else, but it did not shock me. I live in a township and I know the extent to which apartheid has murdered human feelings.... Their own people have been killed so often that it has the effect of reducing killing to nothing."

"What can you tell me about the defendants?"

"In every sense, they are children...in fact, lovely children, like any other. Under normal circumstances, they would have had a wonderful, normal life. But they are children of apartheid. Most come from broken homes and from deprived families where no one is working. Education is out of the question.... They have experienced *everything*, been exposed to *everything*."

I knew what she meant, thinking of the way some of the children of the Chris Hani squatter camp play games like "funeral," "shack burning,"

and "shoot-out." Few South African squatter camp children have escaped the scenes of everyday violence: the burnings of shacks, public whippings, premature death, and even the discovery of corpses where garbage should be. In short, they are scenes of war. A vast literature now documents the situation of older youth – their premature recruitment as foot soldiers in a war of liberation that spanned decades and cost them their childhoods, innocence, health, and education, and therefore (and ironically) their freedom. Denied schooling, manipulated by political slogans, arrested and tortured by police, as well as pursued by local death squads, township youth are unfairly referred to as a "lost generation." Rather, they are children who have been violated, whose childhood was not so much "lost" as taken from them.

The violent eruptions of township life are no more "expressive," senseless, irrational, or chaotic than the routinized and strategic violence of the apartheid state against which the youth were and remain mobilized. The death of so many comrades and warriors in the struggle has turned the roar of the Young Lions into Rachel's lament. However, as Renato Rosaldo (1984; and Chapter 17) observed in his anthropological work with Ilongot headhunters (and through his own process of mourning the tragic death of his first wife), grief can readily turn into murderous, *even gleeful*, rage, the "headhunter's rage" (in reference to both himself and the Ilongot). I think again of the chaotic emotions expressed at the Amy Biehl trial.

As for the three boys accused of killing Amy, the history of apartheid is etched on their very bodies, their *social* skin. In defending the confessions taken from Nofemela (defendant no. 2), Major Lester testified that he had personally examined the lad immediately after his confession and found only "old" wounds on his young body, no signs of recent torture. Yet each of Nofemela's nine "old" scars, painstakingly described by the policeman, tells a vivid story of township violence: stab wounds, brick bashings, machete chops, second-degree burns, scars from untreated infections and botched, discriminatory medical care. While Nofemela was an active participant in the trial, defendant no. 1 (Mongezi Manquina) occasionally sucked his thumb and defendant no. 3 (Vusumzi Samuel Ntamo) dozed off and on throughout the painfully boring proceedings. Both boys (no. 1 and no. 3) were sick with chronic respiratory infections; in Ntamo's case, the "infection" was tuberculosis, the recurrent plague of urban township life. When it was his turn to testify, Ntamo was unable to answer even the most basic questions and was confused about minor bibliographic details; thus, he was sent away for psychiatric evaluation to see if he was capable of understanding the court proceedings.

An air of sullen mockery and suspicion permeated the high court as each group – Afrikaner police, district surgeons (humiliated by the "spoiled history" of their past court performances), skittish witnesses, the defense (who were actually on the *offense vis-à-vis* an increasingly discredited "state"), the hamstrung prosecution lawyers, and the accused (who might as well have been the damned) – eyed each other with mistrust and loathing. The defense strategy was to put South African justice (and its police and doctor interrogator-torturers) on trial in place of the suspects. With the comic disappearances of key witnesses for both sides, the brief and troubling presence of Linda Biehl (Amy Biehl's politically confused and grieving mother), and the inverse Greek chorus of laughing PAC youth "acting up" both in the gallery and on the courthouse steps, the Amy Biehl trial was a drama of mockery, defiance, and refusal. It was a burlesque court that revealed the fissures and the illegitimacy of the apartheid state and the near impossibility of justice or a fair trial. During the liminal transitional period, consent seemed to have been withdrawn from all sides, so that for all practical purposes the Supreme Court had the appearance of a "kangaroo court," by definition "a court... operated by any improperly constituted body. A tribunal before which a fair trial is impossible; a comic or burlesque court" (see *Chamber's Dictionary*).

No wonder the PAC and APLA boys laughed.

As for the necklacing death of 15-year-old Ernest Mphahlele, what justice will the state provide? In the "informal" settlements and squatter camps of South Africa, both abandoned and misrepresented by the formal justice system, popular forms of justice in the form of local security and discipline committees and "people's courts" substitute state courts and the rule of the lash and the necklace for the "rule of law."

Without wishing to defend a form of justice that grew up in the homelands and squatter camps as an offspring of apartheid, I seek to show (through a single instance) how local justice is argued and contested in one small squatter camp that is desperately trying to establish order, harmony, and dignity among some 650 Black squatters, who are forced to live like dogs in the local community where they labor.

Popular Justice

People's courts and local forms of community surveillance, discipline, and punishment in South African townships and informal settlements emerged after 1984, when the struggle against white domination and the tricameral constitution was expressed in the form of alternative grass-roots structures aligned with radical political movements (the United Democratic Front, PAC, or ANC-affiliated groups) to enforce political morality and to enhance community autonomy.

The informal structures included private police forces (sometimes called peace keepers, vigilantes, or security committees), community rules and discipline codes, and autonomous forms of punishment, including public apologies, fines, community service, brief imprisonment in informally constructed local prisons, up through whippings and floggings, mutilation, and even death (the most publicized of which, of course, was death by necklacing). The latter was reserved for the most heinous of crimes: collaboration with the state and its functionaries, which could be interpreted very broadly.

In light of the political turmoil of the times, the emergent street committees, security and discipline committees, and popular courts mediated between the illegitimate state (the army and the SAP) and comrades – the young Black resistance fighters in the townships. Popular justice was designed to produce a South African version of the "new socialist man," the good comrade who was upright, disciplined, respectful of communal norms and the new social and political values, who was accountable, and, above all, who recognized the true "enemy," the apartheid state and *its collaborators*. The range of infractions judged and punished in the popular courts included drunkenness and disorderly conduct, domestic and extra-domestic fights and conflict, theft, housebreaking, assaults and stabbings, and collaboration with the police or the courts.

In discussing the evolution of people's courts in Cape Town, Schärf and Ngcokoto (1990) comment on the dangers of informal justice when these loose structures become detached from disciplined and organized political organizations. They are cautiously pessimistic about the attempts of township people to create and manage alternative systems of justice and punishment. Although viewing these as the inevitable outcome of the apartheid state, they remain critical of the punitive excesses to which these informal institutions are sometimes prey.

Media representations of the activities of people's courts are even less charitable, as the "necklacing stories" of young Ernest Mphahlele and of the two witches burned in Nyanga in January 1994 illustrate. The effect of the "negative press" is such that most educated people of the Western Cape across all political parties tend to view people's courts and discipline codes as aberrations and as inevitably tending toward the beastly and horrific. Discussions of popular justice with local civil rights lawyers and members of the regional ANC offices invariably provoked strong, negative reactions and references to mob rule and "kangaroo courts." The origin of the term "kangaroo court"[4] is difficult to ascertain, but dictionaries refer to informal codes of self-policing and discipline among prisoners as permitted and manipulated by prison warders. In all, "kangaroo court" is perhaps an appropriate metaphor for the situation of Black South Africans, disenfranchised by the years of apartheid and virtually imprisoned in homelands, townships, and squatter camps, where they are left alone to police and discipline themselves.

The Necklace

Among the discredited forms of punishment practiced within the context of South African "people's courts," the necklace is the most contentious. Its ability to mobilize panic and horror made references to the necklace an effective strategy in the NP (National Party) campaign against the ANC in the Western Cape. The NP had plenty of "excellent copy" to draw on, such as the following contributed by a British observer and former Labour Party Member of Parliament:

Here is a description I have received of necklace executions which have been imposed on 172 Blacks between 1 March and 5 June this year: "The terrified victim is captured by his (her) executioners. Frequently, his hands are hacked off as a first deterrent to resistance. Barbed wire is used to tie the hapless victim's wrists together. The tyre is placed over the shoulders and filled with petrol or diesel (the latter has been found to stick to the skin when it burns. It is therefore in greater demand). The fuel is ignited with a match (exhibiting boxes of matches is one way the Comrades [Black militants] earn the respect of fear in the townships). The victim (if his hands have not been hacked off) is usually forced to light his own necklace. The fuel ignites the tyre, which rapidly attains a temperature of 400C to 500C. As the tyre burns great black clouds of smoke spiral upwards. Various short-chain hydrocarbon fumes are released, which reach a temperature of 300C. They are inhaled and destroy the lining of the throat and lungs. The rubber melts and the molten rubber runs down neck and torso, burning, as it goes, deeper into the flesh and tissue. (The tyre cannot be removed by others [e.g., the family] at this stage, nor can the fire be doused with water.) The victim is now a living corpse. He may take up to twenty minutes to die. Whilst he endures this agony, the Comrades stand about laughing and ridiculing him." (Wyatt 1986: 63–4)

The "necklacing scandal" was invoked by Hernus Kriel in the National Party rally at the Good Hope Center in Cape Town the weekend before the presidential elections. It was readily picked up and repeated by many "coloured" voters I spoke with on April 27 and 28 near polling stations in Franschhoek, Mowbray, and Mitchell's Plein. I was told repeatedly: "We can't have a necklacer for President"; "Wherever the Blacks go, there's violence, blood, and burning tires"; "The ANC necklaces its own people.... What do you think they will do with us?" and so on. The image of necklacing feeds a kind of moral panic and today functions, as witchcraft used to, as a kind of collective racial nightmare in South Africa. It forms the primary process substratum of the collective unconscious, the "social imaginary" out of which deep racism emerges. When it is used strategically, as it was in the NP campaign – here I refer in particular to the NP "comic book" pamphlet campaign, replete with its racist photo images of Black youth waiting in the bushes to ambush Black and coloured comrades with match books ready in their hands – it is a form of collective racial calumny.

Obviously, reliable statistics on necklacings are hard to come by. Most reports are based on newspaper stories and should be held suspect. In 1986, F. W. de Klerk reported to Parliament that more than 200 "moderate" Blacks had been killed by the necklace that year. However, a review of all burn cases admitted to Cape Town's Salt River State Mortuary between 1991 and 1992 (see Lerer, n.d.) found only 35 of 358 burn-related township deaths in that part of the municipality to be associated with malicious intent. In all but five of the homicidal burnings, the bodies were set afire *after* murder by fatal shooting or stabbing. The postmortem necklace was most likely used in these cases to dispose of incriminating evidence, to cremate an abandoned body, or to humiliate the relatives of the murdered individual. In any event, the "classic" description (above) of burning the victim alive can only be inferred as probable in *five* cases in this key region of the western Cape at a time when news stories circulated the rumor of an "epidemic" of homicidal "necklacings."

The necklacing rumor, with its implication of uncontrolled "black-on-black" violence, has had a devastating effect on the self-perceptions of squatter camp residents. Working closely with the "security committee" of Chris Hani squatter camp, I began to see the extent to which poor Black South Africans are terrorized and (as one resident put it) afraid of their own "shadows." By "shadow" I mean the violent "double" that is foist upon Black South Africans in relentless media images and representations projecting their *barbarity* and *dangerousness*, so that squatter camp people are actually overly mobilized *against* themselves.

The Problem of the Incident

The case study I will now present concerns a "triple necklacing" that was averted, largely through the intercessions of ANC and PAC – politicized youth. I will argue that "undue restraint" – rather than "senseless violence" – is more characteristic of those South Africans who have been geographically and socially excluded in homelands, townships, and grotesque squatter camps. The notions of "mob rule" and "kangaroo court" are unfortunate and unfair descriptions of the difficult negotiations of crime and punishment in the absence of a legitimate state and, therefore, of fair and representative formal institutions of policing and criminal justice.

The incident on January 24, 1994, involved the theft of 400 rands (about US$125) from a *shebeen* (a small, Black-owned pub) owner by three teenage boys of the Chris Hani squatter camp, followed by a collective demand for their punishment – initially their death by necklacing. As the boys sat trembling and awaiting their fate, a few youth leaders, invoking the ANC Bill of Rights, dangerously raised their voices in protest and successfully argued for public whippings over the death penalty. Further debate ensued and the demand for 100 strokes with a *sjambock* (a bull whip very similar to the slave whips kept on display at the Sugar Museum in Recife, Brazil) was skillfully negotiated down to 50 lashes for each boy caught "red handed." The floggings were laid on "collectively" by several designated older men of the community.

FROM FIELD NOTES TAKEN ON JANUARY 27, 1994:
"*We all deserve a lashing*," I had recently written in a despairing letter to friends during a particularly low point in a year of turbulent transitions. "*The sadism of human society demands it.*" Now, visiting three young thieves, their raw and bleeding backsides etched forever in my memory, makes me want to eat those words. It brings to mind the mob and Foucault's image of "the spectacle," with which he opens *Discipline and Punish* – chaos, irrationality, barbarism: all the old racist tropes came marching out like so many gargoyles.

The three boys lived together in shack no. 12 and they had helped me out more than once by pointing out camp leaders and indicating who spoke some English. In all, there was enough interaction for me to sense hearts beating (now in terror) behind those makeshift, newspaper-covered shack walls with headlines displaying stories and photos of Chris Hani, General Holomisa, and Winnie Mandela. My field assistant, 18-year-old Sidney Kumalo, had recently returned (and was still "red") from his month of initiation, isolation, and disciplined hunger in the bushes near Khayelitsha. Circumcised, Sidney is now a man and he steps out to the world fairly beaming in his new suit of clothes, which announces his new status. Post-initiation rules forbid him from going out for 30 days without his derby, and he brushes the dust off carefully before placing it jauntily on his nearly shaved head.

"There is something you need to know," Sidney proposed hesitantly, "about our codes of discipline." He asked me to visit the boys, and I went to their shack with trepidation. Within minutes, word would spread that the "white woman" was in the

camp again, this time nosing around the "prisoners." Taking notes. Taking pictures. Recording for
whom?

The boys were not a pretty sight, though some in
the community thought they had gotten off easy
with just 50 lashes. The penal whip lay limp and
tired against the wall. Kept in isolation and denied
food, water, and human company as a continuation of the punishment, the three prisoners lay
on dirty rags on the dirt floor. Their eyes were dull
and glassy with fever. They could not bend their
legs, sit down, or walk without wincing; three days
later they still had trouble urinating. The smallest,
Michael B., carried the mark of the lash across his
neck and face. He scowled with pain and with
revenge. "I'll kill them," he kept repeating of his
tormentors.

The community did not want anyone (and certainly not me) to see the boys (fear of police involvement was awesome) and so they had refused
the boys medical attention. The boys' parents and
other relatives were nowhere in sight, fearful that
their shacks might be burned were they to show
any concern, care, or sympathy toward their children.

Sidney urged me to take photos ("for evidence")
and to tape record an interview with the boys that
might be useful later (he said) at a community
meeting. Mindful that this was something of a
trap, I nonetheless complied.

THE FOLLOWING IS FROM THE TAPED TRANSCRIP-
TION OF THE ENCOUNTER:

S.K.: You see they stole 400 rands from one
of the people's houses here. And with it they bought
brandy and weapons. When they were caught,
the *pangas* (machetes) were in their hands
and they still had 200 rand between them. Due to
our codes of conduct they were punished this
way. At first the community called for burnings,
the people were waving *pangas* and sticks and
they said that the boys must be burned because
they are thieves. So they were just waiting to get
killed.

N.S-H.: They couldn't escape?

S.K.: They couldn't run away because they were
surrounded by the whole community.

N.S-H.: Do the people ever wait until things are
more calm to take action?

S.K.: No, no, no! If they catch them now, within
five minutes the whole place is filled with people.
It's very quick. But this is not our traditional way.

In Transkei where I come from, you or I don't have
the right to judge. Only a very old man with a lot of
experience can stand up and speak out and give the
punishment. But here it is too simple. If I don't like
someone, I can just say, "Give him 80 lashes."
Other people who like him better may come up
with a smaller number. It is very harsh.

N.S-H.: Would they really kill them for stealing
400 rands?

S.K.: Let me ask the boys. . . . Yes, they say the
punishment was that they must get burned . . . but
some people had sympathy for them and said,
"No, no, just give them the lashes."

N.S-H.: Who wanted to save them?

S.K.: Some of their friends. And a lot of the
young people here are in the PAC and the ANC
youth committees and they are against these discipline codes. The ANC is opposed. We shouldn't
use the lash on ourselves the way the Boer [an
Afrikaner farmer] did.

N.S-H.: What about their relatives?

S.K.: If their relatives speak out, the people here
think, "Oh, so *you* put them up to this, you set
them up to steal." So the parents can't defend their
children. If a mother speaks out for her son, the
people have the right to burn down her shack. The
people are very strict in this discipline. They say
we cannot afford to be soft.

N.S-H.: Has anyone ever been burned [neck-
laced] here?

S.K.: No, not yet. And that's what makes it a
little bit difficult for them to kill. And we in the
youth committee are afraid of what will happen
here after they take that step once.

N.S-H.: Have there been any other murders
here?

S.K.: Yeah, one guy was murdered and the killer
was never found. That's why they are so strict, so
that the criminals will be found right away and
punished, so that others won't try to do the same
thing. But people are people and I think they will
keep on taking chances, they will keep on doing
bad things, and keep on being punished in this
way. So some of us here want there to be a new
system based on human rights.

N.S-H.: Could you ask Michael what he has
learned from this?

S.K. (translating for M.B.): At this moment he
don't think he will steal again, but the only thing
that's going through his mind over and over is
revenge. But I told him that if he takes revenge,
he'll just be punished all over again. Right now he

wants revenge, only he doesn't have the power to do it.

N.S-H.: Since the whole community made the decision to whip him, whom would he take revenge on?

S.K.: He knows who were the people who did this to him, the ones who whipped him, because they don't even cover their faces. He remembers all the faces of those who did this to him.

N.S-H.: Could you ask him why they decided to steal?

S.K.: They say it was because they have no real work, they are just "casual" workers on the farms. The guys say they were hungry and they were sick and tired of having no money and no work....

N.S-H.: Have they been initiated?

S.K.: No, and that is another problem. Here in the camp there are even grown men who have not been initiated! They build their own house, have a child, but they still don't have any rights. If I, as an initiated man, walk into the door of an older man who is not initiated, I can say, "Listen, my man, please step outside because I want to have a word with your wife." And the old man has to do it. Those who are not initiated don't have any rights.

N.S-H.: Why don't they all go through the initiation?

S.K.: In the old days you would just get a goat or a sheep, but today you must spend a lot of money. There is a feast and everyone must be invited. Another thing, the clothes you wore before initiation you must give away, because now you are starting a new life. Even the room you stay in, the newspapers on the wall, must be taken down and new ones put up. Everything goes back to money and these guys don't have any.

The next day I returned with Rose, a medical student intern with considerable courage and stamina (two other male doctors from Cape Town, one white and one Black, declined my invitation, an offer, it seems, they just *could* refuse). After a careful examination and wound-dressing, she said young Michael's wounds required more extensive treatment and antibiotics to prevent a generalized infection.

Sidney and I brought Michael by combi-taxi to the "white" hospital in Paarl, where he was attended by a young Afrikaner, Dr. McK., who agreed not to ask any questions, though he could

not refrain from whistling his disapproval on seeing Michael's wounds and commenting loudly while he set up an intravenous antibiotic. "And these are the people who are going to be ruling us soon.... Shame! They'll send us all back into the Stone Age." In contrast to the "brutal" and "unsanitary" squatter camp floggings, the doctor explained the "proper procedure" used by local white police, who brought their prisoners to the clinic for a medical examination and approval before administering the lash. The attending doctor decided how many lashes the prisoner could "safely" sustain. "But *this*," Dr. McK. said, gesturing to Michael's exposed buttocks, "this is totally barbaric." He diagnosed an infection-related fever and recommended that Michael be kept in the hospital for a few days for observation and treatment. The boy's general health was poor: he was severely anemic, malnourished, and dehydrated.

Later that night at "The Anchor" Bed & Breakfast, my safe little ship's cabin of a room in rural Franschhoek, I received an anonymous phone call warning me to stay away from Chris Hani squatter camp. "This is a friend calling," the heavily accented brown Afrikaner voice said. "Don't return to Chris Hani squatter camp. Your safety cannot be assured." Two days later, I cautiously dropped Michael B. off at the bottom of the hill leading into Chris Hani, not knowing whether *his* safety could be assured. If Michael was frightened, he certainly wasn't going to tell me.

Who's the Killer? The Funeral of a Comrade

I returned to Chris Hani the following Saturday to attend the political funeral of a young ANC "comrade" who (less fortunate than Michael) had died on the way to the emergency room of Paarl hospital a few days earlier. His wife's relatives said he had a heart spasm and died because the combi-taxi had run out of gas. Anonymous residents said the young man died of a drug "overdose." Neighbors noted that the young father of four children had been sick for a very long time with recurrent and resistant tuberculosis. His young widow was mute with grief and uninterested in the cause of her husband's death.

Sidney's little sister shyly led me to the back of the camp, where a "chapel" was hastily constructed of zinc and plywood and covered by a large tarpaulin that was painted red, green, and black, the ANC colors. A fierce "Cape Doctor" wind blew into the lean-to and rocked its walls while the tent roof waved about like the flag it was meant to be. As the long service drew to an end, the congregation was invited to dance in a single-file line around the coffin, which was raised on its bier, each person holding onto the waist of the one in front. I felt a heavy weight dragging at me as the woman behind me fell into a dead faint, limp as a rag doll. After various desperate attempts to revive her, several women came to my rescue. I took the opportunity to dance out the tent door for air. Just then, the procession to the graveyard began. Sidney fussed with a static-filled ancient sound system that blared the MK (*Umkhonto we Sizwe*) military anthem, complete with the sound of rifle and cannon shots. At the grave site, all the adult men were called on to take up shovels and collectively bury their comrade. Just as we were turning to leave, Duncan, a Rastafarian and close friend of the deceased, came alive and lead the uniformed ANC–PAC youth in a high-stepping and militant *toyi-toyi*, stamping their feet on the earth and chanting, this time in English, while staring fixedly in my direction: "*Who's the Killer? Who's the Killer? Who's the Killer?*" (Who, indeed?)

Civic Association Meetings

On the following day, Sunday, February 6, 1994, a community-wide civic association meeting was held to discuss the question of justice and security at Chris Hani. As people arrived, they took their seats on the ground or on folding chairs positioned in a semicircle under a large tree. The "incident," as it came to be called, had provoked a crisis. The security guards had quit their posts outright in a fit of pique and there had been disorder in the camp with no one to call on for help. People were frightened. Leaders of the local civic association solicited the opinions of everyone present. Should the security guard be reconstituted, or should regular (mostly white and coloured, but no Black) village police be invited to patrol and "discipline" the community?

One by one, the people of Chris Hani stepped forward to express their views. Everyone wanted the local security system, but they wanted the rules and regulations to be more clear.

"Who are the security guards anyway? We don't always know their faces."

"People give us orders and we do not know if they are really our security or not. They ought to wear identity badges."

"What about the rights of the security themselves? They don't feel they have the full support of the community. Everyone wants protection, everyone in the heat of the moment calls for punishment, but afterwards everyone wants to criticize them."

"We need to consider the punishments. It shouldn't happen that older people with 'strong' families in the camp get off easier than young people or single people, but that often happens. Justice for one should be be justice for all."

"What does the ANC say about discipline?"

"The ANC says no more than five lashes should be given!"

"Nonsense! The ANC says there should be no lashes ... and Madiba [Mandela] is opposed to the necklace."

"Who can resolve this?"

"In Khayelitsha (township), they don't whip people anymore. They have built a small jail for thieves and drunkards."

"Do we want to build a jail here in Chris Hani?"

"No, we need toilets, water pumps, and a school first."

"But we still have to take care of disorder when it happens."

"Can't we just wait until April 27th, and after the elections everything will be better?"

"You are like those who think the elections will be a miracle! We still have to figure out how to live with each other, even after elections. Do you think Madiba [Mandela] is going to come here and help us discipline our thieves?" [laughter]

Finally, I was called up to make an accounting of myself, to explain why I had intervened. As I walked up to the microphone, my knees shook. My friend Temba (a member of the striking security committee) translated, and his presence bolstered me up, although I knew well that he was one of the floggers and he personally believed that the boys should have been necklaced. I apologized to the community, saying I was a stranger and had no right to speak, let alone to meddle in community affairs.

"Um, Um ...," people assented angrily.

I said that I understood why people rejected the police and why they needed to have their own justice. I interfered, I said, not to give aid to three boys who had wronged the community. People were right when they said that stealing from poor people who have no locks on their doors or windows is also a human rights violation, one that even the ANC Bill of Rights failed to recognize. Yet I still felt bad for the mothers of the boys who were ashamed of what their sons had done, but who were afraid to feed them or to visit them after the whippings. (Here the row of older women nodded their heads in approval.) I noted that many people in the camp wanted to talk about alternatives to whippings and burnings. Most of the young people and many of the women thought it might be better to put the thieves to work for the community digging ditches, cleaning up garbage, sewage, or fetching water. Some said that thieves should be sent away, losing their right to live in Chris Hani, while others thought that young people needed to have a second chance, maybe even two chances, because it was so easy for young people without money to get into trouble in a squatter camp.

During the meeting, it was decided to form a committee with representatives from all groups in the camp – old and young, men and women, sports groups, political groups and parties, and the security committee members themselves – to draw up alternative proposals for policing and protecting the community and for punishing violators. In the interim, there would be no more whippings. Civic leaders asked for help from the Community Peace Foundation located at the University of the Western Cape and two representatives attended subsequent meetings to help the community draft less punitive community rules. One of the representatives, a charismatic Puerto Rican lawyer and community organizer, used humor and improvised skits to help residents address common fears and to question the tendency to "over-police" and "over-discipline" themselves. The self-imposed nighttime curfew was relaxed and, for the time being, floggings were suspended.

What happened to the three young thieves? Michael B. could not get over his anger and his hot-headed desire for revenge. He was advised to leave the squatter camp and was given help in locating a new home. The other two boys accepted their punishment and they were reintegrated into the camp. Nothing more was said about their crime. Several more youth, following Sidney's lead, entered Xhosa initiation in the bush outside Franschhoek. Among them was one of the former

thieves. The last time I saw the boy, he was slathered with white clay and smiling broadly, though he told me (through Sidney) that his circumcision "cut" hurt very badly, even worse, he maintained, than his whipping.

Discipline and Punish

South Africa has been and remains a violent state. The elections have come and gone, but the legacy of apartheid remains and it includes the many defensive and "renegade" social institutions created by African people who tried to survive as best they could *outside* and *in spite* of the apartheid state. The temptation is great today, even among ANC officials and leaders, to dismiss the alternative systems of policing and popular justice that govern everyday life in South Africa's townships and squatter camps and to view them as anachronisms and obstacles to the building of a democratic civil society. To the contrary, however, civil society in the new South Africa will depend on using the local democratic structures that are already in place, including the popular tribunals, civic associations, and security and discipline committees that have been struggling with questions of law and order, justice and fairness, discipline and punishment over the past 20 years as poor and marginalized people struggled on their own to create some semblance of dignified and orderly social life under inhumane conditions. In any event, these institutions cannot simply be abolished by fiat or by a new constitution and a universal Bill of Rights.

A common charge against grassroots legal systems is that "legitimate" institutions of *popular* justice can all too readily become deformed and degenerate into *populist* justice, the latter referring both to spontaneous outbreaks of "mob rule" (the "lynching mentality") and to private and decidedly undemocratic "vigilante" justice (control by self-appointed mafia or township "totsies"). However, as the "incident" at Chris Hani camp is meant to illustrate, the boundaries between what may be considered legitimate, formal, and orderly popular justice and its supposed polar opposite, "populist" justice, are fluid, especially in the newer urban settlements and squatter camps, where self-government is often invented on the spot and in response to specific crises. In the absence of clear and well-established leadership roles, regular tribunals, legal precedents, written laws and textbooks, and local prisons or jail houses, the only way for serious offenses to be handled at all is through fairly immediate, graphic, and physical means. That is to say, through the mob, the spectacle, and the whip, or worse yet, the "necklace." These means – often the only ones available – consistently convey to outsiders and "educated people" the impression – and sometimes the fact – of miscarriages of justice and the abuse of power.

The strength of popular justice, exemplified by the incident at Chris Hani, is that justice is meted out collectively and, even in the heat of the moment, what may initially appear to be unreflexive and reactive mob rule (i.e., the initial demand for necklacing) may well be open, as it was in this case, to negotiation based on argument and appeals to reason, mercy, and human "rights." What made the initial scene look like an angry, irrational, and undifferentiated "mob" is, in part, a function of the lack of any communal structure or public house large enough to contain the adult members of the new camp. All civic association meetings and popular tribunals in Chris Hani camp take place outdoors and under the tree. So, too, were the events recorded here. Moreover, the apparent "mob" scene that formed around the thieves contained individuals and factions who expressed differences of opinion. Men and women, older adults and youth, Zionist Christians and atheist Marxists, ANC and PAC, residents from Transkei and residents from Natal, those speaking Afrikaans as a second language and those who spoke English as a second language took different positions during the incident and/or in the endless community discussions that followed it.

Popular justice and people's courts are vulnerable on many counts, of course. They are dependent on volunteers and have a high turnover following criticism of their activities. Many concerned residents of good will are afraid to serve, fearing intimidation by relatives of the accused and the punished, paving the way for "strong men" with connections to usurp these roles. These grassroots institutions are not very good at fact-finding and they rely heavily on the rhetoric of accusations and counter-accusations as well as on confessions of guilt.

Even more problematic, perhaps, are the means of discipline and punishment especially for serious crimes: the tire, the whip, and the imposition of physical discomforts – hunger, heat, and thirst. The use of the body as the primary site of social control is rejected by all "modern" codes of individual rights, including the draft Bill of Rights of the ANC. The necklace and the lash have particularly loathsome connotations. The necklace (as discussed above) is depicted as barbaric and as a particular perversion of "Black" people in Southern Africa and in the Caribbean. (Haiti is mentioned most frequently in news reports, and Aristide, like Mandela, has been accused of promoting the necklace among his supporters.)

Representations and images of the lash are more ambiguous, for its use has been and remains more universal. Floggings were part of African colonial history, associated with slavery and later with the culture of public and church-linked schools. In fact, wherever the British colonial system went – the American South, the Caribbean, Ireland, or Africa – it arrived with the cane or the whip in hand. (For Ireland, see the autobiographies of Thomas O'Crohan and Maurice O'Sullivan.) Internalization of the rule of the lash can be seen in the defense of "canings" or floggings by school headmasters and Catholic priests in County Kerry, Ireland (see Scheper-Hughes 1979), by white farm owners in the Western Cape, prison warders and district surgeons in Cape Town, and headmasters in African schools. The men and women of Chris Hani squatter camp likewise defend the practice of whipping and were perplexed and angry about attempts to question or interfere with their system of discipline and punishment.

In 1992, 36,000 young people under the age of 21 were sentenced to be whipped in South African courts (Pinnock 1995: 8). Insofar as flogging is still meted out as a legitimate sentence by the official courts, the heavy censure of its use in popular courts is open to question. As with the infamous case in Botswana in 1933 concerning the flogging of a white man, Phineas McIntosh, living in a Black community by the young local Chief Tsekedi, who was in charge of the jurisdiction (see Crowder 1988; Comaroff 1990), the real issue seems to be the "bodily politics of colonialism." This refers to the unquestioned right of whites to act upon Black bodies, but not the reverse. The concern of even well-meaning outsiders about the "abuse of power" and cruel and unusual punishments in people's courts could also be seen and criticized as an extension of this colonial bodily politics – as questioning the right of Black people to act on Black bodies. Yet in the context of the nonracial politics of the ANC and its commitment to individual rights, including conventional post-Enlightenment notions of the individual subject and rights to bodily sovereignty, children's, women's, and prisoners' rights, and the rejection of capital and most corporal punishment, the real dilemma today is how to balance the extension of these fairly universal, democratic ideas against traditional mores and the practice of popular and revolutionary justice, especially now that the immediate revolution is over. Cultural relativism, of the sort generally practiced by anthropologists in the past, is less appropriate in the vexed and contested pluralistic world in which we and our "subjects" live.

In the glow of the first democratic elections, amid the terrible beauty of South Africa, there is still much to be hopeful for. In the necessary "settling of accounts" that lies ahead, the wounded Young Lions of South Africa deserve special consideration. Their heroism needs to be recognized, their losses mourned, and their bodies mended. Above all, their wandering souls need to be captured and firmly anchored in a new moral economy where the roar of the young lions is an assertion of life and not a cry of danger.

NOTES

1   The term "coloured," under the perverse apartheid laws (and in common usage) refers to all people of mixed (mostly white and Black) "race." Indians in Durban and Malays in the Cape are also referred to as "coloured," although they contest the designation.

2   *Comrade*, a term similar to *compaheiro*, implies political solidarity through membership in the ANC (African National Congress), the more radical and Black separatist PAC (Pan African Congress), or other affiliated youth groups such as APLA (Azanian Peoples Liberation Army) and PASO (Pan African Student Association).

3   The *toyi-toyi* is a spirited dance of defiance and rebellion that is found throughout Southern Africa, Zimbabwe, and Namibia.

4   "A court operated by a mob; by prisoners in jail, by any improperly constituted body. A tribunal before which a fair trial is impossible; a comic or burlesque court" (*Chambers Dictionary*). "Improperly constituted, illegal court held by strikers; a mock court"; "... most jails have a court run by prisoners in which every new prisoner is assessed and tobacco and other property divided.... [I]nfractions [are] punished by spankings... [and] while not legal as such, its oper-

ation is passively accepted by the jailers" (*Oxford Concise Dictionary*).

REFERENCES

African National Congress. 1993. ANC Draft Bill of Rights. Centre for Development Studies (Feb.).

Arendt, Hannah. 1970. *On Violence*. New York: Harcourt, Brace & World.

Basaglia, Franco. 1986. "Peace-Time Crimes." In Nancy Scheper–Hughes and Anne Lovell, eds., *Psychiatry Inside Out: Selected Writings of Franco Basaglia*. New York: Columbia University Press.

Comaroff, John. 1990. "Bourgeois Biography and Colonial Historiography." *Journal of Southern African Studies* 16:3 (Sept.): 550–62.

Crapanzano, Vincent. 1985. *Waiting: The Whites of South Africa*. New York: Vintage Books.

Crowder, Michael. 1988. *The Flogging of Phineas McIntosh: A Tale of Colonial Folly and Justice*. New Haven: Yale University Press.

du Toit, André. 1994. "Dealing with the Past and the Politics of Violence: Some Historical and Comparative Perspectives." Paper read at the "Democracy and Difference" conference, University of Cape Town (May 5–7).

Keller, Bill. 1993. "A Short, Violent Life in South Africa." *The New York Times* (International, Nov. 17): 4.

Kleinman, Arthur and Robert Desjarlais. 1993. "Violence and Demoralization in the New World Disorder." Paper read at the Meetings of the Society for Psychological Anthropology, Montreal, Canada.

Lerer, Leonard B. n.d. "Homicide-Associated Burnings in Cape Town, South Africa." From the Department of Forensic Medicine and Toxicology, University of Cape Town.

Lévi–Strauss, Claude. 1963. "The Sorcerer and His Magic." In *Structural Anthropology*. New York: Doubleday, pp. 161–80.

Pinnock, Don. 1995. "Suffer the Little Children." *Democracy in Action*: 8–9.

Rosaldo, Renato. 1984. "Grief and a Headhunters' Rage: On the Cultural Force of Emotions." In Edward Bruner, ed., *Text, Play, and Story: The Reconstruction of Self and Society*. Washington, DC: American Ethnological Society, pp. 179–95.

Schärf, Wilfried and Baba Ngcokoto. 1990. "Images of Punishment in the People's Courts of Cape Town. From Prefigurative Justice to Populist Violence." In N. Chabani Manganyi and André du Toit, eds., *Political Violence and the Struggle in South Africa*. South Africa: Southern Book Publishers.

Scheper–Hughes, Nancy. 2000 [1979]. *Saints, Scholars, and Schizophrenics: Mental Illness in Rural Ireland*.

Berkeley and Los Angeles: University of California Press.

———. 1992. *Death Without Weeping: The Violence of Everyday Life in Brazil*. Berkeley and Los Angeles: University of California Press.

———. 1994a. "Embodied Knowledge: Thinking with the Body in Medical Anthropology." In Robert Borofsky, ed., *Assessing Cultural Anthropology*. New York: McGraw-Hill, pp. 229–42.

———. 1994b. "Demilitarization and Death Squads in Post-Democratic Transition Brazil." Paper read at the "Democracy and Difference" conference, University of Cape Town (May 5–7).

Wittgenstein, Ludwig. 1969. *On Certainty*. New York: Harper and Row.

Wyatt, Woodrow. 1986. "A Necklace for Azania." *Encounter* 67:3: 63–7.

Part VII

Peacetime Crimes: Everyday Violence

Plate 9: Shooting Gallery, San Francisco, California 1998. Photo © Jeffrey Schonberg, the photographer.

31

Terror as Usual: Walter Benjamin's Theory of History as State of Siege

Michael Taussig

Terror as the Other

A question of distance – that's what I'd like to say about talking terror, a matter of finding the right distance, holding it at arm's length so it doesn't turn on you (after all it's just a matter of words), and yet not putting it so far away in a clinical reality that we end up having substituted one form of terror for another. But having said this I can see myself already lost, lost out to terror you might say, embarked on some futile exercise in Liberal Aesthetics struggling to establish a golden mean and utterly unable to absorb the fact that terror's talk always talks back – super-octaned dialogism in radical overdrive, its talk presupposing if not anticipating my response, undermining meaning while dependent on it, stringing out the nervous system one way toward hysteria, the other way toward numbing and apparent acceptance, both ways flip-sides of terror, the political Art of the Arbitrary, as usual.

Of course, that's elsewhere, always elsewhere, you'll want to say, not the rule but the exception, existing in An-Other Place like Northern Ireland, Beirut, Ethiopia, Kingston, Port au Prince, Peru, Mozambique, Afghanistan, Santiago, the Bronx, the West Bank, South Africa, San Salvador, Colombia, to name but some of the more publicized from the staggering number of spots troubling the course of the world's order. But perhaps such an elsewhere should make us suspicious about the deeply rooted sense of order here, as if their

dark wildness exists so as to silhouette our light, the bottom line being, of course, the tight and necessary fit between order, law, justice, sense, economy, and history – all of which them elsewhere manifestly ain't got much of. Pushed by this suspicion I am first reminded of another sort of History of another sort of Other Within, a history of small-fry rather than of the Wealth of Nations, as for example in a letter in the *Village Voice* in 1984 from an ex-social worker in the state of Colorado, in the USA, commenting on an article on Jeanne Anne Wright who killed her own children. The social worker notes that it was axiomatic that the "deeper you dig, the dirtier it gets; the web of connections, the tangled family histories of failure, abuse, and neglect spread out in awesomely unmanageable proportions." When the social worker asked a young mother about the burn marks on her nine-year old daughter, she replied in a passive futile voice that her husband used a cattle prod on the girl when she was bad. Then she smiled, "as if it was the oddest thing," saying "It hurts too. I know 'cos he uses it on me sometimes." They lived "anonymous and transitory" in a refurbished chicken coop on a canal-lined road. One afternoon this social worker was taking the last of another woman's four children from her home when the woman leapt up and pulled down her pants to show him where her ex-husband had stabbed her in the buttocks. "Just as suddenly," he writes, the woman "realized what she had done and began to cry and to laugh, somehow at the same time, and somehow to mean both." And he concludes by saying "I am left with the impression of lives as massive, dense, and impenetrable as those nodes of collapsed matter out of which nothing escapes and whose only measure is what they absorb and conceal."

But what about the histories of the Big Fry, the Histories of Success? Are they so removed from this violent world whose only measure is what it absorbs and conceals? In talking terror's talk are we ourselves not tempted to absorb and conceal the violence in our own immediate life-worlds, in our universities, workplaces, streets, shopping malls, and even families, where, like business, it's terror as usual? In particular, as we zig-zag between wanting to conceal and wanting to reveal, might we not suddenly become conscious of our own conventions of coordinating power and sense-making and realize, as Walter Benjamin put it in his last writings written on the eve of the Second World War, that:

The tradition of the oppressed teaches us that the "state of emergency" in which we live is not the exception but the rule. We must attain to a conception of history that is in keeping with this insight. Then we shall clearly recognize that it is our task to bring about a real state of emergency, and this will improve our position in the struggle against Fascism. One reason why Fascism has a chance is that in the name of progress its opponents treat it as a historical norm. The current amazement that the things we are experiencing are "still" possible in the twentieth century is *not* philosophical. This amazement is not the beginning of knowledge – unless it is the knowledge that the view of history which gives rise to it is untenable. ("Theses on the Philosophy of History")

In other words what does it take to understand our reality as a chronic state of emergency, as a Nervous System? Note the concept; please take care to note the issue before us. Not a knee-jerk application of postmodern antitotalitarianism bent on disrupting an assumed complicity between terror and narrative order, but an opportunistic position-less position which recognizes that the terror in such disruption is no less than that of the order it is bent on eliminating.

Terror is what keeps these extremes in apposition, just as that apposition maintains the irregular rhythm of numbing and shock that constitutes the apparent normality of the abnormal created by the state of emergency. Between the order of that state and the arbitrariness of its emergency, what then of the center – and what of its talk?

I had been invited by one of our more august institutions of the higher learning to talk on the terror associated with the Peruvian Amazon Company in the early twentieth-century rubber boom in the Putumayo area of Colombia. Before the talk I lunched with my host, a scholar, older than myself. With remarkable verve and flair for detail he compared different historical epochs for their amount of terror, concluding, over dessert, that our century was the worst. There was something weighty, even sinister, about this. We were drawing a balance sheet not just on history but on its harvest of terror, our intellect bending under the weight of fearful facts, and our epoch had come in first. We felt strangely privileged, in so far as we could equate our epoch with ourselves, which is, I suppose, what historical judgment turns upon. And in drawing our grim conclusion, were we not deliberately making ourselves afraid, in ever so sly a way enjoying our fear? But I myself find I am now a little frightened even suggesting this possibility. It seems plausible, yet oversophisticated, mocking both fear and intelligence.

Tennis balls thwacked. The shadows thrown by the Gothic spires lengthened as the afternoon drew on. One could not but feel a little uneasy about the confidence with which terror was being mastered over linen napkins, a confidence shielding the unspoken fear the university community had of the ghetto it had disappeared several years back – "disappeared," a strange new word-usage in English as well as in Spanish, as in El Salvador or Colombia when someone just vanishes off the face of the map due to paramilitary death squads. The university in the USA is of course remote from that sort of thing. Death squads, I mean. But it is well known that some 25 years back this particular university, for instance, had applied relentless financial pressure on the surrounding ghetto-dwellers and that during that time there were many strange fires burning buildings down and black people out. There was hate. There was violence. Nobody forgot the dead white professor found strung up on the school fence. The university came to own the third largest police force in the state. Together with the city administration it changed the traffic pattern, impeding entry to the area by means of a labyrinth of one-way streets. An invisible hand manipulated what it could of public culture and public space. It became unlawful to post certain sorts of flyers on university notice boards, thus preventing certain sorts of people from having any good reason for being in the vicinity. Thus, in time, while preserving the semblance of democratic openness, the university came to reconstruct the ghetto into a middle-class, largely white, fortress within an invisible *cordon sanitaire*. Terror as usual, the middle-class way, justified by the appeal to the higher education, to the preservation of Civilization itself, played out right there in the fear-ridden blocks of lofty spires, the fiery figures of the burning buildings, and the calm spotlights of policemen with their watchful dogs. We remember Walter Benjamin: "no document of civilization which is not at the same time a document of barbarism."

My thoughts drifted to a late nineteenth-century story written by Joseph Conrad's close friend, the larger than life eccentric Robert Bontine Cunninghame Graham. In this story, "A Hegira," Cunninghame Graham relates how on a trip to Mexico City in 1880 he visited eight Apache Indians imprisoned in a cage and on public view in the castle of Chapultepec. As he left the city to return to his ranch in Texas, he heard they had escaped, and all the long way north he witnessed elation and pandemonium as in town after town drunken men galloped off, gun in hand, to track down and kill, one by one, these foot-weary Indians – half-human, half-beast, decidedly and mysteriously Other – slowly moving north through the terrain of Mexico, constituting it as a nation and as a people in the terror of the savagery imputed to the Apache. Yet when I'd finished telling the tale my host looked at me. "Do you know how many people the Apaches killed and how many head of cattle they stole between 1855 and 1885?" he asked. It was as much a challenge as a question, the sort of question you asked looking down the sights of a gun where reality equals a target. The implication was clear; there was "good reason" to fear and kill those Apaches. "But there were only eight of them, in the whole of Mexico, alone and on foot," I replied. "And a dog they'd picked up."

But later on, to my surprise, when the seminar got under way, my host, once so fiery and eloquent on the topic of terror, so in command of his vast history-machine, fell silent as the grave, slumped into the furthest recess of his padded chair. A young tenured professor chaired the occasion in a don't-mess-with-me manner, refusing to allow me to begin with the summary I'd prepared. "That won't be necessary!" he repeated archly, asking nearly all the questions which, like the host's reaction to the Apache story, were not only aimed at making sense of terror as somebody's profit, but in doing so furthered the terror he purported to be explaining. The sad grayness of the late afternoon spread through the room. Pale and forbiddingly silent, the graduate students sat as sentinels of truth for oncoming generations. Why were they so frightened? What did they feel? Maybe they felt nothing?

Reluctantly I met my host for a cup of coffee two days later at the university. He was insistent and invoked all sorts of nostalgia to smooth over unstated tensions. But what a climax! Where was the genteel comfort of his imagined past of heroic intellectuals in the sub-basement of what was said to be a perfect copy of an Oxford college where we now sat holding undrinkable coffee from a slot machine while four or five gangling young men from the ghetto horsed around menacing one another, and the clientele, teasing of course, as they played unbearably loud music from the jukebox? The host leaned forward against the noise. The arteries pulsed in his stout neck. "Have you read Bordovitch's work on the Stalin trials, published in Paris in the fifties?" he shouted.

"No," I had to confess.

He leaned forward again. "Do you know why the prisoners admitted to crimes they hadn't committed?" he demanded with a sharp edge to his voice. "Because they were deprived of sleep – for weeks at a time," he thundered. "In white cells with the light on all the time!"

He sat back, glowing like a white light himself, grimly satisfied, even a little exultant and happy now that he had pushed terror's dark murk well away from those politically staged performances where confusion and confession worked to each other's benefit. He insisted on driving me the five blocks to where I was staying. "Here your car is your tank," he said.

REFERENCES

Benjamin, Walter. 1969. "Theses on the Philosophy of History." In *Illuminations*, ed. Hannah Arendt, tr. Harry Zohn, pp. 253–64. New York: Schocken.

32

Symbolic Violence

Pierre Bourdieu and Loïc Wacquant

Symbolic violence, to put it as tersely and simply as possible, is the *violence which is exercised upon a social agent with his or her complicity.*[1] Now, this idiom is dangerous because it may open the door to scholastic discussions on whether power comes "from below," or why the agent "desires" the condition imposed upon him, etc. To say it more rigorously: social agents are knowing agents who, even when they are subjected to determinisms, contribute to producing the efficacy of that which determines them insofar as they structure what determines them. And it is almost always in the "fit" between determinants and the categories of perception that constitute them as such that the effect of domination arises. (This shows, incidentally, that if you try to think domination in terms of the academic alternative of freedom and determinism, choice and constraint, you get nowhere.)[2] I call *misrecognition* the fact of recognizing a violence which is wielded precisely inasmuch as one does not perceive it as such.

What I put under the term of "recognition," then, is the set of fundamental, prereflexive assumptions that social agents engage by the mere fact of taking the world for granted, of accepting the world as it is, and of finding it natural because *their mind is constructed according to cognitive structures that are issued out of the very structures of the world.* What I understand by misrecognition certainly does not fall under the category of influence; I never talk of influence. It is not a logic of "communicative interaction" where some make propaganda aimed at others that is operative here. It is much more powerful and insidious than

that: being born in a social world, we accept a whole range of postulates, axioms, which go without saying and require no inculcating.[3] This is why the analysis of the doxic acceptance of the world, due to the immediate agreement of objective structures and cognitive structures, is the true foundation of a realistic theory of domination and politics. Of all forms of "hidden persuasion," the most implacable is the one exerted, quite simply, by the *order of things.* [...]

To try to unravel the logic of gender domination, which seems to me to be the paradigmatic form of symbolic violence, I chose to ground my analysis in my ethnographic research among the Kabyle of Algeria and this for two reasons. First, I wanted to avoid the empty speculation of theoretical discourse and its clichés and slogans on gender and power which have so far done more to muddle the issue than to clarify it. Second, I use this device to circumvent the critical difficulty posed by the analysis of gender: we are dealing in this case with an institution that has been inscribed for millennia in the objectivity of social structures and in the subjectivity of men-mental structures, so that the analyst has every chance of using as *instruments* of knowledge categories of perception and of thought which he or she should treat as *objects* of knowledge. This mountain society of North Africa is particularly interesting because it is a genuine cultural repository that has kept alive, through its ritual practices, its poetry, and its oral traditions, a system of representations or, better, a system of principles of vision and di-vision common to the entire Mediterranean civilization, and which survives to this day in our mental structures and, for a part, in our social structures. Thus, I treat the Kabyle case as a sort of "aggrandized picture" on which we can more easily decipher the fundamental structures of the male vision of the world: the "phallonarcissistic" cosmology of which they give a collective and public (re)presentation haunts our own unconscious.

This reading shows, first of all, that male order is so deeply grounded as to need no justification: it imposes itself as self-evident, universal (man, *vir*, is this particular being which experiences himself as universal, who holds a monopoly over the human, *homo*). It tends to be taken for granted by virtue of the quasi-perfect and immediate agreement which obtains between, on the one hand, social structures such as those expressed in the social organization of space and time and in the sexual division of labor and, on the other, cognitive structures inscribed in bodies and in minds. In effect, the dominated, that is, women, apply to every object of the (natural and social) world and in particular to the relation of domination in which they are ensnared, as well as to the persons through which this relation realizes itself, unthought schemata of thought which are the product of the embodiment of this relation of power in the form of paired couples (high/low, large/small, inside/outside, straight/crooked, etc.), and which therefore lead them to construct this relation from the standpoint of the dominant, i.e., as natural.

The case of gender domination shows better than any other that *symbolic violence accomplishes itself through an act of cognition and of misrecognition that lies beyond – or beneath – the controls of consciousness and will*, in the obscurities of the schemata of habitus that are at once gendered and gendering.[4] And it demonstrates that we cannot understand symbolic violence and practice without forsaking entirely the scholastic opposition between coercion and consent, external imposition and internal impulse. (After 200 years of pervasive Platonism, it is hard for us to think that the body can "think itself" through a logic alien to that of theoretical reflection.) In this sense, we can say that gender domination consists in what we call in French a *contrainte par corps*, an imprisonment effected via the body. The work of socialization tends to effect a progressive somatization of relations of gender domination through a twofold operation: first by means of the social construction of the vision of biological sex which itself serves as the foundation of all mythical visions of the world; and, second, through the inculcation of a bodily hexis that constitutes a veritable *embodied politics*. In other words, male sociodicy owes its specific efficacy to the fact that it legitimates a relation of domination by inscribing it in a biological which is itself a biologized social construction.

This double work of inculcation, at once sexually differentiated and sexually differentiating, imposes upon men and women different sets of dispositions with regard to the social games that are held to be crucial to society, such as the games of honor and war (fit for the display of masculinity, virility) or, in advanced societies, all the most valued games such as politics, business, science, etc. The masculinization of male bodies and feminization of female bodies effects a somatization of the cultural arbitrary which is the durable construction of the unconscious. Having shown this, I shift from one extreme of cultural space to the other to explore this originary relation of exclusion from the standpoint of the dominated as expressed in Virginia Woolf's 1927 novel *To the Lighthouse*. We find in this novel an extraordinarily perceptive analysis of a paradoxical dimension of symbolic domination, and one almost always overlooked by feminist critique, namely the domination of the dominant by his domination: a feminine gaze upon the desperate and somewhat pathetic effort that any man must make, in his triumphant unconsciousness, to try to live up to the dominant idea of man. Furthermore, Virginia Woolf allows us to understand how, by ignoring the *illusio* that leads one to engage in the central games of society, women escape the *libido dominandi* that comes with this involvement, and are therefore socially inclined to gain a relatively lucid view of the male games in which they ordinarily partake only by proxy.

NOTES

1   Bourdieu's writings on religion, law, politics, and intellectuals offer different angles on the same basic phenomenon. He treats law, for instance, as "the form par excellence of the symbolic power of naming and classifying that creates the things named, and particularly groups; it confers upon the realities emerging out of its operations of classification all the permanence, that of things, that a historical

institution is capable of granting to historical institutions" (Bourdieu 1987: 233–4, translation modified).

2 "Any symbolic domination presupposes on the part of those who are subjected to it a form of complicity which is neither a passive submission to an external constraint nor a free adherence to values.... The specificity of symbolic violence resides precisely in the fact that it requires of the person who undergoes it an attitude which defies the ordinary alternative between freedom and constraint" (Bourdieu 1982: 36).

3 This is one of the main differences between Bourdieu's theory of symbolic violence and Gramsci's (1971) theory of hegemony: the former requires none of the active "manufacturing," of the work of "conviction" entailed by the latter. Bourdieu (1989: 21) makes this clear in the following passage: "Legitimation of the social order is not...the product of a deliberate and purposive action of propaganda or symbolic imposition; it results, rather, from the fact that agents apply to the objective structures of the social world structures of perception and appreciation which are issued out of these very structures and which tend to picture the world as evident."

4 The immediate agreement of a gendered habitus with a social world suffused with sexual asymmetries explains how women can come to collude with and even actively defend or justify forms of aggression which victimize them, such as rape. Lynn Chancer (1987) provides a vivid demonstration of this process in her case study of the negative reactions of Portuguese women to the highly publicized group rape of another Portuguese woman in Bedford, Massachusetts, in March of 1983. The following comments by two women who marched in defense of the six rapists on trial reveal the deeply taken-for-granted nature of assumptions about masculinity and femininity as they are socially defined within this community: "I am Portuguese and proud of it. I'm also a woman, but you don't see me getting raped. If you throw a dog a bone, he's gonna take it – if you walk around naked, men are just going to go for you." "They did nothing to her. Her rights are to be at home with her two kids and to be a good mother. A Portuguese woman should be with her kids and that's it" (Chancer 1987: 251).

REFERENCES

Bourdieu, Pierre. 1982. *Ce que parler veut dire. L'économie des échanges linguistiques.* Paris: Arthème Fayard.

——.1987 [1986]. "The Force of Law: Toward a Sociology of the Juridical Field." *Hastings Journal of Law* 38: 209–48.

——. 1989 [1988]. "Social Space and Symbolic Power." *Sociological Theory* 7(1) (June): 18–26.

Chancer, Lynn S. 1987. "New Bedford, Massachusetts, March 6, 1983–March 22, 1984: The 'Before' and 'After' of a Group Rape." *Gender and Society* 1(3) (Sept.): 239–60.

Gramsci, Antonio. 1971. *Selections from the Prison Notebooks.* New York: International Publishers.

Woolf, Virginia. 1987 [1927]. *To the Lighthouse.* New York: Harvest/HBJ Books.

33

Two Feet Under and a Cardboard Coffin: The Social Production of Indifference to Child Death

Nancy Scheper-Hughes

A child died today in the favela. He was two months old. If he had lived he would have gone hungry anyway.

Carolina Maria de Jesus (1962: 108)

The opposite of love is not hate, but indifference.

Elie Wiesel (1990: 174)

Forebodings

"Why do the church bells ring so often?" I asked Nailza de Arruda soon after I had moved into a corner of her tiny mud-walled hut near the top of the Alto do Cruzeiro. It was the dry and blazingly hot summer of 1964, the months following the military coup, and save for the rusty, clanging bells of Nossa Senhora das Dores Church, an eerie quiet had settled over the town. Beneath the quiet, however, were chaos and panic.

"It's nothing," replied Nailza, "just another little angel gone to heaven." Nailza had sent more than her share of little angels to heaven, and sometimes at night I could hear her engaged in a muffled, yet passionate, discourse with one of them: 2-year-old Joana. Joana's photograph, taken as she lay eyes opened and propped up in her tiny cardboard coffin, hung on a wall next to the photo of Nailza and Zé Antônio taken on the day the couple had eloped a few years before. Zé Antônio, uncomfortable in his one good, starched, white shirt, looked into the camera every bit as startled as the uncanny wide-eyed toddler in her white dress.

Nailza could barely remember the names of the other infants and babies who came and went in close succession. Some had died unnamed and had been hastily baptized in their coffins. Few lived more than a month or two. Only Joana, properly baptized in church at the close of her first year and placed under the protection of a powerful saint, Joan of Arc, had been expected to live. And Nailza had dangerously allowed herself to love the little girl. In addressing the dead child, Nailza's voice would range from tearful imploring to angry recrimination: "Why did you leave me? Was your patron saint so greedy that she could not allow me one child on this earth?" Zé Antônio advised me to ignore Nailza's odd behavior, which he understood as a kind of madness that, like the birth and death of children, came and went. [. . .]

Throughout Northeast Brazil, whenever one asks a poor woman how many children she has in her family, she invariably replies with the formula, "X children, y living." Sometimes she may say, "Y living, z angels." Women themselves, unlike the local and state bureaucracies, keep close track of their reproductive issue, counting the living along with the dead, stillborn, and miscarried. Each little angel is proudly tabulated, a flower in the mother's crown of thorns, each the sign of special graces and indulgences accumulating in the afterlife. There are a great many angels to keep track of. It is just as well that so many women are doing the counting.

When I first began in 1982 to try documenting the extent of infant and child mortality in the *município*, I was stymied by the difficulty in finding reliable local statistics. I was referred by various public officials of Bom Jesus to the office of the local IBGE, the national central statistics bureau. This was a small rented room across the hall from a local dentist's office in "downtown" Bom Jesus and was closed each time I went there. Finally, one afternoon I encountered a civil servant sleeping in a chair in the otherwise empty office. There was not so much as a typewriter or a file cabinet. "No," I was told, "there are no statistics kept here – no numbers at all." Everything, I was told, was tabulated and sent off to the central office in Recife.

The application of some local political pressure, however, yielded summaries of vital statistics for the community for selected years in the 1970s. In 1977, 761 live births (599 in hospital, 162 at home) and 311 deaths of infants were recorded, yielding an IMR (infant mortality rate) of 409/1,000. In 1978, 896 live births (719 in hospital, 177 at home) and 320 infant deaths yielded an infant mortality rate of 357/1,000. If these statistics were reliable, they indicated that between 36 percent and 41 percent of all infants in the *município* were dying in the first 12 months of their lives, a state of affairs that was immediately and roundly denied by the mayor as an absurdity. "My *município* is growing, not declining," he insisted, and Seu Félix sent me to the local hospital to corroborate the IBGE statistics with the records on births and deaths kept there.

The Barbosa Hospital and Maternity Center is one of three hospitals serving the entire region of the *zona da mata – norte* of Pernambuco and Paraíba. Although privately owned by the Barbosa family, the hospital primarily serves the needs of the rural popular classes, many of whom receive medical services without charge. Hence, the hospital attracts a large clientele that extends far beyond the limits of the municipality, and its statistics reflected a regional, not a municipal, pattern. Nonetheless, the head nurse gave me access to her records. For 1981 a total of 3,213 deliveries were recorded, of which 807 were of indigent, or non-

paying, patients. The remaining deliveries were covered by the national health care security system or by the rural workers health fund. There were 98 (3.1 percent) stillbirths and 38 (1.2 percent) perinatal deaths in the maternity wing for that year. When I returned in 1987 the figures for the previous year were 2,730 deliveries, of which 68 (2.5 percent) were stillborn and 27 (1 percent) died within 48 hours postpartum. Official death certificates were issued in the name of attending physicians, but these were generally filled out by a nurse or hospital functionary. And the causes of death, when given at all, were perfunctory: "prematurity" and "heart and respiratory failure" were the most common diagnoses. One hospital physician had a disproportionately high number of stillbirths and perinatal deaths in his practice at the maternity wing. But no one seemed to be keeping track too closely or carefully.

After I had begun, through various and sometimes creative means, to assess the extent of child mortality in Bom Jesus, I made a visit to the first and newly appointed secretary of health for Bom Jesus. Responding to inquiries about the greatest health risks to the population of the *município*, the debonair and energetic Dr. Ricardo offered without a moment's hesitation, "Stress." And he began to outline his proposals for a stress-reduction education program that would target the substantial business and professional class of the community. Heart problems and cancer were, the secretary of health continued, the two greatest causes of death in the bustling little metropolis. When confronted with the data painstakingly culled from the civil registry office in Bom Jesus indicating that almost a half of all deaths in the *município* each year were of children under the age of 5 and that diarrhea, not heart disease, and hunger, not stress, were the main pathogens, Dr. Ricardo sighed and raised his eyes to the heavens: "Oh, child mortality! If we were to talk child mortality . . . an absurdity, surely. And unknowable as well."

"What do you mean?"

"When I took over this office last August, the municipal administration had no figures on child mortality, none whatsoever. I had to send for them from the state, and they were unusable: an infant mortality of 120 percent!"

"How can that be?"

"And why not? It's quite straightforward. The official figures said that of every 100 infants born in Bom Jesus, 120 of them died before they reached the age of one year! What a disaster! No wonder we are so underdeveloped in Brazil – more of us die than are even born!"

"Surely there are other ways of counting the dead," I suggested. "For example, how many charity baby coffins does the mayor's office distribute each month?"

"Oh, there's no limit there, no limit at all. We give the people as many as they want. In fact, the more they want, the better! It's one of the things we take care of very efficiently and well."

The doctor was pulling my leg, of course, but his remarks captured both the social embarrassment and the bureaucratic indifference toward child mortality as a premodern plague in a self-consciously modernizing interior town.

Later that day I stopped in again to visit Seu Moacir, the municipal "carpenter," although what he "carpenters" for the city are poor people's coffins, mostly baby coffins. Nonetheless, Moacir strongly objected to being called the municipal coffin maker or having his crowded annex to the back of the municipal chambers referred to as a coffin workshop or a *casa funerária*. And so the discreet sign over his door read, "Municipal Woodworks." But even here there was some deception at play, for the media in which Moacir worked were as much cardboard and papier-mâché as plywood and pine. His "product," he told me, cost the city between 2 and 8 dollars apiece, depending on size.

Yes, he was quite busy, Moacir said, but he could answer a few questions. He has been the municipal carpenter since 1965, when Seu Félix decided that every citizen had the right to a decent burial. There were more than twice as many baby coffins requested as adult ones. February and March were the "busiest" months for his work. Why? Perhaps it was, he hazarded a guess, because people liked to marry in June after the *festas juninas* were over and boys and girls on the Alto had begun to "pair up." Moacir was a man of few words, and his own curiosity in the matters I was raising was limited. But the craftsman in him readily agreed to pose for pictures, and he held up both an adult coffin and a baby one, pointing out that the style was similar for both – a cardboard top and a plywood bottom.

All adult coffins, regardless of sex, were painted a muddy brown ("Earth tone," said Moacir), and all children's coffins, males and females, to the age of 7 were painted "sky blue, the favorite color of the Virgin." Moacir noted a detail: there were no fasteners on the children's coffins because parents preferred to put their angels into the ground as unencumbered as possible so that the children's spirits were free to escape their premature graves. Moacir found it difficult to estimate how many coffins "left" the workshop each week: "Some days as many as five or six will leave the shop. And then there are days when there are no requests at all." But, he added, "this doesn't affect my productivity. I just keep on working steadily so that coffins are never lacking in the *município*. I don't like to fall behind in my work; even on a holiday a comrade can find me, and I will have a coffin in stock that will serve his needs."

I asked Moacir if he would be willing to go over his requisitions for the previous few weeks, and, somewhat reluctantly, he agreed. We moved over to a cluttered desk with slips of paper in small, untidy piles. "Here," he said picking up one pile, "I'll read them out to you. But I warn you, things are a little chaotic. Here's one: baby, female, three months, June 22, 1987." And he continued, "Newborn, male, June 17, 1987. Female, about six months, June 11, 1987. Male, four months, June 17, 1987."

Then something had him stumped, and he had a hard time reading the slip of paper. As I approached him to look at it myself, he put it down abruptly: "This has nothing to do with anything. It's an order for seventeen sacks of cement! I warned you that everything was all mixed up here."

When I learned that all the requisition orders were referred back to Seu João in the town hall, I approached João himself for access to the records on all materials furnished by the *prefeitura*. Grumbling, Seu João got down the ledger books, but he warned me not to trust any of them: "If you want numbers," he suggested, "just double everything that's put down here – our inventory is incomplete." In the books that documented in neat columns the "movement" of all supplies in and out of the *prefeitura*, the data on baby coffins were there, interspersed with data on Brillo pads, light bulbs, chlorine bleach, kerosene, toilet paper, cement, alcohol, and soap. In a six-month period in 1988 the *prefeitura* had distributed 131 free infant and child coffins.

When I asked Seu João, who was delighted to get his books back so quickly, why the data on baby coffins were not kept separately, he replied, "Because it wouldn't be of interest to anyone." The deaths of these children, like their brief lives, are invisible and of little or no account.

Finally, I was referred to the *cartório civil* of Bom Jesus, a small, airless, and windowless office privately owned and run by the formidable Dona Leona and her humorless 20-year-old son. Here, for a small fee, the vital statistics of the community – births, deaths, marriages, and (since 1986) divorces were registered by hand in one of several large ledger books. I was invited to borrow one of the two chairs and a small space at a desk to count the entries for selected years, an occupation that took the greater part of many mornings in Bom Jesus da Mata in 1987 and later again in 1988 and 1989.

Dona Leona has maintained the *cartório* for 30 years, and she worked in "cooperation" with the mayor's office. The town hall furnishes a space in the municipal cemetery and a charity coffin only to those who have registered a death at the *cartório civil*. Consequently, the data on child deaths since 1966 are fairly complete, with the exception of stillbirths and perinatal deaths, many of which are neither registered nor buried in the municipal graveyard. Late abortions and stillbirths, many of them occurring at home on the Alto do Cruzeiro, are buried privately in the *mato* or in the backyard, and there is no question of a medical record or a death certificate. Moreover, until relatively recently, the deaths of unbaptized babies of any age went unregistered. As "pagan" infants they were stigmatized creatures and were buried covertly by their parents at a crossroads in the country, the place where Exu, the Afro-Brazilian deity, and his host of unbaptized spirit infants congregate to serve as messengers for good and ill in the world.

In addition to these, about one-fifth of all Alto births today still take place at home, keeping the half dozen elderly midwives (called *parteiras* or *curiosas*) fairly regularly employed. The *parteiras* who work today in virtual isolation from the medical institutions of Bom Jesus (following years of unsuccessful attempts to regulate them and to incorporate them into the extension work of the state health post) especially fear running afoul of the "bureaucracy" and the medical profession in Bom Jesus. Consequently, the *parteiras* do not encourage registration of infant births or deaths in which they were involved. Moreover, stillbirths and perinatal deaths are roundly denied by the midwives, who actively compete with each other for an ever-constricting market.

Although, with these exceptions, the data on infant mortality at the *cartório civil* can be taken as fairly complete and reliable, there is no possibility of ascertaining a reliable infant mortality *rate*. Although universal birth registration is mandatory today, there is no way to enforce it at the local level. In practice, most poor families delay registration until the child has to confront the "state" for the first time – usually on registering for primary school. Otherwise, an individual may not be registered until he or she wants to enter the work force, marry, join the military, or receive some medical or social benefit from the state. Moreover, although all registrations of infant deaths (to age one) also require birth certificates, registrations of child deaths older than one year do not require that the births of the children also be registered. Somewhat more reliable, then, is a calculation of the proportion of child to adult deaths for the community as a whole for the years selected for study. I selected the three years advisedly: 1965, the year following the Brazilian military coup and, as I recalled it, the year of the great die out of Alto babies; 1985, 20 years later and following the crash of the great economic miracle; and 1987, the period of democratization and preparation for the transfer of authority from military to civilian rule, also the year of the cruzado novo and significant fiscal reforms aimed at restructuring the economy with respect to inflation and the debt crisis.

Public records, whether official censuses, birth or baptismal certificates, marriage or divorce records, or death or burial certificates, are obviously not "neutral" documents. They are not in any sense "pure" sources of data. Censuses and other public records count only certain things, not others. They count some things better than others, as in this instance they count infant and child deaths better than births. They reveal a society's particular system of classification. So they are not so much mirrors of reality as they are filters, or "collective representations," as Émile Durkheim might put it. It is just those images and collective representations – in this case, of the child and of child death – that I am after. How are the records kept? What events are kept track of? What is thought hardly worth noting or counting at all? And what can this tell us about the collective invisibility of women and children in particular?

Those relatives who arrive at the *cartório civil* to register the death of a child in Bom Jesus are briefly interviewed by Dona Leona according to the following formula. They are asked to testify, "on their honor," to the time and date of the death, the place of death (usually the home address), the sex of the child, the child's "color," the name of the child's mother and father, the father's (but not the mother's) birthplace, the father's (but not the mother's) profession, and the name of the cemetery. The reporting relative is then asked to sign the form or to affix his or her mark (an X), and two other individuals are asked to testify as "witnesses" to the accuracy of the account.

What we can learn from this particular record is the following: the sex, age, name, and "race" of the child; the marital status of the parents; the neighborhood or street in which they live; the father's occupation; and the place of death. In those few instances where the child died in the hospital and was also issued a death certificate, Dona Leona noted the name of the attending physician and his or her diagnosis.

While copying the birth and child death data at the registry office, I was able to observe many interactions between Dona Leona and the people of Bom Jesus, especially the poor of the Alto, who appeared each day to register the death of a child. Most often it was the father of the child who appeared, but occasionally it was a grandmother, a grandfather, an aunt, a godparent, or even an older sibling. Mothers, however, never appeared in the *cartório* to register the death of one of their own children. The registration and burial of the child usually took place within 12 to 24 hours of the child's death.

Dona Leona was generally distant and officious; if provoked, she could be gruff and dismissive, especially if the relative was uncertain of basic "details," such as the name of the child, the complete names of the child's parents, the marital status of the parents, or the exact time and location of the death. Many of these seemingly obvious and necessarily bureaucratic details were anathema to the people of the Alto and had little relevance to their everyday lives. "Name of the deceased?" Dona Leona snapped. And I saw a father turn anxiously to his sister-in-law to ask her, "Whatever *is* the name of our little Fiapo [a common nickname meaning little bit of nothing]?" Explaining where one lived in response to the bureaucratic question "Street and house number?" could be taxing. There were no official house numbers and only descriptive and informal nicknames for many of the dirt paths and hillside ledges on which *moradores* had

built their homes on the Alto do Cruzeiro. Living arrangements were often informal, and couples frequently did not know each other's surnames. On one occasion, when a father could not produce the full name of his common-law wife, his *compadre* whispered to him, "Well, just let it be Araújo da Silva, then" and so "married" the couple on the spot. Dona Leona was not amused by these "lapses" of memory in her clients, and she was not above giving them an occasional dressing down.

As the end of the day approached, Dona Leona could be testy; her work kept her busy, and she liked to have her books in order by 4 p.m. so that she could go home early. Those who rushed in at the last minute, as did Dona Aparecida of the Rua dos Magos, could face an impassive and bureaucratic wall of resistance. Aparecida had just run from the Barbosa Hospital at one end of Bom Jesus to the *cartório civil* at the other end to register the death of a premature grandson who had been born and who had died earlier that day. Her daughter, the infant's mother, was doing poorly in the hospital and had begun to hemorrhage. The baby's father was away working on a distant plantation and knew nothing of the events that had transpired. It fell to Aparecida to bury her grandson, but in her anxiety over her deathly ill daughter, she had forgotten to register the death earlier in the day, and now Seu Moacir refused to give her the little coffin until she had done so.

"But where is the marriage certificate?" Dona Leona inquired, as the older woman attempted to register her grandson as the "legitimate" son of her daughter and son-in-law. "And how would I know where my daughter keeps such things?" replied the grandmother, who was sent away in search of the document and told to return with it the following day. And so Dona Leona got to go home early, as usual. The infant, meanwhile, wrapped in its *mortália* (winding sheet), lay overnight in a hospital storage room that served on occasion as a morgue for indigent patients.

Dona Leona tried hard to run a tight ship, but she was often frustrated. "Color of the deceased?" she asked. And here the relatives were often puzzled. Some fathers pointed to their own skin, saying, "Well, she was my child." In other words, "Judge for yourself, if you wish." Another young father, when asked the color of his deceased 4-month-old infant, replied, "It was just a baby – it didn't have any color yet." Usually Dona Leona simply designated the color of the infant based on a local cultural category: poor equaled "brown." She never asked the parents to supply the missing "cause of death," however. In the absence of an official death certificate and a medical diagnosis, there was, she said, no way to know, and she was content to leave that space blank on most of the forms.

The state, then – represented in the personages of minor civil servants such as Moacir and Dona Leona – contributes to the routinization and normalization of child death by its implacable opacity, its refusal to comprehend, and its consequent inability to act responsively to the human suffering that presents itself. Bureaucrats and civil servants respond to pain and difference with a studied indifference – *la belle indifférence*. Normally, this is expressed in the bureaucracy's "deaf ear," its interminable off-putting delays and postponements, its failure to note the dire consequences of its indecisiveness. But there is another side to bureaucratic indifference that is more characteristic in this instance: the rapid dispatch. It conveys that nothing of any consequence, nothing worth noting, has really taken place. Two or three minutes to "process" each dead infant or child should suffice.

"But look at this," I spoke (out of turn) from my perusal of the death registry books in the *cartório* on one occasion. "Here is the name of a woman on the Rua dos índios of the Alto do Cruzeiro who has lost three small children within the space of a few months. What do you think could be going on? Shouldn't someone look into it?"

"I wouldn't know," Dona Leona replied coolly. "My job is only to record the dead, not to hold an inquest once they're gone."

I was sufficiently abashed to go quietly back to my "clerking" of the records, scratching away in my copybooks, a modern-day Bartleby the Scrivener, refusing to leave where I was decidedly unwanted and just barely tolerated.

In 1965 a total of 497 child deaths (of those born live through age 5 were recorded. Three hundred seventy-five, or 78 percent, of the deaths were of infants in the first 12 months of life. These infant deaths came from a total of 760 recorded births for 1965, a figure that included all children born in that year and registered in that year or born in 1965 but registered in subsequent years. Even if we assume that some born in that year escaped registration altogether, 1965 (with an infant mortality rate of 493/1,000 live births) was a year the bells of Nossa Senhora das Dores tolled incessantly. And when they tolled, it was for the "holy innocents" of Bom Jesus and its rural surrounds, the most immediate victims of Brazil's "quiet and bloodless" military coup. Quiet, indeed, but perhaps not quite so bloodless after all. Of all deaths in Bom Jesus in 1965, 44.5 percent were of children younger than 5 years.

34

On Suffering and Structural Violence: A View from Below

Paul Farmer

Everyone knows that suffering exists. The question is how to define it. Given that each person's pain has a degree of reality for him or her that the pain of others can surely never approach, is widespread agreement on the subject possible? Almost all of us would agree that premature and painful illness, torture, and rape constitute extreme suffering. Most would also agree that insidious assaults on dignity, such as institutionalized racism and sexism, also cause great and unjust injury.

Given our consensus on some of the more conspicuous forms of suffering, a number of corollary questions come to the fore. Can we identify those most at risk of great suffering? Among those whose suffering is not mortal, is it possible to identify those most likely to sustain permanent and disabling damage? Are certain "event" assaults, such as torture or rape, more likely to lead to late sequelae than are sustained and insidious suffering, such as the pain born of deep poverty or of racism? Under this latter rubric, are certain forms of discrimination demonstrably more noxious than others?

Anthropologists who take these as research questions study both individual experience and the larger social matrix in which it is embedded in order to see how various large-scale social forces come to be translated into personal distress and disease. By what mechanisms do social forces ranging from poverty to racism become *embodied* as individual experience? This has been the focus of most of my own research in Haiti, where political and economic forces have structured risk for AIDS, tuberculosis, and, indeed, most other infectious and parasitic diseases. Social forces at work there have also structured risk for most forms of extreme suffering, from hunger to torture and rape.

Working in contemporary Haiti, where in recent years political violence has been added to the worst poverty in the hemisphere, one learns a great deal about suffering. In fact, the country has long constituted a sort of living laboratory for the study of affliction, no matter how it is defined. "Life for the Haitian peasant of today," observed anthropologist Jean Weise some 25 years ago, "is abject misery and a rank familiarity with death."[1] The situation has since worsened. When in 1991 international health and population experts devised a "human suffering index" by examining measures of human welfare ranging from life expectancy to political freedom, 27 of 141 countries were characterized by "extreme human suffering." Only one of them, Haiti, was located in the Western hemisphere. In only three countries in the world was suffering judged to be more extreme than that endured in Haiti; each of these three countries is currently in the midst of an internationally recognized civil war.

Suffering is certainly a recurrent and expected condition in Haiti's Central Plateau, where everyday life has felt like war. "You get up in the morning," observed one young widow with four children, "and it's the fight for food and wood and water." If initially struck by the austere beauty of the region's steep mountains and clement weather, long-term visitors come to see the Central Plateau in much the same manner as its inhabitants: a chalky and arid land hostile to the best efforts of the peasant farmers who live here. Landlessness is widespread and so, consequently, is hunger. All the standard measures reveal how tenuous the peasantry's hold on survival is. Life expectancy at birth is less than fifty years, in large part because as many as 2 of every 10 infants die before their first birthday. Tuberculosis is the leading cause of death among adults; among children, diarrheal disease, measles, and tetanus ravage the undernourished.

But the experience of suffering, it is often noted, is not effectively conveyed by statistics or graphs. The "texture" of dire affliction is perhaps best felt in the gritty details of biography, and so I introduce the stories of Acéphie Joseph and Chouchou Louis. The stories of Acéphie and Chouchou are anything but "anecdotal." For the epidemiologist as well as the political analyst, they suffered and died in exemplary fashion. Millions of people living in similar circumstances can expect to meet similar fates. What these victims, past and present, share are not personal or psychological attributes – they do not share culture, language, or race. Rather, what they share is the experience of occupying the bottom rung of the social ladder in inegalitarian societies.

Acéphie Joseph's and Chouchou Louis's stories illustrate some of the mechanisms through which large-scale social forces crystallize into the sharp, hard surfaces of individual suffering. Such suffering is structured by historically given (and often economically driven) processes and forces that conspire – whether through routine, ritual, or, as is more commonly the case, these hard surfaces – to constrain agency. For many, including most of my patients and informants, life choices are structured by racism, sexism, political violence, *and* grinding poverty.

Acéphie's Story

For the wound of the daughter of my people is my heart wounded, I mourn, and dismay has taken hold of me.
Is there no balm in Gilead? Is there no physician there?
Why then has the health of the daughter of my people not been restored?
O that my head were waters, and my eyes a fountain of tears, that I might weep day and night for the slain of the daughter of my people!
Jeremiah 8:22–9.1

Kay, a community of fewer than 1,500 people, stretches along an unpaved road that cuts north and east into Haiti's Central Plateau. Striking out from Port-au-Prince, the capital, it can take several hours to reach Kay. The journey gives one an impression of isolation, insularity. The impression is misleading, as the village owes its existence to a project conceived in the Haitian capital and drafted in Washington, DC: Kay is a settlement of refugees, substantially composed of peasant farmers displaced more than 30 years ago by Haiti's largest dam.

Before 1956, the village of Kay was situated in a fertile valley, and through it ran the Rivière Artibonite. For generations, thousands of families had farmed the broad and gently sloping banks of the river, selling rice, bananas, millet, corn, and sugarcane in regional markets. Harvests were, by all reports, bountiful; life there is now recalled as idyllic. When the valley was flooded with the building of the dam, the majority of the local population was forced up into the stony hills on either side of the new reservoir. By all the standard measures, the "water refugees" became exceedingly poor; the older people often blame their poverty on the massive buttress dam a few miles away, and bitterly note that it brought them neither electricity nor water.

In 1983, when I began working in the Central Plateau, AIDS, although already afflicting an increasing number of city dwellers, was unknown in most areas as rural as Kay. Acéphie Joseph was one of the first villagers to die of the new syndrome. But her illness, which ended in 1991, was merely the latest in a string of tragedies that she and her parents readily linked together in a long lamentation, by now familiar to those who tend the region's sick.

The litany begins, usually, down in the valley hidden under the still surface of the lake. Acéphie's parents came from families making a decent living by farming fertile tracts of land – their "ancestors' gardens" – and selling much of their produce. M. Joseph tilled the soil, and his wife, a tall and wearily elegant woman not nearly as old as she looked, was a "Madame Sarah," a market woman. "If it weren't for the dam," M. Joseph assured me, "we'd be just fine now. Acéphie, too." The Josephs' home was drowned along with most of their belongings, their crops, and the graves of their ancestors.

Refugees from the rising water, the Josephs built a miserable lean-to on a knoll of high land jutting into the new reservoir. They remained poised on their knoll for some years; Acéphie and her twin brother were born there. I asked them what induced them to move up to Kay, to build a house on the hard stone embankment of a dusty road. "Our hut was too near the water," replied M. Joseph. "I was afraid one of the children would fall into the lake and drown. Their mother had to be away selling; I was trying to make a garden in this terrible soil. There was no one to keep an eye on them."

Acéphie attended primary school – a banana-thatched and open shelter in which children and young adults received the rudiments of literacy – in Kay. "She was the nicest of the Joseph sisters," recalled one of her classmates. "And she was as pretty as she was nice." Acéphie's beauty and her vulnerability may have sealed her fate as early as 1984. Though still in primary school, she was already 19 years old; it was time for her to help generate income for her family, which was sinking deeper and deeper into poverty. Acéphie began to help her mother by carrying produce to a local market on Friday mornings. On foot or with a donkey it takes over an hour and a half to reach the market, and the road leads right through Péligre, the site of the dam and, until recently, a military barracks. The soldiers liked to watch the parade of women on Friday mornings. Sometimes they taxed them with haphazardly imposed fines; sometimes they taxed them with flirtatious banter.

Such flirtation is seldom unwelcome, at least to all appearances. In rural Haiti, entrenched poverty made the soldiers – the region's only salaried men – ever so much more attractive. Hunger was again a near-daily occurrence for the Joseph family; the times were as bad as those right after the flooding of the valley. And so when Acéphie's good looks caught the eye of Captain Jacques Honorat, a native of Belladère formerly stationed in Port-au-Prince, she returned his gaze.

Acéphie knew, as did everyone in the area, that Honorat had a wife and children. He was known, in fact, to have more than one regular partner. But Acéphie was taken in by his persistence, and when he went to speak to her parents, a long-term liaison was, from the outset, seriously considered:

What would you have me do? I could tell that the old people were uncomfortable, worried; but they didn't say no. They didn't tell me to stay away from him. I wish they had, but how could they have known? . . . I knew it was a bad idea then, but I just didn't know why. I never dreamed he would give me a bad illness, never! I looked around and saw how poor we all were, how the old people were finished . . . What would you have me do? It was a way out, that's how I saw it.

Acéphie and Honorat were sexual partners only briefly – for less than a month, according to Acéphie. Shortly thereafter, Honorat fell ill with unexplained fevers and kept to the company of his wife in Péligre. As Acéphie was looking for a *moun prensipal* – a "main man" – she tried to forget about the soldier. Still, it was shocking to hear, a few months after they parted, that he was dead.

Acéphie was at a crucial juncture in her life. Returning to school was out of the question. After some casting about, she went to Mirebalais, the nearest town, and began a course in what she euphemistically termed "cooking school." The school – really just an ambitious woman's court-yard – prepared poor girls like Acéphie for their inevitable turn as servants in the city. Indeed, domestic service was one of the rare growth industries in Haiti, and as much as Acéphie's proud mother hated to think of her daughter reduced to servitude, she could offer no viable alternative.

And so Acéphie, at age 22, went off to Port-au-Prince, where she found a job as a housekeeper for a middle-class Haitian woman working for the US embassy. Acéphie's looks and manners kept her out of the backyard, the traditional milieu of Haitian servants: she was designated as the maid who, in addition to cleaning, answered the door and the telephone. Although Acéphie was not paid well – she received US$30 each month – she tried to save a bit of money for her parents and siblings, recalling the hunger gnawing at her home village.

Still looking for a *moun prensipal*, Acéphie began seeing Blanco Nerette, a young man with origins identical to her own: Blanco's parents were also "water refugees" and Acéphie had known him when they were both attending the parochial school in Kay. Blanco had done well for himself, by Kay standards: he chauffeured a small bus between the Central Plateau and the capital. In a setting characterized by an unemployment rate of greater than 60 percent, his job commanded considerable respect. He easily won the attention of Acéphie. They planned to marry, and started pooling their resources.

Acéphie had worked as a maid for over three years when she discovered that she was pregnant. When she told Blanco, he became skittish. Nor was her employer pleased: it is considered unsightly to have a pregnant servant. So Acéphie returned to Kay, where she had a difficult pregnancy. Blanco came to see her once or twice; they had a disagreement, and then she heard nothing from him. Following the birth of her daughter, Acéphie was sapped by repeated infections. She was shortly thereafter diagnosed with AIDS.

Soon Acéphie's life was consumed with managing drenching night sweats and debilitating diarrhea, while attempting to care for her first child. "We both need diapers now," she remarked bitterly towards the end of her life, faced each day not only with diarrhea, but also with a persistent lassitude. As she became more and more gaunt, some villagers suggested that Acéphie was the victim of sorcery. Others recalled her liaison with the soldier and her work as a servant in the city, both locally considered risk factors for AIDS. Acéphie herself knew that she had AIDS, although she was more apt to refer to herself as suffering from a disorder brought on by her work as a servant: "All that ironing, and then opening a refrigerator."

But this is not simply the story of Acéphie and her daughter. There is Jacques Honorat's first wife, who each year grows thinner. After Honorat's death, she found herself desperate, with no means of feeding her five hungry children, two of whom were also ill. Her subsequent union was again with a soldier. Honorat had at least two other partners, both of them poor peasant women, in the Central Plateau. One is HIV positive and has two sickly children. Blanco is still a handsome young man, apparently in good health and plying the roads from Mirebalais to Port-au-Prince. Who knows if he carries the virus? As an attractive man with a paying job, he has plenty of girlfriends.

Nor is this simply the story of those infected with the virus. The pain of Mme. Joseph and Acéphie's twin brother was manifestly intense, but few understood the anguish of her father. Shortly after Acéphie's death, M. Joseph hanged himself.

Chouchou's Story

History shudders, pierced by events of massive public suffering. Memory is haunted, stalked by the ghosts of history's victims, capriciously severed from life in genocides, holocausts, and extermination camps. The cries of the hungry, the shrieks of political prisoners, and the silent voices of the oppressed echo slowly, painfully through daily existence.

Rebecca Chopp, The Praxis of Suffering

Chouchou Louis grew up not far from Kay in another small village in the steep and infertile highlands of Haiti's Central Plateau. He attended primary school for a couple of years but was obliged to drop out when his mother died. Then in his early teens, Chouchou joined his father and an older sister in tending their hillside gardens. In short, there was nothing remarkable about Chouchou's childhood; it was brief and harsh, like most in rural Haiti.

Throughout the 1980s, church activities formed Chouchou's sole distraction. These were hard years for the Haitian poor, beaten down by a family dictatorship well into its third decade. The Duvaliers, father and son, ruled through violence, largely directed at people whose conditions of existence were similar to that of Chouchou Louis. Although many of them tried to flee, often by boat, US policy maintained that Haitian asylum-seekers were "economic refugees." As part of a 1981 agreement between the administrations of Ronald Reagan and Jean-Claude Duvalier, refugees seized on the high seas were summarily returned to Haiti. During the first 10 years of the accord, 24,559 Haitians applied for political asylum in the United States; 8 applications were approved.

A growing Haitian pro-democracy movement led, in February 1986, to the flight of Duvalier. Chouchou Louis must have been about 20 years old when "Baby Doc" fell, and he shortly thereafter acquired a small radio. "All he did," recalled his wife years later, "was work the land, listen to the radio, and go to church." It was on the radio that Chouchou heard about the people who took over after Duvalier fled. Like many in rural Haiti, Chouchou was distressed to hear that power had been handed to the military, led by hardened *duvaliéristes*. It was this army that the US government, which in 1916 had created the modern Haitian army, termed "Haiti's best bet for democracy." In the 18 months following Duvalier's departure, over $200 million in US aid passed through the hands of the junta.

In early 1989, Chouchou moved in with Chantal Brisé, who was pregnant. They were living together when Father Jean-Bertrand Aristide – by then considered the leader of the pro-democracy movement – declared his candidacy for the presidency in the internationally monitored elections of 1990. In December of that year almost 70 percent of the voters chose Father Aristide from a field of 10 presidential candidates.

Like most rural Haitians, Chouchou and Chantal welcomed Aristide's election with great joy. For the first time, the poor – Haiti's overwhelming majority, formerly silent – felt they had someone representing their interests in the presidential palace. These are the reasons why the military coup d'état of September 1991 stirred great anger in the countryside, where the majority of Haitians live. Anger was soon followed by sadness, then fear, as the country's repressive machinery, dismantled during the 7 months of Aristide's tenure, was hastily reassembled under the patronage of the army.

In the month after the coup, Chouchou was sitting in a truck enroute to the town of Hinche. Chouchou offered for the consideration of his fellow passengers what Haitians call a *pwen*, a pointed remark intended to say something other than what it literally means. As they bounced along, he began complaining about the conditions of the roads, observing that, "if things were as they should be, these roads would have been repaired already." One eyewitness later told me that at no point in the commentary was Aristide's name invoked. But Chouchou's complaints were recognized by his fellow passengers as veiled language deploring the coup. Unfortunately for Chouchou, one of the passengers was an out-of-uniform soldier. At the next checkpoint, the soldier had him seized and dragged from the truck. There, a group of soldiers and their lackeys – their *attachés*, to use the epithet then in favor – immediately began beating Chouchou, in front of the other passengers; they continued to beat him as they brought him to the military barracks in Hinche. A scar on his right temple was a souvenir of his stay in Hinche, which lasted several days.

Perhaps the worst after-effect of such episodes of brutality was that, in general, they marked the beginning of persecution, not the end. In rural Haiti, during this time, any scrape with the law (i.e., the military) led to blacklisting. For men like Chouchou, staying out of jail involved keeping the local attachés happy, and he did this by avoiding his home village. But Chouchou lived in fear of a second arrest, his wife later told me, and his fears proved to be well-founded.

On January 22, 1992, Chouchou was visiting his sister when he was arrested by two attachés. No reason was given for the arrest, and Chouchou's sister regarded as ominous the seizure of the young man's watch and radio. He was roughly marched to the nearest military checkpoint, where he was tortured by soldiers and the attachés. One area resident later told us that the prisoner's screams made her children weep with terror.

On January 25, Chouchou was dumped in a ditch to die. The army scarcely took the trouble to circulate the canard that he had stolen some bananas. (The Haitian press, by then thoroughly muzzled, did not even broadcast this false version of events.) Relatives carried Chouchou back to Chantal and their daughter under the cover of night. By early on the morning of January 26, when I arrived, Chouchou was scarcely recognizable. His face, and especially his left temple, was misshapen, swollen, and lacerated; his right temple was also scarred. His mouth was a pool of dark, coagulated blood. His neck was peculiarly swollen, his throat collared with bruises, the traces of a gun butt. His chest and sides were badly bruised, and he had several fractured ribs. His genitals had been mutilated.

That was his front side; presumably, the brunt of the beatings came from behind. Chouchou's back and thighs were striped with deep lash marks. His buttocks were macerated, the skin flayed down to the exposed gluteal muscles. Some of these stigmata appeared to be infected.

Chouchou coughed up more than a liter of blood in his agonal moments. Given his respiratory difficulties and the amount of blood he coughed up, it is likely that the beatings caused him to bleed, slowly at first, then catastrophically, into his lungs. His head injuries had not robbed him of his faculties, although it might have been better for him had they done so. It took Chouchou three days to die.

Explaining versus Making Sense of Suffering

The pain in our shoulder comes
You say, from the damp; and this is also the reason

For the stain on the wall of our flat.
So tell us:
Where does the damp come from?

Bertholt Brecht

Are these stories of suffering emblematic of something other than two tragic and premature deaths? If so, how representative is each of these experiences? Little about Acéphie's story is unique; I have told it in detail because it brings into relief many of the forces constraining not only her options, but those of most Haitian women. Such, in any case, is my opinion after caring for dozens of poor women with AIDS. There is a deadly monotony in their stories: young women – or teenaged girls – who were driven to Port-au-Prince by the lure of an escape from the harshest poverty; once in the city, each worked as a domestic; none managed to find financial security. The women interviewed were straightforward about the nonvoluntary aspect of their sexual activity: in their opinions, they had been driven into unfavorable unions by poverty.[2] Indeed, such testimony should call into question facile notions of "consensual sex."

What about the murder of Chouchou Louis? International human rights groups estimate that more than 3,000 Haitians were killed in the year after the September 1991 coup that overthrew Haiti's first democratically elected government. Nearly all of those killed were civilians who, like Chouchou, fell into the hands of military or paramilitary forces. The vast majority of victims were poor peasants, like Chouchou, or urban slum dwellers. (The figures cited here are conservative estimates; I am quite sure that no journalist or observer ever came to count the body of Chouchou Louis.)

Thus, the agony of Acéphie and Chouchou was, in a sense, "modal" suffering. In Haiti, AIDS and political violence are two leading causes of death among young adults. These afflictions were not the result of accident or of force majeure; they were the consequence, direct or indirect, of human agency. When the Artibonite Valley was flooded, depriving families like the Josephs of their land, a human decision was behind it; when the Haitian army was endowed with money and unfettered power, human decisions were behind that, too. In fact, some of the same decisionmakers may have been involved in both cases.

If bureaucrats and soldiers seemed to have unconstrained sway over the lives of the rural poor, the agency of Acéphie and Chouchou was, correspondingly, curbed at every turn. These grim biographies suggest that the social and economic forces that have helped to shape the AIDS epidemic are, in every sense, the same forces that led to Chouchou's death and to the larger repression in which it was eclipsed. What is more, both were "at risk" of such a fate long before they met the soldiers who altered their destinies. They were both, from the outset, victims of structural violence.

While certain kinds of suffering are readily observable – and the subject of countless films, novels, and poems – structural violence all too often defeats those who would describe it. There are at least three reasons why this is so. First, there is the "exoticization" of suffering as lurid as that endured by Acéphie and Chouchou. The suffering of individuals whose lives and struggles recall our own tends to move us; the suffering of those who are distanced, whether by geography, gender, "race," or culture, is sometimes less affecting.

Second, there is the sheer weight of the suffering, which makes it all the more difficult to render: "Knowledge of suffering cannot be conveyed in pure facts and figures, reportings that objectify the suffering of countless persons. The horror of suffering is not only its immensity but the faces of the anonymous victims who have little voice, let alone rights, in history."[3]

Third, the dynamics and distribution of suffering are still poorly understood. Physicians, when fortunate, can alleviate the suffering of the sick. But explaining its distribution requires more minds, more resources. Case studies of individuals reveal suffering, they tell us what happens to one or many people; but to explain suffering, one must embed individual biography in the larger matrix of culture, history, and political economy.

In short, it is one thing to make sense of extreme suffering – a universal activity, surely – and quite another to explain it. Life experiences such as those of Acéphie and Chouchou – who as Haitians living in poverty shared similar social conditions – must be embedded in ethnography if their representativeness is to be understood. These local understandings are to be embedded, in turn, in the larger-scale historical system of which the fieldwork site is a part. The social and economic forces that dictate life choices in Haiti's Central Plateau affect many millions of individuals, and it is in the context of these global forces that the suffering of individuals receives its appropriate context of interpretation.

Similar insights are central to liberation theology, which takes the suffering of the poor as its central problematic. In *The Praxis of Suffering*, Rebecca Chopp notes that, "In a variety of forms, liberation theology speaks with those who, through their suffering, call into question the meaning and truth of human history."[4] Unlike most previous theologies, and unlike much modern philosophy, liberation theology has attempted to use social analysis to both explain and deplore human suffering. Its key texts bring into relief not merely the suffering of the wretched of the earth, but also the forces that promote that suffering. The theologian Leonardo Boff, in commenting on one of these texts, notes that it "moves immediately to the structural analysis of these forces and denounces the systems, structures, and mechanisms that 'create a situation where the rich get richer at the expense of the poor, who get even poorer.'"[5]

In short, few liberation theologians engage in reflection on suffering without attempting to understand its mechanisms. Theirs is a theology that underlines connections. Robert McAfee Brown has these connections and also the poor in mind when, paraphrasing the Uruguayan Jesuit Juan Luis Segundo, he observes that "the world that is satisfying to us is the same world that is utterly devastating to them."[6] [...]

The Conflation of Structural Violence and Cultural Difference

Awareness of cultural differences has long complicated discussions of human suffering. Some anthropologists have argued that what seem to outside observers to be obvious assaults on dignity may in fact be long-standing cultural institutions highly valued by a society. Often-cited examples range from female circumcision in the Sudan to head-hunting in the Philippines. Such discussions are invariably linked to the concept of cultural relativism, which has a long and checkered history in anthropology. Is every culture a law unto itself and a law unto nothing other than itself? In recent decades, confidence in reflex cultural relativism faltered as anthropologists turned their attention to "complex societies" characterized by extremely inegalitarian social structures. Many found themselves unwilling to condone social inequity merely because it was buttressed by cultural beliefs, no matter how ancient. Cultural relativism was also questioned as a part of a broader critique of anthropology by citizens of the former colonies.

But this rethinking has not yet eroded a tendency, registered in many of the social sciences but perhaps particularly in anthropology, to confuse structural violence with cultural difference. Many are the ethnographies in which poverty and inequality, the end results of a long process of impoverishment, are conflated with "otherness." Very often, such myopia is not really a question of motives, but rather, as Talal Asad has suggested, our "mode of perceiving and objectifying alien societies."[7] Part of the problem may be the ways in which the term "culture" is used. "The idea of culture," explains one authority approvingly in a book on the subject, "places the researcher in a position of equality with his subjects: each 'belongs to a culture.'"[8] The tragedy, of course, is that this equality, however comforting to the researcher, is entirely illusory. Anthropology has usually "studied down" steep gradients of power.

Such illusions suggest an important means by which other misreadings – most notably the conflation of poverty and cultural difference – are sustained. They suggest that the anthropologist and "his" subject, being *from* different cultures, are *of* different worlds and *of* different times. These sorts of misreadings, innocent enough within academia, are finding a more insidious utility within elite culture, which is becoming increasingly *transnational*. Concepts of cultural relativism, and even arguments to reinstate the dignity of different cultures and "races," have been easily assimilated by some of the very agencies that perpetuate extreme suffering. Abuses of cultural concepts are particularly insidious in discussions of suffering in general and of human rights abuses more specifically: cultural difference is one of several forms of essentialism used to explain away assaults on dignity and suffering in general. Practices, including torture, are said to be "in their culture" or "in their nature" – "their" designating either the victims or the perpetrators, or both, as may be expedient.

Such analytic abuses are rarely questioned, even though systemic studies of extreme suffering would suggest that the concept of culture should have an increasingly limited role in explaining the *distribution* of misery. The interpretation of – and justifications for – suffering is usually patterned along cultural lines, but this, I would argue, is another question.

Structural Violence and Extreme Suffering

[...] Leonardo Boff and Clodovis Boff, writing from Brazil, insist on the primacy of the economic:

We have to observe that the socioeconomically oppressed (the poor) do not simply exist *alongside* other oppressed groups, such as blacks, indigenous peoples, women – to take the three major categories in the Third World. No, the "class-oppressed" – the socioeconomically poor – are the infrastructural expression of the process of oppression. The other groups represent "superstructural" expressions of oppression and because of this are deeply conditioned by the infrastructural. It is one thing to be a black taxi-driver, quite another to be a black football idol; it is one thing to be a woman working as a domestic servant, quite another to be the first lady of the land; it is one thing to be an Amerindian thrown off your land, quite another to be an Amerindian owning your own farm.[9]

None of this is to deny the ill effects of sexism or racism, even in the wealthy countries of North America and Europe. The point is merely to call for more fine-grained and systemic analyses of power and privilege in discussions of who is likely to suffer and in what ways.

The capacity to suffer is, clearly, part of being human. But not all suffering is equal, in spite of pernicious and often self-serving identity politics that suggest otherwise. One of the unfortunate sequelae of identity politics has been the obscuring of structural violence, which metes out injuries of vastly different severity. Careful assessment of severity is important, at least to physicians, who must practice triage and referral daily. What suffering needs to be taken care of first and with what resources? It *is* possible to speak of extreme human suffering, and an inordinate share of this sort of pain is currently endured by those living in poverty. Take, for example, illness and premature death, in many places in the world the leading cause of extreme suffering. In a striking departure from previous, staid reports, the World Health Organization now acknowledges that poverty is the world's greatest killer: "Poverty wields its destructive influence at every stage of human life, from the moment of conception to the grave.

It conspires with the most deadly and painful diseases to bring a wretched existence to all those who suffer from it."[10]

As the twentieth century draws to a close, the world's poor are the chief victims of structural violence – a violence which has thus far defied the analysis of many seeking to understand the nature and distribution of extreme suffering. Why might this be so? One answer is that the poor are not only more likely to suffer, they are also more likely to have their suffering silenced. As Chilean theologian Pablo Richard, noting the fall of the Berlin Wall, has warned, "We are aware that another gigantic wall is being constructed in the Third World, to hide the reality of the poor majorities. A wall between the rich and poor is being built, so that poverty does not annoy the powerful and the poor are obliged to die in the silence of history."[11]

The task at hand, if this silence is to be broken, is to identify the forces conspiring to promote suffering, with the understanding that these will be differentially weighted in different settings. In so doing, we stand a chance to discern the *forces motrices* of extreme suffering. A sound analytic purchase on the dynamics and distribution of such affliction is, perhaps, a prerequisite to preventing or, at least, assuaging it. Then, at last, there may be hope of finding a balm in Gilead.

NOTES

1 Jean Weise, "The Interaction of Western and Indigenous Medicine in Haiti in Regard to Tuberculosis," Ph.D. dissertation, Department of Anthropology, University of North Carolina at Chapel Hill, 1971.

2 Paul Farmer, "Culture, Poverty, and the Dynamics of HIV Transmission in Rural Haiti," in Han ten Brummelhuis and Gilbert Herdt, eds., *Culture and Sexual Risk: Anthropological Perspectives on AIDS* (New York: Gordon and Breach, 1995), 3–28.

3 Rebecca Chopp, *The Praxis of Suffering* (Maryknoll, NY: Orbis, 1986), 2.

4 Chopp, *The Praxis of Suffering*, 2. See also the works of Gustavo Gutiérrez, who has written a great deal about the meaning of suffering in the twentieth century: for example Gustavo Gutiérrez, *A Theology of Liberation* (Maryknoll, NY: Orbis, 1973) and Gustavo Gutiérrez, *The Power of the Poor in History* (Maryknoll, NY: Orbis, 1983).

5 From the Puebla document, cited in Paul Farmer, "Medicine and Social Justice: Insights from Liberation Theology," *America* 173(2) (1995): 14.

6 Robert McAfee Brown, *Liberation Theology: An Introductory Guide* (Louisville, KY: Westminster, 1993), 44.

7 Talal Asad, ed., *Anthropology and the Colonial Encounter* (London: Ithaca Press, 1975), 17.

8 Roy Wagner, *The Invention of Culture* (Englewood Cliffs, NJ: Prentice-Hall, 1975), 2.

9 Leonardo Boff and Clodovis Boff, *Introducing Liberation Theology* (Maryknoll, NY: Orbis Books, 1987), 29.

10 World Health Organization, *Bridging the Gaps* (Geneva: World Health Organization, 1995), 5.

11 Cited by Jack Nelson-Pallmeyer, *Brave New World Order: Must We Pledge Allegiance?* (Maryknoll, NY: Orbis, 1992), 14.

35

Suffering Child: An Embodiment of War and Its Aftermath in Post-Sandinista Nicaragua

James Quesada

no hay dolor que dure cien anos,
ni cuerpo que lo resista,
...no hay dolor mas grande que el dolor de ser vivo

there is no pain that lasts a hundred years,
nor a body that will endure it,
...there is no pain greater than the pain of being alive

a Nicaraguan saying

[...] This article examines a child's lived experience of the far-reaching effects of war and its aftermath, endemic poverty, political instability, and despair. This article, however, is more than just about Daniel; it is about his family as well. Yet by focusing on the experience of a young boy, perhaps we can more appreciably understand the consequences of chronic stress and the legacy of violence, endemic deprivation, and protracted uncertainty on individuals and society. Daniel's family includes his mother Maria del Carmen, 33; his sole younger brother Omar, 8; and his stepfather Pablo, 31. Pablo occasionally resides with them, but primarily chooses to stay with his mother who resides nearby. Maria and Pablo are "historic combatants," individuals who participated in the Sandinista insurrection against the dictator Anastasio Somoza prior to the triumph of the Sandinista revolution in 1979. In the last 18 years, their daily lives have been affected by insurrection, revolution, war, trade embargoes, economic collapse, an International Monetary Fund (IMF)-induced shock therapy, hurricanes, homelessness, and unemployment. [...]

Daniel is a small, gangly 10-year-old who is an eloquent witness to the suffering of his family. I analyze Daniel's plight not as a single exceptional case study, but as an example of the predicament that many Nicaraguans endure in face of the Sandinista's loss of political power. The sudden displacement of family homes, unstable family life, poor living conditions, and uncertain futures contribute to the very conditions of family and community disorganization that are pervasive throughout Nicaragua and remain highly visible today.

Family Ties: Maria del Carmen and Daniel

Youth confronts us with the simple truth...
that every individual life is bound up with the whole of human history.

Robert Jay Lifton, *In a Dark Time:*
Images for Survival

[...] I first became acquainted with Daniel and his family from a distance. I had watched from the porch of my rented house, opulent by Nicaraguan standards, the transformation of the mountain upon which Maria del Carmen's home was located. Her house was part of a small hilltop settlement of 8 houses that became a full-fledged barrio of more than 80 ramshackle homes in the space of three months. When I met Maria del Carmen, she was living with her two sons on top of a hill in a dilapidated wooden, cardboard, plastic, and zinc two-room dwelling. She had been a strong, resourceful woman and mother during the Sandinista revolution; since the 1990 Nicaraguan presidential elections, however, she had suffered an abrupt reversal of fortunes. Now unemployed, at times physically ailing and living in near total destitution, she was willing to share the poignancy of her current situation with me. I became a regular visitor to her humble house.

Although Maria del Carmen was often a loud and ebullient individual, this demeanor alternated with one that was more quiet, somber, and gray. And though she never referred to her embodied distress as *nervios* (Lock 1989; Scheper-Hughes 1992: 185), she appeared to be suffering from this condition. I grew familiar with the host of symptoms associated with nervios during my clinical ethnographic work in the local public mental health clinic, and I became increasingly certain that her mood swings and somatic complaints strongly indicated nervios. She seemed to teeter between occasional anger, which appeared to be out of control, and periods of dejection, which were marked by sudden fits of agitation, yelling, or crying. She would rail against individuals, political parties, and organizations. Although these mercurial displays alternated with a more purposeful and steady demeanor, it was not uncommon for Maria to succumb to horrible headaches and general fatigue. She would complain about bodily pains and would be unable to get out of bed. Since it was generally known that I also worked in the mental health clinic, she often solicited my advice and assistance. As I came to know her better, she seemed increasingly on the verge of losing all emotional control.

Maria del Carmen had participated in the war of insurrection that led to the defeat of the Dictator Somoza in 1979. Beginning in 1976, she became a FSLN (Sandinista National Liberation Front) collaborator and combatant. [...]

The transition that followed the defeat of the Sandinistas in the 1990 Presidential elections resulted in changes in property rights (Jonakin 1997:100–101). The former property owner of Maria's house was able to successfully evict her family from their home following his victory in the first national court rulings that allowed former property owners to reclaim their original property. This was particularly traumatizing because their eviction was one of the first forced evictions by authorities to follow the Sandinista electoral defeat. The police actually physically forced them out of their home and threw out all of their personal and household belongings. Now jobless, homeless, and openly humiliated, Maria del Carmen and her family first lived with different friends before having to squat on the large hill northeast of the house where my family and I lived.

Pablo began to drink steadily and their relationship became increasingly estranged. He stayed with his mother who lived nearby and only occasionally gave his wife money, food, or help around the house. Maria was engaged in a daily, sometimes desperate, search for work. At her request, I often gave her aspirin and Tylenol when she came by; she coveted this pharmaceutical to ease her chronic headaches.

When she felt well, she was constantly looking for work. She worked spot jobs as a housecleaner, clothes cleaner, and seamstress, doing almost anything to make ends meet. Although her employment was erratic, she was able to maintain a subsistence minimum by piecing together odd jobs in the informal economic sector. Yet she confided to me her occasional desire to run away and abandon her children. Although she loved her boys, she was extremely troubled by the fact that she did not have consistent work. Often she expressed her doubts about being a good mother. Maria's general presentation of self was as a strong, assertive, and forceful woman. But the more I got to know her it became obvious that her public persona sharply contrasted with her private distress.

I witnessed the considerable love between Maria and her boys. In spite of poor housing, lack of amenities, and low income, there was a palpable sense of "pulling together." Daniel and Omar would dig a ditch around their house to prevent flooding and transforming the dirt-packed floor to mud. They collected fire wood and hauled precious water from a communal spigot a half mile from their home. The boys carried their clothes to a nearby stream where Maria would hand wash them. They showed incredible initiative in scavenging for anything that could be put to use. In spite of their wretched conditions, the entire family appeared, on the whole, to be surviving well. This was Daniel's milieu.

He resided sometimes in respectable inner-city wood and mortar homes, and other times in precariously built wood and plastic shacks with dirt-packed floors. He knew good days and bad days, depending on fortune and weather. He knew intimately dislocation, lack of food, and loss of warmth. He directly experienced the material and social consequences of political conflict and economic warfare. [. . .] Daniel did not share with his mother the glorious memories and the ignoble decline of the revolution (Schirmer 1993). He was often present when I interviewed Maria and he was thoroughly familiar with her life story. Although his experience of life during war and times of economic misery was largely filtered by his mother (Fraser 1983), his experience was not synonymous with hers. His scavenging and persistent angling indicated his resourcefullness in attempting to make things better. Yet he appeared to have no master plan, no long-term goal, and no strong ambition other than to improve his family's immediate situation. [. . .]

Life of War

War is not new to the residents of Matagalpa. It was the site of street fighting and aerial bombardment during the insurrection, and although the threat of direct violence during the contra war took on a new character, fear and insecurity were endemic. Daniel was born in Matagalpa in 1981, the year the contra war (1981–90) began in earnest (Sklar 1988). That year, US President Ronald Reagan allocated funds to train an anti-Sandinista military force, popularly known in Nicaragua as contras or counterrevolutionaries, and initiated a devastating economic blockade against Nicaragua. Given its proximity to the Honduran border to the north and the sparsely populated, tropical Atlantic coastal region to the east, Matagalpa became one of the principal military staging grounds during the war. Because the northern contra forces, the Fuerza

Democratica Nacional (FDN), were concentrated in the rural northern and eastern areas, Matagalpa was thrust into the war and transformed into a Sandinista military garrison town. Helicopters shuttled to and from the constantly shifting war front, transporting fresh troops and supplies, and returning with bodies and battle-worn soliders. I was told repeatedly that it was not uncommon in the 1980s to see military trucks laden with pine coffins, or to stumble across slow-moving funeral processions. [. . .]

The specter of uniformed men and women and funeral processions, in addition to persistent electrical blackouts and periodic shortages of food and goods, contributed to an unsettling hyperawareness of the fact that one resided in the heart of troubled terrain. This was brought home by the fact that the city was encircled by shanty settlements.

The 1980s saw the rise and fall of the Sandinista revolution. this was due in large part to the US government, which sought all along to inflict a total war at the grassroots level (Kornbluh 1988). US policies encouraged disaffected Nicaraguans to organize politically and militarily and to destabilize the Sandinistas, if not to topple them outright (Kornbluh and Bryne 1993). The reverberations of the contra war were felt throughout society and exacted a mixed effect that had real lived consequences for practically all Nicaraguans. As expected, the numerous Nicaraguan investigations (ENVIO 1987; Whitford et al. 1985, 1987, 1988) conducted during the war consistently indicated high levels of anxiety and depression among the general population. But of interest to me was the longer-term effects of the suffering brought about by "low-intensity war" (Kornbluh 1988; Summerfield and Toser 1991). For those who lived close to the war, life could be terrifying. The strategy of this low-intensity warfare was "to paralyze . . . life, to silence individuals and communities, to deny hope that personal struggle could ever bear fruit and to insist that the revolution could not live up to its promises" (Summerfield and Toser 1991: 85). For Maria del Carmen's family, the war resulted in repeated separations between parents and children, continuous shortages of food and goods, rampant inflation, faltering infrastructures, limited life options, and a state of chronic uncertainty.

Being Young in Times of Revolution, War, and Imposed Scarcity

Daniel embodies the degradation, difficulties, and deprivations that his family, his generation, and indeed his nation have endured in his short ten years. Like many other children who have been negatively affected by war and its harsh aftermath, and whose comprehension of the Sandinista revolution and the contra war is largely a memory of physical and emotional hardship, Daniel was ultimately left to make the past and present meaningful on his own (Martin-Baro 1994: 130–5). His loneliness is indicative of the fragility and lack of strong social support systems that buffer or ameliorate the negative effects of chronic instability and uncertainty wrought by war and economic despair. Interviews with Nicaraguan mental health professionals and child care workers who served orphans, runaways, and street kids often included references to the resourcefulness of youth that were in contrast to their sense of profound loneliness and abandonment. While their resourcefulness indicates a will to survive, it has its limits (Fields 1980: 55). Children without adequate social support systems often exhibit prolonged reactions to war, even in its aftermath. These difficulties include sleep problems, pessimism, lack of trust, emotional detachment, and even symptoms of posttraumatic stress disorder. [. . .]

As much as he is able to withstand daily stressors and recurrent crises, Daniel must contend with the constancy and weight of these occurrences. Although the lived experience of these difficulties become to some degree internalized and routinized, the sheer chronicity and burden of these difficulties pose existential dilemmas for children in Nicaragua (Martin-Baro 1994: 130). In the face of "normal abnormality" (Martin-Baro 1994: 132), the conditions experienced by children in the context of war, scarcity, destruction, and lack of food and affection, the options available to act freely are limited. Children must make Manichean choices between picking up arms or running away, resisting or giving in. For children and youth living in war, political instability, and poverty, the results include, among other things, emotional trauma, developmental impairment, and altered moral development (Garbarino et al. 1991: 378). [. . .]

Following the triumph of the revolution in 1979, the Sandinista government proceeded to direct some of its diminished resources to rural areas to help women who were both mothers and workers (Donahue 1986; Garfield and Williams 1992). In 1980, the Sandinista government set up subsidized child development centers (CDIs) in neighborhoods all over the country. The CDIs, which remained in operation for the next 10 years, became one of the Sandinistas' most successful and popular programs. Daniel and his brother attended CDIs most of their lives. Although the Sandinista state strove to establish and maintain child care centers throughout the country, they were unable to provide a sufficient supply of centers to meet the overwhelming demand. Women were left to find "individual solutions . . . which for many meant having to leave [their children] in nondesirable situations . . . " (Smith 1993: 213–14).

In Daniel's case, he was variously cared for by his maternal grandmother, his stepfather's mother, friends of Maria del Carmen, and workers at several CDIs. Although I did not focus on Daniel's upbringing during my fieldwork, I noted that he was often referred to as a resourceful and independent boy who was rarely considered troublesome. On the contrary, he was called *hombrecito* (little man).

Suffering Child

Often the boys came to visit me on their way home from school in the early afternoon. They usually arrived shortly after siesta with the excuse of asking for glasses of water. They often left my house with gifts of food, pencils, or other things for which I suspected they had really come. Daniel did the asking. Sometimes I thought he was rather forward and overly aggressive in his attitude. He had a way of asking for things that was more of a demand than a request, and I sometimes became irritated with him. He was always looking for things that I was either not using or throwing away. One afternoon, after I changed the oil in my car, Daniel asked me for the empty oil cans. As he dutifully cleaned them out, I asked him why he wanted them, and he explained, "oh, I can use them for a lot of things. I can keep water in them, I can make flower pots and make our house look nice. Or I might ask you," he said with a wink, "to keep these in your freezer so to make ice." I ended up sharing part of the freezer compartment with Daniel. His younger brother, on the other hand, rarely spoke and dutifully followed his older brother's lead. He always had a grin on his face, which I came to regard as a mask that disguised what he really felt. I never got as close to Omar as I did to Daniel.

One afternoon, Daniel and Omar came to visit after school. As was their habit, they asked for water. I offered them a piece of birthday cake, which they gladly accepted. As Daniel accompanied me to the kitchen to get dishes and forks, he mentioned quite matter of factly that he felt like dying. I stopped immediately and turned to face him. Daniel displayed neither sadness nor alarm. I asked him to repeat what he had said, and he calmly told me that sometimes he felt like dying. I responded that this was a pretty serious sentiment, and I asked him to explain. We were alone in the kitchen, and Daniel quietly, yet flippantly, told me that everyone would be better off with him dead:

Look at me, I'm all bones anyway, I'm already dying. I'm too small and I've stopped growing and I am another mouth to feed. My mother can't keep taking care of my brother and me, and I can't keep taking care of her. I can't do anything. So it would be better if I just died since that would help everyone.

[. . .] Daniel began to describe how he regularly rationed his meals. His family's daily fare was meager at best. For breakfast they usually had sweetened coffee and tortillas, and the rest of the day they subsisted on *gallo pinto* (mixed rice and beans) with tortilla, which was sometimes accompanied by a piece of *cuajada* (salty dry white cheese). He did not remember the last time he had eaten beef or chicken although he ate eggs approximately once a week. Daniel explained that he routinely served himself small portions while generously serving his mother and brother, assuring them that he had served them all equal portions. He explained that sometimes he hid his food, and when his mother was bedridden, he took his food to her. Daniel gave his brother a tortilla a day because Daniel thought his younger brother was the stronger of the two of them, and he wanted to make sure his brother got enough food. In fact, Omar did appear more robust than his older brother.

Daniel said that he was physically exhausted from not sleeping well. He lay awake trying to think of ways to make money such as shoe shining or selling newspapers. He protected his brother from the leaking roof by moving him or holding up a flap of plastic from the wall whenever it rained. Sometimes he stoically allowed himself to get wet, because he did not want to worry his mother or make her get up and go outside to fix the roof. He engaged in daily improvised rituals of sacrifices to contribute in whatever way he could to keep his family from falling apart. Daniel mentioned that he had thought of running away, but to him that would be too cowardly and a betrayal of his mother and brother. So in the end, he thought it would be best to die. He looked at me squarely and said, raising his arm and pinching the skin of his forearm, "besides, I'm already withering away." [. . .]

Daniel's concern for his mother and brother, as well as the daily rituals of sacrifice he enacted, symbolized his preoccupation with, and sense of responsibility to, the very integrity of his family. As the eldest son, he had already assumed the bearing and burden of the mythic "man of the house." Yet he was unable to fulfill the cultural expectations of this imaginary archetype, given both the concrete limitations of everyday life and the Nicaraguan construction of the "new man." His talk of death suggests that he understood this. Still, he persisted and did what he could. He endured. He engaged in numerous acts and rituals that sought to ease or at least make tolerable the situations in which he and his family found themselves.

On one night, during the rainy season, when a storm had continued unabated for days and threatened to destroy Daniel's home, I spent a couple hours after dark in the driving rain helping them repair their roof. The dirt floor had turned to mud after nearly a third of their roof had blown away. Maria, Pablo, and the boys were completely soaked, muddy, and cold. They worked tirelessly, and when the repair job was completed, it was nearly midnight. Had they not returned to my home afterward for a chance to towel dry and drink something hot, they would have remained wet and cold that night. The next day Daniel returned to my home and asked me to drive him to sites where he would be able to scavenge building materials. As it turned out, he did this on his own initiative. He did not want his mother or brother to know what he was doing; if he failed to find anything, no one would feel bad as a result of dashed expectations.

Such sophisticated reasoning suggests a heightened sense of responsibility, which while commendable, indicates how intensely Daniel was trying to shield his family from pain. He was as inseparable from his mother and brother as he was exposed to the contingencies of a harsh environment. Under a leaking plastic roof, at night, on top of a hill, the wind howling, with no electricity, and a dirt floor that quickly turned to mud, Daniel adopted a stoic stance that allowed him to merely withstand and endure. He still strategized to make everything better for his family. He constantly summoned energy even when there was little left. His body exposed to hunger, pain, the physical elements, and little hope for change, he was still a body charged with social and family responsibility. While he endured the elements collectively with his mother and brother, and may have taken some solace in withstanding the rain, there was little joy in the momentary victory of having preserved his home. What is the price of endurance, particularly when the spectrum of hardships seem unrelenting, indeed chronic, and the immediate social resources to endure and overcome such hardships are stretched too thin? Where could Daniel turn for help? [...]

Daniel's desire to die could be viewed as his last act of selflessness, aid, and protection for his family. Objectively, Daniel is imperiled simply by living under conditions of scarcity that are particularly difficult for older children (McDonald et al. 1994). These conditions of scarcity were socially produced and were not merely the product of a dysfunctional family or maternal neglect. In a society where over 50 percent of the population are unemployed, and the state has withdrawn from a commitment to social welfare (FIDEG 1992; Walker 1997), the negative consequences of these circumstances have immediate and direct effects on people. Daniel was very conscious of his predicament, of his "skin and bones." [...] He was primarily concerned about his body's relation to his family. His was another mouth to feed in the face of chronic scarcity. Giddens has written that "ontological security" (1984) is a secure sense of oneself and the world around one, which can be threatened by social ruptures and chaos. Hence when Daniel's web of meaningful social relationships were threatened by violence, scarcity, rapid change, or uncertainty, his particular knowledge about his

body and others' became insecure (Featherstone 1987). This can result in a Manichean way of perceiving (Shneidman 1982). Perhaps Daniel sometimes saw his dilemma as a condition of his physical body versus the family body. [...]

Daniel's stated desire to die may be a flirtation with the "space of death," which Franco (1992: 112) reminds us is also a space of immortality, communal memory, and connections between generations. Franco, discussing Taussig's use of the space of death, sees it as a site of necessary and ethical struggle in the colonized areas of the world (Taussig 1987). In this regard Daniel's body has been colonized through filial piety and loyalty to the notion of an ideal "new man," and to the struggle not to succumb to the extreme social, economic, and physical duress. The Sandinistas, like other revolutionary cultures, did not consider the limits of sacrifice or the vulnerabilities of their power and rule. Daniel's physical anguish was an ironic expression of revolutionary idealism that was both affirmed and negated by his expressed desire to die. His anguish was further increased by the deliberate and callous post-Sandinista state strategy of selective social neglect. The postrevolutionary administration of Dona Violeta Chamorro imposed a state-crafted and deliberate policy of unequal social sacrifice on those who were historically vulnerable, disempowered, and disorganized. Children, who traditionally rank among the most unprotected of assailable populations, bore the brunt of the suffering that was imposed by the postrevolutionary administrations and US-supported neoliberal structural-adjustment programs of international lending institutions. [...]

The analysis of Daniel's situation provides an opportunity to read clearly the costs children pay for the actions of war and its devastating aftermath, conditions that are often neglected simply because they are not perceived as a direct mortal threat. The fact is, they are.

REFERENCES

Donahue, John. 1986. *The Nicaraguan Revolution in Health: From Somoza to Sandinistas*. South Hadley, MA: Bergin and Garvey.

Envio (Monthly Magazine of Analysis of Central America). 1987. Salud Mental: Atras Quedo el Pasado. *Envio* 6(7): 12–23.

Featherstone, Michael. 1987. Leisure, Symbolic Power and the Life Course. In *Sport, Leisure and Social Relations*. J. Horne, D. Jary, and A. Tomlinson, eds. Pp. 113–38. London: Routledge.

Fideg (Fundacion Internacional Para El Desafio Economico Global). 1992. *El Impacto Diferenciado de Genero de las Politicas de Ajuste Sobre Las Condiciones de Vida en el Area Rural y Concentraciones Urbanas Intermedias*. Feb. 1992. Managua, Nicaragua: Norad.

Fields, Rona. 1980. *Society under Siege: A Psychology of Northern Ireland*. Philadelphia: Temple University Press.

Franco, Jean. 1992. Gender, Death, and Resistance: Facing the Ethical Vacuum. In *Fear at the Edge: State Terror and Resistance in Latin America*. J. E. Corradi et al., eds. Pp. 104–18. Berkeley: University of California Press.

Fraser, Morris. 1983. Childhood and War in Northern Ireland: A Therapeutic Response. Paper presented to the Seminar on Children and War, Siuntio Baths, Finland, March 24–7.

Garbarino, James. 1991. What Children Can Tell Us about Living in Danger. *American Psychologist* 46(4): 376–83.

Garfield, Richard and Glen Williams. 1992. *Health Care in Nicaragua: Primary Care under Changing Regimes*. Oxford: Oxford University Press.

Giddens, Anthony. 1984. *The Constitution of Society*. Cambridge: Polity Press.

Kornbluh, Peter. 1988. Nicaragua: U.S. Proinsurgency Warfare against the Sandinistas. In *Low Intensity Warfare*. M. Klare and P. Kornbluh, eds. Pp. 136–57. New York: Pantheon Books.

——and Malcom Byrne, eds. 1993. *The Iran-Contra Scandal: The Declassified History*. New York: The New Press.

Lock, Margaret. 1989. Words of Fear, Words of Power: Nerves and the Awakening of Political Consciousness. *Medical Anthropology* 2: 79–90.

Martin-Baro, Ignacio. 1994. *Writings for a Liberation Psychology*. A. Aron, tr. Cambridge: Harvard University Press.

McDonald, Mary, Marian Sigman, Michael Espinosa, and Charlotte Neumann. 1994. Impact for a Temporary Food Shortage on Children and Their Mothers. *Child Development* 65(2): 404–15.

Scheper-Hughes, Nancy. 1987. The Cultural Politics of Child Survival. In *Child Survival*. N. Scheper-Hughes, ed. Pp. 1–29. Boston: D. Reidel.

——.1992. *Death without Weeping: The Violence of Everyday Life in Northeast Brazil*. Berkeley: University of California Press.

Schirmer, Jennifer G. 1993. Chile: The Loss of Childhood. In *Surviving beyond Fear: Women, Children and Human Rights in Latin America*. M. Agosin, ed. Pp. 162–7. Fredonia, NY: White Pine Press.

Shneidman, Edwin. 1982. *Voices of Death*. New York: Harper and Row.

Sklar, Holly. 1988. *Washington's War on Nicaragua*. Boston: South End Press.

Smith, Hazel. 1993. *Nicaragua: Self-Determination and Survival*. London: Pluto Press.

Summerfield, D. and L. Toser. 1991. "Low Intensity" War and Mental Trauma in Nicaragua: A Study in a Rural Community. *Medicine and War* 7: 84–99.

Taussig, Michael. 1987. *Shamanism, Colonialism, and the Wild Man: A Study in Terror and Healing*. Chicago: University of Chicago Press.

Walker, Thomas, ed. 1997. *Nicaragua without Illusions: Regime Transition and Structural Adjustment in the 1990s*. Wilmington, DE: Scholarly Resources Books.

Whitford, Jaime, Joan Corea Levy, and Martha Ramirez Largaespada. 1985. *Niveles de Ansiedad y Formas de Manifestacion. Estudio Exploratorio en Algunas Sectores de la Poblacion de Managua*. Managua, Nicaragua: Universidad CentroAmericana (UCA), Facultad de Humanidades, Escuela de Psicologia.

——. 1987. *Niveles de Ansiedad y Formas de Manifestacion. Estudio Realizado en la Cuidades de Matagalpa y Jinotega, Region VI, Nicaragua*. Managua: Impesin (Instituto Medico Psicologico Nicaraguense), UCA (Universidad CentroAmericana).

——. 1988. *Depresion y Ansiedad: Identificacion de "Casos." Estudios Realizado en la Cuidad de Juligalpa, Region V, Nicaragua*. Managua: Impesin, UCA.

36

"The Lower Classes Smell," from *The Road to Wigan Pier*

George Orwell

I was born into what you might describe as the lower-upper-middle class. The upper-middle class, which had its heyday in the 1880s and 1890s, with Kipling as its poet laureate, was a sort of mound of wreckage left behind when the tide of Victorian prosperity receded. Or perhaps it would be better to change the metaphor and describe it not as a mound but as a layer – the layer of society lying between £2,000 and £300 a year: my own family was not far from the bottom. You notice that I define it in terms of money, because that is always the quickest way of making yourself understood. Nevertheless, the essential point about the English class-system is that it is *not* entirely explicable in terms of money. Roughly speaking it is a money-stratification, but it is also interpenetrated by a sort of shadowy caste-system; rather like a jerry-built modern bungalow haunted by medieval ghosts. Hence the fact that the upper-middle class extends or extended to incomes as low as £300 a year – to incomes, that is, much lower than those of merely middle-class people with no social pretensions. Probably there are countries where you can predict a man's opinions from his income, but it is never quite safe to do so in England; you have always got to take his traditions into consideration as well. A naval officer and his grocer very likely have the same income, but they are not equivalent persons and they would only be on the same side in very large issues such as a war or a general strike – possibly not even then.

Of course it is obvious now that the upper-middle class is done for. In every country town in Southern England, not to mention the dreary wastes of Kensington and Earl's Court, those who knew it in the days of its glory, are dying, vaguely embittered by a world which has not behaved as it ought. I never open one of Kipling's books or go into one of the huge dull shops which were once the favourite haunt of the upper-middle class, without thinking "Change and decay in all around I see." But before the war the upper-middle class, though already none too prosperous, still felt sure of itself. Before the war you were either a gentleman or not a gentleman, and if you were a gentleman you struggled to behave as such, whatever your income might be. Between those with £400 a year and those with £2,000 or even £1,000 a year there was a great gulf fixed, but it was a gulf which those with £400 a year did their best to ignore. Probably the distinguishing mark of the upper-middle class was that its traditions were not to any extent commercial, but mainly military, official, and professional. People in this class owned no land, but they felt that they were landowners in the sight of God and kept up a semi-aristocratic outlook by going into the professions and the fighting services rather than into trade. Small boys used to count the plum stones on their plates and foretell their destiny by chanting "Army, Navy, Church, Medicine, Law"; and even of these "Medicine" was faintly inferior to the others and only put in for the sake of symmetry. To belong to this class when you were at the £400 a year level was a queer business, for it meant that your gentility was almost purely theoretical. You lived, so to speak, at two levels simultaneously. Theoretically you knew all about servants and how to tip them, although in practice you had one or, at most, two resident servants. Theoretically you knew how to wear your clothes and how to order a dinner, although in practice you could never afford to go to a decent tailor or a decent restaurant. Theoretically you knew how to shoot and ride, although in practice you had no horses to ride and not an inch of ground to shoot over. It was this that explained the attraction of India (more recently Kenya, Nigeria, etc.) for the lower-upper-middle class. The people who went there as soldiers and officials did not go there to make money, for a soldier or an official does not make money; they went there because in India, with cheap horses, free shooting, and hordes of black servants, it was so easy to play at being a gentleman.

In the kind of shabby-genteel family that I am talking about there is far more *consciousness* of poverty than in any working-class family above the level of the dole. Rent and clothes and school-bills are an unending nightmare, and every luxury, even a glass of beer, is an unwarrantable extravagance. Practically the whole family income goes in keeping up appearances. It is obvious that people of this kind are in an anomalous position, and one might be tempted to write them off as mere exceptions and therefore unimportant. Actually, however, they are or were fairly numerous. Most clergymen and schoolmasters, for instance, nearly all Anglo-Indian officials, a sprinkling of soldiers and sailors and a fair number of professional men and artists, fall into this category. But the real importance of this class is that they are the shock-absorbers of the bourgeoisie. The real bourgeoisie, those in the £2,000 a year class and over, have their money as a thick layer of padding between themselves and the class they plunder; insofar as they are aware of the Lower Orders at all they are aware of them as employees, servants, and tradesmen. But it is quite different for the poor devils lower down who are struggling to live genteel lives on what are virtually working-class incomes. These last are forced into close and, in a sense, intimate contact with the working class, and I suspect it is from them that the traditional upper-class attitude towards "common" people is derived.

And what is this attitude? An attitude of sniggering superiority punctuated by bursts of vicious hatred. Look at any number of *Punch* during the past thirty years. You will find it everywhere taken for granted that a working-class person, as such, is a figure of fun, except at odd moments when he shows signs of being too prosperous, whereupon he ceases to be a figure of fun and becomes a demon. It is no use wasting breath in denouncing this attitude. It is better to consider how it has arisen, and to do that one has got to realize what the working classes look like to those who live among them but have different habits and traditions.

A shabby-genteel family is in much the same position as a family of "poor whites" living in a street where everyone else is a negro. In such circumstances you have got to cling to your gentility because it is the only thing you have; and meanwhile you are hated for your stuck-up-ness and for the accent and manners which stamp you as one of the boss class. I was very young, not much more than six, when I first became aware of class-distinctions. Before that age my chief heroes had generally been working-class people, because they always seemed to do such interesting things, such as being fishermen and blacksmiths and bricklayers. I remember the farm hands on a farm in Cornwall who used to let me ride on the drill when they were sowing turnips and would sometimes catch the ewes and milk them to give me a drink; and the workmen building the new house next door, who let me play with the wet mortar and from whom I first learned the word "b——"; and the plumber up the road with whose children I used to go out bird-nesting. But it was not long before I was forbidden to play with the plumber's children; they were "common" and I was told to keep away from them. This was snobbish, if you like, but it was also necessary, for middle-class people cannot afford to let their children grow up with vulgar accents. So, very early, the working class ceased to be a race of friendly and wonderful beings and became a race of enemies. We realized that they hated us, but we could never understand why, and naturally we set it down to pure, vicious malignity. To me in my early boyhood, to nearly all children of families like mine, "common" people seemed almost subhuman. They had coarse faces, hideous accents and gross manners, they hated everyone who was not like themselves, and if they got half a chance they would insult you in brutal ways. That was our view of them, and though it was false it was understandable. For one must remember that before the war there was much more *overt* class-hatred in England than there is now. In those days you were quite likely to be insulted simply for looking like a member of the upper classes; nowadays, on the other hand, you are more likely to be fawned upon. Anyone over thirty can remember the time when it was impossible for a well-dressed person to walk through a slum street without being hooted at. Whole quarters of big towns were considered unsafe because of "hooligans" (now almost an extinct type), and the London gutter-boy everywhere, with his loud voice and lack of intellectual scruples, could make life a misery for people who considered it beneath their dignity to answer back. A recurrent terror of my holidays, when I was a small boy, was the gangs of "cads" who were liable to set upon you five or ten to one. In term time, on the other hand, it was we who were in the majority and the "cads" who were oppressed; I remember a couple of savage mass-battles in the cold winter of 1916–17. And this tradition of open hostility between upper and lower class had apparently been the same for at least a century past. A typical joke in *Punch* in the 1860s is a picture of a small, nervous-looking gentleman riding through a slum street and a crowd of street-boys closing in on him with shouts of "'Ere comes a swell! Let's frighten 'is 'oss!" Just fancy the street boys trying to frighten his horse now! They would be much likelier to hang round him in vague hopes of a tip. During the past dozen years the English working class have grown servile with a rather horrifying rapidity. It was bound to happen, for the frightful weapon of unemployment has cowed them. Before the war their economic position was comparatively strong, for though there was no dole to fall back upon, there was not much unemployment, and the power of the boss class was not so obvious as it is now. A man did not see ruin staring him in the face every time he cheeked a "toff," and naturally he did cheek a "toff" whenever it seemed safe to do so. G. J. Renier, in his book on Oscar Wilde, points out that the strange, obscene bursts of popular fury which followed the Wilde trial were essentially social in character. The London mob had caught

a member of the upper classes on the hop, and they took care to keep him hopping. All this was natural and even proper. If you treat people as the English working class have been treated during the past two centuries, you must expect them to resent it. On the other hand the children of shabby-genteel families could not be blamed if they grew up with a hatred of the working class, typified for them by prowling gangs of "cads."

But there was another and more serious difficulty. Here you come to the real secret of class distinctions in the West – the real reason why a European of bourgeois upbringing, even when he calls himself a Communist, cannot without a hard effort think of a working man as his equal. It is summed up in four frightful words which people nowadays are chary of uttering, but which were bandied about quite freely in my childhood. The words were: The lower classes smell.

That was what we were taught – *the lower classes smell*. And here, obviously, you are at an impassable barrier. For no feeling of like or dislike is quite so fundamental as a *physical* feeling. Race-hatred, religious hatred, differences of education, of temperament, of intellect, even differences of moral code, can be got over; but physical repulsion cannot. You can have an affection for a murderer or a sodomite, but you cannot have an affection for a man whose breath stinks – habitually stinks, I mean. However well you may wish him, however much you may admire his mind and character, if his breath stinks he is horrible and in your heart of hearts you will hate him. It may not greatly matter if the average middle-class person is brought up to believe that the working classes are ignorant, lazy, drunken, boorish, and dishonest; it is when he is brought up to believe that they are dirty that the harm is done. And in my childhood we *were* brought up to believe that they were dirty. Very early in life you acquired the idea that there was something subtly repulsive about a working-class body; you would not get nearer to it than you could help. You watched a great sweaty navvy walking down the road with his pick over his shoulder; you looked at his discolored shirt and his corduroy trousers stiff with the dirt of a decade; you thought of those nests and layers of greasy rags below, and, under all, the unwashed body, brown all over (that was how I used to imagine it), with its strong, bacon-like reek. You watched a tramp taking off his boots in a ditch – ugh ! It did not seriously occur to you that the tramp might not enjoy having black feet. And even "lower-class" people whom you knew to be quite clean – servants, for instance – were faintly unappetizing. The smell of their sweat, the very texture of their skins, were mysteriously different from yours.

Everyone who has grown up pronouncing his aitches and in a house with a bathroom and one servant is likely to have grown up with these feelings; hence the chasmic, impassable quality of class-distinctions in the West. It is queer how seldom this is admitted. At the moment I can think of only one book where it is set forth without humbug, and that is Mr. Somerset Maugham's *On a Chinese Screen*. Mr. Maugham describes a high Chinese official arriving at a wayside inn and blustering and calling everybody names in order to impress upon them that he is a supreme dignitary and they are only worms. Five minutes later, having asserted his dignity in the way he thinks proper, he is eating his dinner in perfect amity with the baggage coolies. As an official he feels that he has got to make his presence felt, but he has no feeling that the coolies are of different clay from himself. I have observed countless similar scenes in Burma. Among Mongolians – among all Asiatics, for all I know – there is a sort of natural equality, an easy intimacy between man and man, which is simply unthinkable in the West. Mr. Maugham adds:

"In the West we are divided from our fellows by our sense of smell. The working man is our master, inclined to rule us with an iron hand, but it cannot be denied that he stinks: none can wonder at it, for a bath in the dawn when you have to hurry to your work before the factory bell rings is no pleasant thing, nor does heavy labour tend to sweetness; and you do not change your linen more than you can help when the week's washing must be done by a sharp-tongued wife. I do not blame the working man because he stinks, but stink he does. It makes social intercourse difficult to persons of sensitive nostril. The matutinal tub divides the classes more effectually than birth, wealth or education."

37

US Inner-city Apartheid: The Contours of Structural and Interpersonal Violence

Philippe Bourgois

> The tradition of the oppressed teaches us that the "state of emergency" in which we live is not the exception but the rule ... it is our task to bring about a real state of emergency ...
>
> Walter Benjamin 1968 [1940]: 257

I did not run fast enough out the door of the video arcade crackhouse to avoid hearing the look-out's baseball bat thud twice against a customer's skull. I had misjudged the harsh words Caesar, the look-out, had been exchanging with a drug-intoxicated customer to be the aggressive, but ultimately playful, posturing that is characteristic of much male interaction on the street. Pausing on the curb in front of the crackhouse, I tried to decide from the continued sound of scuffling inside whether or not I should call for medical emergency. Reassured when I saw the beaten young man crawl out the door amidst a parting barrage of kicks and howling laughter, I walked two doors down the block to the tenement where I was living at the time in the primarily Puerto Rican neighborhood of East Harlem, New York. Angry, scared, and disgusted by the violence committed by my crack-dealer friends, I ended my fieldwork early that night and tried to recover from my rushing adrenaline by going upstairs and putting my new-born son to sleep.

The following evening, I forced myself to return to the crackhouse where I was spending much of my time conducting research for a book on inner-city poverty and social marginalization (Bourgois 1995). I rebuked Caesar for his "overreaction" to the obnoxious customer the night before. Caesar was only too pleased to engage me in a playful argument:

Nah, Felipe, you just don't understand. It's not good to be too sweet sometimes to people, man, because they're just gonna take advantage of you.

That dude was talking shit for a long time, about how we weak; how he control the block; and how he can do whatever he wants.

I mean, we were trying to take it calm like, until he starts talkin' this'n'that, about how he gonna drop a dime on us [report us to the police].

That's when I grabbed the bat – I looked at the axe that we keep behind the Pac-Man but then I said, "No; I want something that's going to be short and compact. I only gotta swing a short distance to clock him.

[Now shouting out the video arcade doorway for anyone who might be passing by on the sidewalk outside to hear] You don't control nothin', because we rocked your bootie. Ha! Ha! Ha!

[Turning back to me] When you ran out the door Felipe. You missed it. I had gotten wild.

You see, Felipe, you can't be allowing people to push you around in this neighborhood, or else you get that reputation, like: "That homeboy's soft."

Primo, the manager of the crackhouse, further confirmed Caesar's story and raised the credibility of his violent persona by noting with a chuckle that he had only barely managed to subdue Caesar after the second blow of the baseball bat to keep Caesar from killing the offending customer while he lay semiconscious on the floor.

Violence as Cultural Capital

Most readers might interpret Caesar's behavior and public rantings and ravings to be those of a dysfunctional antisocial psychopath. In the context of the underground economy, however, Caesar's braggadocio celebration of masculine violence is good public relations. Periodic public displays of aggression are crucial to his professional credibility. The French sociologist Pierre Bourdieu would identify them as representing valuable symbolic and cultural capital in the field of power defined by the drug economy within inner-city street culture (Bourdieu and Wacquant 1992). Caesar's reputation for violence ensures his long-term job security. When Caesar shouted his violent story out the door of the crackhouse for everyone in the vicinity to hear, he was not bragging idly or dangerously. On the contrary, he was advertising his effectiveness as a look-out, and confirming his capacity for maintaining order at his work site. Another side benefit that Caesar derives from his inability to control his underlying rages is a lifelong monthly Social Security Insurance check for being – as he puts it – "a certified nut case." He periodically reconfirms his emotional disability by occasional suicide attempts.

In short, at age 19, Caesar's brutality has allowed him to mature into an effective career as crackhouse look-out. Aside from providing him with what he considers to be a decent income, it also allows him on a personal and emotional level to overcome the terrified vulnerability he endured growing up in East Harlem. Born to a 16-year-old heroin addict, he was raised by a grandmother who beat him regularly, but whom he loved dearly. Sent to reform school for striking a teacher with a chair, Caesar admitted,

I used to cry every day; be a big sucker. I was thinking suicide. I missed my moms. I mean 'buela [Granma] – you've met her.

Plus I was a little kid back then – like about 12 or 13 – and I'd get BEAT down by other kids and shit. I was getting my ass kicked. I used to get hurt.

It was a nasty reform school. I used to see the counselors holding down the kids naked outside in the snow.

Being smart and precocious Caesar soon adapted to the institutionalized violence of his school and developed the skills that eventually allowed him to excel in the underground economy:

So then, I just learned. I used to fight so wild that they wouldn't bother me for awhile. I would go real crazy! Real crazy, every time I would fight. Like I would pick up a chair or a pencil or something and really mess them up. So they'd think I was wild and real crazy.

I mean, I always got into fights. Even if I lost, I always started fights. That let me relax more, because after that nobody messed with me.

Anthropological Approaches to Poverty and the Inner City

Caesar and his immediate supervisor, Primo, were merely two members out of a network of some 25 Puerto Rican retail crack sellers who I befriended in the over four years that I lived and worked in East Harlem at the height of what is now referred to as the "height of the US crack epidemic," extending roughly from 1985 to 1991.

Before even being able to initiate my research formally, I had to confront the overwhelming reality of racial- and class-based segregation in urban America. Initially, it felt as if my white skin signaled the terminal stage of a contagious disease sowing havoc in its path. Busy street corners emptied amidst a hail of whistles whenever I approached as nervous drug dealers scattered in front of me, certain that I was an undercover narcotics agent. Conversely, the police made it clear to me that I was violating unconscious apartheid laws by throwing me spread-eagled against building walls to search me for weapons and drugs. From their perspective, the only reason for a "white boy" to be in the neighborhood after dark was to buy drugs. As a matter of fact, the first time the police stopped me, I naively tried to explain to them in a polite voice that I was an anthropologist studying social marginalization. Convinced I was making fun of them, they showered me with a litany of curses and threats, while escorting me to the nearest bus stop and ordering me to leave East Harlem: "and go buy your drugs in a white neighborhood ya' dirty motherfucka!"

Historically, inner-city poverty research has been more successful at reflecting the biases of an investigator's society than at analyzing the experience of poverty or documenting the structural violence of race and class apartheid. The state of poverty and social marginalization research in any given country emerges almost as a litmus for gauging contemporary social attitudes towards inequality and social welfare. This is particularly true in the United States, where discussions of poverty and interpersonal violence almost immediately become polarized around moralistic value judgments about individual self-worth, and frequently degenerate into stereotyped conceptions of race. In the final analysis, most people in the United States – rich and poor alike – believe in the Horatio Alger myth of going from rags to riches. They are also intensely moralistic about issues of wealth; perhaps this stems from their Puritanical/Calvinist heritage. I suspect that even progressive leftist academics in the United States sometimes secretly worry that the poor may actually deserve their fate. This may explain why they often feel compelled to portray the inner city in an artificially positive manner that is not only unrealistic but is also theoretically and analytically flawed (see critique by Wacquant 2002). The result is that the damage wreaked by structural violence on the intimate lives of the poor is minimized.

When I moved into East Harlem, I was determined to avoid psychological reductionist and cultural essentialist analyses that blame victims. I was determined to focus instead on structural inequality. At the same time, I wanted to document the full force of structural violence by revealing the ways oppression is painfully internalized and becomes expressed as what Nancy Scheper-Hughes (1992) calls "the violence of everyday life" among the persistently poor. Striving to develop a political economy perspective that takes culture and gender seriously, and which also recognizes the link between intimate individual actions and social/ structural determination, I focus on how an oppositional street culture of resistance to exploitation and social marginalization is contradictorily self-destructive to its participants. In fact, street dealers, addicts, and criminals become the local agents administering the destruction of their surrounding community. On a daily level they perpetrate interpersonal violence, usually against their friends and loved ones, as well as against themselves in the form of substance abuse. They frequently engage in more instrumental criminal and delinquency violence to control the drug trade or to steal from the elderly and the weak. Through this everyday interpersonal and criminal violence, they help spawn what the anthropologist Michael Taussig (1984 and Chapter 2) has referred to as a "culture of terror" that exaggerates the impetus of its own horror and confounds discourse. These cultures of terror can be understood as forming what the holocaust survivor Primo Levi (Chapter 8) calls "the gray zone" where moral distinctions between victims and perpetrators lose their meaning under the not necessarily logical practices of everyday violence that have been institutionalized by an oppressive enemy. As a result, on the intimate level the violence is administered as much by the victims as it is by the powerful. Inhabitants of the gray zone are condemned to a dehumanizing rat's-nest struggle for personal advantage.

The Dollars and Sense of Drugs

In the United States during the late twentieth century the crack/cocaine and heroin industries were the only dynamically growing equal-opportunity employers for inner-city men. Furthermore, this multibillion-dollar economy was located right in the neighborhoods where youth with no realistic access to upward mobility in the legal economy resided.

Just on the block where I lived, for example, many millions of dollars of trade was taking place, all within sight of the youths growing up in squalid tenements and decrepit housing projects. Drug dealing in the underground economy offers youths a career with real possibilities of upward mobility. Like most other people in the United States, drug dealers are merely scrambling to obtain their "piece of the American pie" as fast as possible. In fact, in their pursuit of success they are following the minute details of the classical Yankee model for upward mobility: up-by-the-bootstraps via private entrepreneurship. Perversely, they are the ultimate rugged individualists braving an unpredictable frontier where fortune, fame, and destruction are all just around the corner – and where competitors are ruthlessly hunted down and shot.

Although drug dealers represent only a small minority of the residents in any given inner-city neighborhood they too often manage to set the tone for public life through their combination of expressive violence and conspicuous consumption of the prestigious commodities of youth culture from clothing to cars to jewelry. They force local residents, especially women, the elderly, and the young, to live in fear of being assaulted or mugged. Most importantly, on a daily basis, the street-level drug dealers offer a persuasive, even if violent and self-destructive, alternative lifestyle – what I call street culture – to the youths growing up around them. The drug economy is the material base for an especially violent version of street culture. Its multi-billion-dollar expansion in the late twentieth and early twenty-first centuries unconsciously rendered street culture that much more appealing and fashionable to youths excluded from the legal economy.

On a subtler level, street culture is more than economic desperation or greediness. It is also a search for dignity and a refusal to accept the marginalization that mainstream society imposes on children who grow up in the inner city. As was noted earlier, it can be understood as a culture of opposition – if not resistance – to economic exploitation and cultural denigration. Concretely, this takes the form of refusing low wages, poor working conditions, and racism, and of celebrating marginalization as a badge of pride – even if it is ultimately self-destructive.

History and Political Economy

Any understanding of the violence of street culture in the inner city needs to be placed in its historical and structural context lest it serve to confirm racist stereotypes and psychological-reductionist interpretations that blame victims. Indeed, that is one of the weaknesses of ethnographic accounts of violence and poverty: they sometimes degenerate into voyeuristic constructions of a dehumanized, sensationalized "other" constructed in a political and economic vacuum. Upon closer examination, one can discern that the drug dealers' celebration of unemployment, crime, and substance abuse is integrally related to labor-market forces and historical developments – and even international political confrontations – well beyond their control.

Most fundamentally, in the case of the Puerto Rican crack dealers I befriended, the unfortunate strategic geopolitical location of the island of Puerto Rico in the Caribbean has always made it a military prize for world superpowers, resulting in a particularly distorted legacy of economic and political development. This was as true under Spanish colonialism as it is under the contemporary United States-sponsored political control of the territory. An artifice of the Cold War to thwart the influence of neighboring Cuba, Puerto Rico continued to bear the ambiguous status of "Free Associated Commonwealth" in the 2000s. Puerto Ricans who remained on their native island were forbidden from voting in Federal elections, despite being subject to US military selective service. Soon after the US marines invaded the island in 1898, the economy was taken over by US agro-export corporations and Puerto Rico underwent one of the most rapid and dislocating economic transformations that any Third World nation has ever undergone in modern history. To add insult to injury in the post-Second World War decades, in an attempt to upstage the Cuban state-run socialist experiment, the United States dubbed Puerto Rico's development strategy "Operation Bootstrap" and declared it to be a magnificent success of free-market investment incentives. Perhaps the best index of the human failure of Puerto Rico's economic model, however, is provided by the fact that between a third and half of the island's population have been forced to leave their native island to seek work and sustenance abroad since the late 1940s. More Puerto Ricans live outside Puerto Rico today than inside. Like all new immigrants arriving in the United States throughout history, Puerto Ricans have been confronted by racism and cultural humiliation. This is exacerbated by the phenotypical fact that, unlike the Irish, the Jews, and the Italians who arrived in New York City before them, most Puerto Ricans do not have white skin.

In other words, New York-born Puerto Ricans are the descendants of an uprooted people in the midst of a marathon sprint through economic history propelled by *real politik* forces rather than by humanitarian or even by any straightforward economic logic. In diverse permutations, over the past two or three generations their parents and grandparents went: 1) from semi-subsistence peasants on private hillside plots or local haciendas; 2) to agricultural laborers on foreign-owned, capital-intensive agro-export tropical plantations; 3) to factory workers in export-platform shantytowns; 4) to sweatshop workers in New York City ghetto tenements; 5) to service-sector employees in high-rise inner-city housing projects. Over half of those who remained on the island at the turn of the twenty-first century were so impoverished that they qualified for food stamps. Those who made it to New York City endured the highest family poverty rates of all ethnic groups in the nation, except for Native Americans. These are the contexts of structural violence that promote everyday violence and cultures of terror. They create the backdrop for the gray zone and poison intimate relations.

From Manufacturing to Service and the Crack Alternative

The Puerto Rican experience in New York City has been further exacerbated by the fact that most Puerto Ricans arrived on the US mainland in the post-Second World War period in search of factory work precisely at the historical moment when those kinds of jobs were leaving US metropolitan areas. Over the past three decades, multinational corporations have restructured the global economy by moving their factory production facilities overseas to countries with lower labor costs. The personal disruption of living through the structural transformation of New York's economy as an entry-level laborer was clearly articulated by the crack dealers in their life history tape recordings.

With the replacement of manufacturing jobs by service-sector employment in New York's expanded corporate finance-driven economy, the fastest growing niche for high school drop-outs, or even college graduates, is office support work in the administrative headquarters of the multinational corporations that have moved their production plants overseas. The problem, of course, is that the oppositional street identity that is so effective and appealing in the burgeoning underground economy does not allow for the humble, obedient social interaction that professional office workers demand from their subordinates.

Obedience to the norms of high-rise office corridor culture is interpreted as overwhelmingly humiliating by street culture standards – especially for males. On the street, the trauma of experiencing a threat to one's personal dignity was frozen linguistically in the commonly used phrase "to diss," which is short for "to disrespect." I did not have to dig deeply to obtain stories of deep humiliation due to the loss of personal and cultural autonomy experienced by the dealers in their previous bouts of service-sector employment.

Leroy, a crack dealer who operated his own successful independent sales point in the neighborhood, for example, quit his former job as a messenger when he was humiliated by a white woman who fled from him shrieking down the hallway of a high-rise office building where he was delivering a package. He had ridden in the elevator with the frightened woman and, coincidentally, had stepped off on the same floor as she to make a delivery. Worse yet, he had been trying to act as a debonair man at the time, allowing her to step off the elevator first. In fact, I suspect that he had been somewhat unsettled by the taboo presence of a lone white woman in such close quarters.

She went in the elevator first, but then she just waits there to see what floor I press.

She's playing like she don't know what floor she wants to go to, because she wants to wait for me to press my floor. And I'm standing there and I forgot to press the button.

I'm thinking about something else – don't know what was the matter with me. And she's thinking like, "He's not pressing the button; I guess he's following me!"

Leroy struggles to understand the terror that his dark skin inspires in white office workers:

It's happened before. I mean after awhile you become immune to it. Well, when it first happens, it like bugs you, "That's messed up; how they just judge you."

But I understand a lot of them. How should I say it? A lot of white people ... [looking nervously at me] I mean Caucasian people [flustered, putting his hand gently on my shoulder]. If I say white, don't get offended, Felipe.

But those other white people they never even experienced Puerto Rican or black people. So automatically they think something wrong with you. Or you know, they think you out to rob them or something.

It irks me; like, you know, it clicks my mind; makes me want to write a [rap] rhyme. I always write it down.

Of course, by retreating back into his inner-city community to become a crack dealer, Leroy protects himself from having to confront face-to-face these dimensions of class, racial, and gender humiliation.

Polarization around Gender

In addition to their obvious racialized tenor, service-sector confrontations also include a tense gender dynamic. Most of the supervisors at the lowest levels of the service sector are women, and street culture ridicules males who accept public subordination across gender lines. Typically, in their angrier memories of disrespect at work, many of the male crack dealers referred to their female bosses in explicitly sexist language, often insulting their body parts, and dismissing them with street slang's sexualized curses. They also specifically described themselves and the other males around them at work as effeminate.

[Caesar:] I lasted in the mail room for like eight months at this advertising agency that works with pharmaceutical stuff. They used to trust me.

But I had a prejudiced boss. She was a ho' [prostitute]. She was white. I had to take a lot of crap from that fat, ugly ho', and be a wimp.

I didn't like it but I kept on working, because... [shrugging] you don't want to mess up the relationship. So you just be a punk.

Oh my God! I hated that head supervisor. That ho' was REALLY nasty. She got her rocks off on firing people, man. You can see that on her face, boy. She made this one guy that worked with me cry – and beg for his job back.

I used to look at her and want to kill her; wanted to burn her. She used to live in a little trailer thing, I used to want to catch her and – I used to think of all the most miserable shit to do to her.

This structural workplace confrontation polarizing relations between young inner-city men and white-collar upwardly mobile women parallels another profound transformation in traditional gender power relations occurring within working-poor immigrant families. The loss of decently paid factory jobs that provide union family benefits for health and retirement makes it increasingly impossible for men to fulfill old-fashioned patriarchal dreams of being an omnipotent provider for a wife and several children. At the same time, dramatic increases in labor-force participation among Puerto Rican women, as well as the broader cultural redefinition of increased individual rights and autonomy for women occurring throughout all levels of US society since the late 1960s, has thrown into crisis the traditional family model of the conjugal household dominated by an authoritarian man.

Males, however, were not accepting the new rights and roles that women have been carving out for themselves. Instead, they attempted to reassert violently their grandfather's lost autocratic control over their households and over public space. This was exacerbated in the inner-city Puerto Rican case by the persistence of a rural-based memory of large, male-dominated farming households "blessed" with numerous children. Males who were no longer effective heads of households often experienced the rapid historical structural transformations of their generation as a dramatic assault on their sense of masculine dignity.

In the worst-case scenario, as males became impotent economic failures in the service economy, they lashed out against the women and children they could no longer support economically or control ideologically. Concretely, this took the form of fists in the face at home and gang rape in the crackhouse. For example, when Jackie, the 12-year-old daughter of a friend of the crack dealers was gang raped by her boyfriend's best friends, Primo and Caesar criticized the girl for "being a hole out there." They assigned no blame to the rapists and instead hoped Jackie had "learned her lesson," dismissing her with the brutal comment "her pussy itched and it got scratched." When I argued with them that Jackie had been raped, Primo argued back patiently:

Nah Felipe, it looked'ed like she knew what she was doing, 'cause the way I see it, she's always in the window, calling guys from the block.

Jackie wants to be hanging out; she want to be in the street. Besides Jackie's cooling out. She's not like, acting like a victim.

Caesar erased any recognition of the violence done to the child, by interrupting Primo, "What can you do if she fucked out there, and she liked'ed it?" They then went on to blame the girl's rape on her mother, who was one of the few women crack dealers in their network, for being out in the street like a man and even for enjoying sex too much. Ultimately, the women ended up turning their violence upon one another instead of against the rapists. Jackie's mother assaulted the mother of the boyfriend who had engineered Jackie's rape. They left the rapist son completely out of the picture and fought amongst mothers hurling patriarchal insults at one another:

Jackie's mom bashed the boy's moms in the mouth, 'cause she had said, "Your daughter's a ho'."

And Jackie's mom busted her in the lip.

The other mother said, "OK. I'm going to go bring my daughter down, so you can fight me and fight my daughter, too."

This particular incident offers a classic illustration of what Pierre Bourdieu (see Chapter 42, this volume) would call the "symbolic violence of masculine domination," whereby victims actively misrecognize and thereby reproduce and naturalize the power relations destroying their lives.

In Challenge of a Solution

Of all the industrialized nations, the United States is the most extreme with respect to income inequality and ethnic segregation. At the turn of the twenty-first century, only Russia and Rwanda imprisoned larger proportions of their populations than the United States (see Wacquant's Chapter 39, below). No other wealthy industrialized country came close to having such a large proportion of its citizens living below the poverty line.

The inner city represents the United States' greatest domestic failing. The illogical size and cost of its prison industrial complex hangs like an albatross cross on "the land of the free and the home of the brave." The violence of the inner city also dangles like a Damocles sword over the larger society, condemning its population to murder rates that were 4 to 9 times higher than those of comparable industrial nations. This cross and sword, however, remain safely ensconced because the drug dealers, addicts, and street criminals internalize their rage and desperation, converting it into an interpersonal everyday violence that primarily harms them and their loved ones. They direct their brutality against themselves and their immediate community, rather than against their structural oppression. Worse yet, they succumb to symbolic violence by not only failing to see the structural dynamics oppressing them, but by actually blaming themselves for their failure to achieve the American Dream. The everyday interpersonal violence embroiling them blinds them to the racism, economic exploitation, and iatrogenic public policy that sets the stage for their gray zone. Instead, they are forced to secretly suspect that they may be morally – if not culturally, or worse yet, racially – inferior to the wealthy, white world, and that they thereby deserve to be poor and to live in the segregated squalor of the inner city.

There are no simple, technocratic formulas for implementing the public policies that might dismantle US inner-city apartheid and instead provide equitable access to shelter, employment, sustenance, and health instead of easy access to long-term incarceration. Anthropologists, because of their participant-observation methods and their culturally relative sensibilities, can play an important role in fostering a public debate over the human cost of poverty and racism, as well as the nefarious forms of violence that reproduce inequality. The challenge is clearly in front of us. Do we have the intellectual and political energy to confront the gray zone of the US inner city? Can we write against the culture of terror that has normalized the state of emergency?

REFERENCES

Benjamin, Walter. 1968 [1940]. *Illuminations: Essays and Reflections*, ed. Hannah Arendt. New York: Harcourt, Brace & World.

Bourdieu, Pierre and Loïc Wacquant. 1992. *An Invitation to Reflexive Sociology*. Chicago: University of Chicago Press.

Bourgois, Philippe. 1995. *In Search of Respect: Selling Crack in El Barrio*. Cambridge: Cambridge University Press.

Scheper-Hughes, Nancy. 1992. *Death Without Weeping: The Violence of Everyday Life in Brazil*. Berkeley: University of California Press.

Taussig, Michael. 1984. "Culture of Terror – Space of Death: Roger Casement's Putumayo Report and the Explanation of Torture." *Comparative Studies in Society and History* 26(3): 467–97.

Wacquant, Loïc. 2002. "Scrutinizing the Street: Poverty, Morality, and the Pitfalls of Urban Ethnography." *American Journal of Sociology* 107(6): 1468–1532.

38

Denaturalizing Disaster: A Social Autopsy of the 1995 Chicago Heat Wave

Eric Klinenberg

It's hot. It's very hot. We all have our little problems but let's not blow it out of proportion... We go to extremes in Chicago. And that's why people like Chicago. We go to extremes.

Chicago Mayor Richard M. Daley

During my residence in England, at least twenty or thirty persons have died of simple starvation under the most revolting circumstances, and a jury has rarely been found possessed of the courage to speak the truth in the matter... The bourgeoisie dare not speak the truth in these cases, for it would speak its own condemnation... The English working men call this social murder, and accuse our whole society of perpetrating this crime perpetually.

Frederick Engels, *The Condition of the Working Class in England*

On June 30, 1995, the front page of *Morbidity and Mortality Weekly Report*, a journal of the Centers for Disease Control and the US Department of Health and Human Services, featured a report attributing 5,379 American deaths in the 13 years between 1979 and 1992 to excessive heat. Deaths from the heat, the journal concluded, "are readily preventable." Public health experts know the risk factors associated with heat related illness and mortality as well as the procedures responsible parties can take to reduce them. The report lists this information and advises local officials to use it when conditions warrant intervention.[1]

Less than two weeks later an unusual weather system hit Chicago with one of the most severe heat waves in its recorded history. Temperatures reached 106°F; the heat index, or experienced heat, climbed to 120°F: uncommonly "high lows" (daily low temperatures that were them-

selves dangerously high), sparse cloud cover, and a dearth of cooling winds kept the city broiling, without relief, for a full week.[2] Although baseline temperatures were slightly less hot than some of Chicago's heat waves from earlier summers, the combination of these climatic conditions posed a serious threat to the health of the metropolitan community.

Chicago was totally unprepared for this attack of the elements. The heat turned deadly on July 13, and local media stepped up their coverage of the morbid outcome the next day, when two toddlers suffocated after the director of their daycare center inadvertently left them locked inside her truck for hours at a tempeature of 190°F. These deaths initiated a week of suffering so massive that many residents and city officials refused to comprehend or accept that it had happened. By the end of the week, though, few could deny that the city had witnessed a disaster of historical proportion: medical examiners confirmed that over 500 Chicagoans had died directly from the heat, public health workers reported over 700 deaths in excess of the weekly average,[3] and hospitals registered thousands of visits for weather-related problems.

What no one has established, however, is that the processes through which Chicagoans lost their lives followed the entrenched logic of social and spatial division that governs the metropolis.[4] Journalistically constructed and conventionally remembered as the city's most deadly natural disaster, the destructive 1995 heat wave was, in fact, a sign and symptom of the new and dangerous forms of marginality and neglect endemic to contemporary American big cities and notably severe in Chicago, a structurally determined catastrophe for which sociological analysis illuminates not simply the obvious relationship between poverty and suffering, but some of the institutional and social mechanisms upon which extreme forms of American insecurity are built. The Chicago disaster reveals several forms of precariousness as of yet unmentioned or underdeveloped in the emerging debate on the new urban poverty,[5] including the literal social isolation of poor seniors, particularly in the city's most violent areas; the degradation of and rising conflict in urban hotel residences, which constitute a large but generally unmentioned sector of the low-income housing market; the changes in public service delivery and the threats to public health stemming from privatization and other radical shifts in local government administration; and the new social morphological conditions of neighborhoods abandoned by businesses as well as the state and depopulated by residents.[6]

The unprecedentedly high mortality figures in the 1995 heat wave substantiate the dangers of current urban conditions: the excess deaths per 100,000 city residents were greater in July 1995 than in the notable heat waves of 1955, 1983, 1986, and 1988, and only the 1955 heat wave came close to a mortality rate as much as half that of 1995. After nearly thirty years without a significant heat disaster, the series of deadly heat waves that begins in the early 1980s suggests that there is a connection among state retrenchment, rising fear of violence, and vulnerability. The climatic conditions in 1995 were more dangerous than they had been in earlier heat waves, but the 1995 disaster would not have been so deadly unless the conditions of the city's most precarious residents were more dangerous as well. In fact, *scientific studies show that the differences in the mortality rates between the 1995 and earlier heat waves are not natural; that is, they are not attributable to the weather.* [...]

This sociological account of the heat wave shows how the climate, the living conditions of the city's most precarious residents, and the local government, the organization most responsible for protecting the welfare of citizens, interact to determine the level of danger and damage that a disaster such as the heat wave inflicts. In 1995, the city's climatic, sociospatial, and political conditions were all extreme: not only was the weather unprecedentedly severe, in addition the advancing state of poverty and the inadequacy of the state's response created an unusually deadly crisis. [...]

At the heart of this account is the making visible of violence that is otherwise misrecognized, the exposure of a political economy of symbolic violence and thereby opening of new spaces for analytical and political work. This project is most systematically pursued in the work of Pierre Bourdieu, who has empirically shown the obscured machinations of power in such diverse areas as the world of art, the educational system, and the architecture of the home. In his recent work, Bourdieu has focused on two key sites in the production of symbolic domination, both of which are central to the disaster model: the state and the journalistic field. In the early 1990s, when he was developing his work on the political field, Bourdieu argued that state has a unique "power to constitute and to impose as universal and universally applicable ... within the boundaries of a given territory, a common set of coercive norms" and categories.[7] Pushing Weber's famous formulation, Bourdieu claimed that the state is not merely the holder of a monopoly on legitimate physical violence, but over legitimate symbolic violence as well. To trace this violence, Bourdieu departed from most political sociologists by examining the effects of the state outside of formal political institutions and organizations, in the places where it is least recognized but perhaps most potent.[8] Although they seem unlikely subjects for political sociology, naturalized disasters represent a promising domain for locating the work of the state. Bourdieu has also recognized that the media now share the role of legitimating symbolic violence with the state. [...]

Urban Onslaught: The Mounting Spectacle of Death in the City

Chicago: Tuesday, July 12; sunny and still; temperature near 100°F, heat index 102°, the streets ablaze; the air sticky, almost thick enough to chew. The heat came *announced*. Forecasters, watching the warm air rising from the South, predicted a hot spell several days before Chicago cracked 90°, and local television news broadcasts warned of an imminent "summer sizzler" through the night of July 11. [. . .] Some Chicagoans were prepared, others acted quickly to protect themselves. Stores carrying air conditioners and fans sold out their supplies by the afternoon, leaving teams of eager shoppers on long, fruitless searches for home cooling systems. City dwellers swarmed the beaches: 90,000 crammed a modestly sized downtown beach alone. [. . .]

But Chicagoans needed air conditioning to survive such extreme heat, and as the city got its fix on artificial cooling its demand for electricity reached an all-time high, totally overwhelming the normal capacity of Chicago's utilities provider, Commonwealth Edison (Com Ed). Com Ed was not adequately prepared for this soaring use of power and its equipment broke down precisely when its customers most needed energy. Com Ed's generators began failing on Wednesday and continued to malfunction through the weekend. Friday, after the three consecutive days of record-breaking energy consumption and a sweeping series of power failures around the city, two large circuit breakers went out at the Northwest station within an hour. Disarray at the utility company left some communities without electricity – and therefore without air conditioning, fans, elevators, refrigeration, and television and radio for two days or more, and the temperature never moderated.

Thursday the thirteenth was Chicago's most uncomfortable day. Some regions of the city reported temperatures of 106° and heat indices as high as 126°; indoor temperatures in high-rise apartment buildings without air conditioning topped 115° even when windows were open; and school buses, trapped in mid-day traffic while carrying children on summer field trips, grew so hot that dozens of young campers, weak and nauseous from heat exhaustion, had to be pulled out of the stuffy vehicles and hosed down by fire department workers to prevent them from passing out. Massive water treatments were a survival technique the

emergency workers might have borrowed from inhabitants, especially the young, of the poorest and most underserved areas of the city. These Chicagoans, the most likely to lack access to cool spaces, had no choice but to open their neighborhood fire hydrants, creating public fountains and turning the streets into waterparks, oases where the able-bodied could transform deadly conditions into spaces for frolic and relief.

But this popular survival strategy among disadvantaged urban dwellers otherwise trapped in the heat has a dangerous unintended effect: massive use of fire hydrants as cooling devices depletes local water supplies – enough, in extreme cases, to leave entire communities without running water for extended periods. On Thursday, the hottest day in city history, Chicagoans opened over 3,000 fire hydrants, consuming so much water that several neighborhoods lost almost all of their pressure for hours or more. Television news reported that the city was fighting a "water war": over 100 crews circulated through Chicago to close the hydrants and police threatened anyone caught tampering with emergency water sources with a $500 fine, but people in the streets persisted, using acetylene torches, sledgehammers, power drills, and saws to generate a flow of water. Threatened with the possibility of losing their best source of relief from the heat, groups of youths "showered nine water department trucks with gunfire, bricks or rocks . . . and caused minor injuries to four workers" who tried to seal the hydrants.[9] This violent struggle for such a basic resource was truly tragic, for these deprived communities would lose no matter what the final result. If sealing the hydrants would have helped overheated residents regain water pressure, it also would have meant submitting to the more dangerous pressures imposed by the limited resources of the neighborhood and the intensity of the heat. [. . .]

Saturday was massively deadly: 365, or 293 over the norm, died in one day; Sunday, with 241 mortalities, was almost as bad; Monday the rate had dropped, but only to 193; Tuesday it hovered 34 above the norm, at 106; and for the next two days it remained 20 above average (see Figure 38.1).

This profusion of death overwhelmed the morgue, where on average medical examiners see 17 bodies a day and storage facilities as well as staffing levels are designed to accommodate this

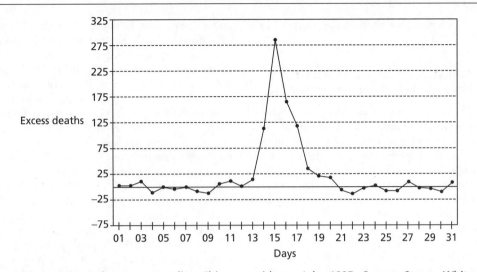

Figure 38.1 Estimated excess mortality, Chicago residents, July, 1995. *Source*: Steven Whitman, Chicago Department of Health

load. [...] Recognizing that the soaring death toll could bring chaos to his office, Dr. Edmund Donoghue, the county's Chief Medical Examiner, made emergency arrangements to handle the excess bodies: a fleet of 48-foot-long refrigerated meat-packing trucks, volunteered by a civic-minded owner of a local trucking company, was brought in to hold the bodies as medical workers raced to complete their autopsies. At the height of the heat wave's destructiveness 10 large trucks, along with a traffic jam of ambulances, police wagons, and fire department vehicles used to deliver bodies from around the city, television and radio vans, and health workers' cars crammed the area surrounding the morgue, forming a parade of death so enormous, so surreal, that it seemed impossible to believe that this was happening in the center of the city.

Locating the Symptoms: An Anatomy of Urban Suffering

During the heat wave, geography was linked to destiny. The processes that killed so many city residents were concentrated around the low-income, elderly, African-American, and more violent regions of the metropolis, the neighborhoods of exclusion in which the most vulnerable Chicagoans make their homes. Similarities between maps of the heat wave's deaths and maps of ethnoracial and class division reveal the social and structural underpinnings of the event. [...] Read

against the history of ethnoracially driven battles for control of space at both the state and street levels – ranging from Chicago's urban renewal and public housing programs to the race riots in which white communities attacked African Americans who tried to move into predominantly white neighborhoods[10] – this ring of death perfectly expresses the human cost of long-standing ethnoracial exclusion in the metropolis. [...]

The demographics of mortality also fit a pattern – this one familiar to public health researchers and practitioners – predicated on the age, gender, and ethnoracial status of city residents. (See Table 38.1.) Seventy-three percent of the 525 Chicagoans whose deaths were medically confirmed as "heat-related" during the month of July were over 65 years old; the death rate for seniors above 65 was 16 times higher than the rate for those under 65. Race and ethnicity mattered also: non-Latino blacks were almost twice more likely than non-Latino whites to die of the heat. Although African Americans make up 39 percent of the city population and African-American seniors represent less than one-third of Chicago residents over 65, black seniors constituted 45 percent of the deaths for Chicagoans 65 and over, and non-elderly blacks, who accounted for 59 percent of all deaths among those under 65, died even more disproportionately. Latinos, though, who number about 19 percent of the city population, represented only 2 percent of the overall mortality. Men died in greater numbers than women; they were 2.5 times more likely to die because of the heat.[11] [...]

"Government alone cannot do it all": City Services in the Empowerment Era

[...] Given the entrenched American history of city governments' unresponsiveness to the needs of poor communities, it would have been surprising if the local Chicago government had effectively protected local residents during the crisis. As organizations, city governments function poorly to secure the welfare of people in need, and they do so only in unusual circumstances.[12] In the current structure and spirit of local government, the state is even less willing and able to provide key services to marginalized residents. [...] Chicago's political machinery all but broke down when its most precarious patrons needed it most.

During the heat wave several city departments failed to provide services that, had they been activated, would have saved hundreds of lives. [...] The Mayor's Commission on the heat wave insists, "government alone cannot do it all,"[13] and residents themselves must take responsibility for securing their own welfare and keeping themselves out of hospitals and other places that provide public assistance. In most American cities, local governments now claim that their role should no longer be that of universal provider, but of enabler.[14] Appropriating the discourse of empowerment as a moral justification to abandon poor communities, state administrators and politicians, convinced that the best way to protect the poor is to force them to protect themselves, are relinquishing responsibility for many of their services to the people least able to provide them. The rapid introduction of market operating principles

and discourse into the public sector has facilitated this process. People in need are now considered consumers of public goods in a competitive market rather than citizens entitled to benefits because they are members of a political community. As consumers, they are expected to provide for themselves in the available market of services. Yet poor, infirm communities are likely to be poor consumers of public services, in part because they have less access to information and thus a limited set of choices from which to choose. [...]

Between July 13 and 16, 23 of 45 hospitals in the city network went on bypass status, whereby they refused to accept new patients for emergency care because they were using all their urgent-care facilities. In one period 18 hospitals went on bypass status at the same time, making it impossible for residents in the most affected areas to receive timely medical attention. [...] With so many emergency rooms shut down and no central program to notify ambulances when and where hospitals closed or reopened, people in need of emergency treatment were shuttled from area to area until their driver could find an available facility, and ambulances were so tied up that at least 55 emergency cases went unattended for more than 30 minutes, a response time the city itself considers totally unacceptable. The medical systems in poorer areas of the city, long insufficient for the needs of the local population but reduced even further by cuts in public health programs since the 1980s, all but collapsed under the pressure of the heat.

Many of the Chicagoans who died or required emergency care during the heat wave were no doubt among those who, failing to master the system, became, in the state's logic, their own victims.

Table 38.1: Total heat-related deaths by age and ethnoracial status, Chicago residents

Age	Non-Latino white	Non-Latino black	Non-Latino other	Latino	Total
< 55	27	39	0	1	67
55–64	25	45	1	4	75
65–74	62	64	0	1	127
75–84	90	66	2	1	159
85+	28	42	1	2	93
Total	252	256	4	9	521

Source: Chicago Department of Public Health.

Home Alone, Home Afraid, Home Sick: The Rise of Literal Social Isolation

In the city's official view, however, real fault for the health crisis lay in the hands of the poor and isolated seniors who, when contacted by neighbors or service agencies, did not heed the instruction to leave their apartments and find air conditioning or at least to open their windows and doors. According to the Mayor's Commission, this showed "that those most at risk may be least likely to want or accept help from government,"[15] but in fact it exemplified the extent to which public agencies and officials, who by out-sourcing service provisions to private contractors increasingly distance themselves from impoverished areas of the city, have failed to recognize the level of insecurity and the depth of deprivation in the most distressed communities. Ground-level scrutiny of the everyday world of Chicago's most precarious residents reveals that they did not refuse to leave their homes because they do not want or are unwilling to accept help from government, but because the proximate social and spatial conditions in which they live make it unacceptably difficult or risky to leave their apartments.

The advancing deterioration of neighborhood infrastructure has been particularly damaging to the city's poor elderly, thousands of whom have responded to the environmental changes by barricading themselves in their small homes, using their walls to protect themselves from a world they perceive as too threatening to enter, all but abandoning a society that has thoroughly abandoned them. Seniors who are trapped within their own residential units represent an emerging group of thoroughly marginalized city residents – the *literally socially isolated* – who, according to several case managers who work with them, rarely leave their residential units, have little contact with family and friends, and, because of cutbacks in public health and transportation programs (essential for bringing them to health providers), are unable to receive many of the basic services they need to stay healthy. While the size and demographic composition of this group is unclear – three case managers at Metropolitan Family Services independently estimated that 90 percent of their clients are socially isolated, and a recent study found that 48 percent of the city's elderly have no one available to help them[16] – it is significant enough to constitute a major problem in the life of the city. [. . .]

The silent deaths of Chicagoans living alone and out of touch with members of their communities signal the dire reality of an emerging, emergency social condition – social life constrained by infirmity or fear and reduced to the boundaries of a tiny apartment – whose features and consequences have received scant attention from scholars and policy-makers.

During the heat wave, researchers from the Division of Epidemiological Studies at the Illinois Department of Public Health report, the high correlation between community area heat-related death rates and community area homicide rates indicated both the depth and the dangerousness of fear itself. High levels of violent crime in concentrated areas, the researchers explain, "can create fears influencing people's desire to open windows, leave home, or stay away from home for extended periods. Even during a heat wave, these fears may cause additional reluctance to go to cooling centers or to open windows."[17]

This problem can be particularly onerous for seniors living in senior public housing units, where changes in city housing policy have forced many to give up not only the public parks and streets that once framed their communal lives but the public spaces within their own apartment buildings as well. [. . .] A client of a social worker I shadowed has wired his door-knob to an electrical current so that it shocks everyone who touches it unless he disconnects the wiring. By 1996 the CHA had acknowledged the problem its housing policy has created, and it has pledged to remove people with substance abuse problems from the senior buildings within the next few years. Until then, however, insecurity will rule the lives of many seniors living in public housing.

Down and Out in Uptown: An Urban Inferno on SRO "Death Row"

The single-room-occupancy dwellings (SROs) that house thousands of Chicagoans on the edge of homelessness represent the last option of insulation from the dangers of life on the streets but impose their own set of threats to the security of residents. SROs vary greatly in quality and form: several hundred units are funded with federal housing grants, well kept, staffed by trained social workers and busy with programs for job training, substance abuse treatment, and habilitation to working life. But most for-profit buildings lack these services entirely and function instead as little more than low-grade shelters for the marginal or mentally ill. [. . .]

By the 1970s, SROs had become homes for some of the most precarious of the elderly and poor, but demand for them remained high because of the lack of other housing options. [. . .] These SROs, as the clerk in one of Uptown's most dilapidated hotels told me, serve as places "where people come to maintain their addictions, live alone, and die." This was never more true than during the heat wave, when the architectural and social conditions in the SROs made them the most dangerous places in the city, more dangerous, even, than the streets.

In the large Wilson Club Hotel it seems a miracle that only a few residents died in the heat. Managers there have used thin wood to subdivide the former industrial building into hundreds of units large enough to fit only a bed, a dresser, and a chair. The wood divisions stop several feet below the high, concrete ceilings, but residents and their property are protected by a keylock door and chicken wire pleated atop the wooden walls to serve as ceilings where none other exists. There are a few windows on the exterior walls and fire escapes on every floor, but these offer little ventilation to the residents lodged in the belly of the building; and there is no air conditioning in the dim public space on the ground floor, which was always empty when I visited.[18] [. . .]

Naturalizing Disaster: The Politics of Representing Death

[. . .] Journalistic and political representations of the heat wave deemphasized the social and political determinants of the disaster. Local political officials had obvious incentives to portray the heat wave as either a non-event or as a natural, and therefore uncontrollable, disaster, one that no one could have anticipated or done anything to prevent. [. . .]

The local media initially considered the heat wave to be a trivial story and covered it with light features such as one about the difficulty of finding air conditioners, but when the mortality levels began to rise the press shifted its coverage to the story of the deaths.[19] Yet the immediate visi-

bility of the crisis did not prevent Mayor Daley from attempting to conceal or deflect attention away from the city's morbid condition. Daley, holder of the mayorship his father had made the throne of machine politics, had won his seat in 1989 on the grounds that, "We can't close our eyes to [Chicago's] problems any longer. Being accountable starts in City Hall. Because the responsibility for managing the city lies with the mayor . . . I won't wait until disaster strikes."[20] But under the heat he changed his message. Refusing to acknowledge that the city had failed to protect the health of its citizens. Daley, who had neglected to issue a Heat Emergency Warning and to activate several possible emergency procedures during the city's deadliest week, groped wildly for alternative explanations or scapegoats he could blame for causing the crisis.

Confronted with early reports of the soaring death rates, Daley's initial response coupled denial with naturalization. "Every day," he lectured the press, "people die of natural causes. You can't put everything as heat-related. . . . Then everybody in the summer that dies will die of the heat."[21] His skepticism was a challenge not only to the empirical connection between the weather and the overload at the morgue and in the hospitals, but also to the medical and scientific credibility of Dr. Edmund Donoghue, whose tenure as the county's chief medical examiner long outdates that of the mayor and whose professional reputation is outstanding. Public denial thus proved an untenable, even embarrassing, official position for the city – especially when the body count mounted and Dr. Donoghue, told of Daley's criticisms, defended his claim to the media and received the support of his colleagues in the field. "The mayor is entitled to raise questions," the medical examiner explained diplomatically, but "If anything, we're underestimating the number of heat-related deaths."[22] [. . .]

Invoking the bi-partisan logic of personal responsibility now ubiquitous within the American political field, Daley and his administrators blamed the victims of the heat waves themselves, as well as their families and friends, for failing to take care of themselves and each other. [. . .] The heat wave deaths, in other words, were caused by behavioral deficiencies rather than structural conditions or political failures. "We're talking about people who die because they neglect themselves," argued Daniel Alvarez, the city Commissioner of

Human Services. "We publicized common sense ideas, what the mayor was saying, drink plenty of water. These are people who don't read the newspapers, who don't watch television"; and Daley cautioned that "we need to be sure seniors do not become victims of their own independence."[23] [...]

During the heat wave, the frame of the "natural disaster" provided the city government with a perfect vehicle for defining the event in an explicitly nonpolitical and commonsensical vocabulary with which its constituency and other observers would be comfortable and familiar. [...] The naturalizing frame, however, only partly explains why Mayor Daley's political reputation survived the crisis so well. Given Mayor Bilandic's political demise in the aftermath of the blizzard, the question – which should be accompanied by the reminder that disaster management was not the only issue in Bilandic's mayorship[24] – remains: how is it that a natural disaster that kills hundreds of residents is less politically damaging than a disaster whose most significant effect was to block roads, stall public transportation, close schools and businesses, and restrict movement in the city? The answer is, in part, that the blizzard was much more damaging to Chicagoans with political clout than the heat wave, which, while killing hundreds, had almost no impact on elites and did relatively little harm to businesses.[25] [...]

The heat wave is now becoming a central part of Chicago folklore,[26] but much of the popular discourse on the event lacks the insights into the structure of the city that the disaster might have exposed. If the heat wave's mythical obituary conceals the very processes that produced its effects, though, the story of its largest funeral speaks its deepest truth. For far from being "the great equalizer," the deaths of the Chicagoans for whom no one cared only reinforced and made permanent the degradation of their lives.[27] At the end of August 1995, over a month after the week of death had passed, the bodies of 41 heat wave victims remained unclaimed at the morgue, leaving the city to care for them. On August 25, Chicago buried these neglected corpses, along with 27 other unclaimed bodies in the city, in a row of plywood boxes marked only by medical case numbers and yellow paper tags tacked onto the side. A Catholic priest who helped officiate the funeral – which was so brief that two of the ministers invited to participate arrived minutes late and missed it entirely – found the discordance of the gruesome event in a city brimming with pride and anticipating renewed international praise too much to bear. "You always hear about mass burials around the world, in war and disaster," he lamented. "And this was home. This was Chicago." Yet there was no one, save a few reporters and a smattering of curious bystanders, to witness the city dispose of the remains, and now they have settled into the earth without stirring up much attention at all. The large grave, which is over 160 feet long, has no tombstone, no sign, nothing to show that the bodies buried therein testify to the expendability of life on the margins of a major American metropolis at the close of the millennium. For the city, the presence of the mass, anonymous grave matters little: almost no one is interested in a reminder of what is otherwise so easy to forget.

NOTES

1 US Centers for Disease Control and Prevention. "Heat-Related Illnesses and Deaths – United States, 1994–1995," *Morbidity and Mortality Weekly Report* 44/25 (1995): 465–8.

2 The heat index measures both temperature and humidity, which together determine how a typical person experiences the heat. It is analogous to the wind-chill factor, which measures experienced cold during the winter. Scientists have long associated high temperatures in cities with the urban "heat island" phenomenon, but only recently have some environmental scientists found that much of the modern warming of the earth takes place at night.

3 Excess death rates measure the number of deaths for a given period of time in relation to the baseline death rate. The Chicago Department of Public Health reported 739 excess deaths during the week of the heat wave, 696 excess deaths for the month of July. Note furthermore that Chicago's mortality rates did not dip in the months following the heat wave; the heat, then, did not (as some initially conjectured) simply kill people who would have died soon thereafter anyway. According to Whitman and his colleagues, heat-related death rates measure the absolute number of cases in which examiners attributed mortality to one of these criteria: "1) a measured body temperature of > 105 °F (> 40.6 °C) before or immediately after death; 2) evidence of high environmental temperature at the scene of death, usually greater than 100 °F; or 3) the body was decomposed and investigation disclosed that the person was last seen alive during the heat wave and that the

environmental temperature at the time would have been high." Steven Whitman et al., "Mortality in Chicago Attributed to the July 1995 Heat Wave," *American Journal of Public Health* 87/9 (Sept. 1997): 1515–18.

4 Here I use "logic" to refer to the structure and course of the disaster as well as to the social order of the city, since it is the latter that largely determined the former.

5 Among the major statements in this discussion are Peter Marcuse, "What's So New About Divided Cities?" *International Journal of Urban and Regional Research* 17/3 (1993): 355–65; Peter Marcuse, "The Enclave, the Citadel, and the Ghetto: What Has Changed in the Post-Fordist U.S. City," *Urban Affairs Review* 33/2 (1997): 228–64; Loïc J. D. Wacquant, "The Rise of Advanced Marginality: Notes on its Nature and Implications," *Acta Sociologica* 39 (1996): 121–39; Douglas Massey, "The Age of Extremes: Concentrated Affluence and Poverty in the Twenty-First Century," *Demography* 33/4 (1996): 395–412; and Manuel Castells, *End of Millennium* (Oxford: Blackwell, 1998).

6 There are several reasons to think that these conditions are not unique to Chicago, and in fact the heat wave provided some of them. Milwaukee, about 100 miles away, experienced 91 heat-related deaths during the week. As in Chicago, this mortality level cannot be explained by the heat alone.

7 Pierre Bourdieu and Loïc J. D. Wacquant, *An Invitation to Reflexive Sociology* (Chicago: University of Chicago Press, 1993), 112.

8 For his most recent analysis of the hidden effects of the state, see Pierre Bourdieu, *The State Nobility* (Palo Alto: Stanford University Press, 1996).

9 *The Chicago Tribune*, July 17, 1995, p. (2)5.

10 See Arnold Hirsch, *Making the Second Ghetto* (Cambridge: Cambridge University Press, 1983).

11 See Steven Whitman, "Mortality and the Mid-July Heat Wave in Chicago," presentation to the Chicago Board of Health (Sep. 20, 1995); and Whitman et al., "Mortality in Chicago Attributed to the July 1995 Heat Wave."

12 See Charles Perrow and Mario Guillén, *The AIDS Disaster* (New Haven: Yale University Press, 1990), for a discussion of the ways in which the least politically powerful people with AIDS, poor people of color who were intravenous drug users, were neglected by the organizations who managed the AIDS crisis. Perrow and Guillen affirm a central claim of urban regime scholars, that lack of resources makes poor and minority communities least able to mobilize the government to support their needs, thus triggering a vicious cycle in which they are deprived further and made even more politically expendable. For statements of this position from urban regime theorists, see, among others, Clarence

Stone. *Regime Politics: Governing Atlanta, 1946–1988*, (Lawrence: University of Kansas Press, 1989); and Steven Elkin, *City and Regime in the American Republic* (Chicago: University of Chicago Press, 1987).

13 City of Chicago, *Mayor's Commission on Extreme Weather Conditions*.

14 Robin Hambleton, "Future Directions for Urban Government in Britain and America," *Journal of Urban Affairs* 12/1 (1990): 75–94.

15 City of Chicago, *Mayor's Commission on Extreme Weather Conditions*, 4.

16 Interviews with social workers. Metropolitan Family Services, June 1996; and M. Fleming-Moran et al., *Illinois State Needs Assessment Survey of Elders Aged 55 and Over* (Bloomington: Heartland Center on Aging. Disability and Long Term Care, School of Public and Environmental Affairs, Indiana University, 1991).

17 Tiefu Shen et al., "Executive Summary: Community Characteristics Correlated with Heat Related Mortality, Chicago, Illinois, July 1995," unpublished MS.

18 The conditions in the worst SROs resemble the "cattle-sheds for human beings" described by Frederick Engels. Engels's remark that "such a district exists in the heart of the second city of England, the first manufacturing city of the world," has an ironic resonance for the case of Chicago, America's own "second city" and historical manufacturing center. See Frederick Engels, *The Condition of the Working Class in England* (Chicago: Academy Chicago Publishers, 1984).

19 Interviews with Chicago journalists.

20 *Chicago Sun Times*, July 25, 1995: 25.

21 *Chicago Tribune*, July 25, 1995: (7) 1.

22 *Chicago Tribune*, July 20, 1995: 1; and *Los Angeles Times*, July 23, 1995: A1.

23 Perhaps the most familiar case in which the political economy and structural morphology of vulnerability determined disaster mortality is the Titanic accident. First-class passengers, whose wealth allowed them to obtain positions at the higher (and in this case safer) levels of the ship and gave them priority in the rescue, survived at a much higher rate than passengers seated in lower-class positions. Passengers with the lowest class tickets suffered the highest mortality rates. Yet wealth does not always protect against disaster damage. Note, for example, that earthquakes in modern cities might be most disastrous for wealthy home-owners who accept the risk of building expensive homes on mountain cliffs, or that forest fires might affect only residents wealthy enough to build homes in expensive, greener areas, such as the Oakland and Berkeley hills. In these crises, however, the order of assistance, organization, and reconstruction is often determined by the

wealth and political power of the communities affected: more elite areas are rebuilt and repaired much more quickly than disadvantaged areas. See William Cronon. "Introduction: In Search of Nature," *Uncommon Ground: Toward Reinventing Nature* (New York: W. W. Norton, 1995).

24 For a thorough discussion of Bilandic's electoral loss to Jane Byrne, see Paul Kleppner, *Chicago Divided: The Making of a Black Mayor* (DeKalb: Northern Illinois University Press, 1985), ch. 5.

25 Some stores and businesses that lost their electricity, particularly those that stocked frozen perishables, and local agriculture were more damaged by the heat wave. Nonetheless, the overall effect of the heat wave on business was less severe than the blizzard.

26 "Now and for the rest of our lives," says one member of Chicago's severe-weather commission, "we'll be telling our grandchildren about the summer of 1995. People will be talking about this forever."

27 For an analysis of the social and symbolic significance of funeral rituals and burial conditions, see Nancy Scheper-Hughes, *Death Without Weeping* (Berkeley: University of California Press, 1992; and Chapter 33).

39

The New "Peculiar Institution": On the Prison as Surrogate Ghetto

Loïc Wacquant

Not one but several "peculiar institutions" have operated to define, confine, and control African-Americans in the history of the United States. The first is *chattel slavery* as the pivot of the plantation economy and inceptive matrix of racial division from the colonial era to the Civil War (Stampp 1956; Berlin 1998). The second is the *Jim Crow system* of legally enforced discrimination and segregation from cradle to grave that anchored the predominantly agrarian society of the South from the close of Reconstruction to the Civil Rights revolution which toppled it a full century after abolition (Woodward 1957; Litwack 1999). America's third special device for containing the descendants of slaves in the Northern industrial metropolis is the *ghetto*, corresponding to the conjoint urbanization and proletarianization of African-Americans from the Great Migration of 1914–1930 to the 1960s, when it was rendered partially obsolete by the concurrent transformation of economy and state and by the mounting protest of blacks against continued caste exclusion, climaxing with the explosive urban riots chronicled in the Kerner Commission Report (Spear 1968; Kerner Commission 1988). The fourth, I contend here, is the novel institutional complex formed by the *remnants of the dark ghetto and the carceral apparatus* with which it has become joined by a linked relationship of structural symbiosis and functional surrogacy.

Viewed against the backdrop of the full historical trajectory of racial domination in the United States, the glaring and growing "disproportionality" in incarceration that has afflicted African-Americans over the past three decades[1] can be understood as the result of the "extrapenological" functions that the prison system has come to shoulder in the wake of the crisis of the ghetto. Not crime, but the need to shore up an eroding caste cleavage, along with buttressing the emergent regime of desocialized wage labor to which most blacks are fated by virtue of their lack of marketable cultural capital, and which the most deprived among them resist by escaping into the illegal street economy, is the main impetus behind the stupendous expansion of America's penal state in the post-Keynesian age and its *de facto* policy of "carceral affirmative action" towards African-Americans (Wacquant 1998 and 1999: 71–94).

Beyond the specifics of that recent US phenomenon, this chapter suggests that there is much to be learned from an historical-cum-analytic comparison between ghetto and prison. For both belong to the same class of organizations, namely, *institutions of forced confinement*: the ghetto is a manner of "social prison" while the prison functions as a "judicial ghetto." Both are entrusted with enclosing a stigmatized population so as to neutralize the material and/or symbolic threat that it poses for the broader society from which it has been extruded. And, for that reason, ghetto and prison tend to evolve relational patterns and cultural forms that display striking similarities and intriguing parallels deserving of systematic study in diverse national and historical settings.

Vehicles for Labor Extraction and Caste Division

America's first three "peculiar institutions," slavery, Jim Crow, and the ghetto, have this in common, that they were all instruments for the conjoint *extraction of labor* and *social ostracization* of an outcast group deemed unassimilable by virtue of the indelible threefold stigma it carries. African-Americans arrived under bondage in the land of freedom. They were accordingly deprived of the right to vote in the self-appointed cradle of democracy (until 1965, for residents of the Southern states). And, for lack of a recognizable national affiliation, they were shorn of ethnic honor, which implies that, rather than simply standing at the bottom of the rank ordering of group prestige in American society, they were barred from it *ab initio*.

Slavery is a highly malleable and versatile institution that can be harnessed to a variety of purposes (Drescher and Engerman 1998) but in the Americas property-in-person was geared primarily to the provision and control of labor. Its introduction in the Chesapeake, Middle Atlantic, and Low Country regions of the United States in the seventeenth century served to recruit and regulate the unfree workforce forcibly imported from Africa and the West Indies to cater to their tobacco, rice, and mixed-farming economy. (Indentured laborers from Europe and native Indians were not enslaved because of their greater capacity to resist and because their servitude would have impeded future immigration as well as rapidly exhausted a limited supply of labor.) By the close of the eighteenth century, slavery had become self-reproducing and expanded to the fertile crescent of the southern interior, running from South Carolina to Louisiana, where it supplied a highly profitable organization of labor for cotton production and the basis for a plantation society distinctive for its feudal-like culture, politics, and psychology (Wright 1978; Kolchin 1993).

An *unforeseen byproduct* of the systematic enslavement and dehumanization of Africans and their descendants on North American soil was the creation of a racial caste line separating what would later become labeled "blacks" and "whites." As Barbara Fields (1990) has shown, the American ideology of "race," as putative biological division anchored by the inflexible application of the "one-drop rule" together with the principle of hypodescent, crystallized to resolve the blatant contradiction between human bondage and democracy. The religious and pseudoscientific belief in racial difference reconciled the brute fact of unfree labor with the doctrine of liberty premised on natural rights by reducing the slave to live property – three-fifths of a man according the sacred scriptures of the Constitution.

Racial division was a consequence, not a precondition, of US slavery, but once it was instituted it became detached from its initial function and acquired a social potency of its own. Emancipation thus created a double dilemma for Southern white society: how to secure anew the labor of former slaves, without whom the region's economy would collapse, and how to sustain the cardinal status distinction between whites and "persons of color," i.e., the social and symbolic distance needed to prevent the odium of "amalgamation" with a group considered inferior, rootless, and vile. After a protracted interregnum lasting into the 1890s, during which early white hysteria gave way to partial if inconsistent relaxation of ethnoracial strictures, when blacks were allowed to vote, to hold public office, and even to mix with whites to a degree in keeping with the intergroup intimacy fostered by slavery, the solution came in the form of the "Jim Crow" regime. It consisted of an ensemble of social and legal codes that prescribed the complete separation of the "races" and sharply circumscribed the life chances of African-Americans (Woodward 1955) while binding them to whites in a relation of suffusive submission backed by legal coercion and terroristic violence.

Imported from the north, where it had been experimented with in cities, this regime stipulated that blacks travel in separate trains, streetcars, and waiting rooms; that they reside in the "darktown" slums and be educated in separate schools (if at all); that they patronize separate service establishments and use their own bathrooms and water fountains; that they pray in separate churches, entertain themselves in separate clubs, and sit in separate "nigger galleries" in theaters; that they receive medical care in separate hospitals and exclusively from "colored" staff; and that they be incarcerated in separate cells and buried in separate cemeteries. Most crucial of all, laws joined mores in condemning the "unspeakable crime" of interracial marriage, cohabitation, or mere sexual congress so as to uphold the "supreme law of self-preservation" of the races and the myth of innate white superiority. Through continued white ownership of the land and the generalization of sharecropping and debt peonage, the plantation system remained virtually untouched as former slaves became a "dependent, propertyless peasantry, nominally free, but ensnared by poverty, ignorance, and the new servitude of tenantry" (McMillen 1990: 126). While sharecropping tied African-American labor to the farm, a rigid etiquette ensured that whites and blacks never interacted on a plane of equality, not even on the athletics field or in a boxing ring – a Birmingham ordinance of 1930 made it unlawful for them to play at checkers and dominoes with one another. Whenever the "color line" was breached or even brushed, a torrent of violence was unleashed in the form of periodic pogroms, Ku Klux Klan and vigilante raids, public floggings, mob killings and lynchings, this ritual caste murder designed to keep "uppity niggers" in their appointed place. All this was made possible by the swift and near-complete disenfranchisement of blacks as well as by the enforcement of "Negro law" by courts which granted the latter fewer effective legal safeguards than slaves had enjoyed earlier by dint of being both property and persons.

The sheer brutality of caste oppression in the South, the decline of cotton agriculture due to floods and the boll weevil, and the pressing shortage of labor in northern factories caused by the outbreak of the First World War created the impetus for African-Americans to emigrate en masse to the booming industrial centers of the midwest and northeast (over 1.5 million left in 1910–30, followed by another 3 million in 1940–60). But as migrants from Mississippi to the Carolinas flocked to the northern metropolis, what they discovered there was not the "promised land" of equality and full citizenship but another system of racial enclosure, the ghetto, which, though it was less rigid and fearsome than the one they had fled, was no less encompassing and constricting. To be sure, greater freedom to come and go in public places and to consume in regular commercial establishments, the disappearance of the humiliating signs pointing to "Colored" here and "White" there, renewed access to the ballot box and protection from the courts, the possibility of limited eco-nomic advancement, release from personal subservience and from the dread of omnipresent white violence, all made life in the urban North incomparably preferable to continued peonage in the rural South: it was "better to be a lamppost in Chicago than President of Dixie," as migrants famously put it to Richard Wright. But restrictive covenants forced African-Americans to congregate in a "Black Belt" which quickly became overcrowded, underserved, and blighted by crime, disease, and dilapidation, while the "job ceiling" restricted them to the most hazardous, menial, and underpaid occupations in both industry and personal services. As for "social equality," understood as the possibility of "becoming members of white cliques, churches, and voluntary associations, or marrying into their families," it was firmly and definitively denied (Drake and Cayton [1945] 1962, vol. 1: 112–28).

Blacks had entered the Fordist industrial economy, to which they contributed a vital source of abundant and cheap labor willing to ride along its cycles of boom and bust. Yet they remained locked in a precarious position of structural economic marginality and consigned to a secluded and dependent microcosm, complete with its own internal division of labor, social stratification, and agencies of collective voice and symbolic representation: a "city within the city" moored in a complexus of black churches and press, businesses and professional practices, fraternal lodges and communal associations that provided both a "milieu for Negro Americans in which they [could] imbue their lives with meaning" and a bullwark "to 'protect' white America from 'social contact' with Negroes" (Drake and Cayton [1945] 1962, vol. 2: xiv). Continued caste hostility from without and renewed ethnic affinity from within converged to create the ghetto as the third vehicle to extract black labor while keeping black bodies at a safe distance, to the material and symbolic benefit of white society.

The era of the ghetto as paramount mechanism of ethnoracial domination had opened with the urban riots of 1917–19 (in East St. Louis, Chicago, Longview, Houston, etc.). It closed with a wave of clashes, looting, and burning that rocked hundreds of American cities from coast to coast, from the Watts uprising of 1965 to the riots of rage and grief triggered by the assassination of Martin Luther King in the summer of 1968 (Kerner Commission 1988). Indeed, by the end of the sixties, the ghetto was well on its way to becoming functionally obsolete or, to be more precise, increasingly *unsuited* to accomplishing the twofold task historically entrusted to America's "peculiar institutions." On the side of *labor extraction*, the shift from an urban industrial economy to a suburban service economy and the accompanying dualization of the occupational structure, along with the upsurge of working-class immigration from Mexico, the Caribbean, and Asia, meant that large segments of the workforce contained in the "Black Belts" of the northern metropolis were simply no longer needed. On the side of *ethnoracial closure*, the decades-long mobilization of African-Americans against caste rule finally succeeded, in the propitious political conjuncture of crisis stemming from the Vietnam war and assorted social unrest, in forcing the federal state to dismantle the legal machinery of caste exclusion. Having secured voting and civil rights, blacks were at long last full citizens who would no longer brook being shunted off into the separate and inferior world of the ghetto.[2]

But, while whites begrudgingly accepted "integration" in principle, in practice they strove to maintain an unbridgeable social and symbolic gulf with their compatriots of African descent. They abandoned public schools, shunned public space, and fled to the suburbs in the millions to avoid mixing and ward off the specter of "social equality" in the city. They then turned against the welfare state and those social programs upon which the collective advancement of blacks was most dependent. *A contrario*, they extended enthusiastic support for the "law-and-order" policies that vowed to firmly repress urban disorders connately perceived as racial threats (Edsall and Edsall 1991; Quadagno 1994; Beckett and Sasson 2000: 49–74). Such policies pointed to yet another special institution capable of confining and controlling, if not the entire African-American community, at least its most disruptive, disreputable, and dangerous members: the prison.

The Ghetto as Ethnoracial Prison, the Prison as Judicial Ghetto

The ghetto operates as an *ethnoracial prison*: it encages a dishonored category and severely curtails the life chances of its members in support of the "monopolization of ideal and material goods or opportunities" by the dominant status group (Weber 1978: 935) dwelling on its outskirts. Recall that the ghettos of early modern Europe were typically delimited by high walls with one or more gates which were locked at night and within which Jews had to return before sunset on pain of severe punishment (Wirth 1928: 32), and that their perimeter was subjected to continuous monitoring by external authorities. Note next the structural and functional homologies with the prison conceptualized as a *judicial ghetto*: a jail or penitentiary is in effect a reserved *space* which serves to forcibly confine a legally denigrated *population* and wherein this latter evolves its distinctive *institutions*, culture, and sullied identity. It is thus formed of the same four fundamental constituents – stigma, coercion, physical enclosure, and organizational parallelism and insulation – that make up a ghetto, and for similar purposes.

Much as the ghetto protects the city's residents from the pollution of intercourse with the tainted but necessary bodies of an outcast group in the manner of an "urban condom," as Richard Sennett (1994: 237) vividly put it in his depiction of the "fear of touching" in sixteenth-century Venice, the prison cleanses the social body from the temporary blemish of those of its members who have committed crimes, that is, following Durkheim, individuals who have violated the sociomoral integrity of the collectivity by infringing on "definite and strong states of the collective conscience." Finally, both prison and ghetto are authority structures saddled with inherently dubious or problematic legitimacy whose maintenance is ensured by intermittent recourse to external force.

By the end of the seventies, then, as the racial and class backlash against the democratic advances won by the social movements of the preceding decade got into full swing, the prison abruptly returned to the forefront of American society and offered itself as the universal and simplex solution to all manners of social problems. Chief among these problems was the "breakdown" of social order in the "inner city," which is scholarly and policy euphemism for the patent incapacity of the dark ghetto to contain a dishonored and supernumerary population henceforth viewed not only as deviant and devious but as downright dangerous in light of the violent urban upheavals of the mid-sixties. As the walls of the ghetto shook and threatened to crumble, the walls of the prison were correspondingly extended, enlarged, and fortified. Soon the black ghetto, converted into an instrument of naked exclusion by the concurrent retrenchment of wage labor and social protection, and further destabilized by the increasing penetration of the penal arm of the state, became bound to the jail and prison system by a triple relationship of functional equivalency, structural homology, and cultural syncretism, such that they now constitute a single *carceral continuum* which entraps a redundant population of younger black men (and increasingly women) who circulate in closed circuit between its two poles in a self-perpetuating cycle of social and legal marginality with devastating personal and social consequences.

Now, the carceral system had already functioned as an *ancillary* institution for caste preservation and labor control in America during one previous transition between regimes of racial domination, that between slavery and Jim Crow in the South. On the morrow of Emancipation, Southern prisons turned black overnight as "thousands of ex-slaves were being arrested, tried, and convicted for acts that in the past had been dealt with by the master alone" (Oskinsky 1996: 32) and for refusing to behave as menials and follow the demeaning rules of racial etiquette. Soon thereafter, the former confederate states innovated "convict leasing" as a response to the moral panic of "Negro crime" that presented the double advantage of generating prodigious funds for the state coffers and furnishing abundant bound labor to till the fields, build the levees, lay down the railroads, clean the swamps, and dig the mines of the region under murderous conditions. Indeed, penal labor, in the form of the convict-lease and its heir, the chain gang, played a major role in the economic advancement of the New South during the Progressive era, as it "reconciled modernization with the continuation of racial domination" (Lichtenstein 1999: 195).

What makes the racial intercession of the carceral system different today is that, unlike slavery, Jim Crow, and the ghetto of mid-century, it does not carry out a positive economic mission of recruitment and disciplining of the workforce: it serves only to warehouse the precarious and deproletarianized fractions of the black working class, be it that they cannot find employment owing to a combination of skills deficit, employer discrimination, and competition from immigrants, or that they refuse to submit to the indignity of substandard work in the peripheral sectors of the service economy – what ghetto residents commonly label "slave jobs." But there is presently mounting financial and ideological pressure, as well as renewed political interest, to relax restrictions on penal labor so as to (re)introduce mass unskilled work in private enterprises inside of American prisons (Wacquant 1999: 82–3): putting most inmates to work would help lower the country's "carceral bill" as well as effectively extend to the inmate poor the workfare requirements now imposed upon the free poor as a requirement of citizenship. The next decade will tell whether the prison remains an appendage to the dark ghetto or supersedes it to go it alone and become America's fourth "peculiar institution."

NOTES

1 Three brute facts need only be recalled here: the ethnic composition of the inmate population of the United States has been virtually inverted in the last half-century, going from about 70% (Anglo) white at the mid-century point to less than 30% today; the black/white incarceration gap has jumped from 1 for 5 to 1 for 8.5 in just the past 20 years; the lifetime cumulative probability of "doing time" in a state or federal prison based on the imprisonment rates of the early 1990s is 4% for whites, 16% for Latinos, and 29% for blacks. Michael Tonry (1995) provides a systematic analysis of the increasing enmeshment of African-Americans in the criminal justice system over the past two decades.

2 This was the meaning of Martin Luther King's "Freedom Campaign" in summer of 1966 in Chicago: it sought to apply to the ghetto the techniques of collective mobilization and civil disobedience used with success in the attack on Jim Crow in the South to reveal and protest "the slow, stifling death of a kind of concentration camp life" to which blacks were condemned in the Northern metropolis (M. L. King, cited by Oates 1982: 373).

REFERENCES

Beckett, Katherine and Theodore Sasson. 2000. *The Politics of Injustice*. Thousand Oaks, CA: Pine Forge Press.

Berlin, Ira. 1998. *Many Thousands Gone: The First Two Centuries of Slavery in North America*. Cambridge: Harvard University Press.

Drake, St. Clair and Horace Cayton. 1945. *Black Metropolis: A Study of Negro Life in a Northern City*. New York: Harper and Row, 1962.

Drescher, Seymour and Stanley L. Engerman. 1998. *A Historical Guide to World Slavery*. New York: Oxford University Press.

Edsall, Thomas Byrne and Mary D. Edsall. 1991. *Chain Reaction: The Impact of Race, Rights, and Taxes on American Politics*. New York: W. W. Norton.

Fields, Barbara Jeanne. 1990. "Slavery, Race, and Ideology in the United States of America." *New Left Review* 181 (May–June): 95–118.

Kerner Commission. 1988. *The Kerner Report: The 1968 Report of the National Advisory Commission on Civil Disorders*. New York: Pantheon; orig. ed. 1968.

Kolchin, Peter. 1993. *American Slavery: 1619–1877*. New York: Hill and Wang.

Lichtenstein, Alex. 1999. *Twice the Work of Free Labor: The Political Economy of Convict Labor in the New South*. New York: Verso.

Litwack, Leon F. 1998. *Trouble in Mind: Black Southerners in the Age of Jim Crow*. New York: Knopf.

McMillen, Neil R. 1990. *Dark Journey: Black Mississippians in the Age of Jim Crow*. Urbana: University of Illinois Press.

Oates, Stephen B. 1982. *Let the Trumpet Sound: The Life of Martin Luther King*. New York: New American Library.

Oshinsky, David M. 1996. *Worse Than Slavery: Parchman Farm and the Ordeal of Jim Crow Justice*. New York: Free Press.

Quadagno, Jill. 1994. *The Color of Welfare: How Racism Undermined the War on Poverty*. Oxford: Oxford University Press.

Sennett, Richard. 1994. *Flesh and Stone: The Body and the City in Western Civilization*. London: Faber.

Spear, Allan H. 1968. *Black Chicago: The Making of a Negro Ghetto, 1890–1920*. Chicago: University of Chicago Press.

Stampp, Kenneth M. 1956. *The Peculiar Institution: Slavery in the Ante-Bellum South*. New York: Vintage Books, rep. 1989.

Tonry, Michael. 1995. *Malign Neglect: Race, Class, and Punishment in America*. New York: Oxford University Press.

Wacquant, Loïc. 1998. "Crime et châtiment en Amérique de Nixon à Clinton." *Archives de politique criminelle* 20 (Spring): 123–38.

——. 1999. *Les Prisons de la misère*. Paris: Editions Raisons d'agir.

Weber, Max. 1978. *Economy and Society*, eds. Guenter Roth and Claus Wittich. Berkeley: University of California Press.

Wirth, Louis. 1928. *The Ghetto*. Chicago: University of Chicago Press.

Woodward, C. Vann. 1955. *The Strange Career of Jim Crow*. New York: Oxford University Press; 3rd rev. ed. 1989.

Wright, Gavin. 1978. *The Political Economy of the Cotton South*. New York: W. W. Norton.

Part VIII

Gendered Violence

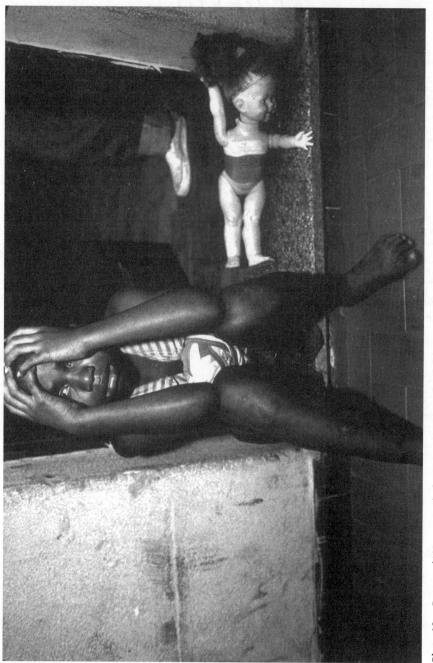

Plate 10: Battered Women's Shelter, Recife, Brazil 1991. Photo © Viviane Moos.

40

Language and Body: Transactions in the Construction of Pain

Veena Das

The very moment of the birth of India as a nation free from colonial domination was also the scene of unprecedented collective violence. One of the earliest studies of this violence stated that history had not known a fratricidal war of such dimensions: "Decrepit old men, defenseless women, helpless young children, infants in arms by the thousands were done to death by Muslim, Hindu and Sikh fanatics."[1] One of the signatures of this violence was the large-scale abduction and rape of women. The earliest estimates put the figure of abducted women from both sides of the border at close to 100,000. In the legislative debates in the Constituent Assembly it was stated, on December 15, 1949, that 33,000 Hindu or Sikh women had been abducted by Muslims, while the Pakistan Government had claimed that 50,000 Muslim women had been abducted by Hindu or Sikh men. [...] I want to reenter this scene of devastation to ask how one should inhabit such a world that has been made strange through the desolating experience of violence and loss. Stanley Cavell describes this as the Emersonian gesture of approaching the world through a kind of mourning for it.[2]

In the work of mourning in many societies it is the transactions between language and body, especially in the gendered division of labor, by which the antiphony of language and silence recreates the world in the face of tragic loss. It is not that in turning to these transactions I expect to find direct answers to the questions on violence and the prob-

lem of meaning, but I do want to reenter some of the texts with which I have engaged earlier to make the dialogue deeper on two questions: 1) How is it that the imaging of the project of nationalism in India came to include the appropriation of bodies of women as objects on which the desire for nationalism could be brutally inscribed and a memory for the future made? 2) Did forms of mourning find a place in the recreation of the world in, for instance, the discursive formations in post-Independence India? [...]

Brutal rape and abduction of women, and painful inscriptions of nationalist slogans on the bodies of women made sudden appearances. [...] Yet, one must ask what this brutalization did to the experiences of self, community, and nation. At the very least these scenes of violence constitute the (perhaps metaphysical) threshold within which the scenes of ordinary life are lived. [...]

In the genre of lamentation, women have control both through their bodies and through their language – grief is articulated through the body, for instance, by infliction of grievous hurt on oneself, "objectifying" and making present the inner state, and is finally given a home in language. Thus the transactions between body and language lead to an articulation of the world in which the strangeness of the world revealed by death, by its non-inhabitability, can be transformed into a world in which one can dwell again, in full awareness of a life that has to be lived in loss. This is one path towards healing – women call such healing simply the power to endure.

Was it possible for women and men to take this image of healing and recreate that which died when the desire for nationalism and autonomy from colonial subjugation became metamorphosed into sexual violation? Could that which died be named, acknowledged, and mourned? Or would one be condemned to dwell alone and nameless in the ruins of memory.[3]

Some realities need to be fictionalized before they can be apprehended. This is apparent in the weight of the distinction between the three registers of the real, the symbolic, and the imaginary in the work of Lacan, and in Castoriadis's formulation of the necessity of working on the register of the imaginary for the conceptualization of society itself.[4] I shall allow myself two scenes, or phantasms, that provide a theoretical scaffolding to the issues I address. In these two scenes I call upon the words of the philosopher Wittgenstein and the short story writer Sadat Hasan Manto, as persons who responded to the call of the world in the register of the imaginary. Manto is important to me for he answered in the sounds and senses of the Indian languages to the scenes of devastation; Wittgenstein because he showed the possibilities of imagination of pain within a rigorous philosophical grammar. In placing their texts within mine, I can simultaneously be there and not be there. I hope I shall be evoking these texts not in the manner of a thief who has stolen another voice but in the manner of one who pawns herself to the words of this other.

I

The first scene is from Wittgenstein's *The Blue and Brown Books* on the question of how my pain may reside in another body:

In order to see that it is conceivable that one person should have pain in another person's body, one must examine what sorts of facts we call criteria for a pain being in a certain place.... Suppose I feel a pain which on the evidence of the pain alone, e.g. with closed eyes, I should call a pain in my left hand. Someone asks me to touch the painful spot with my right hand. I do so and looking around perceive that I am touching my neighbor's hand.... This would be pain *felt* in another's body.[5]

In this movement between bodies, the sentence "I am in pain" becomes the conduit through which I may move out of an inexpressible privacy and suffocation of my pain. This does not mean that I am understood. Wittgenstein uses the route of a philosophical grammar to say that this is not an indicative statement, although it may have the formal appearance of one. It is the beginning of a language game. Pain, in this rendering, is not that inexpressible something that destroys communication or marks an exit from one's existence in language. Instead, it makes a claim asking for acknowledgment, which may be given or denied. In either case, it is not a referential statement that is simply pointing to an inner object.

What is fascinating for me is that in drawing the scene of the pathos of pain, Wittgenstein creates language as the bodying forth of words. Where is my pain – in touching you to point out the location of that pain – has my pointing finger – there it is – found your body, which my pain (our pain) can inhabit, at least for that moment when I close my eyes and touch your hand? And if the language for the inexpressibility of pain is always falling short of my need for its plenitude, then is this not the sense of disappointment that human beings have with themselves and the language that is given to them? But also, does the whole task of becoming human, even of becoming perversely human, not involve a response (even if this is rage) to the sense of loss when language seems to fail? Wittgenstein's example of my pain inhabiting your body seems to me to suggest either the institution that the representation of shared pain exists in imagination but is not experienced, in which case one would say that language is hooked rather inadequately to the world of pain. Or, alternately, that the experience of pain cries out for this response of the possibility that my pain could reside in your body and that the philosophical grammar of pain is an answer to that call.

II

[...] In the modern project of building a nation the bodies of women are violently appropriated for the cause as nationalism gives birth to its double – communalism. If one deified women so that the nation could be imagined as the beloved, the other makes visible the dark side of this project by making the bodies of women the surfaces on which their text of the nation is written. Body and language both function here as simulacrums in which collective desire and collective death meet. [...]

III

The second phantasm I want to evoke is from a story by Sadat Hassan Manto entitled "Khol Do," which I first analyzed in 1986.[6] The setting is the Partition of India and the riots, though we never gaze at the violence directly. An aged father and his daughter take a journey from one side of the border to the other. On reaching his destination, the father cannot find his daughter. He goes berserk searching for her. He comes across some young men who are acting as volunteers to help trace lost relatives. He tells them about his daughter and urges them to find her. They promise to help.

The young men find Sakina, the daughter, hiding in a forest half crazed with fear. They reassure her by telling her how they had met her father. She climbs into the jeep with them. One of them, seeing how embarrassed she is because she does not have her *duppata* (veil), gives her his jacket so that she can cover her breasts.

We next see a clinic. A near dead body is being brought on a stretcher. The father, Sarajjudin, recognizes the corpse. It is his daughter. Numbly he follows the stretcher to the doctor's chamber. Reacting to the stifling heat in the room, the doctor points to the window and says *"khol do"* ("open it").

There is a movement in the dead body. The hands move towards the tape of the *salwar* (trouser) and fumble to unloosen (lit. open) it. Old Sarajjudin shouts in joy "my daughter is alive – my daughter is alive." The doctor is drenched in sweat.

As I understood this story in 1986, I saw Sakina condemned to a living death. The normality of language has been destroyed, as Sakina can hear words conveying only the "other" command. Such a fractured relation to language has been documented for many survivors of prolonged violence, for whom it is the ordinariness of language that divides them from the rest of the world. I noted that even Sakina's father cannot comprehend the nonworld into which she has been plunged, for he mistakes the movement in the body as a sign of life

whereas in truth it is the sign of her living death. Only the doctor as the off-the-center character in the story can register the true horror.

On deeper meditation, I think there is one last movement that I did not then comprehend. In giving the shout of joy and saying "my daughter is alive," the father does not speak here in personalized voices of tradition. In the societal context of this period, when ideas of purity and honor densely populated the literary narratives, as well as family and political narratives, so that fathers willed their daughters to die for family honor rather than live with bodies that had been violated by other men, *this father wills his daughter to live even as parts of her body can do nothing else but proclaim her brutal violation.*

In the terms set by the example from Wittgenstein's *The Blue and Brown Books*, one may ask if the pain of the female body so violated can live in a male body. One can read in Manto a transaction between death and life, body and speech, in the figures of the daughter and the father. In the speech of the father, at least, the daughter is alive, and though she may find an existence only in his utterance, he creates through his utterance a home for her mutilated and violated self. Compare this with hundreds of accounts purporting to be based on direct experience in which the archetypal motif was of a girl finding her way to her parents' home after having been subjected to rape and plunder, and being told, "why are you here – it would have been better if you were dead." As I have argued elsewhere, such rejections may not have occurred as often as they were alleged to have happened in narratives. But the widespread belief in such narrative truths of sacrificing the daughter to maintain the unsullied purity and honor of the family attests to the power of this myth. To be masculine when death was all around was to be able to hand death to your violated daughter without flinching – to obliterate any desire for the concreteness and uniqueness of this human being who once played in your family yard. In the background of such stories, a single sentence of joy uttered by old Sarajjudin transforms the meaning of being a father. [...]

In Manto, the sentence, "my daughter is alive," is like Wittgenstein's, "I am in pain." Although it has the formal appearance of an indicative statement, it is to beseech the daughter to find a way to live in the speech of the father. And it happens not at the moment when her dishonor is hidden from the eyes of the world but at the moment when her body proclaims it. This sentence is the beginning of a relationship, not its end.

At this moment I want to present the glimpse of a later argument. I have written elsewhere that in the gendered division of labor in the work of mourning, it is the task of men to ritually create a body for the dead person and to find a place in the cosmos for the dead. This task, which is always a very difficult one for the mourner, may even become repulsive, as when members of the Aghori sect, who live on cremation grounds, state that in the cases when someone has died an unnatural or violent death, they have to consume parts of the dead body so as to free the dead person from living the fate of a homeless ghost. I wonder if Sarajjudin performed this terrifying task of accepting the tortured relationship with the daughter whom other fathers may have simply cast away as socially dead. And instead of the simplified images of healing that assume that reliving a trauma or decathecting desire from the lost object and reinvesting it elsewhere, we need to think of healing as a kind of relationship with death. [. . .]

V

In the literary imagination in India, the violence of the Partition was about inscribing desire on the bodies of women in a manner that we have not yet understood. In the mythic imagination in India, victory or defeat in war was ultimately inscribed on the bodies of women. The texts on the *vilap* (mourning laments of Gandhari in the *Mahabharata* or of Mandodari in the *Ramayana*, all whose kin were slain in the epic battles) are literary classics. This is a metaphoric transformation of the role of witnessing death in everyday life. Yet, the violence of the Partition was unique in the metamorphosis it achieved between the idea of appropriating a territory as nation and appropriating the body of the women as territory. [. . .]

Thus, we have the interweaving of two strands. First, the idea that women must bear witness to death, which is found in the classical Indian literature and the everyday life, gets transformed into the notion that the woman's body must be made to bear the signs of its possession by the enemy. The second strand seems to come from a narrative trope established at the time of the mutiny that equates the violation of the nation with the violation of its women. It is not clear whether during the riots nationalist slogans were physically imprinted on women, although the most horrific stories about such violations are commonly believed.[7] What is clear is that at least one hundred thousand women from both sides of the border were forcibly abducted and raped. The figures given in the Legislative Assembly during the Constituent Assembly debates in 1949 confirm this. It also affirmed that processions of women who were stripped naked were organized with the accompaniment of jeering crowds in cities like Amritsar and Lahore.[8] Family narratives abound on men who were compelled to kill their women to save their honor. Such sacrificial deaths are beatified in family narratives, while women who were recovered from their abductors and returned to their families or who converted to the other religion and made new lives in the homes of their abductors hardly ever find a place in these narratives, although they occur frequently in the literary representations.

When women's bodies were made the passive witnesses of the disorder of the Partition in this manner, how did women mourn the loss of self and the world? It is in considering this question that we find startling reversals in the transactions between body and language. In the normal process of mourning, grievous harm is inflicted by women on their own bodies, while the acoustic and linguistic codes make the loss public by the mourning laments. When asking women to narrate their experiences of the Partition I found a zone of silence around the event. This silence was achieved either by the use of language that was general and metaphoric but that evaded specific description of any events so as to capture the particularity of their experience, or by describing the surrounding events but leaving the actual experience of abduction and rape unstated. It was common to describe the violence of the Partition in such terms as rivers of blood flowing and the earth covered with white shrouds right unto the horizon. Sometimes a woman would remember images of fleeing, but as one woman warned me, it was dangerous to remember. These memories were sometimes compared to poison that makes the inside of the woman dissolve, as a solid is dissolved in a powerful liquid (*andar hi andar ghul ja rahi hai*). At other times a woman would say that she is like a discarded exercise book in which the accounts of past relationships were kept – the body, a parchment of losses. At any rate, none of the metaphors used to describe the self that had become the repository of poisonous knowledge emphasized the need to give expression to this hidden knowledge.

This code of silence protected women who had been brought back to their families through the efforts of the military evacuation authorities after they were recovered from the homes of their abductors, or who had been married by stretching norms of kinship and affinity since the violation of their bodies was never made public. Rather than bearing witness to the disorder that they had been subjected to, the metaphor that they used was of a woman drinking the poison and keeping it within her: "Just as a woman's body is made so that she can hide the faults of her husband deep within her, so she can drink all pain – take the stance of silence." And as one woman told Ritu Menon and Kamla Bhasin, "what is a woman – she is always used?" Or, as was told to me, "what is there to be proud in a woman's body – everyday it is polluted by being consumed." The sliding of the representations of the female body between everyday life into the body that had become the container of the poisonous knowledge of the events of the Partition perhaps helped women to assimilate their experiences into their everyday lives.

Just as the relation between speech and silence is reversed in the act of witnessing here, so is the relation between the surface and depth of the body. In the fantasy of men, the inscription of nationalist slogans on the bodies of women (Victory to India, Long live Pakistan), or proclaiming possession of their bodies (This thing, this loot – *ye mal* – is ours), would create a future memory by which men of the other community would never be able to forget that the women as territory had already been claimed and occupied by other men. The bodies of the women were surfaces on which texts were to be written and read – icons of the new nations. But women converted this passivity into agency by using metaphors of pregnancy – hiding pain, giving it a home just as a child is given a home in the woman's body. Kriesteva's description of pregnancy – it happens but I am not there – may also be used to describe such violence. But the subsequent act of remembering only through the body makes the woman's own experience displace being from the surface to the depth of the body. The only difference is that unlike the child, which the woman will be able to offer to the husband, this holding of the pain inside must never be allowed to be born. This movement from surface to depth also transforms passivity into agency.

It was again Sadat Hasan Manto who was able to give literary expression to this. In his story *Fundanen* (Pompoms), a woman is sitting in front of a mirror. Her speech is completely incoherent, but like many strings of nonsense used in rhymes or musical compositions, its phonetic properties are like theatrical or musical representations. Interspersed between the strings of nonsense syllables are meaningful sentences with precise information such as the bus number that brought her from one side of the border to the other. The woman is drawing grotesque designs on her body, registering these only in the mirror. She says she is designing a body that is appropriate for the time, for in those days, she says, women had to grow two stomachs – one was the normal one and the second was for them to be able to bear the fruits of violence within themselves. The distortion of speech and the distortion of body seems to make deep sense. The language of pain could only be a kind of hysteria – the surface of the body becomes a carnival of images and the depth becomes the site for hysterical pregnancies – the language having all the phonetic excess of hysteria that destroys apparent meanings. When Tagore's Bimala said that she wondered if Sandip could see the power of the nation in her, she seems to have prefigured Manto's women in whom one could see the completion of that project of making the nation visible by a surrealist juxtaposition of images.

So, if men emerged from colonial subjugation as autonomous citizens of an independent nation, then they emerged simultaneously as monsters. What kind of death rituals could have been performed for these wandering ghosts to be given a place in the cosmos? We have to again turn to the register of the imaginary. Intizar Hussain described this in his story "The City of Sorrow," in which three nameless men are having a conversation. The story opens with the first man saying, "I have nothing to say. I am dead." The story then moves in the form of a dialogue on the manner of his dying. One of his companions asks how he actually died. Did he die when he forced a man on the point of his sword to strip his sister naked? No, he remained alive. Then perhaps when he saw the same man forcing another old man to strip his wife naked? No, he remained alive. Then, when he was himself forced to strip his own sister naked? Then too he remained alive. It was only when his father gazed at his face and died that he heard in his wife's voice the question, "don't you know it is you who are dead?" and he realized that he had died. But he was condemned to carry his own corpse with him wherever he went.

It appears to me that just as women drank the pain so that life could continue, so men longed for an unheroic martyrdom by which they could invite the evil back upon themselves and humanize the enormous looming images of nation and sexuality. But it was not through the political discourse that this was achieved. The debates in the Constituent Assembly on the issue of abducted women were full of the imagery of restoring national honor by recovering the women who had been abducted from the other side and returning "their" women back to the Muslims. Mahatma Gandhi, writing about the exchange of women and the exchange of prisoners on the same page of his Delhi diary, said that it had pained him to learn that many Hindu men were reluctant to return the Muslim women. He urged them to do so as a form of repentance. Jawaharlal Nehru urged Hindu men to accept the women who were recovered and to not punish them for the sins of their abductors. In this entire discourse of exchange of women from both sides, it was assumed that once the nation had claimed back its women, its honor would have been restored. It was as if you could wipe the slate clean and leave the horrendous events behind.

VI

It was on the register of the imaginary that the question of what could constitute the passion of those who occupied this unspeakable and unhearable zone was given shape. The zone between the two deaths that the women had to occupy did not permit of any speech, for what "right" words could be spoken against the wrong that had been done them. Hence, Manto's Sakina can only proclaim the terrible truth of this society by a mute repetition – *murde main kuch jumbish hui* (there was a movement in the corpse). The task of mourning for the men was to hear this silence, to mold it by their presence. Hence the joyful cry of the father that his daughter was alive. This being alive in the zone of the two deaths, and this witnessing of the truth of the women's violation, is how mourning in this zone could be defined. Here the issue is not that

of an Antigone, mourning for her dead brother in defiance of the law of Creon, proclaiming that the register of someone who has been named must be preserved, as Lacan makes us witness it in his interpretation of Antigone's famous passage that she would not have died for a husband or a child but that this concerned her brother, born of the same father and the same mother (the product of criminal desire and criminal knowledge).[9] Here it is the issue of the women drinking poisonous knowledge and men molding the silences of the women with their words. [...]

It is often considered the task of historiography to break the silences that announce the zones of taboo. There is even something heroic in the image of empowering women to speak and to give voice to the voiceless. I have myself found this a very complicated task, for when we use such imagery as breaking the silence, we may end by using our capacity to "unearth" hidden facts as a weapon. Even the idea that we should recover the narratives of violence becomes problematic when we realize that such narratives cannot be told unless we see the relation between pain and language that a culture has evolved. I have found it important to think of the division of labor between men and women in the work of mourning as a model on which the further work of transforming could be done in thinking about the relation between pain, language, and the body. Following Wittgenstein, this manner of conceptualizing the puzzle of pain frees us from thinking that statements about pain are in the nature of questions about certainty or doubt over our own pain or that of others. Instead, we begin to think of pain as asking for acknowledgment and recognition; denial of the other's pain is not about the failings of the intellect but the failings of the spirit. In the register of the imaginary, the pain of the other not only asks for a home in language but also seeks a home in the body.

It is not that there is a seamless continuity between the distant shore and the everyday shore, between the registers of the imaginary and the real, but one can only understand the subtle transformations that go on as we move from one shore to the other, if one keeps in mind the complex relation between speaking and hearing, between building a world that the living can inhabit with their loss and building a world in which the dead can find a home. It worries me that I have been unable to name that which died when autonomous citizens of India were simultaneously born as monsters.

But then I have to remind myself and others that those who tried to name it, such as Manto, themselves touched madness and died in fierce regret for the loss of the radical dream of transforming India, while those who found speech easily, as in the political debates on abducted women in the Constituent Assembly, continue to talk about national honor when dealing with the violence that women have had to endure in every communal riot since the Partition.

NOTES

1 G. D. Khosla, *Stern Reckoning* (Delhi: Oxford University Press, 1989; first published in 1951), 3.

2 Stanley Cavell, *Philosophical Passages: Wittgenstein, Emerson, Austin, Derrida* (Oxford: Blackwell, 1995).

3 Lawrence Langer, *Holocaust Testimonies: The Ruins of Memory* (New Haven, CT: Yale University Press, 1991).

4 C. Castoriadis, *The Imaginary Institution of Society* (Cambridge: Polity Press, 1987).

5 Ludwig Wittgenstein, *The Blue and Brown Books* (London: Blackwell, 1958).

6 This story is included in an anthology of stories on the Partition translated by Alok Bhalla, ed., *Stories about the Partition of India*, vols. I, II, III (Delhi: Indus Publications, 1994), but there are many problems with the translation as I have pointed out elsewhere. See Veena Das, *Review of Stories about the Partition of India*, vols. I, II, and III, ed. Alok Bhalla (Delhi: Indus Publications, 1994).

7 Khwja Ahmed Abbas, "Prastavna," in Ramananda Sagar, *Aur insan mar gaya* (Delhi: Rakjamal Prakashan, 1977, in Hindi); and Das, *Critical Events: An Anthropological Perspective on Contemporary India*.

8 Das, *Critical Events: An Anthropological Perspective on Contemporary India*; Uruashi Butalia, "Community, State and Gender: On Women's Agency during Partition," *Economic and Political Weekly* 17 (1993): WS12–WS24; Ritu Menon and Kamla Bhasin, "Surviving Violence: Some Reflections on Women's Experience of Partition," paper presented at IV Conference of the Indian Association of Women Studies, 1990; and Ritu Menon and Kamla Bhasin, "Recovery, Rupture, Resistance. Indian State and Abduction of Women during Partition," *Economic and Political Weekly* 17 (1993): WS2–WS12.

9 J. Lacan, "The Essence of Tragedy," in J. A. Miller, ed., *The Seminar of Jacques Lacan, Book VII*, trans. Dennis Porter (London: Norton & Co., 1992).

41

From *The Massacre at El Mozote: A Parable of the Cold War*

Mark Danner

It was growing dark, and soon flames were rising from the house of Israel Márquez, highlighting the soldiers' faces and the trunk of the tree. It grew so hot that Rufina began to fear that the tree would catch and she would be forced to run. She had remained perfectly still, hardly daring to breathe, and her legs had begun to fall asleep. And the soldiers, still close enough to touch, remained where they were, smoking cigarettes and watching the fire.

"We'll just stay here and wait for the witches of Mozote to come out of that fire," one said.

The soldiers watched the fire and talked, and Rufina, frozen in her terror a few feet away, listened. "Well, we've killed all the old men and women," one said. "But there's still a lot of kids down there. You know, a lot of those kids are really good-looking, really cute. I wouldn't want to kill all of them. Maybe we can keep some of them, you know – take them with us."

"What are you talking about?" another soldier answered roughly. "We have to finish everyone, you know that. That's the colonel's order. This is an *operativo de tierra arrasada* here" – a scorched-earth operation – "and we have to kill the kids as well, or we'll get it ourselves."

"Listen, I don't want to kill kids," the first soldier said.

"Look," another said. "We have orders to finish everyone and we have to complete our orders. That's it."

At about this time, up on the hill known as El Pinalito, Captain Salazar was shrugging off a guide's timid plea for the children's lives. "If we don't kill them now," he said angrily, "they'll just grow up to be guerrillas. We have to take care of the job now."

Meanwhile, the soldiers sat and gazed at the burning house. Finally, one stood up. "Well, no witches came out," he said. "There are no witches. Let's go see what kind of food they have in that store."

With that, the other men got to their feet, picked up their rifles, and trudged off. A few minutes later, Rufina could hear, from the store of Marcos Díaz, "bottles clinking – you know, as if they were drinking sodas."

The fire was still burning furiously, but the big crab-apple tree, which some miracle had kept from igniting, shielded Rufina from the heat. Over the crackling of the fire she could still hear, coming from the hill called La Cruz, the screams of the girls. Now and again, she heard a burst of gunfire.

After a time, when the soldiers seemed to have finished drinking their sodas, Rufina heard crying and screaming begin from the house of Alfredo Márquez: the screaming of the children. "They were crying, 'Mommy! Mommy! They're hurting us! Help us! They're cutting us! They're choking us! Help us!'

"Then I heard one of my children crying. My son, Cristino, was crying, 'Mama Rufina, help me! They're killing me! They killed my sister! They're killing me! Help me!' I didn't know what to do. They were killing my children. I knew that if I went back there to help my children I would be cut to pieces. But I couldn't stand to hear it, I couldn't bear it. I was afraid that I would cry out, that I would scream, that I would go crazy. I couldn't stand it, and I prayed to God to help me. I promised God that if He helped me I would tell the world what happened here.

"Then I tied my hair up and tied my skirt between my legs and I crawled on my belly out from behind the tree. There were animals there, cows and a dog, and they saw me, and I was afraid they would make a noise, but God made them stay quiet as I crawled among them. I crawled across the road and under the barbed wire and into the maguey on the other side. I crawled a little farther through the thorns, and I dug a little hole with my hands and put my face in the hole so I could cry without anyone hearing. I could hear the children screaming still, and I lay there with my face against the earth and cried."

Rufina could not see the children; she could only hear their cries as the soldiers waded into them, slashing some with their machetes, crushing the skulls of others with the butts of their rifles. Many others – the youngest children, most below the age of 12 – the soldiers herded from the house of Alfredo Márquez across the street to the sacristy, pushing them, crying and screaming, into the dark tiny room. There the soldiers raised their M-16s and emptied their magazines into the roomful of children.

Not all the children of El Mozote died at the sacristy. A young man now known as Chepe Mozote told me that when the townspeople were forced to assemble on the plaza that evening he and his little brother had been left behind in their house, on the outskirts of the hamlet, near the school. By the next morning, Chepe had heard plenty of shooting, and his mother had not returned. "About six o'clock, around ten soldiers in camouflage uniforms came to the house," Chepe told me. "They asked me where my mother was. I told them she had gone to the plaza the night before. I asked them if I could see my mother, and they said I couldn't but I should come with them to the playing field" – near the school. "They said when we got there they would explain where my mother was."

Carrying his little brother, Chepe went with the soldiers and walked along with them as they searched house to house. "We found maybe fifteen kids," he says, "and then they took us all to the playing field. On the way, I heard shooting and I saw some dead bodies, maybe five old people."

When they reached the playing field, "there were maybe thirty children," he says. "The soldiers were putting ropes on the trees. I was seven years old, and I didn't really understand what was happening until I saw one of the soldiers take a kid he had been carrying – the kid was maybe three years old – throw him in the air, and stab him with a bayonet.

"They slit some of the kids' throats, and many they hanged from the tree. All of us were crying now, but we were their prisoners – there was nothing we could do. The soldiers kept telling us, 'You are guerrillas and this is justice. This is justice.' Finally, there were only three of us left. I watched them hang my brother. He was two years old. I could see I was going to be killed soon, and I thought it would be better to die running, so I ran. I slipped through the soldiers and dived into the bushes. They fired into the bushes, but none of their bullets hit me."

Lying amid the maguey that night, Rufina Amaya heard the chorus of screams dwindle to a few voices, and listened as it grew weaker and weaker and finally ceased. She heard the officers order that fire be put to the house of Alfredo Márquez and the church and the sacristy, and from the maguey she saw the flames rise and then she heard faint cries start up again inside the buildings and the short bursts of gunfire finishing off a few wounded, who had been forced by the flames to reveal that they were still alive.

Soon the only sounds were those which trickled down from the hills – laughter, intermittent screams, a few shots. On La Cruz, soldiers were raping the young girls who were left. On El Chingo and El Pinalito, other soldiers busied themselves making camp. Down in the hamlet, a few troops walked about here and there, patrolling. Not far from the still burning house of Israel Márquez, two soldiers halted suddenly, and one of them pointed to the patch of maguey. He lowered his rifle and fired, and after a moment his companion fired, too. In the patch of brush, the stream of bullets sent a dark-green rain of maguey shreds fluttering to the earth. Then the soldiers charged forward and began poking among the weeds.

"She was right here," one said, pulling at some maguey. "I saw her, I know it."

Up on the hills, the soldiers listened to the shots, exchanged glances, and waited. Then they went on with what they had been doing: watching the flames rise from the burning houses and talking quietly among themselves, telling tales of the day's work.

They spoke wonderingly about the evangelicals, those people whose faith seemed to grant them a strange power.

"They said maybe some of the people believed in God so strongly that they just delivered themselves up, they didn't resist," the guide told me. "They said some of the people were singing even as they were killed."

There was one in particular the soldiers talked about that evening (she is mentioned in the Tutela Legal report as well): a girl on La Cruz whom they had raped many times during the course of the afternoon, and through it all, while the other women of El Mozote had screamed and cried as if they had never had a man, this girl had sung hymns, strange evangelical songs, and she had kept right on singing, too, even after they had done what had to be done, and shot her in the chest. She had lain there on La Cruz with the blood flowing from her chest, and had kept on singing – a bit weaker than before, but still singing. And the soldiers, stupefied, had watched and pointed. Then they had grown tired of the game and shot her again, and she sang still, and their wonder began to turn to fear – until finally they had unsheathed their machetes and hacked through her neck, and at last the singing had stopped.

Now the soldiers argued about this. Some declared that the girl's strange power proved that God existed. And that brought them back to the killing of the children. "There were a lot of differences among the soldiers about whether this had been a good thing or whether they shouldn't have done it," the guide told me.

As the soldiers related it now, the guide said, there had been a disagreement outside the schoolhouse, where a number of children were being held. Some of the men had hesitated, saying they didn't want to kill the children, and the others had ridiculed them.

According to one account, a soldier had called the commanding officer. "Hey, Major!" he had shouted. "Someone says he won't kill children!"

"Which son of a bitch says that?" the Major had shouted back angrily, striding over. The Major had not hesitated to do what an officer does in such situations: show leadership. He'd pushed into the group of children, seized a little boy,

thrown him in the air, and impaled him as he fell. That had put an end to the discussion.

Now, up on the hills, the soldiers talked and argued and watched the burning houses, while the two men down below still searched among the maguey, cursing at the sharp thorns.

"I know she was here," the first soldier said. "I saw her. She was right here."

"No, no," his companion finally said. "There's no one here. You're just seeing the dead. You're seeing ghosts. The ghosts of the people you killed are frightening you." With that, the soldiers looked at each other, then turned and trotted back to the center of the hamlet. Amid the maguey, Rufina Amaya closed her eyes, remained motionless. After a time, she reached out a hand and began groping about in the weeds, slowly pulling the thorny strips to her, gathering them into a pile and heaping them over her body.

She lay there still when the stars began to disappear from the lightening sky. She heard sounds of movement from the hills, rising voices as the men woke, urinated, ate, prepared their equipment. Shots echoed here and there, interspersed with the barking and howling of dogs and the lowing of cows as the soldiers killed the animals one by one. From up on La Cruz came a burst of high-pitched screaming and begging, followed by a prolonged chorus of gunfire, and, at last, silence. And then the men of the Atlacatl, having completed the operation in El Mozote, moved out.

Hours earlier, when the chill of the night came on, Rufina Amaya had shivered, for the maguey had badly ripped her blouse and skirt. The thorns had torn the flesh of her arms and legs, but at the time she hadn't noticed. Now she could feel the cuts, swelling and throbbing, and the blood, dried and prickly, on her limbs. And as she lay sobbing amid the thorns, listening to the soldiers pass, her breasts ached with the milk that had gathered there to feed her youngest child.

Marching past the church, which was burning still, past the carcasses of cows and dogs, and out of El Mozote, the men of the Atlacatl did not see the dark shape in the maguey patch, the heap of dark-green leaves. Their minds were on their work, which on that Saturday morning in December lay ahead in the hamlet of Los Toriles.

In Los Toriles, "the soldiers pulled people from their houses and hustled them into the square," the guide told me, "and went down the line taking money and anything of value out of people's pockets. Then they just lined the people up against a wall and shot them with machine guns. The people fell like trees falling."

Even so, the killing in Los Toriles took much of the day. Some of the residents, having seen the columns of smoke rising the afternoon before from El Mozote, had fled their homes and hidden in caves above the hamlet. But most had stayed, wanting to protect their homes: they remembered that on a previous operation soldiers had set fire to houses they found empty, claiming that they belonged to guerrillas.

By afternoon, the streets of Los Toriles were filled with corpses. "It was so terrible that we had to jump over the dead so as not to step on them," the guide told me. "There were dogs and cows and other animals, and people of all ages, from newborn to very old. I saw them shoot an old woman, and they had to hold her up to shoot her. I was filled with pity. I wished we had gone out and fought guerrillas, because to see all those dead children filled me with sadness."

As night fell, the soldiers walked through the town setting fire to the houses. It was dark by the time they left Los Toriles, to march south toward the guerrilla stronghold of La Guacamaya. They made camp in open country, rose at dawn, and, as they prepared to move out again, Captain Salazar motioned them over. The men of the Atlacatl gathered in a circle, sitting cross-legged on the ground as he stood and addressed them.

"¡Señores!" the Captain said angrily. "What we did yesterday, and the day before, this is called war. This is what war is. War is hell. And, goddammit, if I order you to kill your mother, that is just what you're going to do. Now, I don't want to hear that, afterward, while you're out drinking and bullshitting among yourselves, you're whining and complaining about this, about how terrible it was. I don't want to hear that. Because what we did yesterday, what we've been doing on this operation – this is war, gentlemen. This is what war is." And for perhaps half an hour the Captain went on speaking in his angry voice, and the men shifted uneasily.

"There had been a lot of talk about whether it was right," the guide said, "and this had clearly got back to the Captain." Finally, the tirade over, the men got to their feet. Soon they were marching south again.

Late that afternoon, they reached La Guacamaya. They found nothing there but dead animals; the guerrillas had long since departed. The soldiers spent two nights there, resting and cleaning their equipment. Helicopters landed, bringing Colonel Flores and other top officers, who met with the Atlacatl officers for "evaluation and coordination." The operation was now winding down.

"It was a walk-through by then, a joke," the lieutenant involved in the operation told me. "The guerrillas were long gone, and everybody knew it."

On the second morning, the men of the Atlacatl marched west, heading for the black road. On their way, they passed the hamlet of La Joya. "Everything was dead there – animals and people all mixed together," the guide said. "Vultures were everywhere. You couldn't stand to be there, because of the stink."

Above the hamlet, in the caves and ravines and wooded gullies, those who had managed to escape the troops shivered and waited, and tried to keep their children still. Some had left their homes before the soldiers came; others had managed to flee when men from the Atlacatl, on the day some of their comrades were "cleansing" El Mozote, stormed La Joya. "Suddenly, there was shooting and explosions all over," Andrea Márquez, who had been 20 years old at the time, said. "We didn't even see the soldiers at first. There were bullets flying everywhere. I grabbed my little girl – she was one and a half – and put her on my back, and we started crawling through the brush with bullets flying and explosions all around." She showed me an ugly scar from a shrapnel wound on her knee. "We crawled and then we ran and ran, and after a while my baby made sounds as if she were thirsty, and I pulled her around and then I saw there was a wound in her head, and I realized I was covered with blood."

No one else was around – the people had scattered at the soldiers' assault – and Andrea Márquez was too terrified to go back toward La Joya. Holding her child in her arms, she climbed higher into the mountains, found a cave, and tried to care for her daughter's wound with leaves and with water from a stream. Eight days later, she found a stick and dug a hole and buried her little girl. Then, delirious with grief and shock and terror, she wandered high into the northern mountains.

Months later, the surviving villagers, those few who remained in Morazán, began to murmur fearfully to one another that a witch had come to haunt the mountains – a savage woman, who could be glimpsed from time to time late at night by moonlight, naked but for her waist-length hair, as she crouched by a stream and stripped the flesh from a wriggling fish with long, sharp fingernails. The villagers were frightened of her, for they knew that it was after the *matanza*, the great killing of El Mozote, that the witch had come to haunt the mountains.

42

Gender and Symbolic Violence

Pierre Bourdieu

appears benevolent

I would like to warn against the radical misinterpretations often made of the notion of symbolic violence, which all arise from a more or less reductive understanding of the adjective 'symbolic', which is used here in a sense that I believe to be rigorous, and whose theoretical basis I set out in an article two decades ago.[1] Taking 'symbolic' in one of its commonest senses, people sometimes assume that to emphasize symbolic violence is to minimize the role of physical violence, to forget (and make people forget) that there are battered, raped and exploited women, or worse, to seek to exculpate men from that form of violence – which is obviously not the case. Understanding 'symbolic' as the opposite of 'real, actual', people suppose that symbolic violence is a purely 'spiritual' violence which ultimately has no real effects. It is this naive distinction, characteristic of a crude materialism, that the materialist theory of the economy of symbolic goods, which I have been trying to build up over many years, seeks to destroy, by giving its proper place in theory to the objectivity of the subjective experience of relations of domination. Another misunderstanding: the reference to ethnology, of which I have tried to show the heuristic functions here, is suspected of being a way of restoring the myth of the 'eternal feminine' (or masculine) or, worse, of eternalizing the structure of masculine domination by describing it as unvarying and eternal. On the contrary, far from asserting that the structures of domination are ahistorical, I shall try to establish that they are *the product of an incessant (and therefore historical) labour of reproduction*, to which singular agents (including men, with weapons such as physical violence and symbolic violence) and

institutions – families, the church, the educational system, the state – contribute.

The dominated apply categories constructed from the point of view of the dominant to the relations of domination, thus making them appear as natural. This can lead to a kind of systematic self-depreciation, even self-denigration, visible in particular, as has been seen, in the representation that Kabyle women have of their genitals as something deficient, ugly, even repulsive (or, in modern societies, in the vision that many women have of their bodies as not conforming to the aesthetic canons imposed by fashion), and, more generally, in their adherence to a demeaning image of woman. Symbolic violence is instituted through the adherence that the dominated cannot fail to grant to the dominant (and therefore to the domination) when, to shape her thought of him, and herself, or, rather, her thought of her relation with him, she has only cognitive instruments that she shares with him and which, being no more than the embodied form of the relation of domination, cause that relation to appear as natural; or, in other words, when the schemes she applies in order to perceive and appreciate herself, or to perceive and appreciate the dominant (high/low, male/female, white/black, etc.), are the product of the embodiment of the – thereby naturalized – classifications of which her social being is the product.

Being unable to evoke here with sufficient subtlety (it would take a Virginia Woolf to do so) sufficiently numerous, varied, and cogent examples of concrete situations in which this gentle and often invisible violence is exerted, I shall simply refer to observations which, in their objectivism, are more persuasive than description of the minutiae of inter-actions. Surveys show, for example, that a large majority of French women say they want a husband who is older and also (quite coherently) taller than themselves; two-thirds of them even explicitly reject the idea of a husband shorter than them-selves. What is the meaning of this refusal to see the disappearance of the ordinary signs of the sexual 'hierarchy'? 'Accepting an inversion of appearances,' replies Michel Bozon, 'is to suggest that it is the woman who dominates, which, para-doxically, lowers her socially; she feels diminished with a diminished man.'[2] So it is not sufficient to note that women generally agree with men (who, for their part, prefer younger women) when they accept the external signs of a dominated pos-ition; in their representation of their relation with the man to which their social identity is (or will be) attached, they take account of the representation that men and women as a whole will inevitably form of him by applying to him the schemes of perception and appreciation universally shared (within the group in question). Because these common principles tacitly and unarguably demand that, at least in appearances and seen from outside, the man should occupy the dominant position within the couple, it is for him, for the sake of the dignity that they recognize *a priori* in him, but also for themselves, that they can only want and love a man whose dignity is clearly affirmed and attested in and by the fact that he is visibly 'above' them. This takes place, of course, without any calculation, through the apparent arbitrariness of an inclination that is not amenable to discussion or reason but which, as is shown by observation of the desired, and also real, differences, can only arise and be fulfilled in the experience of the super-iority of which age and height (justified as indices of maturity and guarantees of security) are the most indisputable and universally recognized signs.

To follow through the paradoxes that only a dis-positionalist view can make intelligible, one only has to note that those who show themselves to be most submissive to the 'traditional' model – by saying that they wish for a larger age-gap – are found mostly among the social categories of self-employed crafts-men, shopkeepers, farmers and manual workers, in which marriage remains, for women, the prime

means of acquiring a social position – as if, being the product of an unconscious adjustment to the probabilities associated with an objective structure of domination, the submissive dispositions that are expressed in these preferences produced the equiva-lent of what could be a calculation of enlightened self-interest. By contrast, these dispositions tend to weaken – with, no doubt, effects of *hysteresis* which would emerge from analysis of variations in practices not only according to the position occupied, but also according to trajectory – with the objective depend-ency that helps to produce and maintain them (the same logic of adjustment of dispositions to the object-ive chances also explaining why it can be observed that women's access to employment is a major factor in their access to divorce). This tends to confirm that, contrary to the romantic representation of love, choice of partner is not exempt from a form of ration-ality that owes nothing to rational calculation, or, to put it another way, that love is often partly *amor fati*, love of one's social destiny.

So the only way to understand this particular form of domination is to move beyond the forced choice between constraint (by forces) and consent (to reasons), between mechanical coercion and vol-untary, free, deliberate, even calculated submis-sion. The effect of symbolic domination (whether ethnic, gender, cultural or linguistic, etc.) is exerted not in the pure logic of knowing consciousnesses but through the schemes of perception, appreci-ation and action that are constitutive of habitus and which, below the level of the decisions of con-sciousness and the controls of the will, set up a cognitive relationship that is profoundly obscure to itself. Thus, the paradoxical logic of masculine domination and feminine submissiveness, which can, without contradiction, be described as both *spontaneous and extorted*, cannot be understood until one takes account of the *durable effects* that the social order exerts on women (and men), that is to say, the dispositions spontaneously attuned to that order which it imposes on them.

Symbolic force is a form of power that is exerted on bodies, directly and as if by magic, without any physical constraint; but this magic works only on the basis of the dispositions deposited, like springs, at the deepest level of the body.[3] If it can act like the release of a spring, that is, with a very weak expenditure of energy, this is because it does no more than trigger the dispositions that the work of inculcation and embodiment has deposited in those who are thereby primed for it. In other words, it finds its conditions of possibility, and its economic equivalent (in an expanded sense of the word 'economic'), in the immense preliminary labour that is needed to bring about a durable transformation of bodies and to produce the permanent dispositions that it triggers and awakens. This transformative action is all the more powerful because it is for the most part exerted invisibly and insidiously through insensible familiarization with a symbolically structured physical world and early, prolonged experience of interactions informed by the structures of domination.

The practical acts of knowledge and recognition of the magical frontier between the dominant and the dominated that are triggered by the magic of symbolic power and through which the dominated, often unwittingly, sometimes unwillingly, contribute to their own domination by tacitly accepting the limits imposed, often take the form of *bodily emotions* – shame, humiliation, timidity, anxiety, guilt – or *passions* and *sentiments* – love, admiration, respect. These emotions are all the more powerful when they are betrayed in visible manifestations such as blushing, stuttering, clumsiness, trembling, anger, or impotent rage, so many ways of submitting, even despite oneself and 'against the grain' [*à son corps défendant*], to the dominant judgment, sometimes in internal conflict and division of self, of experiencing the insidious complicity that a body slipping from the control of consciousness and will maintains with the censures inherent in the social structures.

The passions of the dominated habitus (whether dominated in terms of gender, ethnicity, culture, or language) – a somatized social relationship, a social law converted into an embodied law – are not of the kind that can be suspended by a simple effort of will, founded on a liberatory awakening of consciousness. If it is quite illusory to believe that symbolic violence can be overcome with the weapons of consciousness and will alone, this is because the effect and conditions of its efficacy are durably and deeply embedded in the body in the form of dispositions. This is seen, in particular, in the case of relations of kinship and all relations built on that model, in which these durable inclinations of the socialized body are expressed and experienced in the logic of feeling (filial love, fraternal love, etc.) or duty, which are often merged in the experience of respect and devotion and may live on long after the disappearance of their

social conditions of production. Thus it is observed that when the external constraints are removed and formal liberties – the right to vote, the right to education, access to all occupations, including politics – are acquired, self-exclusion and 'vocation' (which 'acts' as much negatively as it does positively) take over from explicit exclusion. Exclusion from public places, which, when it is explicitly laid down, as it is among the Kabyles, consigns women to separate spaces and makes approaching a male space, such as the edges of the assembly place, a terrifying ordeal, may elsewhere be achieved almost as effectively through the *socially imposed agoraphobia* which may persist long after the abolition of the most visible taboos and which leads women to exclude themselves from the *agora*.

To point to the marks that domination durably imprints in bodies and the effects it exerts through them does not mean that one is offering support to that particularly vicious way of ratifying domination which consists in making women responsible for their own domination by suggesting, as people sometimes do, that they *choose* to adopt submissive practices ('women are their own worst enemies') or even that they love their own domination, that they 'enjoy' the treatment inflicted on them, in a kind of masochism inherent in their nature. It has to be acknowledged both that the 'submissive' dispositions that are sometimes used to 'blame the victim' are the product of the objective structures, and also that these structures only derive their efficacy from the dispositions which they trigger and which help to reproduce them. Symbolic power cannot be exercised without the contribution of those who undergo it and who only undergo it because they *construct* it as such. But instead of stopping at this statement (as constructivism in its idealist, ethnomethodological, or other forms does) one has also to take note of and explain the social construction of the cognitive structures which organize acts of construction of the world and its powers. It then becomes clear that, far from being the conscious, free, deliberate act of an isolated 'subject', this practical construction is itself the effect of a power, durably embedded in the bodies of the dominated in the form of schemes of perception and dispositions (to admire, respect, love, etc.) which *sensitize* them to certain symbolic manifestations of power.

Although it is true that, even when it seems to be based on the brute force of weapons or money, recognition of domination always presupposes an act of knowledge, this does not imply that one is entitled to describe it in the language of consciousness, in an intellectualist and scholastic fallacy which, as in Marx (and above all, those who, from Lukács onwards, have spoken of 'false consciousness'), leads one to expect the liberation of women to come through the immediate effect of the 'raising of consciousness', forgetting – for lack of a dispositional theory of practices – the opacity and inertia that stem from the embedding of social structures in bodies. [. . .]

These critical distinctions are not at all gratuitous: they imply that the symbolic revolution called for by the feminist movement cannot be reduced to a simple conversion of consciousnesses and wills. Because the foundation of symbolic violence lies not in mystified consciousnesses that only need to be enlightened but in dispositions attuned to the structure of domination of which they are the product, the relation of complicity that the victims of symbolic domination grant to the dominant can only be broken through a radical transformation of the social conditions of production of the dispositions that lead the dominated to take the point of view of the dominant on the dominant and on themselves. Symbolic violence is exercised only through an act of knowledge and practical recognition which takes place below the level of the consciousness and will and which gives all its manifestations – injunctions, suggestions, seduction, threats, reproaches, orders, or calls to order – their 'hypnotic power'. But a relation of domination that functions only through the complicity of dispositions depends profoundly, *for its perpetuation or transformation*, on the perpetuation or transformation of the structures of which those dispositions are the product (and in particular on the structure of a market in symbolic goods whose fundamental law is that women are treated there as objects which circulate upwards).

NOTES

1 Cf. P. Bourdieu, 'Sur le pouvoir symbolique', *Annales*, no. 3 (May–June 1977), pp. 405–11.
2 M. Bozon, 'Les femmes et l'écart d'âge entre conjoints: une domination consentie', I: 'Types d'union et attentes en matière d'écart d'âge', *Population*, 2 (1990), pp. 327–60; II: 'Modes d'entrée dans la vie adulte et représentations du conjoint', *Population*, 3 (1990), pp. 565–602; 'Apparence physique et choix du conjoint', *INED* [Institut National des Études Démographiques], *Congrès et colloques*, 7 (1991), pp. 91–110.
3 It is possible to understand in these terms the symbolic efficacy of religious messages (Papal bulls, preaching, prophecy, etc.), which is clearly based on previous religious socialization (catechism, churchgoing and, above all, immersion from an early age in a universe imbued with religiosity).

43

The Everyday Violence of Gang Rape

Philippe Bourgois

Most of the crack dealers I befriended in East Harlem expressed an ambivalent *ex post facto* sense of guilt over their careers of delinquency. Their life stories revealed, however, that crime and violence had been normalized into their daily lives, becoming an integral part of youthful common sense and self-respect. At first their childhood reminiscences contained accounts of acceptable forms of petty delinquency and petty violence: car burglaries, gang fights, and mugging. It was not until after two more years of fieldwork that I was exposed to a more brutal and even more gendered dimension of teenage socialization: gang rape.

I remember vividly the first night Primo, the manager of the crackhouse located next to where I lived, told me that his older cousins, Ray and Luis, who ran the franchise of crackhouses I studied, used to organize gang rapes upstairs in the abandoned building where the crackhouse was located. He approached the subject casually in a conversation near closing time, catching me unprepared. At the time, these childhood stories of violently forced sex spun me into a personal depression and a research crisis. Furthermore, the voyeuristic bonding and sexual celebration performed by Caesar, the lookout at the crackhouse, in response to Primo's brutal account made me even more disgusted with my new "friends." I felt betrayed, especially by Primo, whom I had grown to like and genuinely respect by that time:

[Primo] I'm hanging out by myself; nobody's on the block; I'm wandering down the street; the block is quiet. The club's here; [hand motions] the corner's up here; on the last floor they had an apartment.

Standing in the corner, Luis looks out the window, and yells, "Primo, you wanna eat?" I thought he had like a pie – a pizza – something. I said, "Bet!" When he said that, I got the munchies real quick.

But when he looks out the window, he goes like that, with his cock out the window, and I'm like, "Oh shit! Motherfucker!"

So they threw the keys down; I went upstairs, it was Sapo, Luis, Tootie, Shorty, Ray, probably Negro; five or six guys there. And that girl.

She was naked in the room, she was naked there with a beer in her hand, a big 40 ounce, getting boned and laughing. They were holding her down.

[Caesar] Yeah! Yeah! The bitch was wit'it, though.

[Primo] When I opened the door, she was getting fucked by Shorty. He was dogging her, and all of us were there looking.

[To me, nervously noticing my horror] It wasn't really all that critical. I'm telling you Felipe! The bitch was laughing with a quart in her hand.

[Caesar] Yeah! Mah' man dicked her with STRENGTH AND ANIMOSITY.

[Primo] After he left – since he wasn't used to hanging out with us and he couldn't concentrate – we locked the door; turned on the light; she was there, free meat. It was just the fellows.

[Caesar] You niggas was training her!

[Primo, concerned again by my expression] She didn't give a fuck. She just ain't nothin'; everybody was there with their cocks all different sizes and widths and everything. All naked; with their pants halfway down; just waiting. Niggas showing off with their dicks.

[Caesar, turning to me and misunderstanding my negative reaction for incomprehension] They just was training her, Felipe. All six niggas boning her in the same room, at the same time.

[Primo, looking back at me] Not me! They wanted me to do it, but I said, "Fuck that! I don't want you niggas' leftovers. Don't want to catch no fucking gonorrhea, herpes."

[Caesar] Training her!

[Primo] She was there stark naked, and them niggas was saying, "Go ahead Primo." She was there like a hole. They were holding her there.

[Caesar] Training that bitch!

[Primo] She had a nice body, man. She was great. But I didn't want someone with . . . shit like that.

I finally grabbed some tits and felt her body. She felt'ed good. I felt with my fingers in her hole and that shit felt nice and tight. But I ain't gonna put my dick in that bitch.

[Caesar] They were training that bitch!

[Primo] I stuck my thumb in her pussy, and my finger in her ass, while they were sucking her tits. It was crazy. I washed my hands after that, but it felt'ed'ed good though.

[Caesar, trying again to bring me into the conversation] Them niggas used to bone some good looking girls.

[Primo] She was 17 years old. She was already a woman; she wasn't a virgin. She's a piece of meat – already fucked up.

Despite the three years that I had already spent on the street at the time of this particular conversation, I was unprepared to face this dimension of gendered brutality. I kept asking myself how it was possible that I had invested so much energy into "taking these psychopaths seriously." On a more personal level, I was confused because the rapists had already become my friends. With notable individual exceptions, I had grown to like many of the veteran rapists presented in Primo's account. I was living with the enemy; it had become my social network. The crack dealers had engulfed me in the "common sense" of street culture until their rape accounts forced me to draw the line.

From an analytical and a humanistic perspective, it was too late for me to avoid the issue, or to dismiss their sociopathology as aberrant. I had to face the prevalence and "normalcy" of rape in street culture and adolescent socialization. In any case, Primo and Caesar would not let me escape it, and over the next year, as if peeling off layers from an onion's core, they gave dozens of accounts and versions of their direct participation in sexual violence during their earliest adolescent years. Few people talk about rape – neither the perpetrators nor the victims. In fact, rape is so taboo that I was tempted to omit this discussion, including their accounts of it from the book I wrote on the crack dealers (Bourgois 1995). I feared that readers would become too disgusted and angry with the protagonists of the book and deny them a human face. As a man, of course, even as I write this short discussion I am also worried about the politics of representation. Most of the dozens of tape recordings that I collected on the subject came from the perspectives of the perpetrators. I tape-recorded several accounts by survivors to obtain alternative perspectives, but I did not have the same kinds of long-term relationships with these individuals to allow for the detail and confidence of a meaningfully contextualized life history interview or conversation (see Bourgois and Dunlap 1993).

From a political perspective, I am concerned about creating a forum for a public humiliation of the poor and powerless. Readers, especially those in the United States, are so unconsciously subjected to the racialized "common sense" of their society that they might be tempted to interpret these passages as some kind of cultural reflection on "the Puerto Rican community." Such an "airing-of-dirty-laundry" interpretation runs counter to my theoretical and political arguments. There is obviously nothing specifically Puerto Rican about gang rape (cf. Sanday 1990). To avoid pushing unconscious taboo buttons it would have been easier as a white male researcher to eliminate this discussion of gang rape. I feel, however, that if I failed to address sexual violence in street culture, I would be colluding with the sexist status quo. Rape runs rampant around us in a terrifying conspiracy of silence. It becomes a public secret (Taussig 1999) that enforces an important dimension of the oppression of women in everyday life.

Learning to be a rapist was very definitely part of Primo's coming of age. Tagging after the "big boys" on the street, he was repeatedly excluded for being too young – or for not wanting – to participate.

Primo: Back in those days I was younger. My dick wouldn't stand up. It was like nasty to me; I wasn't down with it. I can't handle that.

So they be goin' upstairs with a girl, and of course they already knew that I'm not going to be down with it, so they ask me, "What'cha gonna do man? Go home or what?"

So fuck it, the best thing I could do is break out. "See you guys tomorrow", or else, I just wait downstairs in the bar, or something.

The alternative was for Primo to bond with his older peer group by participating actively in this violent male ritual. It was only later that Primo learned to become sexually aroused.

Primo: I wasn't really with it, but I used to act wild too, because the bitch is gonna have to pass through the wild thing. And sometimes, it could be me acting stupid with a bat or something, so that she has got to stay in the room with whoever is there.

Sometimes the older guys, they would play the nice role for awhile with the girl, but once they get that piece of pussy, she gets dissed. It's like psshhht, pssht [making slapping motions]. She gets beat down: "I own you now, bitch."

I used to play that shit before man: There is always the good one, and then the bad one. My man, here [grabbing Caesar by the shoulders], be the meanest one, and you and me [putting his arm around my shoulder], be the good sweet ones ... that we don't, like, wanna bother her. Then Luis over here [putting his arm around Luis who had just walked into the crackhouse to deliver a fresh supply of drugs and retrieve the mid-shift's receipts], is like both good and bad; but Ray [pointing to the doorway] is the meanest one.

So this way, the bitch get comforted, and we explain to her, that we just want some pussy. "That's what you have to give up; it's the price for freedom." And the whole posse be there; they are like saying, "Yeah, Yeah!"

That was back in the days. Nobody is with that shit no more. Pussy is too easy to get nowadays.

The rapists were careful to develop a logic for justifying their actions. For example, Primo separated the women who his peer group raped into categories of worthy versus unworthy victims. He also projected onto them the sexual depravity of his male companions. Despite his attempt to reconstruct some of the women as voluntarily submitting to the gang rape – or even enjoying it as in the case of his original account at the beginning of this chapter – when specifically confronted on the issue, Primo admitted that ultimately

violent force and physical terror were the organizing mediums. Ironically, the particular conversation recorded below was interrupted by gunshots, as if to illustrate the extent to which life-threatening violence permeates, in an explicitly less gendered manner, much of day-to-day street interaction:

[Primo] I mean the way I remember it, I was so fucking young. I looked at it like, most likely, whoever never came back to hang out at the club, passed through some trauma, and it's gonna be hidden within their life, for the rest of their life, and they're never gonn'a hang again. Instead they go home, and chill the fuck out, and keep a dark secret for the rest of their life. [Looking at me defensively] I used to feel sorry, sometimes too, for them.

But some bitches was more suitable, and used to just come back and hang. 'Cause I guess it was like they was on the streets, and they passed through their first shit, and now fuck it: "*Voy a hangear.*" [I'm going to hang out.]

[Philippe, interrupting] Come on, man, get real! Nobody likes going through that shit.

[Primo, speaking slowly] Well ... It was their decision, Felipe. I mean, the first time, maybe they weren't into it. Sometimes there be tears in their eyes. They didn't want to be forced.

[Caesar, laughing at Primo's confusion and my anger] But they were forced; but they liked'ed it; and they come back for more; 'cause they're with it. They just get used to the fact: "We own you now bitch!"

[Philippe] You motherfuckers are sick! [Loud gunshots followed by the sound of someone running]

[Primo] No! You gotta understand Felipe, even when they say no, they're loving it.

[Caesar, interrupting from the doorway of the Game Room, where he was looking out] Yo! Yo! Check this out! Felipe, give me that [grabbing my tape recorder]. I'm gonna say into the mic, that someone shot someone, and just ran by us.

[Primo, ignoring the interruption] Sometimes the girls would end up staying with like, one guy, and maybe having a kid from him. And this is after the whole fuckin' posse – everybody – had fucked her.

I remember this one bitch, she wanted to stay with Luis because he gave her like a tremendous cock fuck. She was a young bitch; she liked'ed that huge cock of Luis', boy. She fell in love with Luis' cock.

Luis busted out a lot of virgins. He used to soup up the girls, and bone them instantly. If not today, then the next day. he used to "DA, DA, DA, BOOM, BANG THEM!"

I used to get my nuts off watching that shit there. Word! It was good. Hell, yeah. It was exciting because after awhile a girl gets into it.

Luis' favorite was: he fucks and we watch. And I know, I used to get off on that!

[Philippe, interrupting again] Shut up man! What the hell is the matter with you?!

Primo ignored my response and continued with an exceedingly explicit account of how Luis would angle his body to maximize the visibility of his actions for the voyeuristic benefit of his gang rape companions. The pornographic detail of Primo's description supports the interpretation that there is a homoerotic dimension to the male sexual bonding that occurs among gang rapists.

Grappling for a confrontational response that would shock Primo into an awareness of the pain he and his friends inflicted on the girls around them, I tried to jostle his conscience by appealing to the patriarchal logic of family honor.

[Philippe] Did you ever worry about this happening to your sisters?

[Primo] Hell yeah!

But I knew my sisters were innocent. Me and Luis used to talk about it. We used to be in the streets, and we said, "We got those sisters, man."

[Caesar] That's why I couldn't handle having a baby. If it's a girl and then I have to see her being a ho'! I would probably kill myself. If I was going to have a baby girl, I don't want nothing to do with it. I don't even want to touch it. Word!

[Primo, trying to reassure me] Put it this way, Felipe, these bitches were young, dumb, and full-a-cum. If they are hanging out too much, and they start seeing that we are wild, and if they are still hanging out, then we know that we can take them.

[Philippe] That is some sick shit you're saying. You motherfuckers were nothin' but a bunch of perverts.

[Primo, frustrated that he could not convince me] I mean look at their attitude; if they hang out too long, believe me, then they know what's happening. If the girl is gonna hang then she's gonna get dicked. I mean these bitches, they would just keep hanging out, and hanging out. They be coming back to the bar everyday, so then we know that they really want a dick.

So Ray and them guys, they would take the bitch aside, because we had her *confianza* [trust]; and by then it was easy to force her into doing it with all of us.

Besides the bitch get smacked, or something, if she don't.

In some conversations, especially when Caesar was not present, Primo responded to my open condemnations by claiming repentance. Even when he was responding in a socially desirable manner so as not to offend me, however, he still remained trapped in the profoundly patriarchal logic of his peer group.

[Primo] Now, every time that I think about those times it makes me feel weak. Because I used to, like, not be with it. And I used to feel SORRY when I would go back to my house and see my mom and my sisters.

Those fucking girls used to go through shit, and if they were good girls, then we used to ruin their lives. Now I think about the ages of those girls. They might have been 15 or 13 or 12 or 14 or 15 or 16, and that's some crazy shit. They looked exactly like the little girls we see now.

[Philippe] Bothers you now?

[Primo] There was never a time that it didn't bother me, Felipe. I never liked that. I hated it. I was like the kinda' person that pleads, "Don't! Stop!"

It was happening all the fucking time. All over. But I never said nothing [morosely]. I wished that I had told them to stop raping her.

I used to be a fuckin' psychiatrist for these girls. Word, Felipe. I shoulda' got paid, because they used to talk to me, like, I used to give them advices and shit. Like: "Get the fuck out of here before your life really gets more fucked up."

But then again, like you said [nodding at Caesar who had just walked inside the Game Room from the doorway to listen more carefully], they liked'ed it.

Ultimately, the violence against women orchestrated by Primo's older role models, reflected itself back on a sense of internalized worthlessness that the misogyny of their frustrated patriarchal dreams was not able to placate:

[Primo] We used to talk between each other, that these women are living fucked up, because they want to hang out with us.

And what the fuck we got to offer? Nothing! We used to wonder.

[Caesar] We don't be doing nothing! Bitch be stupid to go with a nigga' like us.

That's why I don't really want a daughter. I can't stand the feeling of another man touching my daughter. I got like a prejudice against women because of that shit.

REFERENCES

Bourgois, Philippe. 1995. *In Search of Respect: Selling Crack in El Barrio*. New York: Cambridge University Press.

—— and Eloise Dunlap. 1993. "Exorcising Sex-For-Crack Prostitution: An Ethnographic Perspective From Harlem." In *Crack Pipe as Pimp: An Eight-City Ethnographic Study of the Sex-For-Crack Phenomenon*, ed. Mitchell Ratner. Lexington, MA: Lexington Books, pp. 97–132.

Sanday, Peggy Reeves. 1990. *Fraternity Gang Rape: Sex, Brotherhood, and Privilege on Campus*. New York: New York University Press.

Taussig, Michael. 1999. *Defacement: Public Secrecy and the Labor of the Negative*. Stanford, CA: Stanford University Press.

44

Hooking Up: Protective Pairing for Punks

Stephen Donaldson

Note: this advice article was written for incarcerated heterosexual male survivors of prisoner rape, but provides a good description of a unique form of sexual relationship which is an important part of the culture of confinement.

As long ago as 1826, shortly after the building of the first penitentiaries, Louis Dwight described the practice prisoners now call "hooking up" and we call protective pairing, an informal arrangement which has remained ever since the collective response of prisoners to the problem of ongoing sexual assault in confinement. There is historical evidence for similar relationships among the ancient Romans, medieval Vikings, and the Caribbean pirates of the seventeenth century. In most joints the overwhelming majority of rape survivors who remain in or go back to general population do become hooked up as members of such pairs, however distasteful they may find the idea, because they believe it to be the least damaging way to survive in custody.

One reason why this custom has survived for so long is that the alternatives for the known rape victim are usually even more unacceptable. These are a series of very serious and bloody fights, and maybe a lot more time; suicide (a permanent "solution" to a temporary problem); repeated exposure to gang rapes; paying someone for protection; and permanent consignment to "protective custody" in Seg. This last option, p.c., may not even be safe, staff may not allow you to stay there indefinitely, and solitary can drive you crazy if endured for too long. If you're short or only in jail for a short time or a real hermit, you might as well do the rest of your time in p.c. and you don't need to read this. Otherwise, as the authors of *Men Behind Bars: Sexual Exploitation in Prison*, who studied the problem at length, concluded: "For the majority of these 'targets' the best and safest coping strategy is to 'hook up' with a jocker." Still, it is your choice as to which path, none of them good, you want to take.

This brochure is written for those rape survivors who are in and want to stay in population, or who are in p.c. and considering going back into population; who are considering getting hooked up or are already hooked up; and who are punks (we do not use the term "punk" as a put-down, just as the most common and widely understood term for prisoners, usually straight or bisexual youths, who have been forced or pressured into an unwanted passive sexual role), rather than gays. Much of this information also applies to queens, but since gays usually have more experience and fewer problems relating sexually to males, this is written specifically for punks.

General Description of Protective Pairing

Prisoners take hooking up very seriously, for it involves a commitment on the part of both partners, which neither can break (as long as they remain hooked up) without major consequences. The quality of these relationships ranges enormously, from virtual slavery and complete exploitation at one end to a mutually supportive, tender, and human exchange of affection at the other.

The senior partner, or "man" in prisoner slang (also called "daddy," "old man," "jocker," "pitcher," and other terms), in a protective pair is most often not a rapist himself, though he may take advantage of the consequences of a rape by offering protection to a new punk. Sometimes a rapist will try to hook up with his victim. In any case he obligates himself to provide complete protection for his punk or junior partner (also called "kid", "boy," "sweet boy," "fuckboy," "catcher," and other terms) from further sexual assaults from anyone else, from violence, from theft, and from other forms of disrespect. Usually as soon as it becomes known that you are hooked up (and the news will spread like wildfire), everyone else will back off and stop hassling you, and deal with you only through your "man." Any "daddy" who fails to protect you will be seen as weak and may thereby make himself a target for sexual assault. Sometimes two or more buddies will share the "daddy" role, and in many joints a whole gang will take control of a punk.

These "pitchers" are usually straight, sometimes bisexual; they consider their punks to be substitutes for women, and they usually do not consider their own penetrative sexual acts or their relationships with punks to be "homosexual," just masculine, though they may think that what you have to do for them is "homosexual." In a broad sense, they habitually treat their punks the way they are used to treating their women on the Street.

The punk has to give up his independence and his control over his own body to his "man" as the price for this protection. He has to put out sexually in a passive role, giving up head or ass or both. This deal is never totally voluntary for the punk: it is often coercive, the alternatives are frightful, and it is motivated above all by the need to survive in a place where the punk has been marked as a perpetual target for gang rape and other forms of abuse. But it is still very different from a series of violent gang rapes, and, in the age of AIDS, far safer. We call these relationships "survival-driven" from the punk's perspective.

A punk often is able to choose his protector from among various candidates, especially if he is willing to put up a fight (even knowing he'll lose) or is not in a particularly rough joint, and he may be able to establish a relationship of mutual concern, which is a far cry from the pure exploitation of the sexual assaulter. It must be understood, however, that the "pitcher" makes the rules and

the "catcher" follows them. In a particularly tough joint, a punk may be no more than a slave, but usually the relationship allows you some leverage or room to maneuver and have your wishes considered, as long as you respect the basic rules of the relationship.

While a jocker will never tolerate open rebellion, he usually seeks to get along with his punk and avoid an atmosphere of constant tension. He would rather relax around his punk, and over time he can and often does develop genuine affection for him and allow a considerable degree of give-and-take in the nonsexual aspects of the partnership. But the sexual part is pretty fixed and you can't really hope to get out of it.

It may be very hard for you to deal with belonging to somebody else and having to substitute for a girl and satisfy a guy sexually, but at least you only have to do it with one guy or a small number, rather than anybody who can catch you. Your risk of infection with the AIDS virus is greatly reduced, often to zero. You don't have to fight at all and can avoid physical injury, and it is some comfort knowing that a dead punk is of no value to anybody. Often hooking up will improve your financial situation as well, since a jocker is expected to see that his punk gets the canteen necessities of life.

Hooking up means you have definitely become a punk and will be considered a punk for as long as you stay in the joint, so if you decide to hook up, you might as well get used to that status. Your "old man" will control all sexual access to you, and will expect you to do what he tells you. Some daddies share their punks with their buddies. Others will make you turn tricks for canteen goods, drugs, or other favors.

You may well be given duties other than sex: for example, doing laundry, cleaning his cell, making up his bunk, fixing coffee for him, or giving him backrubs.

The advantage of protective pairing with one guy is that the two of you can get to know each other very well, especially if you cell together (which is to your advantage), and that makes for a more human relationship. You are less likely to be seen as an object to be used and exploited, and more like a junior partner. Much depends on the jocker, because guys vary enormously in the way they treat punks: some beat their punks and mistreat them, others get very affectionate and take good care of you, and there is everything in between.

A small partnership among 2 to 5 jocks who are friends and cooperate harmoniously with each other is pretty secure for you, and means you aren't as dependent on the whims of one person, but such arrangements are not as common and may not be stable.

The advantage of hooking up with a gang or tip is that their protection from people outside the gang is a pretty sure thing, and they can keep you in canteen goods. The disadvantage is that you have to sexually service the entire gang, which may seem like just a gentler form of gang rape, and it is harder to develop a personal relationship because your time and attention are so divided. In some joints, gangs may be so strong that you have no choice but to accept a gang's claim on you. Many gangs will force punks into prostitution.

If one of the other prisoners does try to put pressure on you after you've hooked up, tell your daddy about it right away; he'll handle the matter.

The whole compound will know as soon as you get hooked up that you are someone's kid. It's an essential part of the system, so don't fight it. All the booty bandits and other jockers have to be warned off. It isn't always verbal, and a lot or all of the staff may never find out. For instance, you may eat all your meals together with your "old man"; people will notice and draw the right conclusion. Once you are hooked up, you will be respected to the same degree that your jocker is respected. Nobody will be allowed to hassle you or dis you, for that would be seen as the equivalent of dissing your jock. Once you are hooked up and seen as belonging to someone, a rape by anyone else is cause for a very serious fight, so it is rare.

It works best if you are housed together with your jock because then he can protect you better. If you're in different blocks, it's hard for him to look out for you. If you share a double cell with each other, then nobody can enter that cell without permission from him or you, and you'll have more privacy and plenty of time to talk with each other and keep misunderstandings from arising. On the other hand, if you share a double with someone else, strange guys may not refrain from entering it, and it can lead to tensions between your partner and your cellie.

Staff Attitudes

The attitudes of the keepers towards pairs vary a great deal. Most veteran guards and administrators are realistic enough to recognize that protective pairing minimizes the violence in the joint, and that you don't really have much in the way of alternatives, so they won't press the protective pair very hard, often not at all. But officially they still consider your sexual activity a violation of disciplinary codes, so you have to be discreet and careful to keep sex out of sight of the cops. See our handout on dealing with staff. Rookies often try to enforce every rule in the book, and cops may be prejudiced and homophobic and go out of their way to catch you. And sometimes you'll run into higher-ranking officers or staffers with a homophobic bee up their ass about sex between prisoners and you'll have to really watch out. You don't want to get caught having sex, so you should always pay attention to security and don't be foolish. Fortunately, security is mainly your "man's" job and you can generally leave it up to him to make sure you don't get busted. It doesn't hurt to remind him of that duty from time to time, since horny guys sometimes do get carried away and start thinking with their dicks instead of their heads.

Understanding Jockers

The basic fact of the matter is that most males, when separated from females, and especially when they're young and full of sex hormones which make them horny all the time, can become sexually aroused at the thought of penetrating anyone, regardless of their real sex. The nerves which produce pleasure in the dick don't ask if it's a girl's mouth, a boy's mouth; an ass or a pussy. For these guys to be turned on and horny doesn't really require any kind of feminine qualities in you, though the jockers usually prefer to imagine such qualities so they won't have to think of their attraction as homosexual. That's why they'll try to tell you you have feminine qualities even if it's not true.

When locked up, men get bored with beating off and lonesome and start looking for someone else to provide sexual relief. Also there's an unexpressed human need for touch and intimacy and prisoners don't recognize any other way to meet that need. It is also a question of men feeling a need to confirm their own sense of their masculinity, which they feel is somewhat compromised by the fact that they're locked up, by functioning in their accustomed male sexual roles as penetrators and dominant controllers. Prisoners all have to constantly take orders from the authorities, which makes them feel like slaves of the state. As a compensation they like to find a way to be the boss with someone else and give orders themselves. Sex is a vehicle for a jocker to express all these nonsexual needs.

At the same time, only a very small fraction of prisoners, the queens, enjoy being sexually passive, taking care of another guy's dick. This tremendous imbalance between the demand for catchers by most of the fellows and the very small or nonexistent supply of available willing partners is extremely important to understanding the way prisoners relate to each other. There's no way to increase the supply of queens, so all the effort goes into trying to "turn out" new punks. Unfortunately, the main means by which they turn out punks is rape and the threat of it.

Jockers frequently loan out their punks to their friends, usually as a way of ensuring their loyalty to him or to reinforce his position as a leader. In a way, this is good for you, since the more backup he has, the safer you'll be. And when he's not around, you can turn to his friends in an emergency. Sometimes it is just a way to repay a favor. Jockers know you won't get pregnant by someone else. They may, however, be afraid that you could get infected with AIDS and for that reason keep you, or at least your ass, to themselves. You should encourage them to do so.

Since many jockers have very little money, those who are poor are very tempted to use you as an asset with which to make money or get canteen goods. In fact, some jocks (especially professional pimps from the Street) will hook up with a punk for no other reason. In effect they continue their pimp trade on the inside. Avoid them if you can. When you're put "on the block," your old man lets other guys know that you are available for a price and the other guys negotiate with your "owner" and then he tells you what to do and with whom and when. If you have a chance to negotiate with a jocker over this, try to get a veto over particular customers, and especially try to limit it to head jobs, in order to keep the risk of AIDS low. Some jockers will keep everything they get this way to themselves, more will share it with you 50/50, and there is every possibility in between. If you can possibly do so, find a jocker who will not rent you out at all.

Jockers will almost never switch roles with you or let you penetrate them, and they may

get very upset if you even suggest it. Some of them may be willing to jerk you off, but most don't want to be reminded that you even have a dick. It is very important to them that they stay within what they consider the "man" role. They may, however, be willing to consider other human needs of yours, such as the need for affection, for touch, for comforting, and they will often try to see to it that you are as comfortable as possible while having sex. Within the rules of the game, most jockers try to get along with their kids as well as possible, so as long as you live up to your part of the deal they won't get mean or hurt you. If you make them happy, you are even likely to find that over time they'll become grateful, and try to keep you relatively happy, too. But don't expect that gratitude will ever go to the extent of relieving you of your sexual obligations.

Jocks can treat you like a slave and sell you to some other jock whenever they get tired of you or run out of money. They can also fall in love with you and get very jealous of anyone else. It takes all kinds. Some of the jocks who play the gorilla game and act extremely tough, callous, and cold-hearted will relax once they get hooked up and learn to trust you and show a whole different and unexpected side of themselves.

You have to understand that for jockers the world of confinement is one of constant competition, with everyone looking for a weakness. So guys put up a false front which never admits any vulnerability. But this makes them less human. When they get hooked up, they have someone to relate to, who is no longer an actual or potential competitor. Especially when you've accepted their claim, they can feel you're on the same team. Thus they can relax, and become very gentle if they want, and as they learn to trust you and you show you can keep confidences to yourself, they may tell you things about themselves that they would never tell other jockers. They may share their own anxieties and fears and their deepest feelings, and they will listen to you as you learn to trust them and can talk about your own feelings. Thus you have a good chance at developing a human relationship where each of you really cares about the other and you work together to keep the relationship smooth. Generally the older the jocker is, the more likely he is to want to develop a real partnership with you rather than just get his rocks off.

Choosing a Daddy

This usually has to be done pretty quickly or events will overwhelm you and you may get gang raped or forced to hook up before you can make a choice. But if you want to have a choice, as soon as you decide to hook up you should tell the other prisoners; the word will get around fast and guys will then start to talk with you about it. It can get pretty hectic. [. . .]

You'll want to know if the jocker wants to "put you on the block" (which unfortunately is pretty common), whether he has ever shot up drugs (and therefore might carry the AIDS virus), whether he'll settle for head or insists you give up your ass as well, whether he'll allow anyone else to fuck your ass or keep it for himself, whether he'll loan you out to his buddies, whether he wants to cell with you, and what the relationship means to him.

Check out how serious the guy is. Protective pairing is a very serious matter for him as well, since it obligates him to put his life on the line if necessary to keep you from harm, and if you are foolish or stupid and fuck up, he may have to suffer for your mistake. Ask him about any previous catchers he's had and how they managed together and why they split. If any of them are still around, talk with them. Ask him what he feels his responsibilities would be and what yours would be. Also ask about canteen arrangements. [. . .]

Ask jockers how they treat their women, because most jockers treat their punks the same way. If they form real partnerships with their women, they are more likely to do the same with you.

Nitty-gritty Details

As a new punk you won't know diddly-squat about your sexual duties, so here are a few practical tips: to avoid AIDS, learn to suck dick. In fact, learn it so well you can do deep throat and he'll forget all about your ass. The trick is relaxation, not easy at first, to be sure, when you feel the whole thing is absolutely disgusting, but for your own good, you need to learn to relax using any technique that works for you. In order to avoid gagging, wait til your stomach is empty, so there's nothing to barf. If you do throw up, do it on the floor and not him! Train yourself gradually. Meditate, say mantras, anything that gets you to relax. Stop thinking of the dick as an invading foreign

object; if you can get over that perception, you'll be OK. Try to take deep breaths whenever you can and breathe through your nose. Practice holding your breath like a swimmer. If he fucks your skull so hard you think you're about to pass out from asphyxiation, you should grab his legs and signal your distress. Most likely he'll be about to come and won't let up, but it'll be over real soon.

The first few times you get fucked in the ass, it hurts bigtime. If you have to get fucked in the ass, again try to relax as much as possible and get him to slow down. It will hurt less, and if it keeps happening you will get used to it and it won't hurt at all. Be sure to use some kind of greasy stuff (vaseline, hair cream, etc.) as a lubricant, and a condom if at all possible. If you are hooked up, your jocker will usually try to minimize any pain that might be involved. After all, he wants to keep your resentment and complaints to a minimum.

A dick up your ass may well physically stimulate your prostate gland, and you may experience that as pleasurable. You may even get a hard-on while being fucked, just as a physical reaction. And some punks will find the sexual experience arousing. Many guys have some homosexual feelings even though they are basically straight. You don't have to put a label on yourself just because you have a variety of feelings.

Punks sometimes agree to switch out with each other or "take turns" sexually, since this is about the only way you can take a penetrative role instead of a passive one. As a punk you come under a lot of pressure to act less masculine, and you will naturally resent this pressure inside and feel a strong need to act in masculine ways whenever you can get away with it. This need can make the urge to experience what a lot of people call "the male role" in sex very powerful. It is an understandable compensation, a way of proving to yourself that you're still a man, so if you do it, don't feel guilty about it. If you want to take turns with another punk, it is best to clear it with your jockers first. The jocks usually don't object since they know the other punk is not a rival for them. [. . .]

Adaptation

Human beings are remarkably adaptable creatures. It is true that if you become a punk and are locked up for a long time, you will get somewhat used to the punk role. This varies a lot from one punk to another. Some still hate every sex act after a decade of doing it every day. Others focus on other aspects of it and find some value in those aspects. Some treasure the security it brings. Many punks who have good relationships actually become fond of their jockers. It is not even so uncommon, in the unusual conditions of confinement, for two straight guys to fall in love with each other over time. Psychologists generally consider adaptation to be a healthy reaction to a situation which you cannot change, so don't worry about it if you find yourself adapting to the role. Once you are out you can reverse the process and work on reclaiming the full expression of your masculine identity.

Unfortunately, many (if not most) jockers will try to get their punks to be as feminine in appearance and behavior as possible. That is because they are more comfortable pretending they are relating sexually to some kind of female than to another male. But they also know that you are a punk, not a queen, and that such things don't come naturally to you. You should ask about such things before accepting a claim, and make it clear that retaining your masculine identity is important to you. Some jockers don't care; I was hooked up once with a guy who let me grow a moustache! Most will still call you "him" and use your male name. Others may insist that you shave your legs and grow long hair and get a feminine nickname.

No matter what you have to do, remember that it is all an act and you can go back to your normal behavior as soon as you get out.

Sex is a very complex experience. It has many aspects which have nothing to do with lust. Being penetrated is an intense experience; it can give you an adrenaline rush. Being touched can be a pleasant experience, regardless of the sex of the person touching you. Being held has been a comforting experience for most people since they were babies, and it can seem very protective in an environment where gang rape is a grim reality. Being desired can seem like a tempting alternative to being ignored, especially if you've been ignored all your life. Intimacy itself can be very powerfully attractive if you feel isolated and lonely. It is quite possible that you may delve further into these feelings, which are general human feelings. That doesn't mean you are sexually turned on to the guy, it doesn't mean there's lust or sexual arousal or homosexual inclinations. Besides, if experiences alone determined a person's sexuality, we'd all be in love with our hands.

That's a lot of advice, but if it's a whole new world for you, you'll need it. Good luck finding a decent man, and remember you will leave it all behind (except for a much better understanding of men and of women!) when you walk out the front gate.

45

Sex and Death in the Rational World of Defense Intellectuals

Carol Cohn

Stage I: Listening

Clean bombs and clean language

Entering the world of defense intellectuals [at a university's center on defense technology and arms control – hereafter "the Center"] was a bizarre experience – bizarre because it is a world where men spend their days calmly and matter-of-factly discussing nuclear weapons, nuclear strategy, and nuclear war. The discussions are carefully and intricately reasoned, occurring seemingly without any sense of horror, urgency, or moral outrage – in fact, there seems to be no graphic reality behind the words, as they speak of "first strikes," "counterforce exchanges," and "limited nuclear war," or as they debate the comparative values of a "minimum deterrent posture" versus a "nuclear war-fighting capability."

Yet what is striking about the men themselves is not, as the content of their conversations might suggest, their cold-bloodedness. Rather, it is that they are a group of men unusually endowed with charm, humor, intelligence, concern, and decency. Reader, I liked them. At least, I liked many of them. The attempt to understand how such men could contribute to an endeavor that I see as so fundamentally destructive became a continuing obsession for me, a lens through which I came to examine all of my experiences in their world.

In this early stage, I was gripped by the extraordinary language used to discuss nuclear war. What hit me first was the elaborate use of abstraction and euphemism, of words so bland that they never forced the speaker or enabled the listener to touch the realities of nuclear holocaust that lay behind the words.

Anyone who has seen pictures of Hiroshima burn victims or tried to imagine the pain of hundreds of glass shards blasted into flesh may find it perverse beyond imagination to hear a class of nuclear devices matter-of-factly referred to as "clean bombs." "Clean bombs" are nuclear devices that are largely fusion rather than fission and that therefore release a higher quantity of energy, not as radiation, but as blast, as destructive explosive power.

"Clean bombs" may provide the perfect metaphor for the language of defense analysts and arms controllers. This language has enormous destructive power, but without emotional fallout, without the emotional fallout that would result if it were clear one was talking about plans for mass murder, mangled bodies, and unspeakable human suffering. Defense analysts talk about "counter-value attacks" rather than about incinerating cities. Human death, in nuclear parlance, is most often referred to as "collateral damage"; for, as one defense analyst said wryly, "The Air Force doesn't target people, it targets shoe factories."

Some phrases carry this cleaning-up to the point of inverting meaning. The MX missile will carry ten warheads, each with the explosure power of 300–475 kilotons of TNT: *one* missile the bearer of destruction approximately 250–400 times that of the Hiroshima bombing. Ronald Reagan has dubbed the MX missile "the Peacekeeper." While this renaming was the object of considerable scorn in the community of defense analysts, these very same analysts refer to the MX as a "damage limitation weapon."

These phrases, only a few of the hundreds that could be discussed, exemplify the astounding chasm between image and reality that characterizes technostrategic language. They also hint at the terrifying way in which the existence of nuclear devices has distorted our perceptions and redefined the world. "Clean bombs" tells us that radiation is the only "dirty" part of killing people.

To take this one step further, such phrases can even seem healthful/curative/corrective. So that we not only have "clean bombs" but also "surgically clean strikes" ("counterforce" attacks that can purportedly "take out" – i.e., accurately destroy – an opponent's weapons or command centers without causing significant injury to anything else). The image of excision of the offending weapon is unspeakably ludicrous when the surgical tool is not a delicately controlled scalpel but a nuclear warhead. And somehow it seems to be forgotten that even scalpels spill blood.

White men in ties discussing missile size

Feminists have often suggested that an important aspect of the arms race is phallic worship, that "missile envy" is a significant motivating force in the nuclear build-up. I have always found this an uncomfortably reductionist explanation and hoped that my research at the Center would yield a more complex analysis. But still, I was curious about the extent to which I might find a sexual subtext in the defense professionals' discourse. I was not prepared for what I found.

I think I had naively imagined myself as a feminist spy in the house of death – that I would need to sneak around and eavesdrop on what men said in unguarded moments, using all my subtlety and cunning to unearth whatever sexual imagery might be underneath how they thought and spoke. I had naively believed that these men, at least in public, would appear to be aware of feminist critiques. If they had not changed their language, I thought that at least at some point in a long talk about "penetration aids," someone would suddenly look up, slightly embarrassed to be caught in such blatant confirmation of feminist analyses of What's Going On Here.[1]

Of course, I was wrong. There was no evidence that any feminist critiques had ever reached the ears, much less the minds, of these men. American military dependence on nuclear weapons was explained as "irresistible, because you get more bang for the buck." Another lecturer solemnly and scientifically announced "to disarm is to get rid of all your stuff." (This may, in turn, explain why they see serious talk of nuclear disarmament as perfectly resistable, not to mention foolish. If disarmament is emasculation, how could any real man even consider it?) A professor's explanation of why the MX missile is to be placed in the silos of the newest Minuteman missiles, instead of replacing the older, less accurate ones, was "because they're in the nicest hole – you're not going to take the nicest missile you have and put it in a crummy hole." Other lectures were filled with discussion of vertical erector launchers, thrust-to-weight ratios, soft lay downs, deep penetration, and the comparative advantages of protracted versus spasm attacks – or what one military adviser to the National Security Council has called "releasing 70 to 80 percent of our megatonnage in one orgasmic whump."[2] There was serious concern about the need to harden our missiles and the need to "face it, the Russians are a little harder than we are." Disbelieving glances would occasionally pass between me and my one ally in the summer program, another woman, but no one else seemed to notice. [. . .]

Sexual imagery has, of course, been a part of the world of warfare since long before nuclear weapons were even a gleam in a physicist's eye. The history of the atomic bomb project itself is rife with overt images of competitive male sexuality, as is the discourse of the early nuclear physicists, strategists, and SAC commanders.[3] Both the military itself and the arms manufacturers are constantly exploiting the phallic imagery and promise of sexual domination that their weapons so conveniently suggest. A quick glance at the publications that constitute some of the research sources for defense intellectuals makes the depth and pervasiveness of the imagery evident.

Air Force Magazine's advertisements for new weapons, for example, rival *Playboy* as a catalog of men's sexual anxieties and fantasies. Consider the following, from the June 1985 issue: emblazoned in bold letters across the top of a two-page advertisement for the AV-8B Harrier II – "Speak Softly and Carry a Big Stick." The copy below boasts "an exceptional thrust to weight ratio" and "vectored thrust capability that makes the . . . unique rapid response possible." Then, just in case we've failed to get the message, the last line reminds us, "Just the sort of 'Big Stick' Teddy Roosevelt had in mind way back in 1901."[4]

An ad for the BKEP (BLU-106/B) reads:

The Only Way to Solve Some Problems is to Dig Deep.
THE BOMB, KINETIC ENERGY
PENETRATOR
"Will provide the tactical air commander with efficient power to deny or significantly delay enemy airfield operations."
"Designed to maximize runway cratering by optimizing penetration dynamics and utilizing the most efficient warhead yet designed."[5]

[...] Another, truly extraordinary, source of phallic imagery is to be found in descriptions of nuclear blasts themselves. Here, for example, is one by journalist William Laurence, who was brought to Nagasaki by the Air Force to witness the bombing. "Then, just when it appeared as though the thing had settled down in to a state of permanence, there came shooting out of the top a giant mushroom that increased the size of the pillar to a total of 45,000 feet. The mushroom top was even more alive than the pillar, seething and boiling in a white fury of creamy foam, sizzling upward and then descending earthward, a thousand geysers rolled into one. It kept struggling in an elemental fury, like a creature in the act of breaking the bonds that held it down."[6]

Given the degree to which it suffuses their world, that defense intellectuals themselves use a lot of sexual imagery does not seem especially surprising. Nor does it, by itself, constitute grounds for imputing motivation. For me, the interesting issue is not so much the imagery's psychodynamic origins, as how it functions. How does it serve to make it possible for strategic planners and other defense intellectuals to do their macabre work? How does it function in their construction of a work world that feels tenable? Several stories illustrate the complexity.

During the summer program, a group of us visited the New London Navy base where nuclear submarines are homeported and the General Dynamics Electric Boat boatyards where a new Trident submarine was being constructed. At one point during the trip we took a tour of a nuclear powered submarine. When we reached the part of the sub where the missiles are housed, the officer accompanying us turned with a grin and asked if we wanted to stick our hands through a hole to "pat the missile." *Pat the missile?*

The image reappeared the next week, when a lecturer scornfully declared that the only real reason for deploying cruise and Pershing II missiles in Western Europe was "so that our allies can pat them." [...] What is all this "patting"? What are men doing when they "pat" these high-tech phalluses? Patting is an assertion of intimacy, sexual possession, affectionate domination. The thrill and pleasure of "patting the missile" is the proximity of all that phallic power, the possibility of vicariously appropriating it as one's own.

But if the predilection for patting phallic objects indicates something of the homoerotic excitement suggested by the language, it also has another side. For patting is not only an act of sexual intimacy. It is also what one does to babies, small children, the pet dog. One pats that which is small, cute, and harmless – not terrifyingly destructive. Pat it, and its lethality disappears. [...]

The imagery can be construed as a deadly serious display of the connections between masculine sexuality and the arms race. At the same time, it can also be heard as a way of minimizing the seriousness of militarist endeavors, of denying their deadly consequences. A former Pentagon target analyst, in telling me why he thought plans for "limited nuclear war" were ridiculous, said, "Look, you gotta understand that it's a pissing contest – you gotta expect them to use everything they've got." What does this image say? Most obviously, that this is all about competition for manhood, and thus there is tremendous danger. But at the same time, the image diminishes the contest and its outcomes, by representing it as an act of boyish mischief.

Male birth and creation

There is one set of domestic images that demands separate attention – images that suggest men's desire to appropriate from women the power of giving life and that conflate creation and destruction. The bomb project is rife with images of male birth. In December 1942, Ernest Lawrence's telegram to the physicists at Chicago read, "Congratulations to the new parents. Can hardly wait to see the new arrival."[7] At Los Alamos, the atom bomb was referred to as "Oppenheimer's baby." One of the physicists working at Los Alamos, Richard Feynman, writes that when he was temporarily on leave after his wife's death, he received a telegram saying, "The baby is expected on such and such a day."[8] At Lawrence Livermore, the hydrogen bomb was referred to as "Teller's baby," although those who wanted to disparage Edward Teller's contribution claimed he was not the bomb's father but its mother. They claimed that Stanislaw Ulam was the real father; he had the all important idea and inseminated Teller with it. Teller only "carried it" after that.[9] [...]

In light of the imagery of male birth, the extraordinary names given to the bombs that reduced Hiroshima and Nagasaki to ash and rubble – "Little Boy" and "Fat Man" – at last become intelligible. These ultimate destroyers were the progeny of the atomic scientists – and emphatically not just any progeny but male progeny. In early tests, before they were certain that the bombs would work, the scientists expressed their concern by saying that they hoped the baby was a boy, not a girl – that is, not a dud.[10] General Grove's triumphant cable to Secretary of War Henry Stimson at the Potsdam conference, informing him that the first atomic bomb test was successful read, after decoding: "Doctor has just returned most enthusiastic and confident that the little boy is as husky as his big brother. The light in his eyes discernible from here to Highhold and I could have heard his screams from here to my farm."[11] Stimson, in turn, informed Churchill by writing him a note that read, "Babies satisfactorily born."[12] In 1952, Teller's exultant telegram to Los Alamos announcing the successful test of the hydrogen bomb, "Mike," at Eniwetok Atoll in the Marshall Islands, read, "It's a boy."[13] The nuclear scientists gave birth to male progeny with the ultimate power of violent domination over female Nature. The defense intellectuals' project is the creation of abstract formulations to control the forces the scientists created – and to participate thereby in their world-creating/destroying power.

The entire history of the bomb project, in fact, seems permeated with imagery that confounds man's overwhelming technological power to destroy nature with the power to create – imagery that inverts men's destruction and asserts in its place the power to create new life and a new world. It converts men's destruction into their rebirth. [...]

Stage 2: Learning to Speak the Language

The first task was training the tongue in the articulation of acronyms. [...] First, in speaking and hearing, a lot of these terms can be very sexy. A small supersonic rocket "designed to penetrate any Soviet air defense" is called a SRAM (for short-range attack missile). Submarine-launched cruise missiles are not referred to as SLCMs, but "slick'-ems." Ground-launched cruise missiles are "glick'-ems." Air-launched cruise missiles are not sexy but magical – "alchems" (ALCMs) replete with the illusion of turning base metals into gold. [...]

Part of the appeal was the thrill of being able to manipulate an arcane language, the power of entering the secret kingdom, being someone in the know. It is a glow that is a significant part of learning about nuclear weaponry. Few know, and those who do are powerful. You can rub elbows with them, perhaps even be one yourself.

That feeling, of course, does not come solely from the language. The whole set-up of the summer program itself, for example, communicated the allures of power and the benefits of white male privileges. We were provided with luxurious accommodations, complete with young black women who came in to clean up after us each day; generous funding paid not only our transportation and food but also a large honorarium for attending; we met in lavishly appointed classrooms and lounges. Access to excellent athletic facilities was guaranteed by a "Temporary Privilege Card," which seemed to me to sum up the essence of the experience. Perhaps most important of all were the endless allusions by our lecturers to "what I told John [Kennedy]" and "and then Henry [Kissinger] said," or the lunches where we could sit next to a prominent political figure and listen to Washington gossip. [...]

By the time I was through, I had learned far more than a set of abstract words that refers to grisly subjects, for even when the subjects of a standard English and nukespeak description seem to be the same, they are, in fact, about utterly different phenomena. Consider the following descriptions, in each of which the subject is the aftermath of a nuclear attack:

Everything was black, had vanished into the black dust, was destroyed. Only the flames that were beginning to lick their way up had any color. From the dust that was like a fog, figures began to loom up, black, hairless, faceless. They screamed with voices that were no longer human. Their screams drowned out the groans rising everywhere from the rubble, groans that seemed to rise from the very earth itself.[14]

[You have to have ways to maintain communications in a] nuclear environment, a situation bound to include EMP blackout, brute force damage to systems, a heavy jamming environment, and so on.[15]

There are no ways to describe the phenomena represented in the first with the language of the second. Learning to speak the language of defense analysts is not a conscious, cold-blooded decision to ignore the effects of nuclear weapons on real live human beings, to ignore the sensory, the emotional experience, the human impact. It is simply learning a new language, but by the time you are through, the content of what you can talk about is monumentally different, as is the perspective from which you speak. [...]

Finally, then, I suspect that much of the reduced anxiety about nuclear war commonly experienced by both new speakers of the language and long-time experts comes from characteristics of the language itself: the distance afforded by its abstraction; the sense of control afforded by mastering it; and the fact that its content and concerns are that of the users rather than the victims of nuclear weapons. In learning the language, one goes from being the passive, powerless victim to the competent, wily, powerful purveyor of nuclear threats and nuclear explosive power. The enormous destructive effects of nuclear weapons systems become extensions of the self, rather than threats to it.

Stage 3: Dialogue

It did not take very long to learn the language of nuclear war and much of the specialized information it contained. My focus quickly changed from mastering technical information and doctrinal arcana to attempting to understand more about how the dogma was rationalized. [...]

What I found was that no matter how well-informed or complex my questions were, if I spoke English rather than expert jargon, the men responded to me as though I were ignorant, simpleminded, or both. It did not appear to occur to anyone that I might actually be choosing not to speak their language.

A strong distaste for being patronized and dismissed made my experiment in English short-lived. I adapted my everyday speech to the vocabulary of strategic analysis. I spoke of "escalation dominance," "preemptive strikes," and, one of my favorites, "subholocaust engagements." Using the right phrases opened my way into long, elaborate discussions that taught me a lot about technostrategic reasoning and how to manipulate it.

I found, however, that the better I got at engaging in this discourse, the more impossible it became for me to express my own ideas, my own values. I could adopt the language and gain a wealth of new concepts and reasoning strategies – but at the same time as the language gave me access to things I had been unable to speak about before, it radically excluded others. I could not use the language to express my concerns because it was physically impossible. This language does not allow certain questions to be asked or certain values to be expressed.

To pick a bald example: the word "peace" is not a part of this discourse. As close as one can come is "strategic stability," a term that refers to a balance of numbers and types of weapons systems – not the political, social, economic, and psychological conditions implied by the word "peace." Not only is there no word signifying peace in this discourse, but the word "peace" itself cannot be used. To speak it is immediately to brand oneself as a soft-headed activist instead of an expert, a professional to be taken seriously.

If I was unable to speak my concerns in this language, more disturbing still was that I found it hard even to keep them in my own head. I had begun my research expecting abstract and sanitized discussions of nuclear war and had readied myself to replace my words for theirs, to be ever vigilant against slipping into the never-never land of abstraction. But no matter how prepared I was, no matter how firm my commitment to staying aware of the reality behind the words, over and over I found that I could not stay connected, could not keep human lives as my reference point. I found I could go for days speaking about nuclear weapons without once thinking about the people who would be incinerated by them [...]

So to refer to "limited nuclear war" is already to enter into a system that is de facto abstract and removed from reality. To use more descriptive language would not, by itself, change that. In fact, I am tempted to say that the abstractness of the entire conceptual system makes descriptive language nearly beside the point. In a discussion of "limited nuclear war," for example, it might make some difference if in place of saying "In a counterforce attack against hard targets collateral damage could be limited," a strategic analyst had to use words that were less abstract – if he had to say, for instance, "If we launch the missiles we have aimed at their missile silos, the explosions would cause the immediate mass murder of 10 million women, men, and children, as well as the extended illness, suffering, and eventual death of many millions more." It is true that the second sentence does not roll off the tongue or slide across one's consciousness quite as easily. But it is also true, I believe, that the ability to speak about "limited nuclear war" stems as much, if not more, from the fact that the term "limited nuclear war" refers to an abstract conceptual system rather than to events that might take place in the real world. As such, there is no need to think about the concrete human realities behind the model; what counts is the internal logic of the system. [...]

I was only able to "make sense of it" when I finally asked myself the question that feminists have been asking about theories in every discipline: What is the reference point? Who (or what) is the *subject* here? [...]

If human lives are not the reference point, then it is not only impossible to talk about humans in this language, it also becomes in some sense illegitimate to ask the paradigm to reflect human concerns. Hence, questions that break through the numbing language of strategic analysis and raise issues in human terms can be dismissed easily. No one will claim that the questions are unimportant, but they are inexpert, unprofessional, irrelevant to the business at hand to ask. The discourse among the experts remains hermetically sealed. [...]

Stage 4: The Terror

As a newcomer to the world of defense analysts, I was continually startled by likeable and admirable men, by their gallows humor, by the bloodcurdling casualness with which they regularly blew up the world while standing and chatting over the coffee pot. I also *heard* the language they spoke – heard the acronyms and euphemisms, and abstractions, heard the imagery, heard the pleasure with which they used it.

Within a few weeks, what had once been remarkable became unnoticeable. As I learned to speak, my perspective changed. I no longer stood outside the impermeable wall of technostrategic language and, once inside, I could no longer see it. Speaking the language, I could no longer really

hear it. And once inside its protective walls, I began to find it difficult to get out. The impermeability worked both ways.

I had not only learned to speak a language: I had started to think in it. Its questions became my questions, its concepts shaped my responses to new ideas. Its definitions of the parameters of reality became mine. Like the White Queen [in Carroll's *Through the Looking Glass*], I began to believe six impossible things before breakfast. Not because I consciously believed, for instance, that a "surgically clean counterforce strike" was really possible, but instead because some elaborate piece of doctrinal reasoning I used was already predicated on the possibility of those strikes, as well as on a host of other impossible things.

My grasp on what *I* knew as reality seemed to slip. I might get very excited, for example, about a new strategic justification for a "no first use" policy and spend time discussing the ways in which its implications for our force structure in Western Europe were superior to the older version. And after a day or two I would suddenly step back, aghast that I was so involved with the military justifications for not using nuclear weapons – as though the moral ones were not enough. What I was actually talking about – the mass incineration caused by a nuclear attack – was no longer in my head.

Or I might hear some proposals that seemed to me infinitely superior to the usual arms control fare. First I would work out how and why these proposals were better and then work out all the ways to counter the arguments against them. But then, it might dawn on me that even though these two proposals sounded so different, they still shared a host of assumptions that I was not willing to make (e.g., about the inevitable, eternal conflict of interests between the United States and the USSR, or the desirability of having some form of nuclear deterrent, or the goal of "managing," rather than ending, the nuclear arms race). After struggling to this point of seeing what united both positions, I would first feel as though I had really accomplished something. And then all of a sudden, I would realize that these new insights were things I actually knew *before I ever entered* this community. Apparently, I had since forgotten them, at least functionally, if not absolutely.

I began to feel that I had fallen down the rabbit hole – and it was a struggle to climb back out.

Conclusion

I have been arguing throughout this paper that learning the language is a transformative, rather than an additive, process. When you choose to learn it you enter a new mode of thinking – a mode of thinking not only about nuclear weapons but also, de facto, about military and political power and about the relationship between human ends and technological means.

Thus, those of us who find US nuclear policy desperately misguided appear to face a serious quandary. If we refuse to learn the language, we are virtually guaranteed that our voices will remain outside the "politically relevant" spectrum of opinion. Yet, if we do learn and speak it, we not only severely limit what we can say but we also invite the transformation, the militarization, of our own thinking. [. . .]

When defense intellectuals are criticized for the cold-blooded inhumanity of the scenarios they plan, their response is to claim the high ground of rationality; they are the only ones whose response to the existence of nuclear weapons is objective and realistic. They portray those who are radically opposed to the nuclear status quo as irrational, unrealistic, too emotional. "Idealistic activists" is the pejorative they set against their own hard-nosed professionalism.

Much of their claim to legitimacy, then, is a claim to objectivity born of technical expertise and to the disciplined purging of the emotional valences that might threaten their objectivity. But if the surface of their discourse – its abstraction and technical jargon – appears at first to support these claims, a look just below the surface does not. There we find currents of homoerotic excitement, heterosexual domination, the drive toward competency and mastery, the pleasures of membership in an elite and privileged group, the ultimate importance and meaning of membership in the priesthood, and the thrilling power of becoming Death, shatterer of worlds. How is it possible to hold this up as a paragon of cool-headed objectivity?

I do not wish here to discuss or judge the holding of "objectivity" as an epistemological goal. I would simply point out that, as defense intellectuals rest their claims to legitimacy on the untainted rationality of their discourse, their project fails according to its own criteria. Deconstructing strategic discourse's claims to rationality is, then, in and of itself, an important way to challenge its hegemony as the sole legitimate language for public debate about nuclear policy.

I believe that feminists, and others who seek a more just and peaceful world, have a dual task before us – a deconstructive project and a reconstructive project that are intimately linked. Our deconstructive task requires close attention to, and the dismantling of, technostrategic discourse. The dominant voice of militarized masculinity and decontextualized rationality speaks so loudly in our culture, it will remain difficult for any other voices to be heard until that voice loses some of its power to define what we hear and how we name the world – until that voice is delegitimated.

Our reconstructive task is a task of creating compelling alternative visions of possible futures, a task of recognizing and developing alternative conceptions of rationality, a task of creating rich and imaginative alternative voices – diverse voices whose conversations with each other will invent those futures.

NOTES

1 For the uninitiated, "penetration aids" refers to devices that help bombers or missiles get past the "enemy's" defensive systems; e.g., stealth technology, chaff, or decoys. Within the defense intellectual community, they are also familiarly known as "penaids."

2 General William Odom, "C³I and Telecommunications at the Policy Level," Incidental Paper, Seminar on C³I: Command, Control, Communications and Intelligence (Cambridge, MA: Harvard University, Center for Information Policy Research, Spring 1980), 5.

3 This point has been amply documented by Brian Easlea, *Fathering the Unthinkable: Masculinity, Scientists and the Nuclear Arms Race* (London: Pluto Press, 1983).

4 *Air Force Magazine* 68, no. 6 (June 1985): 77–8.

5 Ibid.

6 William L. Laurence, *Dawn over Zero: The Study of the Atomic Bomb* (London: Museum Press, 1974), 198–9.

7 Lawrence is quoted by Herbert Childs in *An American Genius: The Life of Ernest Orlando Lawrence* (New York: E. P. Dutton, 1968), 340.

8 Feynman writes about the telegram in Richard P. Feynman, "Los Alamos from Below," in *Reminiscences of Los Alamos, 1943–1945*, eds., Lawrence Badash, Joseph O. Hirshfelder, and Herbert P. Broida (Dordrecht: D. Reidel, 1980), 130.

9 Hans Bethe is quoted as saying that "Ulam was the father of the hydrogen bomb and Edward was the mother, because he carried the baby for quite a while" (J. Bernstein, *Hans Bethe: Prophet of Energy* [New York: Basic Books, 1980], 95).

10 The concern about having a boy, not a girl, is written about by Robert Jungk, *Brighter Than a Thousand Suns*, trans. James Cleugh (New York: Harcourt, Brace & Co., 1956), 197.

11 Richard E. Hewlett and Oscar E. Anderson, *The New World, 1939/46: A History of the United States Atomic Energy Commission*, 2 vols. (University Park: Pennsylvania State University Press, 1962), 1:386.

12 Winston Churchill, *The Second World War*, vol. 6., *Triumph and Tragedy* (London: Cassell, 1954), 551.

13 Quoted by Easlea, 130.

14 Hisako Matsubara, *Cranes at Dusk* (Garden City, NY: Dial Press, 1985). The author was a child in Kyoto at the time the atomic bomb was dropped. Her description is based on the memories of survivors.

15 General Robert Rosenberg (formerly on the National Security Council staff during the Carter Administration), "The Influence of Policymaking on C^{3}I," Incidental Paper, Seminar on C^{3}I (Cambridge, MA: Harvard University, Center for Information Policy Research, Spring 1980), 59.

Part IX

Torture

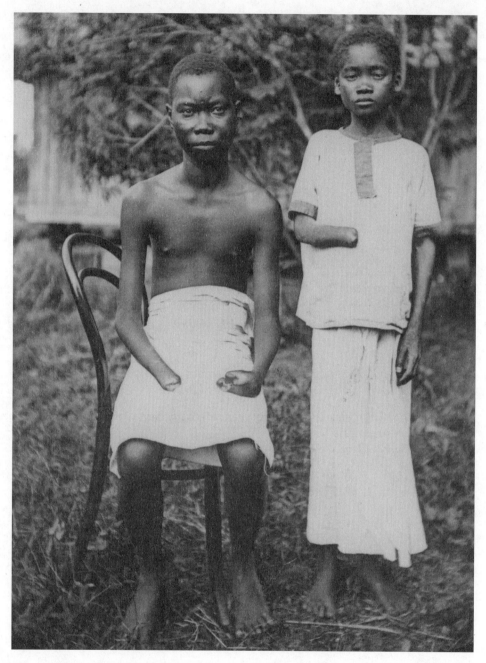

Plate 11:   Mola and Yoka, Belgian Congo circa 1905. Photo courtesy Anti-Slavery International.

46

From *The Body in Pain: The Making and Unmaking of the World*

Elaine Scarry

The Inexpressibility of Physical Pain

When one hears about another person's physical pain, the events happening within the interior of that person's body may seem to have the remote character of some deep subterranean fact, belonging to an invisible geography that, however portentous, has no reality because it has not yet manifested itself on the visible surface of the earth. Or alternatively, it may seem as distant as the interstellar events referred to by scientists who speak to us mysteriously of not yet detectable intergalactic screams or of "very distant Seyfert galaxies, a class of objects within which violent events of unknown nature occur from time to time."

Vaguely alarming yet unreal, laden with consequence yet evaporating before the mind because not available to sensory confirmation, unseeable classes of objects such as subterranean plates, Seyfert galaxies, and the pains occurring in other people's bodies flicker before the mind, then disappear.

Physical pain happens, of course, not several miles below our feet or many miles above our heads but within the bodies of persons who inhabit the world through which we each day make our way, and who may at any moment be separated from us by only a space of several inches. The very temptation to invoke analogies to remote cosmologies (and there is a long tradition of such analogies) is itself a sign of pain's triumph, for it achieves its aversiveness in part by bringing about, even within the radius of several feet, this absolute split between one's sense of one's own reality and the reality of other persons.

Thus when one speaks about "one's own physical pain" and about "another person's physical pain," one might almost appear to be speaking about two wholly distinct orders of events. For the person whose pain it is, it is "effortlessly" grasped (that is, even with the most heroic effort it cannot *not* be grasped); while for the person outside the sufferer's body, what is "effortless" is *not* grasping it (it is easy to remain wholly unaware of its existence; even with effort, one may remain in doubt about its existence or may retain the astonishing freedom of denying its existence; and, finally, if with the best effort of sustained attention one successfully apprehends it, the aversiveness of the "it" one apprehends will only be a shadowy fraction of the actual "it"). So, for the person in pain, so incontestably and unnegotiably present is it that "having pain" may come to be thought of as the most vibrant example of what it is to "have certainty," while for the other person it is so elusive that "hearing about pain" may exist as the primary model of what it is "to have doubt." Thus pain comes unsharably into our midst as at once that which cannot be denied and that which cannot be confirmed.

Whatever pain achieves, it achieves in part through its unsharability, and it ensures this unsharability through its resistance to language. "English," writes Virginia Woolf, "which can express the thoughts of Hamlet and the tragedy of Lear has no words for the shiver or the headache.... The merest schoolgirl when she falls in love has Shakespeare or Keats to speak her mind for her, but let a sufferer try to describe a pain in his head to a doctor and language at once runs dry." True of the headache, Woolf's account is of course more radically true of the severe and prolonged pain that may accompany cancer or burns or phantom limb or stroke, as well as of the severe and prolonged pain that may occur unaccompanied by any nameable disease. Physical pain does not simply resist language but actively destroys it, bringing about an immediate reversion to a state anterior to language, to the sounds and cries a human being makes before language is learned.

Though Woolf frames her observation in terms of one particular language, the essential problem she describes, not limited to English, is characteristic of all languages. This is not to say that one encounters *no* variations in the expressibility of pain as one moves across different languages. The existence of culturally stipulated responses to pain – for example, the tendency of one population to vocalize cries; the tendency of another to suppress them – is well documented in anthropological research. So, too, a particular constellation of sounds or words that make it possible to register alterations in the felt-experience of pain in one language may have no equivalent in a second language: thus Sophocles's agonized Philoctetes utters a cascade of *changing* cries and shrieks that in the original Greek are accommodated by an array of formal words (some of them twelve syllables long), but that at least one translator found could only be rendered in English by the uniform syllable "Ah" followed by variations in punctuation (Ah! Ah!!!!). But even if one were to enumerate many additional examples, such cultural differences, taken collectively, would themselves constitute only a very narrow margin of variation and would thus in the end work to expose and confirm the universal sameness of the central problem, a problem that originates much less in the inflexibility of any one language or in the shyness of any one culture than in the utter rigidity of pain itself: its resistance to language is not simply one of its incidental or accidental attributes but is essential to what it is. [...]

Pain and Interrogation

Torture consists of a primary physical act, the infliction of pain, and a primary verbal act, the interrogation. The first rarely occurs without the second. As is true of the present period, most historical episodes of torture, such as the Inquisition, have inevitably included the element of interrogation: the pain is traditionally accompanied by "the Question." Ancient history, too, confirms the insistent coupling; strangers caught by the *yaksha* cults in India, for example, were sacrificed after being subjected to a series of riddles. The connection between the physical act and the verbal act, between body and voice, is often misstated or misunderstood. Although the information sought in an interrogation is almost never credited with being a *just* motive for torture, it is repeatedly credited with being the motive for torture. But for every instance in which someone with critical information is interrogated, there are hundreds interrogated who could know nothing of remote importance to the stability or self-image of the regime. Just as within a precarious regime the motive for arrest is often a fiction (the eggseller's eggs were too small – Greece), and just as the motive for punishing those imprisoned is often a fiction (the men, although locked in their cells, watched and applauded the television report that a military plane had crashed – Chile), so what masquerades as the motive for torture is a fiction.

The idea that the need for information is the motive for the physical cruelty arises from the tone and form of the questioning rather than from its content: the questions, no matter how contemptuously irrelevant their content, are announced, delivered, *as though* they motivated the cruelty, *as if* the answers to them were crucial. Few other moments of human speech so conflate the modes of the interrogatory, the declarative, the imperative, as well as the emphatic form of each of these three, the exclamatory. Each mode implies a radically different relation of speaker to listener, and so the rapid slipping and colliding of these voices and the relations they imply – the independence of the declarative, the uncertain dependence of the interrogatory, the dominance of the imperative, each as though unaccompanied and unqualified by the others, raised to its most absolute in the urgency of the exclamatory – suggest a level of instability so extreme that the questioner might seem involved in the outcome to the very extent of his being. In fact, when this kind of conflation occurs in private, nonpolitical human speech, and where it is unaccompanied by physical brutality, when, say, a jealous lover or a terrified parent asks questions and asserts the answers in a way that rocks between utterly self-sufficient conviction and a pleading need of the listener's crediting or confirmation, the person may well be involved in the response to the very extent of his or her being. But as the content and context of the torturer's questions make clear, the fact that something is asked *as if* the content of the answer matters does not mean that it matters. It is crucial to see that the interrogation does not stand outside an episode of torture as its motive or justification: it is internal to the structure of torture, exists there because of its intimate connections to and interactions with the physical pain.

Pain and interrogation inevitably occur together in part because the torturer and the prisoner each experience them as opposites. The very question that, within the political pretense, matters so much to the torturer that it occasions his grotesque brutality will matter so little to the prisoner experiencing the brutality that he will give the answer. For the torturers, the sheer and simple fact of human agony is made invisible, and the moral fact of inflicting that agony is made neutral by the feigned urgency and significance of the question. For the prisoner, the sheer, simple, overwhelming fact of his agony will make neutral and invisible the significance of any question as well as the significance of the world to which the question refers. Intense pain is world-destroying. In compelling confession, the torturers compel the prisoner to record and objectify the fact that intense pain is world-destroying. It is for this reason that while the content of the prisoner's answer is only sometimes important to the regime, the form of the answer, the fact of his answering, is always crucial.

There is not only among torturers but even among people appalled by acts of torture and sympathetic to those hurt, a covert disdain for confession. This disdain is one of many manifestations of how inaccessible the reality of physical pain is to anyone not immediately experiencing it. The nature of confession is falsified by an idiom built on the word "betrayal": in confession, one betrays oneself and all those aspects of the world – friend, family, country, cause – that the self is made up of. The inappropriateness of this idiom is immediately apparent in any non-political context. It is a commonplace that at the moment when a dentist's drill hits and holds an exposed nerve, a person sees stars. What is meant by "seeing stars" is that the contents of consciousness are, during those moments, obliterated, that the name of one's child, the memory of a friend's face, are all absent. But the nature of this "absence" is not illuminated by the word "betrayal." One cannot betray or be false to something that has ceased to exist and, in the most literal way possible, the created world of thought and feeling, all the psychological and mental content that constitutes both one's self and one's world, and that gives rise to and is in turn made possible by language, ceases to exist.

47

From *Trauma and Recovery: The Aftermath of Violence – From Domestic Abuse to Political Terror*

Judith Herman

PTSD: A New Diagnosis

Most people have no knowledge or understanding of the psychological changes of captivity. Social judgment of chronically traumatized people therefore tends to be extremely harsh. The chronically abused person's apparent helplessness and passivity, her entrapment in the past, her intractable depression and somatic complaints, and her smoldering anger often frustrate the people closest to her. Moreover, if she has been coerced into betrayal of relationships, community loyalties, or moral values, she is frequently subjected to furious condemnation.

Observers who have never experienced prolonged terror and who have no understanding of coercive methods of control presume that they would show greater courage and resistance than the victim in similar circumstances. Hence the common tendency to account for the victim's behavior by seeking flaws in her personality or moral character. Prisoners of war who succumb to "brainwashing" are often treated as traitors.[1] Hostages who submit to their captors are often publicly excoriated. Sometimes survivors are treated more harshly than those who abused them. In the notorious case of Patricia Hearst, for instance, the hostage was tried for crimes committed under duress and received a longer prison sentence than her captors.[2] Similarly, women who fail to escape

from abusive relationships and those who prostitute themselves or betray their children under duress are subjected to extraordinary censure.

The propensity to fault the character of the victim can be seen even in the case of politically organized mass murder. The aftermath of the Holocaust witnessed a protracted debate regarding the "passivity" of the Jews and their "complicity" in their fate. But the historian Lucy Dawidowicz points out that "complicity" and "cooperation" are terms that apply to situations of free choice. They do not have the same meaning in situations of captivity.[3]

Diagnostic mislabeling

This tendency to blame the victim has strongly influenced the direction of psychological inquiry. It has led researchers and clinicians to seek an explanation for the perpetrator's crimes in the character of the victim. In the case of hostages and prisoners of war, numerous attempts to find supposed personality defects that predisposed captives to "brainwashing" have yielded few consistent results. The conclusion is inescapable that ordinary, psychologically healthy men can indeed be coerced in unmanly ways.[4] In domestic battering situations, where victims are entrapped by persuasion rather than by capture, research has also focused on the personality traits that might predispose a woman to get involved in an abusive relationship. Here again no consistent profile of the susceptible woman has emerged. While some battered women clearly have major psychological difficulties that render them vulnerable, the majority show no evidence of serious psychopathology before entering into the exploitative relationship. Most become involved with their abusers at a time of temporary life crisis or recent loss, when they are feeling unhappy, alienated, or lonely.[5] A survey of the studies on wife-beating concludes: "The search for characteristics of women that contribute to their own victimization is futile.... It is sometimes forgotten that men's violence is men's behavior. As such, it is not surprising that the more fruitful efforts to explain this behavior have focused on male characteristics. What is surprising is the enormous effort to explain male behavior by examining characteristics of women."[6]

While it is clear that ordinary, healthy people may become entrapped in prolonged abusive situations, it is equally clear that after their escape they are no longer ordinary or healthy. Chronic abuse causes serious psychological harm. The tendency to blame the victim, however, has interfered with the psychological understanding and diagnosis of a post-traumatic syndrome. Instead of conceptualizing the psychopathology of the victim as a response to an abusive situation, mental health professionals have frequently attributed the abusive situation to the victim's presumed underlying psychopathology. [...]

The tendency to misdiagnose victims was at the heart of a controversy that arose in the mid-1980s when the diagnostic manual of the American Psychiatric Association came up for revision. A group of male psychoanalysts proposed that "masochistic personality disorder" be added to the canon. This hypothetical diagnosis applied to any person who "remains in relationships in which others exploit, abuse, or take advantage of him or her, despite opportunities to alter the situation." A number of women's groups were outraged, and a heated public debate ensued. Women insisted on opening up the process of writing the diagnostic canon, which had been the preserve of a small group of men, and for the first time took part in the naming of psychological reality. [...]

Need for a new concept

Misapplication of the concept of masochistic personality disorder may be one of the most stigmatizing diagnostic mistakes, but it is by no means the

only one. In general, the diagnostic categories of the existing psychiatric canon are simply not designed for survivors of extreme situations and do not fit them well. The persistent anxiety, phobias, and panic of survivors are not the same as ordinary anxiety disorders. The somatic symptoms of survivors are not the same as ordinary psychosomatic disorders. Their depression is not the same as ordinary depression. And the degradation of their identity and relational life is not the same as ordinary personality disorder.

The lack of an accurate and comprehensive diagnostic concept has serious consequences for treatment, because the connection between the patient's present symptoms and the traumatic experience is frequently lost. Attempts to fit the patient into the mold of existing diagnostic constructs generally result, at best, in a partial understanding of the problem and a fragmented approach to treatment. All too commonly, chronically traumatized people suffer in silence; but if they complain at all, their complaints are not well understood. They may collect a virtual pharmacopeia of remedies: one for headaches, another for insomnia, another for anxiety, another for depression. None of these tends to work very well, since the underlying issues of trauma are not addressed. As caregivers tire of these chronically unhappy people who do not seem to improve, the temptation to apply pejorative diagnostic labels becomes overwhelming.

Even the diagnosis of "post-traumatic stress disorder," as it is presently defined, does not fit accurately enough. The existing diagnostic criteria for this disorder are derived mainly from survivors of circumscribed traumatic events. They are based on the prototypes of combat, disaster, and rape. In survivors of prolonged, repeated trauma, the symptom picture is often far more complex. Survivors of prolonged abuse develop characteristic personality changes, including deformations of relatedness and identity. Survivors of abuse in childhood develop similar problems with relationships and identity; in addition, they are particularly vulnerable to repeated harm, both self-inflicted and at the hands of others. The current formulation of post-traumatic stress disorder fails to capture either the protean symptomatic manifestations of prolonged, repeated trauma or the profound deformations of personality that occur in captivity.

The syndrome that follows upon prolonged, repeated trauma needs its own name. I propose to

1. A history of subjection to totalitarian control over a prolonged period (months to years). Examples include hostages, prisoners of war, concentration-camp survivors, and survivors of some religious cults. Examples also include those subjected to totalitarian systems in sexual and domestic life, including survivors of domestic battering, childhood physical or sexual abuse, and organized sexual exploitation.

2. Alterations in affect regulation, including
   - persistent dysphoria
   - chronic suicidal preoccupation
   - self-injury
   - explosive or extremely inhibited anger (may alternate)
   - compulsive or extremely inhibited sexuality (may alternate)

3. Alterations in consciousness, including
   - amnesia or hypermnesia for traumatic events
   - transient dissociative episodes
   - depersonalization/derealization
   - reliving experiences, either in the form of intrusive post-traumatic stress disorder symptoms or in the form of ruminative preoccupation

4. Alterations in self-perception, including
   - sense of helplessness or paralysis of initiative
   - shame, guilt, and self-blame
   - sense of defilement or stigma
   - sense of complete difference from others (may include sense of specialness, utter aloneness, belief no other person can understand, or nonhuman identity)

5. Alterations in perception of perpetrator, including
   - preoccupation with relationship with perpetrator (includes preoccupation with revenge)
   - unrealistic attribution of total power to perpetrator (caution: victim's assessment of power realities may be more realistic than clinician's)
   - idealization or paradoxical gratitude
   - sense of special or supernatural relationship
   - acceptance of belief system or rationalizations of perpetrator

6. Alterations in relations with others, including
   - isolation and withdrawal
   - disruption in intimate relationships
   - repeated search for rescuer (may alternate with isolation and withdrawal)
   - persistent distrust
   - repeated failures of self-protection

7. Alterations in systems of meaning
   - loss of sustaining faith
   - sense of hopelessness and despair

call it "complex post-traumatic stress disorder." The responses to trauma are best understood as a spectrum of conditions rather than as a single disorder. They range from a brief stress reaction that gets better by itself and never qualifies for a diagnosis, to classic or simple post-traumatic stress disorder, to the complex syndrome of prolonged, repeated trauma. [...]

Lawrence Kolb remarks on the "heterogeneity" of post-traumatic stress disorder, which "is to psychiatry as syphilis was to medicine. At one time or another [this disorder] may appear to mimic every personality disorder. ... It is those threatened over long periods of time who suffer the long-standing severe personality disorganization."[7] Others have also called attention to the personality changes that follow prolonged, repeated trauma. The psychiatrist Emmanuel Tanay, who works with survivors of the Nazi Holocaust, observes: "The psychopathology may be hidden in characterological changes that are manifest only in disturbed object relationships and attitudes towards work, the world, man and God."[8]

Many experienced clinicians have invoked the need for a diagnostic formulation that goes beyond simple post-traumatic stress disorder. William Niederland finds that "the concept of traumatic neurosis does not appear sufficient to cover the multitude and severity of clinical manifestations" of the syndrome observed in survivors of the Nazi Holocaust.[9] Psychiatrists who have treated Southeast Asian refugees also recognize the need for an "expanded concept" of post-traumatic stress disorder that takes into account severe, prolonged, and massive psychological trauma.[10] One authority suggests the concept of a "post-traumatic character disorder."[11] Others speak of "complicated" post-traumatic stress disorder.[12] [...]

As the concept of a complex traumatic syndrome has gained wider recognition, it has been given several additional names. The working group for the diagnostic manual of the American Psychiatric Association has chosen the designation "disorder of extreme stress not otherwise specified." The International Classification of Diseases is considering a similar entity under the name "personality change from catastrophic experience." These names may be awkward and unwieldy, but practically any name that gives recognition to the syndrome is better than no name at all.

Naming the syndrome of complex post-traumatic stress disorder represents an essential step toward granting those who have endured prolonged exploitation a measure of the recognition they deserve. It is an attempt to find a language that is at once faithful to the traditions of accurate psychological observation and to the moral demands of traumatized people. It is an attempt to learn from survivors, who understand, more profoundly than any investigator, the effects of captivity.

NOTES

1 A. D. Biderman and H. Zimmer, eds., *The Manipulation of Human Behavior* (New York: John Wiley, 1961), 1–18.

2 P. Hearst and A. Moscow, *Every Secret Thing* (New York: Doubleday, 1982).

3 L. Dawidowicz, *The War Against the Jews* (London: Weidenfeld and Nicolson, 1975).

4 Biderman and Zimmer, *Manipulation of Human Behavior*; F. Ochberg and D. A. Soskis, *Victims of Terrorism* (Boulder, CO: Westview, 1982).

5 G. T. Hotaling and D. G. Sugarman, "An Analysis of Risk Markers in Husband-to-Wife Violence: The Current State of Knowledge," *Violence and Victims* 1 (1986): 101–24.

6 Ibid., 120.

7 L. C. Kolb, letter to the editor, *American Journal of Psychiatry* 146 (1989): 811–12.

8 H. Krystal, ed., *Massive Psychic Trauma* (New York: International Universities Press, 1968), 221.

9 Ibid., 314.

10 J. Kroll, M. Habenicht, T. Mackenzie et al., "Depression and Posttraumatic Stress Disorder in Southeast Asian Refugees," *American Journal of Psychiatry* 146 (1989): 1592–7.

11 M. Horowitz, *Stress Response Syndromes* (Northvale, NJ: Jason Aronson 1986), 49.

12 D. Brown and E. Fromm, *Hypnotherapy and Hypnoanalysis* (Hillsdale, NJ: Lawrence Erlbaum, 1986).

48

The Wet Bag and Other Phantoms

Antjie Krog

"I stand before you – naked and humble. I have decided to stop apologizing for Apartheid and to tell the truth. With this I will betray my people and I will betray myself. But I have to tell the truth. I have made peace with God and the time has come to make peace with the people of KwaZulu-Natal. To make peace with myself. It is this audience which haunts me in the back of my head. Maybe among you are those whom I assaulted, whom I left behind for dead in the field."

Constable William Harrington testifies about the Seven Day War in the area around Pietermaritzburg in the early nineties, when 200 people died, hundreds of houses were burned down, and thousands of refugees were left homeless. He admits that he assaulted more than a thousand people during his short service period of two years and eight months in the police force. This works out to more than one person every day.

Harrington was 18 years old and had been out of the Police Training College for barely a week when he was sent to track down ANC combatants in the dark.

"Richard said I should stick close to him. I was so afraid. We entered an ANC/UDF area. Rick pointed out Dallies – he was fired at by the ANC the previous week. When we descended into a dark valley, whistling started 200 metres from us – it was echoed into the valley. 'They know we are here,' whispered Rick. I tried to run, but it was difficult – with the *haelgeweer* and belt around my waist, trying to prevent the flares and bullets from falling out of my pocket."

In the darkness they came across a group of men, down on their knees to keep out of sight, and signalling to one another by making clicking sounds with their tongues. The unit Harrington was in crouched down silently and crept closer, making the same clicking noises. Five metres from them someone suddenly shouted, "*Amapoyisa!*" ["The police!"] and everybody started to shoot in all directions.

"It was like a movie imprinted on my memory. Flares were fired, people tumbled as they were shot . . . it was like a herd in flight."

After this baptism Harrington learnt quickly. At night, disguised in balaclavas, his unit sowed destruction in ANC areas. They went from home to home, searched for weapons, demanded to see IFP membership cards. If the house was without one, it was burnt down. "I fired on any ANC house or group from my vehicle, I distributed weapons to IFP chiefs, I transported Inkatha members and ammunition. It was days of death and blood."

"It was my war, my personal war against the ANC. My superiors told me: 'You act as if you are a little God.' And they were right. I did exactly as I pleased. At the age of twenty I made my own choices as a constable. I aligned myself with the IFP and up to this day I never had a lecture, letter or pamphlet informing me the ANC is no longer a lot of terrorists."

Harrington's hero was Major Deon Terreblanche – notorious for his killing sprees. "He was actually like my father. He was interested in my work. He always wanted to know how I was. He told me I personally have to fight against the

ANC, because they were communists. He said he would see to it that I never get into trouble."

But a *kitskonstabel* with ANC sympathies killed Terreblanche.

"A few days before the Seven Day War we buried Major Deon. I cried constantly. I drank to forget. I grieved for that man. I carried him at his funeral – how could I not have loved that man? But when I look at what he did, then I know I should not have loved him, but when I think of him with my heart, then I know that man was my father... that man I loved."

And his mother?

"At that stage she was dying of cancer."

The camera picks up the thin line flowing from the corner of Harrington's left eye over his cheek. He raises his right hand stiffly and tries to wipe it inconspicuously from his face.

"I grew up in jail. I was just 21 when I was sentenced. But my fear now belongs to the past. As I leave this stage here today I will be a marked man for the rest of my life. I have just betrayed the police motto: One for all and all for one. I will be stigmatized as a traitor because I have named every individual who worked with me – and when you fight like that, the only thing you have is trust. You trust on each other for your life. And I have betrayed them – all of them... but I beg you for forgiveness and peace."

When Harrington leaves the stage he bursts uncontrollably into tears. He is immediately taken to a special room for psychiatric support.

William Harrington was refused amnesty.

❋

Amnesty application of policeman Hendrik Johannes Petrus Botha

"Under the pretext that he had toilet paper in his backpack, Laurie retrieved his backpack with the weapons and black bag from the combi. The five of us walked through the thick bushes to an opening on the Tugela River bank. Laurie put down his backpack and whilst Laurie, [Mbuso] Shabalala and Charles [Ndaba] were urinating at the river bank, Sam and I took the two silenced weapons out of the backpack.

"In the meantime Laurie had made Charles and Shabalala sit flat on the ground facing the direction of the river. Laurie told them we are taking them to a safe house in northern Natal. Sam and I came from behind and shot them in the back of the

head. After they had fallen we each shot a second time into the body. I shot Charles and Sam shot Shabalala. Sam and I removed their clothes, while Laurie returned to the vehicle to get concrete poles, hessian and wire.

"Laurie cut the wire into lengths and Sam rolled Charles and Shabalala separately in hessian after the concrete pole had been placed over their chest and legs. The wire was then tied around their bodies to keep the hessian and poles in position. Laurie and I then threw Charles's body into the river from the bank. I then assisted Sam in doing the same to Shabalala's body. We put the clothes into the black bag. Branches were broken off the trees and the bloodstains wiped away. We spent about an hour making sure that the area was clean and that the bodies had sunk."

❋

Extract from Darren Taylor's radio interview with Lourens du Plessis

"What is of utmost importance is to examine the backgrounds in which we grew up. I mean that's where we were moulded. I'm not accusing anybody, but people were placed on a pedestal... not, I think, by intent, but it was carried over from the family conversations... What I would have liked to have done is to follow my conscience, because I really did have... the knowledge that we were doing wrong. I could figure it out for myself... those who never experience a prick of conscience, haven't got a conscience. I would really like to have the courage... to live according to my convictions, because during the seventies, I started feeling uncomfortable about things. I said on many occasions to my colleagues: 'You know, we're wrong! We're oppressing these people.' But this is as far as it went. I must say that I had a family to feed..."

(Du Plessis is a former SADF colonel. His name appears on the "death signal" calling for the permanent removal from society of the Cradock Four.)

❋

Extract from Darren Taylor's interview with Gerrie Hugo

"An experiment was done to test the strength of motherhood with a baboon, a female baboon with a baby... where it was put in confinement and the floor started heating up, so as to test how strong motherhood is, to check how far it will go before the baboon drops the baby... and gets on top of the baby to get away from the heat. In the end, the baboon couldn't take the pain any more and dropped the baby and got on top of the baby to get away from the heat. And I feel this is happening within the rank and file of the security forces... where the baby, being the operative, honestly believes that he will be protected by the powers that be, but the powers that be, the designers of the system and the planners, are starting to feel the heat and eventually... they drop the baby... and the operative must take that in mind, that that is going to happen to you. And the only way that you can protect yourself is to come forward now and come clean."

(Hugo is a former Military Intelligence operative in Namibia and South Africa.)

✳

Shame strangles the remembrance of you

It was different before. Victims told their stories to the Truth Commission. In another hall, at another time, in front of another committee, perpetrators explained their deeds. But the amnesty hearing of police captain Jeffrey Benzien seizes the heart of truth and reconciliation – the victim face to face with the perpetrator – and tears it out into the light.

Never before had the double-edged relationship between the torturer and the tortured been depicted as graphically as it was that week in the small, stuffy hall of the Truth Commission in Cape Town. Initially the body language of the tortured was clear: no one else counts, not the Amnesty Committee, not the lawyers, not the audience – what counts today is you and me. And we sit opposite each other, just like ten years ago. Except that I am not at your mercy – you are at mine. And I will ask you the questions that have haunted me ever since.

But it isn't that easy.

The first indication of the complexity of the relationship between an infamous torturer and his victim is the voice of Tony Yengeni. As a Member of Parliament, Yengeni's voice has become known for its tone of confidence – sometimes tinged with arrogance. When he faces Benzien, this is gone. From where I sit taking notes, I have to get up to make sure that it really is Yengeni speaking. He sounds strangely different – his voice somehow choked. Instead of seizing the moment to get back at Benzien, Yengeni wants to know the man.

"...What kind of man...uhm...that uses a method like this one with the wet bag to people...to other human beings...repeatedly...and listening to those moans and cries and groans ...and taking each of those people very near to their deaths...what kind of man are you, what kind of man is that, that can do...what kind of human being can do that, Mr Benzien?...I'm talking now about the man behind the wet bag."

At Yengeni's insistence, Benzien demonstrates the wet bag method. "I want to see it with my own eyes." The judges, who have come a long way from meticulously sticking to court procedures, jump up so as not to miss the spectacle. Photographers come running, not believing their luck. And the sight of this bluntly built white man squatting on the back of a black victim, who lies face down on the floor, and pulling a blue bag over his head will remain one of the most loaded and disturbing images in the life of the Truth Commission.

But for this moment, Yengeni has to pay dearly.

Back at the table, Benzien quietly turns on him and with one accurate blow shatters Yengeni's political profile right across the country.

"Do you remember, Mr Yengeni, that within thirty minutes you betrayed Jennifer Schreiner? Do you remember pointing out Bongani Jonas to us on the highway?"

And Yengeni sits there – as if begging this man to say it all; as if betrayal or cowardice can only make sense to him in the presence of this man.

"A special relationship" is what Benzien says existed between him and Ashley Forbes. Forbes, biting his upper lip, tries to get Benzien to admit to acts which had clearly plunged him into months of hell, driving him to the point of suicide.

BENZIEN: You I can remember especially because I think that the two of us, after weeks of your confinement, really became quite close...I may be mistaken, but I would say relatively good friends in a way...I assaulted you that first day...but then I took you on a trip...and I'm not saying this flippantly...you said that it is the most Kentucky Fried Chicken you've ever ate...and then we went to the Western Transvaal where you pointed out arms caches...Do you remember the time when you saw snow for the first time... what happened in the snow next to the N1... and the trip to Colesberg, how you braaied with me?

FORBES: Is it true that you tortured me every month on the 16th as a kind of anniversary of when you arrested me?

BENZIEN: In the spirit of reconciliation, you are making a mistake...

FORBES: On the second occasion I was wrapped in a carpet... my clothes were removed and the wet bag method used on me... Do you remember that you said you were going to break my nose by putting both your thumbs into my nostrils, ripping them until blood came out of my nose?

BENZIEN: I know you had a nosebleed but I thought that was as a result of the smack I gave you.

Benzien reminds Forbes that he always brought him fruit on Sundays, and how at great risk he smuggled Westerns – Forbes's favourite reading material – into the cell. The images of snow and fruit blend into the relationship of the protector and the vulnerable – a union in which both could live out fantasy and nightmare. When Forbes mentions anal penetration, Benzien purses his lips disapprovingly: "I deny that, and I'm deeply disappointed that you say that."

All this time, Ashley Forbes's wife is sitting in the row behind her husband's torturer. When Benzien mentions the kind way she greeted him that morning, he is overcome with emotion.

A torturer's success depends on his intimate knowledge of the human psyche. Benzien is a connoisseur. Within the first few minutes he manages to manipulate most of his victims back into the roles of their previous relationship – where he has the power and they the fragility. He uses several techniques to achieve this during the amnesty hearings. He sits alone, for three days, in the same grey suit and tie. At a press conference afterwards, the victims remark how strange it was to see him so alone. He constantly drinks water. He tells how in the past his children had to be escorted by police because he was such a hated man. How they knew about the wet blanket kept in the bath in case of a petrol-bomb attack on the house. Benzien remembers his victims' code names, the exact words they spoke, their unique mannerisms. All of them confirm that he was feared nationally –

he could get the information he wanted in less than thirty minutes.

"Cape Town had the same potential as Johannesburg, Pretoria and Durban for shopping-mall bombs – but I, with respect Mr Chairman, did my work well."

Gary Kruser is now a director in the police force, in command of the VIP protection unit. Neatly and professionally, he asks Benzien: "What happened after you arrested me?"

"I didn't arrest you, sir," says Benzien. "Perhaps you confuse me."

Kruser snaps: "I KNOW YOU. It was you!"

But Benzien does not remember.

KRUSER: Is it not true that you and Goosen assaulted me throughout the trip in the combi... that you sat on my head... after you arrested me outside the bioscope?

BENZIEN: I cannot remember the arrest... but if you say we assaulted you in the combi then I would concede that in all probability we did... I don't know how though...

KRUSER: Do you remember when we arrived at Culemborg you hung me up?

BENZIEN: Hung you up! What you refer to as "hanging up" – is that handcuffing you to the burglar-proofing?

KRUSER: Yes... so that my feet do not touch the ground and then hitting me in the stomach...

Then Kruser breaks down and the protruding eyes of Benzien look concerned that this man, who is now his boss, is crying. Considering the whole state of affairs – Benzien's expression might be saying – what happened to you does not seem so bad.

But for Kruser it is too much for flesh and feelings: that this experience, which has nearly destroyed his life, made not the slightest imprint on Benzien's memory.

KRUSER: (in a stern voice) Did you ever get information out of me?

BENZIEN: (snappy) No sir!

KRUSER: Was anybody ever arrested because of me?

BENZIEN: No sir!

Then Kruser sits up straight – the way he was sitting before the hearing started. Behind Benzien sit the victims of his torture – in a row chained by friendship and betrayal. Yengeni betrayed Jonas, Jonas pointed out people in albums, Peter Jacobs betrayed Forbes, Forbes pointed out caches, Yassir Henry betrayed Anton Fransch. During the tea break they stand together in the passages with their painful truths of triumph and shame. As everybody is leaving Benzien grabs the hand of Ashley Forbes tightly in both his own – Forbes smiling shyly under his thin moustache.

＊

SB/TRC/JACOBS

Police captain Jeff Benzien's first torture victim – Peter Jacobs – has accused him of not making a full disclosure to the Amnesty Committee. Jacobs – now a National Crime Intelligence superintendent – says Benzien has only conceded to the truth about his other torture methods following information from his former victims in cross-examination. Antjie Samuel reports:

TRANSCRIPT OF VOICE REPORT: Benzien has not come out with the whole story, says Peter Jacobs. During cross-examination, Benzien admitted that he had shocked Jacobs with an electric device in the nose, ears, genitals and rectum. He also described the so-called "watch ruse", when policemen changed the time on their watches to give Jacobs the impression that he had been interrogated until the afternoon. Benzien said that when they told Jacobs they would continue the next day, he volunteered to show where Ashley Forbes was hiding. Jacobs knew Forbes would be gone by the afternoon. Benzien also admitted telling Jacobs: "I'll take you to the verge of death as many times as I want to." Antjie Samuel – SABC Radio News – Cape Town.

＊

Beyond the Grape Curtain (by Sandile Dikeni)
And so continues the torture of Tony Yengeni. Yengeni broke in under thirty minutes, suffocating in a plastic bag which denied him air and burnt his lungs, under the hands of Benzien. In the mind of Benzien, Yengeni, freedom fighter and anti-apartheid operative, is a weakling, a man that breaks easily...

I said I am not gonna write no more columns like this, but the torture of Yengeni continues, with some of us regarding him as a traitor to the cause, a sell-out, a cheat and, in some stupid twist of faith and fate, his torturer becomes the hero, the revealer, the brave man who informed us about it all.

Tony Yengeni in my eyes remains the hero. Yengeni is one of the many people in the ANC executive who stood by the TRC, knowing that certain issues about the ANC would be revealed in the most mocking and degrading way by their torturers. In my eyes, Yengeni of Guguletu is one of the people who still gives me hope amidst the caprice of the present.

And not only Benzien, but many of us, owe him an apology.

And now, as I look at Yengeni, yes, I see blood, his own blood on the hands of Benzien and the Apartheid state. I see blood. The blood of Yengeni's friends and comrades crushed and sucked out of their lungs by the heroes of Apartheid – in under forty minutes, says the torturer, in his clinically precise "full disclosure".

I said I am not gonna write no more columns like this.

I made a mistake.

(*Cape Times*)

＊

For the first time, the Amnesty Committee calls and cross-examines a psychologist. Ria Kotze, who testifies on the psychological aspects of Captain Jeffrey Benzien's personality, has been counselling Benzien since 1994 when he had a nervous breakdown. Initially Kotze was treating Benzien's wife for depression, but she was called in to treat him too after an attack she describes as an auditory hallucination.

I go to speak to her after her submission. What does "auditory hallucination" mean?

"It means he heard voices, but more I cannot tell you. This was the only thing that Benzien asked me *not* to talk about."

"Now why was that?"

"It's the only thing he has left – this little incident – and it is his pride that he has kept it to himself."

When Benzien comes out for a smoke break, I ask him about the term.

"I can't tell you, except that I thought I was going out of my mind." He smokes shakily.

"But is it accusing voices, new voices, familiar ones...?"

He walks off: "Leave me ... God, just leave me alone."

The clearest description of what Benzien was experiencing comes from Kotze's testimony. She says Benzien was sitting on his veranda one evening, smoking a cigarette, and then he had a flashback – so intense and real that he burst into tears. His wife called Kotze and told her that when she asked Benzien what was wrong, he kept on saying: "I cannot tell you – I'm too ashamed." Kotze says Benzien suffers from a severe form of self-loathing.

The Amnesty Committee uses the opportunity of Kotze's appearance to explore the issue of memory loss. Several perpetrators claim not to remember certain things and the Committee is obviously not sure whether people are genuinely traumatized or whether they are deliberately hiding information and so do not fulfil the amnesty requirement of full disclosure.

The first issue raised by the victims' advocate is the textbook definition of post-traumatic stress: it can only be experienced by a victim. And the fundamental characteristic of the victim is a feeling of helplessness, intense fear, and powerlessness. Surely Benzien cannot be classified as a victim?

(If this definition is accurate, why do the Commissioners, the briefers, the statement takers, the journalists all get psychological treatment?)

Benzien was a victim of his inhumane working conditions, Kotze says. He was a good cop at Murder and Robbery. But he was so good that he was moved to Security where he had to create these torture methods to fulfil the expectations about him. This destroyed his whole sense of self.

The Amnesty Committee wants to know how Benzien can say one minute that he does not remember and insist the next minute that something did *not* happen. Is it possible to forget and be quite sure at the same time?

All of this centers on what advocate Robin Brink describes as "the nasty broom-stick episode".

Famous Western Cape MK member Nicla Pedro was caught on his way to Lesotho, where he was supposed to meet with MK cadres. Their names were in a letter which he was only to open once he had crossed the border. When he was caught he told the security police he had swallowed the letter – "I lied," says Pedro. Benzien then took him to a separate room, spread a newspaper and ordered him to defecate. Then the nationally famous torturer put on surgical gloves and worked through whatever was on the newspaper. When nothing was found, he pushed his finger up Pedro's anus. Then he took a broomstick and told Pedro: "I'll find the letter, even if I go up to your stomach."

Pedro, just released from an institution for alcoholics, testifies in tears before the Committee. Benzien emphatically denies that he ever used a broomstick. He looks quite shocked when the claim is made. He denies it, over and over.

To reconstruct your memory, to beautify it, is an ordinary human trait, says the psychologist. Most people do it. But there are probably three kinds of memory loss. The first is voluntary – you change your memory because you are under threat, because you cannot bear to live with the reality. The second kind is involuntary – something is so traumatic that it rips a hole in your memory, and you cannot remember the incident or what happened just before and after it. But there is also a third kind of memory loss and that occurs when you testify in public. Kotze says Benzien's stress levels were so compounded by having to testify and his anxiety about how this might affect the last bits of life he has with his wife and children, that it is quite possible he remembered even less than usual.

How to distinguish between lies and memory loss?

Slowly, as if speaking to herself: "In my job there are, in a sense, no lies – all of it ties in, reacts to, plays upon the truth ... "

49

The Treatment of Children in the 'Dirty War': Ideology, State Terrorism, and the Abuse of Children in Argentina

Marcelo M. Suarez-Orozco

DEDICATION
To the memory of Juan Carlos Anzorena

Our task here is to decode the messages, both hidden and overt, in the historical rediscovery of torture in the Argentine chambers of death during the Argentine 'Dirty War.' In these ghastly texts, children emerge as valuable commodities to be strategically exploited in a demented 'dirty war' fought between the Security Forces and their phantom, demonic enemies.

The Sociohistorical Setting: The Path to the 'Dirty War'

In the 1970s the Argentine Republic began writing one of the darkest chapters in modern Latin American history. The first half of that decade was characterized by increasing terrorist violence against military and police officers, government officials, diplomats, journalists, industrialists, and intellectuals. The Argentine economy was collapsing. Extreme inflation rates made the Argentine peso a worthless currency. Unemployment soared. Labor unrest and strikes were daily occurrences. The National University of Buenos Aires became increasingly politicized, losing much of its prestige as a great institution for higher learning.

By the late sixties and early seventies high-ranking members of the military and police hier-archies were kidnapped and/or assassinated in ultra-leftist terrorist operations almost weekly. For example, the chief of the Federal Police, Comisario Villar, a man with as much protection as any head of state, was killed by a bomb that exploded in his boat as he was quietly fishing one weekend. Ex-president [*de facto*] General Aramburo, was kidnapped and executed by a terrorist group, the so-called *Montoneros*, a seemingly unique blend of ultra-leftist internationalist and nationalist Peronists. The heads of major international companies in Buenos Aires were also targets of ultra-leftist terrorist attacks. In one such case the head of FIAT Buenos Aires, an Italian executive was kidnapped by a group of young terrorists in a dramatic operation. He was held for ransom for months and was eventually killed. The *Montoneros* also kidnapped a most influential agro-industrial family, the Born brothers and extracted a reported 60 million dollars for their freedom.

By the early 1970s ultra-rightist paramilitary organizations such as the 'Asociación Anticomunista Argentina' [AAA], began to systematically produce their own brand of terror. Union leaders were executed mid-day in downtown Buenos Aires. Leftists politicians were assassinated in one spectacular operation after another. World renowned academics, such as Professor Silvio Frondisi, a self-described 'theoretical Marxist' and brother of the constitutional ex-president of the Republic, Arturo Frondisi, was kidnapped and executed in public. Journalists also became targets of fire from both the ultra-right and the ultra-left.

In brief, members of all sectors of the society were vulnerable to random flying bullets. The state could no longer monopolize the use of violence. The atmosphere of fear was like a thick fog. No one could feel safe, exempted. The killing became ever more pointless. Bodyguards were in high demand. Paying bribes to terrorist groups for immunity became common practice in the industrial sector. As Timerman reports, 'monthly sums were paid by companies to right-wing and left-wing organizations simultaneously to assure that their executives wouldn't be assassinated or kidnapped' (1981: 19).

The chaos reached its peak in early 1976 at the hands of Maria Estela ['Isabelita'] Martinez de Perón, then the constitutional President of the Argentine Republic. Terrorist attacks by highly dedicated and efficient groups of both ultra-leftist and ultra-rightist persuasion became daily events. The increasing discontent of the Argentine people with the *status quo*, set the stage for a military takeover of civilian institutions. When the military, promising 'order,' finally removed 'Isabelita' Perón from the *Casa Rosada* in March of 1976 'the entire country, including the Peronists, breathed a sigh of relief' (Timerman 1981: 26). Instead of order what ensued was one of the most brutal regimes known in a continent already noted for a long history of brutality.

The Argentine Armed Forces had not fought a war during the twentieth century. Historically modeled after Germanic ideals, the military has traditionally seen itself as an isolated entity of superior men entrusted with a historical duty to protect the 'fatherland' from foreign and, particularly, domestic enemies. According to Timerman (ibid.) the degree of the military's segregation from other sectors of the society is remarkable. For example, military men, Timerman notes, would only marry women from military families. A *caste-like* segregation of the military from the civilian order must be emphasized.

In the seventies, for the first time in its history, the military came under systematic and vicious attacks from highly efficient terrorist bands. It is important to keep this background in mind in order to explore the subsequent emergence of the ideological matrix in which some very grotesque crimes against humanity were committed – including assaulting children and unborn fetuses with electrical prods. [...] After the March 1976 coup paramilitary gangs, known as *patotas*, began to operate much more visibly under the direct control of the security forces.

On the 24th of March, 1976, the Argentine military installed a *de facto* junta composed of the chiefs of its three branches: the Army, the Navy and the Air Force. The head of the Argentine Army, General Jorge Rafael Videla became the President of the Argentine Republic. Thus 'El Proceso de Reorganización Nacional' began [The Process of National Reorganization]. In brief, the self-stated objective of the junta was to 'reorganize' the Argentine nation. Their 'reorganizational' agenda is of critical importance to understand the fate of families and children in the context of the 'dirty war.' [...]

Upon the return to democracy in the early 1980s, following the disastrous adventure of the Argentine military in its attempt to take over the Malvinas Islands, the Argentine people began more fully to realize the extent of the crimes committed on the name of 'saving' the fatherland from leftist 'subversives.' Some victims who were allowed to survive told of their ordeals to the world. [For a moving account of his personal nightmare see Timerman 1981.] The Argentine people finally publicly confronted what the rest of the world had long suspected: that thousands of innocent Argentine citizens, including children, had been kidnapped, brutally tortured, and ruthlessly executed without any pretense at due process of law.

The military regime had responded to terrorist attacks of the left with one of the most grotesque examples of uncontrollable repression known in recent Western history. The state-controlled terrorist machinery assumed a life of its own. Death squads became autonomous units taking full initiative in seeking out victims. Clandestine detention camps had been set up in military, police, and other installations throughout the country to house and torment the kidnapped [see Amnesty International 1984: 143–5; Comisión Nacional Sobre la Desaparición de Personas 1984, and Timerman 1981].

In December of 1983 the democratically elected government of President Raúl Alfonsín responded to the public outcry of horror by creating the Comisión Nacional sobre la Desaparición de Personas [CONADEP]. Prominent Argentines became members of the CONADEP. Ernesto Sabato was appointed the commission's president. Argentine scientists, congressmen, distinguished reporters, business and industry leaders, etc., also were members of the commission.

Their objective was to systematically document the nature and extent of the repression unleashed following the military take over of 1976. For months the commission received and recorded the painful testimony of those who for one reason or another had survived the ordeal of clandestine imprisonment. However, the degree collective fear is still so pervasive that the commission believes that even under present democratic rule the *relatives* of many 'disappeared' dare not come forth to relate their cases. In short, not all has yet been revealed.

The 20th of September 1985, the commission presented their report, entitled *Nunca mas* [Never Again], to President Raul Alfonsin. *Nunca Mas* is one of the important documents printed this decade. It presents a detailed, graphic view of a monstrous system for death.

The CONADEP report concluded that *at least* 8,960 citizens, including 127 children, remain 'disappeared' and should be considered dead (CONADEP 1984: 16). That is not counting the children that were kidnapped, systematically abused by the security forces and then returned to their relatives [see below]. I should point out that many regard the CONADEP estimate of 8,960 as much too conservative. Some argue that close to 15,000 persons were disappeared. The assault on children was so systematic that the *Abuelas de la Plaza de Mayo* [Grandmothers of the Plaza de Mayo] formed to find out and make public the savagery inflicted upon children and to help locate those still missing.

Security officers rationalized the necessity of the systematic savage torture 'sessions' as the only viable way to combat 'leftist terrorism' in an urban setting [see Timerman 1981; CONADEP 1984: 26–54; Amnesty International 1984: 143–5; El Diario del Juicio vols. I through XV; The Economist 1985: 37–8]. Yet, I emphasize that it is now generally agreed that most of the terrorists died in actual military confrontations with security forces, or committed suicide just prior to capture. In fact, by mid-1976 the terrorists could no longer

pose a serious military threat (see Cabeza 1985: 170). In brief, the majority of those brutalized by the repression were sought out and tormented after ultra-leftist violence had been exterminated.

Many of those latter victims were professionals from 'suspected occupations' such as psychologists, psychiatrists, sociologists, welfare workers, and journalists judged to be 'critical' of the regime [see CONADEP 1984: 293–441; Timerman 1981: 93–9]. The irony is that the military specifically sought out these professionals which Foucault (1979) considers to be the 'social regulators' which replaced jailers and torturers as consensus agents in post-nineteenth-century Europe. Foucault's model may explain the historical shift in European social control from focusing on the 'body' to the 'soul,' but it obviously fails to account for the recurrence of torture in the postcolonial world.

During the 'dirty war' attorneys working of behalf of 'disappeared' persons, themselves were made to 'disappear' [CONADEP 1984: 416–24]. Members of human rights groups working on behalf of 'disappeared' persons, themselves 'disappeared' [CONADEP 1984: 424–6]. Students and labor organizers were 'disappeared.' Other innocent civilians were kidnapped simply 'by mistake.' Dagmar Ingrid Hagelin, a 17-year-old Swedish tourist, was mistaken for a 'subversive.' She was kidnapped by security officers, tortured, and then was killed. Others were picked up, tortured, and 'disappeared' after an anonymous call to the security forces identified them as 'subversive.' No questions were asked. One such a call could mean a death sentence. The randomness characterizing the 'dirty war' was the key to the establishment of a collective fear.

At the peak of the nightmare entire families were kidnapped [see CONADEP 1984; Timerman 1981]. Pregnant women were kidnapped [see CONADEP 1984: 299–323]. Old men, in some cases over 70 years old, were kidnapped [see Timerman 1981: 143]. Children were kidnapped [see CONADEP, ibid.; Guthmann 1986: 23–4].

Children in the 'Dirty War'

Let us turn to a more systematic exploration of the various forms of use and abuse to which children were submitted to during the so-called 'dirty war.' In order to fully appreciate the meaning of the atrocities committed, as well as the contexts in which these atrocities recur, we also briefly analyze the very nature of torture. Torture today continues to play a central role in the theatrics of political and religious orthodoxy [Amnesty International 1984, 1973; Bacry and Ternisien 1980]. State sponsored torture is an old and widespread phenomenon [see for example Mellor 1961; Tomas y Valiente 1973; Ruthven 1978; Foucault 1979]. We will explore the meaning of the torturers' assault on children and the family unit in the context of the 're-organizational' fantasies of the *Reorganización Nacional* junta. After delineating the anatomy of terror, and its uses for social control, we turn to explore the ideological blueprint by means of which the atrocities occurred. In certain historical contexts and armed with totalizing ideological agendas human beings have shown themselves to be capable of treating other human beings most atrociously. Yet to understand the degree of the madness created in the Argentine torture chambers, we need to explore how a collective delusion could be mobilized in the creation, and subsequent exorcism, of the demonic 'subversive.' Finally, we turn to a consideration of the instrumental aspects of state sponsored terrorism and abuse as a form of political discourse.

Alicia B. Morales de Galanba related the following case to the CONADEP:

I lived in Mendoza with my children, Paula Natalia and Mauricio. They were a year and a half and two months old. My friend, Maria Luisa Sanchez de Vargas and her two children Josefina, a five year old, and Soledad, a one and a half year old, also lived with us.

On the 12th of June, 1976 at about 11PM, Maria Luisa and I were in the kitchen when we heard knocks and suddenly saw our kitchen invaded by a group of men. Before we could even realize what was going on, they beat us to the floor and blind-folded us. With all the screaming and noise, the children woke up and began crying frantically. The men searched and destroyed each room of the house. As they proceeded, they repeatedly asked me where my husband was. They would also stop and click their weapons as if they were going to kill us. The terror was already within us and would not let me breathe. It was a terror that grew with the crying of the little children, increasingly more dementing.

When we could Maria Luisa and I took the children in our arms and tried to calm them down. After about twenty minutes or so, they took us out of the house and shoved us in to a car, probably a Ford. They took us to a place I was later to recognize as Mendoza's Police Headquarters. They put us in an empty room and they took away my two month old baby, Mauricio. I felt that my world was collapsing. I did not wish to live. I soon stopped even crying. I threw myself in the floor and remained in a fetal position. After several hours they returned my two month old baby, Mauricio. Slowly I began to recuperate. For the next two days we kept all four children with us. Josefina and Paula could not tolerate being locked up. They cried constantly, kicking the door, and asking the jailer to let us go.

Then one of the jailers took Josefina [the 5-year-old] away. Again we felt aware of the terror. We did not know what they wanted to do with the little girl. About two hours later they returned her to us. Josefina told us that they had taken her to the bus terminal to identify people. A while after they came by and took all four children away from us. Eventually the children were taken back to their respective grandparents. After that, they separated Maria Luisa and I, though we were both kept at the same installation. One day the jailer told me that they were going to bring Maria Luisa to my cell. I was happy that I would see her again, although I feared what I would see.

Indeed Maria Luisa was another person. The pain she had suffered made her age. She told me in tears that through a prostitute she was able to see her husband, Jose Vargas, soon after we had been separated. He is now disappeared. When they saw each other Jose told his wife that their daughter, Josefina, was taken to witness a torture session. They had made her witness his torture so that he would talk. This must have been between the 12th and 14th of June, after they took Josefina from our cell. But Maria Luisa's story did not end there. What I heard next was so horrible that even today I feel like I felt then, that of all the tragedies a person may live through, nothing could be worse than this... Maria Luisa next told me that a few days before, she was taken to her parents house, in San Juan. She said that she really thought that it was to give her parents the pleasure of seeing that she was alive and to make her renew contact with her girls. Then she said: 'But no, instead they took me to a funeral. And you know whose? It was the funeral of my daughter, Josefina,' the five year old. When Maria Luisa asked her father, Dr. Sanchez Sarmiento, a federal attorney, how such a thing happened, he told her that a few days after arriving to their house, the girl took a weapon from her grandfather's drawer and shot herself. [CONADEP 1984: 319–20]

During the years of terror after March of 1976 the children of those who were suspected of 'subversive activities' became victims of brutal and systematic abuse. Today 127 children remain 'unaccounted for,' or in the Argentine vocabulary of terror, *desaparecidos* [see CONADEP 1984: 299–323]. Other children were kidnapped, brutalized, and then returned to relatives. As in Josefina's case, the children were often picked up by security officers in the course of capturing the parents [see Slavin 1985: 1–7]. In some cases, if lucky, the children were allowed to remain behind, at times to stay at home all alone through the night. In other cases children were taken to a neighbor who was told to keep them and to keep quiet. Other children died in captivity [see CONADEP 1984: 99–323].

Children became very valuable pawns in the psychotic war that engulfed Argentina into the early 1980s. There is widespread evidence that children were brought into torture sessions to witness how a parent was tortured with electroshocks, drowning, burning, etc. (CONADEP 1984: 99–323). This is what they did to Josefina, a 5-year-old. She could only erase the atrocities she witnessed by killing herself soon after witnessing the grotesque spectacle involving her father.

Children were tortured in front of the parents commonly to make the adults 'talk,' sign a confession, or to implicate others in 'subversive activities.' CONADEP reports a number of such cases [see CONADEP 1984: 20 and 299–323]. The torture of small children, particularly in front of their parents, had been systematic. For example, a doctor who was detained and put to work in a military hospital reported that a renowned torturer was very interested in finding out from medical experts how big would a child need to be to survive systematic electric shocks. The torturer asked a military physician, another renowned torturer, 'how much should a child weigh before we can torture him. Vidal [the Doctor] responded "after 25 kilos you can run electrical charges through their bodies"' [El Diario de Juicio 1985: (vol. 12) p. 4]. The Argentine agents of death by no means hold monopoly over the political tormenting of children. For example, Amnesty International's eerie document *Torture in the Eighties* (1984) reports that state sponsored torture of children has been reported in both El Salvador (1984: 155–6) and in Iraq (1984: 99).

In Argentina, family torture sessions were not uncommon [see CONADEP 1984: 20; Timerman 1981: 148–9]. For example, a man reports that after answering a number of questions negatively, security officers began brutally kicking and hitting with a belt his wife and their children, a 13-year-old, an 8-year-old, and a 3-year-old who were witnessing the inferno. Then, he said, the officers turned to their 20-day-old daughter and, to their horrified disbelief, they started shaking her violently and holding her head down by her feet, yelling 'if you don't talk, we'll kill her.' Next they filled the tub with water and submerged the mother several times, drowning her in front of her children (CONADEP 1984: 320).

The children were used for other instrumental purposes. For example, Josefina, a 5-year-old, was taken by the torturers to a bus terminal to identify friends and acquaintances of her parents (CONADEP 1984: 323). In other words, children were used as 'informants' to single out 'subversives' to be picked up and tormented. It was apparently easier to make the children 'cooperate' after showing them how their parents were tortured.

In other cases children were used as 'bait' by the security forces to entrap other 'subversives.' For example, Fernando, a 13-year-old boy, was used to single out friends of his parents. He was then ordered by his captors to set up a meeting with two friends of his parents. At that meeting the friends were kidnapped by security forces in front of the boy [see CONADEP 1984: 324].

The abuse of children was thus theatrically organized to force information out of the parents, to have the parents admit to 'subversion,' and/or to have them sign confessions. In other cases, children became innocent tools in the reproduction of terror. Actively working to capture 'subversives' is one such example. The mechanism seemed to work effectively and was based on the fact that the children were induced to expect that by cooperating they would earn their parents' freedom or at least better treatment for them. The scene was so morbid that there are reports that older children, particularly girls, would try to seduce guards in hope that their parents would be treated less brutally (Timerman 1981: 149). Seldom, if ever, did such sexual 'favors' result in better treatment.

The instrumental exploitation of children went beyond the immediate 'war-related' scenario.

Children of *desaparecidos*, particularly babies, were commonly taken as 'war booty' [see Chavez 1985a: 19–20; El Diario del Juicio 1985 (vol. 11): 254]. An Uruguayan woman, whose husband and nursing infant disappeared, related:

The 13th of July, 1976 between 11 and 11:30PM, they knocked on the door of our home in Barrio Belgrano in this Capital [Buenos Aires]. At that moment I was breast feeding my baby, Simon. They broke down the door and about 10 to 15 people, in civilian clothing, identified themselves as members of the Argentine Army and the Uruguayan Army. One of the officers introduced himself as Major Gavazzo of the Uruguayan Army. They searched the home and they found written materials which showed them that I worked for the cause of freedom in my country [Uruguay]; then they began torturing me. When they took me away, I asked them what would happen to my baby. They told me that I should not worry about that that they would keep him... That was the last time I saw Simon. [CONADEP 1984: 20]

Simon was probably sold in a lucrative black market or placed with a sterile military or upper-class couple. The moving film entitled *La historia oficial* treats the plight of a child so 'adopted' into an upper-middle-class family. And the documentary 'Las Madres: The Mothers of the Plaza de Mayo,' considers the pain of a group of mothers who silently marched around the national plaza for the last 7 years,' demanding to know the fate of their sons and daughters who were 'disappeared' during the 'dirty war.'

Thus the torturers discovered and manipulated the value of children as the *priceless cathected appendix of the 'subversive.'* Children became a commodity to be exploited for information in the halls of death and were subsequently placed with families sympathetic to the regime. Yet before a child could be placed with a 'proper' family the torturers deemed necessary to radically sever his/her bonds with the 'contaminated subversive.' Thus assaulting children with electrical prods *in the presence of their parents* should be seen as serving both instrumental and expressive aims.

We have already explored the instrumental aspects of the abuse. Expressively torturing children, or torturing parents in front of the children, can also be seen as a *ritual of separation* in which

the torturers proceed to 'surgically remove' with electrical prods the subversive's precious 'appendix' before turning him/her to a security or upper-class family for proper Christian upbringing. We shall return to the implications of this in the following section.

The magnitude of the children's market was such that upon return to democracy the 'Grandmothers of the Plaza de Mayo' contacted a number of scientists from the Massachusetts Institute of Technology, the University of California, etc., to identify disappeared children through studies establishing the genetic relatedness between a child and his or her biological relatives [see Slavin 1985: 1–7]. Neighbors who saw a childless couple 'adopt' a child under obscure circumstances during the 'dirty war' years are now encouraged to come forth to denounce them.

Pregnant women were treated like all other 'subversives.' That is, they were routinely tortured and often raped [see CONADEP 1984: 299–323]. Some military men eventually were compelled to confess crimes [see also Victor 1981]. A sergeant told the CONADEP that 'as a nurse he worked at the Hospital Campo de Mayo [a military installation] between 1976 and 1977. He reported that in the epidemiology wing of the hospital there were a number of pregnant women about to give birth. Their hands and feet were tied and they were given serum to accelerate the delivery. The nurse himself saw four or five women in this condition. He thought they were extremists...' (CONADEP 1984: 308–9). He also reported that a guard named Falcon had raped a number of pregnant women (ibid.).

Pregnant women, or their husbands, were made to 'talk' by placing electric prods inside them, close to the uterus, to discharge electrical currents on the fetus. For example, one pregnant woman who survived her calvary reported that she was brutally tortured during the sixth month of her pregnancy. Subsequent to her release she gave birth to an abnormal child diagnosed as having brain damage (CONADEP 1984: 317–18).

In other cases, the strategy was to keep the mother alive until the birth of her child. The babies were then taken away from the mothers to be sold or placed with sterile couples. The mother could then be executed [see Slavin 1985: 1–7]. The military would fabricate illegal birth certificates, almost always signed by military physicians, in order to place a child with a new couple. Schools are now alerted to report any suspicious birth certificates, particularly if signed by a military physician (ibid.)[1]

The Body, Children, and the 'Reorganization' of Society

The difficult question of why entire families and specifically children entered the stage of terror as key protagonists requires further elaboration. Any satisfactory explanation should relate to both the instrumental and the expressive nature of a terrorist act.

On the instrumental level we have documented how children emerged as priceless commodities to be fully exploited in the politics of pain. Directly torturing a child, or torturing a parent in front of a child, seemed to be a facile way to elicit information from a 'subversive.' It is much harder to explore the possible symbolic dimensions of the politics of torture.[. . .]

A partial answer to *why children* can be explored in the context of the stated wishes of many high ranking officers in charge of the operation. In fact, there are a number of printed reports [see CONADEP 1984: 20] that high ranking officers of the security forces did specifically tell their men that *the war was not on the children* and that children should *not* be taught to grow up to hate the flag and the armed forces [See El Diario del Juicio 1985 vol. v]. Rather, their expressed wishes were that the children be *removed* from the 'subversives' and placed in 'proper' homes. When a desperate mother asked her tormenters what they would do with her nursing infant as he was being taken away, one said 'The war is not on children, we'll keep him' (CONADEP 1984: 20).

Yet we have documented that children of suspected 'subversives' were systematically abused regardless of the 'official policy.' We have also argued that any specific act of torture can be analyzed as a cultural and psychological metamessage conveying a multitude of meanings. I thus argue that the symbolics of political pain underlined the destructive and *reorganizational* agenda on the military operation.

The assault on children and the calculated collective spectacles of torture in which entire families participated are literalization of the military's fantasy of 'reorganizing' the Argentine social landscape. The agenda for reorganizing the social land-

scape was at the heart of why the children had to be removed from 'subversive' homes and placed elsewhere. The collective torture session themselves are viewed as a *rite de separation* (Van Gennep 1960). Before a child could be placed with a military or an upper-class family for a good Christian education all ties with his/her tainted family had to be severed. Thus collective rituals of pain flourished before placing a child with an acceptable family. A sort of 'ideological surgery' was required to sever all bonds.

Indeed, the entire military operation had a very noted reorganizational tone. The very term 'Proceso de Reorganización Nacional' under which the military organized its campaign forcefully conveys this imagery. The entire nation needed a 'reorganization' according to the military. The assault on children and the family unit represents a most perverse translation of this fantasy of control and the 'reorganization' of life through death.

Terror as Social Control

Thus was forged what Taussig and others have appropriately termed a 'culture of terror' (see Taussig 1984: 467–97; Fagen 1985). Thousands of Argentines 'were disappeared' by security officers. The term came to capture the power of collective terror as brutal social control. Introducing the word *desaparecido* even in the security of a family discussion, produced a chilling effect. The relatives of *desaparecidos* often knew that a loved one was taken by the security forces. The term itself encouraged a form of prerational, magical thinking: just as a son or daughter magically 'disappeared' one day, they could so 'reappear' another. The networks of horror operated on what soon became a sacred currency, silence. Relatives were often contacted by the captors. Yet these contacts remained in closed secrecy. Money and possessions were extracted from relatives of 'disappeared' ones [see CONADEP 1984; 22–3], sometimes even after the *desaparecido* had been killed.

In some cases the *desaparecido* was allowed to talk to his or her relatives, usually over the telephone or through an intermediary. Expectations that the end of the nightmare was possible were thus implanted in the hearts and minds of relatives. The message was monothematic: 'be quiet,' 'don't talk to anyone or for sure she or he will be killed,' *Collective silence thus became part of the madness as if it intervened in the causality of events.* Families of *desaparecidos* came to believe that should the rumor begin that a son or daughter was 'disappeared,' it would mean certain death. In truth, people died regardless of the code of strict silence.

Psychologically it is very hard to mourn without a corpse. Death, in the abstract, can never be as convincing as the body of a loved one. Without concrete evidence of death, there is always hope. Thus the networks of terror and control were firmly established. A collective hysterical denial permeated the atmosphere. In the midst of the horror, many people let themselves believe that there were some minor 'abuses,' but only of those who were 'implicados en algo' [involved in something]. How otherwise could they live with the knowledge that members of the security forces were torturing even children and pregnant women? Such reports were dismissed as part of an exaggerated 'international propaganda campaign' against Argentina.

The code of silence was fostered by other fears. To have a *desaparecido* in the family was like having a contagious disease. Life-long friends broke relationships for fear of being caught in the madness. They of course were active participants in the madness. A major fear was that should a person's name be in the private telephone book of a *desaparecido*, that name would become a target. Indeed, many other innocent people were thus recruited to the stage of terror. [...]

The Assault on Life: Torture and Child Abuse as Political Discourse

Instrumentally, torture became an intrinsic part of the military's political mission. Prisoners were routinely tortured before and during interrogation, before execution or before regaining freedom. In other cases people were tortured and let go free *without ever been interrogated.* The human body became the canvas in which the 'anatomists of pain' (Foucault 1979: 11) dramatized an ancient discourse on power and orthodoxy. Indeed a new inquisition was unleashed. The Christian and occidental way of life was to be saved by finally removing all atheist subversives from the landscape. The perverse medical – hygienic and surgical – imagery which accompanied the crusade again points to the paranoid atmosphere that emerged in the midst of the 'dirty war.' An infection had penetrated and was growing, spreading throughout the 'fatherland.' A 'dirty' war was required to 'cleanse' the country of political contamination. Indeed, political killings were commonly referred to as 'cleanings.' 'Los vamos a limpiar' [we will clean you], was a common phrase out of the lips of the torturers. In fact, 'limpiar' [to clean] means to kill in Argentine slang, just as 'to waste' does in American English slang. It took a 'dirty' war to *limpiar* Argentina.

This imagined growth required radical surgical and hygienic intervention. The enemy must be completely extirpated from the fatherland. The new inquisition was thus framed in medical and sanitary symbolism over political orthodoxy. This metaphorical system also helps explain the prominent role physicians played during the 'dirty war.' In fact, many survivors reported that often during torture sessions, a military or police physician would come in, take their vital signs and proceed to inform the torturers whether to continue torturing, or whether to give the 'patient' a break. In fact the torture chambers themselves were known as the *quirofano*, or the 'operating room.'

The extermination took a very specific, indeed patterned, tone. Again, I argue that we must explain the torture, as well as the *specific* forms the torture took. Torture is never merely an instrumental act. Even when it is routine, as it certainly was in Argentina, each time a torturer discharges an electrical current through his prisoner's body, they become intimate partners in a poly-semantic ritual.

The expressive symbolism of torture is of fundamental importance to explore the unconscious agenda of the torturer. The phallus of men was routinely assaulted with electricity. The castration metaphor is unmistakable. In clandestine *quirofanos* the ideological surgeons thus emasculated godless 'subversives', *turning the feared enemy into passive, castrated beings.* The *macho* army men were turning 'dangerous subversives,' who had given them so much anxiety, indeed for the first time genuine fear, into harmless eunuchs. In the torturer's mind assaulting the penis was always related to the masculinity of their victim. For example, an 'ex-torturer' reported a torture session in which an officer ordered him to systematically place the electric prods in the testicles of a victim 'to see if he is such a *macho*' (Victor 1981: 67).

Women's generativity was also routinely assaulted. Running electro-shocks through the sources of life, the vagina, uterus, and breasts was standard practice. Pregnant women were systematically tortured and raped [see CONADEP 1984: 309]. Systematically electrocuting the symbols of life was necessary to turn the mothers of potential dissidents into helpless beings to be sexually used and discarded. The keepers of the faith were symbolically assaulting the essence of dissident life.

The systematic electrical assault on the genitals is the kind of surgical intervention required for the society the agents of terror wished to carve out: a society of ruling *machos* and obedient, harmless *mansos*, castrated beings, that would not question orders but would just obey. This is the political agenda the repression advocated. In the halls of death, torture became the form through which they created the conforming citizens they wished to govern. In this case the body was the medium in which the 'reorganizing' fantasy surfaced.

The 'reorganization' of society required 're-organizing' the basic social unit, the family. The family's affective bond was manipulated in skillfull games of horror. Torturing a child may have been done to make a parent talk or sign a confession, but symbolically the torture ritual was the ultimate perversion in the universe of the pain: the surgical severing of the child from the 'contaminating' subversive, to violently break the intense affective bond that makes up the Argentine family. In all modern police states – whether rightist or leftist – children are used to get at the parents; as spies, informants, or to torture. *Divide et impera* is the rule of thumb. Indeed the torturers in Argentina concentrated on literally and symbolically 'dividing' families.

The Argentine journalist Jacobo Timerman, who himself was brutally tortured, reflected on his encounters with absolute horror in several clandestine prisons. The obscenities enacted in the chambers of death produced the destruction on the units of life:

Of all the dramatic situations I witnessed in clandestine prisons, nothing can compare to those family groups who were tortured often together, sometimes separately but in view of one another, or in different cells, while one was aware of the other being tortured. The entire affective world, constructed over the years with utmost difficulty, collapses with a kick in the father's genitals, a smack on the mother's face, an obscene insult to the sister, or the sexual violation of

a daughter. Suddenly an entire culture based on familial love, devotion, the capacity for mutual sacrifice collapses. Nothing is possible in such a universe, and that is precisely what the torturers know.

The fathers' glances: of desperation at first, then of apology, and then of encouragement. Seeking some way to mutually help one another – sending an apple, a glass of water. Those fathers, thrown on the ground, bleeding, endeavoring for their children to find the strength to resist the tortures still in store for them. The impotence, that impotence that arises not from one's failure to do something in defense of one's children but from one's inability to extend a tender gesture. From my cell, I'd hear the whispered voices of children trying to learn what was happening to their parents, and I'd witness the efforts of daughters to win over a guard, to arouse a feeling of tenderness in him, to incite the hope of some lovely future relationship between them in order to learn what was happening to her mother, to have an orange sent to her, to get permission for her to go to the bathroom. (Timerman 1981; 148–9)

Torture and death of 'subversives' was the magical treatment against the spread of an infectious way of life. To simplify their thinking and to focus energy, the armed left, the democratic left, intellectuals, artists, psychiatrists, psychologists, sociologists, children, pregnant women, and other deviants were bunched together as representatives, or potential representatives, or sympathizers with an international assault penetrating the fatherland from the outside and growing, spreading within.

Conclusion

In early 1985, following the return to democratic rule, and responding to a worldwide outcry over the horrors committed by the military, an unprecedented phenomenon occurred in Argentina. For the first time in Latin American history, members of a prior *de facto* government were brought to civilian justice. For reasons of space, I can only briefly refer to the trial of the 9 commanders [for a full description of this trial see, El Diario del Juicio 1985]. Technically the six-man court was a court-martial, although under civilian control.

At the trial the military leaders continued to hide any remorse behind the ideological shield. General Videla dismissed all accusations asserting that 'terrorism is a global phenomena which will one day show that Argentina continues to be a priority target' [see El Diario del Juicio 1985 (vol. 15): 351]. The battle goes on, the invisible enemy is everywhere, because it is within. Others, either hysterically or psychopathically, deny that any abuses took place and view the trial as the beginning of the end for the Christian and occidental way of life in Argentina.

These millitary leaders refuse to accept the legitimacy of the trial. According to them 'corrupted,' myopic politicians and civilians lack the moral authority and strength to pass judgment on their righteous crusade against the very essence of evil. General Videla, for example, 'ignores the court and reads, apparently from a book of spiritual meditations' (The Economist 1985: 38). In fact, right-wing military and paramilitary groups have already been found planting bombs to simulate a major leftist guerrilla comeback, and thus create the atmosphere in which another military takeover would be possible. The more recent revolts by younger officers in Campo de Mayo, Cordoba, and Salta over the jurisprudence and legitimacy of civilian courts over crimes committed during the 'Dirty War' again point to the military's caste-like attitude of depreciation of civilian institutions. Heuristically, it might prove fruitful to approach these new 'dirty wars' in reference not just to older models relating Latin authoritarianism to oligarcho-militaristic alliances to international interests, but also in terms of an internal structural logic of castelike stratification and depreciation of the civico-democratic order.

On the 9th of December 1985, the civilian court found five of the former top military leaders guilty of crimes committed during the 'dirty war' [see Chavez 1985b: 1–2; Montalbano 1985; 1–2]. General Jorge Videla, President of the first junta and Admiral Emilio Massera, also a junta member, were given life sentences. General Roberto Viola, President of the second military junta, received a 17-year sentence. Admiral Armando Lambruschini, the second junta's Navy representative received 8 years; and Brigadier General Orlando Agosti, head of the Air Force and member of the first junta received a four-and-a-half year sentence. Four other military heads were acquitted (Chavez 1985b: 1–2).

REFERENCES

Amnesty International. 1973. *Amnesty international report on torture*. London: Gerald Duckworth & Co. Ltd.

——. 1984. *Torture in the eighties: an amnesty international report*. London: Amnesty international publications.

Bacry, Daniel and Michel Ternisien. 1980. *La torture: la nouvelle inquisition*. Paris: Fayard.

Cabeza, Carlos. 1985. Entrevista a José Deheza, Ex Ministro de Defensa. El Diario del Juicio. Anõ I – No 7. July 9th, pp. 170–1.

Chavez, Lydia. 1985a. Argentine Children Who Became 'War Booty.' *The San Francisco Chronicle*. September 10th, pp. 18–19.

——. 1985b. Five from Juntas are Found Guilty in Argentine Trial. *The New York Times*. December 10th, pp. 1–2.

Colson, Elizabeth. 1985. Using Anthropology in a World on the Move. *Human Organization* 44, 3: 191–6.

Comisión Nacional Sobre la Desaparición de Personas [CONADEP]. 1984. *Nunca Mas: Informe de la Comisión Nacional Sobre la Desaparición de Personas*. Buenos Aires: Editorial Universitaria de Buenos Aires.

El Diario del Juicio. 1985. Volumes I through XV. Buenos Aires.

Fagen, Patricia W. 1985. The Culture of Fear: Responses to State Terrorism in the Southern Cone. Paper Presented at the Center for Latin American Studies, University of California, Berkeley, October 28th.

Foucault, Michel. 1979. *Discipline & Punish: The Birth of the Prison*. Translated from the French by Alan Sheridan. New York: Vintage Books.

Gennep, Arnold van. 1960. *The Rites of Passage*. Translated from the French by Vizedom and Caffee. Chicago: University of Chicago Press.

Guthmann, Edward. 1986. 'My Child is Missing.' *The San Francisco Examiner*, January 12th, pp. 23–4.

Mellor, Alec. 1961. *La torture: son histoire, son abolition, sa reapparition au XXe siècle*. Paris: Mame.

Montalbano, William. 1985. Argentina's Ex-Leader Gets Life. *Los Angeles Times*, December 10th, pp. 1–2.

Ruthven, Malise. 1978. *Torture: The Grand Conspiracy*. London: Weidenfeld and Nicolson.

Slavin, J. P. 1985. Argentine grandmothers seek lost kids. *The Daily Californian*, vol. XVII, no. 112. Monday, July 15th, pp. 1–7.

Taussig, Michael. 1984. Culture of Terror – Space of Death: Roger Casement's Putumayo Report and the

Explanation of Torture. *Comparative Studies of Society and History,* 26, 3: 467–97.

The Economist. 1985. Argentina Discovers its Past, with Horror. London, September 28th, pp. 37–8.

Timerman, Jacobo. 1981. *Prisoner without a Name, Cell without a Number.* New York: Alfred A. Knopf.

Tomas y Valiente, Francisco. 1973. *La Tortura en España, Estudios Historicos.* Barcelona: Editorial Ariel.

Victor, J. 1981. *Confesiones de un torturador.* Barcelona: Editorial Laia.

Vidal-Naquet, Pierre. 1963. *Torture: Cancer of Democracy.* Baltimore, MD: Penguin Books.

Part X

Witnessing/Writing Violence

From *Maus: A Survivor's Tale, II:* And Here My Troubles Began

Art Speigelman

SPECIAL PRISONERS WORKED HERE SEPARATE. THEY GOT BETTER BREAD, BUT EACH FEW MONTHS THEY ALSO WERE SENT UP THE CHIMNEY. ONE FROM THEM SHOWED ME EVERYTHING HOW IT WAS.

Missing the Revolution: Anthropologists and the War in Peru

Orin Starn

On 17 May 1980, Shining Path guerrillas burned ballot boxes in the Andean village of Chuschi and proclaimed their intention to overthrow the Peruvian state. Perhaps playing on the Inkarrí myth of Andean resurrection from the cataclysm of conquest, the revolutionaries had chosen the 199th anniversary of the execution by the Spanish colonizers of the neo-Inca rebel Tupac Amaru. Chuschi, though, prefigured not rebirth but a decade of death. It opened a savage war between the guerrillas and government that would claim more than 15,000 lives during the 1980s.

For hundreds of anthropologists in the thriving regional subspecialty of Andean studies, the rise of the Shining Path came as a complete surprise. Dozens of ethnographers worked in Peru's southern highlands during the 1970s. One of the best-known Andeanists, R. T. Zuidema, was directing a research project in the Río Pampas region that became a center of the rebellion. Yet no anthropologist realized a major insurgency was about to detonate, a revolt so powerful that by 1990 Peru's civilian government had ceded more than half the country to military command.

The inability of ethnographers to anticipate the insurgency raises important questions. For much of the twentieth century, after all, anthropologists had figured as principal experts on life in the Andes. They positioned themselves as the "good" outsiders who truly understood the interests and aspirations of Andean people; and they spoke with scientific authority guaranteed by the firsthand experience of fieldwork. Why, then, did anthropologists miss the gathering storm of the Shining Path? What does this say about ethnographic understandings of the highlands? How do events in Peru force us to rethink anthropology on the Andes? [...]

What I will claim is that most anthropologists were remarkably unattuned to the conditions which made possible the rise of Sendero. First, they tended to ignore the intensifying interlinkage of Peru's countryside and cities, villages and shantytowns, Andean highlands and lowlands of the jungle and coast. These interpenetrations created the enormous pool of radical young people of amalgamated rural/urban identity who would provide an effective revolutionary force. Second, anthropologists largely overlooked the climate of sharp unrest across the impoverished countryside. Hundreds of protests and land invasions testified to a deep-rooted discontent that the guerrillas would successfully exploit.

To begin accounting for the gaps in ethnographic knowledge about the highlands, I consider the concept of Andeanism.[1] Here I refer to representation that portrays contemporary highland peasants as outside the flow of modern history. Imagery of Andean life as little changed since the Spanish conquest has stretched across discursive boundaries during the twentieth century to become a central motif in the writings of novelists, politicians, and travelers as well as the visual depictions of filmmakers, painters, and photographers. I believe

Andeanism also operated in anthropology, and helps to explain why so many ethnographers did not recognize the rapidly tightening interconnections that were a vital factor in the growth of the Shining Path.

Andeanism, though, was not the only influence on anthropologists of the 1960s and 1970s. The growing importance of ecological and symbolic analysis in international anthropology theory of the period also conditioned ethnographic views of the Andes. I argue that the strong impact of these two theoretical currents produced an intense preoccupation with issues of adaptation, ritual, and cosmology. This limited focus, in turn, assists in accounting for why most anthropologists passed over the profound rural dissatisfaction with the status quo that was to become a second enabling factor in Sendero's rapid rise. [...]

I feel a certain unease about writing on the Andes and the Shining Path. "Senderology" – the study of the guerrillas – is a thriving enterprise. In my view, a sense of the intense human suffering caused by the war too often disappears in this work. The terror becomes simply another field for scholarly debate. This essay is open to criticism for contributing to the academic commodification of Peru's pain. But I offer the account in a spirit of commitment. No outside intervention – and certainly not by anthropologists – is at present likely to change the deadly logic of the war. I hope, though, that sharper anthropological views of the situation will help others to understand the violence and to join the struggle for life. [...]

It was precisely as a consequence of their emphasis on the immutability of Andean traditions that anthropologists tended to ignore the fluid and often ambiguous quality of Andean personal identity. The popular typology of Indian, cholo, and mestizo suggested three separate spheres of personhood. This contravened the far less clear-cut experience of hundreds of thousands of highland-born people. From 1940 to 1980, poverty drove at least a quarter of a million Andean farmers to settle in the jungle and more than a million more to Lima (cf. Martinez 1980). Seasonal migrations took thousands of others on frequent journeys between the mountains and the Amazon and coast. This mass mobility meant that many people in the most "remote" highland hamlets had visited the bustling coast. Conversely, many inhabitants of the sprawling shantytowns of Lima, La Paz, Quito, Ayacucho, Cuzco, and Huancayo kept strong bonds to the countryside. The distance between thatch-roofed adobe Andean peasant dwellings and city shacks of tin, cardboard, and straw mats was not that between "indigenous" Andean society and "Westernized" modernity. Rather, it was the space between different points on a single circuit that was integrated by family ties, village loyalties, and constant circulation of goods, ideas, and people. Indian, cholo, and mestizo were not discrete categories, but partly overlapping positions on a continuum.

The rise of the Shining Path highlighted the continuities between different locations along the city/country circuit. Urban intellectuals led by Abimael Guzmán founded the movement during the late 1960s at Ayacucho's University of Huamanga. But university and high school students of mostly peasant origin were the cadre of the revolution. These young people had friends and family in their home communities; yet most had studied in the city of Ayacucho and been politically radicalized by exposure to a revolutionary discourse that answered to their own experience of poverty and lack of opportunity. They became the guerrillas who fanned across the countryside during the 1970s to begin underground organizing, and then took up arms in the 1980s.

The ability of these cadres to start a major upheaval testified to the interpenetrations of different positions along the rural/urban loop. Education and the language of Marxism separated the young revolutionaries from peasants in the countryside. But most of the Senderistas were also poor people with dark skin, knowledge of Quechua, and familiarity with the physical geography and cultural textures of mountain life. "Sendero advances," as the Ayacucho-born historian Jaime Urrutía pointed out in a recent interview,

because they are the ones there [in the mountains] who are the equal with the population. They aren't the middle class, they aren't physically different, they speak the same language and the people feel close to them.[2]

Urrutía underplays how the arrival of the Shining Path in a village by force of arms can be a sudden and often violent intrusion. Yet he also explodes the favorite counterinsurgency metaphor of the Peruvian authorities, familiar from Vietnam, El Salvador, and wherever governments fight guerrilla uprisings, that the Shining Path are "infiltrators" and "subversives," a force completely external to the peasantry. What distinguishes Sendero from the failed Peruvian guerrilla movements of the 1960s is precisely the close connections of so many Senderistas to the mountains. The Lima intellectuals of Luis de la Puente Uceda's Cuban-inspired National Liberation Army were quickly wiped out by the army. But the young women and men of the Shining Path know the hidden trails of the mountains, how to survive the cold nights, how to dodge army patrols, how to blend with the civilian population and regroup when the security forces withdraw. The guerrillas, in short, frequently have a double status in the peasant communities of Ayacucho. They are part "insiders" and part "outsiders." [. . .]

If the thick interchange between city and country made possible the spread of the Shining Path across Ayacucho from the gray-stoned University of Huamanga, the immediate successes of the revolutionaries in winning support in the countryside testified to the explosive discontent of many peasants. It is vital from the start to point out that the Shining Path also depends on violence. The revolutionaries have killed campesinos for reasons from breaking decrees against voting to participating in compulsory Army-directed civil patrols. In September 1984, guerrillas slaughtered 21 villagers in Huamanguilla, Ayacucho, on the suspicion of "collaboration" with the government (Amnesty International 1989: 5). "Violence is a universal law," as Abimael Guzmán himself proclaims, " . . . and without revolutionary violence one class cannot be substituted for another, an old order cannot be overthrown to create a new one."[3]

At the same time, though, persuasive evidence exists for a degree of genuine rural backing of the revolution. In mid-1982, inquiries about Sendero in Ayacucho by journalist Raul Gonzalez (1982: 47) elicited a near unanimous reply: "It's a movement supported by the youngest peasants. The older ones are resigned to their lot, but do back their kids." In early 1983, peasant leaders in Huancayo told political scientist Cynthia McClintock (1984: 54) "that substantial majorities [of peasants] were supportive." David Scott Palmer (1986: 129) concluded that Sendero retained a "substantial reservoir of support" in rural Ayacucho. By 1985, Senderistas had also found a profitable new niche in the upper Amazon as the defenders of smallholding coca-growers, mostly migrants from the highlands, against rapacious

Colombian buyers and government officials. It was in part because of popular support that Sendero grew so fast in the 1980s. Nine of Peru's 181 provinces were declared military-controlled Emergency Zones in December 1982. The number had jumped to 56 by mid-1989 (Amnesty International 1989: 2).

The Senderistas used a similar strategy in communities across Ayacucho, Huancavelica, Andahuaylas, and Junin. They arrived preaching the overthrow of the government and often redistributing land and animals from state-administered cooperatives. The call for radical change appealed to many villagers. The young guerrillas, who sometimes had relatives in the communities where they went to organize, had the knowledge of Quechua and mountain life that enabled them to bear the revolutionary doctrine effectively. Executions of corrupt bureaucrats and cattle rustlers were generally greeted with enthusiasm. They bolstered the Shining Path's popularity. Torture and massacres by the security forces could scare off support. But it was also clear by the end of 1980s that the tactics of terror often backfired. Resentful villagers had another reason to back the Shining Path.

Signs of the discontent that Sendero exploited abounded in the southern highlands during the 1960s and 1970s. Growing pressure from peasants for the breakup of haciendas was one reason behind the decision in 1969 of the Velasco government to carry out agrarian reform. The 1960s brought an outpouring of land invasions, strikes, and the strengthening of regional and national peasant unions. In 1963 alone, political scientist Howard Handelman (1975: 121) estimated that campesinos staged between 350 and 400 land seizures in Peru's southern mountains. Thousands of peasants continued to mobilize through the decade, even though police usually sided with landowners and many farmers died in invasions under fire from the security forces. The reform did not stop the unrest. Many haciendas were not divided, and new cooperatives proved inefficient. The state failed to provide money for loans or technical assistance even as official rhetoric during the early Velasco years of equality and campesino pride further radicalized many peasants. In Ayacucho and Apurímac, peasant protest intensified (Isbell 1988: 7). Campesinos now invaded not only undivided haciendas, but also the cooperatives. Agrarian leagues first formed by the Velasco government became independent, and by the late

1970s a mosaic of militant regional federations stretched across the highlands. [...]

Many Andeanists, however, ignored the widespread strikes, invasions, and campesino unionism across not just the Peruvian Andes, but also in Bolivia, Colombia, and, to a lesser extent, Ecuador. Studying peasant movements was left largely to political scientists, journalists, and lawyers. The only well-known ethnography devoted to protest, June Nash's (1977) fine *We Eat the Mines and the Mines Eat Us*, dealt not with the countryside, but the proletarianized Bolivian tin mines. Of the 464 publications cited by Frank Salomon (1982) in his thorough review of Andean ethnology in the 1970s, only 5 dealt directly with peasant organizing. Anthropologists, in short, almost entirely bypassed one of the most crucial issues of the time.

Part of the explanation rests with the state of anthropological theory in the 1960s and 1970s. Until the florescence of political economy in the mid-1970s, much of the thinking in these years sorted into the general camp of either cultural ecology or symbolic anthropology. This alignment carried into studies of the Andes. A large body of scholarship arose on issues of adaptation; another gathered around cosmology, kinship, and ritual. The analysis of mobilization and protest did not have a real place on either side.

The disappearance of politics was most marked in the work of ecological anthropologists. With the rapid growth of cultural ecology in North American anthropology during the late 1960s, anthropologists like Stephen Brush, Glynn Custred, Jorge Flores Ochoa, R. Brooke Thomas, and Bruce Winterhalder made the study of Andean ecosystems into popular specialty. These scholars recognized that modern highland life reflected the experience of Spanish conquest and contact with capitalism. A few, most notably Benjamin Orlove, combined interests in the environment and political economy to fashion creative historically sensitive ethnography. Most of the literature, though, followed the line of leading ecological anthropologists like Marvin Harris and Roy Rappaport. It emphasized the development by Andean people of stable adaptations to their rugged environment. The more biologically minded scholars documented the large lungs of mountain peasants, and their success in developing strains of grains and potatoes suited to the cold. Others, like Brush and Flores Ochoa, analyzed how highland land tenure and pastoral management in Andean villages were especially suited to the ecology. The precise nature of Andean "vertical ecology" – the term coined by John Murra to describe how pre-Inca states controlled lands at varying altitudes – became an issue of special debate. Stressing the self-regulating and distinctive character of Andean ecology, the ecological literature fit with the premise of Andeanism about a discrete and stable Andean tradition. The authors, in long collections like *Man in the Andes* (Baker and Little 1976) and *Pastores de Puna* (Flores Ochoa 1977), could discuss in painstaking detail the special character of adaptation in places like Puno, Ayacucho, and Huancayo even amidst political tumult and an imminent revolution.

There was marginally more interest in politics on the culturally focused side of Andeanist ethnography. The structuralism of Lévi-Strauss and interpretive anthropology of Clifford Geertz were variously brought to the classic Andeanist topics of ritual, reciprocity, kinship, and cosmology by ethnographers like Joseph Bastien, Leslie Brownrigg, Olivia Harris, Luis Millones, Tristan Platt, and R. T. Zuidema. New studies analyzed Andean cultures in terms of "structural oppositions," "ritual transformations," "webs of meaning." Where the ecologists made "vertical ecology" a particular concern, the nature of the ayllu became the focus for many of the scholars concerned with symbol and structure. Anthropologists such as Michael Taussig (1980) and Nathan Wachtel (1977) elucidated highland culture in the context of conquest or the arrival of capitalism. But they preserved a vision of unchanging beliefs that dovetailed with the assumptions of Andeanism. Like that on cultural ecology, debate over the structure of Andean culture became such an absorbing project that it was possible to miss the signs of the nearing upheaval. Efforts in the mid-1970s to join ecological and structural perspectives – Isbell subtitled her book "ecology and ritual" in the spirit of synthesis – only perpetuated anthropological insensitivity to the political agency of Andean peasants.

Beyond their narrow and partly distorting theoretical lenses, a further factor in the oversight of rural unrest was the general orientation of Andeanists toward their ethnographic subjects. In the 1950s, paternal views of Andean people as backward agriculturalists who would have to become modern farmers still prevailed. The renowned ecological anthropologist Julian Steward

(1963: xxix) coupled Andeanist imagery of highlanders as non-Westernized "Indians" with the rhetoric of modernization typical of the 1950s:

As the Indians' slight understanding of European systems leaves them poorly equipped to solve their own problems, great efforts are being made to rehabilitate them economically, through restoration of lands and improved farm methods, and to reintegrate them culturally, through education and other means designed to facilitate their fuller participation in national life.

The conviction that peasants needed a dose of Western initiative and modern technology guided the Cornell anthropologists in the 1950s who bought the hacienda of Vicos in the central highlands to supervise the process through which the exserfs were to enter the modern age.

This unabashed paternalism had largely disappeared by the mid-1960s with the decline of modernization theory. The flavor of Andeanist anthropology in the 1960s and 1970s was increasingly redemptive. Some ethnographers highlighted problems of intracommunal feuding and conflict (Bolton 1973, 1974; Stein 1962). But most unilaterally stressed the resilience and value of Andean traditions. While often edging into a condescending presumption about their right to "speak for" highland people, anthropologists sent an important message to government bureaucrats and development administrators about the need to respect the practices and opinions of campesinos. Peasants were shown to posses sophisticated knowledge of their environment, to have elaborate ritual calendars and astronomical systems, to possess rich memories of their past. An entire literature sprang up on the physiological benefits of coca-chewing, a practice once considered a sign of Andean backwardness.

At the same time, though, the project of redeeming *lo andino* helped lead Andeanists to downplay the underside of highland life: the grinding poverty that led so many peasants into angry action. All Andeanists recognized poverty. But the stress on ecological adaptations and sophisticated symbolism had as a consequence a tendency to minimize the full extent of the economic suffering across the countryside. Ethnographers usually did little more than mention the terrible infant mortality, minuscule incomes, low life expectancy, inadequate diets, and abysmal health care that

remained so routine. To be sure, peasant life was full of joys, expertise, and pleasures. But the figures that led other observers to label Ayacucho a region of "Fourth World" poverty would come as a surprise to someone who knew the area only through the ethnography of Isbell, Skar, or Zuidema. They gave us detailed pictures of ceremonial exchanges, Saint's Day rituals, weddings, baptisms, and work parties. Another kind of scene, just as common in the Andes, almost never appeared: the girl with an abscess and no doctor, the woman bleeding to death in childbirth, a couple in their dark adobe house crying over an infant's sudden death.

In sum, Andeanist anthropology did not recognize the explosive pain and discontent in the highlands. This anger did not, of course, neatly translate into backing for the Shining Path. Campesinos in the southern department of Puno and the northern departments of Cajamarca and Piura have rejected guerrilla overtures. Even in the Sendero strongholds of Ayacucho, Apurímac, Huancavelica, Junin, many rural people have refused to collaborate.

One of the many places where the Shining Path found a warm reception was the village of Chuschi, the subject of Isbell's (1977) classic ethnography. Chuschinos almost universally approved of the Sendero execution of two cattle thieves, the public whipping of two others, and the expulsion of five corrupt bureaucrats. In August 1982, many Chuschinos were among the 2,000 peasants from 9 villages who joined a Sendero-led invasion of a University of Huamanga agricultural station. In December, the communities converged in Chuschi for an enthusiastic march to celebrate the birth of a Shining Path-organized popular army. Ten blocks of peasants waved red flags, shouting *vivas* to the revolutionary war.

In the short final section of *To Defend Ourselves* about Chuschi's future prospects, Isbell (1977: 244–5) had written that "consumerism and new cultural values due to increased out-migration and education may in time cause changes in the perspective of the community." But her main contention was that change had not yet happened, and that villagers would in the near future "retain their conservative attitudes" and continue "efforts to resist incorporation into the national economy and culture." The impact of radical mestizos would "be minimal because, as discussed earlier, they do not share the political concerns of the comuneros, who are attempting to protect their cultural isolation."

Like other Andeanists, Isbell had drastically underestimated the desires of impoverished Ayacuchans for change. Far from rejecting radical ideology and "attempting to protect their cultural isolation," many Chuschinos and other Andean peasants proved ready to embrace the concept of revolution. The price Chuschinos would pay for welcoming Sendero proved incalculably high. In 1983–4, government forces disappeared 6 peasants from Chuschi and 46 from the neighboring community of Quispillacta. A detachment of Sinchis, black-sweatered police commandos who are the most self-avowedly savage of the counterinsurgency forces, blew apart an elderly Chuschino with hand grenades in the village square. By 1985, the Army had burned down much of Chuschi. Most of the comuneros fled to Lima's brown shantytowns.[4] [...]

As for anthropologists, most have retreated from Peru. Only a handful still work in the highlands, and none in Ayacucho's countryside. Only one remains of the more than 10 major Andean archaeology projects that operated at the end of the 1970s. Graduate students interested in the Andes now opt for Ecuador or Bolivia. [...]

Active anthropological work for life and peace ought, I believe, to accompany the break from Andeanism. If the effects may be small, our efforts can at least help to bring Peru's situation to public attention and to build pressure on the Peruvian government to respect human rights. We can also support the courageous peasant federations, women's organizations, shantytown soup kitchens, mineworker unions, and human rights groups which stand between the fire of the Shining Path and the government. [...]

Let me end, then, with an appeal rather than a conclusion. ANFASEP and two other Peruvian human rights organizations have urgent need for support. They work under great danger to monitor violations and to assist victims of the terror. Please consider sending them a donation:

Committee for the Defense of Human Rights in Apurímac
CODEH, Apartado 26, Abancay, Apurímac, Peru

Association of the Families of Disappeared in Ayacucho
ANFASEP, Apartado 196, Ayacucho, Peru

Center for Research and Action for Peace
CEAPAZ, Costa Rica 150, Lima 11, Peru, tel. 63501

NOTES

1 My thinking owes a great debt to Said's (1979) controversial writing on Orientalism.
2 The interview is in *Quehacer*, no. 57, Feb./March 1989, pp. 42–56.
3 This comes from an interview with Guzmán in *El Diario*, 31 July 1988, p. 15. There remains some doubt about the interview's authenticity, as there is about whether Guzmán is still alive. But most Sendero-watchers in Lima believed the interview was indeed authentic; for their opinion, see *La Republica*, 31 July 1988, pp. 12–15.
4 This information comes from Isbell's introductory note to the 1985 reprinting of *To Defend Ourselves*.

REFERENCES

Amnesty International. 1989. *Caught Between Two Fires, Peru Briefing*. London: Amnesty International.
Baker, Paul, and Michael Little, eds. 1976. *Man in the Andes: A Multidisciplinary Study of the High-Altitude Quechua*. US/IBP Synthesis Series, 1. Stroudsburg: Dowden, Hutchinson, and Ross Inc.
Bolton, Ralph. 1973. Aggression and Hypoglycemia among the Qolla: A Study in Psychobiological Anthropology. *Ethnology* 12: 227–57.
——. 1974. To Kill A Thief: A Kallawya Sorcery Session in the Lake Titicaca Region of Peru. *Anthropos* 69: 191–215.
Flores Ochoa, Jorge. 1977. *Pastores de Puna*. Lima: IEP.
Gonzalez, Raul. 1982. Por los caminos de Sendero. *Quehacer* 19: 39–77.
Handelman, Howard. 1975. *Struggle in the Andes*. Austin: University of Texas Press.
Isbell, Billie Jean. 1977. *To Defend Ourselves: Ecology and Ritual in an Andean Village*. Austin: University of Texas Press.
——. 1985. Reprinting of *To Defend Ourselves*. Prospect Heights, IL: Waveland Press.
——. 1988. The Emerging Patterns of Peasants' Responses to Sendero Luminoso. Paper presented at

Patterns of Social Change in the Andes Research Conference sponsored by NYU and Columbia University LAS Consortium, New York City.

Martinez, Hector. 1980. *Migraciones internas en el Peru*. Lima: IEP.

McClintock, Cynthia. 1984. Why Peasants Rebel: The Case of Peru's Sendero Luminoso. *World Politics* 27(1): 48–84.

Nash, June. 1977. *We Eat the Mines and the Mines Eat Us*. New York: Columbia University Press.

Palmer, David Scott. 1986. Rebellion in Rural Peru: The Origins and Evolution of Sendero Luminoso. *Comparative Politics* 18(2): 127–46.

Said, Edward. 1979. *Orientalism*. New York: Vintage Books.

Salomon, Frank. 1982. Andean Ethnology in the 1970s: A Retrospective. *Latin American Research Review* 17(2): 75–128.

Stein, William. 1962. *Hualcan: Life in the Highlands of Peru*. Ithaca, NY: Cornell University Press.

Steward, Julian. 1963. Preface. In *Handbook of South American Indians*, vol. 2. New York: Cooper Square Publications.

Taussig, Michael. 1980. *The Devil and Commodity Fetishism in South America*. Chapel Hill: University of North Carolina Press.

Wachtel, Nathan. 1977. *The Vision of the Vanquished*. Hassocks: Henson Press.

52

From *War Stories: The Culture of Foreign Correspondents*

Mark Pedelty

I was visiting a member of the Salvadoran Foreign Press Corps Association (SPECA) when suddenly the shout "Un muerto! Un muerto!" ("a corpse") rang out in the halls of the Camino Real Hotel.[1] The reporters spent most of their time at the Camino – writing, talking, playing, but most of all, waiting in their rented offices. They waited for interviews, press conferences, and if really lucky, a corpse. It was the fall of 1991 and the war in El Salvador was coming to an end, but the battlefield death toll remained as high as ever as both sides fought for territory and increased leverage at the negotiating table. The number of "political" killings had been steadily decreasing, however, so this corpse excited the journalists.

"Un Muerto!" The members of the corps poured into the hall, smiling and laughing, hoping this one would be news. Like disciplined firemen they jammed into the elevators, ran through the lobby, jumped into their vehicles and were off. They would not have to go far. The body had been dumped just blocks away.

The photographers took the lead, moving towards the body *en masse* while searching for the most dramatic angle. They began shooting immediately. Rather than anarchic competition, the photographers performed a disciplined dance they had developed and perfected during countless other encounters with the dead. They moved slowly around the body, synchronizing their movements in silence. Alonzo, a Salvadoran journalist, explained: "You look at things with the view of the press, not that of a man. To see the dead, you look at the corpse from different angles and then do interviews of the survivors. 'How did it happen? Who was killed?' This is not normal." Not normal for them, but necessary.

The young, tired-looking Green Cross worker standing near the body had taken part in this performance just as often. He had already done his initial body work, measuring the man's corpse as well as his relative location to the curb and corner – a forensic archaeologist conducting a surface survey. He held a blanket, but dared not cover the body until the photographers' dance ended. He stared at the photographers with contempt while other journalists approached to interview him.

A small crowd gathered on each side of the street. They stared at the dead man, comparing his corpse with others they had witnessed first-hand or in the daily paper. I looked for some emotion in their eyes. There was none. The adults and even the children had that stone-faced stare so common among Salvadorans. Emotion, passion, allegiance are too dangerous to exhibit in public.

I too was dancing with the photographers, so as not to get in their way or in their photographs. As they continued their "soft murder" (Sontag 1977: 15) of the corpse, I scribbled meaningless notes, anything to avoid looking at the dead man. "You know how it is," wrote Vietnam correspondent Michael Herr, "you want to look and you don't want to look" (1968: 18). This is a common attitude among reporters, a near-addiction to violence. Participant-observation, the great lie of Anthropology, betrayed me in this regard. Unlike my research subjects, I could not get over my initial feeling of basic revulsion, disbelief, and incomprehension looking at these macabre images. It takes much more practice.

Everyone has some relationship with terror. For many it is anesthetized distance, violence via remote control, voyeurism. Others are more directly involved in the sort of violence that characterizes contemporary El Salvador, unwilling participants in a culture of unarticulable fear and terror. War correspondents have a unique relationship to terror, however, a hybrid condition that combines both voyeurism and direct participation. For these "participant observers" violence is not a matter of "values" in the moral sense of the term, but instead "value" in the economic. They need terror to realize themselves in both a professional and spiritual sense, to achieve and maintain their culture identity as "war correspondents."

"He is laid out like Jesus," I wrote in my note pad, "his arms outstretched, legs crossed at the ankles, a bullet hole in the open palm resembling a nail wound." I wrote that and other senseless words; anything to keep busy, anything to keep from thinking about the cooling flesh in front of me as human, as a person who minutes before got shot while attempting to steal a woman's purse. That was, in fact, the story. The corpse was the culmination of a failed robbery attempt on a bus, an ex-combatant trying to steal food money from others who also barely had enough to eat. A vigilante foiled the thief's attempt, killing him with a shot to the head, and somehow, one through the hand. The driver stopped the bus long enough to open the door and shove the man's body out on the street before continuing his route. It is a common saying among Salvadorans that "through ten years of war, El Salvador has not stopped working."

As the formal conflict came to an end, the fundamental structures of social injustice and daily violence, which first gave rise to the war, continued without interruption. As the combatants began returning to civilian life, the violence simply became more dispersed and less organized. Therefore, this corpse represented a typical Salvadoran story. Too typical, too confused, and ultimately, too complicated for news. [...]

This body, the corpse of a Salvadoran thief-ex-soldier, would not become currency in the aforementioned battle. It lacked sufficient "political value." It would neither be highlighted on a government billboard condemning FMLN (Farabundo Marti National Liberation Front) "terrorism," advertised in the "urgent action" alerts of the left, nor splashed across the front page of the world's newspapers. The messy nature of the incident would provide political capital to no one, because it would not fit easily into the two dimensional discourse of terrorism and human rights. Wrong body, wrong story. This corpse served no journalistic purpose and was soon forgotten.

As the journalists moved back toward their vehicles, they spoke of an upcoming party and made jokes at each others' expense. This was a normal scene for them. Respect for the dead is not a cultural universal, at least not during war and not for journalists. But, reporters are a community in and of themselves. They work together, play together, and often, live together. They share an integrated set of myths, rituals, and behavioral norms. They are, in short, a culture – as coherent as any in the postmodern world. This work is an ethnography about this seemingly familiar, yet oddly alien and exotic culture. [...]

News production is more than a question of "censorship," a form of repression easily identified and relatively simple to resist. Whereas, regimes of censorship attempt to silence dissent (and usually fail), disciplinary regimes overwhelm, co-opt, incorporate, and transform it. Censorship is a simple, negative state – a significant silence. Discipline is an active, productive, and creative form of power, a more subtle, sophisticated, penetrant, and effective means of control than that which is implied by the term "repression." [...]

Most US media organizations are large corporations or subsidiaries thereof. As Ben Bagdikian explains in *The Media Monopoly* (1990: 4):

Today fifty corporations own most of the output of daily newspapers and most of the sales and audience in magazines, broadcasting, books, and movies. The fifty men and women who head these corporations would fit in a large room. They constitute a new Private Ministry of Information and Culture.

To a significant degree, the ideological content of news texts is representative of the worldview of the stockholders, executives, owners, and especially advertisers who produce, manage and profit from news production (Herman and Chomsky 1988).[2] [...]

News organizations do not function alone in the productive role, however. Sources are also extremely influential. Foreign correspondents routinely rely upon elite authorities and powerful institutions as news sources. The most important of these in El Salvador include (in declining order of importance): the US Embassy, the Salvadoran government press office (SENCO), both FMLN radio stations (*Radio Venceremos* and *Radio Farabundo Marti*), The Armed Forces Press Service (COPREFA), and finally, the University of Central America (UCA). This is not to say that SPECA journalists are more sympathetic to the US Embassy than the UCA. In fact, the reverse is usually true. However, the selective pressures of editors and the weight of traditional press practices prompt them to privilege the voices of US and allied elites.

In addition to institutional influences, there is the more inclusive question of ideology. Ideology is often defined as an explicit sociopolitical program, propaganda aimed at legitimating a clearly defined system of domination. This definition of ideology is most appropriately applied to totalitarian states such as the former USSR, where both the means of coercion and the rationalizations thereof lay on the surface. The citizens of the USSR consciously recognized the products of PRAVDA and other state organs as propaganda. PRAVDA never claimed otherwise. The situation is considerably different in advanced capitalist democracies, especially the US, where the dominant means of communication are rationalized in an obfuscational idiom of neutrality, independence, and objectivity.

The journalistic ideal of objectivity began developing in the last century. Objective journalism did not become the dominant mode, however, until well into this century. In addition to providing a hedge against tendentious reporting, the objective code also guided the incipient mass media in their production of news sufficiently "acceptable to all of its members and clients" (Schudson 1978: 4). Objectivity was partially a marketing tool.

The positivistic pretenses of US news media have created a set of irresolvable contradictions for working journalists. While the rules of objective journalism prohibit reporters from making subjective interpretations, their task *demands* it. A "fact," itself a cultural construct, can only be communicated through placement in a system of meaning shared by reporter and reader.

Journalists cannot resolve this contradiction between professional myth and practice, only manage it through judicious use of news *frames*. Frames are "persistent patterns of cognition, inter-

pretation, and presentation, of selection, emphasis and exclusion by which symbol-handlers routinely organize discourse, whether verbal or visual" (Gitlin 1980: 6–7, Goffman 1974). Mainstream journalists tend to adopt frames whose logic is drawn from the most penetrant and unquestioned cultural values, myths, and ideologies – perspectives least likely to be challenged, or perhaps even identified, by audience and journalist (Hallin 1983: 22–5). News frames that contain our most deeply held cultural subjectivities will therefore appear as "natural" expositions of reality (Gitlin 1980: 6), commonsense portrayals rather than constructed, interpretive frameworks. In other words, the objective reality of news is formed of our most fundamental and intractable subjectivities, what Herbert Gans calls "enduring values" (1980: 41–52). Taking a critical view of these values, or at least the media manipulation thereof, Michael Parenti writes, "The worst forms of tyranny – or certainly the most successful ones – are not those we rail against but those that so insinuate themselves into the imagery or our consciousness and the fabric of our lives as not to be perceived as tyranny" (1986: 7).

In the North American vernacular, "ideology" is considered the antithesis of "objectivity" (McLellan 1986: 50–63, Gans 1979: 29–30, 183–6). The belief in objectivity has itself become an ideology, however, not in the simpler sense of the term, but as a system that both legitimates and *obfuscates* relations of domination. In claiming to be objective, media organizations shield their close affinity for and incorporation within dominant institutions and ruling class structures. Objectivity asks us to accept the world "as it is" (or how it has been constructed for us) rather than take a more active part in the creative process of discovery (Thompson 1990). The ideology of objectivity "serves to inhibit imagination" (Rachlin 1988: 134). Incorporated into this network of knowledge production, we cede much of our creative social power to those with the greatest means to produce "objective" truths and the greatest interest in maintaining them (Gitlin 1980: 6–7).

Because I am challenging the basic premises of positivism, however, I never resort to the banal claim that journalists and their texts are "biased." We all are, regardless of our stake in power. Instead, I will attempt to demonstrate how the particular biases of news are connected to structures of domination, and how they are operationalized in the practices of journalists. Todd Gitlin argues (1980: 10):

I retain Gramsci's core conception: those who rule the dominant institutions secure their power in large measure *directly and indirectly*, by impressing their definitions of the situation upon those they rule and, if not usurping the whole of ideological space, still significantly limiting what is thought throughout the society. The notion of hegemony that I am working with is an active one: hegemony operating through a complex web of social activities and institutional procedures.

That is the general theory of ideology I use here. I examine the "social activities and institutional procedures" of SPECA journalists themselves to delimit the ways in which they are, and are not, patterned by the needs of power.

An Example of Institutional Influence

During the early period of my fieldwork, I was speaking with an experienced European reporter about the issue of institutional influence.[3] As another journalist entered the room and began asking me questions, my informant suddenly disappeared. Rejoining us minutes later, she was holding computer printouts of two reports she had recently written about the same event. One report was produced for a European news institution, the other submitted to a US newspaper. As the author herself pointed out, the difference between the two news articles was quite striking. They are as follows:

The US Report

Leftists rebels in El Salvador have admitted that one of their units may have executed two US servicemen after their helicopter was shot down last Wednesday.

An official FMLN rebel statement issued yesterday said two rebel combatants had been detained, "under the charge of suspicion of assassinating wounded prisoners of war."

The US helicopter was downed in the conflictive eastern province of San Miguel as it was flying back to its base in Honduras. One pilot was killed in the crash, but a Pentagon autopsy team concluded that the other two servicemen in the helicopter were killed execution-style afterwards.

Civilians confirmed that the two servicemen had survived the crash, although no-one actually saw the actual execution.

"The FMLN has concluded that there are sufficient elements to presume that some of the three, in the condition of wounded prisoners, could have been assassinated by one or various members of our military unit," said the rebel statement. It also said that their investigations had determined that their initial information from units on the ground was false.

At first the guerrillas said the bodies of the Americans had been found in the helicopter. Then they said that two of the three had survived the crash but later died of wounds.

Salvadoran officials have said that if the Americans were executed the guerrillas should hand over those responsible. The call was echoed by Rep. Joe Moakley (D-Mass), the Chairman of a congressional special task force on El Salvador.

"We would expect and we would demand that the FMLN turn over to the judicial authorities those responsible, if not this lack of action will have serious consequences," he said.

But the rebel statement made no promise to do that. "If responsibility for the crime is proved, the FMLN will act with all rigor, in conformity with our normal war justice," read the statement. The rebels said that because of the nationality of the victims, the investigations would be carried out publicly.

The rebels also defended shooting down the helicopter which they said was flying in "attack position" in a conflicted zone. The UH1H Huey helicopter is the same model as those used by the Salvadoran army and was flying very low to evade anti-aircraft missiles.

The rebel statement did not say whether those detained were in charge of the guerrilla unit which shot down the helicopter. Western diplomats believe it unlikely the unit would have time to radio for orders. The hilly terrain also makes radio communication over any distance difficult.

A US embassy spokesman in San Salvador said State Department and embassy officials are studying the rebel statement.

In the last few days the rebels have privately sounded out United Nations officials about the possibility of setting up an independent commission made up of US and UN investigators as well as the FMLN, according to a senior rebel source. However, no public proposal has been made.

The killings have opened up a debate in Washington as to whether $42.5 million in military aid to El Salvador, frozen by congress last October, should be released. The money was withheld in protest at the lack of progress in investigating the murders of six Jesuit priests by elite army soldiers a year ago. [the final four paragraphs concern the Jesuit murder case]

The European Report
Nestled amid the steep mountains of Northern Chalatenango province, a simple wooden cross on a small hill marks the grave of a teenage guerrilla fighter. There is no name on the grave. None of the villagers from the nearby settlement of San Jose Las Flores who buried his body two years ago knew what he was called.

In life the young guerrilla had little in common with three North American servicemen who were killed last month after the rebels shot down their helicopter. They were enemies on opposite sides of a bitter war. But they shared a common death. They were all killed in cold blood after being captured.

When the young rebel was killed two years ago, I remember taking cover behind the wall of a church of San Jose Las Flores. One moment I was watching two adolescent guerrilla fighters sipping from Coke bottles and playing with a yo-yo. Then I remember seeing soldiers running, crouching, and shooting across the square. The crack of automatic rifle fire and the explosion of grenades was deafening in the confined space.

The whole incident lasted about twenty minutes. As soon as the soldiers left, whooping and yelling victory cries, we ran across the square to find the body of one of the teenage guerrillas still twitching. The villagers said that he had been wounded and surrendered. The soldiers had questioned him – and then finished him off at close range in the head. The bullet had blown off the top of his skull.

I remember clearly the reaction of the then US ambassador when asked about the incident. "That kind of incident cannot be condoned," he said, "but I was a soldier, I can understand – it happens in a war." In a country where tens of thousands have been killed, many of them civilians murdered by the US backed military or by right wing death squads, there was no suggestion of any investigation for the execution of a prisoner.

At the beginning of January this year a US army helicopter was shot down by rebel ground fire in Eastern El Salvador. The pilot died in the crash. But two other US servicemen were dragged badly wounded from the wreckage by the rebels. Before the guerrillas left they finished off the two wounded Americans execution style with a bullet in the head.

The present US ambassador referred to the guerrillas in this incident as "animals."

The killings made front page news internationally and provided the climate needed by President Bush to release forty-two and a half million dollars of military aid, which was frozen last October by Congress. US lawmakers wanted to force the Salvadoran army to make concessions in peace talks and clean up its human rights record.

The two incidents highlight a fact of political life in El Salvador, recognized by all, that it is not worth killing Americans. Until the helicopter incident, in more than a decade of civil war the rebels have only killed six US personnel. They have a deliberate policy of not targeting Americans, despite the fact that most guerrillas have a deep hatred of the US government. As many have been killed by the US's own allies. Extreme groups in the military, who resent US interference, murdered four US church workers and two government land reform advisers in the early 1980s.

In fact the rebels, because of the outcry and the policy implications in Washington, have had to admit guilt in the helicopter incident. They have arrested two of their combatants and say they will hold a trial. They have clearly got the message.

Up until the Gulf War El Salvador has easily seen the most prolonged and deepest US military commitment since Vietnam. However, it is a commitment for which few Americans have felt the consequences.

The first is a rather typical US news report, a set of basic facts and elite source quotes strung together in a dispassionate and "balanced" narrative. The second is typically European (with the caveat that there are significant differences among various European news media). As opposed to her US-bound writing, the author presents her own voice in the European report. The frame is mostly of her own making. Featuring just two quotes, both from like-minded sources, the European report is not "balanced" like its American twin. Furthermore, the reporter offers critical comment in her European article, signaling the reader that her sources' statements are disingenuous. Authorial intervention of that sort is generally considered taboo in US journalism, a fact that led another European "stringer" (reporters who write for several client institutions or "strings") to complain that the American system "goes against the whole point of having a correspondent in the first place."

As for news frames, the American report validates the anger of US officials and legitimates the predicted release of aid. As the European report ironically concludes: "The killings made front page news internationally and provided the climate needed by President Bush to release forty-two and a half million dollars of military aid." That critique applies frighteningly well to the author's other article. The editors of the US newspaper in which her article appeared wrote an editorial supporting the administration's subsequent release of military aid.

There are, however, subversive aspects to the US report. The author's clever quote of the ubiquitous "Western diplomat" makes it clear the FMLN high command was probably not involved in the killing ("Western diplomats believe it unlikely the unit would have time to radio for orders"). Likewise, her addition of information concerning the Jesuit murders calls the potential release of aid into question. In other words, underneath the objective text and the source-dominated frame, lies the author's critical voice, subsumed but not completely silenced.

The author has a very good reputation among the corps. One colleague referred to her as "the reporter of record." Indeed, her work is often exceptional. Why then did this reporter write two very different, even contradictory reports? The answer is simple: she had to. Every journalist must conform to the criteria of her clients. A system of sanctions and rewards – employment policies, prestige endowments, and monetary compensation – facilitate this disciplinary training process. [. . .]

When the war began, only a handful of stringers from Europe, Latin America, and the United States were reporting El Salvador. Journalists flocked to the country soon thereafter, however, when President Ronald Reagan proclaimed "America's economy and well being are at stake" in the war (Reagan in Gettleman et al. 1986: 11–14, Heertsgard 1988: 109–15, Herman and Chomsky 32–3, 107–9). The permanently stationed press corps increased to over 200 journalists. The presence of "parachuters" (journalists who fly in for short periods to cover major events and crises) swelled their ranks to include more than 700 reporters during the 1982, 1984, and 1989 elections, and once again during the FMLN November offensive of 1989 (Massing 1982: 49; 1989).

Long before the war was over, however, the administration's public discourse shifted to other parts of the world, and the media began to abandon El Salvador. The *New York Times* in 1985 published 360 news reports and editorials, 239 fewer than 1984. The decline was even more dramatic in the following years. There were fewer stories written during the next three years, 1986–8 (121, 134, and 107 respectively), than in 1985 alone. What one journalist referred to as "the third generation of Salvador journalists" came to the country during this period of declining interest. This change-over caused a major disjuncture in corps consciousness. Those who witnessed the overt public terror of the early 1980s were replaced by newcomers who would experience a period of more discreet and carefully targeted violence. Greater restrictions were placed on press movement during the latter period, further removing the correspondents from the worst effects of the war. One of the few to have reported the entire war, stated: "They don't know what it was like."

The Offensive of 1989 provided a "book-end," in the words of one reporter, to both the war and the news coverage thereof. Recognizing the war might soon be over, the press corps began its rapid withdrawal from the region. Like most other third world nations, El Salvador is now rarely covered at all. Even the landmark presidential elections of 1994 received scant news attention. [. . .]

The *war correspondent*, is like the accountant who rides a Harley. He projects a renegade identity to himself and the world in a desperate attempt to live up to the American myth of the independent man. Instead of simply accepting the routines and his status as a paid professional, always at the beck and call of his employer, the *Salvador* reporter casts the image of a maverick investigator, poised to uncover the hidden truths of corruption and conspiracy.

In reality, most war correspondents are no more independent or free from discipline and censure than their domestic colleagues. Therefore, I challenge the view that news is reported by independent, tenacious, and objective journalists who function as watchdogs against the abuses of power. Rather, I have concluded that reporters play a relatively small role in the creative process of discovery, analysis, and representation involved in news production. Instead, they are mainly conduits for a system of institutions, authoritative sources, practices, and ideologies that frame the events and issues well before they, the mythical watchdogs, have a chance to do anything resembling independent analysis or representation.

Daniel Hallin argues that the "ideology of the journalist" is, among other things, "myth" (1986: 23). He explains: "It is, in short, a 'myth' – but in a particular sense of that word. Far from being a mere lie or illusion, it is a deeply held system of consciousness that profoundly affects both the structure of the news organization and the day-to-day practice of journalism." The "Salvador" identity is a social manifestation of the myth to which Hallin refers, a claim to independence and neutrality, a wondrous creation that imbues the rather mundane practice of objective journalism with a sense of adventure, poetry, and romance.

Journalists are not the first North Americans to bring these notions to El Salvador. Before the war, thousands of *gringo* surfers came to pay homage to El Salvador's famed Pacific surf. They too found El Salvador an excellent medium for their foreign fantasies. The war correspondents came seeking more than mere adventure, however. They sought truth. Yet, like the weekend warriors who preceded them, most SPECA journalists barely skimmed El Salvador's surface. Their institutions, professional conventions, and other disciplinary structures encouraged them to produce surface texts, to describe violence, politics, and society as if such things are caused by the same seemingly random forces as earthquakes, floods, and hurricanes. We, the news audience, are caught up in this whirlwind adventure as well; places, images and events flash by in rapid succession, an unintelligible pastiche of terror whose effect is to unsettle rather than enlighten.

Eric Wolf argues the goal of anthropology should be "the creation of an image of [humanity] that is adequate to the experience of our time" (1964: 94). Surely, the goal of journalists should be similar – to provide an adequate definition of events, the context in which they take place, their underlying causes, and most importantly, our connection to them – to engender what sociologist C. Wright Mills calls "The Sociological Imagination," a sense of knowledge and interconnectedness linking individuals to the larger world in which they live (1959). Unfortunately, the international news system is currently inadequate to the task.

NOTES

1 SPECA is normally abbreviated as "SPCA" According to press corps lore, the name and acronym were decided upon in a drinking session during the early part of the war. As a joke, journalists borrowed the acronym from the Society for the Prevention of Cruelty to Animals (SPCA). I have added a written "e" to increase textual flow and match the verbalized form.
2 Roach 1993: 17–21, describes the current form and function of the "military-industrial-communication complex."
3 In order to provide nominal anonymity to my research subjects, I will use pseudonyms, will limit my use of their published work, and will not provide citations thereof. Although very few of my subjects requested anonymity, I feel obligated to offer its limited protection to all.

REFERENCES

Bagdikian, Ben H. 1990. *The Media Monopoly*. Boston: Beacon.
Gans, Herbert J. 1980. *Deciding What's News*. New York: Vintage Books.
Gettleman, M., P. Lacefield, L. Menashe, and D. Mermelstein, eds. 1986. *El Salvador: Central America in the New Cold War*. New York: Grove Press.
Gitlin, Todd. 1980. *The Whole World is Watching: Mass Media in the Making and the Unmaking of the New Left*. Berkeley: University of California Press.
Goffman, Erving. 1974. *Frame Analysis: An Essay on the Organization of Experience*. New York: Harper and Row.
Hallin, Daniel C. 1983. "The Media Go to War: From Vietnam to Central America." *NACLA Report on the Americas* 17(4): 2–26.
——. 1986a. *The "Uncensored War": The Media and Vietnam*. Berkeley: University of California Press.
——. 1986b. "We Keep America On Top of the World." In *Watching Television*, ed. Todd Gitlin. New York: Pantheon Books.
Herman, Edward S. and Noam Chomsky. 1988. *Manufacturing Consent: The Political Economy of the Mass Media*. New York: Pantheon.
Herr, Michael. 1968. *Dispatches*. New York: Avon.
Hertsgaard, Mark. 1988. *On Bended Knee: The Press and the Reagan Presidency*. New York: Schocken Books.
McLellan, David. 1986. *Ideology: Concepts in Social Thought*. Minneapolis: University of Minnesota Press.

Massing, Michael. 1982. "Central America: A Tale of Three Countries." *Columbia Journalism Review*, July/Aug.: 47–52.

——. 1989. "When More Means Less." *Columbia Journalism Review*, July/Aug.: 42–4.

Mills, C. Wright. 1959. *Sociological Imagination*. Oxford: Oxford University Press.

Parenti, Michael. 1986. *Inventing Reality: The Politics of the Mass Media*. New York: St. Martin's Press.

Rachlin, Allen. 1988. *News as Hegemonic Reality: American Political Culture and the Framing of News Accounts*. New York: Praeger.

Roach, Colleen, ed. 1993. *Communication and Culture in War and Peace*. Newbury Park, CA: Sage.

Schudson, Michael. 1978. *Discovering the News: A Social History of American Newspapers*. New York: Basic Books.

Sontag, Susan, 1977. *On Photography*. New York: Doubleday.

Thompson, John B. 1990. *Ideology and Modern Culture: Critical Social Theory in the Era of Mass Communications*. Stanford, CA: Stanford University Press.

Wolf, Eric. 1959. *Sons of the Shaking Earth*. Chicago: University of Chicago Press.

53

With Genet in the Palestinian Field

Ted Swedenburg

Two unavoidable risks confront me when I discuss the dangers of the "field" of Palestine. The first is that a sensational or heroic aura might, without justification, become attached to me because I have worked in treacherous, frontline field sites. I admit that when I agreed to write this piece, I planned to spend the spring and summer of 1992 in the West Bank and thought I would be able to write a first-hand report on the quandaries of fieldwork during the intifada. As it turns out, I was only there during August 1992, a period of relative quiescence. Not that my stay was devoid of stimulating episodes. I witnessed *shabab* (young men) burning tires and throwing stones at Israeli soldiers, I was teargased, and I encountered both *mulaththamin* (the famous "masked men" who soldiers have orders to shoot on sight) patroling a village and Israeli soldiers senselessly harassing pedestrians and vendors in East Jerusalem. But such incidents have become thoroughly routine and unremarkable. No Palestinian in downtown Ramallah who noticed this unitedstatesian visitor weeping and gagging from CS gas made-in-the-USA considered the sight uncommon or bothered to console him. Moreover, while Palestinians are loath to characterize the current situation as "postintifada," they will say that the struggle has entered a new stage. Many people were weary, worn down, introspective, pessimistic about the outcome of "peace" negotiations, preoccupied by the dull grind of economic hardships, alarmed by the growing constraints on the activities of women. [...]

The other peril is that a researcher can sometimes be tainted with the dangerous images associated with his or her informants. This hazard seems particularly acute when one chooses to consort with Palestinians and, by some contagious magic, one is contaminated with their "terrorist" or "anti-Semitic" reputation. "To choose to focus your research on a Palestinian subject," a recent report in the *Chronicle of Higher Education* gently put it, "was not always a wise career move" for aspiring academics (Coughlin 1992: A8). I hope that someday someone will document how aspiring graduate students, from various disciplines, were warned by advisers not to do research on Palestinians, how guilt by association with Palestinian "terrorists" affected academic hiring and promotion, how the taboo on this subject severely circumscribed academic discussion of the issues, and so on. Yet the inescapable trap in the context of this discussion is that when a researcher explains how she faced real or imagined difficulties in the academy due to her Palestinian affiliations, *she* will be seen as a victim, and attention will thus be deflected away from her relative privilege and away from the more serious, although certainly related, suffering. [...]

So I would like to avoid the issues of the ersatz heroism and/or victimization of the ethnographer who ventures into hazardous territory. Instead I want to consider the instructive account of another Western adventurer. It is still not well known in the United States that, while stricken with throat cancer, Jean Genet devoted the last years of his life to completing a book based mainly on his experiences with the Palestinians, with additional material on the Black Panthers, with whom he stayed in spring 1970. This marvelously quirky text from one of the century's greatest writers, *Un Captif amoureux*, appeared in France a little over a month after Genet's death in 1986. [. . .]

I am personally drawn to this text not merely by its literary merits – although very different from Genet's earlier *oeuvre*, it is fully that works' stylistic equal – but because it represents a kind of ethnography that resonates with my own experience. *Prisoner of Love* recounts, principally, the time Genet spent, between 1970 and 1972, among Palestinian fedayeen in Jordan. Of course, his sojourn did not constitute "professional" ethnography. Genet was, as is well known, a thief, a homosexual, a prisoner, a novelist, and a playwright. When he visited the Palestinians he was over 60 and his writings of the last decade or so had consisted primarily of the occasional journalistic piece and political statement. He was still a celebrated if somewhat scandalous political figure. But he was not an ethnographer. Genet admits, for instance, that his knowledge of Arabic was rudimentary (how many professional fieldworkers could afford to make such an admission?); he stayed with the guerrillas at the invitation of the Palestine Liberation Organization (PLO) leadership – hardly a prescription for "objectivity"; and he makes no pretense of writing a scholarly book. Nonetheless – and perhaps precisely *because* of the absence of "academic" constraints – the work contains many astute observations regarding doing ethnography in dangerous fields.

Fieldwork?

The first issue *Un Captif amoureux* raises for me concerns the very definition of fieldwork. Genet's rendering of his experiences among the fedayeen in the hills of ʿAjlun and of his encounters with Palestinian leaders in Amman and Beirut manifests an acute and sensitive self-awareness about the limits of its own subject position. I will return to these issues below. But, more significant, it brings to mind the time I spent in many of the same spots between 1961 and 1976. Genet's work leads me to wonder whether there is a legitimate(d) way for me to discuss, in an "academic" context, my long prefieldwork experiences in the Arab world, the time I passed, living, studying, working, playing, and traveling there. Is lapsing into this sort of autobiography merely a narcissistic exercise? Do only the 14 months I spent in the Occupied Territories

in 1984–5, traveling to villages to interview veterans of the 1936–9 revolt with notebook and tape recorder in hand, sanctified by Ph.D. candidacy and a Social Science Research Council (SSRC) grant, qualify as "fieldwork," as the only database for all my future academic writing on Palestinian memory, identity, and culture?

Perhaps many ethnographers who are similarly motivated to work in "treacherous" sites face similar questions. I have been forced to confront this issue whenever sympathetic colleagues have asked me how I manage to cope with working in and writing about a geographic/academic area that seems so emotionally and politically overcharged and so excessively violent. I can only begin to make sense of how *natural* it feels for me to be involved in this field by referring to personal history. Probably I have been there/here, emotionally, at least since I was twelve. My family first visited the West Bank – during the course of an extended pilgrimage to the "Holy Land" – in the winter of 1961–2, when it was still ruled by the Hashemite Kingdom of Jordan. One day a US Christian relief worker took us to Twayni, a "border village" in the Hebron district. We made our way from Hebron (al-Khalil) by Land Rover, over a poorly marked and rugged goat track. Twayni's inhabitants, we learned, had lost their farmlands, located in the nearby plains, to the Jewish state when Israel was created in 1948. Since the villagers still retained their dwellings in the highlands, they could not be classified as "refugees" and therefore – although they had no means of livelihood – they were ineligible for assistance from the United Nations Relief and Works Agency (UNRWA). Coming from the Santa Clara Valley, I was astonished and appalled by the stark poverty. My memory (since refreshed by slides my father took) is of a bleak grayish brown atmosphere, the rocky hills, the ground, and the mud-and-stone houses all hewn from the same monotonous color, unrelieved by the greenery of trees or plants. I recall buzzing flies, scrawny animals, urchins in shabby dress, an absence of plumbing, sewage, or electricity. We quickly departed Twayni when we learned that the villagers, ever the hospitable and friendly Arabs despite their destitution, were rounding up the few stringy chickens we had noticed earlier, scrabbling around on the rugged ground, so that they could honor us with dinner. Perhaps, ever since, I have wanted to repay those generous, desperate villagers who the world had ignored, for their offer of roasted chickens. [. . .]

During the time I lived in Beirut, between 1964 and 1976, the significance and stakes of the Palestine question only intensified, especially after Israel occupied the West Bank and Gaza in 1967 and Palestinians took up arms, thereby transforming their global image from one of hapless refugees to, depending on your point of view, terrorists or freedom fighters. Events in Palestine and its diaspora were especially crucial for my life once I enrolled at the American University of Beirut (AUB) in 1969 and made friends and allies with Palestinians who were active in student politics and in various factions of the resistance movement. These relationships made the escalating violence of the 1970s tangible and personal. I will never forget one Palestinian friend, the gentle and unassuming Nabil Saʿd. Nabil was the child of refugees from the Galilee who, after 1948, had taken up residence with their Maronite Christian coreligionists in Ashrafiya (East Beirut). Although active in student politics, Nabil was never a particularly prominent figure; after receiving his BA, he began teaching in a local secondary school. In fall 1975, early in the Lebanese civil war, rightwing Phalangist militiamen kidnapped Nabil, tortured him with knife blades and glowing cigarettes, shot him through the head, and discarded his body in a vacant lot. The only apparent motive was that Nabil was a Palestinian. Nabil's parents' flat in Ashrafiya was plundered and burned, and the family was left with no photographs of Nabil except for the snapshot taken in the morgue. I will never forget the hours I spent with Nabil's younger brother, trying to lend comfort and to convince him of the folly of attempting revenge. [...]

The point is simply that my Beirut friendships and experiences were crucial for my subsequent fieldwork project in the West Bank – because they ensured support networks and thus enabled my understanding of, and capacity to manage, life under military occupation. Many researchers, I assume, have a similar complex mix of attachments, investments, relations, experiences, emotions, or understandings that connect them to the trouble spots in which they work. Such links usually cannot be defined as "academic," and we have therefore not been encouraged to speak about them. The usual assumption is that the "field" is "virgin territory" for the researcher, and therefore ethnographic accounts are full of fables of "first contact." But others of us may have prior contacts

with people in the areas where we work, ties that are crucial to understanding our motivations and capacities for undertaking "dangerous" fieldwork. To speak of such ties is not merely a self-indulgent conceit.

Fieldwork as Fun?

The second suggestion that Genet offers is that we admit, moreover, that we might actually be *attracted* to such perilous sites. "It was for *fun* as much as anything," he informs us, "that I'd accepted the invitation to spend a few days with the Palestinians. But I was to stay nearly two years ... neither afraid nor surprised, but *amused* to be there" (1989: 9; emphasis added). Genet returns to the theme of enjoyment several times. During a shootout between fedayeen and King Hussein's army, he informs us, he experienced a kind of "idiotic delight" crouching against a wall while bullets sprayed nearby, watching the "happy smiles" and "calm" on the faces of the Palestinian fighters (ibid., 53). Genet also speaks of his great passion for the guerrillas: "From late 1970 to late 1972, more than anything or anyone else I loved the fedayeen" (ibid., 373). The Palestinian revolt in the hills of ʿAjlun, he declares, was a "party that lasted nine months," and he compares it to "the freedom that reigned in Paris in May 1968" – except, he notes, "the fedayeen were armed" (ibid., 247).

Strange motivations. What could they have to do with ethnography? Is doing ethnography in a hazardous field really supposed to be a question of fun, or love? Aren't we supposed to be attracted to intriguing intellectual problems? Isn't it magnanimity that compels us to live with the wretched of the earth? Yet maybe if we admitted that struggles sometimes exude a party atmosphere and exert a magnetic pull, the heroism sometimes associated with our dangerous ethnography would be diminished.

I recall my visit to Jordan in spring 1970, partly for the purpose of researching a paper for a sociology course with Samir Khalaf, on the topic, "Is the Palestinian resistance a force for modernization?" I found Amman's atmosphere, during those days of Palestinian mobilization and gunslinging guerrillas in the streets, exhilarating, the promise of radical change inspiring, the spirit of defiance contagious. I was particularly moved by a performance I witnessed at Baqaʿ refugee camp, where young women and children danced the *dabka* and sang nationalist songs with transcendent joy and determination. And it was discussions with some astute leaders and members of the Popular Democratic Front for the Liberation of Palestine that originally sparked my interest in Marxism.

The ambience at AUB in the late 1960s and early 1970s was equally electric and frequently scary: strikes, occupations of buildings and demonstrations, bloody fights between rival student groups, endless political arguments and Marxist study groups, militancy, foolish excesses, work camps in refugee camps, and Stalinist demagogy. Although I also spent a year and a half in the United States during this period, for me "the sixties" was primarily a Beirut experience; and armed revolt and brutal repression were an integral part of that political reality. Like Genet, I was enamored of the Palestinian revolution, ensnared by its charms and dangerous allure. So when talking about dangerous ethnography, I must admit the appeal, the thrills inherent in projects for social change. I feel extraordinarily lucky to have tasted something of the joys of insurrection, the – if I may *détourn* Durkheim's phrase – "collective effervescence" of revolt.

Not a Laudable Occupation

[...] Under such conditions *participant-observation* is impossible. And how absurd this paradoxical anthropological conceit seems, when you are among men shouldering Kalashnikovs who are slated for death, prison, torture (ibid., 97). Genet may be full of love, chaste desires, and identification, but ultimately he is simply an outside observer. He even has doubts about what the fedayeen *really* felt about him, what they truly thought his role was (ibid., 302). This is no fable of ethnographic "rapport." Genet always recognizes the difference, the gap separating him from the fighters (ibid., 344). And he actively shuns the notion of any heroism on his part. "My whole life," he asserts, "was made up of unimportant trifles cleverly blown up into acts of daring" (ibid., 148). A rather remarkable statement given the legendary outsider status of the man who asserted in 1974, "It was completely natural for me to be attracted to the people who are not only the most unfortunate but also crystallize to the highest degree the hatred of the West."[1]

Genet admits of other complications in his relationship to the Palestinians. After the 1973 war, his "passionate love" faded and "the typical lover's weariness" set in. "I was still charmed," he writes, "but I wasn't convinced; I was attracted but not blinded. I behaved like a prisoner of love" (ibid., 188). A prisoner of love who continues to exercise great care and caution in depicting the Palestinians because he is well aware of the West's antipathy. He constantly underscores the fedayeen's bravery, the nobility of their cause of liberation. [...]

When I write I make a constant effort to balance my interest in exposing the seams and cracks in nationalist history with the need to safeguard the nationalist history from vilification by its powerful opponents. Genet's example suggests that such solidarities are necessary, that they have their price, and that they must be undertaken self-consciously.

But he does not advocate cheerleading. His depictions of the PLO leadership, for instance, are scathing. "I found the manners of almost all the ordinary Palestinians, men and women, delightful," he writes. "But their leaders were a pain in the neck" (ibid., 243); many were guilty of corruption. The legs of the guerrilla chiefs "often wilted," he asserts, "at the sight of heaps of gold or the sound of new banknotes" (ibid., 164). His descriptions of the Palestinian bourgeoisie, the "Leading Families," are equally caustic. Nor does Genet shy away from blasting the PLO's illusory military strategy. He labels the poorly defended fedayeen positions in the hills of 'Ajlun, where he stayed in 1971, "Potemkin" bases (ibid., 125). The United States and Israel "were in no danger," he asserts, from such PLO "sham[s]," from "defeats presented as victories, withdrawals as advances – in short, from a shifting dream floating over the Arab world, capable only of such unsubtle acts as killing a plane-load of passengers" (ibid., 149). Fedayeen, Genet maintains, were often sent off on "operations without really knowing from start to finish what their objective was" (ibid., 289). Even his beloved fighters were not all innocents. Fateh, the organization that welcomed him into its camps, seemed to attract youths "who delighted in scrapping and looting and guns ... more hooligans than heroes" (ibid., 202). Genet witnesses fedayeen lording it over Jordanian peasants (ibid., 340) and other fighters who were "glad to be able to pilfer cars, cameras, discs, books and trousers with impunity" and who excused their actions as revolutionary (ibid., 227). Such biting critiques are unusual for a partisan account.

Leapfrogging over Corpses

But what, you might now object, about the *real* issues? What is all this talk of love and play? What about the horror and terror, what about all those people killed, wounded, tortured? Genet does deal with death and suffering, somehow managing to sustain a kind of impassioned coolness of tone. In particular, he discusses the carnage at the Beirut refugee camp of Shatila, which he wandered through in September 1982 shortly after the Phalangist-inflicted massacres there and at Sabra camp. "I've gone down the main street in Chatila having almost to leapfrog over the corpses blocking the streets," he tells us. "The number of obstacles I've had to jump over in my life. The smell of decomposition was so strong it was almost visible, and insurmountable as a rampart" (ibid., 338). Other horrific images from Shatila are interspersed throughout. And, he tells us, "when I hear the word Palestinian, I shudder and have to recall the image of a grave waiting like a shadow at the feet of every fighter" (ibid., 329). [. . .]

Reading this and other similar passages, I too want to personalize the violence and oppression. I think of Ahmad Kilani, assassinated by Israel's "special forces" during the first year of the intifada. I think of my friend Sam'an Khuri, who spent three and one-half years in jail during the intifada. Sometimes I feel that involvement in this field has also required me to hop over corpses, with all the pain and privilege attendant on the outsider who inevitably survives the struggle and feels compelled to bear witness.

The first time I sat down to write about the personal effects of experiencing such violence and horror – albeit at second hand – I was paralyzed with pain, nausea, and depression. Whenever I think of this issue, a troubling jumble of images assaults me. I lived through the first months of the Lebanese civil war in Beirut (until January 1976), going to sleep every night to the music of machine guns, bombs, and rocket-propelled grenades in the distance, and losing a number of friends and acquaintances in the process. For years I was virtually unable to talk about Beirut, and I am still beset by violent dreams about the civil war. My fieldwork in 1984–5, unlike my "sixties" experiences in Beirut and Amman, was mostly not "fun." This

was a period when West Bank Palestinians were building grassroots institutions that laid the basis for the intifada, but it was also a period of repression, of the security forces' "Iron Fist," and a time when many friends were rounded up. I was often frightened, depressed, and nervous. After I returned to the United States, I twice came close to mental collapse; both times memories of West Bank violence (plus my mother's death and the breakup of my marriage) played a major part in the breakdown. [. . .]

Perhaps the hardest thing is how impossible it is to convey the everyday *normality* of the violence to anyone living in our safe middle-class US enclaves. It is extremely difficult to convince anyone of Walter Benjamin's insight, that such a "'state of emergency' . . . is not the exception but the rule" (1969: 257). So one usually shies away from speaking about the horror, since most people respond with looks of shocked disbelief and exaggerated compassion (both for you and for the Palestinians) but rarely with the realization that the "state of emergency" connects to their own lives.

Fabulous Images

Perhaps this is why, even though images like corpses, severed digits, and mutilated bodies are scattered throughout the pages of *Un Captif amoureux*, they are not Genet's principal focus. His chief concern is to capture the life, the humor, amid the blood and suffering. He recognizes, of course, how tricky this task is. "To depict the Palestinian resistance as a game or a party," Genet maintains, "doesn't mean one is taking it lightly. The Palestinians have been denied houses, land, passports, a country, a nation – everything! But who can deny laughter and a light in the eye?" (ibid., 305). [. . .]

I do not know if Genet would urge us on, given that he left so many projects uncompleted. But witnessing the holocaust at Shatila in September 1982 was what set him to writing *Un Captif amoureux*, which was completed 25 years after the publication of his last play, *The Screens* (*Les Paravents*) (see notes to Genet 1991: 406). He felt compelled to write, in part, so that the revolt he had witnessed might leave its mark. For the fedayeen, he asserts, knew that "their persons and their ideas [would] only be brief flashes against a world wrapped up in its own smartness. . . . [T]he fedayeen...are tracer bullets, knowing their traces vanish in the twinkling of an eye" (1989: 179). Genet sees his role as the sender of "fabulous images" of the struggle "into the future, to act in the very long term, after death," images that might be "starting point[s] for actions" (1989: 262). He does not pretend that he is "giving voice" to the Palestinians or acting as the relay of *their* messages. Rather, he accepts responsibility for the fact that the interpretation is all his own. [...]

Genet equally expresses doubts about the ultimate utility of his work. "Perhaps what I write is no use to anyone," he wonders. "'What's the use of talking about this revolution?' It...is like a long-drawn-out funeral, with me occasionally joining in the procession" (ibid., 190). And again, "Any reality is bound to be outside me, existing in and for itself. The Palestinian revolution lives and will live only of itself" (ibid., 374). [...]

Vitalizing the Will

Perhaps, in trying to avoid getting caught up in either the heroic or the terrorist image associated with the Palestinians, I have neglected my own dangerous ethnography. I have mentioned my own investments and experiences, but I have spoken more of Genet – maybe because Genet's text provides a vehicle for me to address issues that are still difficult for academics. After all, the outlaw Genet did not face all the constraints that professional ethnographers usually encounter. He visits the guerrillas at their invitation, openly declaring his partisanship, fearlessly affiliating with "terrorists." (Our affiliations are usually with the Ford and Rockefeller foundations, the National Endowment for the Humanities, the Social Science Research Council.) Moreover, Genet's overt solidarity permits him the paradoxical freedom to be devastatingly critical. (While we have to be cultural relativists.) He also speaks of investments – desire, pleasure, anger – which the academy avoids. And he is concerned principally not with analysis or interpretation but with producing images, images with hoped-for future political and aesthetic value. Perhaps because he is a brilliant writer, the images will be remembered.[2] [...]

Perhaps I continue seeking such images in this ethnographic minefield because I hope, somehow, to prove that I am worthy of having been offered a taste of roasted chicken by dispossessed, but generous, peasants.

NOTES

1 Quoted in Edmund White's introduction to *Prisoner of Love*, in Genet 1989: viii.
2 Genet spent his last years living in Morocco, where he is buried (see Muhammed Choukri's *Genet in Tangier*). He was an active supporter of the rights of Arab immigrants in France and an early champion of Maghrebi authors like Tahar Ben Jelloun writing in French (see Genet 1991). He was always actively disloyal to French, and Western, civilization.

REFERENCES

Benjamin, Walter. 1969. "Theses on the Philosophy of History." In *Illuminations*, ed. Hannah Arendt, trans. Harry Zohn, 253–64. New York: Schocken Books.

Coughlin, Ellen K. 1992. "As Perceptions of the Palestinian People Change, Study of Their History and Society Grows." *Chronicle of Higher Education* (Feb. 19): A8–9, A12.

Genet, Jean. 1986. *Un Captif amoureux*. Paris: Gallimard.

——. 1989. *Prisoner of Love*, trans. Barbara Bray. London: Picador.

——. 1991. *L'Ennemi déclaré: Textes et entretiens*, ed. Albert Dichy. Paris: Gallimard.

Peteet, Julie. 1991. *Gender in Crisis: Women and the Palestinian Resistance Movement*. New York: Columbia University Press.

Swedenburg, Ted. 1992. "Seeing Double: Palestinian-American Histories of the *Kufiya*." *Michigan Quarterly Review* 31(4): 557–77.

54

The Anthropologist as Terrorist

Joseba Zulaika

In the middle of Franco's darkest repression, I was informally asked in London, where I was living for a year, to join the armed organization. The invitation came from two ETA members on a hunger strike in Trafalgar Square protesting the death penalties issued against six Basque activists. There were at the time massive demonstrations in Europe's capitals against Franco's military trial. I was not up to the call then, nor was I later, when, back in the Basque country, the same youths requested again my services and my loyalty. By then my only real interest was anthropology. In 1979, after several years of study in Canada and the United States, I returned to my village to do fieldwork on the very thing I had dodged. It was then that I began to realize the incongruities of my role as ethnographer. They became truly alarming when I visited an old friend who was one of ETA's leaders. Through him I met several members of the group in their hideouts in France. Against all common sense, but conscious of the fieldwork rhetoric of initiation, I expressed willingness to join them so as to gain insight into their lives and organizational circumstances. I made clear to them that I was not interested in any nationalist agenda but only in writing a good ethnography. I did not wish to imitate their thirst for martyrdom, yet unexpectedly I too had fallen under the spell that "the truths we respect are those born of affliction. We measure truth in terms of the cost to the writer in suffering" (Sontag 1978: 49–50). One of the activists pointed out that for me fieldwork and writing seemed to be something similar to what patriotic martyrdom was for them. They

could understand a willingness to sacrifice oneself for political truth, but they were baffled by my disposition for analysis and writing. They did not know what to do and were embarrassed to have to tell me they did not want me around. My time for initiation, with all its distortions, was fortunately over.

A Town Meeting and a Community of Faces

Itziar, a village of 1,000 people, had been shaken by six political murders between 1975 and 1980. ETA was responsible for the killings of two police informers, one civil guard, one industrialist, and a worker mistakenly taken to be an informer; the civil guards killed an ETA operative. Against the background of such violent acts, I attempted to reconstruct, as if in a Homeric tragedy, the conditions under which the actors and their audience created each other and ultimately became each other's dilemma.

Yet what sort of dialogue can a fieldworker establish with groups who practice or support such violence? What kind of "authenticity" can a writer stage for such an encounter? In my ethnographic work, while deriving various types of models and metaphors from the culture, still I dwelled on the sense of tragedy produced by the phenomenon of violence. The ethnographer is like a poet, I concluded, in his attempts to turn into a song what is incomprehensible in human experience. I could not overcome my essential ambivalence toward the violent subjects, nor could I present a firm moral ground from which to

judge the entire historical narrative. If I was nowhere close to discovering any exemplary realm of
intact heroism, neither could I finalize the political
options of my informants as vicious criminality.

At the end of the fieldwork, I was asked by the
villagers to give them a lecture expounding my
"findings." I welcomed the exceptional occasion
of that town meeting, but the ironies of my role as
ethnographer became disturbingly embarrassing
for me. At the outset I had to point out that I had
no answer of any sort to our deeply perplexing
political and moral dilemmas. Nor did I have any
startling new factual information that was of true
concern to them – except, perhaps, that I found
some of our collective assumptions about the village's police informer, killed by ETA, to be false.
My ironic predicament – a specialist who knew
nothing special about the violence and who was
frequently asking his neighbors simple social and
political questions about which they had better
understanding than he – did not pass unnoticed
by my "informants," who, half-jokingly, would
even chide me at times about my alleged knowledge. What had I really been doing during all
those months of fieldwork? What was the purpose
of my writing?

Still, confronted with the town meeting, I was
determined to use the very precariousness of
the ethnographer's position as my greatest asset
when asked to validate my knowledge. Standing
in front of my small but unique audience of people
tormented by two decades of local political violence, all I had was a parable taken from our recent
history: a priest who became secularized and who
then attempted to explain to his former parishioners his sacramental status change. After having
possessed the indelible sacerdotal character, he
had become an ordinary layman. Yet he continued
to be the very same person, and he wanted his
former parishioners to treat him as such. I was
as helpless as the former priest, I told them, if they
wanted me to "explain" what makes people choose
violent martyrdom or decide that it is no longer
necessary. There were no objective grounds to
compare the life of the same man when he was a
priest and when he was not, no ultimate rule with
which to judge the movement back and forth from
sacrament to metaphor, from ritual to theater.
Indeed, we were hardly able to *say* what we knew
about the violence. My audience, who knows and
admires that man, understood at once. The historical analogy between the local former priest and the
local former "terrorist" seemed to capture a crucial
dimension of the violence for all of us. It prompted
a dialogue among the competing political and
moral identities within the village. For a moment
it appeared that local experience, framed as exemplary parable, could be turned into a powerful
source of communal solidarity and tolerance.

Irony was, in fact, the master trope in that village meeting: former members of ETA opposed
violence, while their sympathizers, who had
never undergone the baptism by fire of belonging
to the underground organization, continued to
support it. The exchanges were of this sort:
"I remember I was opposed to your entering
ETA," said the brother of one jailed ETA activist
to a former ETA member. "I thought it was nothing but activism and volunteerism; we argued
and argued about it; my position was that we
should organize the working classes, not leave
the struggle in the hands of an armed elite. And
what about now? Now you are opposed to violence and you are telling me, who was always
against it, that the armed struggle is worthless.
I am now the violent one because I don't think
like you. If it was right for you to do it, why not
for others?" To which the former ETA activist
replied, "It was all right then when Franco was
still alive. Now things have changed a lot. We did
the fighting and I am proud of it. But now we are in
a far different world. If I hadn't taken up arms
when it was the proper time, I wouldn't be as
opposed to it as I am now. Violence makes no
sense whatsoever now. It has become our major
problem as a people. We can go nowhere with
violence." This was, indeed, a face-to-face debate,
on questions that were most vital for the community and reflective of one's intimate personal
thoughts and experiences.

This was certainly not what the terrorism
experts had urged us to do: avoid at all costs
anything having to do with the terrorists. The
community debate was not about a reified and
tabooed abstraction but a face-to-face encounter
with the pronouns "I" and "you" on the line, exploring questions and responsibilities over events
that had taken place in our own village. We could
not find an argument we could all share to soothe
the excessive incongruity of the "But how can that
be?" prompted by politically motivated killing.
But ethnographic perspectivism was at least able
to carve out a communal space in which people
with irreconcilable conceptions could talk to each

other without turning one another into monsters. We as neighbors preferred not to depend on the representations that others – politicians, journalists, experts, social scientists – had made of our lives. But the meeting was even more revelatory in that we realized we could not trust even our own collective representations, as illustrated by our views of the death of the alleged police informer Carlos, well deserved for some, tragically unjust for others (including his political antagonist, Martin).

In that meeting we were worried about something prior to criminality: we wanted to reassure ourselves we were a community, and we looked for the ethical basis supporting our sense of justice. We were not interested in further texts or laws but in the intersubjectivity that had orchestrated the killings. The call not to dehumanize ourselves could be summed up in a commanding duty we were performing: confronting the faces of neighbors to understand the meaning in their silent expressions as well as their words. The daily routine of having to face a neighbor can be evaded in various ways, at times even totally avoided. Yet, at other times, when it radically exposes personal destitution or communal dependency, facing a stark face is the prime burden of solidarity. The message of our meeting was that "the solution" to the problem would not come from further tabooing the faces of the violent subjects but from personally confronting them as revelatory mirrors that can reflect the dilemmas of ethics and politics. [...]

Terrorism and the Face

Whatever the "terrorist" might be, he or she was not a faceless man or woman in those meetings. It was possible to carry on an I–you conversation with them. When one's birthplace decides that one has friends and neighbors belonging to that category of persons, then the immediate problem becomes simply how to react to their presence. No explanation of the moral and political paradox will provide a definitive answer to the "But how can that be?" of violence and death. Yet seeing literally and figuratively the face of the faceless activist may become, rather than a contaminating taboo proscribed in the name of science, a condition necessary for understanding that inferno of action. In those meetings, the face rescued us from allegory and representation.

But in the background of such reciprocal interaction there emerges also the presence of the impersonal witness, the ethical call to help the other gratuitously, what Emmanuel Levinas (1988a: 165) characterized as "the asymmetry of the relation of *one* to the *other*" (emphasis in original). This implies, in Jacques Derrida's (1978: 314 n. 37) commentary, "a summoning of the third party, the universal witness, the face of the world." Martin Buber thought that one individual has nothing to say about another; the only authentic relationship, he held, was the living dialogue with another person. The other cannot be thematized; we must speak *to* him, not just about him. Inquisitors and experts should take the example of the seventeenth-century Spanish inquisitor Salazar who spoke to the alleged witches, not just in order to know about them and accuse them of crime, but to convince them of their own tragic self-deception.

Yet am I my brother's keeper? When Cain's desolate interrogation for the absent brother or friend obtains an existential urgency, no response appears to make much sense. Thinkers as diverse as Alasdair MacIntyre and Richard Rorty appeal in the end to the notions of "community" and "solidarity." But dialogue with terrorists? The premise that, whatever they are, they should be perceived as part of one's own community and not as always the evil, disembodied Other projected on a foreign place, that is the lesson I was taught by Itziar villagers when they – as a community – took responsibility for their sons' actions. The villagers could not rely on the representations created by outsiders – the politicians, the news media – as to how to judge their own lives; they could not even trust their own collective representations, as the case of Carlos turned into a demonic scapegoat made painfully obvious. This was a face-to-face interaction that eliminated the privileging of any representation. As concerned neighbors, we were primarily distressed with something prior to criminality, that is, with the ethics that provides a foundation to justice, with contemplation of the face in order not to become dehumanized. Levinas (1988b: 175) even calls the face "the opposite of justice." For him, the last word is not justice: "There is a violence in justice." Any historical narrative makes us all too aware of the politics of murder (Foucault 1977). Obviously, we must advocate justice, but this does not rescue authority and morality from their internal paradoxes.

The accusation of terrorism, like that of witchcraft and demonic possession in former times, allows us to deface the accused person and thereby deprive his or her most intimate humanity. The presence of the real face, its commanding proximity, shows itself to be more original that any allegory, ritual, or narrative. Knowledge scorns such immediacy, which it knows time and again to be mediated by various kinds of prejudices. But the goal of knowledge is only more knowledge, and reason becomes its most compelling argument, whereas the kind of puzzlement that forces ultimate questions about the paradoxes of violence demands movement beyond reason: the rational justification for killing, either in warfare or capital punishment, is all too banal for such perplexity. This is where ethical philosophies such as the one proposed by Levinas, in the very exorbitance of their claims, come to the aid of the ethnographer, for they invoke the power to contest knowledge and justice in the name of the other's absolute alterity. The villagers' perplexity while witnessing politically motivated murder in their neighborhood was oblique recognition that everybody was partly responsible for it; the confusion led us to question the intersubjective premises of the community that had orchestrated the killings. The inquiry could only begin by appealing to common sense while contemplating indepth people's faces.

REFERENCES

Derrida, Jacques. 1978. *Writing and Difference*. Chicago: University of Chicago Press.

Foucault, Michel. 1977. *Discipline and Punish: The Birth of the Prison*. New York: Pantheon.

Levinas, Emmanuel. 1988a. "Useless Suffering." In *The Provocation of Levinas: Rethinking the Other*, eds. Robert Bernascone and David Wood. New York: Routledge, pp. 156–67.

———. 1988b. "The Paradox of Morality: An Interview with Emmanuel Levinas." In *The Provocation of Levinas: Rethinking the Other*, eds. Robert Bernascone and David Wood. New York: Routledge, pp. 168–80.

Rorty, Richard. 1989. *Contingency, Irony, and Solidarity*. Cambridge: Cambridge University Press.

Sontag, Susan. 1978. *Against Interpretation and Other Essays*. New York: Octagon Books.

55

An Alternative Anthropology: Exercising the Preferential Option for the Poor

Leigh Binford

> To articulate the past historically does not mean to recognize it as "the way it really was" (Ranke). It means to seize hold of a memory as it flashes up at a moment of danger.
>
> Walter Benjamin, *Illuminations*

Visitors to northern Morazán and to El Mozote often enjoy the hospitality of the little concrete-block hotel at the visitors' center in Segundo Montes. [. . .]

One of the few persons they regularly seek out is Rufina Amaya, whose account of the El Mozote massacre was first broadcast by Radio Venceremos and appeared in abbreviated form several weeks later in the *New York Times* and the *Washington Post*. Since 1990, Rufina has shared her story dozens of times. On various occasions she has even guided visitors around El Mozote, pointing out the former site of the Alfredo Márquez house in which she was interned with the other women and children. Then she retraces the route down the main street, around a corner, and up the little footpath to the home of Israel Márquez, toward which the soldiers marched her along with other adult women to a certain death. The tree behind which she crouched grows a little larger each year. It is rooted only a hundred meters from the slopes of Cerro Chingo, where Rufina hid in a patch of maguey before she finally made her escape from the smoldering ruins of El Mozote.

But most visitors are unaware that the wooden shacks located a few meters from their sleeping quarters are home to at least a half dozen other former residents of El Mozote, each with a story about the community and about flight and survival that is as affecting, if not quite as graphic or shocking, as the story told by Rufina Amaya. Nor do they know, or are many of them interested to know, that the pitted sheetmetal roofing and loosely boarded walls throughout the five settlements that compose Segundo Montes house thousands of other people who survived assassinations, massacres, captures, and bombings. These survivors – there is no better word to signify their situation – are working to construct a new community out of the ruins of numerous destroyed ones. Visitors to the region are much more interested in the social experiment in progress than they are in the tragedies that engendered it. Thus, few of the stories actually get told to foreigners, not because of a deficit of storytellers, but because listeners are so few and far between. [. . .]

Wouldn't it be preferable if, instead of reading my narrative about El Mozote, we could listen directly to those who lived there recount the pride that they had in their community, the joy of the fiestas, the difficulty of making a living, the hard work involved in securing the cemetery and school and in organizing the agricultural cooperative? They would tell us of the bodies that showed up one day in the cemetery, the sounds of the shells that fell on La Guacamaya on the other side of the hill, and the rumors of an impending invasion of army troops who would exterminate the population. We would want to hear from those who fled [...] – impoverished but hopeful – to a devastated land where instead of salvation they found more tribulation: continuing military repression and harassment (until the war ended), barren soil, a lack of employment opportunities, and rudimentary shelter.

It would be best, I think, if we were shucking corn, sorting beans, or engaged in some other repetitive task that relaxes the mind. "Boredom," Walter Benjamin (1968: 91) tells us, "is the dream bird that hatches the egg of experience. A rustling in the leaves drives him away." Then, perhaps, we would drive the ticking hands of the clock back to zero and learn again how to let the words of the storyteller fill our heads. Therein lies the danger of this account of El Mozote's people and their history, and of analogous accounts of other peoples and events: the conversion of stories, vibrant and living, into information, dead and self-contained, through their inscription and analysis. But if I have taken stories told to me and transformed them into information for reproduction, consumption, and disposal, I have at least sought to mitigate the worst of the effects by organizing that information in a way that owes more to the oral historian than to the archivist, more to the testimonial than to the ethnography. I have assumed (I think) a consistent political register marked by an identification with the plight of the poor and a cynicism regarding the claims of power; and I have tried to show how the El Mozote massacre, a short episode in a long civil war, draws people and relationships together over vast distances and decades of time. It is linked in a complex chain of causalities to Cortés and Pedro de Alvarado; it references the violent dispossession of peasants from the fertile volcanic uplands during the last quarter of the nineteenth century and the first quarter of the twentieth (it is likely that some of the refugees from those displacements settled in northern Morazán); El Mozote descends from the great matanza of 1932, when several thousand desperate peasants challenged the oligarchical system and tens of thousands were indiscriminately slaughtered by its defenders. And without doubt "El Mozote" is a call for reflection upon the human dimension of the US counterin-

surgency strategies launched at the beginning of the 1960s. El Mozote is one tragic chapter in the long, bloody history of capitalism, [...] as well as a portent of those histories that are to come and the brutalities that will surely accompany them. On the other hand, I have also suggested an alternative future in which El Mozote, to borrow a phrase from the epigraph to this chapter, becomes one of those memories that future generations "seize hold of ... at a moment of danger."

The "Preferential Option" and the Limits of Anthropology

Benjamin states that "there is no story for which the question as to how it continued would not be legitimate" (1968: 100). The testimonial – which provides the architectural framework for my narrative – is a type of story distinguished from other categories of stories by the intimate relationship between the teller and the account. For nontestimonial stories, a storyteller's audience can become storytellers in their own right – simplifying, embellishing, or restructuring what they have heard as they see fit before sharing it with others. But the testimonial loses its moral force and much of its truth value when recounted by anyone other than the witness who lived the experiences that are at the heart of the narrative. It is at that point that my effort to model *this* story on the testimonial encounters its limits.

As a storyteller in the generic sense rather than a witness to a lived experience, I have been able to do no more than share the testimonies that northern Morazanians shared with me during interviews and conversations. Invariably, I have translated their accounts in ways that might not please every one of the people who contributed to the construction of this narrative, but such is the contradiction between the speaker and the scribe, the telling and its translation. In anthropology this contradiction – between those who are at liberty to describe the cultures of others and those others less able to contest their objectification, whose beliefs and practices are described – lies at the heart of the ethnographic enterprise; it will exist as long as some people have the desire and, more significantly, the opportunity and the power to make objects of the lives of others. [...]

There exists no contradiction between anthropology and imperialism per se; the majority of anthropologists only object when imperialist intervention threatens the physical existence of the subjects who are the bearers of the ideas and practices that they study. In El Salvador those prospective subjects – "exotic" Native Americans – were mostly killed off during the 1932 matanza, with the result that El Salvador never developed a reputation in the United States or Europe as a desirable field site for anthropological work. With notable exceptions few US anthropologists protested in print the slaughter perpetrated by their government and the Salvadoran military on tens of thousands of mestizo peasants, workers, and students. On the other hand, more anthropologists responded to the Guatemalan military's scorched-earth policies that were wiping out thousands of highland Mayans who had for decades served up the ethnographic "raw material" for the molding of academic reputations. But even in Guatemala, the response was muted; only a handful of the dozens of anthropologists who had carried out research there got involved. [. . .]

Anthropology's historic subjects have, as defined by that "tradition," been among the oppressed, so why haven't the various dimensions of oppression (social, economic, political) assumed a more prominent role within anthropological discourse? And more importantly, why haven't more anthropologists committed themselves to political *engagement* on behalf of their subjects, rather than confining most of their energies to sharing materials with like-minded colleagues through specialist books and journals? [. . .]

Some in the field argue that extreme cultural relativism or a rigid commitment to science and "objectivity" account for some anthropologists' political passivity before human rights violations. Radical cultural relativists cannot agree on a universal code of human rights (Schirmer 1988: 92; Dundes Renteln 1990; cf. Messer 1993: 224), while some science-oriented anthropologists hide behind a self-imposed "neutral observer status" and professional division between research and application to justify their lack of involvement. [. . .]

Anthropologists are "establishment" products, and those who have found jobs within the system have made their peace with it: most are locked into a comfort zone of middle-class rewards, reveling in their "liberalism" and parrying the stickier moral questions that occasionally confront them as they jet back and forth between materially under-stocked field settings in the South and materially overstocked homes in the North. A significant percentage are now employed outside academia. For most (not all, of course) of these "practicing anthropologists," anthropology has become a job for which the parameters and constraints (what can and cannot be investigated and said) are set by their employers. "[T]he educated and cultured of the world, the well-born and well-bred, and even the deeply pious and philanthropic" cannot escape the contradiction that they "receive their training and comfort and luxury, the ministrations of delicate beauty and sensibility, on condition that they neither inquire [too closely] into the real source of their income and the methods of distribution nor interfere with the legal props which rest on a pitiful human foundation of writhing white and yellow and brown and black bodies" (Du Bois 1986).

Is Du Bois's thesis so radical? *Should* we expect otherwise? *Should* we expect an entire category of mostly European American, "accommodated" intellectuals to develop a trenchant critique of the system that feeds them, and, more importantly, to work actively toward both a national and global redistribution of wealth, power, and privilege, *including their own?* Could anthropology survive in a worldwide system of social and economic equality in which the ethnographer toils without the support of either the imperial headquarters or a neocolonial subsidiary and in which the erstwhile "informants" have *the absolute right of refusal* to serve as subjects of anthropological projects? [. . .]

Anthropology will doubtlessly persist as long as do the inequalities that enable its practice. And those inequalities are growing both inside the capitalist "centers" and in the "peripheries" into which capital is expanding (Asia, Latin America) or from which it is retracting (e.g., large areas of West Africa). My encounters with the survivors of El Mozote, and with many other people in northern Morazán and elsewhere, lead me to suggest, therefore, that anthropologists hesitant to abandon the discipline follow the lead of liberation theology and adopt a "preferential option for the poor." [. . .]

Practicing the preferential option for the poor means struggling and working closely with grassroots organizations in the investigation of human rights abuses; it means scrutinizing the institutions and agencies that are at the forefront of the "New World Order"; it means anthropologists working actively in their own communities to oppose the growing assault on social programs such as welfare, public education, and public housing; it means dedicating more time to translation and dissemination of materials produced by people who have little or no access to a larger public in the decision-making imperial centers and sponsoring, as well, speaking tours in which witnesses testify directly to the chaos being wreaked upon them as well as to their resistance to it; and finally, it means working within colleges, universities, and other institutions to increase the representation on faculties and staffs of people of color *beyond the token level* so as to sharpen anthropology's internal critique, politicize the discipline, and hasten the arrival of a day when anthropology will die a dignified death rather than the unseemly one toward which it lurches at present. Whether intercultural investigation and knowledge production would proceed on the basis of another set of relationships, methods, and procedures; whether people would assume all responsibility for explaining themselves to others; or whether, in the future, such explanation would even be warranted or desirable, I cannot say. I can only say that the practice of anthropology *as we now know it* would be inconceivable. [...]

The violations of basic human rights are regular and predictable products of capitalism, and they define what Nancy Scheper-Hughes (1992) calls "the violence of everyday life." The maintenance of such violence is only possible through the use of state-sponsored violence that "tries to hinder the struggle against injustice by taking preventive measures" (Ellacuría 1991a: 40). As a result the human rights of the majority of Salvadorans are doubly violated: in their daily intercourse workers and peasants are deprived of the essentials to life; and when they protest and organize to seek redress, they are murdered, beaten, tortured, and disappeared. Pacifists eschew violence in favor of nonviolent routes to change, but the history of El Salvador and many other countries demonstrates that revolutionary violence is but the original violence of the ruling classes and their supporters turned back upon them – the violence that derives from exploitation, political repression, and ideological depreciation. "The rebel armed resistance," stated Edward Herman and Frank Brodhead, "was an *effect* not a *cause* of violence" (1984: 10). Without the original sources of violence, revolutionary violence (of the FMLN and opposition

groups in other countries) would not exist; it would have no rationale.

The Peace Accords, demobilization of the FMLN, and the general elections of March 1994 have not stemmed the violence of everyday life in El Salvador, which will continue to grow in magnitude unless there is a two-fold redistribution of wealth: a redistribution from North (imperialist capitalist centers) to South (neocolonies) and an internal redistribution of wealth from that small minority of immensely wealthy Salvadoran capitalists to the large majority of struggling workers, peasants, and unemployed whose labor was the source of their fortunes. Drawing on material from a wide variety of sources, the Human Rights Committee of El Salvador, Nongovernmental, summarized the dismal state of social and economic rights almost two years after the end of the civil war. El Salvador's literacy rate remained unchanged at 67 percent; infant mortality was 50 per 1,000 live births, one of the highest rates in Latin America; over half the children under the age of 5 showed signs of malnutrition; and 44 percent of the population lacked access to health services. Sixty percent of the population was classified as "impoverished," and 28 percent lived in "conditions of extreme poverty nationally" (CDHES-NG 1993: 21–2). The authors concluded, "All these 1993 statistics show the persistence of structural conditions that could, at some moment in El Salvador's future as they did in the past, become the immediate cause of widening internal social conflicts and even military conflicts" (23). In other words, a radical reconfiguration of Salvadoran society is the sine qua non for a reduction in the everyday violence from which most other forms of violence originate.

Since 1993 income distribution has worsened despite hundreds of millions of dollars in international assistance for reconstruction and $700–800 million in annual remittances from Salvadorans living outside the country. [...] Right now in Latin America the wealthy make war on the poor through free-trade agreements and structural adjustment programs (see NACLA 1993), while in the United States, welfare recipients, public schools, and affirmative action policies are among the major targets of domestic structural adjustment. ("Structural adjustment," whether the International Monetary Funds-sponsored version or the domestic government-sponsored version, has the goal of "readjusting" income distribution to the benefit of the wealthiest 5 to 10 percent of the population.) In the long run in El Salvador the campaign now under way to reduce the state's role in the economy and to channel all exchanges of goods and services through the market will cause more pain and suffering than did the 12-year civil war concluded in February 1992. Everyday life will become increasingly violent for the vast majority of the population. But impelled by the depredations of the present and drawing on the reservoirs of past struggles, Salvadorans will continue to organize and struggle to create an alternative future. There is no option to this. It behooves those of us who identify with the preferential option for the poor to listen, to learn, and to struggle at their sides, for in this very intertwined global economy that capital has configured to the benefit of the few, their future – the future of the masses there and here – is the future of us all.

REFERENCE

Benjamin, Walter. 1968. *Illuminations*, ed. Hannah Arendt. New York: Schocken.

CDHBS-NG (Comité de Derechos Humanos de El Salvador, No (obernamental), 1993. "Report on the Human Rights Situation in El Salvador." *La Viz*. Special edition. San Salvador.

Du Bois, W. E. B. 1986. "'To the World' (Manifesto of the Second Pan-African Congress)," In W. E. B. Du Bois, *Pamphlets and Leaflets*, comp. and ed. Herbert Aptheker, pp. 194–9. White Plains, NY: Kraus-Thompson.

Dundes Renteln, Alison, 1990. *International Human Rights: Universalism versus Relativism*, Newbury Park, CA: Sage.

Ellacurfa, Ignacio. 1993. "Liberation Theology and Socio-historical Change in Latin America." In Hassell and Lacey, eds., *Towards a Society That Serves Its Peoples*, pp. 19–43.

Hassell, John, and Hugh Lacey, eds. 1991. *Towards a Society That Serves Its People: The Intellectual Contribution of El Salvador's Murdered Jesuits*, Washington, DC: Georgetown University Press.

Herman, Edward S. and Frank Brodhead. 1984. *Demonstration Elections: U.S.-Staged Elections in the Dominican Republic, Vietnam and El Salvador*. Boston: South End.

Messer, Ellen. 1993. "Anthropology and Human Rights." *Annual Review of Anthropology* 22: 221–49.

NACLA. 1993. "A Market Solution for the Americas". NACLA 26, no. 4: 16–46.

Scheper-Hughes, Nancy. 1992. *Death without Weeping: The Violence of Everyday Life in Brazil*. Berkeley: University of California Press.

Schirmer, Jennifer. 1988. "The Dilemma of Cultural Diversity and Equivalency in Universal Human Rights Standards." In *Human Rights and Anthropology*, eds. Theodore Downing and Gilbert Kushner, pp. 91–113. Cambridge, MA: Cultural Survival.

56

The Continuum of Violence in War and Peace: Post-Cold War Lessons from El Salvador

Philippe Bourgois

When the bombardments and strafing began, I was told to crouch beside a tree trunk and, whatever I did, not to move. They shot at anything that moved.

During the first four days about 15 women and children were wounded, shrapnel was removed and amputations were performed with absolutely no pain medicine. The government troops encircling us were pressing in on foot, killing whoever they encountered.

On the fourth night we found ourselves running along a rocky path when we reached the government's line of fire. The babies the women were carrying began shrieking at the noise of the shooting and as soon as we got within earshot of the government soldiers they turned their fire on us.

It was pandemonium, grenades were landing all around; machine guns were firing; we were running; stumbling; falling; trying to make it through the barrage of bullets and shrapnel. A little boy about 20 yards ahead of me was blown in half when a grenade landed on him. His body lay in the middle of the narrow path. I had to run right over him to escape. [*Washington Post*, Dec. 28, 1982b]

In the first 13 months I spent in Spanish Harlem I witnessed:

– A deadly shooting, outside my window, of the mother of a 3-year-old child, by an assailant wielding a sawed-off shotgun.

– A bombing and a machine-gunning of a numbers joint, once again within view of my apartment window.

– A shoot-out and a police-car chase scene in front of a pizza parlor where I happened to be eating a snack.

– The aftermath of the firebombing of a heroin house.

– A dozen screaming, clothes-ripping fights.

– Almost daily exposure to broken-down human beings, some of them in fits of crack-induced paranoia, some suffering from delirium tremens, and others in unidentifiable pathological fits screaming and shouting insults to all around them.

Perhaps the most poignant expression of the pervasiveness of the culture of terror was the comment made to me by a 13-year-old boy in the course of an otherwise innocuous conversation about how his mother's pregnancy was going. He told me he hoped his mother would give birth to a boy "because girls are too easy to rape." [*New York Times Magazine*, Nov. 12, 1989]

These paragraphs are excerpted from newspaper pieces that I wrote in the 1980s to call attention to violence in two very different settings where I was then conducting fieldwork: the first is among revolutionary peasants in rural El Salvador and the second among second-generation Puerto Rican crack dealers in East Harlem, New York City. Moving from one site to the next, I became interested in differentiating the forms and meanings assumed by violence in war and peace in order to document the ways in which it either challenges or buttresses inequalities of power.

The political context in which I was operating in the 1980s deeply affected what I was able to document empirically and analyze theoretically. In Central America, I labored under an unconscious Cold-War imperative that led me to sanitize my depictions of political violence and repression among revolutionary peasants. On a theoretical level, this obscured the multisided character of violence and the commonalities among its various subtypes of violence across historical, cultural, and political settings. Most importantly, my Cold-War lenses led me to underreport and misrecognize the power of violence to buttress patterns of social inequality in the public's eye, and to depoliticize attempts to oppose oppression in wartime El Salvador. By contrast, in the racialized urban core of the United States, I was able to critique the demobilizing effects of everyday violence by showing how it resulted from the internalization of historically entrenched structural violence as expressed in a banalized maelstrom of interpersonal and delinquent aggression.

To unravel the interrelated strands of violence that complicated my understanding of revolutionary El Salvador as compared to the declining US inner city, I have found it useful to distinguish between four types of violence, namely political, structural, symbolic, everyday violence:

Direct Political: Targeted physical violence and terror administered by official authorities and those opposing it, such as military repression, police torture, and armed resistance.

Structural: Chronic, historically entrenched political-economic oppression and social inequality, ranging from exploitative international terms of trade to abusive local working conditions and high infant mortality rates. Term brought into academic debates by Galtung (1969, 1975).

Symbolic: Defined in Bourdieu's (1997) work as the internalized humiliations and legitimations of inequality and hierarchy ranging from sexism and racism to intimate expressions of class power. It is "exercised through cognition and misrecognition, knowledge and sentiment, with the unwitting consent of the dominated" (Bourdieu 2001; see also Bourdieu and Wacquant 1992: 162–73, 200–5).

Everyday: Daily practices and expressions of violence on a micro-interactional level: interpersonal, domestic and delinquent. Concept adapted from Scheper-Hughes (1992, 1996) to focus on the individual lived experience that normalizes petty brutalities and terror at the community level and creates a common sense or ethos of violence.

This reinterpretation of my ethnographic data reveals how I was unable to recognize the distinctiveness of everyday violence in revolutionary El Salvador and therefore failed to discern it to be a product of political and structural violence, despite the fact that I had effectively understood everyday violence to be at the interface of structural and symbolic violence in the US inner city.

The Cold-War Politics of Representation in El Salvador

The opening vignette depicting the military repression of revolutionary peasants in El Salvador was written in 1981 during the final escalation of the Cold War. El Salvador was then in the midst of a civil war pitting a right-wing military government against a coalition of socialist guerilla organizations known as the Farabundo Marti National Liberation Front (FMLN). For most of the twentieth century the United States had invoked a rhetoric of defending the free world from communism to justify supporting a succession of military regimes in the country. In 1981, at the time of my fieldwork, an average of almost 800 people were being killed every month by the Salvadoran military and its affiliated death squads (Americas Watch 1985; United Nations 1993). During this period, the Salvadoran government depended upon US military, political, and economic support for its survival, receiving a total of over 4 billion dollars during the 1980s, more than any other nation except Egypt and Israel (Wallace 2000).

While conducting exploratory fieldwork for my dissertation in rural El Salvador among supporters of the FMLN guerrillas, I found myself caught with the local residents in the middle of a government scorched-earth campaign. Army troops surrounded and carried out aerial bombardment of a 40-square-mile region that was home to a dozen pro-FMLN small-farmer villages. They followed up with infantry destroying as much of the infrastructure as possible – crops, livestock, houses. They killed and sometimes tortured the people they captured. Alongside the civilian population of approximately 1,000 peasants, I ran for my life for 14 days before finally reaching safety as a refugee in neighboring Honduras. Accompanied by no more than a hundred armed FMLN fighters, we hid during the day and fled at night. The guerrillas, most of whom were born and raised in the area, moved along our flanks in an attempt to protect us, but we were continually strafed, bombed, and pursued by the Salvadoran military's airplanes, helicopters, and ground troops. Government soldiers were guided by especially brutal paramilitary fighters recruited from among the neighboring villagers.

At the time, it appeared to me that state repression of the civilian population was backfiring. The pain, fear, and anguish caused by the military campaign was strengthening the ideological and emotional commitment of the civilian population to rebellion. In short, repression was radicalizing the marginalized small farmers. Their mobilization into armed struggle appeared to be socially as well as individually liberating – similar to the dynamic heralded by Frantz Fanon (1963) and Sartre (1963) during the anticolonial war of Algerians against France. The Salvadoran peasants were organizing around an ideology that syncretized Catholic liberation theology, marxist class struggle, romantic socialist populism, and, finally, social vengeance and personal dignity (Bourgois 1982a). Most significant was the quasi-messianic quality of their rejection of humiliation and exploitation by landlords and the rural paramilitaries. They were inverting a symbolic violence that, for generations, had naturalized the abuse of dark-skinned, illiterate *campesinos*. I described the Salvadoran peasants as metamorphosing,

from being the most despised creatures on earth (i.e., landless or land-poor laborers, giving obligatory days worth of labor to overbearing landowners) to becoming the leaders of history: the people the Bible prophesies about. They felt honored to die for their cause because before its advent they had been half dead – and it hurt. (Bourgois 1982a: 24)

My fieldwork notes from the days just prior to the military invasion in 1981 report that a surprisingly high number of the Salvadoran guerrilla fighters had repented past histories of alcoholism and domestic violence. In a politically engaged article published at the height of the war, I quoted the emblematic words of one guerrilla fighter: "We used to be *machista*. We used to put away a lotta drink and cut each other up. But then the Organization showed us the way, and we've channeled that violence for the benefit of the people" (Bourgois 1982a: 24–5). In other words, political violence among FMLN supporters was decreasing major dimensions of interpersonal everyday violence – including drunken brawling and wife beating.

The Neoliberal Politics of Representation in El Barrio, USA

In contrast to the liberating dynamic of political violence in El Salvador, I understood the everyday violence that pervades the US inner city described in the second opening vignette as strictly oppressive

and demobilizing. In the late 1980s, I spent nearly five years living in a tenement with my family next to a crackhouse in East Harlem, New York City. There, I befriended a group of Puerto Rican street-level crack dealers, reconstructed their life stories, and observed their daily struggles for sustenance and self-respect (see Chapters 37 and 43 in this volume). The frequent beatings and periodic shootings and stabbings between the young men I spent most of my time with, and the ongoing fracas within their families, was more challenging for me to analyze theoretically and politically than the violence of wartime El Salvador. The crack commerce scene offered a window onto the mechanisms whereby structural and symbolic violence fuse to translate themselves into an everyday violence. Extreme segregation, social inequality, and material misery express themselves at ground level in interpersonal conflicts that the socially vulnerable inflict mainly onto themselves (via substance abuse), onto their kin and friends (through domestic violence and adolescent gang rape), and onto their neighbors and community (with burglaries, robberies, assaults, drive-by shootings, etc.). The result is a localized "culture of terror," (Taussig 1987), or a heightened level of everyday violence that enforces the boundaries of what I call US inner-city apartheid (Bourgois 1995). More subtly, it turns the social suffering of US-style neoliberal capitalism into a public secret and allows symbolic violence to prevail: blaming the poor – and getting the poor to blame themselves for their poverty.

As a member of the dominant culture and class in the United States, I worried about the political as well as scholarly implications of my ethnographic depiction of Puerto-Rican crack dealers. I feared contributing to a "pornography of violence" that submerges the structural causes of urban destitution under lurid details of blood, aggression, and gore. As noted long ago by Laura Nader (1972), anthropological accounts based on participant-observation among the powerless risk publicly humiliating them. This is especially true in the context of the hegemonic US neoliberal ideology which, by definition, considers the poor as morally suspect. Yet I was theoretically and politically committed to fully documenting the social suffering caused by extreme social and economic marginality in East Harlem. This quandary encouraged me to focus on structural violence and later symbolic violence, which are concepts that by definition shift attention onto the broader, macro-level power inequalities that condition everyday violence.

By the end of my sojourn in East Harlem, just as the Cold War was coming to a close, I presented a paper at a session of the American Anthropological Association in which I attempted to compare patterns and experiences of violence in wartorn rural El Salvador and the peacetime US inner city (Bourgois 1992). In highlighting the difference between direct political violence and invisible structural violence in that paper, I thought I was transcending Cold War ideology, but instead I mimicked it. For, throughout my analysis, I maintained a moral opposition between "worthy" political violence that rallies the subordinate in the face of repression by an authoritarian state versus "unworthy" violence that confuses and demobilizes the socially vulnerable in neoliberal democratic societies. My concern with differentiating all-good from all-bad violence, and for separating out politically progressive from self-destructive and irresponsible violence, prevented me from understanding how violence operates along multiple, overlapping planes along a continuum that ranges from the interpersonal and delinquent to the self-consciously political and purposeful. It also encompasses structural, institutional, and historical forms as well as symbolic, cultural, and ideological ones. Specifically, I failed to see how political repression and resistance in wartime reverberate in a dynamic of everyday violence akin to that produced by the fusing of structural and symbolic violence during peacetime. I was unprepared to recognize the "gray zone" that the Auschwitz survivor, Primo Levi (see Chapter 8, this volume), describes. Those who are condemned to survive under conditions of extreme hierarchy and cruelty jockey for survival at one another's expense. The gray zone itself is a continuum permeating to a greater or lesser extent any social setting where inequality and suffering is imposed by structural and symbolic forces.

Instead, I constructed a Gramscian-inspired explanation for why the guerrilla experience of repressive political violence in El Salvador could be interpreted as humanly uplifting and politically liberating through the physical pain and anger it generated. I contrasted that dynamic to the everyday acts of violence that I had witnessed in East Harlem, which I interpreted as the expression of false consciousness in a structurally and symbolically oppressive society that no longer needs to wield political violence to buttress its structures of inequality. Gramsci's theory of hegemony is a valuable tool, but the ways in which I categorized violence as worthy versus unworthy in that paper directly shaped what I was able to see, hear and believe; what I interpreted as "data" and what I took fieldwork notes on; and which debates I viewed as pertinent and sought to engage. On an empirical level, whereas I amply documented the range of suffering caused by structural and symbolic violence in a socially polarized society during peacetime, I oversimplified and understated the ramifications of terror in a repressive society torn by civil war. By failing to recognize the continuum of violence in war and peace I was unprepared in the case of El Salvador for the rapidity and ease of the transition from political violence to delinquent and interpersonal violence during peacetime in the neoliberal context of ongoing structural and symbolic violence. I had failed to recognize the ongoing everyday violence that had operated at the height of the civil war camouflaged in political violence that was mimetic of state repression.

Rewriting Fieldnotes from the Salvadoran Civil War

Referring back to the opening vignette, I can still vividly remember that night of November 14, 1981, when I found myself running through the military's line of fire with about 1,000 terrified men, women, and children. I have a different vocabulary to describe the victims, however. For example, I might now refer to the mutilated "little boy" writhing in front of me with his torso severed as a "teenage fighter," since he was carrying an automatic weapon even though he was no more than 14 years old. The political strictures of the Cold War, however, made it important, indeed imperative, to label him "little boy" rather than "teenage fighter," because, in the martial vision of that conflict prevalent in the early eighties, adolescents carrying automatic weapons deserved to be killed. The human pathos of a child dying in face-to-face combat while defending his family from marauding government soldiers would have been missed.

More subtly, and perhaps more importantly, I have different memories of the moments before

I ran over the body of that boy fighter. I rewrote an *ex-post-facto* fieldwork excerpts 18 years after the fact emphasizing what I now remember. When I prepared the original newspaper piece in 1981, I had not been able to fully remember or analyze these events. Perhaps I thought these details were unimportant. Once again, in the context of the Cold War, my primary concern was to spotlight the more objectionable power vectors aimed at small farmers in El Salvador, namely, the repressive military regime maintained by US foreign policy. I may also have omitted these memories from my fieldnotes because I sensed that they might reveal a personal character flaw on my part:

When the grenade landed on the teenage fighter up ahead, I dove into the dirt behind some bushes. I accidentally jostled a young mother who was already crouching behind the bushes where I landed. I startled her six-month-old baby and it began to cry. With me panting next to them, huge, foreign, and stinking of strange sweat and panic, the baby's cries spiraled into wailing shrieks.

The mother hissed in my ear, "<u>Vete! Vete de aqui!</u> <u>Rapido!</u>" [Get out of here! Scram!]. At first, shocked, I thought she was angry at me and was being cruel, pushing me off into the hail of bullets. Suddenly, it dawned on me that she was trying to save my life: her baby's cries were beginning to cut through the sound of the gunfire. I jumped to my feet and sprinted forward, just as another barrage of machine guns fired into the shrieks of mothers and babies that I left behind me.

This was my first participant-observation exposure to the kind of human betrayal that survivors commit in counterinsurgency warfare. Making a baby cry and then running from it when one realizes that those cries will attract gunfire forced me to fail my own sense of human dignity and masculinity, and to question my self-esteem. It also bordered on symbolic violence by causing me to be angry at both myself and the FMLN for making the civilians the target of government repression.

I do not know for sure if the mother and baby died in the bullets directed at the infant's cries. I suspect that they were both killed. Had I not startled that baby, it would have turned 20 as this article goes to press. Maybe if I had been smarter and sprinted away sooner when the baby's mother begged me to, then the infant's wailing would not

have escalated into shrieking and the government soldiers may not have heard it. A decade later, conversations with guerrilla fighters and their families demonstrate that those kinds of blames and feelings of betrayal over human failures abound in counterinsurgency warfare. They are an inevitable part of surviving military repression and they contribute to a form of symbolic violence whereby survivors focus their recriminations on their fellow victims' as well as their own character flaws, rather than on the agents who actually perpetrated terror. The result is often a traumatized silencing of the brutal events by witnesses who blame themselves for what they had to do to survive. It provides a glimpse of the basis for what psychologists call "survivor guilt" – fallout from the gray zone.

During that same night when we ran through the government troops encircling us, I passed parents and older siblings stumbling under the weight of terrified children or wounded family members. I wondered as I fled if I was supposed to stop and do something to help them. Convinced that we were all going to die, I ran for my life feeling that I was betraying those left behind. As dawn rose, most of us managed to reassemble at the bottom of a ravine to hide together. We hoped that the guerrilla fighters might be able to offer us some protection and we prayed that the government helicopters and ground troops combing the area would not find us. As my photograph from that moment illustrates, a few well-aimed grenades or rounds of automatic fire directed into our hiding place would have sufficed to kill several hundred of us. Luckily, when a helicopter did fly over the ravine, only a couple dozen feet immediately above us, it strafed the fighters who had stationed themselves on the hillside and it failed to detect us. The guerrillas above us dispersed rapidly and successfully drew the enemy fire away from us.

For the next eight days almost 1,000 of us stayed close together, striving to minimize our noise at night as we moved to new hiding places and scavenged for food in the underbrush. On several occasions we were spotted by Salvadoran troops and strafed by US-supplied gunships or chased by ground patrols. Each time we ran as fast as possible to hide behind trees or boulders, hoping that those carrying weapons were decoying the enemy away from us.

It was the young, healthy, and fleet-footed, consequently, who had the best chance of surviving. At sunset, on the eighth day of our flight (twelfth day after the start of the attack), under particularly heavy bombardment, I found myself chasing after a small group of men who appeared to know their way. Most of them were fighters who had thrown away the guns with which they were supposed to be protecting their families. Instead, we ran fast all night in what felt like selfish terror. Further and further behind us, we could hear the sounds of crying children drawing the bulk of the fire. We escaped alive as refugees into neighboring Honduras before the sun rose and listened for the rest of the day as government helicopters blasted the slower moving, noisy mass of civilians we had left behind. If my companions from that final night of flight survived until the end of the war, they likely still feel survivor guilt today.

Throughout the civil war, US and Salvadoran government propaganda denounced the guerrillas for hiding amidst the civilians and thereby causing them to be killed in the crossfire. The FMLN leadership itself was divided over its policy of encouraging – and at times demanding – civilians and family members of fighters to remain in the war zones. Spouses were often in bitter disagreement over this issue. In retrospect, mothers sometimes hold husbands responsible for the death of their children because the latter insisted on remaining in their home village to support the FMLN. By 1983, a little over a year after this scorched-earth campaign, the guerrillas changed their tactics and evacuated the majority of nonfighters from the most actively contested war zones. The point here is that the boundary between protector and coward is often ambiguous and inconsistent in counterinsurgency warfare. Such a "liminal space of death" (Taussig 1987) or gray zone obfuscates responsibility from those primarily responsible for the terror – in this case the US-trained and supported Salvadoran military. Instead, the snares of symbolic violence – in the form of confused feelings of inadequacy, guilt, and mutual recriminations – deflect attention away from the repressive political violence that created the conditions of terror which imposed a bitter choice between survival and betrayal.

Violence in War and Peace

During the summer of 1994, with the Cold War over, I revisited the same resettled villages of guerrilla fighters and supporters where I had been trapped during the military attack of 1981. Most immediately tangible was the silent brutality of economic oppression. My first set of fieldnotes from that visit describe the intersection of the scars of structural and political violence on the local ecology and the bodies of residents:

July, 1994
Due to land scarcity the villagers are forced to farm steep, rocky terrain. As if to add insult to injury, badly healed wounds from the war make it difficult for many of the young men to even hobble up to their awkwardly pitched milpas [farm plots]. Even the earth appears disabled and angry: carved by rivulets of runoff from exposure to the heavy rain and pock-marked by sharp protruding stones.

Tito, the son of the woman whose house we are staying in, fought for almost ten years with the FMLN. Now, he limps up the incline to the eroded hillside where he tries to scrape together a crop of corn and sorghum with only his machete and a digging stick. He uses his digging stick as a cane to keep from falling in his field, and he occasionally grimaces from the shrapnel still lodged in his calf and knee.

No one is particularly sympathetic to Tito, however, because he now has an alcohol problem. It is whispered that he was not a particularly brave fighter during the war.

I had hoped that this return visit would be a cathartic reunion with the people I had bonded with during the 14-day military raid of 1981. It turned out to be an awkward and at times disillusioning experience of tip-toeing around minefields of misdeeds, deception, and disloyalty. My friends insisted upon telling me about what military mistakes had been made; which wounded person had been abandoned and left to the enemy; that a particular undersized and cognitively challenged child had been permanently damaged by the five-pill valium overdose given to him by his mother to quiet his crying during the flight; which fighters had deserted; how it felt to shoot a friend in the head when he was wounded so that the enemy would not capture and torture him into revealing the identity and location of guerrillas; how it felt to be a father who forced his scared 14-year-old son to join the guerrilla only have him killed by airborn gattling guns in his very first sortie. Thirteen years after the armistice, my closest friend, José, was troubled by the fact that he had planted over 150 homemade land mines on the hillside paths leading to his guerrilla encampment. He was convinced that most of these mines had mutilated a soldier's foot, and that his former enemies were now hobbling up and down a steep hillside in a neighboring village, trying to eke out a harvest of corn to keep their families alive, just as he and his father were.

The notes from my first day of fieldwork also include a description of the infected cut on the foot of Tito's 10-year-old little brother. Ridden with fever, he moaned listlessly in a hammock in the house of the family sheltering me. There was no access to medical care in the entire region. I feared that this little boy was going to die from blood poisoning due to this simple cut. But he survived and five years later, in 1999, I learned that he killed Tito, whose alcoholism had escalated. At the murder trial of her 15-year-old, the mother, who had lost her husband during the civil war to military repression, begged the judge – unsuccessfully – not to incarcerate the only surviving male of her household: she beseeched mercy on grounds that the teenager had only tried to protect her from her oldest son, Tito, who beat her savagely when he drank too much.

One of the most disturbing stories I collected during this return visit was that of a mother who suffocated two of her infants while hiding in a cave with a dozen other villagers. They had not followed us during the night when we broke through the government troops surrounding us. Fearing that the Salvadoran military would otherwise detect their presence, her companions gave her the choice of either leaving the cave or stuffing rags into the mouths of her hysterically crying children. Over a decade later, there was disagreement over whether the father, who had made it through the line of fire that night, was justified in subsequently abandoning the mother for killing their two offspring. Some hailed the mother as a hero for having chosen to sacrifice her babies in an attempt to safeguard the lives of her companions in the cave. They condemned the father for having left her behind that night. It was taken for granted that she would have been captured, had she left the cave with her crying children, and under torture she likely would have revealed the location of her hidden companions. Nevertheless, years later, doubts persist over the moral worth of the hapless mother and the angry father, yet again blurring the boundary between hero and villain in counterinsurgency war.

Finally I began hearing stories of executions of fighters and even of pro-guerrilla civilians who were erroneously accused of being government spies. The wisdom of hindsight allows one to see clearly how the revolutionary movement in El Salvador was traumatized and distorted by the very violence it was organizing against. Through an almost mimetic process, the government's brutality was transposed into the guerrilla's organizational structures and internal relations, as violence became a banal instrumental necessity. There are several well-known prominent examples of internecine killings within the FMLN leadership. Most famously, Roque Dalton, El Salvador's most famous poet, was killed by the guerrilla organization he belonged to in the 1970s for being a "revisionist." He disagreed with his comrades over technical political strategy with respect to the timing for engaging in armed struggle. In the mid-1980s, the woman who was the second-in-command of one of the largest guerrilla factions within the FMLN coalition was killed in a leadership dispute over a strategy of continued armed struggle versus negotiation. She was reportedly stabbed 68 times by the bodyguard of Cayetano Carpio, the head of her faction, who himself is believed to have committed suicide in Nicaragua a few months later, after the assassination was finally made public. The normalization of internecine violence in the broader context of political violence makes sense if the extent of the pain and terror that political repression causes is fully appreciated as a "pressure cooker" generating everyday violence through the systematic distortion of social relations and sensibilities. It also helps explain why El Salvador had the highest per capita homicide rate in the western hemisphere during the 1990s *after* the end of the Civil War. 6,250 people per year perished from direct political violence during the civil war in the 1980s, compared to 8,700 to 11,000 killed every year by criminal violence in the 1990s following the peace accords of New Year's Eve of 1990/1 (De Cesare 1998: 23–4; Wallace 2000).

The Cold War in Academia

Writing about repression and resistance in the Salvadoran civil war for the American Anthropological Association meetings in 1992, I would not have known how to deal with internecine violence among the guerrillas. I am not sure that I could even have heard these accounts of murderous revolutionary justice – much less have tape-recorded them and written them up in my fieldnotes. Even as late as 1992, most Salvadorans who had been supportive of the FMLN during the 1980s may not have discussed internal killings with me. Indeed, I have hesitated publishing this account for several years after presenting it at an academic conference in Canada in 1997 (Bourgois 1997). I was worried that this new data might fan smoldering embers of Cold War rhetoric. But by 2002 they were openly discussed as a given of the revolutionary process. They are referred to as isolated errors, interpersonal betrayals, or systemic policy depending upon the political perspective and/or personality trait of the interlocutors.

A decade ago, I knew very well how to deal intellectually, emotionally, and politically with the fact of machine-guns shooting into the sound of crying babies in the darkness of night. With special care, I documented the human rights violations of civilians by the Salvadoran government military. The killing of some 75,000 people in El Salvador during the 1980s was directly attributable to US military, economic, and logistical support for the Salvadoran army. There is no pre- or post-Cold War questioning of that fact. Of the 22,000 denunciations of human rights violations investigated by the United Nations Truth Commission only 5 percent were found to have been committed by the FMLN compared to 85 percent by the army and 10 percent by army-linked death squads (Binford 1996: 117).

In the 1980s, my understanding of the political violence generated by US foreign policy was further truncated by the fact that my attempts to write on it and to publicize it came up against the neo-McCarthyism that pervaded public debate. Popular unrest in Central America was widely suspected of being the result of calculated communist machinations. This built-in censorship operated routinely not only in the media but in academe as well: when I gave a press conference in 1981 describing the killing of civilians in the counterinsurgency campaign I had witnessed, my university's anthropology department formally considered expelling me for what it called "unethical professional behavior" (Bourgois 1991). After I testified before the US Congress on how military aid and US military trainers were assisting in the slaughter of civilians in El Salvador, the Central Intelligence Agency circulated a report to the members of Congress who had listened to me

depicting me as a communist propagandist for the FLMN guerrillas (US Congress 1982).

In this Cold War atmosphere, it was difficult for me to perceive and portray the revolutionary Salvadoran peasants as anything less than innocent victims, at worst, or as noble resistors at best. The urgency of documenting and denouncing state violence and military repression blinded me to the internecine everyday violence embroiling the guerrillas and undermining their internal solidarity. As a result I could not understand the depth of the trauma that political violence imposes on its targets, even those mobilized to resist it. This is not to deny, however, that the peasants also took pride in mobilizing in support of the FMLN to demand their rights (cf. Wood 2000). Certain forms of everyday violence decreased in the revolutionary setting, namely drunken stabbings and wife-beating, others increased, such as killings over political disagreements and sexual jealousies.

Beyond a Pornography of Violence

In *Pascalian Meditations*, Bourdieu (1997: 233) warns that the particularly degrading "effects of symbolic violence, in particular that exerted against stigmatized populations, ... makes it ... difficult to talk about the dominated in an accurate and realistic way without seeming either to crush them or exalt them." He identifies "the inclination to violence that is engendered by early and constant exposure to violence" as "one of the most tragic effects of the condition of the dominated" and notes that the "active violence of people" is "often [directed against] one's own companions in misfortune." He sketches the following causal chain:

> The *violence exerted everyday* in families, factories, workshops, banks, offices, police stations, prisons, even hospitals and schools ... is, *in the last analysis, the product of the "inert violence"* of economic structures and social mechanisms relayed by the active violence of people. (Bourdieu 1997: 233, emphasis added)

Political, economic, and institutional forces shape micro-interpersonal and emotional interactions in all kinds of ways by supporting or suppressing modes of feeling and manifestations of love or aggression, definitions of respect and achievement, and patterns of insecurity and competition. In post-Cold War, end-of-the-century Latin America, neoliberalism actively dynamizes everyday violence. In the United States, the fusing of structural and symbolic violence produces especially destructive but persistent patterns of interpersonal violence that reinforce the legitimacy of social inequality.

Through gripping descriptions, harrowing photographs, and seductive poetics, ethnographers risk contributing to a pornography of violence that reinforces negative perceptions of subordinated groups in the eyes of unsympathetic readers. But, conversely, the imperative of painting positive portraits of the inner-city poor in the United States or of revolutionary guerrillas in El Salvador diminishes the real human devastation wrought by political repression in war and by political-economic inequality under neoliberal capitalism and obfuscates an understanding on a theoretical level of the grayness of violence. People do not simply "survive" violence as if it somehow remained outside of them. Those who confront violence with resistance – whether it be cultural or political – do not escape unscathed from the terror and oppression they rise up against. The challenge of ethnography, then, is to check the impulse to sanitize, and instead to clarify the chains of causality that link structural, political, and symbolic violence in the production of an everyday violence that buttresses unequal power relations and distorts efforts at resistance. In the post-Cold War era, a better understanding of these complex linkages is especially important because it is international market forces rather than politically-driven repression or armed resistance that is waging war for the hearts and minds of populations.

REFERENCES

Americas Watch. 1985. *Managing the Facts: How the Administration Deals with Reports of Human Rights Abuses in El Salvador.* New York: The Americas Watch Committee.

Binford, Leigh. 1996. *The El Mozote Massacre: Anthropology and Human Rights.* Tucson: University of Arizona Press.

Bourdieu, Pierre. 1997. *Pascalian Meditations.* Stanford, CA: Stanford University Press.

——. 2001. *Male Domination.* Oxford: Blackwell Publishers.

—— and Loïc Wacquant. 1992. *Invitation to Reflexive Sociology.* Chicago: University of Chicago Press.

Bourgois, Philippe. 1982a. 'What U.S. Foreign Policy Faces in Rural El Salvador: An Eyewitness Account,' *Monthly Review* 34(1): 14–30.

——. 1982b. "Running for My Life in El Salvador: An American caught in a Government Attack that Chiefly Killed Civilians," pp. C1, C5 in *The Washington Post*, Feb. 14.

——. 1989. 'Just Another Night on Crack Street,' pp. 52–3, 60–5, 94 in *New York Times Magazine*, Nov. 12.

——. 1991. 'The Ethics of Ethnography: Lessons From Fieldwork in Central America,' pp. 110–26 in Faye Harrison, ed., *Decolonizing Anthropology: Moving Further Toward an Anthropology for Liberation.* Washington, DC: Association of Black Anthropologists and American Anthropological Association.

——. 1992. 'The Pornography of Violence: Fieldwork in El Barrio and Beyond,' paper presented at the 91st Annual Meeting of the American Anthropological Association, San Francisco, Dec. 2–6.

——. 1995. *In Search of Respect: Selling Crack in El Barrio.* New York: Cambridge.

——. 1997. 'The Pornography of Violence: Fieldwork in El Salvador and the U.S. Inner City,' paper presented at the plenary session of the Canadian Anthropology Society/Congress of Learned Societies, St. John's, Newfoundland, June 13.

DeCesare, Donna. 1998. 'The Children of War: Street Gangs in El Salvador,' *NACLA* 32(1): 21–9.

Fanon, Frantz. 1963. *The Wretched of the Earth.* New York: Grove Press.

Galtung, Johan. 1969. 'Violence, Peace, and Peace Research,' *Journal of Peace Research* 6: 167–91.

——. 1975. "Peace: Research, Education, Action," *Essays in Peace Research.* Copenhagen: Christian Ejlers, Vol. 1.

Nader, Laura. 1972. 'Up the Anthropologist – Perspectives Gained from Studying Up,' pp. 284–311 in Dell Hymes, ed., *Reinventing Anthropology.* New York: Pantheon.

Sartre, Jean-Paul. 1963. 'Preface,' pp. 7–31 in Frantz Fanon, *Wretched of the Earth.* New York: Grove Press.

Scheper-Hughes, Nancy. 1992. *Death without Weeping: The Violence of Everyday Life in Brazil.* Berkeley: University of California Press.

——. 1996. 'Small Wars and Invisible Genocides,' *Social Science and Medicine* 43(5): 889–900.

Taussig, Michael. 1987. *Shamanism, Colonialism, and the Wild Man: A Study in Terror and Healing.* Chicago: University of Chicago Press.

United Nations. 1993. 'From Madness to Hope: The 12-Year War in El Salvador. Report of the Commission on the Truth for El Salvador,' Document no. S/25500.

United States Congress. 1982. 'U.S. Intelligence Performance on Central America: Achievements and Selected

Instances of Concern,' *Staff Report Subcommittee on Oversight and Evaluation-98-805 O (97th Congress, 2nd Session)*. Washington, DC: US Government Printing Office.

Wallace, Scott. 2000. 'You Must Go Home Again: Deported L.A. Gangbangers Take over El Salvador,' *Harper's Magazine* 301(1803): 47–56.

Wood, Elisabeth. 2000. 'Insurgent Collective Action and Civil War: Redrawing Boundaries of Class and Citizenship in Rural El Salvador,' Unpublished manuscript, 223 pages.

Part XI

Aftermaths

Plate 13: School in Nyarubuye Village, Rwanda, 1995. Photo © Sebastião Salgado, Contact Press Images.

57

The Witness

Giorgio Agamben

1.1   In the camp, one of the reasons that can drive a prisoner to survive is the idea of becoming a witness. "I firmly decided that, despite everything that might happen to me, I would not take my own life ... since I did not want to suppress the witness that I could become" (Langbein 1988: 186). Of course, not all deportees, indeed only a small fraction of them, give this reason. A reason for survival can be a matter of convenience: "He would like to survive for this or that reason, for this or that end, and he finds hundreds of pretexts. The truth is that he wants to live at whatever cost" (Lewental 1972: 148). Or it can simply be a matter of revenge: "Naturally I could have run and thrown myself onto the fence, because you can always do that. But I want to live. And what if the miracle happens we're all waiting for? Maybe we'll be liberated, today or tomorrow. Then I'll have my revenge, then I'll tell the whole world what happened here – inside there" (Sofsky 1997: 340). To justify one's survival is not easy – least of all in the camp. Then there are some survivors who prefer to be silent. "Some of my friends, very dear friends of mine, never speak of Auschwitz" (Levi 1997: 224). Yet, for others, the only reason to live is to ensure that the witness does not perish. "Others, on the other hand, speak of it incessantly, and I am one of them" (ibid.).

1.2   Primo Levi is a perfect example of the witness. When he returns home, he tirelessly recounts his experience to everyone. He behaves like Coleridge's Ancient Mariner:

You remember the scene: the Ancient Mariner accosts the wedding guests, who are thinking of the wedding and not paying attention to him, and he forces them to listen to his tale. Well, when I first returned from the concentration camp I did just that. I felt an unrestrainable need to tell my story to anyone and everyone! ... Every situation was an occasion to tell my story to anyone and everyone: to tell it to the factory director as well as to the worker, even if they had other things to do. I was reduced to the state of the Ancient Mariner. Then I began to write on my typewriter at night. ... Every night I would write, and this was considered even crazier! (Levi 1997: 224–5)

But Levi does not consider himself a writer; he becomes a writer so that he can bear witness. In a sense, he never became a writer. In 1963, after publishing two novels and many short stories, he responds unhesitatingly to the question of whether he considers himself a writer or a chemist: "A chemist, of course, let there be no mistake" (Levi 1997: 102). Levi was profoundly uneasy with the fact that as time passed, and almost in spite of himself, he ended up a writer, composing books that had nothing to do with his testimony: "Then I wrote. ... I acquired the vice of writing" (Levi 1997: 258). "In my latest book, *La Chiave a stella*, I stripped myself completely of my status as a witness. ... This is not to deny anything; I have not ceased to be an ex-deportee, a witness" (ibid.: 167).

Levi had this unease about him when I saw him at meetings at the Italian publisher, Einaudi. He could feel guilty for having survived, but not for

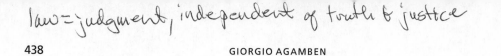
having borne witness. "I am at peace with myself because I bore witness" (ibid.: p. 219).

1.3   In Latin there are two words for "witness." The first word, *testis*, from which our word "testimony" derives, etymologically signifies the person who, in a trial or lawsuit between two rival parties, is in the position of a third party (**terstis*). The second word, *superstes*, designates a person who has lived through something, who has experienced an event from beginning to end and can therefore bear witness to it. It is obvious that Levi is not a third party; he is a survivor [*superstite*] in every sense. But this also means that his testimony has nothing to do with the acquisition of facts for a trial (he is not neutral enough for this, he is not a *testis*). In the final analysis, it is not judgment that matters to him, let alone pardon. "I never appear as judge"; "I do not have the authority to grant pardon....I am without authority" (ibid.: 77, 236). It seems, in fact, that the only thing that interests him is what makes judgment impossible: the gray zone in which victims become executioners and executioners become victims. It is about this above all that the survivors are in agreement: "No group was more human than any other" (ibid.: 232). "Victim and executioner are equally ignoble; the lesson of the camps is brotherhood in abjection" (Rousset, cf. Levi 1997: 216).

Not that a judgment cannot or must not be made. "If I had had Eichmann before me, I would have condemned him to death" (ibid.: 144). "If they have committed a crime, then they must pay" (ibid.: 236). The decisive point is simply that the two things not be blurred, that law not presume to exhaust the question. A non-juridical element of truth exists such that the *quaestio facti* can never be reduced to the *quaestio iuris*. This is precisely what concerns the survivor: everything that places a human action beyond the law, radically withdrawing it from the Trial. "Each of us can be tried, condemned and punished without even knowing why" (ibid.: 75).

1.4   One of the most common mistakes – which is not only made in discussions of the camp – is the tacit confusion of ethical categories and juridical categories (or, worse, of juridical categories and theological categories, which gives rise to a new theodicy). Almost all the categories that we use in moral and religious judgments are in some way contaminated by law: guilt, responsibility, innocence, judgment, pardon. . . . This makes it difficult to invoke them without particular caution. As jurists well know, law is not directed toward the establishment of justice. Nor is it directed toward the verification of truth. Law is solely directed toward judgment, independent of truth and justice. This is shown beyond doubt by the *force of judgment* that even an unjust sentence carries with it. The ultimate aim of law is the production of a *res judicata*, in which the sentence becomes the substitute for the true and the just, being held as true despite its falsity and injustice. Law finds peace in this hybrid creature, of which it is impossible to say if it is fact or rule; once law has produced its *res judicata*, it cannot go any further.

In 1983, the publisher Einaudi asked Levi to translate Kafka's *The Trial*. Infinite interpretations of *The Trial* have been offered; some underline the novel's prophetic political character (modern bureaucracy as absolute evil) or its theological dimension (the court as the unknown God) or its biographical meaning (condemnation as the illness from which Kafka believed himself to suffer). It has been rarely noted that this book, in which law appears solely in the form of a trial, contains a profound insight into the nature of law, which, contrary to common belief, is not so much rule as it is judgment and, therefore, trial. But if the essence of the law – of every law – is the trial, if all right (and morality that is contaminated by it) is only tribunal right, then execution and transgression, innocence and guilt, obedience and disobedience all become indistinct and lose their importance. "The court wants nothing from you. It welcomes you when you come; it releases you when you go." The ultimate end of the juridical regulation is to produce judgment; but judgment aims neither to punish nor to extol, neither to establish justice nor to prove the truth. Judgment is in itself the end and this, it has been said, constitutes its mystery, the mystery of the trial.

One of the consequences that can be drawn from this self-referential nature of judgment – and Sebastiano Satta, a great Italian jurist, has done so – is that punishment does not follow from judgment, but rather that judgment is itself punishment (*nullum judicium sine poena*). "One can even say that the whole punishment is in the judgment, that the action characteristic of the punishment – incarceration, execution – matters only insofar as it is, so to speak, the carrying out of the judgment" (Satta 1994: 26). This also means that "the sentence of acquittal is the confession of a judicial error," that "everyone is inwardly innocent," but that the only truly innocent person "is not the one who is acquitted, but rather the one who goes through life without judgment" (ibid.: 27).

1.5   If this is true – and the survivor knows that it is true – then it is possible that the trials (the twelve trials at Nuremberg, and the others that took place in and outside German borders, including those in Jerusalem in 1961 that ended with the hanging of Eichmann) are responsible for the conceptual confusion that, for decades, has made it impossible to think through Auschwitz. Despite the necessity of the trials and despite their evident insufficiency (they involved only a few hundred people), they helped to spread the idea that the problem of Auschwitz had been overcome. The judgments had been passed, the proofs of guilt definitively established. With the exception of occasional moments of lucidity, it has taken almost half a century to understand that law did not exhaust the problem, but rather that the very problem was so enormous as to call into question law itself, dragging it to its own ruin.

The confusion between law and morality and between theology and law has had illustrious victims. Hans Jonas, the philosopher and student of Heidegger who specialized in ethical problems, is one of them. In 1984, when he received the Lucas Award in Tübingen, he reflected on the question of Auschwitz by preparing for a new theodicy, asking, that is, how it was possible for God to tolerate Auschwitz. A theodicy is a trial that seeks to establish the responsibility not of men, but of God. Like all theodicies, Jonas's ends in an acquittal. The justification for the sentence is something like this: "The infinite (God) stripped himself completely, in the finite, of his omnipotence. Creating the world, God gave it His own fate and became powerless. Thus, having emptied himself entirely in the world, he no longer has anything to offer us; it is now man's turn to give. Man can do this by taking care that it never happens, or rarely happens, that God regrets his decision to have let the world be."

The conciliatory vice of every theodicy is particularly clear here. Not only does this theodicy tell us nothing about Auschwitz, either about its victims or executioners; it does not even manage to avoid a happy ending. Behind the powerlessness of God peeps the powerlessness of men, who continue to cry "May that never happen again!" when it is clear that "that" is, by now, everywhere.

1.6   The concept of responsibility is also irremediably contaminated by law. Anyone who has tried to make use of it outside the juridical sphere knows this. And yet ethics, politics, and religion have been able to define themselves only by seizing terrain from juridical responsibility – not in order to assume another kind of responsibility, but to articulate zones of nonresponsibility. This does not, of course, mean impunity. Rather, it signifies – at least for ethics – a confrontation with a responsibility that is infinitely greater than any we could ever assume. At the most, we can be faithful to it, that is, assert its unassumability.

The unprecedented discovery made by Levi at Auschwitz concerns an area that is independent of every establishment of responsibility, an area in which Levi succeeded in isolating something like a new ethical element. Levi calls it the "gray zone." It is the zone in which the "long chain of conjunction between victim and executioner" comes loose, where the oppressed becomes oppressor and the executioner in turn appears as victim. A gray, incessant alchemy in which good and evil and, along with them, all the metals of traditional ethics reach their point of fusion.

What is at issue here, therefore, is a zone of irresponsibility and *"impotentia judicandi"* (Levi 1989: 60) that is situated not *beyond* good and evil but rather, so to speak, *before* them. With a gesture that is symmetrically opposed to that of Nietzsche, Levi places ethics before the area in which we are accustomed to consider it. And, without our being able to say why, we sense that this "before" is more important than any "beyond" – that the "underman" must matter to us more than the "overman." This infamous zone of irresponsibility is our First Circle, from which no confession of responsibility will remove us and in which what is spelled out, minute by minute, is the lesson of the "terrifying, unsayable and unimaginable banality of evil" (Arendt 1992: 252).

1.7   The Latin verb *spondeo*, which is the origin of our term "responsibility," means "to become the guarantor of something for someone (or for oneself) with respect to someone." Thus, in the promise of marriage, the father would utter the formula *spondeo* to express his commitment to giving his daughter as wife to a suitor (after which she was then called a *sponsa*) or to guarantee compensation if this did not take place. In archaic Roman law, in fact, the custom was that a free man could consign himself as a hostage – that is, in a state of imprisonment, from which the term *obligatio* derives – to guarantee the compensation of a wrong or the fulfillment of an obligation. (The term *sponsor* indicated the person who substituted himself for the *reus*, promising, in the case of a breach of contract, to furnish the required service.)

The gesture of assuming responsibility is therefore genuinely juridical and not ethical. It expresses nothing noble or luminous, but rather simply obligation, the act by which one consigned oneself as a prisoner to guarantee a debt in a context in which the legal bond was considered to inhere in the body of the person responsible. As such, responsibility is closely intertwined with the concept of *culpa* that, in a broad sense, indicates the imputability of damage. (This is why the Romans denied that there could be guilt with respect to oneself: *quod quis ex culpa sua damnum sentit, non intelligitur damnum sentire*: the damage that one causes to oneself by one's own fault is not juridically relevant.)

Responsibility and guilt thus express simply two aspects of legal imputability; only later were they interiorized and moved outside law. Hence the insufficiency and opacity of every ethical doctrine that claims to be founded on these two concepts. (This holds both for Jonas, who claimed to formulate a genuine "principle of responsibility" and for Lévinas, who, in a much more complex fashion, transformed the gesture of the *sponsor* into the ethical gesture par excellence.) This insufficiency and opacity emerges clearly every time the borders that separate ethics from law are traced. Let us consider two examples, which are very far from each other as to the gravity of the facts they concern but which coincide with respect to the *distinguo* they imply.

During the Jerusalem trial, Eichmann's constant line of defense was clearly expressed by his lawyer, Robert Serviatus, with these words: "Eichmann feels himself guilty before God, not the law." Eich-

mann (whose implication in the extermination of the Jews was well documented, even if his role was probably different from that which was argued by the prosecution) actually went so far as to declare that he wanted "to hang himself in public" in order to "liberate young Germans from the weight of guilt." Yet, until the end, he continued to maintain that his guilt before God (who was for him only a *höherer Sinnesträger*, a higher bearer of meaning) could not be legally prosecuted. The only possible explanation for this insistence is that, whereas the assumption of moral guilt seemed ethically noble to the defendant, he was unwilling to assume any legal guilt (although, from an ethical point of view, legal guilt should have been less serious than moral guilt).

Recently, a group of people who once had belonged to a political organization of the extreme Left published a communiqué in a newspaper, declaring political and moral responsibility for the murder of a police officer committed twenty years ago. "Nevertheless, such responsibility," the document stated, "cannot be transformed . . . into a responsibility of penal character." It must be recalled that the assumption of moral responsibility has value only if one is ready to assume the relevant legal consequences. The authors of the communiqué seem to suspect this in some way, when, in a significant passage, they assume a responsibility that sounds unmistakably juridical, stating that they contributed to "creating a climate that led to murder." (But the offense in question, the instigation to commit a crime, is of course wiped out.) In every age, the gesture of assuming a juridical responsibility when one is innocent has been considered noble; the assumption of political or moral responsibility without the assumption of the corresponding legal consequences, on the other hand, has always characterized the arrogance of the mighty (consider Mussolini's behavior, for example, with respect to the case of Giacomo Matteotti, the member of the Italian parliament who was assassinated by unknown killers in 1924). But today in Italy these models have been reversed and the contrite assumption of moral responsibilities is invoked at every occasion as an exemption from the responsibilities demanded by law.

Here the confusion between ethical categories and juridical categories (with the logic of repentance implied) is absolute. This confusion lies at the origin of the many suicides committed to escape trial (not only those of Nazi criminals), in which the tacit assumption of moral guilt attempts to compensate for legal guilt. It is worth remembering that the primary responsibility for this confusion lies not in Catholic doctrine, which includes a sacrament whose function is to free the sinner of guilt, but rather in secular ethics (in its well-meaning and dominant version). After having raised juridical categories to the status of supreme ethical categories and thereby irredeemably confusing the fields of law ethics, secular ethics still wants to play out its *distinguo*. But ethics is the sphere that recognizes neither guilt nor responsibility; it is, as Spinoza knew, the doctrine of the happy life. To assume guilt and responsibility – which can, at times, be necessary – is to leave the territory of ethics and enter that of law. Whoever has made this difficult step cannot presume to return through the door he just closed behind him.

1.8   The extreme figure of the "gray zone" is the *Sonderkommando*. The SS used the euphemism "special team" to refer to this group of deportees responsible for managing the gas chambers and crematoria. Their task was to lead naked prisoners to their death in the gas chambers and maintain order among them; they then had to drag out the corpses, stained pink and green by the cyanotic acid, and wash them with water; make sure that no valuable objects were hidden in the orifices of the bodies; extract gold teeth from the corpses' jaws; cut the women's hair and wash it with ammonia chloride; bring the corpses into the crematoria and oversee their incineration; and, finally, empty out the ovens of the ash that remained. Levi writes:

Concerning these squads, vague and mangled rumors already circulated among us during our imprisonment and were confirmed afterward.... But the intrinsic horror of this human condition has imposed a sort of reserve on all the testimony, so that even today it is difficult to conjure up an image of "what it meant" to be forced to exercise this trade for months.... One of them declared: "Doing this work, one either goes crazy the first day or gets accustomed to it." Another, though: "Certainly, I could have killed myself or got myself killed; but I wanted to

survive, to avenge myself and bear witness. You mustn't think that we are monsters; we are the same as you, only much more unhappy."...One cannot expect from men who have known such extreme destitution a deposition in the juridical sense, but something that is at once a lament, a curse, an expiation, an attempt to justify and rehabilitate oneself....Conceiving and organizing the squads was National Socialism's most demonic crime. (Levi 1989: 52–3)

And yet Levi recalls that a witness, Miklos Nyszli, one of the very few who survived the last "special team" of Auschwitz, recounted that during a "work" break he took part in a soccer match between the SS and representatives of the *Sonderkommando*. "Other men of the SS and the rest of the squad are present at the game; they take sides, bet, applaud, urge the players on as if, rather than at the gates of hell, the game were taking place on the village green" (Levi 1989: 55).

This match might strike someone as a brief pause of humanity in the middle of an infinite horror. I, like the witnesses, instead view this match, this moment of normalcy, as the true horror of the camp. For we can perhaps think that the massacres are over – even if here and there they are repeated, not so far away from us. But that match is never over; it continues as if uninterrupted. It is the perfect and eternal cipher of the "gray zone," which knows no time and is in every place. Hence the anguish and shame of the survivors, "the anguish inscribed in everyone of the 'tohu-bohu,' of a deserted and empty universe crushed under the spirit of God but from which the spirit of man is absent: not yet born or already extinguished" (Levi 1989: 85). But also hence our shame, the shame of those who did not know the camps and yet, without knowing how, are spectators of that match, which repeats itself in every match in our stadiums, in every television broadcast, in the normalcy of everyday life. If we do not succeed in understanding that match, in stopping it, there will never be hope.

REFERENCES

Arendt, Hannah. 1992. *Eichmann in Jerusalem: A Report on the Banality of Evil* (London: Penguin).

Langbein, Hermann. 1988. *Auschwitz: Zeugnisse und Berichte*, eds. H. G. Adler, Hermann Langbein, and Ella Lingens-Reiner (Frankfurt am Main: Athenäum).

Levi, Primo. 1989. *The Drowned and the Saved*, trans. Raymond Rosenthal (New York: Random House).

——. 1997. *Conversazioni e interviste* (Turin: Einaudi).

Lévinas, Emmanuel. 1982. *De l'évasion* (Montpellier: Fata Morgana).

Lewental, S. 1972. *Gedenkbuch, Hefte von Auschwitz* 1 (Oswiecim: Staatliches Auschwitz-Museum).

Satta, Sebastiano. 1994. *Il mistero del processo* (Milan: Adelphi).

Sofsky, Wolfgang. 1997. *The Order of Terror: The Concentration Camp*, trans. William Templer (Princeton: Princeton University Press).

Spinoza, Baruch. 1925. *Compendium grammatices linguae hebraeae*, in *Opera*, ed. Carl Gebhardt, vol. 3 (Heidelberg: C. Winter).

58

Colonial War and Mental Disorders

Frantz Fanon

But the war goes on; and we will have to bind up for years to come the many, sometimes ineffaceable, wounds that the colonialist onslaught has inflicted on our people.

That imperialism which today is fighting against a true liberation of mankind leaves in its wake here and there tinctures of decay which we must search out and mercilessly expel from our land and our spirits.

We shall deal here with the problem of mental disorders which arise from the war of national liberation which the Algerian people are carrying on. [...]

Today the war of national liberation which has been carried on by the Algerian people for the last seven years has become a favorable breeding ground for mental disorders, because so far as the Algerians are concerned it is a total war. [...] It seems to us that in the cases here chosen the events giving rise to the disorder are chiefly the bloodthirsty and pitiless atmosphere, the generalization of inhuman practices, and the firm impression that people have of being caught up in a veritable Apocalypse.[1] [...]

The observations noted here cover the period running from 1954–9. Certain patients were examined in Algeria, either in hospital centers or as private patients. The others were cared for by the health divisions of the Army of National Liberation. [...]

Case No. 1: Impotence in an Algerian following the rape of his wife.

B—is a man 26 years old. He came to see us on the advice of the Health Service of the FLN for treatment of insomnia and persistent headaches. A former taxi-driver, he had worked in the nationalist parties since he was eighteen. Since 1955 he had been a member of a branch of the FLN. He had several times used his taxi for the transport of political pamphlets and also political personnel. When the repression increased in ferocity, the FLN decided to bring the war into the urban centers. B— thus came to have the task of driving commandos to the vicinity of attacking points, and quite often waited for them at those points to bring them back.

One day however, in the middle of the European part of the town, after fairly considerable fighting a very large number of arrests forced him to abandon his taxi, and the commando unit broke up and scattered. B—, who managed to escape through the enemy lines, took refuge at a friend's house. Some days later, without having been able to get back to his home, on the orders of his superiors he joined the nearest band of Maquis.

For several months he was without news of his wife and his little girl of a year and eight months. On the other hand he learned that the police spent several weeks on end searching the town. After two years spent in the Maquis he received a message from his wife in which she asked him to forget her, for she had been dishonored and he ought not to think of taking up their life together again. He was extremely anxious and asked his commander's leave to go home secretly. This was refused him, but on the other hand measures were taken for a member of the FLN to make contact with B—'s wife and parents.

Two weeks later a detailed report reached the commander of B—'s unit.

His abandoned taxi had been discovered with two machine-gun magazines in it. Immediately afterward French soldiers accompanied by policemen went to his house. Finding he was absent, they took his wife away and kept her for over a week.

She was questioned about the company her husband kept and beaten fairly brutally for two days. But the third day a French soldier (she was not able to say whether he was an officer) made the others leave the room and then raped her. Some time later a second soldier, this time with others present, raped her, saying to her, "If ever you see your filthy husband again don't forget to tell him what we did to you." She remained another week without undergoing any fresh questioning. After this she was escorted back to her dwelling. When she told her story to her mother, the latter persuaded her to tell B— everything. Thus as soon as contact was reestablished with her husband, she confessed her dishonor to him. Once the first shock had passed, and since moreover every minute of his time was filled by activity, B— was able to overcome his feelings. For several months he had heard many stories of Algerian women who had been raped or tortured, and he had occasion to see the husbands of these violated women; thus his personal misfortunes and his dignity as an injured husband remained in the background.

In 1958, he was entrusted with a mission abroad. When it was time to rejoin his unit, certain fits of absence of mind and sleeplessness made his comrades and superiors anxious about him. His departure was postponed and it was decided he should have a medical examination. This was when we saw him. He seemed at once easy to get to know; a mobile face: perhaps a bit too mobile. Smiles slightly exaggerated; surface well-being: "I'm really very well, very well indeed. I'm feeling better now. Give me a tonic or two, a few vitamins, and I'll build myself up a bit." A basic anxiety came up to break the surface. He was at once sent to the hospital.

From the second day on, the screen of optimism melted away, and what we saw in front of us was a thoughtful, depressed man, suffering from loss of appetite, who kept to his bed. He avoided political discussion and showed a marked lack of interest in everything to do with the national struggle. He avoided listening to any news which had a bearing on the war of liberation. Any approach to his difficulties was extremely long, but at the end of several days we were able to reconstruct his story.

During his stay abroad, he tried to carry through a sexual affair which was unsuccessful. Thinking that this was due to fatigue, a normal result of forced marches and periods of undernourishment, he again tried two weeks later. Fresh failure. Talked about it to a friend who advised him to try vitamin B-12. Took this in form of pills; another attempt, another failure. Moreover, a few seconds before the act, he had an irresistible impulse to tear up a photo of his little girl. Such a symbolic liaison might have caused us to think that unconscious impulsions of an incestuous nature were present. However, several interviews and a dream, in which the patient saw the rapid rotting away of a little cat accompanied by unbearably evil smells, led us to take quite another course. "That girl," he said to us one day, speaking of his little daughter, "has something rotten about her." From this period on, his insomnia became extremely marked, and in spite of fairly large doses of neuroleptics, a state of anxiety excitation was remarked which the Service found rather worrying. Then he spoke to us for the first time about his wife, laughing and saying to us: "She's tasted the French." It was at that moment that we reconstructed the whole story. The weaving of events to form a pattern was made explicit. He told us that before every sexual attempt, he thought of his wife. All his confidences appeared to us to be of fundamental interest.

I married this girl although I loved my cousin. But my cousin's parents had arranged a match for their daughter with somebody else. So I accepted the first wife my parents found for me. She was nice, but I didn't love her. I used always to say to myself: "You're young yet; wait a bit and when you've found the right girl, you'll get a divorce and you'll make a happy marriage." So you see I wasn't very attached to my wife. And with the troubles, I got further apart than ever. In the end, I used to come and eat my meals and sleep almost without speaking to her.

In the Maquis, when I heard that she'd been raped by the French, I first of all felt angry with the swine. Then I said "Oh, well, there's not much harm done; she wasn't killed. She can start her life over again." And then a few weeks later I came to realize that they'd raped her *because they were looking for me.* In fact, it was to punish her for keeping silence that she'd been violated. She could have very well told them at least the name of one of the chaps in the movement, and from that they could have searched out the whole network, destroyed it, and maybe even arrested me. That wasn't a simple rape, for want of something better to do, or for sadistic reasons like those I've had occasion to see in the villages; it was the rape of an obstinate woman, who was ready to put up with everything rather than sell her husband. And the husband in question, *it was me.* This woman had saved my life and had protected the organization. It was because of me that she had been dishonored. And yet she didn't say to me: "Look at all I've had to bear for you." On the contrary, she said: "Forget about me; begin your life over again, for I have been dishonored."

It was from that moment on that I made my own decision to take back my wife after the war; for it must be said that I've seen peasants drying the tears of their wives after having seen them raped under their very eyes. This left me very much shaken; I must admit moreover that at the beginning I couldn't understand their attitude. But we increasingly came to intervene in such circumstances in order to explain matters to the civilians. I've seen civilians willingly proposing marriage to a girl who was violated by the French soldiers, and who was with child by them. All this led me to reconsider the problem of my wife.

So I decided to take her back; but I didn't know at all how I'd behave when I saw her. And often, while I was looking at the photo of my daughter, I used to think that she too was dishonored, like as if everything that had to do with my wife was rotten. If they'd tortured her or knocked out all her teeth or broken an arm I wouldn't have minded. But that thing – how can you forget a thing like that? And why did she have to tell me about it all?

He then asked me if his "sexual failing" was in my opinion caused by his worries.

I replied: "It is not impossible."

Then he sat up in bed.

"What would you do if all this had happened to you?"

"I don't know."

"Would you take back your wife?"

"I think I would..."

"Ah, there you are, you see. You're not quite sure..."

He held his head in his hands and after a few seconds left the room.

From that day on, he was progressively more willing to listen to political discussions and at the same time the headaches and lack of appetite lessened considerably.

After two weeks he went back to his unit. Before he left he told me:

"When independence comes, I'll take my wife back. If it doesn't work out between us, I'll come and see you in Algiers."

Case No. 2: Undifferentiated homicidal impulsions found in a survivor of a mass murder.

S—, 37 years old, a *fellah.* Comes from a village in the country around Constantine. Never took any part in politics. From the outset of the war, his district was the scene of fierce battles between the Algerian forces and the French army. S—thus had occasion to see dead and wounded. But he continued to keep out of things. From time to time however, in common with the people as a whole, the peasantry of his village used to come to the aid of Algerian fighting men who were passing through. But one day, early in 1958, a deadly ambush was laid not far from the village. After this the enemy forces went into operation and besieged the village, which in fact had no soldiers in it. All the inhabitants were summoned and questioned; nobody replied. A few hours after, a French officer arrived by helicopter and said: "There's been too much talk about this village. Destroy it." The soldiers began to set fire to the houses while the women who were trying to get a few clothes together or save some provisions were driven away by blows with rifle-butts. Some peasants took advantage of the general confusion to run away. The officer gave the order to bring together the men who remained and had them brought out to near a watercourse where the killing began. Twenty-nine men were shot at point-blank range. S—was wounded by two bullets which went through his right thigh and his left arm respectively; the arm injury gave rise to a fracture of the humerus.

S—fainted and came to find himself in the midst of a group of ALN. He was treated by the Health Service and evacuated as soon as it was possible to move him. While on the way, his behavior became more and more abnormal, and worried his escort continually. He demanded a gun, although he was helpless and a civilian, and refused to walk in front of anybody, no matter who they were. He refused to have anyone behind him. One night he got hold of a soldier's gun and awkwardly tried to fire on the sleeping soldiers. He was disarmed rather roughly. From then on they tied his hands together, and it was thus that he arrived at the Center.

He began by telling us that he wasn't dead yet and that he had played a good trick on the others. Bit by bit, we managed to reconstruct his story of the assassination he had attempted. S—was not anxious, he was in fact rather overexcited, with violent phases of agitation, accompanied by screaming. He did not break anything much, but tired everybody out by his incessant chatter, and the whole Service was permanently on the alert on account of his declared intention of "killing everybody." During his stay in the hospital he attacked about eight patients with makeshift weapons. Nurses and doctors were not spared either. We almost wondered whether we were not witnessing one of those masked forms of epilepsy which is characterized by a wholesale aggressivity which is nearly always present.

Deep sleep treatment was then tried. From the third day on, a daily interview made it possible for us to better understand the moving force of the pathological process. The patient's intellectual confusion progressively toned down. Here are some extracts from his statements:

God is with me ... but he certainly isn't with those who are dead.... I've had hellish good luck.... In life you've got to kill so as not to be killed.... When I think that I knew nothing at all about all that business.... There are Frenchmen in our midst. They disguise themselves as Arabs. They've all got to be killed. Give me a machine-gun. All these so-called Algerians are really Frenchmen...and they won't leave me alone. As soon as I want to go to sleep they come into my room. But now I know all about them. Everyone wants to kill me. But I'll defend myself. I'll kill them all, every single one of them. I'll cut their throats one after the other, and yours with them. You all want to kill me but you should set about it differently. I'd kill you all as soon as look at you, big ones and little ones, women, children, dogs, birds, donkeys...everyone will be dead. And afterward I'll be able to sleep in peace....

All this was said in jerks; the patient's attitude remained hostile, suspicious, and aloof.

After three weeks, his state of excitement had disappeared, but a certain reticence and a tendency to seek solitude gave us grounds for fearing a more serious evolution of his disorder. However after a month he asked to be let out in order to learn a trade that would be compatible with his disability. He was then entrusted to the care of the Social Service of the FLN. We saw him six months after, and he was going on well. [...]

Case No. 3. A European policeman in a depressed state meets while under hospital treatment one of his victims, an Algerian patriot who is suffering from stupor.

A—, 28 years old, no children. We learnt that for several years both he and his wife underwent treatment, unfortunately with no success, in order to have children. He was sent to us by his superiors because he had behavior disturbances.

Immediate contact seemed fairly good. The patient spoke to us spontaneously about his difficulties. Satisfactory relations with his wife and parents-in-law. His trouble was that at night he heard screams which prevented him from sleeping. In fact, he told us that for the last few weeks before going to bed he shut the shutters and stopped up all the windows (it was summer) to the complete despair of his wife, who was stifled by the heat. Moreover, he stuffed his ears with cotton wool in order to make the screams seem less piercing. He sometimes even in the middle of the night turned on the wireless or put on some music in order not to hear this nocturnal uproar. He consequently explained to us at full length the whole story that was troubling him.

A few months before, he had been transferred to an anti-FLN brigade. At the beginning, he was entrusted with surveying certain shops or cafés; but after some weeks he used to work almost exclusively at the police headquarters. Here he came to deal with interrogations; and these never occurred without some "knocking about." "The thing was that they never would own up to anything." He explained:

Sometimes we almost wanted to tell them that if they had a bit of consideration for us they'd speak out without forcing us to spend hours tearing information word by word out of them. But you might as well talk to the wall. To all the questions we asked they'd only say "I don't know." Even when we asked them what their name was. If we asked them where they lived, they'd say "I don't know." So of course, we have to go through with it. But they scream too much. At the beginning that made me laugh. But afterward I was a bit shaken. Nowadays as soon as I hear someone shouting I can tell you exactly at what stage of the questioning we've got to. The chap who's had two blows of the fist and a belt of the baton behind his ear has a certain way of speaking, of shouting, and of saying he's innocent. After he's been left two hours strung up by his wrists he has another kind of voice. After the bath, still another. And so on. But above all it's after the electricity that it becomes really too much. You'd say that the chap was going to die any minute. Of course there are some that don't scream; those are the tough ones. But they think they're going to be killed right away. But we're not interested in killing them. What we want is information. When we're dealing with those tough ones, the first thing we do is to make them squeal; and sooner or later we manage it. That's already a victory. Afterward we go on. Mind you, we'd like to avoid that. But they don't make things easy for us. Now I've come so as I hear their screams even when I'm at home. Especially the screams of the ones who died at the police headquarters. Doctor, I'm fed up with this job. And if you manage to cure me, I'll ask to be transferred to France. If they refuse, I'll resign.

Faced with such a picture, I prescribed sick leave. As the patient in question refused to go to the hospital, I treated him privately. One day, shortly before the therapeutic treatment was due to begin, I had an urgent call from my department. When A—reached my house, my wife asked him to wait for me, but he preferred to go for a walk in the hospital grounds, and then come back to meet me. A few minutes later as I was going home I passed him on the way. He was leaning against a tree, looking overcome, trembling and drenched with sweat: in fact having an anxiety crisis. I took him into my car and drove him to my house. Once he was lying on the sofa, he told me he had met one of my patients in the hospital who had been questioned in the police barracks (he was an Algerian patriot) and who was under treatment for "disorders of a stuporous nature following on shock." I then learnt that the policeman had taken an active part in inflicting torture on my patient. I administered some sedatives which calmed A—'s anxiety. After he had gone, I went to the house in

the hospital where the patriot was being cared for. The personnel had noticed nothing; but the patient could not be found. Finally we managed to discover him in a toilet where he was trying to commit suicide: he on his side had recognized the policeman and thought that he had come to look for him and take him back again to the barracks.

Afterward, A—came back to see me several times, and after a very definite improvement in his condition, managed to get back to France on account of his health. As for the Algerian patriot, the personnel spent a long time convincing him that the whole thing was an illusion, that policemen were not allowed inside the hospital, that he was very tired, that he was there to be looked after, etc.

Case No. 4: A European police inspector who tortured his wife and children.

R—, 30 years old. Came of his own accord to consult us. He was a police inspector and stated that for several weeks "things weren't working out." Married, had three children. He smoked a lot: five packets of cigarettes a day. He had lost his appetite and his sleep was frequently disturbed by nightmares. These nightmares had no special distinguishing features. What bothered him most were what he called "fits of madness." In the first place, he disliked being contradicted:

Can you give me an explanation for this, doctor: as soon as someone goes against me I want to hit him. Even outside my job, I feel I want to settle the fellows who get in my way, even for nothing at all. Look here, for example, suppose I go to the kiosk to buy the papers. There's a lot of people. Of course you have to wait. I hold out my hand (the chap who keeps the kiosk is a pal of mine) to take my papers. Someone in the line gives me a challenging look and says "Wait your turn." Well, I feel I want to beat him up and I say to myself, "If I had you for a few hours my fine fellow you wouldn't look so clever afterwards."

The patient dislikes noise. At home he wants to hit everybody all the time. In fact, he does hit his children, even the baby of 20 months, with unaccustomed savagery.

But what really frightened him was one evening when his wife had criticized him particularly for hitting his children too much. (She had even said to him, "My word, anyone'd think you were going mad.") He threw himself upon her, beat her, and tied her to a chair, saying to himself "I'll teach her once and for all that I'm master in this house."

Fortunately his children began roaring and crying. He then realized the full gravity of his behavior, untied his wife and the next day decided to consult a doctor, "a nerve specialist." He stated that "before, he wasn't like that"; he said that he very rarely punished his children and at all events never fought with his wife. The present phenomena had appeared "since the troubles." "The fact is" he said:

nowadays we have to work like troopers. Last week, for example, we operated like as if we belonged to the army. Those gentlemen in the government say there's no war in Algeria and that the arm of the law, that's to say the police, ought to restore order. But there *is* a war going on in Algeria, and when they wake up to it it'll be too late. The thing that kills me most is the torture. You don't know what that is, do you? Sometimes I torture people for ten hours at a stretch....

"What happens to you when you are torturing?"

You may not realize, but it's very tiring.... It's true we take it in turns, but the question is to know when to let the next chap have a go. Each one thinks he's going to get the information at any minute and takes good care not to let the bird go to the next chap after he's softened him up nicely, when of course the other chap would get the honor and glory of it. So sometimes we let them go; and sometimes we don't.

Sometimes we even offer the chap money, money out of our own pockets, to try to get him to talk. Our problem is as follows: are you able to make this fellow talk? It's a question of personal success. You see, you're competing with the others. In the end your fists are ruined. So you call in the Senegalese. But either they hit too hard and destroy the creature or else they don't hit hard enough and it's no good. In fact, you have to be intelligent to make a success of that sort of work. You have to know when to lay it on and when to lay it off. You have to have a flair for it. When the chap is softened up, it's not worth your while going on hitting him. That's why you have to do the work yourself; you can judge better how you're getting on. I'm against the ones that have the chap dealt with by others and simply come to see every hour or so what state he's in. Above all, what you mustn't do is to give the chap the impression that he won't get away alive from you. Because then he wonders what's the use of talking if that won't save his life. In that case you'll have no chance at all of

getting anything out of him. He must go on hoping; hope's the thing that'll make him talk.

But the thing that worries me most is this affair with my wife. It's certain that there's something wrong with me. You've got to cure me, doctor.

His superiors refused to give him sick leave, and since moreover the patient did not wish to have a psychiatrist's certificate, we tried to give him treatment "while working full time." The weaknesses of such a procedure may easily be imagined. This man knew perfectly well that his disorders were directly caused by the kind of activity that went on inside the rooms where interrogations were carried out, even though he tried to throw the responsibility totally upon "present troubles." As he could not see his way to stopping torturing people (that made nonsense to him for in that case he would have to resign) he asked me without beating about the bush to help him to go on torturing Algerian patriots without any prickings of conscience, without any behavior problems, and with complete equanimity.[2] [...]

Case No. 5: The murder by two young Algerians, 13 and 14 years old respectively, of their European playmate.

We had been asked to give expert medical advice in a legal matter. Two young Algerians 13 and 14 years old, pupils in a primary school, were accused of having killed one of their European schoolmates. They admitted having done it. The crime was reconstructed, and photos were added to the record. Here one of the children could be seen holding the victim while the other struck at him with a knife. The little defendants did not go back on their declarations. We had long conversations with them. We here reproduce the most characteristic of their remarks:

a) The boy thirteen years old:

"We weren't bit cross with him. Every Thursday we used to go and play with catapults together, on the hill above the village. He was a good friend of ours. He usn't to go to school any more because he wanted to be a mason like his father. One day we decided to kill him, because the Europeans want to kill all the Arabs. We can't kill big people. But we could kill ones like him, because he was the same age as us. We didn't know how to kill him. We wanted to throw him into a ditch, but he'd only have been hurt. So we got the knife from home and we killed him."

"But why did you pick on him?"

"Because he used to play with us. Another boy wouldn't have gone up the hill with us."

"And yet you were pals?"

"Well then, why do they want to kill us? His father is in the militia and he said we ought to have our throats cut."

"But he didn't say anything to you?"

"Him? No."

"You know he is dead now."

"Yes."

"What does being dead mean?"

"When it's all finished, you go to heaven."

"Was it you that killed him?"

"Yes."

"Does having killed somebody worry you?"

"No, since they want to kill us, so . . . "

"Do you mind being in prison?"

"No."

b) The boy fourteen years old:

This young defendant was in marked contrast to his schoolfellow. He was already almost a man, and an adult in his muscular control, his appearance, and the content of his replies. He did not deny having killed either. Why had he killed? He did not reply to the question but asked me had I ever seen a European in prison. Had there ever been a European arrested and sent to prison after the murder of an Algerian? I replied that in fact I had never seen any Europeans in prison.

"And yet there are Algerians killed every day, aren't there?"

"Yes."

"So why are only Algerians found in the prisons? Can you explain that to me?"

"No. But tell me why you killed this boy who was your friend."

"I'll tell you why. You've heard tell of the Rivet business?"[3]

"Yes."

"Two of my family were killed then. At home, they said that the French had sworn to kill us all, one after the other. And did they arrest a single Frenchman for all those Algerians who were killed?"

"I don't know."

"Well, nobody at all was arrested. I wanted to take to the mountains, but I was too young. So X— and I said we'd kill a European."

"Why?"

"In your opinion, what should we have done?"

"I don't know. But you are a child and what is happening concerns grown-up people."

"But they kill children too . . . "

"That is no reason for killing your friend."

"Well, kill him I did. Now you can do what you like."

"Had your friend done anything to harm you?"

"Not a thing."

"Well?"

"Well, there you are . . . "

Case No. 6: Accusatory delirium and suicidal conduct disguised as "terrorist activity" in a young Algerian 22 years old.

This patient was sent to our hospital by the French judicial authorities. This measure was taken after medical and legal advice given by French psychiatrists practicing in Algeria.

The patient was an emaciated man in a complete state of aberration. His body was covered with bruises and two fractures of the jaw made all absorption of nourishment impossible. Thus for more than two weeks the patient was fed by various injections.

After two weeks, the blank in his thoughts receded; we were able to establish contact and we managed to reconstruct the dramatic history of this young man.

During his youth he went in for scouting with unusual enthusiasm. He became one of the main leaders of the Moslem Scout Movement. But when he was 19 years old he dropped scouting completely in order to have no preoccupation other than his profession. He was a multicopying-machine maker; he studied hard and dreamt of becoming a great specialist in his profession. The first of November, 1954, found him absorbed by strictly professional problems. At the time he showed no interest at all in the national struggle. Already he no longer frequented the company of his former companions. He defined himself at that time as "completely bent on increasing [his] technical capacity."

However, about the middle of 1955, when spending the evening with his family, he suddenly had the impression that his parents considered him a traitor. After a few days this fleeting impression became blunted but at the back of his mind a certain misgiving persisted, a sort of uneasiness that he did not understand.

On account of this, he decided to eat his meals quickly, shrinking from the family circle, and shut himself into his room. He avoided all contacts. It was in these conditions that catastrophe intervened. One day, in the middle of the street at about half-past twelve, he distinctly heard a voice calling him a coward. He turned round, but saw nobody. He quickened his pace, and decided that from then on he would not go to work. He stayed in his room and did not eat any dinner. During the night the crisis came on. For three hours he heard all sorts of insults coming from out of the night and resounding in his head: "Traitor, traitor, coward...all your brothers who are dying,... traitor, traitor..."

He was seized with indescribable anxiety: "For eighteen hours my heart beat at the rhythm of 130 pulsations to the minute. I thought I was going to die."

From that time on, the patient could no longer swallow a bite. He wasted away almost visibly; he shut himself up in complete darkness, and refused to open the door to his parents. Around the third day he took refuge in prayer. He stayed kneeling, he told me, from 17 to 18 hours on end each day. On the fourth day, acting on impulse "like a madman," with "a beard that was also enough to make [him] be taken for a madman," wearing neither coat nor tie, he went out into the town. Once in the street, he did not know where to go; but he started walking, and at the end of some time he found himself in the European town. His physical appearance (he looked like a European) seemed then to safeguard him against being stopped and questioned by the police patrols.

As a contrast to this, beside him Algerian men and women were arrested, maltreated, insulted, and searched. Paradoxically, he had no papers on him. This uncalled-for consideration toward him on the part of the enemy patrols confirmed his delusion that "everybody knew he was with the French. Even the soldiers had their orders; they left him alone."

In addition, the glances of the arrested Algerians, who were waiting to be searched with their hands behind their necks, seemed to him to be full of contempt. The prey of overwhelming agitation, he moved away, striding rapidly. It was at this moment that he happened to walk in front of the building which was the French Staff Headquarters. In the gateway stood several soldiers armed with machine-guns. He went toward the soldiers, threw himself upon one of them and tried to snatch his machine-gun, shouting "I am an Algerian."

He was quickly overcome and was brought to the police, where they insisted on making him confess the names of his "superiors" and the different members of the network to which he (supposedly) belonged. After some days the police and the soldiers realized that they were dealing with a sick man. An expert opinion was sought which concluded that he was suffering from mental disorders and that he should be sent to the hospital. "All I wanted to do," he said, "was to die. Even at the police barracks I thought and hoped that after they'd tortured me they would kill me. I was glad to be struck, for that showed me that they considered that I too was their enemy. I could no longer go on hearing those accusing voices, without doing something. I am not a coward. I am not a woman. I am not a traitor."[4] [...]

It remains for us to give the explanation.

Should it be said that war, that privileged expression of an aggressivity which is at last made social, canalizes in the direction of the occupying power all congenitally murderous acts? It is a commonplace that great social upheavals lessen the frequency of delinquency and mental disorders. This regression of Algerian criminality can thus be perfectly explained by the existence of a war which broke Algeria in two, and threw onto the side of the enemy the judicial and administrative machine.

But in the countries of the Magrab which have already been liberated this same phenomenon which was noticed during the conflicts for liberation continues to exist and even becomes more marked once independence is proclaimed. It would therefore seem that the colonial context is sufficiently original to give grounds for a reinterpretation of the causes of criminality. This is what we did for those on active service. Today every one of us knows that criminality is not the consequence of the hereditary character of the Algerian, nor of the organization of his nervous system. The Algerian war, like all wars of national liberation, brings to the fore the true protagonists. In the colonial context, as we have already pointed out, the natives fight among themselves. They tend to use each other as a screen, and each hides from his neighbor the national enemy. When, tired out after a hard sixteen-hour day, the native sinks down to rest on his mat, and a child on the other side of the canvas partition starts crying and prevents him from sleeping, it so happens that it is a little Algerian. When he goes to beg for a little semolina or a drop of oil from the grocer, to whom he already owes some hundreds of francs, and when he sees that he is refused, an immense feeling of hatred and an overpowering desire to kill rises within him: and the grocer is an Algerian. When, after having kept out of his way for weeks he finds himself one day cornered by the caid who demands that he should pay "his taxes," he cannot even enjoy the luxury of hating a European administrator; there before him is the caid who is the object of his hatred – and the caid is an Algerian.

The Algerian exposed to temptations to commit murder every day – famine, eviction from his room because he has not paid the rent, the mother's dried-up breasts, children like skeletons, the building-yard which has closed down, the unemployed that hang about the foreman like crows – the native comes to see his neighbor as a relentless enemy. If he strikes his bare foot against a big stone in the middle of the path, it is a native who has placed it there; and the few olives that he was going to pick, X—'s children have gone and eaten in the night. For during the colonial period in Algeria and elsewhere many things may be done for a couple of pounds of semolina. Several people may be killed over it. You need to use your imagination to understand that: your imagination, or your memory. In the concentration camps men killed each other for a bit of bread. I remember one horrible scene. It was in Oran in 1944. From the camp where we were waiting to embark, soldiers were throwing bits of bread to little Algerian children who fought for them among themselves with anger and hate. Veterinary doctors can throw light on such problems by reminding us of the well-known "peck order" which has been observed in farmyards. The corn which is thrown to the hens is in fact the object of relentless competition. Certain birds, the strongest, gobble up all the grains while others who are less aggressive grow visibly thinner. Every colony tends to turn into a huge farmyard, where the only law is that of the knife.

In Algeria since the beginning of the war of national liberation, everything has changed. The whole foodstocks of a family or a *mechta*[5] may in a single evening be given to a passing company. The family's only donkey may be lent to transport a wounded fighter; and when a few days later the owner learns of the death of his animal which has been machine-gunned by an airplane, he will not begin threatening and swearing. He will not question the death of his donkey, but he will ask anxiously if the wounded man is safe and sound.

Under the colonial regime, anything may be done for a loaf of bread or a miserable sheep. The relations of man with matter, with the world outside, and with history are in the colonial period simply relations with food. For a colonized man, in a context of oppression like that of Algeria, living does not mean embodying moral values or taking his place in the coherent and fruitful development of the world. To live means to keep on existing. Every date is a victory: not the result of work, but a victory felt as a triumph for life. Thus to steal dates or to allow one's sheep to eat the neighbor's grass is not a question of the negation of the property of others, nor the transgression of a law, nor lack of respect. These are attempts at murder. In order to understand that a robbery is not an illegal or an unfriendly action, but an attempt at murder, one must have seen in Kabylia men and women for weeks at a time going to get earth at the bottom of the valley and bringing it up in little baskets. The fact is that the only perspective is that belly which is more and more sunken, which is certainly less and less demanding, but which must be contented all the same. Who is going to take the punishment? The French are down in the plain with the police, the army, and the tanks. On the mountain there are only Algerians. Up above there is Heaven with the promise of a world beyond the grave; down below there are the French with their very concrete promises of prison, beatings-up, and executions. You are forced to come up against yourself. Here we discover the kernel of that hatred of self which is characteristic of racial conflicts in segregated societies.

The Algerian's criminality, his impulsivity, and the violence of his murders are therefore not the consequence of the organization of his nervous system or of characterial originality, but the direct product of the colonial situation. The fact that the soldiers of Algeria have discussed this problem; that they are not afraid of questioning the beliefs fostered among themselves by colonialism; that they understand that each man formed the screen for his neighbor and that in reality each man committed suicide when he went for his neighbor: all these things should have primordial importance in the revolutionary conscience. Once again, the objective of the native who fights against himself is to bring about the end of domination. But he ought equally to pay attention to the liquidation of all untruths implanted in his being by oppression. Under a colonial regime such as existed in Algeria, the ideas put forward by colonialism not only influenced the European minority, but also the Algerians. Total liberation is that which concerns all sectors of the personality. The ambush or the attack, the torture or the massacre of his brothers plants more deeply the determination to win, wakes up the unwary and feeds the imagination. When the nation stirs as a whole, the new man is not an *a posteriori* product of that nation; rather, he co-exists with it and triumphs with it. This dialectic requirement explains the reticence with which adaptations of colonization and reforms of the façade are met. Independence is not a word which can be used as an exorcism, but an indispensable condition for the existence of men and women who are truly liberated, in other words who are truly masters of all the material means which make possible the radical transformation of society.

NOTES

1   In the unpublished introduction of the first two editions of *Year V of the Algerian Revolution*, we have already pointed out that a whole generation of Algerians, steeped in wanton, generalized homicide with all the psycho-affective consequences that this entails, will be the human legacy of France in Algeria. Frenchmen who condemn the torture in Algeria constantly adopt a point of view which is strictly French. We do not reproach them for this; we merely point it out: they wish to protect the consciences of the actual torturers who today have full power to carry on their work; they wish at the same time to try to avoid the moral contamination of the young people of France. As far as we are concerned we are totally in accord with this attitude. Certain notes here brought together [...] are sad illustrations and justifications for this obsession which haunts French believers in democracy. But our purpose is in any case to show that torture, as might well be expected, upsets most profoundly the personality of the person who is tortured.

2   With these observations we find ourselves in the presence of a coherent system which leaves nothing intact. The executioner who loves birds and enjoys the peace of listening to a symphony or a sonata is simply one stage in the process. Further on in it we may well find a whole existence which enters into complete and absolute sadism.

3   Rivet is a village which since a certain day in the year 1956 has become celebrated in the region around Algiers. For on that evening the village was invaded by the militia who dragged 40 men from their beds and afterward murdered them.

4   During the year 1955, cases of this type were very numerous in Algeria. Unfortunately not all the patients had the good fortune to be sent to a hospital.

5   Mountain village in Algeria. – *Trans.*

59

From *The Soft Vengeance of a Freedom Fighter*

Albie Sachs

1

Oh shit. Everything has abruptly gone dark, I am feeling strange and cannot see anything. The beach, I am going to the beach, I packed a frosty beer for after my run, something is wrong. Oh shit, I must have banged my head, like I used to do when climbing Table Mountain in Cape Town, dreaming of the struggle, and cracking my cranium against an overhang. It will go away, I must just be calm and wait. Watered the tropical pot-plants, stared at the ten heads on the giant African sculpture in my beautiful apartment. Oh shit, how can I be so careless? The darkness is not clearing, this is something serious, a terrible thing is happening to me, I am swirling, I cannot steady myself as I wait for consciousness and light to return. I feel a shuddering punch against the back of my neck, and then what seems like another one. The sense of threat gets stronger and stronger, I am being dominated, overwhelmed. I have to fight, I have to resist. I can feel arms coming from behind me, pulling at me under my shoulders. I am being kidnapped, they have come from Pretoria to drag me over the border and interrogate me and lock me up. This is the moment we have all been waiting for, the few ANC members still working in Mozambique, with dread and yet with a weird kind of eagerness.

'Leave me,' I yell out. 'Leave me.'

I jerk my shoulders and thrash my arms as violently as I can. I always wondered how I would react, whether I would fight physically, risking death, or whether I would go quietly and rely on my brain and what moral courage I had to see me through.

'Leave me alone, leave me alone,' I demand violently, aware that I am shouting in both English and Portuguese, the official language of this newly independent state where I have been living for a decade. I've forgotten my Afrikaans after 20 years in exile, I'm screaming for my life yet with some control, some politeness, since after all I am a middle-aged lawyer in a public place.

'I would rather die here, leave me, I'd rather die here.'

I feel a sudden surge of elation and strength as I struggle, making an immense muscular effort to pull myself free. I might be an intellectual but at this critical moment without time to plan or think I am fighting bravely and with the courage of the youth of Soweto even though the only physical violence I have personally known in my life was as a schoolboy being tackled carrying a rugby ball. I hear voices coming from behind me, urgent, nervous voices not talking but issuing and accepting commands, and they are referring to me.

The darkness is total, but still I hear tense staccato speech.

'Lift him up, put him there.'

I am not a him, I am me, you cannot just cart me around like a suitcase. But I am unable to struggle any more, I just have to go along and accept what happens, my will has gone.

We are travelling fast, the way is bumpy, how can they leave me in such discomfort, if they are going to kidnap me at least they could use a vehicle with better springs. I have no volition,

I cannot decide anything or even move any part of me. But I have awareness, I think, therefore I am. The consciousness fades and returns, swirls away and comes back, I am lying down like a bundle, there is a point in my head that is thinking, and then oblivion and then awareness again, no thought related to action, but passive acknowledgment that my body is being transported somewhere, that I exist, even if without self-determination of any sort. I wonder if we have reached the South African border yet, I wonder who my captors are, what their faces look like, do they have names? This darkness is so confusing.

More urgent voices, speaking with rapid energy, treating me as an object, to be lifted and carried and moved this way and that...I feel the muscles and movements of people all around me, above me, at my side, behind me. Nobody engages me as a person, speaks with head directed towards me, communicates with me. I exist as a mass, I have physicality, but no personality, I am simply the object of other people's decision. They point their mouths to each other, never towards my head, I am totally present, the centre of all the energetic talking, but I am never included in the discussion, my will, my existence is being violated, I am banished even while in the group.

All is very still and calm and without movement or voices or muscular activity. I am wrapped in complete darkness and tranquillity. If I am dead I am not aware of it, if I am alive I am not aware of it, I have no awareness at all, not of myself, not of my surroundings, not of anyone or of anything.

'Albie...' through the darkness a voice, speaking not about me but to me, and using my name and without that terrible urgency of all those other voices '...Albie, this is Ivo Garrido speaking to you...' the voice is sympathetic and affectionate, I know Ivo, he is an outstanding young surgeon and a friend '...you are in the Maputo Central Hospital...your arm is in a lamentable condition...' he uses a delicate Portuguese word to describe my arm, how tactful the Mozambican culture is compared to the English one, I must ask him later what that word is '...we are going to operate and you must face the future with courage.'

A glow of joy of complete satisfaction and peace envelops me, I am in the hands of Frelimo, of the Mozambican Government, I am safe.

'What happened?' I am asking the question into the darkness, my will has been activated in response to hearing Ivo's voice, I have a social existence once more, I am an alive part of humanity.

A voice answers, close to my ears, I think it is a woman's, '...a car bomb...' and I drift back, smiling inside, into nothingness.

2

I am elsewhere and other. There is a cool crisp sheet on me, I am lying on a couch, aware that I have a body and that I can feel and think and even laugh to myself, and everything seems light and clean and I have a great sense of happiness and curiosity. This is the time to explore and rediscover myself. What has happened to me, what is left of me, what is the damage? I am feeling wonderful and thinking easily in word thoughts and not just sensations, but maybe there is internal destruction...

Let me see...A joke comes back to me, a Jewish joke from the days when we Jews still told jokes to ward off the pains of oppression and humiliation, from when I was still a young student and my mountain-climbing friend had a new joke for me each week, and I smile to myself as I tell myself the joke, and feel happy and alive because I am telling myself a joke, the one about Himie Cohen falling off a bus, and as he gets up he makes what appears to be a large sign of the cross over his body.

A friend is watching in astonishment. 'Himie,' he says, 'I didn't know you were a Catholic.'

'What do you mean, Catholic?' Himie answers. 'Spectacles...testicles...wallet and watch.'

My arm is free and mobile and ready to respond to my will. It is on the left side and I decide to alter the order a little, I am sure Himie would not mind in the circumstances. Testicles...My hand goes down. I am wearing nothing under the sheet, it is easy to feel my body. My penis is all there, my good old cock (I'm alone with myself and can say the word) that has involved me in so much happiness and so much despair and will no doubt lead me up hill and down dale in the future as well, and my balls, one, two, both in place, perhaps I should call them testes since I am in hospital. I bend my elbow, how lovely it is to be able to want again, and then be able to do what I want; I move my hand up my chest, what delicious self-determination, what a noble work of art is man...Wallet...My heart is there, the ribs over it seem intact, the blood will pump, the center of my physical being, the part you take for granted is okay, I am fine, I will live and live robustly. Spectacles . . . I range my fingers over my forehead, and cannot feel any craters or jagged pieces, and I know I am thinking clearly, the darkness is now feather-light and clean, unlike the heavy, opaque blackness of before. Watch . . . my hand creeps over my shoulder and slides down my upper arm, and suddenly there is nothing there . . . so I have lost an arm, Ivo did not say which one, or even that they were going to cut it off, though I suppose it was implicit in his words, and it's the right one, since it is my left arm that is doing all the feeling . . . So I have lost an arm, that's all, I've lost an arm, that's all. They tried to kill me, to extinguish me completely, but I have only lost an arm. ~~Spectacles, testicles,~~ wallet, and watch. I joke, therefore I am.

3

So this is what it's like. I came close to death and survived. I am in the intensive care ward, there are tubes running into me like I've seen in the films and it always looked so uncomfortable, how could you bear to have a tube going into your nose or into your arm? And yet it is not difficult at all, the whole body feels slightly odd and the tubes are just part of the general strangeness. I know that time has passed, but have no sense of how, long it has been; when you sleep, your body clock keeps going, but not when you are being operated on. Somebody told me that the operation lasted seven hours, that is how they measure ops, and I remember the sense of pride in his voice. They explored all of me, looking for damage everywhere, taking out scores of pieces of shrapnel from all over my body and head, and I was proud of my complicity in this major surgical enterprise.

And now, is it the same day or the next or the next? The darkness has continued, and I suppose I am quite heavily drugged, and I just do not know how long I have been here. I remember Ivo talking to me once, chatting to me with the intimacy of a friend, reestablishing a personal relationship after having cut up my body, and giving me his personal version of the bomb story that has apparently stirred all Maputo, telling me he heard a tremendous explosion shortly after he had got up, and that he dressed quickly and rushed to the hospital without waiting to be called because he knew from the violence of the bang that there would be victims, and then when he got to the hospital he saw someone being carried in and looked closer and was shocked to see it was me in my bathing trunks. And then there was Anatoli, with the gentlest hands of any man I have known. I wonder what he looks like – from his name and the way he speaks Portuguese I guess that he is one of the Soviet doctors at the hospital – all I know is that he peels the bandages off with lovely delicacy, speaking softly as he dresses the wounds on my right side and then winding the bandages on again with equal fingerly kindness.

Someone has given me a rundown of my injuries: it seems there has been no injury to internal organs and no brain damage (I could have told them that, spectacles . . . testicles . . .) and that apart from the loss of the arm I have four broken ribs, a fractured heel on my right leg and a severed nerve in my left leg, lots of shrapnel wounds, ruptured eardrums, and, as for my eyes, they would know as soon as they took the dressing off which would be quite soon, all in all a miracle, if you had seen my car, it is still there, everybody is driving past or walking by, and nobody believes I could have escaped alive, it is just a heap of crumpled metal with two beach chairs peeking out the back.

From time to time I allow the fingers of my left hand to trace the slope of my right shoulder. The whole of that side is heavily bandaged and I do not want to press too hard, but I can feel the shape of the upper part of the arm, and then before I can reach the elbow, the bandages turn inwards and there is nothing more. If I did not feel with my left hand, I would not know that I had lost my right arm, it still seems to be there, it exists in sensation even if not in reality. What puzzles me is something else, and the doctors do not seem to have an explanation for it, and that is, why, after having been through what must have been a terrible experience, and lying in complete darkness with a mass of fractures and wounds, I am feeling so wonderful. [. . .]

Epilogue

Was it worth it?

A long, slow, totally intimate yet highly publicised run was the affirmative way I had chosen to mark my stepping aside from organized political activity. The mayor of Cape Town gave me a kiss and a gentle push with her hands to send me on my 11-kilometer way, the traffic police cleared the road, television crews developed their calf muscles while they ran backwards to capture frontal images of my elated panting, a waiter handed me a small cup of espresso (not a banned substance) when my legs pounded step by slow thudding step into the pavement outside Giovanni's, and the workers at the Arthur's Seat Hotel shouted 'Viva, comrade Albie, viva' as I jogged slowly and heavily past the palm trees on Sea Point promenade. The occasion was a repeat of my run 30 years before from Caledon Square Police Station to the sea. It was 1994, six years after the bomb, four years after my return from exile, and a month before the country's first free and democratic elections, and I needed to do something personal and physical to feel the involvement of my body in the process of transforming South Africa. The intense underfoot churning of the fine white sand of Clifton Beach was as joyous as I had long envisaged. As I eventually threw myself with narcissistic bravura into the cold waves, Basil 'Manenberg' Coetzee, one of the creators of Cape jazz, blew his saxophone loudly – he and I and the gathering crowd celebrated the simultaneous recovery of my body and the revival of our country.

How necessary and yet how sad that my generation of freedom fighters had been compelled to transmute the painful and distinctive ecstasy of our lives into the run-of-the-mill emotions of any other contenders for office. The great and poignant paradox of our lives was that we had fought with all our passion to create a boring society. Although the quest for human rights would never end, the forms it took would now be different. I felt that we had won the right to embark upon new careers that had been unthinkable as long as apartheid was in place, and, much as I admired my colleagues from the struggle who were willing to carry on with political work, I wished to shout my last 'Viva!' and be considered for appointment as a judge or, failing selection, to make movies. At the conference in a hot crowded hall to ballot for persons to be placed on the ANC election list, exhausted by nonstop traveling during the negotiation period, I had gripped the table in front of me and drunk several glasses of water to make sure I stayed awake. My fear had been that I would fall asleep before the Ss were reached and wake up effectively a member of Parliament. I wouldn't enjoy electioneering – vote for us, we've got the finest policies, we're the best, we're the most honest – as if integrity were something capable of calibration. I hadn't wanted to find myself anx-

iously waiting for a telephone call to see if I had been chosen for some high government post. At last I heard the words 'Sachs, Albert Louis,' stood up, and said 'Please take my name off the list,' and with this short sentence weaned myself from 42 years of total personal commitment and disciplined loyalty to the cause. The values would be the same, but the context and format quite different.

As I eventually stood in line to vote I wished I hadn't felt so tired and tense, my sleep destabilized by the weight of history, my waking moments upset by a terror that some madness would overcome me in the voting booth and force my hand perversely and shamefully to put my cross next to (my vote was my secret) instead of next to (my vote was my secret). The elections were meant to be the most joyous period in my life, yet the only moment when I wept with real tears of unforced emotion was when I saw on TV the elderly and the infirm being the first to vote. [Mommy, you must live, we need your vote, there are special assistants for the blind. . . . My mother knew what I was saying: it wasn't the extra vote, it was a reminder of what her life of 90 years had been about, ever since as a rebellious schoolgirl she had sung: God save our gracious King, when we get hold of him . . .] Elderly African men and women stood with a quiet, disciplined sense of achievement and told the interviewers exactly what I knew they would say: we have waited our whole lives for this moment, and we, the crazies, the idealists, the holders of impossible dreams, turned out to be right, our lives were valid after all, our beliefs justified. Suddenly, for three days we had become the normal ones, and the rest of the disbelieving world the oddballs.

Yet the shock of having suddenly reached my life's most wondrous day seemed to have left me disturbed rather than elated. Shuffling forward in a queue to make two anonymous pencil marks, I was about to consummate the most precious asset any person can have, the hope for a glorious future, and at the same time to extinguish it. Could it be that once we achieved our ideals, we could no longer live for them? I felt miserably neutered by the normality for which we had fought, and which had produced not only the desired political equality between black and white but an unsettling equality of emotion and existence between ourselves and those who, offered a choice between human rights and a piece of chocolate, would have selected the chocolate each time.

I thought with amusement, part smug, part wry, about the one previous time I had received a ballot slip. It had been during my second detention, nearly 30 years before, in a doubly-padlocked cell in Roeland Street jail, and I was recovering from torture by sleep deprivation. To save himself the complicated routines required to unlock both padlocks, Captain Rossouw of the Security Police thrust his hand with the ballot slip in it through the bars of the window and said: Advocate Sachs, this is a democratic country and you have the right to vote, and I answered: No thank you, Captain Rossouw (we freedom fighters were well brought up), I would rather not, and I saw the ballot slip float back past the bars.

Now with my left hand which, disappointingly, would produce the identical feeble scrawl of my former right hand, I picked up the pencil provided in the voting booth, and thought of the words of Albert Luthuli, the ANC President who had died in banishment: After decades of knocking patiently and vainly at the door asking for improvement of our conditions, our life is worse than it was before, and the only road to freedom now lies via the cross. The cross on the ballot paper, the cross of sacrifice.

It hadn't just been the solitary confinement, the sleep deprivation torture or the bomb; it had been the surveillance, the bugs, the raids, the informers, the unrelenting pressure wherever we were, every hour of day and night, to wipe us out because we had the vision that one day in South Africa everyone would be equal. ('You mean, you seriously believe in one man one vote?') Truly, whatever else it signified, the Bill of Rights in our new Constitution was the negative biography of our generation, the 'never again' of our lives. Our confrontations had been real and directly experienced: the suppressed panic, the unrelenting tension of underground work, the comradeship of the embattled, the pain of isolation, the constant secrecy that had compelled the most honest amongst us to become the biggest dissemblers. It had been dark and intimately and intensely our own, and, oh, so sharply and personally experienced.

[Albie, I don't know why you want me to dictate my memoirs, I wasn't important.... Mommy, that's exactly why... I was able to get a visit to Albie while he was held in Caledon Square under the ninety day law. Johnny had just undergone an open heart operation in London and I phoned the police and cried over the phone that my one son was in hospital and my other son was detained: so I was able to visit him. I bought a new dress, and had my hair and nails done. I came along looking as bright as I could. I never wore that dress again, only that once. The visit had the opposite effect on Albie to what the police had expected. They thought I would be crying and pleading with him to talk, and what happened was the contrary. He wanted to say something, and I put my hand to my lips because I was sure there would be a microphone somewhere. After that we just spoke about trivialities. Even though it was a chilly day, Albie chose to meet me in the yard rather than in his cell, not only to get fresh air, but to avoid being bugged, yet I was sure there would be a microphone there as well. It didn't matter, though, it was enough just to see him. Later, after his release, Albie wrote to Johnny about me, saying 'poor Mommy, her son the doctor went to hospital, her son the lawyer went to jail.']

Today, I thought with dismay, my life and my smile were becoming more public, while my emotions were growing ever more private. Once upon a time our success had depended on deep secrecy, now it flowed from intense publicity. Instead of putting on gloves to hide fingerprints and be invisible from the police, I would choose attire to make me look handsome, trustworthy, and wise on TV. What mattered was no longer the intrinsic quality of the things we did, but the excellence of the way we presented ourselves. Our emotions, once intensely and rawly our own, were now parasitic on the experiences of others. Fevered by soundbites on the screen or radio or snippets in print, we were unable, even unwilling to immunize ourselves against electoral cholera. We ended up investing the banal exercise of counting ballot slips with the intense and over-furnaced emotions of history. And just as our feelings came from watching and reading about the doings of others, so did the world at large witness with pleasurable disbelief the queues of black and white voters waiting patiently to participate as equals for the first time in our elections, and declare that our negotiated revolution was a miracle.

It wasn't a miracle. It didn't just come to pass. Our transition had been the most willed, thought-about, planned-for event of the late twentieth century. I had once written that all revolutions were impossible until they happened, then they became inevitable. In our case the movement from impossibility to inevitability seemed miraculous to many, particularly to those of little faith, who could only anticipate racial war and mutual ruin. That was the irony – the relationship between history and miracle had been reversed; for the total doubters, it had been a miracle, while for those of intense belief, it had been entirely rational. We believers knew that the transition had been the product of intensely thought-through planning and had been based on meetings and yet more meetings, endless, endless meetings, above-ground, underground, in prison, on Robben Island, in exile, meetings, some boring, some interesting, all with their 'agendas' and 'matters arising' and 'any other business,' meetings, meetings – I used to believe that freedom meant no more meetings, but still they continued, more and more meetings . . . we would have a classless society long before we achieved a meetingless one.

Did things just happen, or did we make things come about? I knew that nothing we were living through had just come to pass. We had willed it all, worked for it, never given up, never let go of the basic ideas. Yes, we had believed – belief had been fundamental – but we had backed it up with endless hard work, and learned how to do things together, and to accommodate the fears and interests of others, and to survive the sarcasm and disbelief of those who regarded themselves as more knowledgeable than ourselves about what they called the real world, and we just kept going on and on until at last the impossible became first feasible then real and finally inevitable.

I marked my clumsy cross next to the photograph of (my vote is my secret) folded it with my teeth, and dropped it in the box. Sufficient unto the day was the banal goodness thereof.

60

Undoing: Social Suffering and the Politics of Remorse in the New South Africa

Nancy Scheper-Hughes

As a very small girl "in training" for my First Confession in preparation for First Communion, I was impressed by the story a nun told to our catechism class. It was about an old woman who went to her priest asking forgiveness for a sin of gossip that had harmed the reputation of a neighbor. The priest accepted the woman's expression of remorse, gave her "conditional" absolution, told her to mend her ways, and gave her the following penance. He ordered the old woman to climb the belfry of the parish church, where she was to cut a small hole in a feather pillow and then shake the feathers loose onto the streets below. Then she was told to go about the village collecting the feathers until she had enough to sew back into the pillow. "But Father," the woman protested, "That would be impossible!" To which the good priest sadly replied: "Yes, and so, too, is it impossible to *undo* the damage caused by malicious acts."

These were wise words, but counterintuitive to the received wisdoms of the day. For the romance with remorse and with reparation, memory, and healing – of the individual and the social body – has emerged as a master narrative of the late twentieth century, as individuals and entire nations struggle to overcome the legacies of suffering ranging from rape and domestic violence (see Winkler 1995; Herman 1994) to collective atrocities of state-sponsored dirty wars and ethnic cleansings (Weschler 1990; Suarez-Orozco 1987; Boraine, Levy, and Scheffer 1994).

The psychologies of remorse, guilt, catharsis, and closure compete today with the theologies of reconciliation, forgiveness, and redemption in another version of what Philippe Rieff (1966) called the triumph of the therapeutic. Michael Ignatieff has hit upon an appropriate generative metaphor for looking at the present contexts of national recovery: *getting over*. The words conjure up biblical images of safe passage, of reaching the other side, and, finally, of *overcoming*. Just what needs to be "gotten over" if South Africa and South Africans are to get safely to the other side? Is reconciliation possible without some kind of powerful, transcendental faith? Surely, as many have argued, a first step in the politics of reconciliation and forgiveness is knowledge seeking, learning exactly what happened to whom, by whom, and why.

"I sometimes wonder," said Fr. Lapsley,

who that man or woman was who typed my name on the envelope that was supposed to kill me. I wonder, what did they tell their spouses or children that night at suppertime about what they did in the office that day? Either they are so dehumanized that they don't care or else they have learned to live comfortably with their guilt....I don't want vengeance, but I think that the names and faces of these people should be known.

The official vehicle to facilitate individual and collective "getting over" and liberating South Africa of the ghosts of its past is the Truth and Reconciliation Commission. In hundreds of hearings around the country, more than 2,000 victims of apartheid-era brutality have told their stories to the independent Commission. A smaller number of perpetrators of the violence have come forward to confess the details of their attacks on civilians, in exchange for political amnesty.

Those seeking truth in South Africa today do not want the partial, indeterminate, shifting truths of the postmodern, which resemble the dissembling, always self-described "complex" truths and realities promoted by the old apartheid state. Instead, they desire the single, sweet, "objective" truth of the moralist and, with it, a restored sense of wholeness and a taste of justice. Yet, as Justice Albie Sachs has noted, South Africans are willing to settle for an agreed-upon, a "good enough" truth – a narrative that will at least place Black and white South Africans, Afrikaners and English-speakers, Xhosas and Zulus, ANC and PAC members on the same map rather than living in different nations across the road from each other.

There are, of course, many critics of the TRC process. Some worry about the focus on the exceptional, extreme, and gross acts of human rights violation, which runs the risk of obscuring, or worse, of normalizing the ordinary, daily, routine acts of apartheid's structural violence: the legal, medical, economic, bureaucratic, and commercial violations of human rights that alienated millions of South Africans from their property, their homes, their families, their labor, their citizenship, and even their own bodies. *Segregation*

Others worry about the dangers of "numbing" South Africans by exposure to televised images of the TRC's invented and routinized public ritual of feigned remorse and forced forgiveness. I recall a chilling scene evoked by anthropologist Michael Taussig when, a few years ago, he was visiting the capital of a South American country (which shall remain anonymous) during a period of official truth- and soul-searching. He was directed to a local municipal office where documents were being filed by those who had been tortured during the previous regime. Taussig described the petty bureaucrats as seated along a bench behind a very long table. In front of each official stood a long line of ordinary – and some very poor and barefooted – people waiting their turn to testify to the suffering they had endured. They were asked to do so following the official form and set formula of questions. Each petitioner was given three or four minutes to answer the questions: When were you abducted? Where were you taken? Were you beaten? Tortured? On which parts of your body? What tools were used? What questions were you asked? How did you reply? The officers might have been tax collectors. As such, the original torture was mimetically reproduced by a new structure of indifferent state interrogators.

Still others – most of the "ordinary" South African whites I have spoken to in malls and shopping centers, in tea rooms and in public gardens, in office buildings and in hospitals, in private homes and large farm estates – worry about "witch-hunting, scapegoating, and persecution." Indeed, it seems that a great many white people in South Africa still fail to get the point behind the TRC. So, time and again, I was told that if General Malan ordered these tortures or that massacre, it was because he *had* to do it for the national security. Those who were detained, tortured, and killed were not "innocent," after all, they were terrorists. In addition, I was reminded, there were border wars going on. Communists were poised to take over all of Southern Africa.

As for the "higher ups," their defenses are well fortified. Mr. Breytenbach, for example, a former Deputy Defense Minister who served within the old apartheid Secretary of Defense under Presidents Botha and De Klerk, is now comfortably retired on a government pension and living out his days as a recovering heart-transplant patient in a luxurious, well-tended, and secured gated community in Sun Valley, outside Cape Town. He remains unrepentant and willing to attribute the atrocities emerging daily through the TRC amnesty hearings to a "few bad apples" in the old security and defense forces. I asked Mr. Breytenbach his opinion of the TRC hearings:

S-H: *You were once in the Ministry of Defense. Do you think that your colleagues are getting a fair shake?*

B: Well, I don't think this [the TRC] is the right thing to do. Instead of reconciling us, it is making the divisions even bigger. The thing now is to join people together. Of course, I think, most people, even I (and I was chairman of my party in the Orange Free State and in the Secretary of Defense for more than seven years) were unaware of what was going on. I was positively shocked out of my mind to hear of the... well, let's just call them atrocities, and that sort of thing. It gives me goose bumps. I just can't believe it. Some of the people standing up there [before the TRC], I know them well. You would never have thought that such things went on. But I have a son in the police, and he was telling me going back all these years, "Dad, you must look at some of these characters on the far right, the AWB, and such." He said the police were infested with them. A person who is not white, well these guys had no respect for him and eventually they had no respect for life itself. So, what is coming out there, well, it shakes me out of my mind every time.

I asked Mr. Breytenbach if he watched the summary of the week's TRC proceedings produced by the SABC (South African Broadcasting Company) on Sunday nights. He replied.

> I watch it. I watch it with disgust, yah. But, you know, I sat in at all the top executive meetings of the Defense Force, which is where all the decisions were taken. There was Magnus Malan, myself, and the whole Defense Council, all the generals and brigadiers and so on, and I swear to you that *never, ever* were these sorts of things discussed. O.K. We said that we must try and achieve something in this area [i.e., torture] to get stability. But these characters went out and slaughtered people like cattle.

Does that mean that discipline had broken down in the security forces?

> I wouldn't say that discipline had broken down so much as. . . . If you read that book, *The Sword and the Swastika*, you can see what the Germans did in the past war to the Jews. It was so sickening, you know, I walked around the house for a few days after I read it. It left such an impression on me. You just can't believe it. And there, too, you find the same thing as happened here. It all boils down to a few individuals, a few rotten apples, small people sitting in big jobs who suddenly think that they can play God. Chaps like these had taken it on their own to do things such as they have done and to thinking that they can just "remove" certain people. But nowhere and at no time were these things ever discussed or hinted at during the executive meetings.

Do you believe that De Klerk and Botha did not know what was happening within their own forces?

They must have known something. When I was a member of the Security Committee, we were five people – the President, Mr. Botha, General Malan, myself, Pik, and Bryon Deplussey, the Minister of Finance. They knew something because we kept asking for a lot of money for developing arms for the border wars and for the security problems at home. I think it was a case of people looking you in the eye and saying one thing while they go out and do another. As far as I am concerned, these people are in for the high jump and let them go. I don't care.

So you are opposed to amnesty then?

No, amnesty is a good thing. If a man has something on his chest, he can come out and confess it and ask amnesty for it. So, I agree with that.

Since all these atrocities were carried out in secret, now that things are coming to the light, what will happen to these men's private lives? I mean, for example, to a son watching his father on TV before the TRC amnesty hearings. Will he say, "Dad, did you really do all those things?" What will it mean for those families?

I don't know too much about that. . . . But some of these characters have just disappeared. They have walked out and left their wives and kids. I know of one specific case in the Orange Free State where neighbors had to take up a collection and pay for food and rent for a family who was deserted by someone who couldn't stand to face the music. Finally, this family was so poor they had to move in with someone else's family. So, I can only imagine . . . but, then, remember you get some of those women in the AWB [right wing] and you can't believe the things they still say. They are some of the worst ones. But I don't think there are very many of these real SS types. I have spoken to another girl whose husband was involved – who tortured and killed a lot of people – and she says that this part is worse for her than death itself. Kids at school point out her children and they say, "Your Daddy did this and this." I often wonder how many of them have had mental problems around all this. *[like you?]*

What were the biggest surprises for you?

[deep sigh] So many. What was going on at the Vlockplas, this de Kock chap. He's unbelievable, a real monster. Some of these characters had access to accounts abroad with millions of rands that they used to do their dirty work. How did they get those funds? But the Vlockplas goings-on, that really shocked me, and the Biko thing. And this other hearing, the Kondile case now going on. The burnings of the bodies and all that. It is terrible. One just doesn't know. But, again, I would go back to the Nazi era. Pretty much the same thing happened there. People lost all sense of humanity and engaged in cold-blooded murder. And, if you want to talk about atrocities, when I was stationed over there in Kenya, it was during the Mau Mau massacres. On my off time, I used to fly and I did some observations from the air. Once I found a small strip about half way up Mt. Kilimanjaro where you could land a small airplane. And from the air, I saw farmers and cattle and small babies slaughtered. You can't sleep for months after seeing something like that. And, if you go even today into KwaZulu-Natal, you will find similar massacres still going on. So, this whole thing is not clear-cut. Both sides [i.e. Blacks and whites] are to blame, and there is more to all this than politics. It's about power. They all want power. And total power corrupts totally.

Do you believe that forgiveness and reconciliation are possible in South Africa?

Yes, I am very optimistic. I have to be. I have a stake in this country. I have six adult children and they have nowhere else to go . . . But what really concerns me now is that the – let's call them the whites of the country, some, not all of them, but a great many, are beginning to think that there is no law and order in the country. When white people see these large numbers of so-called disadvantaged people marching down the street, breaking things, taking and stealing whatever they want, well, they become very negative. They think that there is no good policing any more. And they start to think, well, if *these people* can get away with this, so can we, too. But I try to warn them not to lower their standards, to become like the bad ones . . .

In this extraordinary narrative, Mr. Breytenbach manages to deny and assert his knowledge of, and responsibility for, state-level atrocities, to attribute blame above and below him, and to take comfort in the knowledge that the kinds of atrocities committed by the apartheid state are not unique to South Africa, but have taken place before (as in Nazi Germany) and in other parts of Africa (as in Kenya during the Mau Mau massacres). At the end of his discourse, the *real* "bad guys" in this story turn out to be the "disadvantaged" Blacks who have no respect for law and order and who are corrupting the morals of white people.

Like most whites I have encountered since 1992, Mr. Breytenbach fails to recognize the enormous grace by which he and all white South Africans have been spared.

In light of the aberrant behaviors becoming known through the TRC amnesty hearings, one is inclined to feel that perhaps the "witch-hunting" metaphor is not such a bad trope. The apartheid state was filthy with "witches" at all levels of power and authority and a little "witch-hunting" could clear the air. Among its many horrors, the TRC has provided the world with unforgettable images of culture inverted and a world turned upside-down.

The political assassinations were carried out by trained hit squads, acting – we now know through confessions delivered before the TRC – on explicit orders. Suspected "terrorists" were abducted from their homes by police, blindfolded, kicked and beaten, and tortured in new, improved, and creative ways, some of them similar to the "toilet plunger rape" technique used by New York City police officer Volpe in his handling of a Black suspect. What has come out of the halting, uptight "confessions" are images of the white South African family picnic, the *braii* (barbecue) turned into a cannibalistic political ritual. *[lynchings!]*

For example, at the TRC amnesty hearings in Pretoria in 1997 (TRC hearings; Feldman 1997) former policemen Hennie Gerber and Johan van

Eyk told how they abducted, blindfolded, tortured, and murdered a suspected PAC member, Samuel Kganakga. They took him to an isolated rural setting, kicked and beat him, tied him up and hung his body upside down, pulled his trousers down and applied electric shocks to his private parts. Later they built a fire under his head to "dry him out." While Kganaka's fat splattered and sizzled over the fire, Jack Mkoma, a private guard and police accomplice was sent out to fetch brandy, vodka, and cold cans of soda that were passed around among the men in a signifying cannibalistic ritual of apartheid Afrikaner brotherhood.

No wonder so many family members of those tortured and killed by the police state have rejected the TRC imposed duty to reconcile. "I am not ready to forgive," the mother of Sidizwe Kondile, another victim of a police-orchestrated *braii murder*, told me during a break in the TRC amnesty hearings for her son's murderers in Cape Town in February 1998. Father Michael Lapsley refers to "cheap theologies" of forgiveness and to his extreme discomfort with the idea of blanket amnesty, although he says that for the sake of the "greater good" of the country – and for the nation to be able to close a chapter on the past – he accepts the TRC's version of exchanging full disclosure for *conditional* amnesty. He has also often expressed his resentment of those who seem to demand that he extend an instantaneous, unconditional, "Christian" forgiveness toward his would-be assassins. Michael notes how often his speeches and lectures are misheard by those who come up to him afterwards and thank him for being "so forgiving" toward the people who sent him the bomb, although he has never once mentioned the word forgiveness (Worsnip 1996: 134).

Albie Sachs (cited in Boraine, Levy, and Scheffer 1994: 20–1; and see also Chapter 59) tells the story of his own failure to forgive when, soon after he returned from exile, he was enjoying a night out at a jazz bar on Cape Town's waterfront. His private enjoyment was interrupted by a young, white man in a jacket and tie who approached Sachs' table and in a thickly Afrikaner-accented English asked: "Are you Albie Sachs?"

Annoyed at the intrusion, Sachs replied brusquely, "I am."

"*Verskoon my*" – "Forgive me" – the man said in Afrikaans, his voice almost drowned out by the drummers. Albie Sachs said nothing.

Again, he repeated. "*Verskoon my.*"

Albie tossed off the request with a somewhat callous: "This lovely club is my forgiveness." Later he thought of things he might have said – "Don't ask me for forgiveness – I was a volunteer in the struggle. I chose my fate. What about the millions of Black South Africans who had no choice but to suffer and die under apartheid?" Still later, in an interview with him in 1998, Albie Sachs confided (personal communication): "What I probably should have done was embrace the young man and accepted his forgiveness. But I simply couldn't. Not then."

Witchcraft as Popular Justice

Allow me, then, to play devil's advocate in suggesting that witch-hunting might not only be a fitting metaphor for the collective recovery and healing of South Africa, but also to show the extent to which the South African Truth and Reconciliation Commission has incorporated certain aspects of traditional practices of popular justice into its curiously hybrid formulas and rituals.

Confession is, of course, a central dynamic in all witchcraft-believing societies (see Jeffreys 1952), from the Navajo and Pueblo peoples of the American Southwest to highland New Guinea (Bercovitch 1989), to vast stretches of indigenous Africa (Douglas 1970), to the Bocage region of modern France (Favret-Sada 1980), and to rural western Ireland (Arensberg 1968). Conventional insight suggests that witch-hunts are aberrant and dysfunctional institutions based on the mobilization of "primitive" projections with the identified "witch," chosen as the surrogate ritual scapegoat who represents the group's worst collective nightmare. The processes of fact-finding, guilt determination, the ritualized expressions of remorse, and the demand for immediate, though often symbolic, reparation strike liberal, bourgeois sensibilities as weak, irrational, and unjust.

Yet a great many anthropologists (beginning with Monica Wilson 1951) working on the ground with witch-believing societies have challenged the Western stereotype by showing the positive uses of witchcraft in restoring health to troubled communities. [...]

In South Africa, the power of traditional Zulu medicine (see Berglund 1989; Ngubane 1977) resides in a *sangomas'* (healer's) skill in identifying the social tensions, "hard feelings," and antisocial hostilities that can congeal into sickness, misfortune, and death in the community. "Witches" are asked to identify themselves, to come forward and to "speak out" their "bottled up" envy, hatred, and guilt. A great many "witches" do indeed come forward. From their perspective, confessions are said to be a means of "emptying themselves" of the burden of evil and restoring feelings of lightness and emptiness that signify balance, health, and good relations.

Rarely, however, do such public confessions result in amnesty, of course, and even the most repentant "witches" can be punished by fines, forced labor, and public floggings, not to mention the miscarriages of popular justice that can result in outbreaks of indiscriminate witch-hunting hysterias and witchburnings, such as the much publicized spate of recent witch-hunts in Venda (see Minnaar et al. 1992), the Northern Transvaal (see Niehaus 1997), and in Soweto (see Ashforth 1996; Keller 1994) in the early 1990s. Yet these incidents are anomalies, while the more common and judicious applications of "counter-sorcery" as a traditional form of popular justice are known to few outside the field of anthropology.

During the anti-apartheid struggle years, some of these older practices were transformed into newer institutions of popular justice, including the peoples' courts, security committees, and discipline committees put into place by "the comrades" in urban townships and squatter camps. Peoples' courts meted out a rough sort of popular, revolutionary justice. Apologies and fines were levied for lesser infractions. More serious offenses were punished through public spectacles in which the lash – and less often the infamous necklace – predominated. At times, suspected or confessed police collaborators were punished or even killed as "witches" (see Scheper-Hughes, Chapter 30). [. . .]

The strength of these institutions of popular justice is that they are immediate, public, collective, face-to-face, and relatively transparent. They are based on traditional notions of ubuntu (an ethos of humanism based on collective values), and the power of shame within a context of codes of personal honor and dignity. I once attended an outdoor court meeting on a Sunday morning in 1994, held under a large tree in the Chris Hani squatter camp. One of the petitioners to come before the community that morning had

been accused by his neighbors of public drunkenness and disturbing the peace. The man sent a friend to represent him, explaining his absence due to a job he had to attend to that day. The friend was called to the front and read from a respectful letter of apology written by the man. The court of elder men and women listened attentively, conferred among themselves, and then gave their verdict: the offender could not be forgiven until he appeared in person. The written apology was appreciated, but the man would still have to appear in front of those whom he had offended. He would have to "face" them. Then the next case was heard. [. . .]

Elements of traditional and popular justice have made their way into the uniquely South African version of the late modern idea of the truth commission. Like traditional witch-hunting and the peoples' courts that proliferated during the anti-apartheid years, the TRC is not so terribly concerned with fact-finding and fact checking. It relies more on the power of the dramaturgic moment: public enactments of suffering, confession, remorse, and forgiveness. Written testimonies and formal legalistic petitions are part of the TRC record and process, but these are never completely acceptable without an *appearance* by the petitioners in symbolic face-to-face encounters with their victims and survivors. The TRC places a high premium on apologies offered in person by the perpetrators who are asked to give "eye contact" to those who were hurt and wronged. At the close of each amnesty hearing, the commissioners and trained "briefers" expedite a "closing" ritual by inviting the survivors to come forward and address their former tormentors, raising with them any final, unanswered questions.

And so, Dawie Ackerman, who lost his wife in the St. James Massacre, came forward to tell the young men who killed his wife how he had been made to step over dead bodies to get to his wife, still sitting bolt upright in her front row pew, and how all the while he was hoping against hope, that Marita might just be shell-shocked but still alive, until he had finally crossed that endless expanse and reached her. But just as he touches her back, her body rolls over and falls with a dull thud to the floor, her special Sunday clothes splattered with blood. Dawie continues, his composure now broken, his voice cracking and trembling with tears that have been, he said, a very long time – five years, in fact – in coming:

I've never cried since I lost my wife other than to have silent cries. I've never had an emotional outburst till now. When ... when Mr. Makoma here [the young man who was 17 at the time he took part in the church attack] was testifying, he talked about his own tortures in prison, and that he was suicidal at times, but that he never once cried. I thought to myself – and I passed you [the TRC lawyer] a note – to please bring your cross-examination to an end. Because what are we doing here? The truth, yes. But then I looked at the way in which he, Makoma, answered you. All his anger. What on earth are we doing? And I thought that *he* cannot be reconciled.

Then, in a final and painfully wrenching scene Dawie Ackerman, now openly weeping, asked the three young applicants to turn their averted faces to look at him directly:

This is the first opportunity we have had to look each other in the eye while talking. I want to ask Mr. Makoma, who actually entered the church my ... my wife ... was sitting at the door when you came in. [Dawie weeps and the words seem to be dragged from the roots of his shaking body.] She was wearing a long blue coat. *Please, can you remember if you shot her?*

Makoma looks terrified, as if he is seeing Hamlet's father's ghost. He nervously bites his lower lip and slowly shakes his head. No, he cannot remember, either Marita or her long, blue coat. Nevertheless, all three young men apologize to Dawie. Makoma is the most affected:

We are truly sorry for what we have done. But it was not intentional. It was the situation in South Africa. Although people died, we did not do that out of our own will. It was the situation we were living under. And now we are asking you *please*, do forgive us.

Dawie Ackerman *did* give Mr. Makoma his forgiveness and he withdrew his formal, legal objection to the young men receiving amnesty from the state.

After the formal hearing, Ackerman and several other survivors, including Bishop Reteif, met behind closed doors in an arranged, private meeting with their attackers, each of whom walked around the table addressing each survivor in turn, shaking hands, and asking personal forgiveness. Paul Williams, who is partially paralyzed from a bullet lodged in the small of his back, said, "I have now forgiven the one who shot me, uncondition-

ally. I looked him in the eye and actually had a chat with him. It was a good experience for me. I saw that we could each forgive the other."

Each forgive the other?, I asked.

You have to remember that I am a Coloured man and I know where these guys are coming from. I know how they were wronged and how even my own group [i.e., the mixed-race population] turned away from their suffering.

Brian Smart was most struck by the ages of the PAC militants:

They were only 17 years old, and I could relate to that. When I was 18, I was in the Air Force and sent to Cyprus in defense of the realm, if you like. The only difference between myself and them was that I was operating under a more controlled military order. So an incident like this [the massacre] would not have happened. But in their case, the command structure was very weak and they had the normal soldier's ability to kill, just as I had.

Mary Powers chimed in to say,

I have been thinking about their parents, how it must have been so hard, you know, they were children. And maybe they had gone a way they didn't want them to go. Maybe they pleaded with them, but there were stronger forces at work. Or, maybe, they supported them. I don't know. But I am a mother, too, and I just feel for the parents.

Bishop Reteif, who was not in the church until moments after the attack took place and who subsequently suffered a great deal of pastoral survivor guilt (*Shepherd, why were you not keeping watch over your flocks by night?*), originally opposed the TRC and the granting of amnesty to "terrorists." His initial response to the massacre was to heroize the clergy and congregation and to criminalize the youth, seen hardly as people, but as "instruments" of other evil forces. After the hearings, the bishop is contrite about the "blindness" of his church to the suffering caused by the apartheid state. Moreover, after actually meeting the young men, he felt for the first time since the attack that he could carry on with his normal life. He said:

Something like a weight has been lifted from my heart, something that would be hard for you to understand if you had not been a part of the TRC process yourself. Now, I finally understand why it [the TRC] was necessary to bring about healing in the end.

Young Makoma, serving a more than 20-year sentence for his part in the massacre, returned to Polsmor prison to await the result of his amnesty petition. The other two PAC applicants returned to the Defense Forces, where they have been serving as soldiers since 1994, their trials pending the results of their amnesty pleas. (The Amnesty Committee of the TRC granted amnesty on June 11, 1998, to all three of the PAC "operatives" in the St. James Massacre.) Although Dawie Ackerman, Bishop Reteif, and other church members seem to have experienced a real catharsis through the TRC process, young Makoma has yet to find any such emotional relief. During a SABC media-arranged prison visit between Makoma and Dawie Ackerman's daughter, Leisel, the young man was asked how he felt, upon seeing the graphic police photos at his amnesty hearing "of all the people and all the blood." He replied to the girl whose mother he had killed in the attack:

Yah, I remember that O.K. And I had feelings then. It was bad. But no matter how I feel now, at this moment, that what I did was bad, there is nothing which I can do. The people are dead. How I feel cannot change anything.

As a strong and disciplined PAC militant, Makoma still feels that all these emotional performances are unseemly and just a little bit beside the point.

Remorse and Changes in Spirit

Albie Sachs (personal communication, 1998) expressed the wish that there could be more "felt emotion" by the perpetrators of political violence. He referred to those who seem unmoved by the TRC process, who (like P. W. Botha and Winnie Mandela) have refused the new history, and who remain frozen in the past. The TRC process has, in fact, opened up new emotional spaces where conversations and actions that were once impossible, even unthinkable, are now happening. The unlikely encounters between perpetrators and victims, who are beginning to empathize with each other's situation, is an extraordinary case in point. Soon after Makoma's arrest in 1993, the first time a church member (a divinity student) approached, he chased the young man out of his cell, saying that he would send his "comrades" out to get him. Less than five years later, Makoma

was both gracious and apologetic toward his visitors. After their arranged meeting, Leisel Ackerman was even able to wonder, "Will we ever see each other again? Could we possibly become friends?"

I think of the ordinary Afrikaner couple who, with very concerned looks on their faces, approached me one day on the steps of St. George's Cathedral in Cape Town (Archbishop Tutu's church). "Where could they find the bishop?" they asked.

"Oh, he's a very busy man," I said. "I'm sure he's not here now." They both looked crestfallen. "Well, what did you want to see him about?"

"We want to confess to the Truth Commission. We did not treat Black people very well and now we want to make a fresh start."

I explained that the TRC was a very formal process "with lawyers and official papers" meant for murderers and torturers, not for ordinary people who could have behaved better. Yet the real effects of the TRC will perhaps be felt in small ripple effects like these and, hopefully, in various community circles where people, like this couple, might be able to meet with others to talk about just what happened to them, how they behaved, and how to set the record straight. This is what some of the churches and, in particular, Father Lapsley's "Healing the Memories" forums are doing. At least some of these healing retreats are reserved for those who were neither victims nor perpetrators, but people who, all the same, were hurt, diminished, traumatized, and/or compromised by the apartheid state and the violent struggle against it. After the formal TRC has disbanded and all the counselors return to business as usual, what will be needed still are a multitude of little TRCs, community based, for ordinary citizens who had to live through extraordinary times.

Redemption

So I close with the story of Hennie's redemption. Hennie is an acquaintance, an Afrikaner and a private security guard in Cape Town. During the year we first spent in South Africa in 1993, Hennie frequently dropped by our house to visit. I feared that either he was spying on us or that he had a special fondness for one of our adult daughters. We tolerated his visits as patiently as we could. He seemed honestly curious and well-intentioned. I ran into Hennie in the streets of Cape Town during a spontaneous celebration of South Africa's having won the All-Africa Soccer Cup in February 1996. Hennie was very excited, almost emotionally overwrought, and he didn't know quite how to explain to me the magnitude and significance of that magical moment. "Did you see the game?" he asked. I did, I said, on a big screen in a packed bar.

"*Both* goals?"

"Yes, indeed."

"And did you see our President [Nelson Mandela] right there out on the field?"

"Yes."

"Can you possibly know what this means for us?" Without waiting for an answer, Hennie told me:

It means we are not 100% bad. It means God is willing to forgive us. That He would give to us – of all people! – such great heroes! It is a sign that we are going in a good way now. We are not hated any more. Oh, how can I explain this? It's like before we were Fat Elvis: sick, disgusting, ugly. Now we are like skinny Elvis: young, handsome, healthy. In the New South Africa, we have all been reborn.

REFERENCES

Arensberg, Conrad M. 1968. *The Irish Countryman: An Anthropological Study.* Garden City, NY: Natural History Press.

Ashforth, Adam. 1996. "Of Secrecy and the Commonplace: Witchcraft and Power in Soweto." *Social Research* 63,4 (Winter): 1183–1233.

Bercovitch, E. 1989. "Moral Insights: Victim and Witch in the Nalumin Imagination." In G. Herdt and M. Stephen (eds.), *The Religious Imagination of New Guinea.* New Brunswick: Rutgers University Press: 122–59.

Berglund, Axel-Ivar. 1989. "Confessions of Guilt and Restoration of Health. Some Illustrative Zulu Examples." In *Culture, Experience, and Pluralism: Essays on African Ideas of Illness and Healing.* Department of Anthropology, University of Upsala, Sweden: Upsala Studies in Cultural Anthropology.

Boraine, Alex, Janet Levy, and Ronael Scheffer, eds. 1994. *Dealing with the Past: Truth and Reconciliation in South Africa.* Cape Town: IDASA.

Douglas, Mary, ed. 1970. *Witchcraft Confessions and Accusations.* ASA Monographs No. 9. London: Tavistock.

Favret-Saada, J. 1980. *Deadly Words: Witchcraft in the Bocage.* Cambridge: Cambridge University Press.

Herman, Judith. 1994. *Trauma and Recovery.* New York: Basic Books.

Ignatieff, Michael. 1977. "Digging up the Dead." *The New Yorker* (Nov. 10): 85–93.

Jeffreys, M. D. W. 1952. "Confessions by Africans." *Eastern Anthropologist* 6: 42–57.

Keller, Bill. 1994. "Apartheid's Grisly Aftermath: Witch Burning." *New York Times* (Sunday, Sept. 18):3.

Minnaar, A. de V., D. Offringa, and C. Payze. 1992. *To Live in Fear: Withchburning and Medicine Murder in Venda.* Pretoria: Human Sciences Research Council.

Ngubane, Harriet. 1977. *Body and Mind in Zulu Medicine.* London: Academic Press.

Niehaus, Isak. 1997. *Witchcraft, Power, and Politics: An Ethnographic Study of the South African Lowveld.* Johannesburg: University of Witwatersrand, Department of Social Anthropology.

Rieff, Philip. 1966. *The Triumph of the Therapeutic: Uses of Faith After Freud.* New York: Harper & Row.

Sachs, Albie. 1998. "Violence and Recovery in the New South Africa." Regents Professor Lecture, Department of Anthropology, University of California, Berkeley, February 2, 1998.

Scheper-Hughes, Nancy. 1994. "The Last White Christmas: The Heidleberg Pub Massacre." *American Anthropologist* 96,4 (Dec.): 1–28.

——. 1996. "Small Wars and Invisible Genocides." *Social Science and Medicine* 43, 5: 889–900.

——. 1997. "Peace-Time Crimes," *Social Identities*, 3,3: 471–97.

——. 1998. "The New Cannibalism: The Global Trade in Human Organs." *The New Internationalist* no. 300 (April).

Suarez-Orozco, Marcelo. 1987. "Children in the Dirty War." In N, Scheper-Hughes, ed., *Child Survival.* Dordrechi. Netherlands: D. Reidel.

Weschler, Lawrence-1990. *A Miracle. A Universe; Settling Accounts with Torturers.* New York: Viking.

Wilson, Monica, 1951. "Witch Beliefs and Social Structure." *American Journal of Sociology* 56, 4: 307–13.

Winkler Cathy, 1995. "Rape Attack: Ethnography of the Ethnographer," In Carolyn Nordstrom and Antonius C. G. M. Robben, eds., *Fieldwork Under Fire: Contemporary Studies of Violence and Survival.* Berkeley: University of California Press, 155–85.

Worship, Michael. 1996. *Michael Lapsley; Priest and Partisan,* Melbourne: Ocean Press.

61

From *When Victims Become Killers: Colonialism, Nativism, and the Genocide in Rwanda*

Mahmood Mamdani

A Reconciliation with History

Postgenocide Rwanda presents a sharp contrast to postapartheid South Africa. In the white population in Apartheid South Africa, there were few perpetrators but many beneficiaries. Among the Hutu in Rwanda of the genocide, there were fewer beneficiaries and many more perpetrators. If it is true that hundreds of thousands of Hutu participated directly in the killings, then reconciliation presents a dilemma, morally and politically. Even a cursory visit to postgenocide Rwanda brings one face-to-face with this dilemma. Every time I visited postgenocide Rwanda, I would ask responsible state officials – sometimes a minister – as to how many ordinary civilians they thought had participated in the genocide. Every time, the answer was in the millions. Even more troubling, the estimate grew with each visit. The first time I went, a minister suggested a practical way to apportion blame and mete out justice: "Categorize according to responsibility. Let those with responsibility be shot in the national stadium. Then go ahead and say that for all those who participated, the three to four million, let them say we did the wrong thing."[1] From "three to four million" in 1995, the figure had grown to "four to five million" in 1997, when another minister told me that "80 percent of those [Hutu] alive had participated in the killing."[2] What was the point of these growing estimates? Was it an attempt by those in power to underscore that the majority of Hutu in Rwanda are guilty of genocide? Or, was it also a claim that this guilty majority be deprived of political rights as punishment for its crimes? I am concerned less with the truth of the claim than with its political significance. Rwanda's key dilemma is how to build a democracy that can incorporate a *guilty majority* alongside an aggrieved and *fearful minority* in a single political community.

The Rwandan state generally avoids the use of Hutu and Tutsi as political identities. But it has adopted a "genocide framework" from which to categorize the population politically, meaning that "the 1994 genocide is singled out as an event producing the only politically correct categories for identification and guidelines" for state policy.[3] The state language in Rwanda, the language one hears from all officials, and also from many who are not, divides the population into five categories: returnees, refugees, victims, survivors, and perpetrators. The *returnees* are, first and foremost, the mainly Tutsi (and some Hutu) exiles who returned with the Rwanda Patriotic Front (RPF). The *refugees* are divided into two: the "old caseload" refers to mainly Tutsi pregenocide refugees, whereas the "new caseload" refers to the wholly Hutu postgenocide refugees. The terminology is also used by UN and NGO circles. The *victims* are said to be both Tutsi and Hutu – the latter victims of the massacres of the internal political opposition. But when it comes to identifying living victims, this identification is limited to the "Tutsi genocide survivors" and "old caseload refugees"; "new case-load are not considered victims and as such are often not entitled to assistance for the construction of homes."[4] Finally, *survivor* is a term applied only to Tutsi. This is because the genocide was aimed at only the Tutsi, I was told. From this point of view, the "survivor" is a Tutsi who had been in the country at the time of the genocide and who is alive today. The word is not used for any Hutu then in the country. The assumption is that every Hutu who opposed the genocide was killed. The flip side of this assumption is that every living Hutu was either an active participant or a passive onlooker in the genocide. Morally, if not legally, both are culpable. The dilemma is that to be a Hutu in contemporary Rwanda is to be presumed a *perpetrator.*

Associated with this is another obvious fact: that political violence in the Rwandan genocide had an open, mass, and perversely popular character, as opposed to the secret, cloak-and-dagger nature of political violence in South Africa. Killings in Rwanda were not done by shadowy death squads, but by mobs of machete-wielding citizens. Killings did not happen under cover of darkness, with hardly a witness in sight, and with every effort to destroy the evidence. Instead, they happened in broad daylight, for all to see, and with no effort to destroy the evidence. In a nutshell, while the identity of the perpetrator was not always known in South Africa, it *is* known in Rwanda.

True, there are many more perpetrators than there are beneficiaries in Rwanda, unlike in South Africa, and their identity also tends to be more public. And yet, neither the identity of the perpetrator nor that of the survivor is as transparent in Rwanda as these differences would lead one to think. This is because the identification of both perpetrator and survivor is contingent on one's historical perspective. This is why it is not possible to think of reconciliation between Hutu and Tutsi in Rwanda without a prior reconciliation with history. In a 1996 visit to Kigali, I requested to be taken to a school so I could talk to a history teacher. My host, an aide to the vice-president, said this would be difficult since history teaching in schools had stopped. I asked why. Because there is no agreement on what should be taught as history, was the reply. History in Rwanda comes in two versions: Hutu and Tutsi. Ever since the colonial period, the cycle of violence has been fed by a

victim psychology on both sides. Every round of perpetrators has justified the use of violence as the only effective guarantee against being victimized yet again. For the unreconciled victim of yesterday's violence, the struggle continues. The continuing tragedy of Rwanda is that each round of violence gives us yet another set of victims-turned-perpetrators.

To break the stranglehold of Hutu Power and Tutsi Power on Rwanda's politics, one also needs to break their stranglehold on Rwanda's history writing, and thus history making. This exercise requires putting the truth of the genocide, the truth of mass killings, in a historical context. To find a way out of this cycle, it is necessary to link political outcomes more to political institutions and less to political agency. The tendency has been the opposite: indeed, to so individualize and decontextualize the truth of the genocide – South Africa-style – that it escapes comprehension. What would it mean to contextualize the truth? It would be, *first of all*, to connect it to the civil war. This means to avoid two pitfalls: neither to merge and dissolve the genocide in the civil war, in which case it would cease to exist analytically, nor to sever it so completely from the civil war that the act of killing would become devoid of motivation. To see the genocide as one outcome of defeat in the civil war would be to see it as *political* violence, an outcome of a power struggle between Hutu and Tutsi elites. That would mean both to recognize Hutu and Tutsi as political identities and to recognize that the problem of Rwanda is first and foremost one of political power. There can be no reconcilation without a reorganization of power. [...]

Two Forms of Justice

Victor's justice

To pursue victor's justice would be to follow the example of Israel. It would be to build a Zionist-type state on the ashes of the genocide. This is indeed what is happening in contemporary Rwanda. Three convictions underline the character of postgenocide power in Rwanda. The first is an overwhelming sense of moral responsibility for the very survival of all remaining Tutsi, globally. This gives postgenocide power its first distinguishing characteristic: it is defined by a diasporic, rather than a territorial, notion of political obligation and political community. The second conviction – also a direct outcome of the experience of the genocide – is that Tutsi Power is the minimum condition for Tutsi survival. Tutsi will only be protected if they have a state of their own. I found this conviction shared by both the Congolese Tutsi legal adviser to the secretary-general of the Alliance of Democratic Forces in Kabila's Congo, and the newly appointed Rwandese commander of the Congolese national army in 1997. This point of view marks postgenocide power with yet a third conviction: that the only peace possible between Tutsi and Hutu is an armed peace. It also lends credibility to those in the opposition who argue that the Hutu must be armed if they are not to return to the servile condition of pre-1959 Rwanda.

Thus, even the moderate opposition to the RPF complains that not only are structures of power in Rwanda being Tutsified; civic organizations – from the media to nongovernmental organizations – are being cleansed of any but a nominal Hutu presence.[5] On its part, postgenocide power is determined to remove from the soil of Rwanda any trace of conditions that could possibly lead to a repeat of the genocide. Its unswerving motto recalls the claim that made post-Holocaust power in Israel immune to any moral doubts when it came to atrocities against Palestinians: NEVER AGAIN. Ironically, the conviction that Tutsi Power is the precondition for Tutsi survival means that life itself can be subordinated to this supreme goal, the survival of Tutsi Power.

The founding ideology of Tutsi Power in postgenocide Rwanda is the memory of the genocide and the moral compulsion never to let it happen again. The pursuit of the *génocidaires* is the raison d'être of the postgenocide state, the one permanent part of its agenda. In the real world of state politics, however, the word *génocidaire* may be used to label any Hutu seen as an opponent, or even a critic, of Tutsi Power. Arrests can be made on the basis of denunciation, not investigation. Even if the crowded jails of Rwanda take a daily toll on the lives of those incarcerated within, this does not disturb moral sensibilities.[6] The moral certainty about preventing another genocide imparts a moral justification to the pursuit of power with impunity.

Most recognize that the precondition for victor's justice is, clearly, victory. Few, however, recognize its price. The victor must remain on constant guard, lest the spoils of victory be snatched yet again. Just as a jailer comes to be tied to the jail as much as is the prisoner, so a victor must live in anticipation and fear of the next round of battle, why adversaries often tend to get locked into a single cycle more securely than do friends. The price of victor's justice is either a continuing civil war or a permanent divorce. It is worth remembering that it is not simply German defeat in the Second World War that made Nuremburg possible, but also the effective divorce between Gentiles and Jews in Germany, since most surviving German Jews departed for either America or Israel. In the absence of this effective divorce, anything resembling Zionist power in Germany would have been a recipe for triggering a civil war. In this sense, we need to bear in mind that while the RPF won the war, there has been no divorce between Tutsi and Hutu in Rwanda. The price of victor's justice, in Rwanda, must thus be yet another round of a continuing civil war.

It is also worth remembering a second difference between the Nazi Holocaust and the Rwandan genocide. Though both were designed from above, from within the state, the genocide alone unfolded as wave upon wave of mass killings, where not only victims but perpetrators too were drawn from civil society. As a state project that was carried out by many in society, the Rwandan genocide resembles apartheid more than it does the Holocaust. This is why victor's justice – the Tutsification of state institutions – cannot be an effective guarantee against a repeat of genocidal violence in Rwandan society. If anything, it will keep alive the specter of yet another round of genocidal violence.

Survivor's justice

The form of justice flows from the form of power. If victor's justice requires victor's power, then is not victor's justice simply revenge masquerading as justice? To get away from this dilemma, we need to explore answers to two questions. Is a form of justice possible that is not at the same time victor's justice? Is a form of reconciliation possible that is not at the same time an absence of justice, and thus an embrace of evil? These questions provide a clue to finding a way out of the dialectic of civil war. That way has to be anchored in an alternative form of justice that I will call *survivor's justice*.

The prerequisite for survivor's justice, as for victor's justice, may also be victory. For victory presents alternatives to the victor, which it does not to the vanquished. Only the victor has the choice of reaching out to the vanquished on terms that have the potential of transcending an earlier opposition between the two, by defining both as survivors of the civil war. To transcend the terms of the earlier opposition is to forge a new community of survivors of the civil war. From this point of view, the term "survivor" does not refer to surviving victims – which, as I have pointed out, is how it is used in contemporary Rwanda – but to all those who continue to be blessed with life in the aftermath of the civil war.[7] The notion of survivor seeks to transcend the bipolar notions of victim and perpetrator.

The difference between victor's justice and survivor's justice is clear if we look at the two major postwar paradigms of justice: de-Nazification and de-Sovietization. The former came into being at the onset of the Cold War. The latter marked the end of the Cold War. Simply put, the logic of de-Nazification is to blame the agent, that of de-Sovietization is to blame the system; de-Nazification requires identifying both victims and perpetrators. De-Sovietization is anchored first and foremost in the identity of survivors; it acknowledges victims, but not perpetrators. From this point of view, to identify individuals as perpetrators would be to demonize them. To pursue the logic of de-Nazification in contemporary Rwanda would be to identify the leadership of the genocide so as to hold it accountable. Such, indeed, is the purpose of the international court in Arusha and the local courts inside Rwanda. To pursue the logic of de-Sovietization would be to put emphasis, first and foremost, on the institutions of rule in Rwanda. Where survivors – victims and perpetrators from an earlier round of struggle – must learn to live together, ways must be found to reconcile the logic of reconciliation with that of justice.

Survivor's justice is different from revolutionary justice. It makes sense only in contexts where there have been few beneficiaries in the preceding civil war. I have already commented on the difference between South Africa and Rwanda on this score: one is struck by how few were the perpetrators of apartheid, and how many its beneficiaries, and conversely, how many were the perpetrators in Rwanda's genocide and how few its beneficiaries. Where beneficiaries are many, reconciliation has to be social to be durable, which is the same thing as saying there can be no durable reconciliation without some form of social justice.[8] But where beneficiaries are few, the key to reconciliation is political reconciliation. The prime requirement of political reconciliation is neither criminal justice nor social justice, but *political justice*. It requires not only shifting the primary focus of reform from individuals to institutions, but also recognizing that the key to institutional reform is the reform of institutions of rule. Thus the question: What would it mean to reform institutions of rule so as to give survivors of the genocide another chance?

Reconciling Justice to Democracy

The genocide retrenched Hutu and Tutsi as salient political identities. The dilemma of postgenocide Rwanda lies in the chasm that divides Hutu as a political majority from Tutsi as a political minority. While the minority demands justice, the majority calls for democracy. The two demands appear as irreconcilable, for the minority sees democracy as an agenda for completing the genocide, and the majority sees justice as a self-serving mask for fortifying minority power. To break out of this logjam, I suggest we link both political justice and political democracy to a reform of institutions of rule.

Justice

The question of political justice goes beyond holding the perpetrators of the genocide accountable. Ultimately, it is about the definition of political identities. I have argued that European colonialism in twentieth-century Africa turned indigeneity into the litmus test of rights. Every postindependence regime vowed to change the political world of the settler and the native. Every one of them pledged to deracialize civic rights by making them available to all citizens regardless of color. That is where similarities ended.

While everyone agreed that the settler's prerogative had to go, not everyone was agreed that the native too was a colonial construct that needed to be reformed just as urgently. Could the political identity "settler" be done away with when its bipolar twin "native" was embraced? Anticolonial nationalism was divided on this question. Radical nationalism – as championed by Julius Nyerere, for example – was determined to reform citizenship consistently, both to deracialize and to deethnicize it. From this point of view, it was not enough to do away with just the settler's prerogative; all prerogatives, racial as well as ethnic, would need to be abolished. The predominant trend in African postcolonialism was otherwise: for conservative nationalism, the point of independence was precisely to replace the settler's prerogative by the native's prerogative.

Even though the political prerogative was transferred to the native, the continued legal representation of the indigenous population as *natives* showed that the colonial political legacy had yet to be fully transcended. Where colonial rule had been indirect, as in Uganda and Congo, the native prerogative was defined as ethnic. But where colonialism had imposed a version of direct rule – a halfway house, as I have said, in the case of Rwanda – the prerogative was racial. The 1959 Revolution in Rwanda against the Tutsi, like the 1964 Revolution in Zanzibar against Arabs and the 1972 expulsion of Asians in Uganda, belongs to this second category. Targeted in 1959 as an alien race, the Tutsi were recognized as an indigenous ethnicity by the Second Republic after 1973, but reconstructed as an alien race by the *génocidaires* after the coup of April 1994. As in the 1959 Revolution, so in the 1994 genocide too, the Tutsi were targeted as an alien race. Political justice for the Tutsi cannot mean simply identifying and holding the perpetrators of massacres accountable. By itself, that would return them to the world of the rat and the cat. It also requires a juridical and institutional reform that ceases to make a distinction between two kinds of citizens: one indigenous, the other not.

In contrast to colonial Rwanda, where race was the salient political identity, Congo and Uganda were indirect-rule colonies where *both* race and ethnicity defined political identity. If the settler identity was *racialized*, the native identity was *ethnicized*. Did it not follow that, in indirect-rule colonies such as Uganda and Congo, decolonization would require a combination of deracialization and deethnicization, as indeed Nyerere had championed in Tanzania? On this question, too, nationalism was differentiated. The mainstream – conservative – view was that the world of the "customary" as defined by colonialism was indeed the world of African tradition, and so the conviction that it must be preserved.[9] A reform executed from this point of view did two things. While civic law and civic authority were deracialized in the name of a universal rights culture, an ethnically defined "customary" law and an authority to enforce it were retained as *particular* to the tradition

of those indigenous to Africa. Independent governments also vowed to end the perversion of colonialism by restoring the political prerogative of those indigenous over strangers. The result was to reproduce the bifurcated world created by colonialism: the distinction between indigenous and non-indigenous, abolished in the civic sphere, remained in the ethnic sphere. Even if turned upside-down, the political world remained as designed by the settler.

The antidote to the embrace of colonially constructed custom as authentic African tradition came from among the postindependence oppositional political movements that had to contend with the rights of ethnic strangers. As one would expect, the most promising initiatives came from those that stood to lose the most from an uncritical reproduction of the colonial legacy. Not surprisingly, the most creative departures have come from those movements strongly influenced by Rwandan Tutsi: the Banyamulenge in Congo, and the National Resistance Army in Uganda. Of the two, we have seen that the most radical solution to this dilemma came from the latter, born of the guerrilla struggle in the Luwero Triangle. Luwero had an extremely heterogeneous population: anywhere from a third to a half of its residents had immigrated from outside the area. To continue to define rights on the basis of indigeneity in such a socially heterogeneous context was bound to be politically explosive and disruptive – regardless of whether one leaned in favor of those indigenous or those not. Welding an alliance between locals and migrants required a political identity that could encompass both. The National Resistance Army found this identity in the criterion of resident. When it came to deciding who would be a member of a village council and who could run for office on the ten-person village committee, what mattered was residence, not the circumstances of one's birth or ethnic belonging.

To leave the test of indigeneity for one of residence as the basis for political identity and political rights is to take leave of the world of the rat and the cat, of ethnicity and race, of the native and the settler, as political identities. This, in turn, would require making a clear distinction between cultural and political identities so as to redress the dialectic between the past and the future. To ground political rights in cultural identities is to accent the past – of which a shared culture is one outcome – as a guide to limiting future possibilities. To differentiate political from cultural identities, however, is to accent the commitment to live under a common roof over the recognition of a common history – no matter what the overlap between them – as the real basis for a shared future. [...]

One needs to close with a sense of real political obstacles that will face any attempt to democratize public life in postgenocide Rwanda. Where there is an uneasy coexistence between guilty majorities and fearful minorities, the possibility of a democratic transition is likely to appear more as a threat than a promise to the minorities concerned – why vulnerable minorities tend to fear rather than welcome democracy. The experience of the Tutsi, too, is likely to reinforce an ambivalent attitude to democracy. Were not the Tutsi liberators inside Uganda's NRA sidelined on the morrow of the guerilla victory precisely because they came from a vulnerable minority? Did not the dawn of democracy in Zaire, signified by the coming together of a National Conference of civil and political society in the early 1990s, complete the process leading to the disenfranchising of the Banyarwanda minority? Was not the Rwandan genocide driven forward by the energy of popular mobs mobilized to defend Hutu Power? By itself, majority rule provides no guarantee for minorities that fear majority domination. My point is that if we go by the experience of Banyarwanda – and more specifically Tutsi Banyarwanda – in the African Great Lakes, majority rule can be turned into a bedrock for domination over fragile minorities.

How to foreclose the possibility of a *democratic despotism* remains our toughest challenge yet. While this question is not directly the subject of this book, I believe its subject does bring us a step closer to addressing this question. I began the book with the claim that, even when they mimic preexisting identities – whether cultural or market based – political identities need to be understood as a product of the political process. From this point of view, Hutu and Tutsi need to be understood both as *historical* identities and as *political* identities. As majority and minority, Hutu and Tutsi are not natural identities brought into the political realm; they are political artifacts of a particular form of the state.

If the immediate challenge in Rwanda is to undercut Hutu and Tutsi as political identities,

I have argued that this will not happen so long as the minority monopolizes power. If anything, it will be the surest way of locking the Banyarwanda into the world of the rat and the cat, and giving these identities a longer lease on life. The region provides us two examples of how a minority may give up power. The first is Zanzibar, the second South Africa. For a minority gripped by the fear of extinction, the Zanzibari example is likely to have greater resonance, for at least one reason: it involved longer-term political concessions by both the minority and the majority. Not only did the "Arab" minority cede power, the "African" majority in Zanzibar also ceded full claim on power as the country merged with mainland Tanganyika to form a wider union, Tanzania. The union set in motion a new dynamic tending to dissolve the identities "Arab" and "African" in a wider crucible, over time generating a "Zanzibar" identity. Is a dynamic possible that may undercut the legacy of Hutu and Tutsi as binary political identities, dissolving them in the crucible of a larger Banyarwanda identity in the short run and, other identities we may not imagine today, in the medium run? If yes, it will require us to question the hitherto presumed equation of the democratic project with the national project. Indeed, if it is to be, it will need to draw on energies that go beyond any national assertion. Such a dynamic will need to be the result of a regional initiative, backed up by international support, which in turn needs to be driven by the urgent need to defuse a simmering volcano before it blows up yet again, this time engulfing the wider region.

NOTES

1. I. Inyumba, interview, Kigali, 20 July 1995.
2. Patrick Mazimpaka, interview, Kigali, 11 July 1997; Philip Gourevitch cites several estimates, from a million (Vice-President Kagame) to three million (Dusaidi, aide to the vice-president). See Philip Gourevitch, *We wish to inform you that tomorrow we will be killed with our families: Stories from Rwanda* (New York: Farrar, Straus, and Giroux, 1998), p. 244.
3. Saskia Van Hoyweghen, "The Rwandan Villagisation Programme: Resettlement or Reconstruction?" in Didier Goyvaerts, *Conflict and Ethnicity in Central Africa* (Tokyo: Institute for the Study of Languages and Cultures of Asia and Africa, 2000), p. 212.
4. Ibid.
5. Filip Reyntjens writes:

The tutsisation of the state machinery was further reaffirmed. Even while the government, the country's international "business card" has grosso modo equal representation (14 Hutu, 12 Tutsi, 1 unidentified), out of the 18 general secretaries identified, 14 are Tutsi from the RPF; with the exception of 2 ministers, all the non-RPF ministers are flanked by a general secretary from the RPF. While the National Assembly already has a Tutsi majority, it continues to be subject to purges.... Out of the twelve prefects, nine are Tutsi, two Hutu and one position is vacant. The number of Tutsi mayors is established to be over 80%. Eleven of the fourteen ambassadors are Tutsi, with nine coming from the ranks of the RPF. Among the fourteen officers comprising the high command of the army and gendarmerie, there is only one Hutu.... The tutsisation of the judiciary has been reinforced in a very pronounced manner after the suspension of six Hutu judges of the *Cour de Cassation* and the Council of State on March 24, 1998; they were later dismissed.

See Filip Reyntjens, *Talking or Fighting? Political Evaluation in Rwanda and Burundi, 1998–99*, Current African Issues, no. 21 (Nordiska Afrikainstitutet, 1999), pp. 5, 15.

6   "At the end of 1998, 125,028 persons remained officially detained, though the actual number is probably much higher. According to the Rwandan government, in 1998 several thousand detainees died as a result of AIDS, malnutrition, dysentery and typhus. During the month of November 1998, 400 prisoners died from typhus in the Rilima prison alone." See ibid., p. 14.

7   This is the sense in which Abraham Lincoln used the term in the aftermath of the Civil War in the United States. Though dipped in religious terminology, he called for survivors to be born again, to reconcile. See Robert Meister, "Forgiving and Forgetting," in Carla Hesse and Robert Post, eds., *Human Rights in Political Transitions: Gettysburg to Bosnia* (New York: Zone Books, 1999), pp. 135–76.

8   See Mahmood Mamdani, "The Truth According to the TRC," in Ifi Amadiume and Abdullahi An-Nai'im, eds., *The Politics of Memory: Truth, Healing and Social Justice* (London: Zed Press, 2000).

9   This, indeed, is Basil Davidson's solution to Africa's political problems. See Davidson, *The Black Man's Burden: Africa and the Curse of the Nation-State* (New York: Times Books, 1992).

62

From *The Burden of Memory: The Muse of Forgiveness*

Wole Soyinka

From within the same continent, two strategies of confrontation with one's history. They are off-springs of the same age, sprung from minds of a shared identity, and they appear to complement yet contradict each other. Both depend on a process of baring the truth of one's history in order to exorcise the past and secure a collective peace of mind, the healing of a bruised racial psyche. Both concepts even appear to play a game with each other – in the mind at least – since some form of mental reconciliation appears to be provoked for their cohabitation. How on earth does one reconcile reparations, or recompense, with reconciliation or remission of wrongs? Dare we presume that both, in their differing ways, are committed to ensuring the righting of wrongs and the triumph of justice?

The undeniable differences merely complicate matters – one proposal originates from a history of Africa that has become somewhat remote, attenuated by time and becoming blurred by global relationships, while the other owes its birth to an ordeal that is so immediate that both victims and violators are alive and locked within the necessity of cohabitation. This contrast in itself provides a paradox – in expectations. If anything, it is the latter condition, the contemporary one, that should mandate a call for reparations in one form or another. The victims are alive and in need of rehabilitation while their violators – as a recognizable group – pursue a privileged existence, secure in the spoils of a sordid history. Indeed, it is within the enclosure of that nation called South Africa that the principle of repar-ations presents itself as something quite practical and feasible, indeed, clamorous, unlike the context of slavery that continues to be increasingly contumacious in the determination of responsibilities.

Just to let one's fantasy roam a little – what really would be preposterous or ethically inadmissible in imposing a general levy on South Africa's white population? This is not intended as a concrete proposal, but as an exercise in pure speculation. We are, after all, engaged in identifying all possible routes to social harmonization – from the obvious to the unthinkable. A collective levy need not be regarded as a punitive measure; indeed – since the purpose is reconciliation, such an offer could originate from the beneficiaries of Apartheid themselves, in a voluntary gesture of atonement – it need not be a project of the state. Is such a genesis – from within the indicted group itself – truly beyond conception? If, however, this attribution of self-redeeming possibilities within the psychology of guilt remains within the utopian imagination, and some external prodding proved necessary, the initiative could be taken up by someone of the non-establishment stature of Archbishop Desmond Tutu. The respected cleric and mediator mounts his pulpit one day and addresses his compatriots on that very theme: "White brothers and sisters in the Lord, you have sinned, but we are willing to forgive. The scriptures warn us that the wages of sin are death but, in your case, they seem to be wealth. If therefore you chose to shed a little of that sinful wealth as a first step toward atonement ... etc. etc." [...]

Despite the realization that South Africa is, like any other zone of state-engendered anomie, unique in the intricacy of motions – both internal and external – that led to her liberation, there remains a sense that the adopted formula for the harmonization of that society erodes, in some way, one of the pillars on which a durable society must be founded – Responsibility. And ultimately – Justice.

A fact that is often conveniently ignored is that the territory of culpability in the South African instance was not limited to the state. One of the most courageous admissions that I know of in the aftermath of revolutionary struggles was that of President Nelson Mandela, who openly confronted the ANC with its own dismal record of needless cruelty and abuse of human rights, especially in prisons and detention camps run by the movement within friendly frontline states such as Zambia. Torture and arbitrary executions were, apparently, commonplace, and it is not easy to forget the untidily resolved murder of the luckless "Stompie," beaten to death by members of Winnie [Madikizela] Mandela's football club – in reality, her bodyguards. The murder of the white American volunteer girl, stabbed to death by four Soweto thugs who were later imprisoned for the crime, is an even more harrowing reminder. A recent televised appearance of the four murderers at a meeting with the parents of the victim, exploiting in their turn the rites of open confession with the prospect of an amnesty, actually goes to the heart of a nation's moral dilemma. The parents bestowed their forgiveness, and it does seem likely that, by classifying the crime as a "political" one, the perpetrators may also be deemed to have fulfilled all the conditions that qualify them for a remission of their sentence. Must the psychopathic opportunists of a revolutionary struggle also become beneficiaries of the balm of victory? A cowardly killing, surely, can be defined even by the internal moralities of any liberation struggle, however violent, otherwise, let us, at once and for all time, abandon all concepts of, and the exceptional deeds that attach to, heroism!

Let us, for a brief moment, superimpose the face of Pol Pot over any one of these public applicants for remission in a parallel process in Cambodia. Is it really given to the human mind to accommodate, much less annul, such a magnitude of man-inflicted anguish? The logic of "Truth and Reconciliation," however, demands that the mind prepare itself for the spectacle of a "penitent" Pol Pot, freed, morally cleansed, at liberty to go about his business in a humanely restored milieu!

This risk-free parade of villains, calmly – and occasionally with ill-concealed relish – recounting their roles in kidnappings, tortures, murders, and mutilation, at the end of which absolution is granted without penalty or forfeit, is either a lesson in human ennoblement, or a glorification of impunity. Admittedly, it does constitute at the very least, a revelation of the infinite possibilities of human options in the resolution of social crises – and this perhaps must remain our consolation. Even if judgment comes down eventually on the negative import of such a proceeding, there is still an inherent challenge in it that cannot be denied. It is not, after all, an occurrence in a historic vacuum. [. . .]

And there are other models – like Rwanda, in which the international community has again recognized and pursued a role in a process that establishes that there are certain crimes that have ramifications beyond the borders of any nation and constitute crimes against humanity. The problem with the South African choice is therefore its implicit, *a priori* exclusion of criminality and, thus, responsibility. Justice assigns responsibility, and few will deny that justice is an essential ingredient of social cohesion – indeed, I have asserted elsewhere that justice constitutes "the first condition of humanity." And even as justice is not served by punishing the accused before the establishment of guilt, neither is it served by discharging the guilty without evidence of mitigation – or remorse.

We recognize that the application of what, in effect, is an attribution of mitigation before the proof has, in this case, only one end in view, and that is to encourage revelation, to establish truth. Could it be then that, underlying it all, is the working out of that Christian[1] theological precept: "The Truth shall make you free"? Or do we seek answers, for this unusual lesson of our time, in a humanism that our own poets and philosophers have ascribed, in moments of race euphoria or contestation with the European world, as being uniquely African? Poets and statesmen of the temperament of Léopold Sédar Senghor would, I am certain, endorse this largeness of black generosity. If the government of Nelson Mandela sought vindication among Africa's poets for its "Truth and Reconciliation" option, Senghor's poetry would provide it more than amply; advocating, as it does, a philosophy of wholesale remission. And Senghor would root this, undoubtedly, within that generous earth of Africa's humanity that he regards as an enduring critique of Europe's soullessness. Well, the Africa of Senghor's Muse is hardly recognizable in the realities that surround us today, and with Rwanda hardly a memory beat away from even the most uninformed, we would be wise to tread warily along that path, or at least call to our aid the corrective views of contemporary witnesses – also black – such as Keith Richburg![2]

But will the South African doctrine work, ultimately? Will society be truly purified as a result of this open articulation of what is known? For even while we speak of "revelation," it is only revelation in concrete particulars, the ascription of faces to deeds, admission by individual personae of roles within known criminalities, affirmation by the already identified of what they had formerly denied. Nothing, in reality, is new. The difference is that knowledge is being shared, collectively, and entered formally into the archives of that nation. So, back to the question, this procedural articulation of the known, will it truly heal society? Will it achieve the reconciliation that is the goal of the initiators of this heroic process? For it is heroic – let that value be frankly attributed. Even those of us who, conceding our unsaintliness, distance ourselves from the Christian – or indeed Buddhist – beatitudes, do acknowledge that forgiveness is a value that is far more humanly exacting than vengeance. And so – will this undertaking truly "reconcile" the warring tribes of that community? My inclination is very much toward a negative prognosis. An ingredient is missing in this crucible of harmonization and that ingredient is both material and moral.

The moral element is glaring enough, though it is much too nebulous to assess – that element being remorse and, thus, repentance. Nebulous because one can only observe that an expression of remorse has been made. Is it genuine? Impossible to tell. [...]

I remain convinced that the answer to the missing question – at least one that I never heard put – would be, "Oh yes, given the same circumstances, I would do the same thing all over again." However, let us abandon the hazy zone of remorse for now, and move to the material.

And here, I believe, is where the cry for Reparations for a different and more ancient cause suggests itself as the missing link between Truth and Reconciliation. The actual structuring of Reparations is secondary – in the case of South Africa, it is not too difficult to identify targets – from the collective to the individual – from state agencies to businesses and voluntary associations – be they all-white political parties, segregated clubs and resorts, etc., self-defense militias (the volunteer backbone of the state system)...a host of privileged and/or profit-generating institutions that prospered through Apartheid. The essential is to establish the principle: that some measure of restitution is always essential after dispossession.

NOTES

1 The convention that capitalizes this and other so-called world religions is justified only when the same principle is applied to other religions, among them, the Orisa.

2 Keith Richburg, *Out of America* (Basic Books, 1997).

Index

Notes: Page numbers in *italic* refer to plates. Abbreviations used in subheadings are: NI = Northern Ireland; PTSD = post-traumatic stress disorder; SA = South Africa; US = United States of America.